Implementing VMware Horizon 7.7
Third Edition

Manage and deploy the end-user computing infrastructure for your organization

Jason Ventresco

BIRMINGHAM - MUMBAI

Implementing VMware Horizon 7.7
Third Edition

Copyright © 2019 Packt Publishing

All rights reserved. No part of this book may be reproduced, stored in a retrieval system, or transmitted in any form or by any means, without the prior written permission of the publisher, except in the case of brief quotations embedded in critical articles or reviews.

Every effort has been made in the preparation of this book to ensure the accuracy of the information presented. However, the information contained in this book is sold without warranty, either express or implied. Neither the author, nor Packt Publishing or its dealers and distributors, will be held liable for any damages caused or alleged to have been caused directly or indirectly by this book.

Packt Publishing has endeavored to provide trademark information about all of the companies and products mentioned in this book by the appropriate use of capitals. However, Packt Publishing cannot guarantee the accuracy of this information.

Commissioning Editor: Pavan Ramchandani
Acquisition Editor: Prachi Bisht
Content Development Editor: Sharon Raj
Technical Editor: Prashant Chaudhari
Copy Editor: Safis Editing
Project Coordinator: Drashti Panchal
Proofreader: Safis Editing
Indexer: Tejal Daruwale Soni
Graphics: Tom Scaria
Production Coordinator: Tom Scaria

First published: May 2013
Second edition: June 2016

Third edition: January 2019

Production reference: 1100119

Published by Packt Publishing Ltd.
Livery Place
35 Livery Street
Birmingham
B3 2PB, UK.

ISBN 978-1-78961-784-9

www.packtpub.com

Contributors

About the author

Jason Ventresco is a 19-year veteran of the IT field, currently working for Cohesity as a Senior Implementation Practice Lead. In that role, he both develops and delivers Cohesity product training and creates professional services offerings. Jason previously worked as a Professional Services Offerings Manager for McAfee, an EUC Consultant Solutions Engineer for Dell EMC, a member of the Global Infrastructure team for FHI 360, and an IT consultant for WorkSmart and Xerox Global Services. Jason previously authored the books *Implementing VMware Horizon 5.2*, *VMware Horizon 5.3 Design Patterns and Best Practices*, *VMware Horizon 6.0 Desktop Virtualization Cookbook*, and *Implementing VMware Horizon 7*.

About the reviewer

Fady Fawzy Abdelmalek (VMFCore) is a Senior System Engineer and Solution Architect working at Equinox ME in Egypt. He has been specializing in VMware technologies, from simple vSphere to complex VMware cloud automation, for more than 7 years. He has participated in many large projects as an SME, architect, advisor, implementer, and technical team delivery lead. He is also a freelance consultant, and has been working in the software industry for more than 9 years.

Packt is searching for authors like you

If you're interested in becoming an author for Packt, please visit `authors.packtpub.com` and apply today. We have worked with thousands of developers and tech professionals, just like you, to help them share their insight with the global tech community. You can make a general application, apply for a specific hot topic that we are recruiting an author for, or submit your own idea.

mapt.io

Mapt is an online digital library that gives you full access to over 5,000 books and videos, as well as industry leading tools to help you plan your personal development and advance your career. For more information, please visit our website.

Why subscribe?

- Spend less time learning and more time coding with practical eBooks and Videos from over 4,000 industry professionals

- Improve your learning with Skill Plans built especially for you

- Get a free eBook or video every month

- Mapt is fully searchable

- Copy and paste, print, and bookmark content

Packt.com

Did you know that Packt offers eBook versions of every book published, with PDF and ePub files available? You can upgrade to the eBook version at www.packt.com and as a print book customer, you are entitled to a discount on the eBook copy. Get in touch with us at customercare@packtpub.com for more details.

At www.packt.com, you can also read a collection of free technical articles, sign up for a range of free newsletters, and receive exclusive discounts and offers on Packt books and eBooks.

Table of Contents

Preface	1
Chapter 1: VMware Horizon Infrastructure Overview	9
VMware Horizon components	10
Horizon Connection Server	12
Horizon Security Server	12
Horizon Unified Access Gateway	13
Horizon Enrollment Server	14
VMware vSphere	14
VMware vCenter Server	15
Horizon Composer	16
Horizon Agent	16
Horizon Client	16
VMware App Volumes	17
VMware User Environment Manager	18
VMware ThinApp	19
VMware Horizon licensing	19
VMware Horizon core infrastructure requirements	21
Microsoft infrastructure requirements	21
OS requirements	22
Database requirements	23
vCenter Server requirements	23
Horizon Agent-supported OS	24
VMware Horizon design overview	25
Measuring virtual desktop resource requirements	25
The need for vSphere reserve capacity	26
Providing sufficient Horizon Client bandwidth	28
The importance of a VMware Horizon pilot	29
Performance is the key	31
Summary	32
Questions	32
Further reading	33
Chapter 2: Implementing Horizon Connection Server	35
Overview of VMware Horizon Connection Server	36
Horizon Connection Server requirements	38
Hardware requirements	38
Software requirements	39
Limits of a Horizon Connection Server	39
Load balancing Connection Servers	40

Table of Contents

Load-balancing appliances	41
vCenter Server requirements	41
Horizon installation prerequisites	**42**
Infrastructure and other prerequisites	43
Creating a vCenter role and granting permissions	43
Horizon event database	46
SQL database tutorials	47
Deploying the first Horizon Connection Server	**47**
Installing the first Horizon Connection Server	47
Configuring the first Horizon Connection Server	50
Configuring the Horizon Instant Clone Engine	**55**
Configuring the Instant Clone Engine AD user account	56
Updating the Instant Clone Engine Domain Administrator setting	56
Deploying a Horizon Replica Connection Server	**58**
Installing a Horizon Replica Connection Server	58
Upgrading an existing Horizon Connection Server	**60**
Upgrading prerequisites	60
Backing up the existing Horizon configuration	61
Horizon upgrade process	62
Backing up a Horizon Connection Server	**63**
Backing up the vCenter Server database	63
Backing up the Horizon AD LDS database	64
Horizon Connection Server recovery	**65**
Restoring a single Horizon Connection Server	66
Removing a Horizon Connection Server	66
Restoring the vCenter database	67
Restoring the Horizon Connection Server AD LDS database	67
Summary	**68**
Questions	**68**
Further reading	**69**
Chapter 3: Implementing Horizon Composer	**71**
Overview of VMware Horizon Composer	**72**
Refreshing linked-clone desktops	75
Recomposing linked-clone desktops	76
Horizon Composer requirements	**77**
Hardware requirements	77
Limits of Horizon Composer	**78**
Horizon Composer installation prerequisites	**78**
Horizon Composer service account	79
Horizon Composer vCenter permissions	80
Creating a Horizon Composer vCenter role and granting permissions	81
Horizon Composer AD permissions	82
Delegating permissions for Horizon Composer in AD	82
Horizon Composer database	85
SQL Database tutorials	86

Table of Contents

Deploying Horizon Composer	86
Installing Horizon Composer	87
Configuring Horizon Composer	88
Backing up Horizon Composer	92
Backing up the Horizon Composer database	92
Backing up the Horizon Composer SSL certificates	93
Horizon Composer recovery	94
Restoring the Horizon Composer database	94
Restoring the Horizon Composer SSL certificates	96
Restoring Horizon Composer with a new default SSL certificate	96
Restoring Horizon Composer with a custom SSL certificate	97
Summary	98
Questions	98
Further reading	99
Chapter 4: Implementing Horizon Security Server	**101**
Horizon Security Server overview	102
Horizon Security Server limits	103
Horizon Security Server additional considerations	104
High availability overview	105
Security Server network requirements	106
Installing and configuring Horizon Security Server	108
Installation prerequisites	108
Security Server pairing password	109
Deploying a Horizon Security Server	110
Enabling Blast/PCoIP Secure Gateway	111
Installing a Horizon Security Server	113
Updating the Horizon Security Server settings	117
Horizon Security Server options	118
Horizon Security Server backup	119
Horizon Security Server recovery or upgrade	119
Summary	121
Questions	122
Further reading	122
Chapter 5: Implementing Horizon Unified Access Gateway	**123**
Horizon Unified Access Gateway overview	124
Horizon Unified Access Gateway limits	125
Horizon Unified Access Gateway additional considerations	126
High availability overview	126
Horizon Unified Access Gateway network requirements	128
Preparing the infrastructure for a Horizon Unified Access Gateway	130
Installation prerequisites	130
Deploying a Horizon Unified Access Gateway	133
Configuring the Connection Servers	133

[iii]

Table of Contents

Deploying a Horizon Unified Access Gateway	135
Troubleshooting a Horizon Unified Access Gateway deployment	**138**
Updating the Horizon Unified Access Gateway configuration	**139**
Summary	**140**
Questions	**140**
Further reading	**141**
Chapter 6: Implementing a Horizon Cloud Pod	**143**
Horizon Cloud Pod overview	**144**
Sharing key data in the Horizon Cloud Pod Global Data Layer	146
Sending messages between Horizon pods	146
Cloud Pod port requirements	147
Cloud Pod topology limits	147
Configuring a Horizon Cloud Pod	**148**
Configuring Horizon sites	151
Associating users with Horizon sites	154
Creating Cloud Pod Global Entitlements	**156**
Creating and configuring a Global Entitlement for a Horizon desktop pool	157
Creating and configuring a Global Entitlement for a Horizon application pool	161
Removing a Horizon pod from a Cloud Pod	**163**
Updating the settings of a Global Entitlement	**164**
Editing the general settings of a Global Entitlement	165
Determining the effective home site of a user or security group	**167**
Monitoring Global Entitlement Horizon client sessions	**169**
Summary	**171**
Questions	**171**
Further reading	**172**
Chapter 7: Creating Horizon Desktop Pools	**173**
Horizon desktop pool overview	**174**
Desktop pool common terms	**174**
Horizon desktop pool options	**176**
Horizon Composer-linked clones	177
Instant-clone desktops	178
Full-clone desktops	180
Linux desktops	180
QuickPrep versus Sysprep	**180**
Advantages of Linked or Instant Clone desktops	**182**
Considerations for Linked and Instant Clone desktops	**183**
Creating a Horizon desktop pool	**184**
Creating a pool using Horizon Composer-linked clones	185
Creating a pool using Horizon Instant Clones	196
Creating a pool using full clones	199
Monitoring the desktop creation process	**203**
Horizon Administrator console	203

The vSphere Web client task window	204
Common provisioning problems	205
Managing Horizon Desktop pool entitlements	206
Summary	208
Questions	209
Further reading	209

Chapter 8: Implementing the Microsoft Remote Desktop Services Application and Desktop Pools 211

Configuring a Microsoft RDSH server for use with Horizon	212
Microsoft RDS licensing	213
Microsoft RDSH Server recommended hardware configuration	214
Importing the Horizon RDS AD group policy templates	215
Installing the Horizon Agent on the Microsoft RDS host	219
vSphere customization specification for the Microsoft RDS servers	220
Additional resources related to using Microsoft RDS servers	220
Creating a Microsoft RDS farm in Horizon	221
Creating a Horizon application pool	227
Creating an RDS desktop pool	229
Using the Horizon Client to access application pools	234
Monitoring the status of Horizon application pool clients and RDS servers	235
Modifying or deleting a Horizon application pool	236
Managing a Horizon RDS farm or server	237
Summary	240
Questions	241
Further reading	241

Chapter 9: Performing Horizon Pool Maintenance 243

An overview of instant and linked clone maintenance	244
Instant-clone parent image update	245
Linked clone desktop refresh	245
Linked clone desktop recompose	246
Linked clone desktop rebalance	247
Managing Horizon maintenance tasks	248
Global settings for Horizon maintenance	249
Logoff warning and timeout	250
Concurrent maintenance operations	251
Storage overcommit	253
Updating datastore storage overcommit settings	254
Performing linked clone desktop maintenance	255
Refreshing linked clone desktops	255
Refreshing individual desktops	258
Recomposing linked clone desktops	258
Recomposing individual desktops	260

Rebalancing linked clone desktops	261
Rebalancing individual desktops	262
Performing instant clone desktop maintenance	263
Updating the instant clone desktop parent image	263
Recovering an individual instant clone desktop	265
Managing Horizon Composer persistent disks	266
Detaching persistent disks	266
Recreating a desktop using a persistent disk	268
Attaching a detached persistent disk to an existing desktop	269
Importing a persistent disk	270
Summary	271
Questions	272
Further reading	272
Chapter 10: Creating a Master Virtual Desktop Image	273
The importance of desktop optimization	274
Optimization results – Horizon desktop IOPS	274
Optimization results – CPU utilization	275
Customizing the Windows desktop OS cluster size	276
Customizing the Windows cluster size during the installation process	277
Permanently removing Windows Store applications	278
Windows OS pre-deployment tasks	280
Installing VMware Tools	280
Removing an unwanted application – native update features	281
Disabling the Adobe Acrobat Reader DC update feature	281
Disabling the Java updater utility	283
Windows OS optimizations	283
Disabling Windows Error Reporting	284
Disabling automatic updates	284
Removing unnecessary Windows components	285
Pre-compiling Microsoft .NET Framework assemblies	286
Disabling Windows hibernation	287
Disabling Windows System Restore	287
Sizing virtual machine RAM properly	288
Setting the Windows page file to a fixed size	289
Disabling paging the executive	289
Disabling Content Indexing of the desktop drive	290
Disabling Content Indexing for the remaining file locations	291
Disabling unnecessary services	291
SuperFetch	292
Removing unnecessary scheduled tasks	292
Changing the Group Policy refresh interval	294
Disabling the Windows boot animation	294
Optimizing the Windows profile	295
Adjusting for best performance	296

Turning off system sounds	296
Disabling the Windows background and screen saver	296
Summary	297
Questions	297
Further reading	297
Chapter 11: Implementing App Volumes	**299**
App Volumes overview	300
App Volumes prerequisites	302
vCenter permissions	304
Installing App Volumes Manager server	304
Configuring App Volumes Manager	306
Deploying additional App Volumes Manager servers	311
Installing the App Volumes Agent	312
Configuring native load balancing for the App Volumes Agent software	313
Creating an AppStack	315
Updating an AppStack	320
Assigning AppStacks	321
Deleting AppStacks assignments	323
Enabling Writable Volumes	324
Deleting Writable Volumes	327
App Volumes backup and recovery	329
What to back up	329
Recovery process	330
Summary	330
Questions	331
Further reading	331
Chapter 12: Implementing User Environment Manager	**333**
UEM overview	334
UEM pre-installation tasks	336
Configuration share	337
Persona share	337
Windows user folder redirection share	338
Group policy files	339
Installing the UEM Agent	340
Configuring UEM	341
Installing the UEM management console	342
Easy Start configuration	344
Easy Start defaults	345
UEM group policy settings	347
UEM user policies	347
UEM computer policies	350
Windows folder redirection	352
Advanced UEM configuration examples	354

Table of Contents

Personalization	355
Application profile Import/Export feature	355
User Environment	358
Shortcut management feature	360
Summary	**361**
Questions	**361**
Further reading	**362**
Chapter 13: Implementing the Just-in-Time Management Platform (JMP)	**363**
An Overview of the Horizon Just-in-Time Management Platform	364
Just-in-Time Management Server requirements	365
Hardware requirements	365
Software requirements	365
General requirements	366
Database requirements	366
VMware infrastructure requirements	367
Deploying the JMP Server	369
Installing the JMP Server software	369
Configuring the JMP settings	372
Managing JMP Assignments	379
Creating a JMP Assignment	379
Deleting, duplicating, or editing a JMP Assignment	383
Summary	**384**
Questions	**384**
Further reading	**385**
Chapter 14: Using Horizon PowerCLI	**387**
Enabling remote management in Windows	388
Enabling WinRM	388
Establishing a remote Horizon PowerCLI session	389
Viewing all the PowerCLI commands and their options	391
Listing all Horizon PowerCLI commands	391
Displaying the options for a single PowerCLI command	391
Sample data for Horizon PowerCLI commands	392
Horizon PowerCLI commands not covered in this chapter	393
Configuring the Horizon infrastructure	394
Adding a vCenter server to Horizon	394
Updating the settings of the vCenter server that is linked to Horizon	396
Removing a vCenter server from Horizon	396
Updating the Horizon connection broker settings	396
Updating the Horizon global settings	397
Configuring the Horizon license	398
Administering Horizon desktop pools	398
Creating a dedicated assignment persistent linked clone pool	399

[viii]

Creating a floating assignment (non-persistent) linked clone pool	400
Creating an automatically provisioned full clone desktop pool	400
Creating a manually provisioned desktop pool	401
Updating the configuration of a Horizon desktop pool	402
Updating a linked clone pool	402
Updating an automatically provisioned full clone pool	403
Updating a manually provisioned pool	403
Refreshing a linked clone desktop or pool	403
Recomposing a linked clone desktop pool	404
Rebalancing a linked clone desktop pool	405
Resetting a Horizon desktop	405
Managing Horizon client entitlements and sessions	406
Adding desktop pool entitlements	406
Removing desktop pool entitlements	406
Entitling or unentitling an individual desktop	407
Disconnecting the Horizon client session	407
Logging off the Horizon client session	408
Retrieving information about the Horizon infrastructure	408
Retrieving Horizon composer server information	408
Retrieving a list of the Horizon desktop pools	409
Retrieving the global Horizon configuration data	409
Retrieving the Horizon connection broker information	409
Retrieving a list of virtual machines managed by Horizon	409
Get-DesktopVM - ComposerTask refresh	410
Retrieving the AD user or group information	410
Retrieving information about user persistent data disks	411
Retrieving the Horizon event reports and their descriptions	411
Retrieving the Horizon infrastructure health monitors and their status	412
Retrieving information about remote Horizon sessions	412
Retrieving a list of the vCenter servers linked to the Horizon environment	413
Retrieving the Horizon license information	413
Reviewing the desktop pool entitlement	414
Summary	414
Questions	415
Further reading	415
Chapter 15: Implementing Horizon Group Policies	417
Horizon Group Policy overview	417
Loopback processing for group policies	419
The Horizon Agent Configuration ADM template	421
Agent configuration base settings	422
Viewing USB configuration settings	422
Client Downloadable only Settings	425
Agent Configuration settings	427
Agent Security settings	431

Unity Touch and Hosted App settings	431
VMware FlashMMR Settings	432
The Horizon Client Configuration ADM template	**433**
Client Configuration Base settings	433
Scripting definitions settings	436
Security Settings	438
RDP Settings	441
Horizon USB Configuration settings	444
Settings not configurable by Agent	444
The Horizon Common Configuration ADM template	**445**
Common Configuration Base settings	446
Log Configuration settings	446
Performance Alarm settings	447
Security Configuration settings	448
The Horizon Server Configuration ADM template	**449**
The Server Configuration Base template	449
The PCoIP Session Variables ADM template	**449**
PCoIP Session Variables Base settings	450
The Blast Session Variables ADM template	**455**
Blast Session Variables settings	455
Summary	**456**
Questions	**456**
Further reading	**457**
Chapter 16: Managing Horizon SSL Certificates	**459**
Creating a Local Computer Certificates console	**460**
Requesting a certificate using Microsoft AD Certificate Services	**462**
Requesting a certificate with SANs	**468**
Replacing a Horizon Connection Server certificate	**471**
Replacing a Horizon Security Server certificate	**474**
Replacing a Horizon Composer certificate	**475**
Replacing a Horizon Unified Access Gateway certificate	**477**
Summary	**479**
Questions	**480**
Further reading	**480**
Appendix A: Assessments	**481**
Chapter 1, VMware Horizon Infrastructure Overview	481
Chapter 2, Implementing Horizon Connection Server	481
Chapter 3, Implementing Horizon Composer	482
Chapter 4, Implementing Horizon Security Server	482
Chapter 5, Implementing Horizon Unified Access Gateway	483
Chapter 6, Implementing a Horizon Cloud Pod	483
Chapter 7, Creating Horizon Desktop Pools	484

Chapter 8, Implementing Microsoft Remote Desktop Services Application and Desktop Pools	484
Chapter 9, Performing Horizon Pool Maintenance	485
Chapter 10, Creating a Master Virtual Desktop Image	485
Chapter 11, Implementing App Volumes	486
Chapter 12, Implementing User Environment Manager	486
Chapter 13, Implementing the Just-in-Time Management Platform (JMP)	487
Chapter 14, Using Horizon PowerCLI	487
Chapter 15, Implementing Horizon Group Policies	488
Chapter 16, Managing Horizon SSL Certificates	488
Other Books You May Enjoy	489
Index	493

Preface

Implementing VMware Horizon 7.7 is meant to be a hands-on guide on how to deploy and configure various key features of Horizon, including App Volumes and User Environment Manager. The examples provided in this book focus on 14 different topics, and the book instructs you on their purpose, configuration, and administration. Using the examples provided in this book, you will be able to implement and manage these features in your own VMware Horizon environment.

There are many places in this book that refer to the official VMware Horizon, App Volumes, and User Environment Manager documentation. You are encouraged to review this documentation as it complements the material in this book and contains additional information that can provide a deeper understanding of the technical details and capabilities of the entire VMware Horizon platform.

There are a number of different reasons why an organization may decide to implement VMware Horizon in their own environment. Many organizations are already familiar with the benefits of virtualization, such as the following:

- **Server consolidation**: Less physical hardware is required to service the same quality of workload.
- **Simplified management**: Fewer physical resources to manage.
- **More energy efficient**: Less power and cooling required.
- **Hardware independence**: Virtual machines can run on almost any hardware platform without any changes required.
- **Enhanced capabilities**: Deploy new virtual servers much faster than physical ones, and with less effort.

This is just a small sample of the benefits of virtualization. If you have already implemented virtualization in your organization, you likely have additional reasons of your own.

Preface

Virtual desktops and applications can provide an organization with additional advantages beyond those of virtualization itself. Using VMware Horizon, we can do the following:

- Roll out a new Windows desktop OS across your enterprise without making any changes to the existing desktops, although eventually you will want to retire or repurpose these machines.
- Horizon desktops are live in the data center, and they can be accessed from almost anywhere from a variety of clients. Horizon desktops, as well as the data stored on them, can't be left in airports, stolen from cars, or accidentally left on your desk at the office. Horizon offers the ability to control how data can be copied between the client endpoint and the desktop or application being accessed.
- Stop caring about endpoint hardware. Use existing Windows PCs as desktops if you want or move to a zero client and do away with common endpoint management tasks. Better yet, have users bring their own device and let them use it to access their Horizon desktop. Worry about what's in the data center, not on the desk.
- Microsoft Patch Tuesday redefined. With Horizon instant and linked clones, you patch once and then quickly update the desktops with a whole new master image. No more testing patches across 15 different hardware platforms. No more monitoring patch status across hundreds or thousands of desktops. The same technique can be used to roll out new applications as well.
- Stop troubleshooting random desktop problems. Problems with Windows? Provide the user a new or refreshed desktop in minutes with linked clones, or even seconds with instant clones. With features such as User Environment Manager to manage Windows profiles and App Volumes to deliver applications on demand, the individual desktop doesn't have to matter. If a problem with a persistent desktop will take more than a few minutes to fix, refresh the desktop instead. If using non-persistent desktops, simply ask the user to log off and on again, which will assign them a brand new desktop to use.

These are just some of the advantages of using VMware Horizon, vSphere, App Volumes, and User Environment Manager to move your desktops and applications into a data centre. While reading this book, I encourage you to think of ways that Horizon can change how you provide end user computing resources to your organization. These are just a few examples:

- Don't just simply forklift your desktops into the data center as full virtual machines, consider the benefits of linked or instant clones.
- Rather than create large numbers of master images for different departments or worker types across your organization, create a basic image that you can layer applications on top of using App Volumes.
- Investigate software that is optimized for virtual desktops, such as the vShield Endpoint antivirus platform. Software that is optimized for virtual desktop platforms typically requires fewer per-desktop resources, which may enable you to run more desktops on a given vSphere host.
- Horizon Enterprise has features that make the individual desktop less important, you just need to use them. Use User Environment Manager to manage your users' Windows profiles, and use App Volumes to centrally manage and deliver applications independent of the desktop, and suddenly the individual desktop won't matter as much. This allows you to focus on the only things that actually matter: user data and applications.

VMware Horizon, App Volumes, and User Environment Manager can provide you with much more than just a means of virtualizing your desktops and applications. The more familiar you become each product's features and capabilities, the more you will realize that you can rethink a lot of what you do concerning application and desktop management and delivery, and eventually provide a higher quality experience to your end users.

I certainly hope this is the case.

Who this book is for

If you are a newcomer to system administration and you wish to implement the Horizon environment, then this book is for you. Prior knowledge of Horizon is beneficial.

What this book covers

Chapter 1, *VMware Horizon Infrastructure Overview*, provides a broad overview of VMware Horizon and discusses topics that will influence the design, implementation, and assessment of a VMware Horizon infrastructure.

Chapter 2, *Implementing Horizon Connection Server*, covers the infrastructure requirements, sizing, limits, high availability, deployment, configuration, backup, and recovery of Horizon Connection Server.

Chapter 3, *Implementing Horizon Composer*, covers the infrastructure requirements, deployment, configuration, backup, and recovery of Horizon Composer. The capabilities of Horizon Composer and benefits of using linked-clone desktops are also discussed.

Chapter 4, *Implementing Horizon Security Server*, covers the infrastructure requirements, limits, high availability designs, deployment, configuration, backup, and recovery of Horizon Security Server.

Chapter 5, *Implementing Horizon Unified Access Gateway*, covers the infrastructure requirements, limits, high availability designs, deployment, configuration, and troubleshooting of Horizon Unified Access Gateway.

Chapter 6, *Implementing a Horizon Cloud Pod*, covers how to deploy, configure, and administer a Horizon Cloud Pod, which enables the creation of global client entitlements to resources in multi-site, multi-pod Horizon environments.

Chapter 7, *Creating Horizon Desktop Pools*, covers how to create desktop pools using the Horizon View Manager Admin console. Topics covered include desktop pool options, desktop pool types, monitoring pool creation, user entitlement, and common provisioning problems.

Chapter 8, *Implementing Microsoft Remote Desktop Services Application and Desktop Pools*, covers how to configure Microsoft Windows Remote Desktop Services for use with Horizon, how to deploy and manage Remote Desktop Services farms, how to create Remote Desktop Services-based Horizon Application and Desktop Pools, and how to manage and monitor the status of Windows Remote Desktop Services hosts and Horizon clients who are streaming applications.

Chapter 9, *Performing Horizon Pool Maintenance*, covers how to perform maintenance on Horizon pools that contain linked-clone or instant-clone desktops. Topics include an overview of the different maintenance operations including linked-clone refresh, recompose, and rebalance, instant-clone push image and recovery, and how to manage the optional linked-clone persistent disks.

Preface

Chapter 10, *Creating a Master Virtual Desktop Image*, covers the techniques that should be used when creating a master Horizon desktop image. Topics covered include the importance of optimizing the desktop OS; sample optimization results; examples of how to disable native application update features; and how to optimize the Windows filesystem, Windows OS, and Windows user profiles.

Chapter 11, *Implementing App Volumes*, covers the infrastructure prerequisites, deployment, configuration, and administration of VMware App Volumes. Topics include the deployment and configuration of the App Volumes Manager appliance, the installation and configuration of the App Volumes Agent and AppCapture program, the App Volumes AppStack creation, update, and assignment process, the Writable Volume assignment and creation process; and App Volumes backup and recovery procedures.

Chapter 12, *Implementing User Environment Manager*, covers the implementation and management of the VMware User Environment Manager profile management platform and provides an overview of the capabilities of some of the product's advanced features.

Chapter 13, *Implementing the Just-in-Time Management Platform (JMP)*, covers the implementation of the Horizon Just-in-Time Management Server, the VMware resources required, and how to create JMP Assignments that include access to Horizon desktops, App Volumes AppStacks, and user profile management using User Environment Manager.

Chapter 14, *Using Horizon PowerCLI*, covers the different PowerCLI commands that you can use to configure and administer nearly all aspects of the Horizon platform, and provides examples of how those commands are used.

Chapter 15, *Implementing Horizon Group Policies*, covers how to use the View Active Directory Group Policy templates to customize the different Horizon software components. Topics covered include a detailed description of each of the different Group Policy template settings, an explanation of where the settings should be applied within Active Directory, the location of the Group Policy template files, and the importance Group Policy loopback processing with View desktops.

Chapter 16, *Managing Horizon SSL Certificates*, covers how to replace the default SSL certificates on each of the Horizon components including Connection Server, Composer, Security Server, and Unified Access Gateway. This chapter also discusses how to create the SSL certificate requests and obtain new certificates using a Microsoft Active Directory Certificate Services server.

Preface

To get the most out of this book

You should have a basic understanding of the following concepts, which are integral to the implementation and management of View:

- Microsoft Windows Server
- Microsoft Active Directory:
    - Certificate services
    - DNS
    - Group policies
- VMware vSphere:
    - vCenter Server
    - Virtual machine snapshots
    - Virtual machine templates
    - VMware tools
    - vSphere administration
- Networking:
    - DHCP
    - Protocol and port types
    - Basics of LAN and WAN networking

The following software is required to implement the solutions described in this book:

- VMware Horizon installation media, including all optional components
- VMware App Volumes installation media, including all additional components
- VMware User Environment Manager installation media, including all additional components
- vSphere 6.7 Update 1 installation media, including vCenter Server and vSphere
- Windows Server 2012 R2 installation media
- Installation media for a supported Windows desktop OS

The installation media for the required VMware products can be obtained from the VMware.com website. If you do not have a current license for the products, you can register for a trail to obtain access to the software.

Conventions used

There are a number of text conventions used throughout this book.

`CodeInText`: Indicates code words in text, database table names, folder names, filenames, file extensions, pathnames, dummy URLs, user input, and Twitter handles. Here is an example: "Mount the downloaded `WebStorm-10*.dmg` disk image file as another disk in your system."

Any command-line input or output is written as follows:

```
sviconfig -operation=restoredata -dsnname=Composer_Pod1 -
username=composer -password=Password123 -
backupfilepath="C:\Temp\Backup-2018-1004180731-
horcomp01_vjason_local.SVI."
```

Bold: Indicates a new term, an important word, or words that you see onscreen. For example, words in menus or dialog boxes appear in the text like this. Here is an example: "Select **System info** from the **Administration** panel."

Warnings or important notes appear like this.

Tips and tricks appear like this.

Get in touch

Feedback from our readers is always welcome.

General feedback: If you have questions about any aspect of this book, mention the book title in the subject of your message and email us at `customercare@packtpub.com`.

Errata: Although we have taken every care to ensure the accuracy of our content, mistakes do happen. If you have found a mistake in this book, we would be grateful if you would report this to us. Please visit `www.packt.com/submit-errata`, selecting your book, clicking on the Errata Submission Form link, and entering the details.

Preface

Piracy: If you come across any illegal copies of our works in any form on the Internet, we would be grateful if you would provide us with the location address or website name. Please contact us at `copyright@packt.com` with a link to the material.

If you are interested in becoming an author: If there is a topic that you have expertise in and you are interested in either writing or contributing to a book, please visit `authors.packtpub.com`.

Reviews

Please leave a review. Once you have read and used this book, why not leave a review on the site that you purchased it from? Potential readers can then see and use your unbiased opinion to make purchase decisions, we at Packt can understand what you think about our products, and our authors can see your feedback on their book. Thank you!

For more information about Packt, please visit `packt.com`.

1
VMware Horizon Infrastructure Overview

This chapter will discuss a number of topics that play a critical role in our Horizon design. We will discuss the different components of a Horizon installation, examine the different license levels, and outline the core requirements of a Horizon infrastructure. We will also consider how to measure the resource requirements of a desktop, and how those requirements impact all layers of our infrastructure, including the storage design, network design, and the configuration of our virtual desktop VMware vSphere hosts.

By the end of this chapter, we will have learned about the following:

- The individual components of a VMware Horizon installation
- The role of different components of VMware Horizon
- VMware Horizon license options
- Core infrastructure requirements for VMware Horizon
- An overview of several key VMware Horizon design and pilot project considerations

> Throughout this book, you may see references to components or features of VMware Horizon View made without the word View being included in the name. While this book focuses heavily on components of VMware Horizon View itself, it does include other components that are now part of the larger product that is known as VMware Horizon. So, while these names may be slightly different to the ones that you are used to seeing, be aware that my goal is to match the terms VMware wants us to use for their products, and not necessarily those that we are most familiar with (or that VMware themselves always uses for that matter).

VMware Horizon Infrastructure Overview

VMware Horizon components

VMware Horizon is a family of desktop and application virtualization solutions designed to deliver end user computing services, from both on-premises data centers and from cloud providers such as **Amazon Web Services (AWS)**. The following section will provide a high-level overview of the components in the Horizon family of products that we will cover in this book, which includes the following:

- VMware Horizon Connection Server, Security Server, and Unified Access Gateway
- VMware Horizon Help Desk Tool
- VMware Horizon **Just-in-Time Management Platform (JMP)**
- VMware Horizon Composer
- VMware Horizon Agent
- VMware Horizon Client
- VMware vSphere, including vCenter Server
- VMware App Volumes
- VMware User Environment Manager
- VMware Horizon PowerCLI

 Refer to the VMware Horizon product page for a list of all of the products that are part of the Horizon family (https://www.vmware.com/products/horizon.html).

The following diagram shows where each component of a typical Horizon installation resides within the data center. The only components that are not shown but are discussed in this book are the VMware App Volumes servers and the Windows-based files servers used for hosting VMware User Environment Manager data. If they were to be shown, both of these components would be located on the internal network, along with the Horizon Connection Server, vCenter Server, virtual desktops, and Microsoft Windows **Remote Desktop Session (RDS)** servers.

[10]

Chapter 1

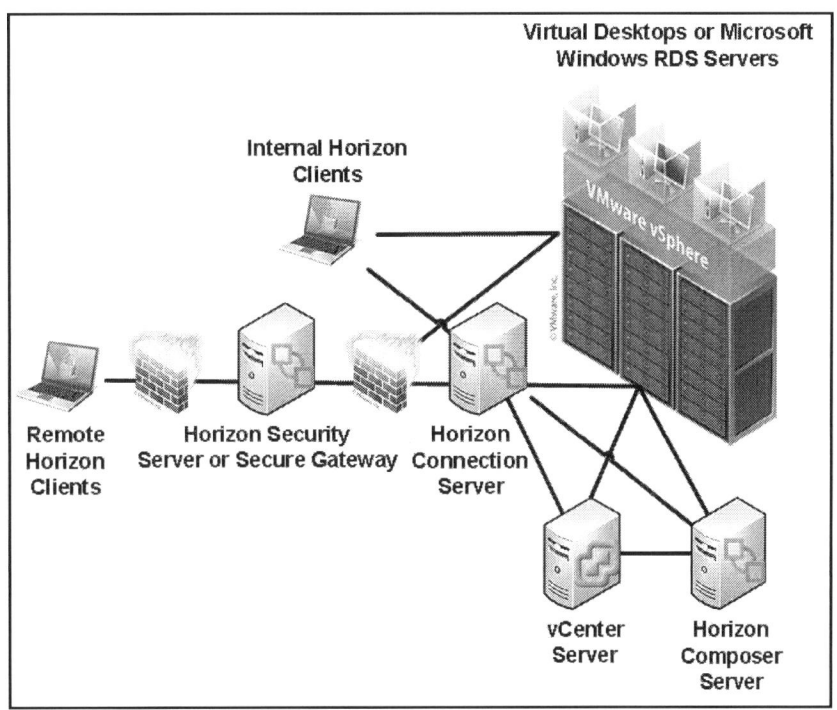

While this book focuses on deploying an on-premises installation of VMware Horizon and other components, VMware has partnered with **Amazon Web Services** (**AWS**) to make it possible to do so in the cloud as well. Consult the VMware document **Deploying Horizon 7 on VMware Cloud on AWS** (`https://www.vmware.com/content/dam/digitalmarketing/vmware/en/pdf/products/vmw-deploy-horizon-seven-on-vmware-cloud-on-aws.pdf`) for examples of how to deploy a vSphere-based **Software Defined Datacenter** (**SDDC**) on AWS, which you would use to host your Horizon infrastructure. Note that VMware does not intend for this to be your only Horizon Pod, but rather one used to expand your existing Horizon infrastructure, meet disaster recovery or business continuity requirements, or for data locality purposes (place applications closer to the resources they rely on). Since you are leveraging vSphere within AWS, the Horizon deployment process is no different.

Horizon Connection Server

VMware Horizon Connection Server is a software service that performs as the broker for Horizon client connections. In this role, it authenticates user connection requests, verifies the desktops or Microsoft Windows **RDS Servers** that the user is entitled to access, and then directs the connection to the appropriate resource. Horizon Connection Server is installed on a dedicated server that is required to be a member of an **Active Directory** (**AD**) domain that is trusted by all Horizon clients. Horizon Connection Server also hosts the Horizon Administrator console, an Adobe Flex-based web application that is used to manage the Horizon environment and perform tasks including the following:

- Deploying virtual desktops
- Creating desktop or Microsoft Windows RDS-based pools
- Controlling access to desktop pools
- Creating and managing Horizon Cloud Pods
- Examining Horizon system events

The Horizon Connection Server is one component that is required in every Horizon environment. `Chapter 2`, *Implementing Horizon Connection Server*, provides the information needed to install and configure a VMware Horizon Connection Server. `Chapter 6`, *Implementing a Horizon Cloud Pod*, provides information regarding the configuration of the Cloud Pod feature that is used to provide Horizon clients with access to desktops across multiple Horizon Pods, with each Pod representing a standalone installation of VMware Horizon. The following chapters provide information about the deployment of Horizon desktops and the management of desktop pools:

- `Chapter 7`, *Creating Horizon Desktop Pools*
- `Chapter 8`, *Implementing Microsoft Remote Desktop Services Application and Desktop Pools*
- `Chapter 9`, *Performing Horizon Pool Maintenance*

Horizon Security Server

VMware Horizon Security Server is a custom instance of the Horizon Connection Server that is designed to be installed in a datacenter **Demilitarized Zone** (**DMZ**), in order to provide strong levels of authentication and secure access for Horizon clients connecting from outside the organization's private network. Multiple Security Servers may be installed to provide load balancing and high availability to these external clients.

The following diagram shows the placement of a Horizon Security Server or **Unified Access Gateway** (discussed next) within a DMZ:

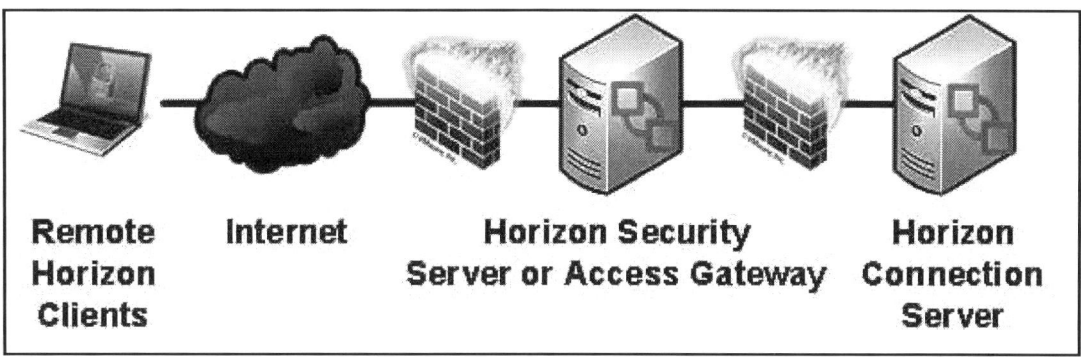

Horizon Security Server is installed on top of a supported version of Microsoft Windows' Server using the same installation package used for Horizon Connection Servers. Horizon Security Server is only required if providing access to Horizon clients residing outside of the company network. `Chapter 4`, *Implementing Horizon Security Server*, provides the information needed to install and configure a VMware Horizon Security Server.

Horizon Unified Access Gateway

VMware Horizon Unified Access Gateway, previously known as Horizon Access Point and first introduced in **VMware Horizon 6.2**, is designed to provide strong authentication, and secure access, for Horizon clients connecting from outside the organization's private network. The diagram in the previous section shows the placement of a Horizon Unified Access Gateway within a DMZ environment, as is typical since it performs similar functions to Horizon Security Server.

Unified Access Gateway is packaged in **Open Virtualization Format (OVF)** and is deployed on vSphere as a hardened, pre-configured Linux-based virtual appliance. Horizon Unified Access Gateway is provided as an option to Horizon Security Server and, like Security Server, it is only required if providing access for external clients. it is designed to be installed in a *DMZ*, and multiple appliances may be installed to ensure high availability and load balancing. `Chapter 5`, *Implementing Horizon Unified Access Gateway*, provides the information needed to install and configure a VMware Horizon Unified Access Gateway.

VMware Horizon Infrastructure Overview

VMware recommends that customers using Security Server today may continue to do so, but they have also indicated that Unified Access Gateway is their primary focus moving forward. New deployments may wish to future-proof their Horizon installation by selecting Unified Access Gateway, as VMware has indicated that Security Server will be deprecated or possibly even phased out in a future Horizon release. Additionally, Unified Access Gateway supports all of the latest Blast Extreme client protocol features, can be deployed (or redeployed) very quickly and with minimal effort, requires fewer ports to be opened between the DMZ and the internal network, and does not require tunneling or secure gateway to be configured on the internal Connection Servers.

Horizon Enrollment Server

The **VMware Horizon Enrollment Server** was first introduced in version 7, is installed as a standalone service, and integrates with the **VMware Workspace ONE Identity Manager** to enable true **Single Sign-On (SSO)** for Horizon clients that are using non-AD-based authentication methods such as **RSA SecureID**. SSO means that, when using non-AD-based authentication methods, users will only need to log into Horizon once to reach their desktop or streamed application. The VMware blog post **Introducing True SSO (Single Sign-On) in VMware Horizon 7** (http://blogs.vmware.com/euc/2016/03/true-sso-single-sign-on-view-identity-manager-authenticate.html) provides an overview of this new Horizon feature.

This feature is only used when Horizon clients use non-AD-based methods for authentication. Implementing solutions, such as SecureID and the VMware Workspace ONE Identity Manager, is outside of our scope. Therefore, the Enrollment Server will not be covered here, so consult the Horizon documentation (https://docs.vmware.com/en/VMware-Horizon-7/index.html) for additional information about the deployment and configuration of the Horizon Enrollment Server.

VMware vSphere

VMware vSphere, also referred to as ESXi or even ESX for earlier versions, is a Type 1 hypervisor that is the virtualization platform used for the vSphere suite of products. Type 1 hypervisors are designed to run directly on the host hardware, whereas Type 2 hypervisors run within a conventional OS environment.

Chapter 1

ESXi is the only hypervisor that is fully supported by VMware for hosting Horizon virtual desktops, as it fully integrates with Horizon for full desktop life cycle management. All of the primary desktop provisioning and maintenance tasks are performed using the Horizon Administrator console; the vSphere Client is not used. Horizon supports multiple versions of vSphere, but **vSphere 6.0 Update 1** and newer are required to leverage many of the latest features of the platform. **vSphere 6.0 Update 2** or newer is required to use the latest version of **Virtual SAN (vSAN)**. Refer to the *VMware vCenter Server* requirements section for examples of some Horizon features that require a specific version of both vSphere and vCenter Server.

VMware vSphere also includes the **vSAN** feature that uses local ESXi server storage to build a highly resilient virtual **Storage Area Network (SAN)** to provide storage for virtual machines. The deployment and configuration of vSAN are outside of our scope, so consult the Horizon documentation (`https://docs.vmware.com/en/VMware-Horizon-7/index.html`) if you require information about using vSAN with Horizon.

VMware vCenter Server

VMware vCenter Server is a software service that provides a central administration point for VMware ESXi servers, as well as other components of the vSphere suite. vCenter Server performs the actual creation and management of virtual desktops, based on instructions received from the Horizon Connection Server and the Horizon Composer Server.

This book includes some information that applies only to the Windows-based version of VMware vCenter, but rest assured that it possible to use the Linux-based **vCenter Server Appliance (vCSA)** for your VMware Horizon deployment if needed, which is the only vCenter Server version provided with vSphere 6.5 and later. The *vCSA* supports up to 10,000 desktops, which is more than enough for most Horizon implementations and represents the maximum recommended number of active sessions per Horizon Pod (a Pod can support up to 20,000 desktops, but VMware recommends no more than half that number). The most significant difference you will encounter (aside from the fact that you will not need to create a separate database for vCenter) is that when you use the *vCSA*, you will be required to deploy a standalone Horizon Composer server. This will be demonstrated in `Chapter 3`, *Implementing Horizon Composer*.

[15]

VMware Horizon Infrastructure Overview

Horizon Composer

VMware Horizon Composer is a software service that works alongside the VMware vCenter and Horizon Connection Servers to deploy and manage linked clone desktops. Horizon Composer can be installed directly on the vCenter Server, or on a dedicated server.

Horizon Composer is only required if linked clone desktops will be deployed. `Chapter 3`, *Implementing Horizon Composer*, provides the information required to install and configure Horizon Composer.

Horizon Composer is not required when using Instant Clone desktops; it is only required if you are using linked clone desktops. The operation methods of Linked Clone and Instant Clone desktops are similar once they have been deployed, but the deployment process of these two desktops itself is quite different.

Horizon Agent

VMware Horizon Agent is a software service that is installed on the systems that will be managed by Horizon. This includes not only a virtual desktop image that will be deployed using Horizon, but also any physical desktops or Microsoft RDS Servers.

The Horizon agent provides services including, but not limited to, support for connecting the virtual desktop to Horizon's client-attached USB devices, client connection monitoring, virtual printing, and single sign-on.

Horizon Client

VMware Horizon Client is a software application that is used to communicate with a Horizon Connection Server, and initiate connections to desktops and Microsoft Windows RDS servers.

The Horizon Client is available for multiple software platforms, including **Microsoft Windows**, **Apple OSX and IOS**, **Android**, and **Linux**. In addition, there are a number of Thin and Zero clients that come preloaded with Horizon-compatible clients.

VMware App Volumes

VMware App Volumes is an optional component of VMware Horizon that provides multiple capabilities, particularly in environments where floating assignment desktops are used, or changes to a virtual desktop are discarded after every session (also known as **non-persistent desktops**). The deployment and configuration of VMware App Volumes are discussed in detail in Chapter 11, *Implementing App Volumes*.

The primary features of VMware App Volumes include the following:

- The ability for applications to be delivered to Horizon desktops or Microsoft Windows RDS servers, immediately and dynamically, in a manner that is transparent to the end user. This feature works both with Horizon desktops and Microsoft Windows **RDS servers**, and is called an **App Volumes AppStack**.
- The ability to roam user-installed applications across Horizon client sessions, even if a different desktop virtual machine is assigned during the next login. This feature is designed for use with Horizon desktops only, and is called **Writable Volumes**.

The following diagram shows the logical layering of multiple **AppStack** and a **Writeable Volume** on top of the host OS. Each of the items is attached to the host virtual machine individually when a user logs in, can be removed individually if changes are required, and will follow a user from one login to the next:

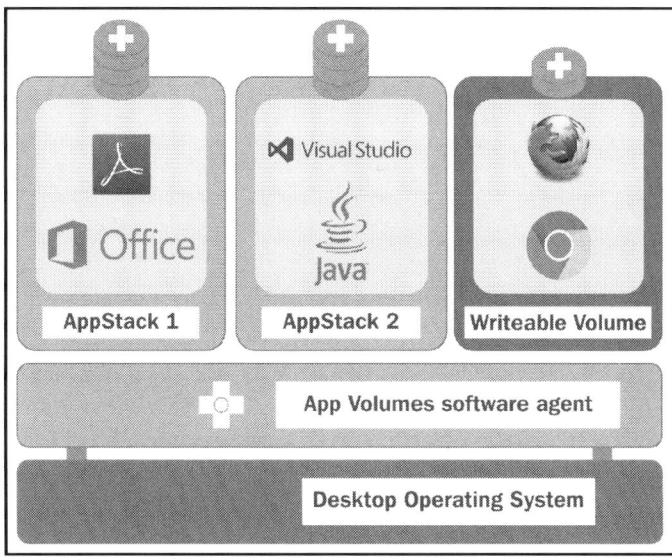

[17]

App Volumes AppStacks are packaged as a **Virtual Machine Disk (VMDK)** file and attached to one or more virtual machines as needed. The App Volumes agent seamlessly integrates this VMDK into the virtual machine's OS so no actual installation is performed. AppVolumes can even capture an application packaged using VMware **ThinApp**, which provides organizations who rely on ThinApp with an additional method for distributing its virtualized application packages.

App Volumes creates a unique Writeable Volume for each user, using a VMDK that is also seamlessly integrated into their current virtual machine. The Writable Volumes is attached to the Horizon desktop when the user logs in, and detached when the user logs off.

The combination of VMware App Volumes and VMware User Environment Manager (discussed next), provides organizations with a way to leverage the efficiencies of floating assignment non-persistent desktops (described in `Chapter 7`, *Creating Horizon Desktop Pools*), while still providing users with a highly personalized desktop experience.

VMware User Environment Manager

VMware **User Environment Manager (UEM)** is an optional component of VMware Horizon that provides the ability to roam end user Windows profile and persona configuration data, including application settings, across different Windows **Operating System (OS)** versions, or even between physical desktops and virtual desktops or Windows **RDS Servers**.

VMware UEM works with all three Microsoft Windows profile types, including mandatory, roaming, or local. UEM is not a replacement for any of these profile types as it does not roam user data across sessions or devices, only across the profile and persona configuration. User data should be saved using techniques such as roaming profiles, or even folder redirection.

Highlights of the benefits of UEM include the following:

- A consistent and personalized end user experience, regardless of where a user logs in or which Windows OS they are using
- Implementation of various settings that previously required AD **group policies**, such as Windows user profile redirection, and some Horizon agent settings
- Customization of user settings, such as printers, based on logon location
- Elimination of the need to perform user profile migrations when moving to a newer version of Windows that has a new profile type (such as from Windows 8.1 to Windows 10)
- Robust design that scales to support over a hundred thousand end users

- Simple design that requires no scripting knowledge, can be implemented rapidly, and requires minimal infrastructure to begin using

Chapter 12, *Implementing User Environment Manager*, provides information regarding the implementation and administration of UEM.

VMware ThinApp

VMware ThinApp is an application virtualization platform that integrates with Horizon to provide users with rapid access to new or upgraded applications without having to perform any changes to the virtual desktops. Applications that have been packaged with ThinApp are delivered as a single executable file that runs in complete isolation to both of the other ThinApp packaged applications, as well as applications that are installed on the desktop itself.

ThinApp provides Horizon customers with a number of powerful capabilities. Two popular scenarios where ThinApp can benefit an organization are as follows:

- It eliminates application conflicts that can occur when specific programs are installed together within the desktop image
- It virtualizes legacy applications to ensure that they will continue to function regardless of the underlying Windows OS

This book does not have a dedicated chapter concerning VMware ThinApp, so consult the VMware ThinApp documentation page for more details about how it is used (https://www.vmware.com/support/pubs/thinapp_pubs.html).

> In Chapter 11, *Implementing App Volumes*, an overview of how you can use ThinApp virtualization within an AppStack will be provided.

VMware Horizon licensing

VMware Horizon offers four different license levels: **Standard**, **Linux**, **Advanced**, and **Enterprise**. Additionally, the Advanced and Enterprise licenses may be purchased as **Named User (NU)** or **Concurrent Connection User (CCU)** as needed. Named user licenses are recommended when your staff needs dedicated access to Horizon; concurrent connection user licenses are recommended when access to Horizon will be shared among many users, but only a portion of them will be connected at any one time.

The license levels are differentiated by several factors, as outlined in the following section. The licenses themselves are sold in packs of 10 or 100:

- All VMware Horizon license levels include VMware Horizon, vCenter, and vSphere Desktop Edition:
    - **vSphere Desktop Edition** is similar to vSphere Enterprise Plus in terms of functionality, but allows an unlimited number of CPU sockets for the desktop ESXi servers.
- **VMware ThinApp** is included with all versions, except the Linux edition
- Standard and Linux offer similar features, the only difference is the desktop OS that they are licensed for:
    - Horizon Enterprise edition supports both Windows and Linux desktop OSes under the same license
- Advanced and Enterprise includes licenses for Fusion Pro, Workspace ONE Identity Manager, application publishing using Windows RDSH servers, **VMware Virtual SAN Advanced**, and **Virtualization pack for Skype for Business**.
- Enterprise includes licenses for Horizon Instant Clones, **Horizon Help Desk Tool**, **VMware App Volumes Enterprise**, User Environment Manager, vRealize Operations for Horizon, and the vRealize Orchestrator Plugin for **VMware Horizon**.

Visit the VMware Horizon website (https://www.vmware.com/products/horizon.html) for the most recent information concerning licensing options and their costs.

> It is important to note that many of the components, particularly those included with either the Advanced or Enterprise licenses, can be licensed separately. When determining which licenses to buy, it may be that you don't need all of the features, for all of your users, and that buying a smaller standalone license for those users makes sense from a cost perspective. Consult with VMware or your VMware system integrator to determine the optimal licensing strategy for your organization.

When listing the different components included with each VMware Horizon license level, you may have noticed that not all of them will be discussed in this book. The primary focus of this book is on VMware Horizon View itself, and those components of VMware Horizon that are most commonly used to extend its capabilities and potential use cases. For more information regarding those components, consult the following VMware resources:

- VMware Fusion (https://www.vmware.com/products/fusion.html)
- VMware Horizon Cloud (https://www.vmware.com/products/horizon-cloud-virtual-desktops.html)
- VMware Workspace ONE Identity Manager (https://www.vmware.com/products/workspace-one/identity-manager.html)
- VMware ThinApp (https://www.vmware.com/products/thinapp.html)
- VMware vRealize Orchestrator Plugin for VMware Horizon (https://docs.vmware.com/en/VMware-Horizon-7/7.6/using-horizon-vro-plugin/GUID-90269DBE-7760-4FF7-9F7D-E42F19A2270C.html)
- VMware vRealize Operations for Horizon (https://www.vmware.com/products/vrealize-operations-horizon.html)

VMware Horizon core infrastructure requirements

There are a number of requirements to contemplate even before the infrastructure needs of the virtual desktops themselves are considered. These include, but are not limited to, the following:

- OS requirements for both vSphere and Horizon components
- Database requirements for vCenter Server, Horizon Composer, and Horizon Connection Server
- Required Microsoft infrastructure services and components

> The online VMware Compatibility Guide (https://www.vmware.com/resources/compatibility/search.php) and Product Interoperability Matrices (https://www.vmware.com/resources/compatibility/sim/interop_matrix.php) maintain an up-to-date listing of supported OSes, hardware platforms, and product compatibility for all VMware products.

Microsoft infrastructure requirements

VMware Horizon requires Microsoft AD to support the virtual desktop infrastructure. VMware Horizon supports all AD domain functional levels, starting with Windows 2003 up to Windows 2016.

VMware Horizon Infrastructure Overview

Horizon also requires **Domain Name System (DNS)** servers that can resolve requests for the standard **Service Record (SRV)** and **Resource Record (RR)** DNS entries. Incomplete or inaccurate DNS entries can lead to issues with tasks, such as virtual desktop deployment and user authentication.

Dynamic Host Configuration Protocol (DHCP) servers are required in the Horizon environment to provide **Internet Protocol (IP)** addresses to the virtual desktops. In situations where the virtual desktops cannot self-register the IP addresses that they have been assigned, the DHCP server should be configured to register the entries with a DNS server that is accessible by the Horizon Connection Server.

OS requirements

The following table shows which 64-bit non-Core Microsoft Windows Server OSes are supported for the each of the different software packages that comprise a Horizon infrastructure. App Volumes host OS requirements will be outlined separately in `Chapter 11`, *Implementing App Volumes*:

Operating System	vCenter Server 6.0 U1 (Windows-based)	Horizon Connection Server, Security Server, and Composer
Windows Server 2008 SP2	Supported	Not supported
Windows 2008 R2 (No SP)	Supported	Not supported
Windows Server 2008 R2 SP1	Supported	Supported
Windows Server 2012	Supported	Not supported
Windows Server 2012 R2	Supported	Supported
Windows Server 2016	Not Supported	Supported

While VMware vCenter and the different Horizon servers support a number of different Windows OSes, use of the newest supported version is recommended to ensure that the servers will not be impacted by any changes in OS support by Microsoft. Additionally, you never know when vSphere or Horizon itself will end support for older OSes, which would impact your ability to perform in-place upgrades.

As Horizon Composer supports only Windows Server 2008 R2 SP1, 2012 R2, and 2016, any Horizon installation that plans on deploying linked-clone desktops and installing Composer directly on the vCenter Server will need to choose that specific version of Windows. Refer to the VMware document **Horizon 7 Installation** (`https://docs.vmware.com/en/VMware-Horizon-7/index.html`) for updated information regarding which Windows OSes are supported.

Database requirements

The following list shows which database types are supported for the core components of a Horizon infrastructure, which includes the Horizon Connection Server and Horizon Composer. Unless otherwise noted, both 32-bit and 64-bit versions of the specified database platform are supported. Database platforms that support some, but not all, of the components will not be listed. App Volumes database requirements will be outlined separately in `Chapter 11`, *Implementing App Volumes*. The databases are as follows:

- Microsoft SQL Server 2017 (Standard and Enterprise; 64-bit is the only version available)
- Microsoft SQL Server 2016 (Standard and Enterprise; through SP1 and 64-bit only)
- Microsoft SQL Server 2014 (Standard and Enterprise; SP1)
- Microsoft SQL Server 2012 (Express, Standard, and Enterprise; 64-bit and SP3 only)
- Microsoft SQL Server 2008 R2 (Express, Standard, and 64-bit Enterprise; SP3)
- Oracle 12C Standard Edition, Release 2 (12.2.0.1.0) - 64-bit

For VMware Horizon, visit the product installation guide (`https://docs.vmware.com/en/VMware-Horizon-7/index.html`) for updated information regarding which databases are supported.

vCenter Server requirements

VMware Horizon supports multiple versions of vSphere. The purchase of Horizon licenses entitles users to use the latest supported version of both vSphere and vCenter Servers, although support is maintained for some older versions due to restrictions that some organizations may be under.

The following versions of vSphere are supported by VMware Horizon:

- vSphere 6.7.0
- vSphere 6.5.0, 6.5 U1, or 6.5 U2
- vSphere 6.0 (Update 1 or newer is required to support the latest Horizon features; Update 2 or newer is required to support VSAN 6.2)
- vSphere 5.5 (Update 3b or newer recommended; SSLv3 must be re-enabled as described in VMware KB article **2139396**) (`https://kb.vmware.com/s/article/2139396`)

Consult the VMware Product Interoperability Matrices for an updated list of the supported versions of vSphere and vCenter Servers. Supporting earlier versions of vSphere and vCenter Servers is important for customers who are already running earlier versions of either software platform, and cannot, or will not, upgrade for some reason. Even with this support, the use of dedicated ESXi servers and vCenter Servers for your Horizon environment is recommended to ensure that all the latest Horizon features are supported.

There are multiple Horizon features that are supported only if certain other prerequisites are met. Examples of these vSphere version-dependent features include the following:

- vSphere 6 is required to use VMware vSAN, or Windows 10 as a desktop OS
- Prior to vSphere 6, the vCenter Server Appliance could not support the maximum number of desktops that can be deployed in a single Horizon Pod
- Some virtual desktop graphics acceleration technologies, such as NVDIA GRID Tesla processor-based server cards (`https://www.nvidia.com/en-us/design-visualization/technologies/virtual-gpu/`), require vSphere 6 or newer.

A complete list of Horizon features that require specific versions of vSphere or vCenter Server may be found in VMware document **Horizon 7 Installation** (`https://docs.vmware.com/en/VMware-Horizon-7/index.html`) or the Horizon 7 Release Notes (`https://docs.vmware.com/en/VMware-Horizon-7/7.6/rn/horizon-76-view-release-notes.html`) that accompany each release of the Horizon platform.

Horizon Agent-supported OS

The VMware Horizon Agent supports multiple versions of the Microsoft Windows desktop OS and Microsoft Windows (RDS) Server. The following table outlines which Windows OSes are currently supported.

Windows OS Version	Product Edition	Service Pack	Notes
Windows 10 (32-bit or 64-bit)	Support varies based on build	None	Consult VMware KB **2149393** (link below)
Windows 8.1 (32-bit or 64-bit)	Enterprise or Professional	Latest update	Instant Clones not supported
Windows 7 (32-bit or 64-bit)	Enterprise or Professional	SP1	Full support
Windows 2016 (64-bit)	Standard or Datacenter	Latest update	Full support
Windows 2012 R2 (64-bit)	Standard or Datacenter	Latest update	Full support (RDS host or desktop)
Windows 2012 (64-bit)	Datacenter	None	As RDS host only
Windows 2008 R2 (64-bit)	Datacenter	SP1	Full support (RDS host or desktop)

To obtain current information about which desktop OSes and Microsoft RDS server versions are supported, please refer to VMware KB articles **2149393** (https://kb.vmware.com/s/article/2149393), **2150305** (https://kb.vmware.com/s/article/2150305), and **2150295** (https://kb.vmware.com/s/article/2150295).

VMware Horizon design overview

The primary focus of this book is to show you how to deploy and configure VMware Horizon. Ultimately, the deployment is only one part of a successful Horizon implementation. Determining the infrastructure requirements of your virtual desktops is critical to ensuring that all your hard work implementing Horizon won't ultimately be a disappointment because you failed to consider what your desktops actually need.

Some organizations that are virtualizing older desktops that lack flash drives, may feel that meeting their users' needs will be easy because expectations are low from the start. Of course, some organizations tend to forget that their users are probably using flash-based devices at home. This means that even with a poor computing experience at work, these users will have some expectation of what it is like when they get a *new computer*, which is what their new Horizon desktop will appear to be. So, even if your Horizon infrastructure is capable of providing performance that is similar to the computers that users have today, that does not mean it will provide an experience that the users will find acceptable.

The goal of this section is to provide some information that you need to consider before you buy your Horizon licenses. Buying those licenses is the easy part, assembling the infrastructure they will be built on, is not. Unfortunately, it isn't possible to put into words everything you need to know in order to build an infrastructure that guarantees a good performance for your users. Therefore, I have suggested a detailed analysis of the network and storage infrastructure that you intend to use with your Horizon infrastructure. This analysis, combined with an understanding of the resources your Horizon infrastructure will require, is integral to delivering a superior end user experience.

Measuring virtual desktop resource requirements

One of the most important aspects of any Horizon design is ensuring that an infrastructure has adequate compute, storage, and network resources to host the required number of virtual desktops. Were it not for troublesome things such as budgets, we could simply purchase an excess of all three of those resources and rest easy at night. In general, our goal is to build an infrastructure that is robust enough to support our average user workload, with some capacity in reserve for growth or maintenance purposes.

Determining the resource requirements of a Horizon environment is a complicated task, and one that could fill a book by itself. While it is possible to collect desktop performance data using free tools such as Windows Performance Monitor, gathering all of the data you need would be difficult, and interpreting it is even harder.

The goal in this section is to introduce you to some tools that were created specifically to help with designing and testing virtual desktop infrastructures so that you understand exactly what is required to ensure a successful implementation.

The following products can assist in determining your resource requirements and ensuring that your vSphere infrastructure has sufficient capacity and the performance capabilities needed to ensure the desktops perform as expected. These are as follows:

- **Lakeside Software SysTrack** (https://www.lakesidesoftware.com/solutions/desktop-transformation) performs an extensive analysis of your existing desktop workloads, including characterizing those that would be difficult to virtualize, and helps determine infrastructure needs and optimal placement.
- **Liquidware Labs Stratusphere UX** (http://www.liquidware.com/products/stratusphere-UX) can assist you in determining virtual desktop resource needs and performs tasks similar to *Lakeside Software SysTrack*.
- **Login VSI** (http://www.loginvsi.com/) has created tools that can be used to test the performance of your Horizon infrastructure. Login VSI is used to run a simulated user workload in as many desktops as you want to test the performance of all layers of your virtual desktop infrastructure.

It is important to note that these software packages are typically used as part of a virtual desktop assessment project led by an outside system integrator. If your user base has varying requirements, products such as SysTrack and Statusphere UX may be the only way to find out exactly what infrastructure resources you need to ensure a successful VMware Horizon deployment.

The need for vSphere reserve capacity

In the event that you choose to determine your own vSphere infrastructure requirements, it is very important to keep in mind the concept of vSphere reserve capacity. I realize that you may choose to do maintenance after hours, so reserve capacity may not be a priority, but what about unplanned downtime, or periods where you can't do maintenance after hours? Many users simply cannot work if they do not have access to their computer, and now that you have virtualized that computer, it is your job to ensure it is available whenever it is needed.

Maintaining reserve ESXi server capacity is critical to ensuring that we can accommodate all of our desktops in the event of an ESXi server failure or host maintenance operation. Consider a vSphere cluster with eight ESXi servers hosting 128 desktops each (1,024 total desktops):

- Desktop requirements:

  > **TIP**
  > Desktop requirements will vary from one environment to the next; these figures are just an example.

    - Each single vCPU desktop requires 10 percent of one ESXi server CPU core
    - Each desktop requires 2,048 MB of memory
- Eight ESXi servers, each running 12.5 percent of the total number of virtual desktops:
    - *1,024 desktops / 8 ESXi servers = 128 desktops per host*
- To continue to run all of the desktops in the event one of the ESXi servers was to become unavailable; we would need to be able to accommodate 18.29 desktops on each of the remaining seven hosts:
    - *128 desktops / 7 remaining vSphere hosts = 18.29 desktops per each ESXi server*
- To continue to run all desktops without any degradation in the quality of service; each server needs to have an excess of capacity that is sufficient to host 18 to 19 desktops. This is entails the following:
    - *19 desktops * 10% of a CPU core = 1.9 available CPU cores required*
    - *19 desktops * 2,048 MB of memory = 38,912 MB or 38 GB of available memory required*
    - *19 desktops * 121.21 MB of memory for virtual machine overhead = 2,303 MB or 2.3 GB of additional available memory required*
    - *19 desktops * 0.75 MB network bandwidth = 14.25 MB of available network bandwidth required*
    - *19 desktops * 0.23 MB storage network bandwidth = 4.37 MB of available storage network bandwidth required*

VMware Horizon Infrastructure Overview

These calculations assume that we want to protect the ability to provide resources for 100 percent of our desktops at all times, which is a very conservative, yet valid, approach to building a Horizon infrastructure.

The final configuration of the ESXi servers should take into account not only what percentage of desktops are actually in use at a given time, but also the cost of purchasing the additional capacity needed to support ESXi server failures or other events that require downtime.

> **TIP**
> Always take into consideration the growth of your Horizon environment. Purchasing equipment that has limited ability to scale may save money today, but could cost you dearly when you need to expand. If a piece of equipment you plan to buy for your Horizon infrastructure barely meets your needs, look into the next larger model or even a competing product, if necessary.

Providing sufficient Horizon Client bandwidth

In the era of affordable 10 **Gigabit Ethernet (GbE)** for servers and 1 GbE for desktops, I realize that bandwidth within a single site is typically not a concern. The following information is something to keep in mind for clients who are connecting to their Horizon desktop remotely, either from over the internet or over a WAN from another company site. Ensuring that sufficient bandwidth is available is just another part of making sure your Horizon clients have an acceptable experience when connecting to the Horizon infrastructure.

The VMware document **Horizon 7 Architecture Planning** (https://docs.vmware.com/en/VMware-Horizon-7/index.html) provides some information about how to determine Horizon Client bandwidth requirements. The following table is built upon information obtained from that document as well as other VMware documentation:

User type	Workload characteristics	Bandwidth in Kilobits per second (Kbps)
Basic office productivity desktop	2D display, typical office applications, no video, default Windows and Horizon 7 settings	100-150 Kbps
Optimized basic office productivity desktop	2D display, typical office applications, no video, optimized Windows and Horizon 7 settings	50-100 Kbps
Knowledge Worker (3D)	3D display (Windows Aero), multiple monitors, and office applications	400-600 Kbps

Knowledge Worker (3D) - High Change Rate	3D display (Windows Aero), multiple monitors, office applications, and frequent screen changes caused by basic video or similar	500 Kbps - 1 Megabits per second (Mbps)
Power User	3D display (Windows Aero), multiple monitors, 480P video, and frequent screen changes	2 Mbps

Bandwidth utilization is heavily dependent on a number of factors, many of which can be controlled with the Horizon PCoIP and Blast GPO settings. Additionally, Windows OS settings, such as display resolution and quality, can also affect bandwidth utilization. Actual bandwidth utilization will vary based on the client usage pattern, the protocol being used, and your GPO settings.

> **TIP**
> Refer to the VMware document **Setting Up Application Pools in View** (`https://docs.vmware.com/en/VMware-Horizon-7/index.html`) for information about the AD group policy templates included with VMware Horizon. The PCoIP protocol was invented by a company called Teradici. For additional information about how the protocol works, visit the Teradici PCoIP technology page (`http://www.teradici.com/what-is-pcoip`).

Even with a careful analysis of user desktop usage patterns, it is important to remember that there will be spikes in usage from time to time. A Knowledge Worker or Task Worker who has a need to use an application with a large number of screen changes, such as viewing images in succession or watching a video, may cause a brief bandwidth spike of between 500 Kbps and 1 Mbps or more. Preparing for these spikes in bandwidth utilization is important in order to preserve the quality of service for all of the Horizon Client connections.

Refer to `Chapter 10`, *Creating a Master Horizon Desktop Image*, for information regarding optimal settings for a Windows desktop, an important topic for those new to virtualizing desktops.

The importance of a VMware Horizon pilot

Up until now, this chapter has been about introducing us to a variety of different concepts that form the basis of architecting our Horizon infrastructure. If we learn anything from this chapter, it is that our goal is to obtain the resources we need to provide an acceptable end user computing experience.

VMware Horizon Infrastructure Overview

Classifying our end users and measuring their resource requirements is a valuable exercise that will help us understand what will be required to transition our end user computing resources from the desktop to the data center. That being said, no amount of planning can possibly replace a properly run pilot that validates not only the configuration of our master Virtual Desktop image, but also the performance of the Horizon infrastructure and the quality of the experience from an end user perspective.

Our Horizon pilot should involve the same types of users as our user analysis did, but not necessarily the same users within each group. The following list includes a number of goals that our Horizon pilot should attempt to achieve:

- Include multiple users from each user classification: Task Worker, Knowledge Worker, and Power User
- Include fully remote users, as well as WAN-connected users at other company sites
- Perform additional performance analysis at all layers of the Horizon infrastructure, including:
    - Storage
    - Network
    - ESXi server
    - Guest operating
- Measure the impact of common Horizon scenarios, such as:
    - User logon storms: Large numbers of users logging on within a short time frame
    - Steady-state user load: Measure Horizon infrastructure performance during a period of steady desktop usage by a significant number of users
    - Antivirus platform performance: Measure the impact of common antivirus platform tasks, such as on-demand scans and pattern file updates
    - Horizon refresh or recompose: Measure the impact of these common Horizon linked-clone desktop maintenance operations, described in detail in `Chapter 9`, *Performing Horizon Desktop Pool Maintenance*
    - A fully populated ESXi server: Measure host performance with higher than normal workloads, such as simulating an outage or another period of higher than usual utilization.

Performance is the key

Performance deficiencies at any layer of the Horizon infrastructure can lead to a poor end user experience, usually in the form of longer than anticipated application response times. This is why it is critical to involve a large cross-section of our users in the pilot process, and to seek their opinion throughout the program.

The performance data that we collect during the pilot program can be used to measure the average of the actual resource utilization, which can then be compared to the estimated average resource utilization from the initial physical desktop analysis. Ideally, the numbers would be rather close to one another, but if they are not, we will want to work to identify the cause. Now that we can measure performance at all layers of the Horizon infrastructure, it should be easy to determine where the higher than expected utilization originates from. Some potential issues to look for include the following:

- The earlier analysis of the users did not include a sufficient number or a wide enough cross-section of users.
- The Virtual Desktop master image was not properly optimized. Refer to `Chapter 10`, *Creating a Master Horizon Desktop Image*, for details on how to optimize the master desktop image.
- A component of the Horizon infrastructure was improperly configured. This problem can affect any number of components of the infrastructure.
- The pilot program is occurring during a period of higher than normal user workload, for example, a recurring event unique to the organization, such as financial reporting.

In summary, the Horizon pilot is your best time to learn about how it will perform within your environment, both from a performance perspective and in terms of user acceptance. Use the pilot program to identify any potential barriers to a successful rollout, and make any changes that are needed in order to minimize the risk of failure as the project moves forward.

Summary

In this chapter, we have been introduced to the different components that comprise a VMware Horizon infrastructure, including the licensing and core infrastructure requirements. Later chapters will discuss how to install and configure each of these components.

We have also been introduced to the basics of what level of research is required even before the first virtual desktop is deployed, including assessing our existing physical desktops, determining bandwidth requirements for remote users, and adjusting our design to accommodate ESXi server maintenance or failure.

We concluded this chapter by learning the basics of running a Horizon pilot, which is critical as it will either validate or invalidate all of the research that we carried out in the early phases of our design.

In the next chapter, we will begin the installation of our VMware Horizon infrastructure, starting with the Horizon Connection Server.

Questions

1. Name the key functions of the Horizon Connection Server.
2. What tasks are a Horizon Composer Server responsible for?
3. What resource should you use to obtain the latest information regarding what OSes are supported for use as Horizon virtual desktops or as a Horizon Connection Server?
4. What are some reasons why you would deploy a Horizon Unified Access Gateway instead of a Horizon Security Server?
5. What versions of vSphere does the latest version of Horizon support?
6. What advantages does VMware User Environment Manager have over traditional roaming profiles?
7. What are some tools you could use to help assess your current end user computing resource requirements?
8. What is the difference between an Instant Clone and Linked Clone desktop?
9. What is the VMware recommended maximum number of desktops that you should deploy in a Horizon Pod?
10. What types of things typically impact the amount of bandwidth needed by Horizon clients?

Further reading

The following resources may be used to learn more about the topics described in this chapter:

- VMware documentation:
    - **VMware Horizon** (https://docs.vmware.com/en/VMware-Horizon-7/index.html)
    - **VMware Horizon Cloud** (https://docs.vmware.com/en/VMware-Horizon-Cloud-Service/index.html)
    - **VMware App Volumes** (https://docs.vmware.com/en/VMware-App-Volumes/index.html)
    - **VMware User Environment Manager** (https://www.vmware.com/support/pubs/uem-pubs.html)
    - **VMware Workspace ONE Identity Manager** (https://docs.vmware.com/en/VMware-Workspace-ONE/index.html)
    - **VMware vRealize Operations for Horizon** (https://www.vmware.com/support/pubs/vcops-view-pubs.html)
        - **VMware Fusion** (https://www.vmware.com/support/pubs/fusion_pubs.html)
- **VMware ThinApp** (https://www.vmware.com/support/pubs/thinapp_pubs.html)
- **VMware vSphere** (https://www.vmware.com/support/pubs/vsphere-esxi-vcenter-server-pubs.html)

2
Implementing Horizon Connection Server

The VMware Horizon Connection Server is a key component of the VMware Horizon infrastructure. In addition to acting as a connection broker between Horizon clients and desktops or Microsoft Windows RDS servers, it also hosts the Horizon Administrator console.

This chapter will discuss multiple topics surrounding the design, deployment, configuration, backup, and recovery of a Horizon Connection Server instance. We will also discuss how to install additional Horizon Connection Server instances, which are known as **replicas**.

In this chapter, we will look at the following topics:

- An overview of a Horizon Connection Server instance
- The virtual machine and OS requirements of a Horizon Connection Server instance
- The connection limits of a Horizon Connection Server instance
- How to determine the number of Horizon Connection Server instances required
- Infrastructure and vCenter installation prerequisites
- How to install the first Horizon Connection Server instance in a Pod
- The initial configuration of a Horizon Connection Server instance
- The configuration of the **Instant Clone Engine Domain Administrator** account
- How to install additional Horizon Replica Connection Server instances in a Pod
- The Horizon Connection Server upgrade process
- How to back up components of a Horizon Connection Server instance and which components to back up
- How to restore a Horizon Connection Server instance from backups or in response to a server failure

Overview of VMware Horizon Connection Server

In `Chapter 1`, *VMware Horizon Infrastructure Overview*, we discussed some of the roles of Horizon Connection Server. These roles include the following:

- Managing connections between end user Horizon client connections and Horizon-managed resources, including Horizon desktops and Microsoft RDS servers
- Authenticating user connection requests and providing access to assigned resources
- Hosting the Horizon Administrator console for the VMware Horizon infrastructure
- Working in tandem with VMware vCenter and Horizon Composer to manage, deploy, and maintain virtual desktops

The following diagram shows the placement of the **Horizon Connection Server** in a simple Horizon environment. For now, only the **Horizon Connection Server** is displayed; later chapters will add respective Horizon Servers to this diagram:

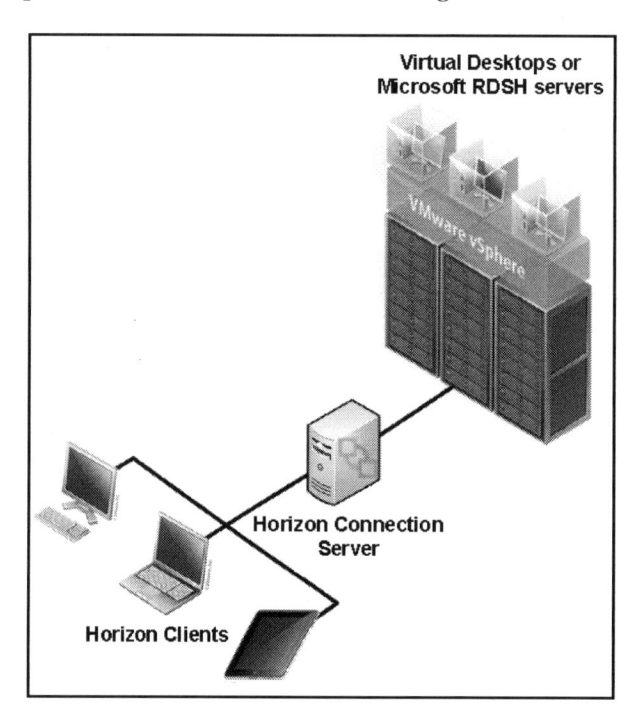

The **Horizon Connection Server** authenticates the clients and provides them with access to the appropriate resources. Depending on the configuration of the **Horizon Connection Server** instance, the clients may connect directly to the remote resource, or the connection may be tunneled through the **Horizon Connection Server** instance. The behavior of a Horizon client connection will be discussed further in this chapter; again in `Chapter 4`, *Implementing Horizon Security Server*, when discussing Horizon Security Server; and once more in `Chapter 5`, *Implementing Horizon Unified Access Gateway*, when discussing Horizon Access Point.

Horizon Connection Server also hosts the Horizon Administrator console, the central management point for Horizon resources. The following screenshot shows the dashboard presented to a Horizon administrator upon login:

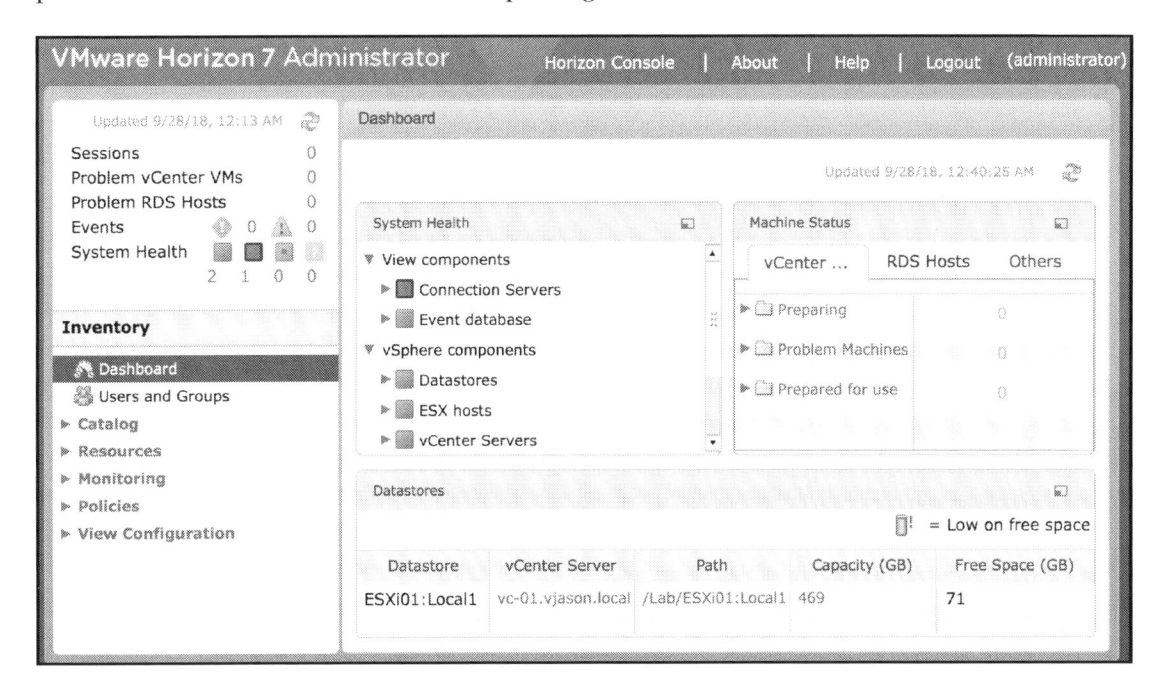

The Horizon Administrator console provides a web-based GUI for performing a variety of tasks, including the following:

- Integrating Horizon with your vSphere infrastructure
- Creating Horizon desktop or application pools, which will then create any required virtual machines within the linked vSphere virtual infrastructure
- Entitling clients with access to the Horizon pools or applications packaged using ThinApp

Implementing Horizon Connection Server

- Performing maintenance on Horizon pools
- Monitoring the status of the Horizon infrastructure

It is important to note that while the virtual machines created by Horizon appear in vSphere in the same format as a typical virtual machine, you should not edit their configuration within vCenter (or any other vSphere administration consoles) directly. Horizon maintains configuration information about the virtual machines within a **Microsoft Active Directory Lightweight Directory Services** (**MS LDS**) database installed on each Horizon Connection Server instance, and any changes made to those virtual machines within the vCenter console may lead to problems that prevent the virtual machine from being managed by Horizon or available for client connections.

The entire life cycle of virtual machines that were created by Horizon must be managed using only Horizon administrative tools.

Horizon Connection Server requirements

Like many other software services, Horizon Connection Server requires a minimum server configuration to ensure adequate performance. To properly support Horizon Connection Server, VMware vCenter Server must also be assigned adequate resources and configured appropriately, based on the projected size of the Horizon infrastructure.

Hardware requirements

The Horizon Connection Server software has specific requirements with regard to the hardware specifications and host operating system. In addition, all Horizon Connection Servers, regardless of the type, should be installed on a dedicated virtual or physical server.

> The first Horizon Connection Server you install will be referred to as a Horizon 7 Standard Server during the installation process. To meet scalability and high-availability needs, up to six additional Horizon Connection Servers can be installed per deployment; each of these is referred to as a Horizon Replica Connection Server during the installation process. The limits of a Horizon Connection Server are discussed later in this section.

The following table outlines both the minimum and recommended hardware specifications of a Horizon Connection Server. The same specifications apply to both Horizon Replica Servers and Horizon Security Servers:

Hardware component	Minimum requirement	Recommended
Processor	Pentium IV 2.0 GHz processor or higher	4 CPUs
Memory	4 GB RAM or higher	A minimum of 10 GB RAM for deployments of 50 or more desktops
Networking	100 Mbps NIC	1 GBps NICs
Hard disk capacity	40 GB	40 GB

Like most other software platforms, the recommended guidelines should be followed to ensure that the Horizon Connection Server performs optimally.

Software requirements

Each of the four different Horizon Connection Server types, which include Standard, Replica, Security, and Enrollment, support 64-bit Windows Server 2008 R2 SP1, 2012 R2, and Windows 2016 as the host OS. Standard, Enterprise, and Datacenter editions of Windows Server 2008 R2 are supported, as well as Standard and Datacenter editions of Windows Server 2012 R2 and 2016.

Limits of a Horizon Connection Server

The limits of a Horizon Connection Server are defined by the maximum number of simultaneous client connections it can support. In Horizon 7, if you create a `locked.properties` file as described in the Horizon 7 Architecture Planning guide (https://docs.vmware.com/en/VMware-Horizon-7/7.6/horizon-architecture-planning.pdf), the maximum number of connections supported is 4,000 per Connection Server. If you do not create that file, the maximum number of connections supported is 2,000 per Connection Server.

Each single Horizon installation supports a maximum of seven Horizon Connection Servers in a 5+2 configuration known as a Pod, supporting a maximum of 10,000 active sessions. The term Pod implies that the Horizon environment is managed as one entity, based on the limitations of the Connection Server. This means that five of the servers are considered active, and two are held in reserve as spares. The spare Horizon Connection Servers maintain an up-to-date copy of the **Horizon AD LDS** database so that they can serve clients immediately in the event they are needed.

> **TIP:** Not every Horizon environment will require seven Horizon Connection Servers, but at the very least they should have two. Even if the number of desktops to be deployed is less than the concurrent connection limit of 4,000 clients per Connection Server, having two Connection Servers ensures that sufficient capacity exists in the event of a server outage or maintenance event. Always build in extra capacity to accommodate events that can impact availability.

In environments where more than 10,000 virtual desktops are required, you will be required to deploy a second Standard Connection Server, which creates another Horizon Pod. This will create a unique Horizon AD LDS database, rather than a replica of the one in your first Horizon installation, enabling support for additional Horizon Connection Servers and an additional 10,000 desktops. Using the Horizon Cloud Pod feature described in Chapter 6, *Implementing a Horizon Cloud Pod*, you can link up to Pods together, and create a global entitlement that grants simultaneous access to Horizon pools in each.

A single-Pod design is suitable for smaller single-site Horizon environments as it is the easiest to manage. If you plan to install Horizon Connection Servers in multiple sites, you are required to create a unique Pod in each site as VMware does not support a single Pod that spans multiple sites due to the amount of communication traffic generated by connection replication.

> **TIP:** In Chapter 6, *Implementing a Horizon Cloud Pod*, we will create a Cloud Pod, which is a collection of up to 25 Horizon Pods located at a maximum of ten distinct sites. While the Pods are still administered individually, using the Cloud Pod feature we can entitle users to Horizon resources located in multiple Pods from a single interface, and regardless of which Pod a user logs into they will be transparently connected to the appropriate Pod where their Horizon resources are located.

Load balancing Connection Servers

VMware Horizon provides no native method to load-balance client requests to Horizon Connection Servers. It is recommended that you implement some sort of load-balancing method to help balance the client connections across all the Horizon Connection Servers in your infrastructure. While methods such Round Robin DNS and Microsoft Windows **Network Load Balancing** (**NLB**) could be used to provide basic load-balancing capabilities, a physical or virtual load-balancing appliance is the preferred method due to the advanced features and capabilities these platforms typically offer. The next section provides an overview of the capabilities of dedicated load-balancing solutions.

Load-balancing appliances

Dedicated load-balancing appliances are available both in physical and virtual formats. The difference between the physical and virtual versions will differ from one vendor to another, so it is important to understand the impact of choosing one over the other.

Dedicated load balancers often have the capability to balance client connections based on a number of different factors. The following load-balancing metrics are not from any specific vendor, but are simply examples of the metrics that various solutions use:

- Server load
- Recent server response times
- Server up/down status
- Number of active connections
- Geographic location
- How much traffic has been assigned to a given host

In addition to any advanced features, dedicated load-balancing appliances do not require additional resources on the servers they are balancing traffic for, which is one additional advantage they have over using Microsoft NLB.

vCenter Server requirements

You should use a dedicated VMware vCenter Server for VMware Horizon wherever possible, particularly if you are using Horizon Composer to deploy linked-clone desktops. For larger Horizon deployments, this will ensure that your vCenter Server is configured based on the exact requirements of your Horizon infrastructure, ensuring optimal performance and providing maximum flexibility when future upgrades or updates are required.

> While Horizon and vCenter supports up to 10,000 desktops per vCenter Server instance, for performance and availability reasons VMware recommends no more than 2,000 desktops per vCenter Server.

Implementing Horizon Connection Server

Using a dedicated vCenter Server for the Horizon provides a number of benefits over using an existing vCenter Server. These benefits include the following:

- A new Horizon deployment that plans to use an existing vCenter Server may require a version of vCenter that is currently not in use, necessitating an upgrade that may not be possible based on environmental or licensing constraints.
- If a Horizon upgrade or patch requires an accompanying vCenter Server upgrade or patch, this operation will not affect the existing vCenter server.
- The existing vCenter Server may not be properly sized to handle the planned number of virtual desktops, and may require changes to CPU, memory, the OS version, or vCenter Server settings.
- For organizations that plan to deploy linked-clone desktops using Horizon Composer, the vCenter Server will be placed under a significant load during various Composer Operations. Isolating these operations to a dedicated vCenter Server ensures that this load does not affect the management of other, non-Horizon related, ESXi servers.

The installation and configuration of VMware vCenter can proceed as outlined in the VMware **vSphere Installation and Setup Guide** (https://docs.vmware.com/en/VMware-vSphere/6.7/vsphere-vcenter-server-67-installation-guide.pdf).

Horizon installation prerequisites

The installation and configuration process for the first Horizon Connection Server, referred to as a Horizon Standard Connection Server during installation, requires some amount of preparation. This section will outline what is required prior to beginning the installation.

> **TIP**
> If your organization requires that a firewall or other network controls be placed between your internal Horizon clients and your Connection Servers, consult the Horizon documentation (https://docs.vmware.com/en/VMware-Horizon-7/index.html) for a comprehensive list of all firewall ports required when implementing a Horizon Connection Server.

Infrastructure and other prerequisites

There are a number of prerequisites that should be addressed prior to installing the first VMware Horizon Connection Server. In addition to the items described in `Chapter 1`, *VMware Horizon Infrastructure Overview*, the following sections will outline what should be prepared in advance for the installation.

Creating a vCenter role and granting permissions

VMware Horizon requires access to the vCenter Server in order to perform tasks related to the creation or management of virtual desktops. To facilitate this access, we first need to create an **Active Directory** (**AD**) user account that the Horizon Connection Server will use to access the vCenter Server; in this chapter, we will use an account named `svc-horizon`. To make it easier to update the Horizon Connection Server AD account in the future, we will create a vCenter role that includes all the required privileges. Once created, the role can be quickly applied to AD user accounts. Perform the following steps to create the role in vCenter:

1. In **vSphere Web Client**, navigate to **Home** | **Administration** | **Roles**, click the green **+** sign indicated by the red arrow, and then enter a role name such as `Horizon Connection Server`, as shown in the following screenshot:

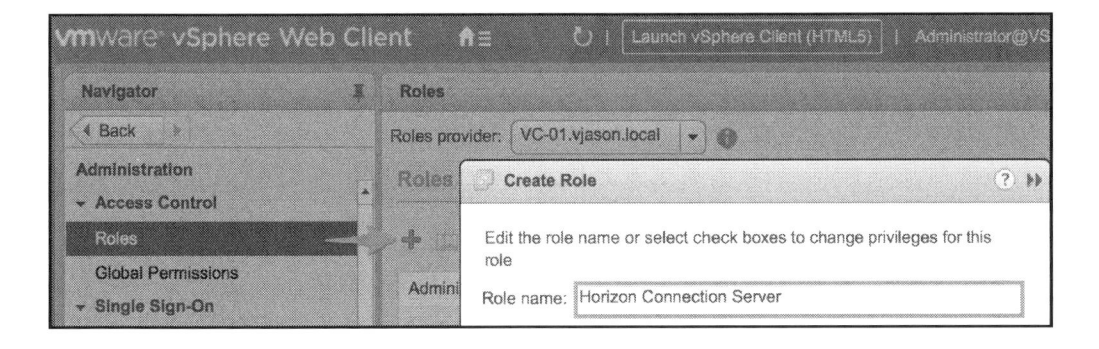

Implementing Horizon Connection Server

2. From within the **Create Role** window, expand each privilege group listed in the following table and check the required privilege items. All listed privileges must be checked in order for the Horizon Connection Server to function properly. Click on **OK** when you have finished creating the role:

vCenter privilege group	Privilege subsection	Privilege
Datastore		Allocate space
Folder		• Create Folder • Delete Folder
Global		Act as vCenter Server
Host	Configuration	Advanced settings
Profile Driven Storage		All
Resource		Assign virtual machine to resource pool
Virtual Machine	Configuration	• Add or remote device • Advanced • Modify device settings
	Interaction	• Perform wipe or shrink operations • Power Off • Power On • Reset • Suspend
	Inventory	• Create new • Create from existing • Remove
	Provisioning	• Clone template • Clone virtual machine • Customize • Deploy template • Read customization specifications

3. In **vSphere Web Client**, click the following in order, **Home | Hosts and Clusters**, the vCenter Server at the top level of the inventory, the **Manage** tab, the **Permissions** section, and finally the green + sign indicated by the red arrow. This will open the **Add Permission** window used in the next step:

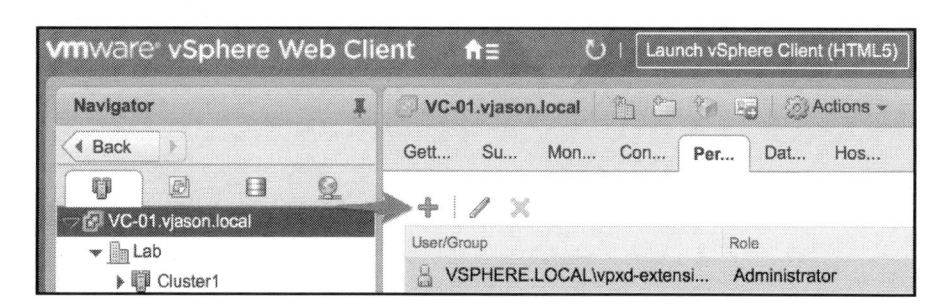

[44]

4. In the **Add Permission** window, click on the **Add...** button to open the **Select Users/Groups** window.
5. In the **Domain:** drop-down menu, select the **AD** domain that contains the Horizon administrator user or security group. In our example, the domain is named **VJASON**.
6. In the **Users and Groups** list, select the **Horizon Connection Server** service account. For our sample environment, we have searched for and selected an account named `svc-horizon`. Once selected, click on the **Add** button as shown in the following screenshot. Click on **OK** to close the **Select Users/Groups** window:

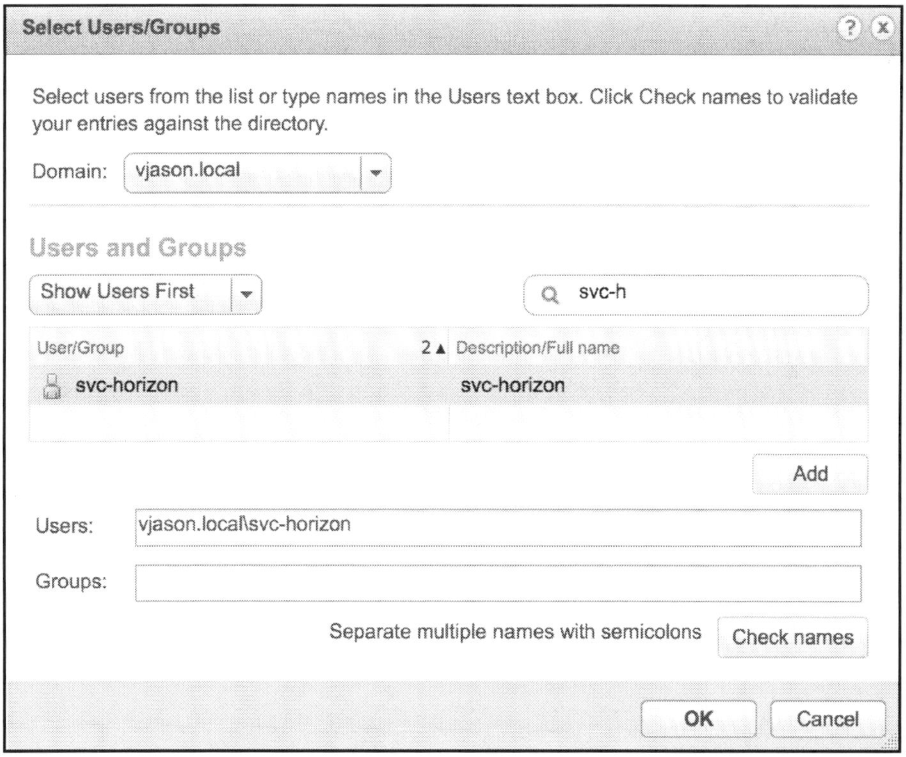

7. In the **Add Permission** window then **Assigned Role** drop-down menu, select the **Horizon Connection Server** role we created in step 2 as shown in the following screenshot, and then click **OK** to close the window and complete the action:

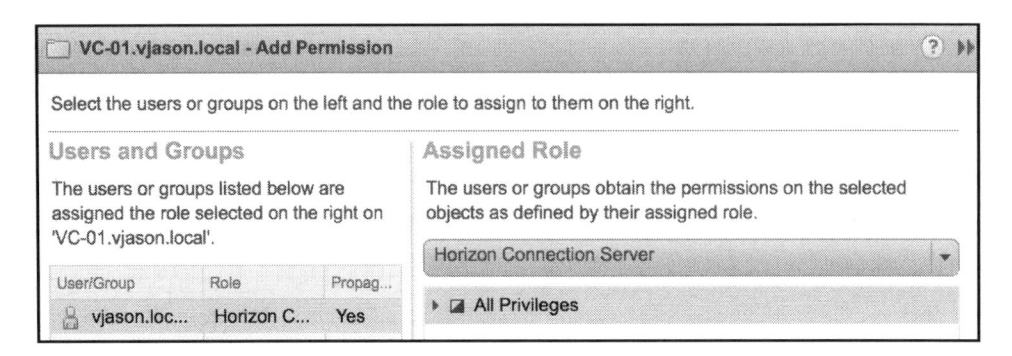

The Horizon Pod now has the sufficient permissions on the vCenter Server that it will use to deploy and manage desktops and Windows RDS servers.

Horizon event database

VMware recommends using an external Horizon Connection Server event database in order to retain detailed, Pod-wide information about any events that occur. Without an event database, only minimal information is recorded within the log files on each individual Horizon Connection Server. It is recommended that you create a database, both to retain historical data about Horizon events, as well as to support any troubleshooting that may need to be done. Only one database is required for each Horizon Pod, and it is possible to share a database among Horizon Pods by using unique database headers for each, as shown later on in this chapter.

Chapter 1, *VMware Horizon Infrastructure Overview*, outlines different database types that can be used to record Horizon Connection Server events. In addition to using a supported database platform, the following database configurations must be done:

- For SQL Server:
    - Horizon requires an account on the database server with SQL Server authentication
    - The Horizon database user account must have permission to read from, write to, and create tables and views

The database schema will be installed when the database is configured within the Horizon Administrator console.

SQL database tutorials

The following Microsoft documentation can assist with creating databases and creating users and granting them access to databases:

- **Create a Database** – `https://docs.microsoft.com/en-us/sql/relational-databases/databases/create-a-database?view=sql-server-2017`
- **Managing Logins, Users, and Schemas How-to Topics** – `https://docs.microsoft.com/en-us/sql/relational-databases/security/authentication-access/managing-logins-users-and-schemas-how-to-topics?view=sql-server-2017`

Deploying the first Horizon Connection Server

Deploying the first Horizon Connection Server is broken down into two stages; the installation of the Connection Server software and the final setup using the Horizon Administrator console.

Installing the first Horizon Connection Server

The Horizon Connection Server software is delivered as a single executable (EXE) file, named in a format similar to `VMware-Horizon-Connection-Server-x86_64-x.x.x-yyyyyy.exe`. This installer is used for all four Horizon Connection Server types, which include Standard, Replica, Security, and Enrollment.

> **TIP:** In step 8 of the installation process you will grant an AD security group administrative access to Horizon. Before you install the Horizon Connection Server software, make sure you add this group to the local administrator group on the host Windows server, and then log off of the server and back on again before beginning the installation. If you do not do this, and proceed to install the Horizon HTML access option, the installation will fail.

Implementing Horizon Connection Server

The following steps outline the installation process:

1. Double-click on the **Horizon Connection Server** installer EXE file to launch the installer.
2. In the **Welcome to the Installation Wizard for VMware Horizon 7 Connection Server** window, click on **Next>**.
3. Review the **License Agreement** section, select the **I accept the terms in the license agreement** radio button, and click on **Next>**.
4. Select the installation directory and click on **Next>**.
5. Highlight the Horizon Connection Server instance type. Since this is the first Horizon Connection Server in the environment, we will choose **Horizon 7 Standard Server** as shown in the following screenshot, and then click on **Next>**:

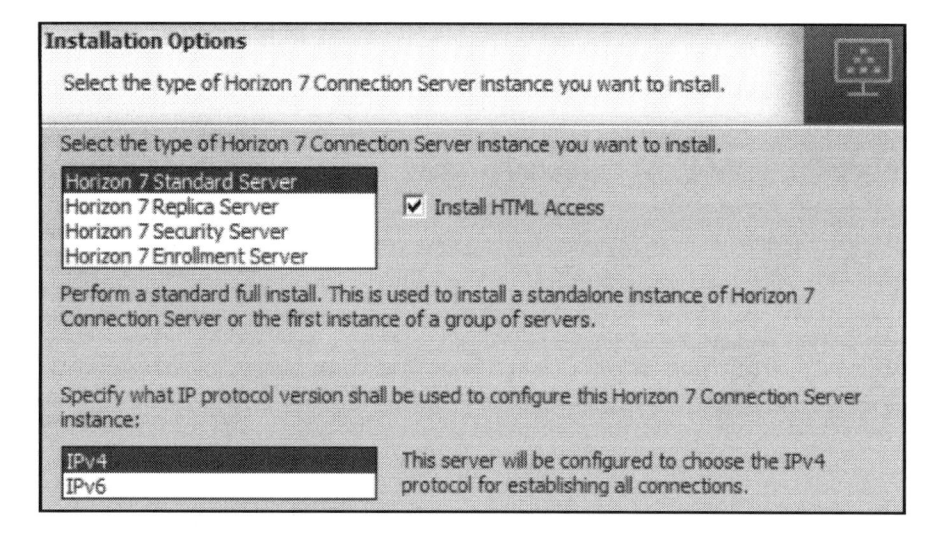

```
Installation Options
Select the type of Horizon 7 Connection Server instance you want to install.

Select the type of Horizon 7 Connection Server instance you want to install.
┌─────────────────────────────┐
│ Horizon 7 Standard Server   │   ☑ Install HTML Access
│ Horizon 7 Replica Server    │
│ Horizon 7 Security Server   │
│ Horizon 7 Enrollment Server │
└─────────────────────────────┘
Perform a standard full install. This is used to install a standalone instance of Horizon 7
Connection Server or the first instance of a group of servers.

Specify what IP protocol version shall be used to configure this Horizon 7 Connection Server
instance:
┌─────────────────────────────┐
│ IPv4                        │   This server will be configured to choose the IPv4
│ IPv6                        │   protocol for establishing all connections.
└─────────────────────────────┘
```

6. Enter a data recovery password and an optional password reminder and click on **Next>**. Record this password, as it will be required for any future restores of this Horizon Connection Server configuration. We will review how to standardize this password across all Horizon Connection Servers in this Pod later on in this chapter.

Chapter 2

7. Select the **Configure Windows Firewall automatically** option and click on **Next >**.

> **TIP:** Windows Firewall must be enabled and properly configured to ensure that communications between Horizon Security Servers and the Connection Server can be encrypted.

8. Select the **Authorize a specific domain user or domain group** radio button, enter either a single AD account or AD security group that is designated as the Horizon Administrator, and click on **Next>**. As shown in the following screenshot, we will use the AD security group titled **Horizon-Admins** in the VJASON domain in the format `domain-name\group-name`:

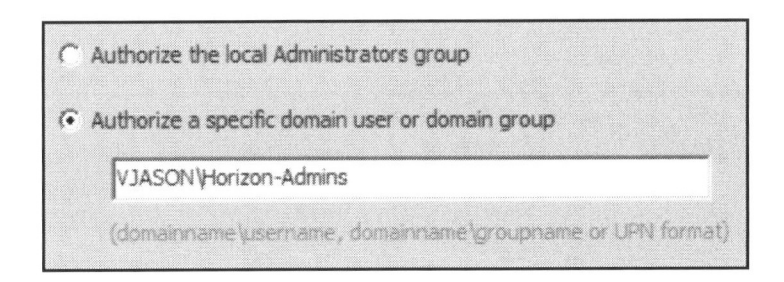

```
○ Authorize the local Administrators group

● Authorize a specific domain user or domain group

  VJASON\Horizon-Admins

  (domainname\username, domainname\groupname or UPN format)
```

9. Configure the drop-down menus for the **User Experience Improvement Program**, or uncheck the **Participate anonymously in the user experience improvement program** checkbox, and click on **Next >**.

10. Review the final installation screen to ensure that the installation directory is correct. If changes are required, click on the **< Back** button to reach the necessary configuration screen and make the required changes. Assuming that the settings are correct, click on **Install** to begin the automated installation process.

11. Click on **Finish** when prompted at the completion of the installation process.

The installation process will install all the components required for a Horizon Standard Connection Server, including the Connection Server software and the AD LDS database used to store configuration information. The final configuration steps will be completed in the Horizon Administrator console, and will be detailed in the next section.

Configuring the first Horizon Connection Server

Once the installation of the first Horizon Connection Server has completed, we need to log in to the Horizon Administrator Console. The console URL will be in the format `https://Connection Server FQDN/admin`. You must use lowercase letters when typing `admin`.

By default, the installation process creates a self-signed SSL certificate to encrypt connections to the Horizon Connection Server. While the server will function with this default self-signed certificate installed, it is recommended you replace the default certificate with one from a trusted internal or commercial certificate authority. Until the default certificate is replaced, Horizon clients will be notified about the untrusted certificate each time they connect. In addition, the Horizon Administrator console will display an informational error. `Chapter 16`, *Managing Horizon SSL Certificates*, will provide the process used to replace the default SSL certificates for all Horizon components.

Complete the following steps to configure the first Horizon Connection Server:

1. Log in to the Horizon Administrator console using an AD account that was granted administrative permissions during the installation process. The following screenshot shows the login page for our sample Horizon Connection Server, which was accessed at the URL: `https://horcon1.vjason.local/admin`.
2. Upon successful login to the first Horizon Connection Server that was installed, the dashboard will open to the **Product Licensing and Usage** window in the **View Configuration** page as shown in the following screenshot. Click on the **Edit License...** button to open the **Edit License** window:

Chapter 2

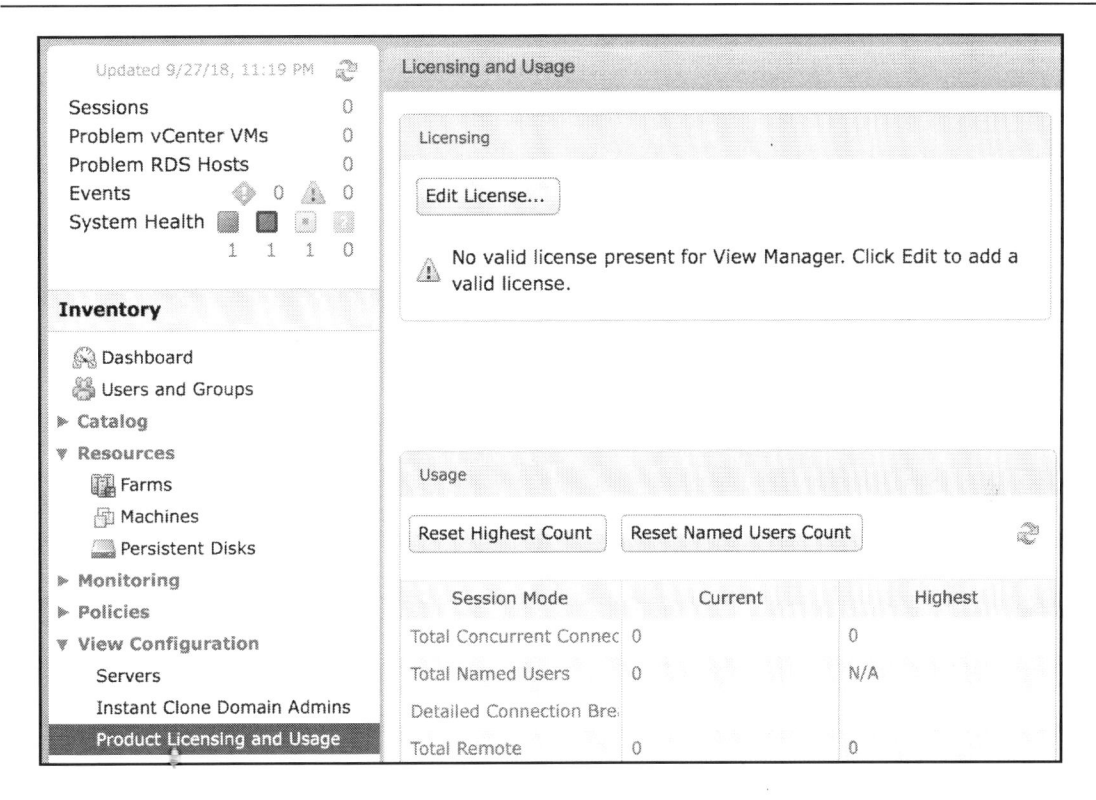

3. Enter the 25-character license key, including the dashes, and click on **OK** to complete the license entry.
4. Open the **Event Configuration** window in the **View Configuration** page within the console. Click on **Edit...** in the **Event Configuration** page to open the **Edit Event Database** window.

Implementing Horizon Connection Server

5. Fill in the information for the Horizon event database configuration including **Database server**, **Database type**, **Port**, **Database name**, **User name**, **Password**, and optionally the **Table prefix**. The **Table prefix** field is used to identify this Horizon installation within the database itself, and would be used when sharing the database among multiple Horizon Pods. The following screenshot shows the database configuration for our sample server. Click on **OK** once all the information has been provided, and Horizon will complete the database configuration assuming the necessary privileges have been granted as outlined earlier in this chapter:

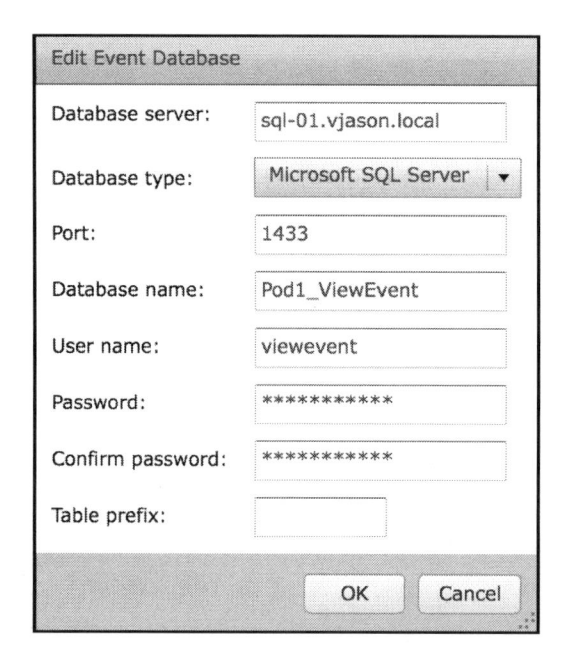

Edit Event Database	
Database server:	sql-01.vjason.local
Database type:	Microsoft SQL Server
Port:	1433
Database name:	Pod1_ViewEvent
User name:	viewevent
Password:	**********
Confirm password:	**********
Table prefix:	

> **TIP**: The console **Event Configuration** page also allows us to customize how events are displayed in the Horizon Administrator console. The VMware Horizon Documentation page (https://docs.vmware.com/en/VMware-Horizon-7/index.html) provides detailed information about these settings, which can be changed at any time.

6. Navigate to **View Configuration** | **Servers** to bring up the **vCenter Servers** tab of the **Servers** window. Click on **Add...** to open the **Add vCenter Server** window.

7. In the **Add vCenter Server | vCenter Server Information** window, fill in the information required to link the vCenter Server that we will be using for desktops to our Horizon Connection Server. The information required includes the vCenter Server address in a **fully qualified domain name (FQDN)** format, the Horizon vCenter AD user name that we created earlier in this chapter in the format `domain-name\user-name`, and the password for the account. Click on **Next>** when the required information has been provided. The following screenshot shows the completed screen for our sample server:

> **TIP**
> The **vCenter Server Information** window also allows us to specify advanced options such whether or not this vCenter Server is hosted on VMware Cloud on AWS, and new limits for number of concurrent vCenter tasks our Horizon Connection Server can initiate. The VMware Horizon documentation (`https://docs.vmware.com/en/VMware-Horizon-7/index.html`) provides detailed information about these settings, which can be changed at any time.

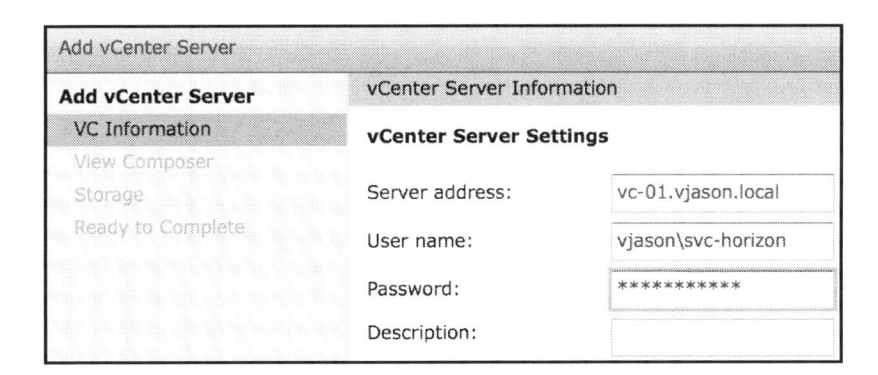

Add vCenter Server	vCenter Server Information
Add vCenter Server	
VC Information	**vCenter Server Settings**
View Composer	Server address: vc-01.vjason.local
Storage	User name: vjason\svc-horizon
Ready to Complete	Password: **********
	Description:

8. Horizon Connection Server will attempt to verify the SSL certificate of the vCenter Server as part of the linking process. If the vCenter Server is still using the default self-signed certificate, a window will open and announce that the identity of the specified vCenter Server cannot be verified. If this happens, click on **View Certificate...** to open the **Certificate Information** window, verify that the certificate information is correct, and click on **Accept** to move to the next window, **View Composer**.
9. `Chapter 3`, *Implementing Horizon Composer*, will outline how to deploy VMware Horizon Composer. Since Composer is not yet installed, select the **Do not use View Composer** radio button and click on **Next>** to open the **Storage** window. Horizon Composer can be enabled within the Horizon Administrator console at any time after it has been installed.

Implementing Horizon Connection Server

10. The **Add vCenter Server | Storage** window is used to enable two different Horizon storage-related features. Click the **Reclaim VM disk space** checkbox, then the **Enable View Storage Accelerator** check box, set the **Default host cache size:** value to 2048, the maximum allowed, and then click **Next >**:

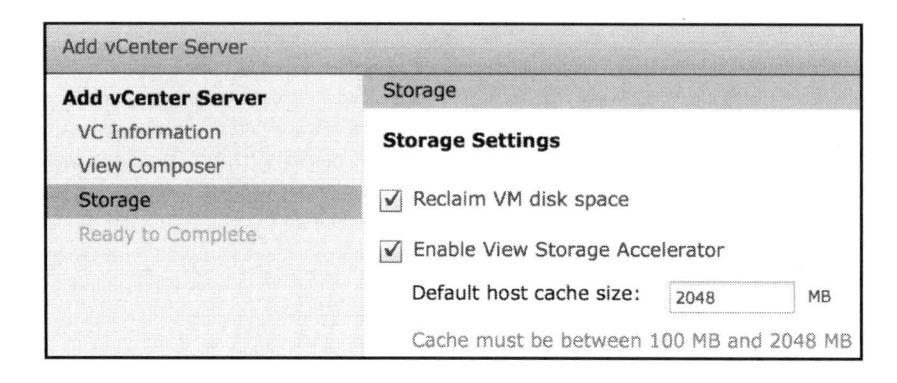

Add vCenter Server	Storage
VC Information	**Storage Settings**
View Composer	
Storage	☑ Reclaim VM disk space
Ready to Complete	☑ Enable View Storage Accelerator
	Default host cache size: 2048 MB
	Cache must be between 100 MB and 2048 MB

    > **TIP:** **Reclaim VM disk space** periodically scans the Horizon desktop VMDK files for blocks that are no longer in use and releases them to the storage array for reuse. This feature is particularly useful when using a storage platform that relies on deduplication to reduce array physical capacity requirements. However, running a reclaim operation can place significant stress on a storage array and should not be enabled without consulting the storage vendor beforehand. Horizon Storage Accelerator caches critical Horizon desktop data in RAM on the ESXi server, which can significantly reduce the amount of read IO that needs to be serviced by the storage array. Consult the VMware Horizon documentation (https://docs.vmware.com/en/VMware-Horizon-7/index.html) for detailed information about both of these features.

11. The **Ready to Complete** window will provide a summary of the options chosen in the previous steps. Review the summary and click on **Finish** to complete the process and link the vCenter Server to the Horizon Connection Server.

12. The vCenter Server will now be displayed in the **View Configuration** | **Servers** | **vCenter Servers** window, as shown in the following screenshot:

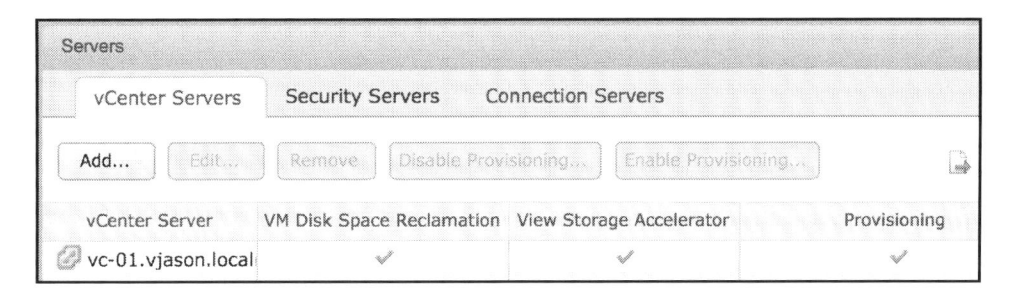

vCenter Server	VM Disk Space Reclamation	View Storage Accelerator	Provisioning
vc-01.vjason.local	✓	✓	✓

13. Repeat steps 6 through 11 as needed to link additional vCenter Servers.

At this point, the basic configuration of the Horizon Connection Server has been completed; if we had a virtual desktop image, we could deploy full-clone virtual desktops. However, before moving forward to the next step it is advisable to set up a second Horizon Connection Server; this one will be a replica of our first one. The *Deploying a Horizon Replica Connection Server* section will outline how to install a Horizon Replica Connection Server.

Configuring the Horizon Instant Clone Engine

While Horizon does not require a Composer Server to deploy and manage instant clone desktops, we are required to provide an AD account that it will use to create and manage the Instant Clone desktop AD computer objects. In this section we will create the AD account, grant it the permissions required in AD, and provide the account details in the Horizon Administrator console.

Configuring the Instant Clone Engine AD user account

Horizon requires an AD account with specific permissions in order to manage the desktop AD computer objects for Instant Clone desktops. Refer to the *Delegating permissions for Horizon Composer in Active Directory* section of `Chapter 3`, *Implementing Horizon Composer*, for the procedure used to delegate these permissions, although refer to the following list of updates to that procedure as the permissions required and AD account used are different. It is assumed that prior to performing this procedure you have already created the AD user account you intend to use (`svc-horizonic` in this example):

- In step 5 of the *Delegating permissions for Horizon Composer in Active Directory* section of `Chapter 3`, *Implementing Horizon Composer*, in the **Select Users**, **Computers**, or **Groups** window, type the name of the Horizon Composer service account (`svc-horizonic`), click **OK** to return to the **Delegation of Control Wizard - Users or Groups** window, and then click **Next >**.

> Note that we are using a dedicated AD account for Instant Clone operations. I recommend using dedicated accounts for Horizon, Horizon Composer, and Horizon Instant Clone (AD operations) for security reasons and to make it easier to troubleshoot any issues that may occur.

- In step 8 of the *Delegating permissions for Horizon Composer in Active Directory* section of `Chapter 3`, *Implementing Horizon Composer*, in the **Delegation of Control Wizard | Permissions** window, click the **General**, **Property-specific**, **Read**, **Read All Properties**, **Write All Properties**, and **Reset password** checkboxes, and then click **Next >**.

Updating the Instant Clone Engine Domain Administrator setting

The following steps outline the procedure used to specify the AD user account we created as our Instant Clone Engine Domain Administrator:

1. Log on to the Horizon Administrator console using an AD account that has administrative permissions within Horizon.
2. Open the **View Configuration | Instant Clone Domain Admins** window within the console.

Chapter 2

3. Click on the **Add...** button in the **Instant Clones Engine Domain Administrators** window to open the **Add Domain Admin** window.
4. Provide the **User Name:** (`svc-horizonic`) and **Password:** as shown in the following screenshot, and then click **OK** to return to the previous window:

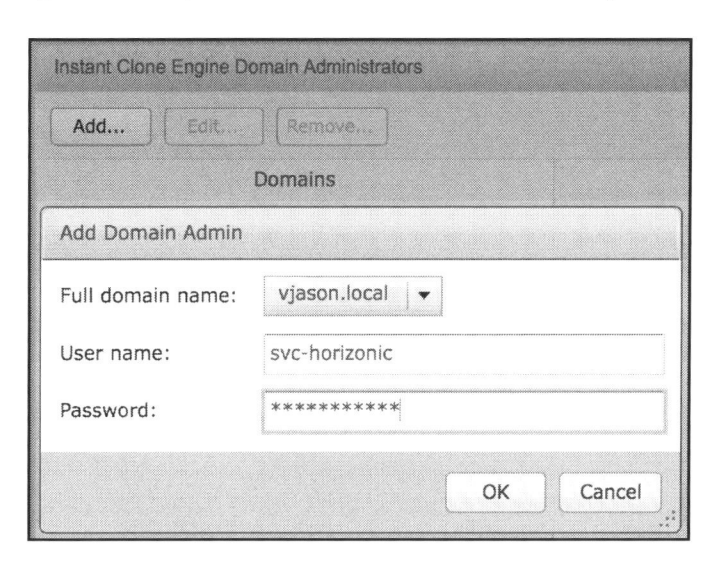

5. Verify that the account was added successfully as shown in the following screenshot:

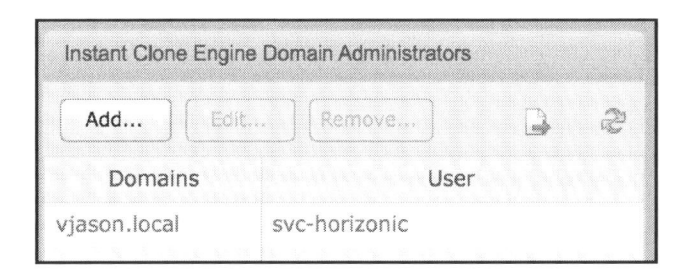

Horizon is now able to deploy Instant Clone desktops using the procedure described in `Chapter 10`, *Creating Horizon Desktop Pools*. Note that if the permissions for this account were not granted correctly, we will likely not notice until we attempt to create an Instant Clone desktop pool.

[57]

Deploying a Horizon Replica Connection Server

The installation process for a Horizon Replica Connection Server is straightforward as the configuration information is copied from the Horizon Standard Connection Server that was installed in the previous section. This section will explain how the installation process differs with regard to options that are chosen during installation.

Installing a Horizon Replica Connection Server

The steps required to install a Horizon Replica Connection Server are largely the same as those for a Standard Connection Server; only a few steps differ. The following list outlines where the installation process differs, using the numbered steps provided within the *Deploying the first Horizon Connection Server* section as a reference:

- In step 5: **Installation Options** | Choose **Horizon 7 Replica Server** as the instance type and click on **Next>**.
- New Step: **Source Server** then provide the FQDN for the Horizon Standard Connection Server deployed in the previous section and click on **Next>**. For our sample server, the FQDN is `horcon1.vjason.local`. Refer to the following screenshot as an example:

> A group of Horizon 7 Connection Server instances that share the same configuration data is called a Horizon 7 Connection Server group. Setup will replicate configuration data from an existing server instance.
>
> Enter the server name of an existing Horizon 7 Connection Server instance to make this server part of that group.
>
> Example server: view.internal.vmware.com.
>
> Server: `horcon1.vjason.local`   (hostname or IP address)

> **TIP:** This installation step is unique to the Horizon Replica Connection Server installation.

- Steps 6, 8, and 9 are not required.

Chapter 2

During the installation process, the Horizon Replica Connection Server will install all the same components as a Standard Connection Server but the AD LDS database will be a replica of the Standard Connection Server AD LDS database. The AD LDS database holds the configuration data for the Horizon environment, so no additional configuration is needed beyond the installation itself.

Once the installation has successfully completed, the Horizon Replica Connection Server will be displayed in the **View Configuration** | **Servers** | **Connection Servers** window in the Horizon Administrator console as shown in the following screenshot:

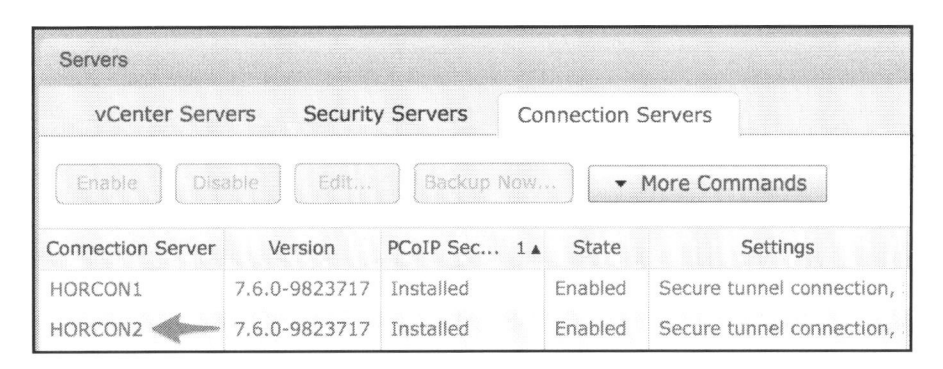

Connection Server	Version	PCoIP Sec...	State	Settings
HORCON1	7.6.0-9823717	Installed	Enabled	Secure tunnel connection,
HORCON2	7.6.0-9823717	Installed	Enabled	Secure tunnel connection,

At this point, the Horizon Connection Server would be available to broker connections to whatever resources have been configured within the Horizon Administrator console.

> Once installed, a Horizon Replica Connection Server is a full peer of all other Horizon Standard Connection Servers and Horizon Replica Connection Servers within the installation. Unlike some software platforms, which have a master-slave or split role architecture, all Horizon Standard Connection Servers and Horizon Replica Connection Servers share the same responsibilities and capabilities.

As previously mentioned, Horizon lacks any native load-balancing capabilities. As a result, unless a load-balancing solution of some sort is deployed, clients will need to manually choose which of the two Horizon Connection Servers they want to connect to. Since this is likely to lead to an unbalanced distribution of client resources, it is recommended that you consider one of the previously mentioned options for load-balancing the Horizon client connections.

Upgrading an existing Horizon Connection Server

Upgrading an existing Horizon Connection Server is a straightforward process that typically requires no more than a few minutes to complete, not counting the time required to plan the operation. Regardless, it is important to block access to the Connection Server while the upgrade is being performed to ensure no Horizon clients attempt to connect to it, or at the very least to perform the upgrade during a period of time in which the Connection Server is not expected to be used.

If you are using a load balancer to distribute traffic among multiple Horizon Connection Servers, the easiest way to block access to the Connection Server is to remove it from the load-balancing group. This prevents connections from being sent to it, while at the same time being transparent to the end users.

> Do not disable the Connection Server network cards during the upgrade to ensure that any needed AD LDS replication will occur.

Upgrading prerequisites

Each release of VMware Horizon includes release notes that summarize the differences between the new release and the previous release. New releases are just as likely to include bug fixes as they are new or deprecated features, so it is important to read these notes prior to performing any upgrade.

> The release notes are available on the VMware Horizon documentation home page (https://docs.vmware.com/en/VMware-Horizon-7/index.html).

The following are items to look for when reviewing Horizon release notes prior to an upgrade:

- Are features I use being removed?
    - One example of this is that Horizon 6 supported Windows XP and Windows Vista if an extended support agreement was purchased, but Horizon 7 does not offer this option.
- Are any other components of my Horizon infrastructure required to be upgraded first?
    - One example of this occurred with Horizon 6.2.1, which removed support for certain older cipher suites used by older Horizon client software. In this case, the Horizon client software should be upgraded first to ensure those clients don't experience any errors or other interruption in service.
- Am I required to update the rest of the Horizon components immediately, or are they backward compatible and therefore can wait until another time?
    - Examples of this include Horizon Composer, the Horizon Agent, and more.

These are just a sample of the things we need to look for prior to performing an upgrade.

Backing up the existing Horizon configuration

By default, each Horizon Connection Server backs up the AD LDS database nightly to a local folder; this backup is key to restoring the configuration of the Pod-wide Horizon AD LDS instance were there problems with the upgrade. Chapter 3, *Implementing Horizon Composer*, talks about backing up the Composer database, which should also be performed prior to an upgrade. The following list summarizes the backups we should make or verify prior to performing an upgrade:

- **Horizon AD LDS database**: Performed by default, but can be done on demand as described later on in this chapter. Each Horizon Connection Server hosts a copy of this backup.
- **Horizon event database**: Backed up using native backup procedures for the hosting database platform.
- **Horizon vCenter databases**: These databases would typically not be impacted by a Horizon upgrade, but as mentioned later in this chapter they are critical to any larger Horizon disaster recovery operations.

Horizon upgrade process

A Horizon Connection Server upgrade is performed using the same installer used to perform new Horizon Connection Server installations. The following steps outline how an upgrade is performed; they should be repeated on each Horizon Connection Server in the Pod until all have been successfully upgraded:

1. Double-click on the Horizon Connection Server installer EXE file to launch the installer.
2. In the **Welcome to the Installation Wizard for VMware Horizon 7 Connection Server** window, click on **Next >**.
3. Review the VMware End User License Agreement section, select the **I accept the terms in the license agreement** radio button, and click on **Next >**.
4. Verify the installation directory (you will not be able to change it) and click on **Install**.
5. Once the upgrade process has been completed, click **Finish** to close the installer window.
6. In the Horizon Administrator console, navigate to **View Configuration | Servers | Connection Servers** window and verify that the Connection Server displays the new version number as indicated by the red arrow in the following screenshot:

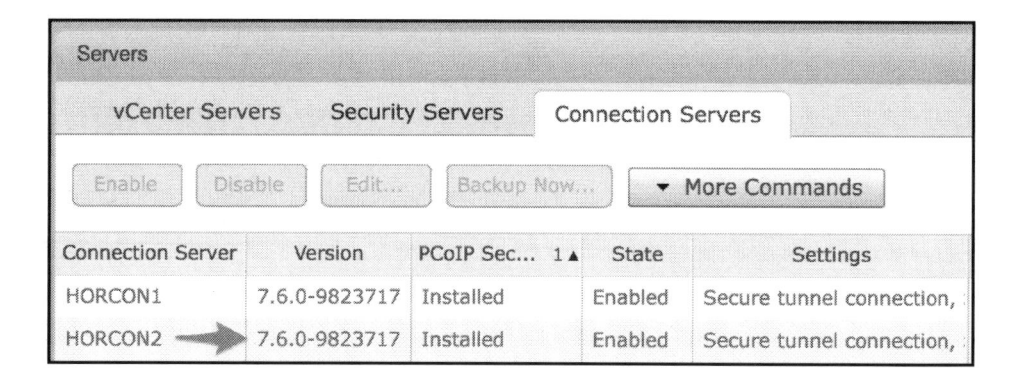

Connection Server	Version	PCoIP Sec...	State	Settings
HORCON1	7.6.0-9823717	Installed	Enabled	Secure tunnel connection,
HORCON2	7.6.0-9823717	Installed	Enabled	Secure tunnel connection,

Once the functionality and compatibility of the upgraded Connection Server has been verified, the remaining Connection Servers in the Pod can be upgraded using the same procedure.

> **TIP**
> In the event that vSphere VM snapshots are used to restore a VMware Horizon Connection Server to a previous state, the Connection Server will stop replicating its AD LDS database to other Connection Servers. In the event you wish to retain the configuration contained within the AD LDS database on the server where the snapshot was reverted, all other Connection Servers within the same Horizon Pod will need their Connection Server software and AD LDS database uninstalled and reinstalled from scratch. Refer to the Horizon 7 Upgrades guide (`https://docs.vmware.com/en/VMware-Horizon-7/index.html`) for additional information about what is required if a Horizon Connection Server is reverted to an earlier snapshot.

Backing up a Horizon Connection Server

The information required to restore a Horizon Connection Server is stored in two different databases:

- Horizon Connection Server AD LDS database
- vCenter Server database

Horizon Composer, described in `Chapter 3`, *Implementing Horizon Composer*, also uses a database that contains critical Horizon configuration information. Horizon installations that utilize Horizon Composer will also need to back up the Composer database as part of their backup and recovery plan.

Backing up the vCenter Server database

The vCenter Server database should be backed up using whatever method is available within your environment. For Windows-based vCenter Servers, this includes options such as the following:

- Native backups based on the capabilities of the database platform, such as Microsoft SQL Server backup
- Third-party database backup solutions

For a vCenter Server appliance (VCSA), the internal vCenter Postgres database should be backed up using the procedure outlined in VMware KB Article 2110031 (`https://kb.vmware.com/s/article/2091961?docid=2110031`).

> **TIP:** VMware KB 2110031 also provides the procedure used to restore the vCenter Postgres database.

There are no specific requirements with regard to database backup methodologies, so long as you can recover the database to a previous state; either to the same database server or an alternative. Consult with your database server or backup software documentation if additional information about performing database backups is required.

Consult the **VMware vSphere Installation and Setup Guide** (`https://docs.vmware.com/en/VMware-vSphere/6.7/vsphere-vcenter-server-67-installation-guide.pdf`) for additional information about how to back up the components of a vSphere installation.

Backing up the Horizon AD LDS database

The VMware Horizon Connection Server AD LDS database contains key Horizon configuration information and should be backed up on a regular basis. By default, a Horizon Standard Connection Server or Replica Connection Server will perform a nightly backup of the AD LDS database at midnight (12:00 AM).

A limited number of changes to the Horizon Connection Server backup policy can be made within the Horizon Administrator console. These changes include the following:

- Backup frequency
- Number of backups to retain
- Data recovery password

These options can be configured using the following steps in the Horizon Administrator console:

1. Navigate to **View Configuration** | **Servers** | **Connection Servers**.
2. Highlight the targeted Horizon Connection Server and click on **Edit...** to open the **Edit Connection Server Settings** window.

3. Click on the **Backup** tab and make any desired changes; refer to the following screenshot for an example . Note that setting the data recovery password on this page will update it for all Connection Servers in the Pod:

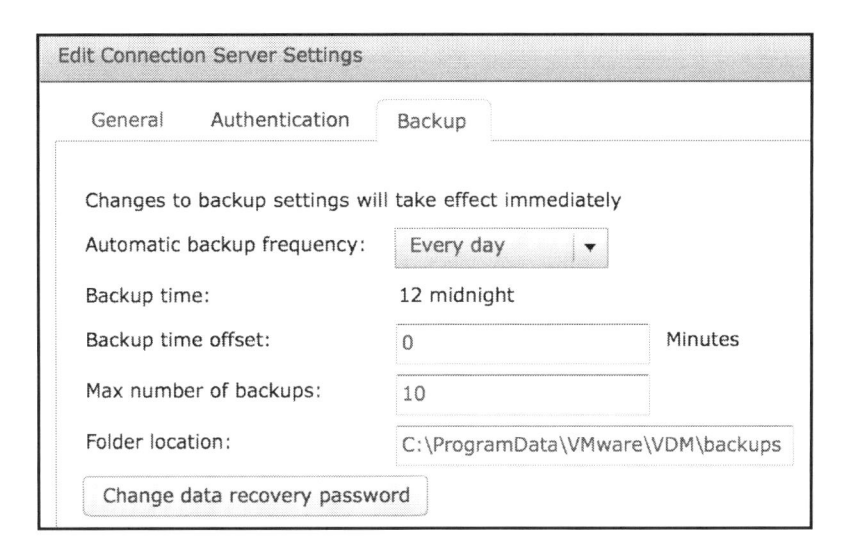

Edit Connection Server Settings	
General Authentication **Backup**	
Changes to backup settings will take effect immediately	
Automatic backup frequency:	Every day
Backup time:	12 midnight
Backup time offset:	0 Minutes
Max number of backups:	10
Folder location:	C:\ProgramData\VMware\VDM\backups
Change data recovery password	

Horizon Connection Server recovery

The process to restore a Horizon Connection Server varies based on the scenario that necessitated the restore.

If you are restoring all of your Horizon Connection Servers from scratch, the Horizon Composer database will need to be restored as part of the recovery process as its contents are tied to those of the Horizon AD LDS database. Refer to the *Restoring the Horizon Composer database* section in `Chapter 3`, *Implementing Horizon Composer*, for additional information about restoring the Composer database.

In situations where it is required to restore multiple Horizon-related databases at once, you should use backups that were taken as closely together as possible when performing the restore. Ideally, backup plans for all Horizon components should coincide as closely as possible to ensure that the data shared between them is consistent. The further apart the backups are taken, the less likely it is that the contents will match when a restore is required. This could lead to issues that require the assistance of VMware Support as items within one or more of the databases may need to be removed or edited.

Restoring a single Horizon Connection Server

Horizon configuration settings are stored in the local AD LDS database on each Connection Server. If the Horizon Connection Server software becomes corrupt, you can simply uninstall and reinstall it without having to perform any additional configuration.

If a Horizon Connection Server cannot be accessed due to a hardware or software failure, and you need to replace it, you must remove it from the AD LDS replication set first. The following steps should be executed from an existing Horizon Connection Server. In this example, we will remove the server named `horcon2` from the AD LDS replication set using the `vdmadmin.exe` utility:

1. Navigate to the `Program Files\VMware\VMware View\Server\tools\bin` directory.
2. Execute the following command:

   vdmadmin.exe -S -r -s horcon2

The failed Horizon Connection server `horcon2` has now been removed from the AD LDS replica set and can now be replaced.

> **TIP:** To learn about all the options available for the `vdmadmin.exe` command, run `vdmadmin.exe /?`.

To restore or replace the server, simply reinstall the Horizon Connection Server on a replacement server and follow the procedure outlined in the *Deploying a Horizon Replica Connection Server* section of this chapter. The software will be installed and the server will be joined to the existing Horizon Pod.

Removing a Horizon Connection Server

To remove a functioning Horizon Connection Server from your environment, perform the following steps:

1. Open the **Windows Programs and Features** control panel on the target Connection Server.
2. Uninstall the **VMware Horizon 7 Connection Server** software.
3. Uninstall the **AD LDS Instance VMwareVDMDS** software.
4. Reboot the server to complete the removal of the Connection Server software.

When performed on a functioning Horizon Connection Server this procedure automatically removes the server from the Pod-wide AD LDS instance, which means that the procedure described in the previous section to forcibly remove the non-functional server from AD LDS is not required.

Restoring the vCenter database

The vCenter database is restored using the same tools used to perform the backup. Consult with the database server or backup software documentation for information about how to perform the restore operation.

Consult the **VMware vSphere Installation and Setup Guide** (`https://docs.vmware.com/en/VMware-vSphere/6.7/vsphere-vcenter-server-67-installation-guide.pdf`) for additional information about how to restore the components of a vSphere installation.

Restoring the Horizon Connection Server AD LDS database

The Horizon Connection Server AD LDS database can be restored using the `vdmimport` utility, located in the VMware Connection Server installation drive in the `Program Files\VMware\VMware View\Server\tools\bin` directory. The utility is a command-line tool and is executed from a Windows Command Prompt. The utility requires administrative access to the Horizon infrastructure, so the AD user account used to run it must have administrative rights within the target Horizon Pod. If the AD account does not have sufficient rights, errors will be displayed during the restore operation.

> **TIP:** To learn about all the options available for the `vdmadmin.exe` command, run `vdmimport.exe /?`.

The AD LDS database is not usually restored unless all the Horizon Connection Servers are lost or the AD LDS database is found to be corrupt. If you are having problems with just a single Horizon Connection Server, you should refer to the *Restoring a single View Connection Server* section in this chapter for instructions on how to restore or remove just that server.

The restore operation requires two commands:

1. Decrypt the AD LDS database backup titled `backup.LDF` to a file titled `decrypted.LDF`, and replace the password with the data recovery password specified during the installation of the first Horizon Connection Server or the global data recovery password set using the Horizon Administrator console:

    ```
    vdmimport -d -p password -f backup.LDF > decrypted.LDF
    ```

2. Restore the decrypted backup:

    ```
    vdmimport -f decrypted.LDF
    ```

Once the restore is complete, the remaining Horizon Connection Servers will replicate the restored data into their local AD LDS databases.

Summary

In this chapter, we have been introduced to the key component of a VMware Horizon installation: the Connection Server. We have learned what is required to deploy a Connection Server, what the limits of a Connection Server are, how to perform the installation and initial configuration, and how to install additional Replica Connection Servers.

We have also discussed how to backup to the Horizon Connection Server configuration, including the vCenter databases.

We concluded this chapter by discussing how to restore the Horizon Connection Server configuration, and how that process varies based on the recovery scenario.

In the next chapter, we will implement Horizon Composer; the component of a Horizon installation that enables the deployment of linked-clone virtual desktops.

Questions

1. What Windows OS can you install the Horizon Connection Server software on?
2. What are the four Horizon Connection Server types?
3. What are the maximum number of Horizon Connection Servers you can install in a single pod?

4. What are the recommended CPU and RAM requirements for a Horizon Connection Server?
5. What is the name of the first Horizon Connection Server you install in a new Horizon pod?
6. What is the term used to describe the second Connection Server you install in an existing Horizon pod?
7. What are the maximum number of client connections supported by a single Horizon Connection Server?
8. If you intend to assign an AD security group administrative permissions during the Horizon Connection Server installation process, what key step must you perform before you begin the installation?

Further reading

The following resources may be used to learn more about the topics described in this chapter:

- VMware documentation:
    - **VMware Horizon** (https://docs.vmware.com/en/VMware-Horizon-7/index.html)
    - **VMware vSphere** (https://www.vmware.com/support/pubs/vsphere-esxi-vcenter-server-pubs.html)

Implementing Horizon Composer

VMware Horizon Composer is a feature of Horizon that enables the rapid provisioning of linked clone virtual desktops. A pool of linked-clone desktops shares the same master image and writes any changes to a dedicated virtual hard disk, also known as a **delta disk**. This drastically reduces the amount of per-virtual desktop storage required compared to full-clone virtual desktops, as each of those requires its own copy of the master image. In addition, linked-clone desktops can be provisioned much more quickly than full clone desktops, which is beneficial in and of itself and also enables new ways of managing desktops throughout their life cycle.

This chapter will discuss benefits, installation, configuration, backup, and recovery of the Horizon Composer component of VMware Horizon.

In this chapter, we will look at the following topics:

- An overview of the capabilities and benefits of Horizon Composer
- The hardware requirements of Horizon Composer
- Horizon Composer pre-installation tasks and other requirements
- How to deploy Horizon Composer
- How to configure Horizon Composer
- How to back up components of Horizon Composer and what components to backup
- How to restore Horizon Composer from backups

> **TIP**
> Horizon Composer requires Microsoft **Key Management Services** (**KMS**) in order to activate linked-clone desktops. **Multiple Active Key** (**MAK**) licenses are not natively supported by Horizon Composer, and if used, the frequent need to reactivate Windows will quickly exhaust the key activation limit. If KMS is not available, VMware KB article 1026556 (https://kb.vmware.com/s/article/1026556) provides details about a registry key that can be set in the master virtual desktop image to skip the Windows activation process during the customization of the linked clone desktop.

Overview of VMware Horizon Composer

Horizon Composer is used to provision linked-clone virtual desktops, which are a type of virtual machine that shares a common virtual desktop master image, sometimes referred to as a golden image. Horizon and vSphere support up to 4,000 desktops for each single replica of the virtual desktop master image, which enables significant storage savings over traditional full-clone virtual desktops.

The concept behind a linked-clone desktop is demonstrated in the following diagram, which shows the relationship between the master **Replica Disk Read Only** and the **Linked-Clone Disk**:

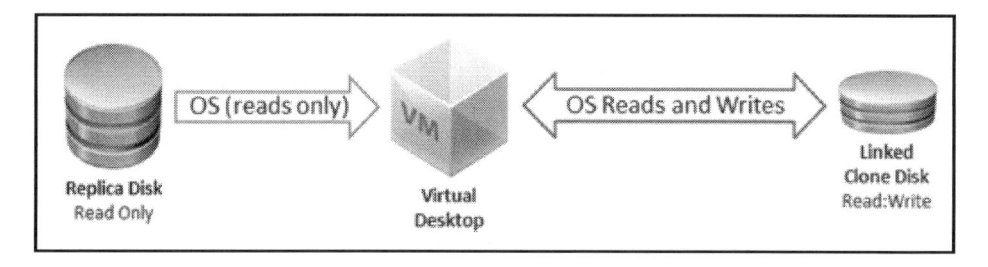

> **TIP**
> This diagram is to illustrate the concept of a linked clone, the actual architecture of a linked clone virtual machine is explained next.

When a pool of linked-clone desktops is provisioned, a replica of the virtual desktop master image is copied to storage accessible by the Horizon ESXi servers. This replica will be used as a read-only copy of the virtual desktop master image; all writes are redirected to unique disks that are attached to each linked-clone. Linked-clones are provisioned using thin virtual disks, the configuration of which varies depending on the desktop pool settings.

> **TIP**: Beginning with Horizon 6.2, Composer gained the ability to create linked-clone Windows RDS servers. Much of the information or language contained in this chapter will refer primarily to linked-clone desktops, but understand that Composer is also required if you wish to use linked-clone Windows RDS servers, and both use the concept of a shared replica.

The following diagram shows the configuration of two linked-clone virtual desktops that share the same virtual desktop master image:

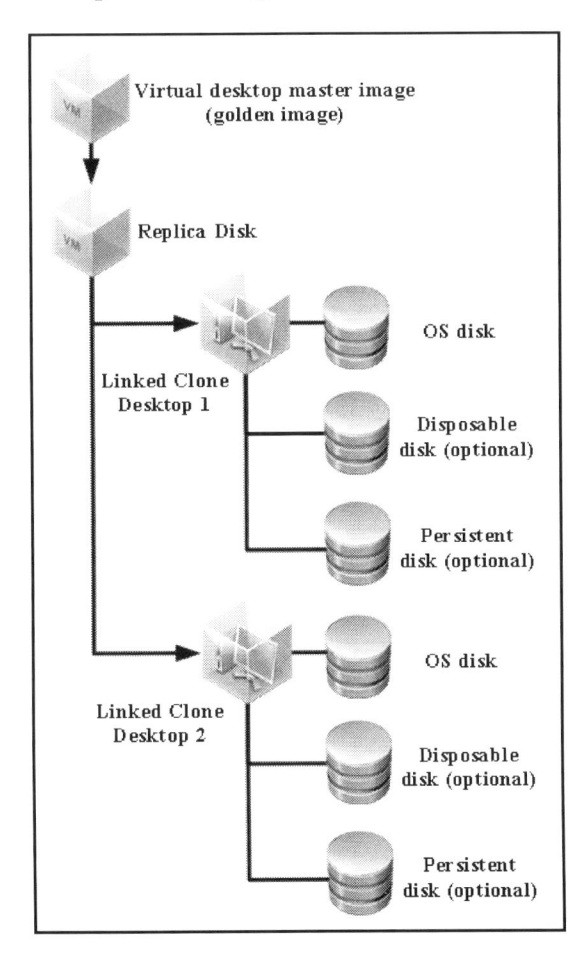

In this diagram, each **Linked-Clone Desktop** is configured with optional disposable disks and persistent disks. `Chapter 7`, *Creating Horizon Desktop Pools*, explains the different options that affect the configuration of these and other linked-clone disks.

When the linked-clone desktops are powered on for the first time, they will begin redirecting any writes to the linked-clone disks and will also create a **virtual swap (vswp)** file of a size equal to the amount of unreserved **virtual RAM (vRAM)** allocated to the virtual machine.

> Controlling the growth of a linked-clone desktop requires an understanding of multiple topics, all of which will be described within this book. The following chapters contain valuable information that can help you control the storage utilization of linked-clone desktops:
>
> - `Chapter 7`, *Creating Horizon Desktop Pools*
> - `Chapter 9`, *Performing Horizon Pool Maintenance*
> - `Chapter 10`, *Creating a Master Virtual Desktop Image*
> - `Chapter 12`, *Implementing User Environment Manager*

Horizon Composer works at the direction of the Horizon Connection Server to provision and manage linked-clone desktops. Horizon Composer uses the vSphere **application program interface (API)** to initiate whatever tasks are required based on the operation that is being performed. To achieve this, Horizon Composer requires specific permissions within vCenter Server, as well as permissions within Microsoft Active Directory, both of which will be described later in this chapter.

Horizon Clients do not come into contact with Horizon Composer; its role as an orchestration tool is to perform actions based on the configuration of the Horizon desktop pool. As such, Horizon Composer is depicted in the following architectural diagram as a stand-alone component that works directly with the vSphere and Horizon infrastructure:

Chapter 3

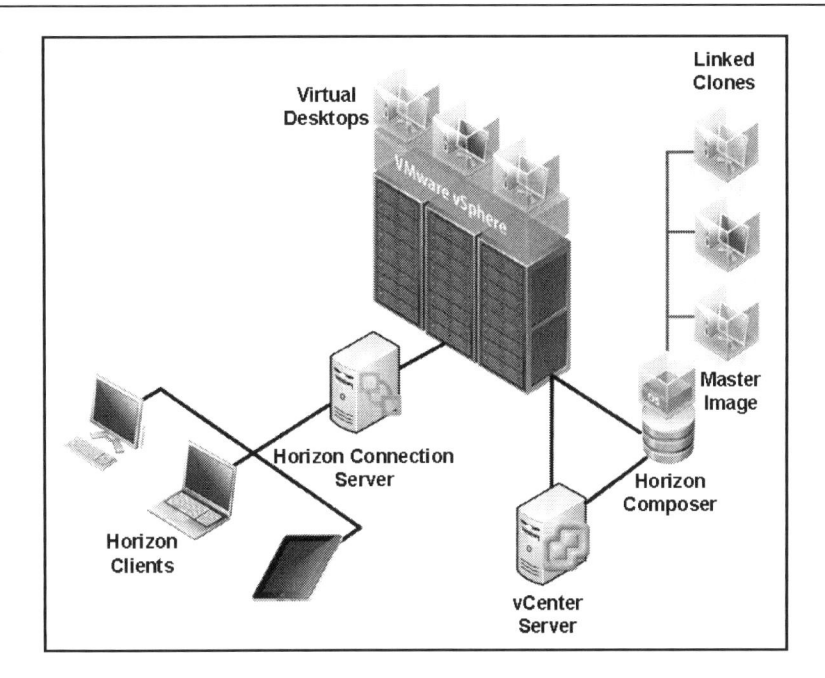

![Diagram showing Horizon Clients connecting through Horizon Connection Server to VMware vSphere hosting Virtual Desktops, with vCenter Server and Horizon Composer managing Linked Clones from a Master Image]

The benefits of Horizon Composer do not start and end with gains in storage efficiency. The following features are just some of the ways with which you can leverage Horizon Composer to change how you manage desktop maintenance.

Refreshing linked-clone desktops

The changes made to a linked-clone desktop can be discarded on demand or upon user logoff. This operation is called a refresh, as it refreshes the desktop back to the exact configuration that it was in when it was first provisioned. User persistent data disks, if used, are not impacted by this action.

> **TIP**: Horizon also supports deleting the desktop as an additional option. After the desktop has been deleted, a new desktop is provisioned to replace it.

[75]

Implementing Horizon Composer

By refreshing desktops you maintain tight control over their storage utilization as all writes to the dedicated linke-clone virtual disk are discarded. In addition, when all changes are discarded, the desktop is returned to the same state it was in when it was provisioned, which enables tight control over the end-user computing experience.

The refresh process is described in detail in Chapter 9, *Performing Horizon Pool Maintenance*.

> **TIP**
> Refer to Chapter 7, *Creating Horizon Desktop Pools*, and Chapter 12, *Implementing User Environment Manager*, for more information about how to preserve user persona data during recompose or refresh operations.

Recomposing linked-clone desktops

A virtual desktop recompose operation is used when you need to update the master desktop replica image. One of the key methods of maintaining the storage efficiencies of linked-clone desktops is to control the amount of data that is written to the linked-clone disks, which if left unchecked will grow in size during the course of regular use. Traditional per-desktop administrative tasks such as installing applications and applying patches can quickly increase linked-clone storage utilization, as the writes would be made to the linked-clone disk of each desktop that was the target of the action. In addition, these operations would need to be repeated on each desktop, which can require significant management overhead.

A recompose operation replaces the linked-clone replica disk with an updated version that uses the same OS. Recomposing to a completely different OS is not supported. During the recompose process, all virtual desktops will be provisioned again and linked to the new replica disk. If the desktop was configured with a persistent disk for storing user profile data—an option for dedicated assignment desktop pools—that disk would be retained and attached to the recomposed desktop.

> **TIP**
> Technically speaking, a recompose operation requires a refresh operation. Either of these operations will temporarily reduce the amount of vSphere datastore capacity your persistent Horizon desktops are using.

Chapter 3

The recompose process is described in detail in `Chapter 9`, *Performing Horizon Pool Maintenance*.

> **TIP**
>
> When a desktop is recomposed, it will maintain the same computer name but will obtain a new DHCP lease. Your DHCP server must have a large enough pool of addresses available to handle these requests. In addition, it is recommended you use a short address lease period so that the now unused leases are quickly removed and the associated addresses are made available for use.

Horizon Composer requirements

Horizon Composer requires a minimum server configuration to ensure adequate performance and to properly support linked clone provisioning and maintenance operations. In this section we will focus on the hardware requirements; the supported OSes were already listed in `Chapter 1`, *VMware Horizon Infrastructure Overview*.

Hardware requirements

The Horizon Composer software has specific requirements with regard to the hardware specifications and host OS. Horizon Composer may be installed on a dedicated virtual or physical server.

The following table outlines both the minimum and recommended hardware specifications of a dedicated Horizon Composer server. Additionally, the server hosting Horizon Composer must have a static IP address:

Hardware component	Minimum requirement	Recommended
Processor	1.4 GHz x64 and 2 CPUs	2 GHz x 64 or faster and 4 CPUs
Memory	4 GB RAM or higher	8 GB RAM or more for deployments of 50 or more desktops
Networking	One or more 100 Mpbs NICs	1 GBps NICs
Hard disk capacity	40 GB	60 GB

Like most other software platforms, the recommended guidelines should be followed to ensure that the Horizon Composer performs optimally.

Limits of Horizon Composer

A single Horizon Composer instance can support only one vCenter Server. A single vCenter Server can support up to 10,000 desktops, which is the maximum number of desktops supported in a single Horizon Pod. As a result, while Horizon can support multiple vCenter Servers, each with its own dedicated Horizon Composer instance, only one of each is actually required to manage up to the maximum number of desktops supported in a single Horizon Pod.

If you still wish to have multiple vCenter Servers in your Horizon environment, you will need multiple instances of Horizon Composer as a single instance can service only one vCenter Server. Each additional instance of Horizon Composer will also require its own database, as the databases cannot be shared between Horizon Composer instances.

Horizon Composer installation prerequisites

There are a number of prerequisites that should be addressed prior to installing Horizon Composer:

- At least one configured Horizon Connection Server with a license key installed
- An **Active Directory** (**AD**) user account or security group that will be granted the necessary permissions within Microsoft AD and the vCenter Server
- A dedicated host server for Horizon Composer, running a supported host OS
- A static IP address for the dedicated Horizon Composer host server (required only if you are using a dedicated server)
- Local administrator access on the host server
- A supported Horizon Composer database as referenced in `Chapter 1`, *VMware Horizon Infrastructure Overview*
- A 64-bit ODBC connection to the Horizon Composer database configured on the Composer host server

> If your organization requires that a firewall or other network controls be placed between your Horizon Composer Server and your Connection Servers, consult the Horizon documentation (`https://docs.vmware.com/en/VMware-Horizon-7/index.html`) for a comprehensive list of all firewall ports required when implementing a Horizon Composer.

In addition to the items described in Chapter 1, *VMware Horizon Infrastructure Overview*, the following sections will outline which items should be prepared in advance of the installation.

> **TIP**
> Starting with the release of vSphere 6.7, VMware no longer provides the option to deploy a Windows-based vCenter Server, which means you can no longer install Horizon Composer directly on the vCenter Server. While Horizon still supports previous version of vSphere that support this option, for the purpose of this chapter we will assume you are deploying a dedicated Horizon Composer server.

Horizon Composer service account

Horizon Composer requires access to the vCenter Server in order to perform tasks related to the creation and management of virtual desktops. To facilitate this access, you can either grant additional permissions to the Horizon Connection Server vCenter user account created in Chapter 2, *Implementing Horizon Connection Server*, or create a dedicated AD user account that Horizon Composer will use to access the vCenter Server and AD.

> **TIP**
> In Chapter 2, *Implementing Horizon Connection Server*, we granted the vSphere permissions required just for the Horizon Connection Server itself. In the examples provided in this chapter, we will use a new dedicated account named Svc-horizoncomp. Similar to Horizon Connection Servers, grant whichever account you use with Composer local administrator access on the Composer host server, as well as the needed privileges in AD and vSphere as outlined in this chapter.

This section assumes that you will use a dedicated AD account for Horizon Composer.

Horizon Composer vCenter permissions

The following table outlines only those vCenter permissions required for Horizon Composer. Using the procedure outlined in `Chapter 2`, *Implementing Horizon Connection Server*, we can create a vCenter role just for the Composer service account, or we could modify the existing role we created to add the permissions as outlined in the following table:

vCenter privilege group	Privilege subsection	Privilege
Datastore		• Allocate space • Browse datastore • Low level file operations
Folder		• Create folder • Delete folder
Global		• Act as vCenter Server • Disable methods • Enable methods • Manage custom attributes • Set custom attribute • System tag
Host	Inventory	Modify Cluster
Network		All
Profile Driven Storage		All
Resource		• Assign virtual machine to resource pool • Migrate powered off virtual machine
Storage views		View
Virtual Machine	Configuration	All
	Interaction	• Device connection • Perform wipe or shrink operations • Power off • Power on • Reset • Suspend
	Inventory	All
	Provisioning	• Allow disk access • Clone template • Clone virtual machine • Customize • Deploy template • Read customization specifications
	Snapshot management	All

The decision on whether or not to use separate AD accounts for the Horizon Connection Servers and Horizon Composer is up to you. In some cases, organizational security policies will require it in order to minimize the permissions any one account has within your down, which makes the decision an easy one.

For the purpose of this chapter, we will create the following:

- AD service account named `svc-horizoncomp`
- vSphere role with the previously listed permissions named `Horizon Composer`

Creating a Horizon Composer vCenter role and granting permissions

The following steps outline how to create a vCenter role for Horizon Composer and grant the permissions. If examples are needed, refer to the screenshots for this process found in *Chapter 2, Implementing Horizon Connection Server*. The process of creating a vCenter role is the same in this case; all that is changed is the role name, vCenter permissions granted, and the target AD account:

1. In vSphere Web Client, navigate to **Home | Administration | Roles**, click the green + sign, and then enter a role name such as `Horizon Composer`.
2. From within the **Create Role** window, expand each privilege group listed in the table provided previously in this section and check the required privilege items. All listed privileges must be checked in order for Horizon Composer to function properly. Click on **OK** when finished with creating the role.
3. In the vSphere Web Client, click the following in order, **Home | Hosts and Clusters**, the vCenter Server at the top level of the inventory, the **Manage** tab, the **Permissions** section, and finally the green + sign. This will open the **Add Permission** window used in the next step.
4. In the **Add Permission** window, click on the **Add...** button to open the **Select Users/Groups** window.
5. In the **Domain:** drop-down menu, select the **AD domain** that contains the Horizon Composer user. In our example, the domain is named `VJASON`.
6. In the **Users and Groups** list, select the **Horizon Composer** service account. For our sample environment, we will search for and select the account named `svc-horizoncomp`. Once selected, click on the **Add** button. Click on **OK** to close the **Select Users/Groups** window.
7. In the **Add Permission** window | **Assigned Role** drop-down menu, select the **Horizon Composer** role we created in step 2, and then click **OK** to close the window and complete the action.

Horizon Composer now has sufficient permissions on the vCenter Server to deploy and manage linked-clone virtual desktops and Windows RDS servers.

Horizon Composer AD permissions

The Horizon Composer AD account requires permission to manage the AD Computer objects for the virtual desktops that it creates. As there is some risk associated with granting accounts direct access to AD in order to create and delete computer objects, it is important to minimize the access granted to the Horizon Composer account.

To minimize risk, the following guidelines are recommended:

- Create an AD **organizational unit** (**OU**) that will be used only to store linked-clone virtual machines created using Horizon Composer.
- Grant the Horizon Composer AD account the minimum permissions required in order to manage the AD computer accounts contained within the OU.

To grant the necessary permissions, you need at a minimum full control over the OU, which will contain the Horizon linked-clone AD computer accounts. This gives you the ability to not only delegate the required permissions for Horizon Composer, but also to create additional child OUs to enable additional control over the various Horizon pools that you provision.

> Separating the AD computer accounts of desktop pools into separate OUs enables us to customize the group policies for each.

Delegating permissions for Horizon Composer in AD

The following steps outline the process used to delegate the minimum permissions required for Horizon Composer. In our example, we will be granting to the `svc-horizoncomp` AD account the necessary permissions for the **Horizon | Computers** OU:

1. From the Windows Start menu, select **Administrative Tools | Active Directory Users and Computers**.

2. Right-click on the parent OU that will contain the virtual desktops created using Horizon Composer and select **Delegate Control...** as shown in the following screenshot to open the **Delegation of Control Wizard**. In our example, the OU is named **Computers**:

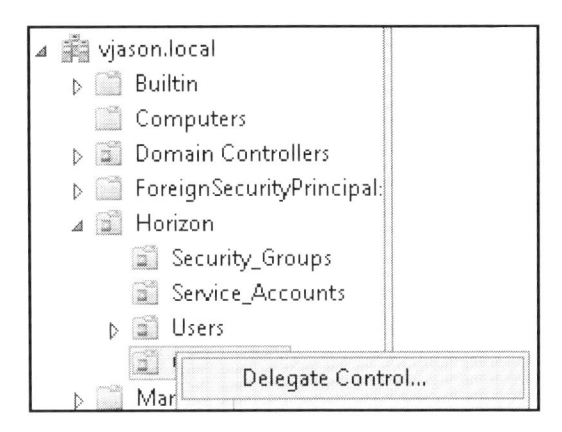

3. In the **Delegation of Control Wizard** window, click **Next >**.
4. In the **Delegation of Control Wizard | Users or Groups** window, click **Add...** to open the **Select Users, Computers, or Groups** window as shown in the following screenshot:

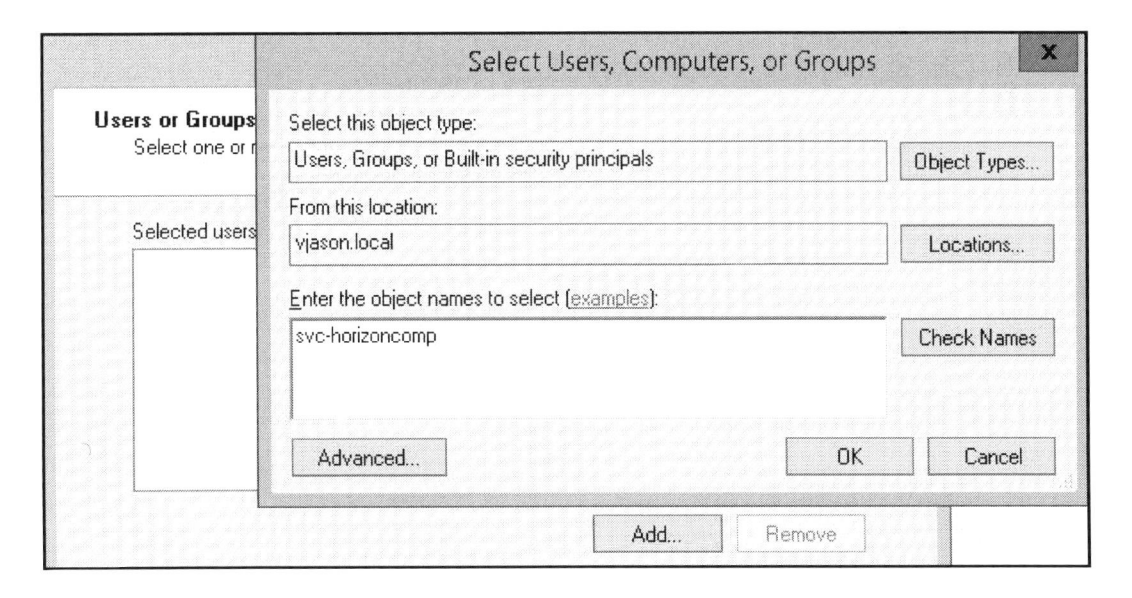

Implementing Horizon Composer

5. In the **Select Users, Computers, or Groups** window, type the name of the Horizon Composer service account (svc-horizoncomp), click **OK** to return to the **Delegation of Control Wizard- Users or Groups** window, and then click **Next >**.
6. In the **Delegation of Control Wizard | Tasks to Delegate** window, click the **Create a custom task to delegate** radio button and then click **Next >**.
7. In the **Delegation of Control Wizard | Active Directory Object Type** window, click the **Only the following objects in the folder** radio button, then click the **Computer objects, Create selected objects in this folder**, and **Delete selected objects in this folder** checkboxes as shown in the following screenshot, and then click **Next >**:

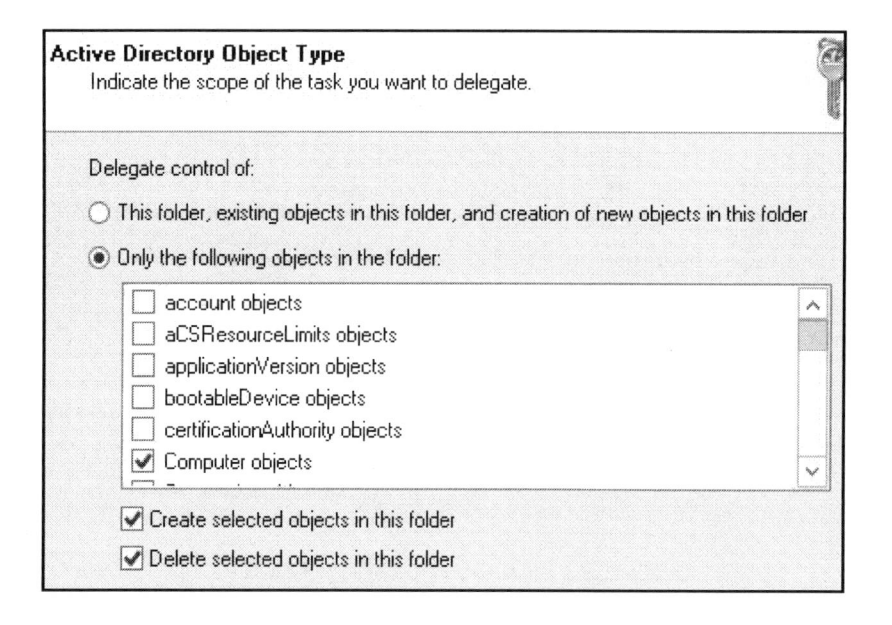

```
Active Directory Object Type
  Indicate the scope of the task you want to delegate.

Delegate control of:
  ○ This folder, existing objects in this folder, and creation of new objects in this folder
  ● Only the following objects in the folder:
      ☐ account objects
      ☐ aCSResourceLimits objects
      ☐ applicationVersion objects
      ☐ bootableDevice objects
      ☐ certificationAuthority objects
      ☑ Computer objects

  ☑ Create selected objects in this folder
  ☑ Delete selected objects in this folder
```

8. In the **Delegation of Control Wizard | Permissions** window, click the **General**, **Property-specific**, **Read**, **Read All Properties**, **Write All Properties**, and **Change password** checkboxes as shown in the following screenshot, and then click **Next >**:

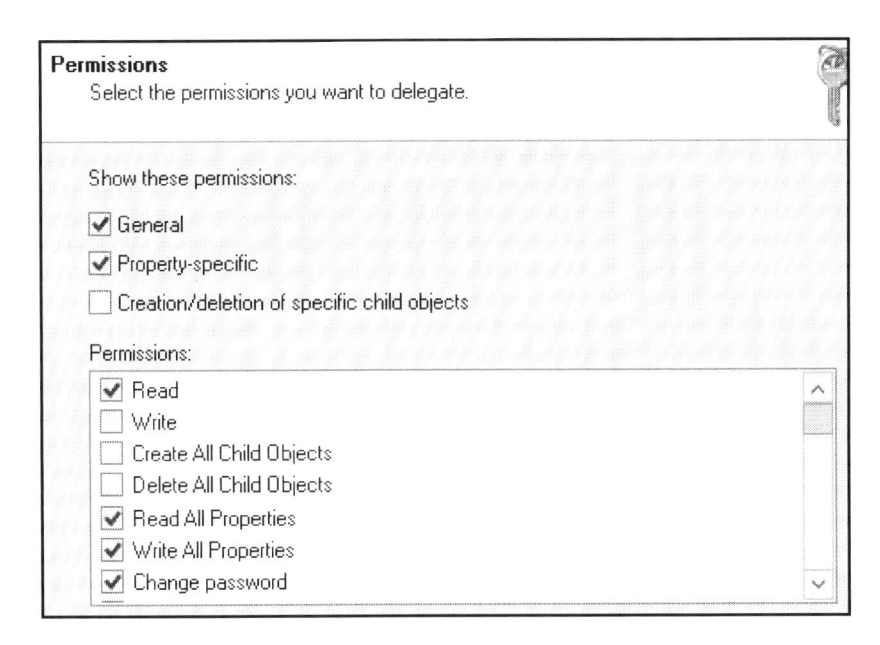

```
Permissions
    Select the permissions you want to delegate.

Show these permissions:
  ☑ General
  ☑ Property-specific
  ☐ Creation/deletion of specific child objects

Permissions:
  ☑ Read
  ☐ Write
  ☐ Create All Child Objects
  ☐ Delete All Child Objects
  ☑ Read All Properties
  ☑ Write All Properties
  ☑ Change password
```

9. In the **Delegation of Control Wizard | Completing the Delegation of Control Wizard** window, review the changes, making any changes if needed, and then click **Finish**.

The Horizon Composer service account now has the permissions needed to manage AD computer objects in the selected OU and any child OUs within it.

Horizon Composer database

Horizon Composer requires an external database in order to store information about vCenter Server connections, AD connections, and linked clone desktops and Windows RDS servers as well as their associated virtual hard disks.

Chapter 1, *VMware Horizon Infrastructure Overview*, outlines the different database types that are supported by Horizon Composer. In addition to using a supported database platform, the following database configuration item must be performed:

- Create a 64-bit **Database Source Name (DSN)** connection for the Horizon Composer database on the Composer host server. This process is outlined in the Microsoft how-to guide titled **Using the ODBC Data Source Administrator** (https://docs.microsoft.com/en-us/sql/odbc/admin/odbc-data-source-administrator?view=sql-server-2017).

When using Horizon Composer with SQL Server databases, the following general requirements must be met:

- **Local SQL instance**: Windows NT authentication is supported; database owner permissions are required if not already present
- **Remote SQL instance**: Requires an SQL Server user account, SQL Server authentication, and the account must have database owner permissions

The database schema will be installed during the installation of Horizon Composer.

SQL Database tutorials

The following Microsoft documentation can assist with creating databases and creating users and granting them access to databases:

- **Create a Database** – https://docs.microsoft.com/en-us/sql/relational-databases/databases/create-a-database?view=sql-server-2017
- **Managing Logins, Users, and Schemas How-to Topics** – https://docs.microsoft.com/en-us/sql/relational-databases/security/authentication-access/managing-logins-users-and-schemas-how-to-topics?view=sql-server-2017

Deploying Horizon Composer

The deployment of Horizon Composer is broken down into two stages: the installation of the Horizon Composer software, and the final setup using the Horizon Administrator console.

Installing Horizon Composer

The Horizon Composer software is delivered as a single executable (EXE) file, named in a format similar to `VMware-viewcomposer-x.x.x-yyyyyy.exe`. The following steps outline the installation process:

> **TIP**: If you plan to use a custom SSL certificate for Horizon Composer, install that certificate prior to installing Composer. If you install the certificate now, you can select it during the installation process. Refer to `Chapter 16`, *Managing Horizon SSL Certificates*, for instructions on how to obtain and deploy a new SSL certificate for Horizon Composer.

1. If it has not already been done, grant the Horizon Composer service account (`svc-horizoncomp`) local administrator access on the Horizon Composer host server.
2. Double-click on the Horizon Composer installer EXE file to launch the installer.
3. In the **Welcome to the Installation Wizard for VMware Horizon 7 Composer** window, click on **Next >**.
4. Review the **License Agreement**. Then select the **I accept the terms in the license agreement** radio button and click on **Next >**.
5. Select the installation directory and click on **Next >**.
6. Provide the name of the Horizon Composer **Data Source Name** (**DSN**), database user, and the password. The following screenshot shows the required information for our sample environment. Click on **Next >** to move on to the next step:

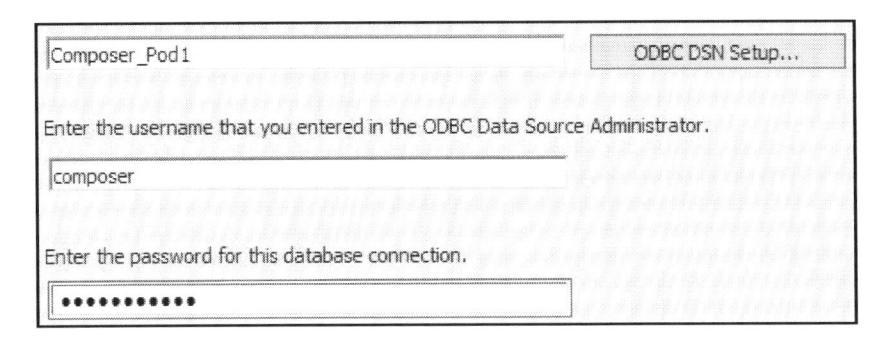

```
Composer_Pod1                                    ODBC DSN Setup...

Enter the username that you entered in the ODBC Data Source Administrator.
composer

Enter the password for this database connection.
••••••••••
```

Implementing Horizon Composer

7. If no SSL certificates were previously installed, select **Next >** to accept the default port settings as shown in the following screenshot. If a SSL certificate was preinstalled, select the **Use an existing SSL certificate** radio button and highlight the desired certificate from the list provided. Click on **Next >** to move on to the next step:

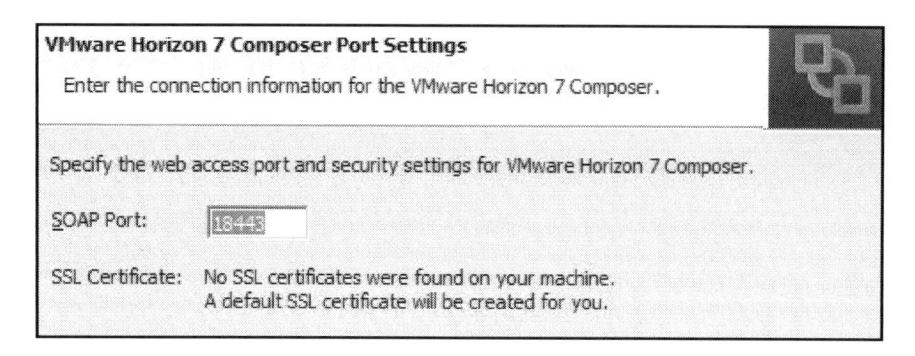

```
VMware Horizon 7 Composer Port Settings
Enter the connection information for the VMware Horizon 7 Composer.

Specify the web access port and security settings for VMware Horizon 7 Composer.

SOAP Port:        18443

SSL Certificate:  No SSL certificates were found on your machine.
                  A default SSL certificate will be created for you.
```

8. Click on **Install** to initiate the installation process and reboot the Composer server as requested when the installation is complete.

Horizon Composer is now ready to be configured, which is done using the Horizon Administrator console.

Configuring Horizon Composer

To link Horizon Composer to the Horizon Pod, you need to log in to the Horizon Administrator console. The console URL will be in the format `https://Connection Server FQDN/admin`. The following steps outline the configuration process:

1. Log in to the Horizon Administrator console using an AD account that has administrative permissions within Horizon.
2. Navigate to **View Configuration** | **Servers** within the console.

[88]

Chapter 3

3. Select the **vCenter Servers** tab in the **Servers** window, highlight the vCenter Server you wish to enable for Horizon Composer, and click on **Edit** to open the **Edit vCenter Server** window. In the following screenshot, we edit the **vc-01.vjason.local** vCenter Server. Note the appearance of the green and yellow vCenter icon to the left of the vCenter Server name; that icon will change once Horizon Composer is enabled:

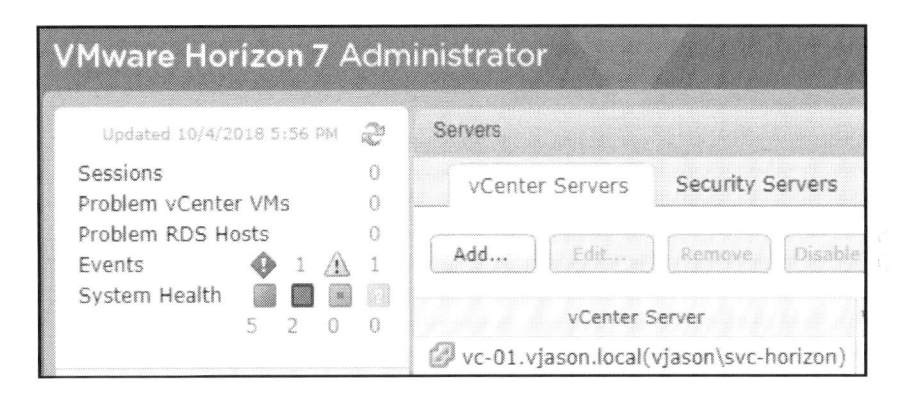

TIP

Any errors that occur during the remaining steps are likely related to insufficient permissions for the Horizon Composer service account to either AD or vCenter. If errors occur, review the *Horizon Composer service account* section and verify that the necessary permissions have been granted.

4. Check the **Standalone View Composer Server** radio button and complete the following tasks:
    1. Populate the **Server address** field with the FQDN of the dedicated Horizon Composer host server.
    2. Provide **User name** and **Password** for the dedicated Horizon Composer AD account. Use the format `domain-name\user-name` for the username.
    3. Since we used the default port when installing Horizon Composer, we do not need to change the **Port** value.

Implementing Horizon Composer

5. Click on **Verify Server Information** shown in the following screenshot to verify Horizon Composer access to the AD domain:

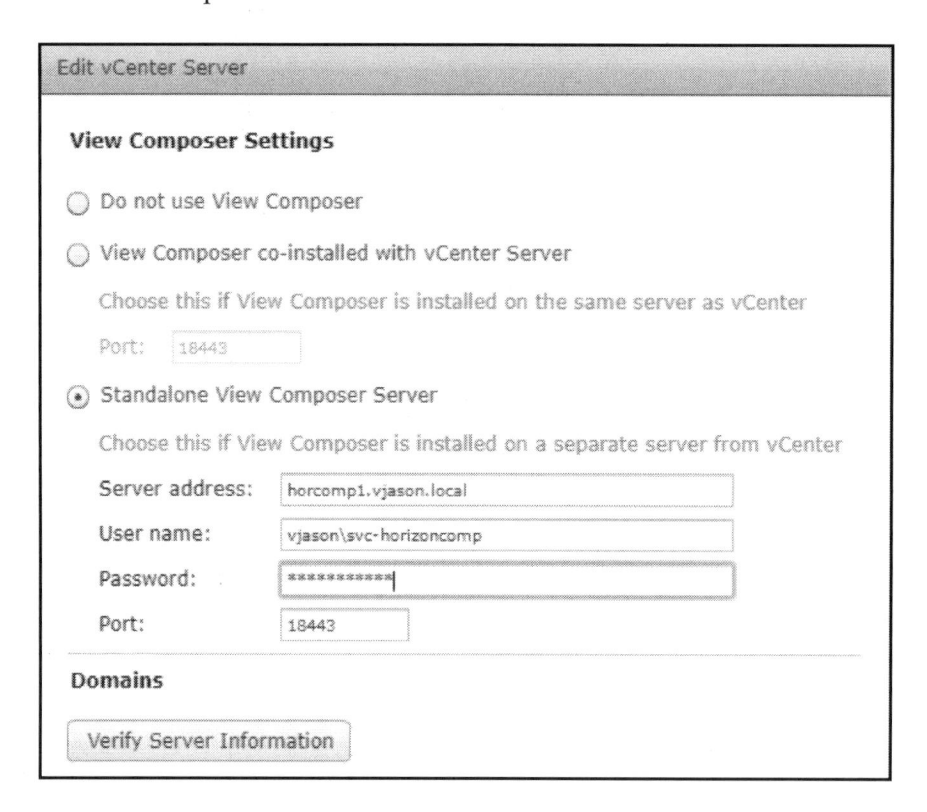

```
Edit vCenter Server

View Composer Settings

○ Do not use View Composer

○ View Composer co-installed with vCenter Server
   Choose this if View Composer is installed on the same server as vCenter
   Port: 18443

● Standalone View Composer Server
   Choose this if View Composer is installed on a separate server from vCenter
   Server address: horcomp1.vjason.local
   User name:      vjason\svc-horizoncomp
   Password:       ***********
   Port:           18443

Domains

[ Verify Server Information ]
```

6. If the Horizon Composer server was installed with the default, untrusted SSL certificate the **Invalid Certificate Detected** window will be displayed. Click the **View Certificate...** button to open the **Certificate Information** window.
7. In the **Certificate Information** window, review the certificate and click **Accept** to return to the **Edit vCenter Server** window.
8. In the **Edit vCenter Server** window under **Domains**, click **Add...** to open the **Edit Domain** window as shown in the following screenshot:

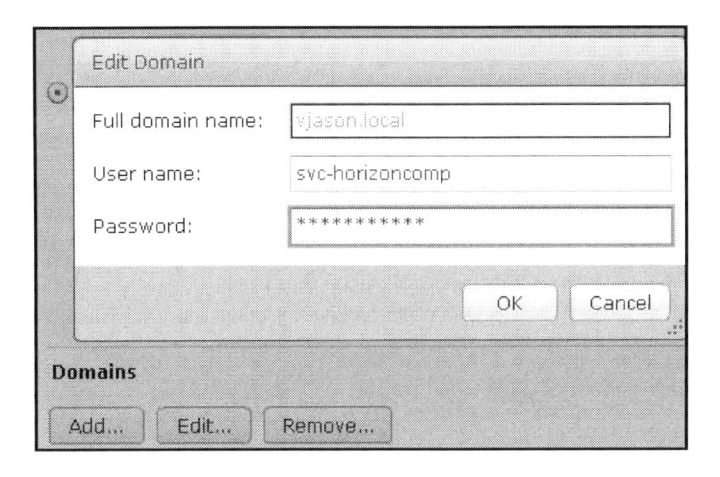

Chapter 3

9. Provide the **User name** and **Password** for the Horizon Composer service account and click **OK** to return to the **Edit vCenter Server** window.
10. Confirm that the **Standalone View Composer Server** and **Domains** fields have been populated as shown in the following screenshot:

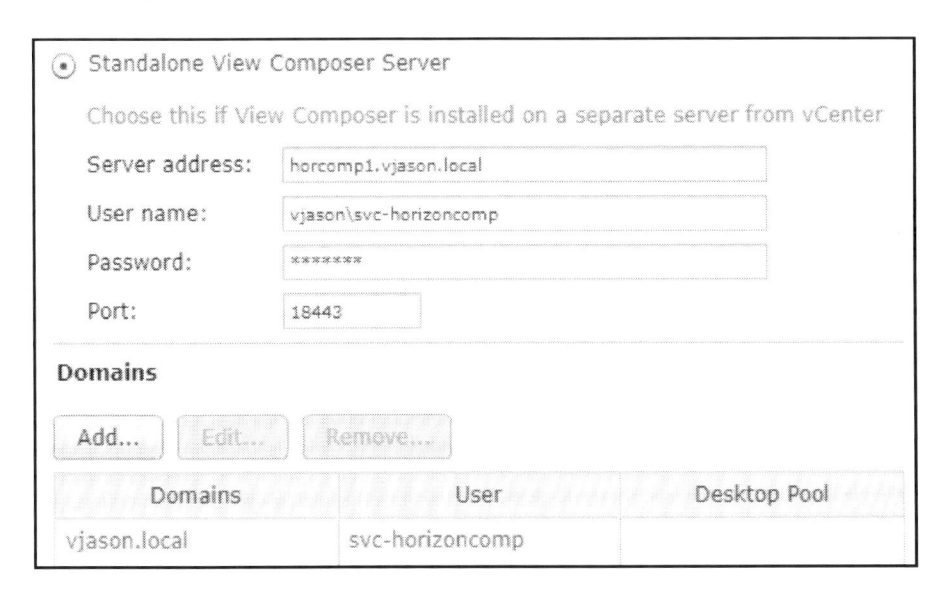

11. Click **OK**, and then **OK** again in the parent **Edit vCenter Server** window to complete the Horizon Composer configuration.

[91]

Implementing Horizon Composer

12. Review the vCenter icon to the left of the vCenter Server name in the **View Configuration** | **Servers** page within the console; as Horizon Composer is now enabled, that icon will be displayed within a yellow square as shown in the following screenshot:

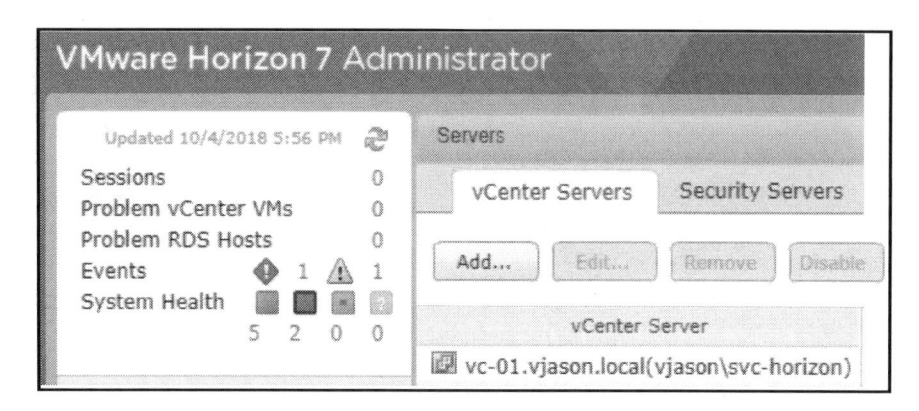

Horizon Composer is now linked to the Horizon Pod, and available to provision linked clone desktops or Windows RDS servers.

Backing up Horizon Composer

The information required to restore Horizon Composer is stored in two different locations:

- Horizon Composer database
- Horizon Composer SSL certificates or RSA key container

The Horizon Composer database should be backed up as part of a larger backup plan that includes the vCenter database, the Horizon Connection Server AD LDS database, and the Horizon Event database. By default, each Horizon Connection Server backs up both the AD LDS database and the Composer database to a folder on the Connection Server.

Backing up the Horizon Composer database

The Horizon Connection Server backs up the Horizon Composer database as part of its own native backup process. This is the preferred method of backing up the Horizon Composer database as it will be backed up at the same time as the Horizon Connection Server AD LDS database. As these databases contain related information, it is critical that they are backed up at the same time.

The default location for the Horizon Connection Server database backups is on any Horizon Connection Server in the `C:\ProgramData\VMware\VDM\backups` folder. The Horizon Composer database backups will have an SVI extension and include the name of the Horizon Composer host server in the filename. In our example, the most recent Horizon Composer database backup file is named `Backup-20181004180731-horcomp01_vjason_local.SVI` and is the name of the dedicated Horizon Composer host server in our sample environment.

The Horizon Composer database may also be backed up using native database backup tools. This includes options such as the following:

- Native backups based on the capabilities of the database platform, such as Microsoft SQL Server backup
- Third-party database backup solutions

> **TIP**: Remember that while native database backups will work, they may not be usable for restore purposes if they were not performed at the same time as the Horizon Connection Server AD LDS database backup. It is recommended you use the backups performed by the Horizon Connection Server, if you need to restore the Horizon Composer database.

Refer to your database server or backup software documentation if additional information about performing database backups is required.

Backing up the Horizon Composer SSL certificates

The process used to back up the default Horizon Composer SSL certificate requires the Microsoft .NET Framework to be installed on the Horizon Composer host server.

The following steps explain how to back up the SSL certificates:

1. From the Command Prompt on the Horizon Composer host server, navigate to the `c:\Windows\Microsoft.NET\Framework\v4.0.xxxxx` directory.
2. Execute the following command to export the Horizon Composer RSA key container to a local file named `keys.xml`:

   ```
   aspnet_regiis -px "SviKeyContainer" "keys.xml" -pri
   ```

Implementing Horizon Composer

The following screenshot shows the expected output if the command was successful:

```
c:\Windows\Microsoft.NET\Framework\v4.0.30319>aspnet_regiis.exe -px "SviKeyConta
iner" "keys.xml" -pri
Microsoft (R) ASP.NET RegIIS version 4.0.30319.34209
Administration utility to install and uninstall ASP.NET on the local machine.
Copyright (C) Microsoft Corporation.  All rights reserved.
Exporting RSA Keys to file...
Succeeded!
```

The `keys.xml` file should be backed up to an alternative location to be used in the event that the Horizon Composer software needs to be installed on a new server.

`Chapter 16`, *Managing Horizon SSL Certificates*, outlines the process by which you can obtain new certificates for all Horizon components. During this process, you obtain a copy of the SSL certificate that can be used when restoring a Horizon Connection server from backups. If you choose to use a custom SSL certificate, you do not need to use the `aspnet_regiis` command to export the Horizon Composer RSA key container. During the creation of your custom SSL certificate, you should have been given a copy of it with the private key intact, which is what is required to perform a restore.

Horizon Composer recovery

The same process is used to recover or move Horizon Composer to a new host server. To retain the current settings, all that needs to be restored is the Horizon Composer database and the RSA key container or custom SSL certificate.

Restoring the Horizon Composer database

The Horizon Composer database should be restored using the native Horizon `sviconfig.exe` command-line tool. This tool is located within the install directory of Horizon Composer, which is at the following location on our sample server: `D:\Program Files (x86)\VMware\VMware View Composer`.

[94]

You will need the following information to restore the database:

- The name of your **Database Source Name** (**DSN**) connection on the Horizon Connection Server. On our sample server, the name is `Composer_Pod1`.
- Horizon Composer database username. On our sample server, the name is `composer`.
- Horizon Composer database password. On our sample server, the password is `Password123`.
- The backup file path location of the `Backup-20181004180731-horcomp01_vjason_local.SVI` file referenced in the *Backing up the Horizon Composer database* section of this chapter. On our sample server, the file is located in `C:\Temp`.

> **TIP**
> The Horizon Composer database and Horizon Connection Server AD LDS databases contain related data. If one is being restored, the other should also be restored, using the restore data from the same backup set. Failure to adhere to this rule can lead to database inconsistencies that will require the assistance of VMware Support in order to fix them.

The following steps outline the process used to restore the database, using the information from our sample server:

1. Stop the VMware Horizon Composer service.
2. From the Command Prompt, navigate to the Horizon Composer installation directory.
3. Execute the following command to restore the Horizon Composer database backup. A screenshot that shows the command input is provided after the command:

   ```
   sviconfig -operation=restoredata -dsnname=Composer_Pod1 -
   username=composer -password=Password123 -
   backupfilepath="C:\Temp\Backup-2018-1004180731-
   horcomp01_vjason_local.SVI."
   ```

```
c:\Program Files (x86)\VMware\VMware View Composer>SviConfig.exe -operation=rest
oredata -dsnname=Composer_Pod1 -username=composer -password=Password123 -backupf
ilepath="C:\Temp\Backup-20181004180731-horcomp1_vjason_local.SVI"_
```

[95]

4. The restore process should output several lines of status information. The last few lines of the output are shown in the following screenshot, the last of which indicates that the restore was successful:

```
Object type AdConfigEntryDo found in the backup
Object type UcConfigEntryDo found in the backup
Object type AuthorizedUserDo found in the backup
Object type SequenceNumDo found in the backup
Object type UmNameDo found in the backup
Object type GuestComputerNameDo found in the backup
Object type ReplicaDo found in the backup
Object type DeploymentGroupDo found in the backup
Object type SimCloneDo found in the backup
Restoring data finished successfully.

c:\Program Files (x86)\VMware\VMware View Composer>
```

5. Start the Horizon Composer service.

Horizon Composer is now operating with the restored database.

Restoring the Horizon Composer SSL certificates

The process to restore Horizon Composer SSL certificates varies depending on the scenario. The following sections explain the procedure you should use based on whether or not you plan to re-use an existing SSL certificate. Both of these procedures assume that you have already restored your Horizon Composer database and configured an ODBC connection to that database on your Horizon Composer host server.

Restoring Horizon Composer with a new default SSL certificate

Prior to installing the Horizon Composer software, restore the RSA key container that was backed up in the section Backing up the Horizon Composer SSL certificates. The following steps outline the full restore process:

1. Copy the `keys.xml` backup file to a location on the new Horizon Composer host server. In our example, the file has been placed within the folder from which we will be executing the restore command.
2. From the Command Prompt on the new Horizon Composer host server, navigate to the `c:\Windows\Microsoft.NET\Framework\v4.0xxxxx` directory.

[96]

Chapter 3

3. Execute the following command to import the Horizon Composer RSA key container. A screenshot that shows the expected output if the command was successful is provided after the command:

   ```
   aspnet_regiis -pi "SviKeyContainer" "keys.xml" -exp
   ```

   ```
   c:\Windows\Microsoft.NET\Framework\v4.0.30319>aspnet_regiis.exe -pi "SviKeyConta
   iner" "C:\Temp\keys.xml" -exp
   Microsoft (R) ASP.NET RegIIS version 4.0.30319.34209
   Administration utility to install and uninstall ASP.NET on the local machine.
   Copyright (C) Microsoft Corporation.  All rights reserved.
   Importing RSA Keys from file..
   Succeeded!
   ```

4. Reinstall Horizon Composer using the steps provided in the section *Installing Horizon Composer*. Since this is a new server, Horizon Composer will note that no SSL certificates are available and will create a new one.

Horizon Composer is now ready to be linked to the Horizon Connection server using the steps provided in the *Configuring Horizon Composer* section. If only Composer was restored, and the link between the Connection Servers and Composer is already present, you will need to re-verify the SSL certificate as described starting with step 5 of *Configuring Horizon Composer*.

Restoring Horizon Composer with a custom SSL certificate

The process used to restore a Horizon Connection server with a custom SSL certificate is straightforward as all the steps are handled within either the Microsoft Certificates MMC Snap-in or during the installation of Horizon Composer. The following steps outline the full restore process:

> **TIP**: Since we are re-using the same SSL certificate, it is important to remember that the new Horizon Composer host server needs to have the same computer name as the old one.

1. Install the custom SSL certificate on the new Horizon Connection server using the procedure outlined in `Chapter 16`, *Managing Horizon SSL Certificates*.
2. Reinstall Horizon Composer using the steps provided in the *Installing Horizon Composer* section. Since the SSL certificate has already been installed, select the option **Use an existing SSL certificate**, and select the designated certificate.
3. Complete the installation and reboot the Horizon Composer host server.

Horizon Composer is now ready to be linked to the Horizon Connection server using the steps provided in the *Configuring Horizon Composer* section. If only Composer was restored, and the link between the Connection Servers and Composer is already present, you may need to re-verify the SSL certificate as described starting with step 5 of *Configuring Horizon Composer*. If the certificate was in fact already trusted by the Connection Server, this step is typically not required.

Summary

In this chapter, you have been introduced to an important and powerful component of the Horizon installation: VMware Horizon Composer. You have learned about what is required to deploy Horizon Composer, what the limits of Composer are, and how to perform its installation and configuration.

We also discussed how to back up the Horizon Composer configuration, which includes the RSA key container and Horizon Composer database.

We concluded this chapter by discussing how to restore the Horizon Composer database and RSA key container or SSL certificate, and how that process varies based on the recovery scenario.

In the next chapter, we will implement Horizon Security Server, the component of a Horizon installation that enables secure access to Horizon resources on your internal network from an external network, such as the internet.

Questions

1. Name the key features that Horizon Composer enables.
2. What option for deploying Horizon Composer no longer exists in vSphere 6.7?
3. What is the only database software that is supported by Horizon Composer (you don't need to list all the versions of that software that are supported)?
4. What additional step must you perform (beyond the native Horizon Connection Server backups of the Horizon database) to ensure you can rebuild a Horizon Composer server after a disaster?

6. Are you required to deploy one Horizon Composer server for every vCenter server you will link to Horizon (assume you will be deploying linked clones on vSphere hosts managed by that server)?
7. What steps must you perform prior to installing the Horizon Composer software?
8. How do you link a Horizon Composer instance with your Horizon Pod?

Further reading

The following resources may be used to learn more about the topics described in this chapter:

- VMware documentation:
    - **VMware Horizon** (https://docs.vmware.com/en/VMware-Horizon-7/index.html)
    - **VMware vSphere** (https://www.vmware.com/support/pubs/vsphere-esxi-vcenter-server-pubs.html)

Implementing Horizon Security Server

VMware Horizon Security Server is a core feature of the Horizon platform that enables secure remote access to applications and desktops, without the need to use a connection or provide direct access from the internet to the Horizon Connection Server. The Horizon Security Server is a specialized installation of the Horizon Connection Server that serves as the connection point between remote Horizon Clients and desktops or applications hosted on a private network.

This chapter will discuss the installation, configuration, backup, and recovery of the Horizon Security Server.

In this chapter, we will look at the following topics:

- An overview of the Horizon Security Server
- The connection limits of a Horizon Security Server
- Horizon Security Server network protocol and port usage
- Horizon Security Server prerequisites
- How to enable the Horizon Blast/PCoIP Secure Gateway setting
- How to install a Horizon Security Server
- How to update the Horizon Security Server and Connection Server settings
- How and what components of the Horizon Security Server to back up
- How to restore or upgrade a Horizon Security Server

Horizon Security Server overview

The Horizon Security Server is a type of Horizon Connection Server that is designed to add an additional layer of security between remote Horizon Clients and Horizon resources that are located on a private network. Rather than provide remote Horizon clients with direct access to the Horizon Connection Server, organizations can deploy a Horizon Security Server within a DMZ or other secure network to provide secure remote access to Horizon-managed resources. Some of the functions and features of the Horizon Security Server include the following:

- Provides remote Horizon Clients with their own dedicated Horizon connection broker, ensuring an optimal user experience
- Brokers connections between remote Horizon Clients and internal Horizon-managed resources
- Authenticates user connection requests
- Supports both **RSA SecureID** and **RADIUS** for enabling optional two-factor user authentication; currently supported RADIUS providers include **VASCO DIGIPASS**, **SMS Passcode**, **SafeNet**, and others
- Can be placed in a DMZ to further isolate the Security Server from the private network
- Does not need to be a member of an **Active Directory** (**AD**) domain

The following diagram shows the placement of a Horizon Security Server in a simple Horizon environment. The Horizon Security Server brokers access to a number of different components of the private Horizon infrastructure, each of which is shown in the diagram:

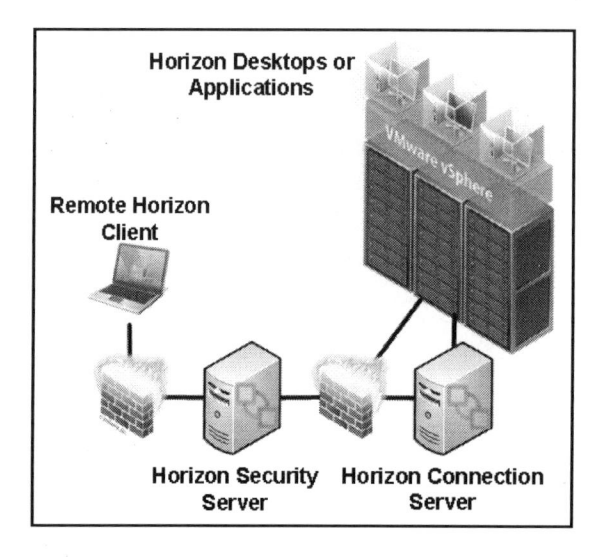

The **Horizon Security Server** authenticates the clients by contacting the **Horizon Connection Server**, and then provides them with access to the entitled resources including **Horizon Desktops or Applications**.

> **TIP**: Horizon Unified Access Gateway is a hardened, Linux-based virtual appliance that provides similar capabilities to a Horizon Security Server. Chapter 5, *Implementing Horizon Unified Access Gateway*, provides details about the installation and configuration of this newer Horizon component, which is an alternative to the Horizon Security Server.

Horizon Security Server limits

A Horizon Security Server can support up to 2,000 simultaneous Horizon client connections, which is half the number that the Connection Server it connects to can support. Due to this, it is important to deploy multiple Security Servers so that both capacity and availability requirements are met.

Each Horizon Security Server is a stand-alone instance; therefore, there is no specific guidance with regard to how many can be deployed. A Horizon Security Server can only be paired with one Horizon Connection Server while a Connection Server can be paired with multiple Security Servers.

> **TIP**: Keep in mind that the more Horizon Connection Servers you deploy, the more Security Servers you will need as well. For example, if you deploy the pod-maximum of 7 active Connection Servers, and intend to pair Security Servers with all of them, you should deploy 14 Security Servers to ensure redundancy, or two per Connection Server. When designing your Horizon infrastructure you will want make all layers of it redundant, as this is the only way to ensure that the high levels of availability and performance that your end users will require.

Horizon Security Server additional considerations

The following are additional considerations that should be kept in mind when deploying a Horizon Security Server:

- If you require Windows IPsec encryption to be applied to the network traffic between the Horizon Security Server and the Horizon Connection Server, the Windows firewall service must be enabled for both hosts in order for Horizon to create the required Windows IPsec policies. The firewall service is enabled by default; if it was disabled, visit the Microsoft TechNet article **Windows Firewall with Advanced Security Overview** (https://technet.microsoft.com/en-us/library/hh831365.aspx) for information about how to manage the feature. It is recommended to enable the firewall service prior to the installation of any Horizon software component, as the installer will then automatically configure the appropriate settings.
- Like Horizon Connection Servers, Horizon Security Servers have no native load-balancing functionality. It is recommended that you implement some sort of load-balancing functionality to help balance the client connections across all the Horizon Security Servers in your infrastructure. Refer to the *Load-Balancing Connection Servers* section in Chapter 2, *Implementing Horizon Connection Server*, for information about load-balancing options.
- When installed, the Horizon Security Server is configured with a self-signed SSL certificate that will not be trusted by Horizon clients. It is recommended that you replace the self-signed certificate with one issued from an internal or commercial certificate authority that the Horizon clients will trust. Chapter 16, *Managing Horizon SSL Certificates* will provide the process used to replace the default SSL certificates for all Horizon components.
- Options such as tunneling connections and two-factor authentication are set on a per-Connection Server basis. If either of these options is going to be used, and you do not want to subject internal Horizon clients to the additional security measures, you are required to deploy additional Connection Servers with these settings enabled to be used solely with the Horizon Security Servers.

High availability overview

When deploying Horizon Security Servers it is important to understand how that impacts our high availability requirements. This section will provide an overview of what a highly available Horizon infrastructure that must service both internal and external clients might look like.

The following diagram illustrates a Horizon infrastructure that meets the following four requirements:

- Internal Horizon clients use load-balanced connections to Connection Servers
- Remote Horizon clients use load-balanced connections to Security Servers
- Security Servers installed in a DMZ
- Two-factor authentication or connection tunneling policies that apply only to remote Horizon clients

The diagram does not show the connections to the Horizon desktops or applications; it is only meant to illustrate the placement of load-balancing appliances, and show how true high-availability might be achieved in an environment that includes multiple Horizon Security Servers. In addition, it shows that additional Connection Servers are being used for internal clients, as these connections do not require the same security settings as the remote clients do:

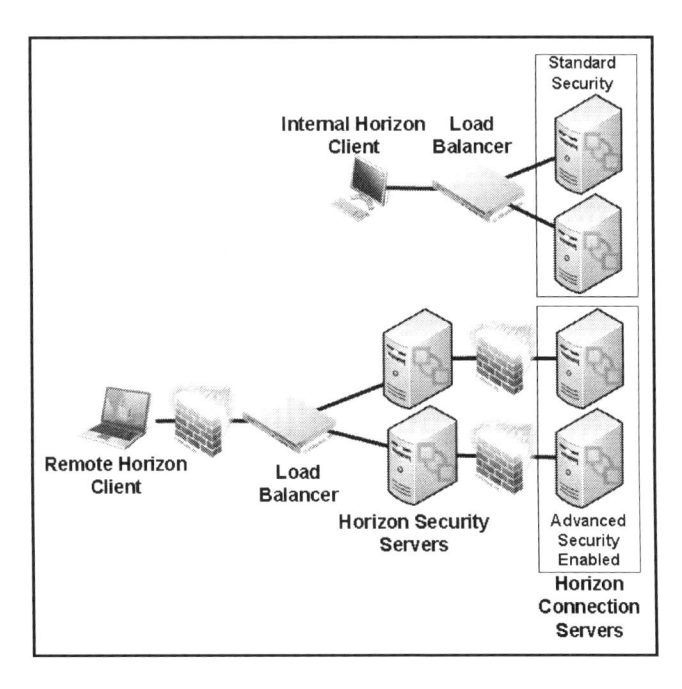

[105]

This Horizon architecture ensures that Horizon clients will be able to connect or reconnect if either of these two scenarios were to occur:

- Failure of any one of the four Connection Servers shown in the diagram
- Failure of any one of the Security Servers

As a single Horizon Security Server cannot be paired with more than one Connection Server, there is no need to place a load balancer between the Security Servers and the Connection Servers. Load balancing the Security Servers ensures that the Horizon client connection will be maintained regardless of which server fails, be it a Security Server or the Connection Server that it is paired to.

Security Server network requirements

The following diagram illustrates how the primary protocols used by the Horizon Security Server work with other components of the Horizon infrastructure. The diagram shows the following components of a Horizon infrastructure:

- Communication between the **Horizon Security Server** and the **Horizon Desktop or Application**
- Communication between the **Horizon Security Server** and the **Horizon Connection Server**

The arrows indicate the direction in which each protocol travels, assuming that the default settings are used:

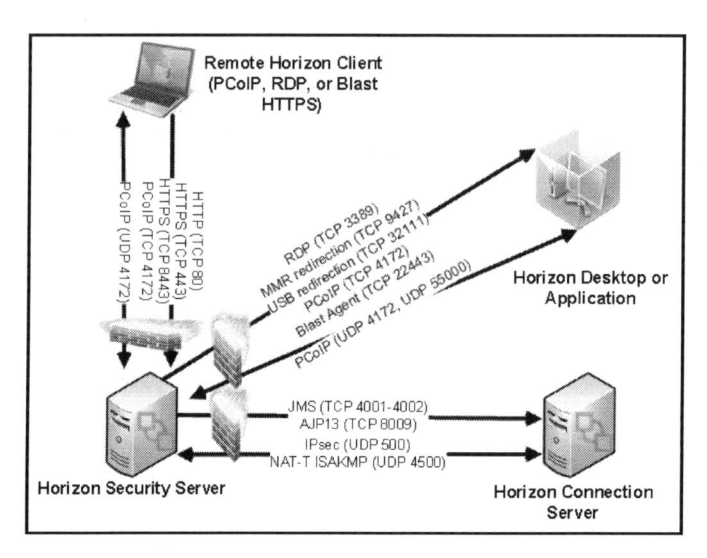

This list of ports used by the core components is outlined in the following table. Additionally, consult the **Firewall Rules for DMS-Based Security Servers** in the VMware document **Horizon Architecture Planning** (https://docs.vmware.com/en/VMware-Horizon-7/7.6/horizon-architecture-planning.pdf) for additional information concerning the function of each component, and when the associated port is actually required to be opened in the firewall:

Protocol or Service	Port	Notes
AJP13 (Apache Tomcat Connector)	TCP 8009	Not used if IPsec is enabled and the DMZ backend firewall uses one-way or two-way NAT.
Blast Agent	TCP/UDP 22443	Used to connect to the Blast (HTML Access) Agent on the desktop or application host
HTTP/HTTPS	TCP 80/443/8443	Port TCP 8443 is only used for HTML Access (web) clients.
JMS (Java Messaging Service)	TCP 4001-4002	If upgrading existing Horizon Security Servers, port TCP 4002 might not be open as it was not previously required.
MMR (Multimedia redirection)	TCP 9427	Used alongside RDP; uses client rather than server resources to render DirectShow-based media and codecs.
NAT-T ISAKMP	UDP 4500	Used to negotiate IPsec security; if the DMZ backend firewall uses one-way or two-way NAT, and IPsec is enabled, UDP port 4500 must be allowed in each direction between the Security Server and the Horizon Connection Server.
PCoIP	TCP/UDP 4172, UDP 55000	
RDP	TCP 3389	
IPsec	UDP 500	
USB Redirection for PCoIP, Blast, and RDP	TCP 32111	TCP 32111 is used to support USB redirection to Horizon clients.

> **TIP**: Consult the Horizon documentation (https://docs.vmware.com/en/VMware-Horizon-7/index.html) for a comprehensive list of all firewall ports required when implementing a Security Server.

Installing and configuring Horizon Security Server

The installation and configuration process for the Horizon Security Server requires some amount of preparation. This section will outline what is required prior to beginning the installation.

Installation prerequisites

There are a number of prerequisites that should be addressed prior to installing a Horizon Security Server:

- At least one configured Horizon Connection Server with a license key must be installed.
- A dedicated 64-bit Windows 2008 R2 SP1, 2012 R2, or 2016 server is needed to host the Horizon Security Server role.
- You must have two network adapters and a static IP address for each on the Security Server host (one adapter will be public facing, the other private facing).
- The Security Server host should be able to resolve the FQDN of the Connection Server it will pair with, either using DNS or the local hosts file.
- You must have a valid Horizon Connection Server pairing password is needed.
- Firewall access is required between the Horizon Security Server and the necessary Horizon components on the private network.
- Firewall access between the Internet and the Horizon Security Server.
- A resolvable public URL that will be used for accessing the Horizon Security Server.
- You must have local administrator access on the host server.

In addition to the items described in `Chapter 1`, *VMware Horizon Infrastructure Overview*, the following items should be prepared in advance of the installation.

Security Server pairing password

The Horizon Security Server is paired to a Horizon Connection Server using a password that is specified in the Horizon Administrator console. This password is entered during the installation of the Security Server, and enables secure communication between it and the Connection Server on the private network. The following steps outline how to generate the password:

1. Log on to the Horizon Administrator console using an AD account that has administrative permissions within Horizon.
2. Navigate to the **View Configuration** | **Servers** page within the console.
3. Select the **Connection Servers** tab in the **Servers** window.
4. Highlight the Connection Server that you wish to pair with the Security Server, click on the **More Commands** button, and select **Specify Security Server Pairing Password...**. In the following screenshot, we have highlighted the **HORCON01** Connection Server:

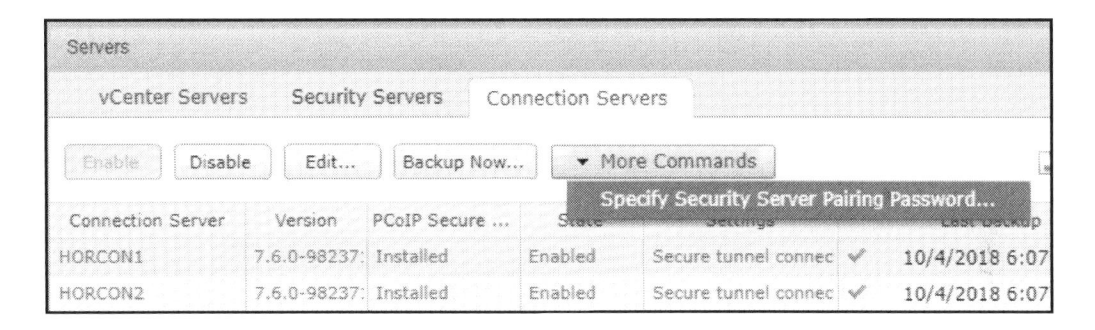

Connection Server	Version	PCoIP Secure ...	State	Settings	Last Backup
HORCON1	7.6.0-98237	Installed	Enabled	Secure tunnel connec ✓	10/4/2018 6:07
HORCON2	7.6.0-98237	Installed	Enabled	Secure tunnel connec ✓	10/4/2018 6:07

Implementing Horizon Security Server

5. In the **Specify Security Server Pairing Password** window, specify a password and the amount of time it will be valid for. Click on **OK** when finished. The following screenshot shows the **Pairing password:**, **Confirm password:**, and **Password timeout:** fields:

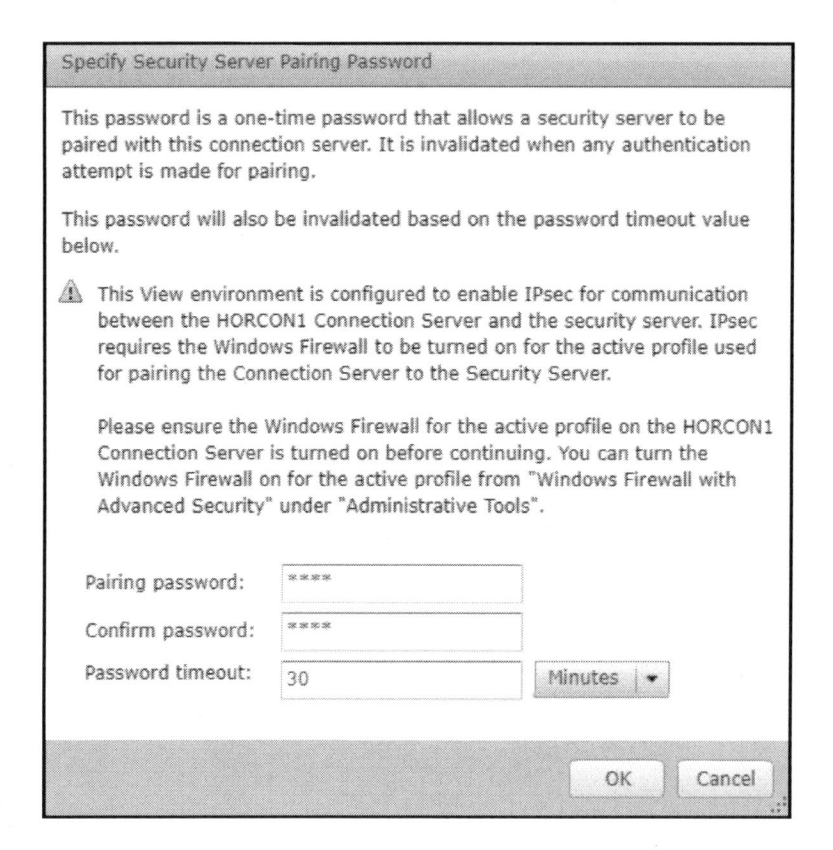

> **Specify Security Server Pairing Password**
>
> This password is a one-time password that allows a security server to be paired with this connection server. It is invalidated when any authentication attempt is made for pairing.
>
> This password will also be invalidated based on the password timeout value below.
>
> ⚠ This View environment is configured to enable IPsec for communication between the HORCON1 Connection Server and the security server. IPsec requires the Windows Firewall to be turned on for the active profile used for pairing the Connection Server to the Security Server.
>
> Please ensure the Windows Firewall for the active profile on the HORCON1 Connection Server is turned on before continuing. You can turn the Windows Firewall on for the active profile from "Windows Firewall with Advanced Security" under "Administrative Tools".
>
> Pairing password: `****`
> Confirm password: `****`
> Password timeout: `30` Minutes ▼
>
> OK   Cancel

With the password specified, the installation of the Security Server can now proceed. In the event that the installation cannot be completed prior to the password expiring, simply generate a new password.

Deploying a Horizon Security Server

Deploying a Horizon Security Server is broken down into two stages: the installation of the Horizon Security Server software, and the final setup using the Horizon Administrator console.

Enabling Blast/PCoIP Secure Gateway

By default, once a Horizon client has authenticated a Horizon Connection Server, it allows a direct connection to their target desktop or server hosting applications. The Connection Server is responsible only for brokering the connection, not maintaining it. While this is the optimal configuration for clients located on the private network where the desktops are located, it is not recommended for clients using public Internet connections as they do not have direct access to their desktops.

In order for external Horizon clients to gain access, the Horizon Connection Server must be configured with the appropriate Blast/PCoIP Secure Gateway settings. External clients are required to tunnel their connections through the Security Server, which, as we know, is designed to be the public internet-facing component of VMware Horizon. The options that control this behavior are known as the **Blast Secure Gateway** and **PCoIP Secure Gateway**, and it is not updated when you pair a Horizon Security Server with the Connection Server.

The Blast/PCoIP Secure Gateway configuration must be changed prior to placing a Security Server into production. The following steps outline how to enable the setting on the Connection Server we will use with our Security Servers. This setting may also be updated after the Security Servers have been installed:

1. Log on to the Horizon Administrator console using an AD account that has administrative permissions within Horizon.
2. Navigate to the **View Configuration** | **Servers** page within the console.
3. Select the **Connection Servers** tab in the **Servers** window.
4. Highlight the Connection Server that we intend to pair with the Security Server, and click on the **Edit...** button shown in the following screenshot to open the **Edit Connection Server Settings** window:

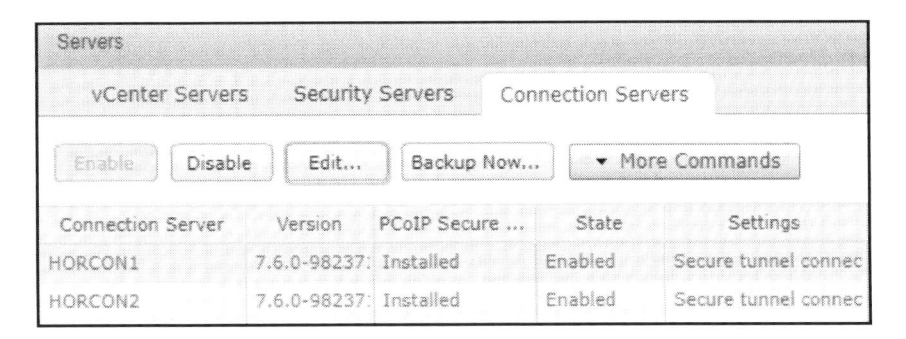

Implementing Horizon Security Server

5. In the **Edit Connection Server Settings** window, check the **Use PCoIP Secure Gateway for PCoIP connections to machine** and **Use Blast Secure Gateway for PCoIP connections to machine** checkboxes as shown in the following screenshot, and then click **OK**:

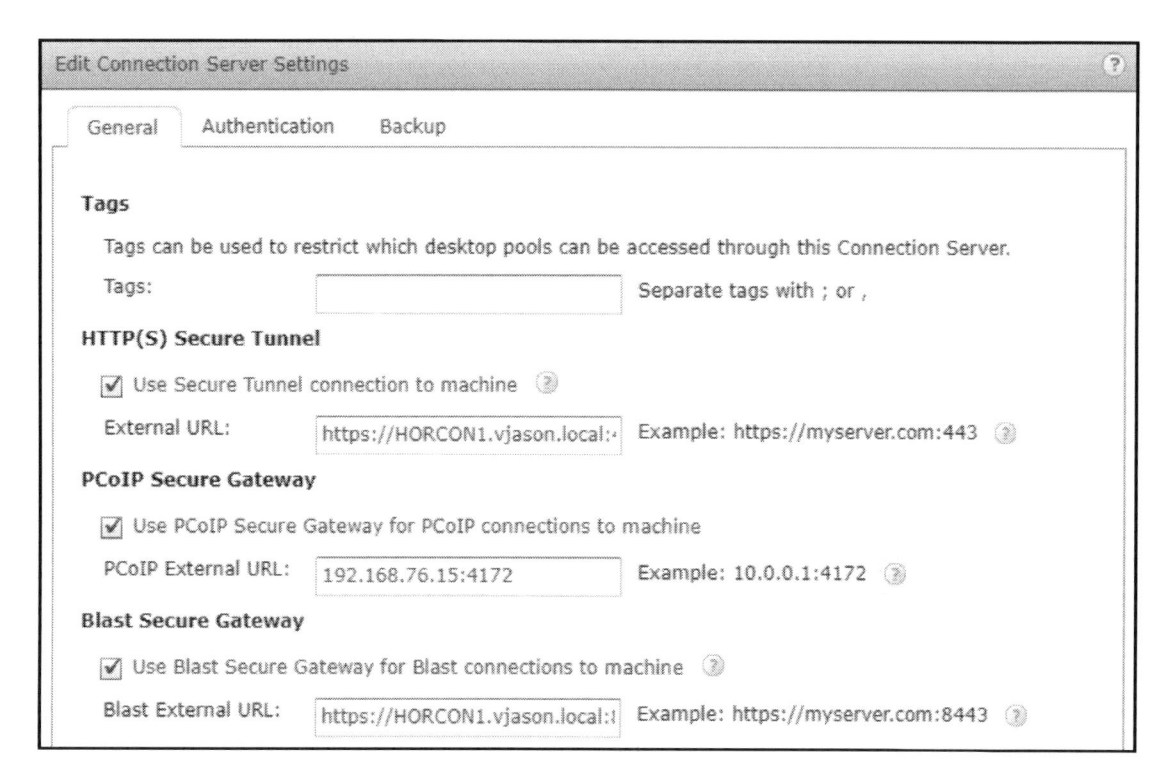

```
Edit Connection Server Settings

  General    Authentication    Backup

  Tags
    Tags can be used to restrict which desktop pools can be accessed through this Connection Server.
    Tags:                [                    ]    Separate tags with ; or ,
  HTTP(S) Secure Tunnel
    [✓] Use Secure Tunnel connection to machine
    External URL:        [https://HORCON1.vjason.local:]    Example: https://myserver.com:443
  PCoIP Secure Gateway
    [✓] Use PCoIP Secure Gateway for PCoIP connections to machine
    PCoIP External URL:  [192.168.76.15:4172]             Example: 10.0.0.1:4172
  Blast Secure Gateway
    [✓] Use Blast Secure Gateway for Blast connections to machine
    Blast External URL:  [https://HORCON1.vjason.local:]  Example: https://myserver.com:8443
```

The Blast/PCoIP Secure Gateway feature is now enabled, and any attempt to connect to Horizon desktops or applications will be tunneled through the Security Server or even through the Connection Server if the connection is made from within the private network.

> **TIP**: A similar settings screen is available for each Horizon Security Server in the **View Configuration** | **Servers - Security Servers** tab in the Horizon Administrator console. That page is shown in the section of this chapter titled *Security Server options*.

Installing a Horizon Security Server

The Horizon Security Server software is delivered as a single executable (EXE) file, named in a format similar to `VMware-Horizon-Connection-Server-x86_64-x.x.xyyyyyy.exe`. The following steps outline the installation process:

1. Double-click the Horizon Connection Server installer EXE file to launch the installer.
2. In the **Welcome to the Installation Wizard for VMware Horizon 7 Connection Server** window, click on **Next >**.
3. Review the **License Agreement**, select the **I accept the terms in the license agreement** radio button, and click on **Next >**.
4. Select the installation directory and click on **Next >**.
5. Select **Horizon 7 Security Server** as shown in the following screenshot, and then click on **Next >**:

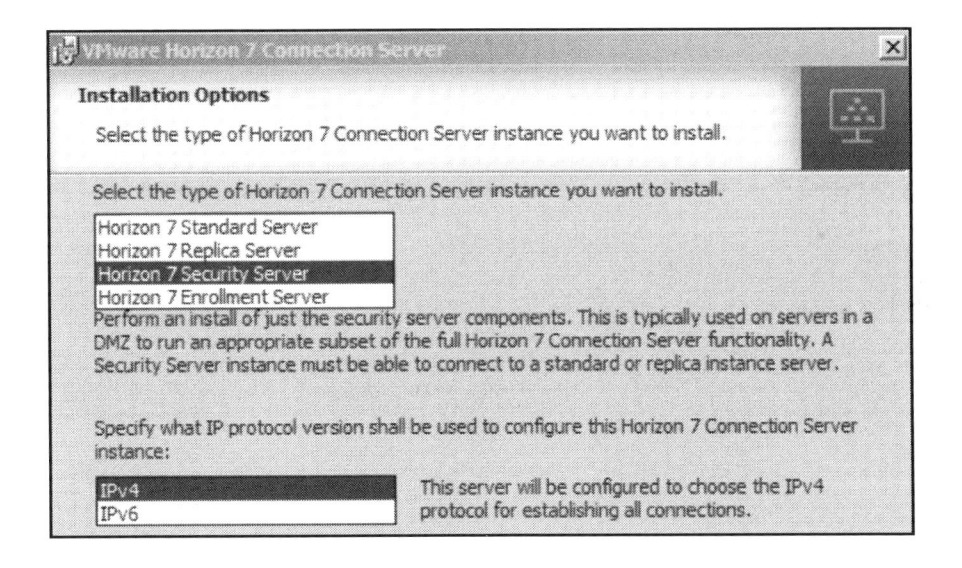

6. Enter the name of the Horizon Connection Server that the Horizon Security Server should be paired with in the **Server:** field and click on **Next >**.

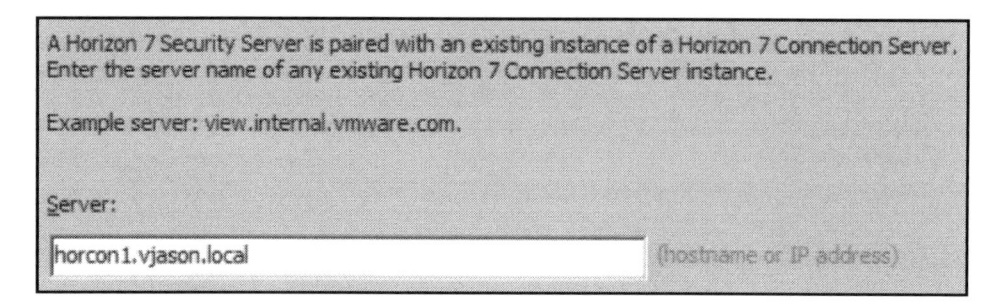

> A Horizon 7 Security Server is paired with an existing instance of a Horizon 7 Connection Server. Enter the server name of any existing Horizon 7 Connection Server instance.
>
> Example server: view.internal.vmware.com.
>
> Server:
>
> `horcon1.vjason.local`   (hostname or IP address)

7. In the **Password:** field, enter the Security Server Pairing Password that was specified earlier and click on **Next >**.

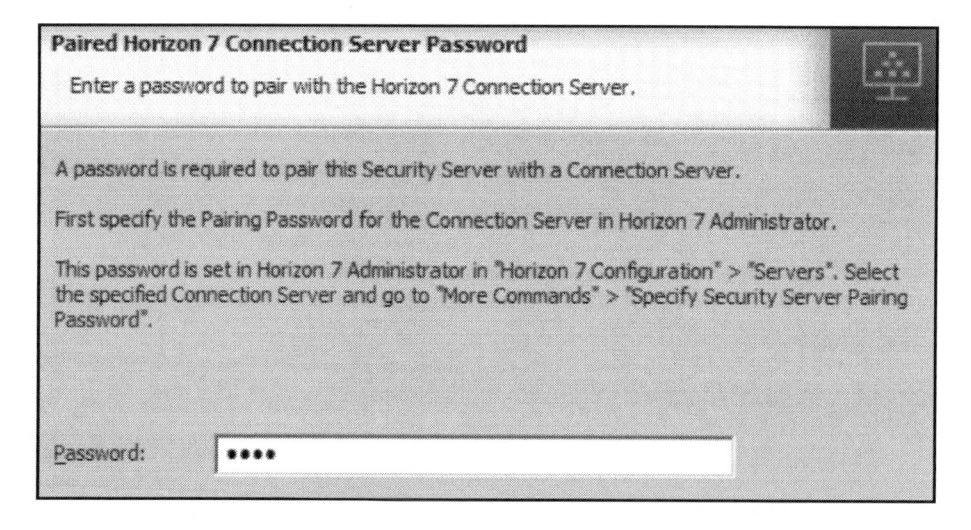

> **Paired Horizon 7 Connection Server Password**
> Enter a password to pair with the Horizon 7 Connection Server.
>
> A password is required to pair this Security Server with a Connection Server.
>
> First specify the Pairing Password for the Connection Server in Horizon 7 Administrator.
>
> This password is set in Horizon 7 Administrator in "Horizon 7 Configuration" > "Servers". Select the specified Connection Server and go to "More Commands" > "Specify Security Server Pairing Password".
>
> Password: ••••

8. Enter each of the publicly resolvable URLs as requested in the **External URL:**, **PCoIP External URL:**, and **Blast External URL:** fields. Click on **Next >** when complete.

Chapter 4

Horizon 7 Security Server Configuration

Specify Security Server settings.

Enter the External URLs for this Security Server.

The External URLs specified are used by Horizon Clients to establish connections to this Security Server for the secure tunnel, PCoIP and Blast protocols respectively. The URL names and IP addresses must not be load balanced.

Note that the hostnames must be resolvable by the Horizon Client and the PCoIP External URL must contain an IP address.

External URL: https://HORSEC1.vjason.local:443

PCoIP External URL: 192.168.76.17:4172

Blast External URL: https://HORSEC1.vjason.local:8443

> The PCoIP External URL must be entered as an IP address that remote clients will use to access the Horizon Security Server. The other values shown may be changed later if required.

9. Select either the **Configure Windows Firewall automatically** or **Do not configure Windows Firewall** radio button and click on **Next >**. If the **Do not configure Windows Firewall** option was selected, configure the firewall manually using the settings provided earlier in the chapter.
10. Review the final installation screen to ensure that the installation directory is correct. If changes are needed, click on the **< Back** button to reach the necessary configuration screen and make the required changes. Assuming that the settings are correct, click on **Install** to begin the automated installation process.

11. Click on **Finish** when prompted at the completion of the installation process.
12. The installation process will install all the components required for the Horizon Security Server. The same process can be used to install additional Horizon Security Servers, although a new Security Server pairing password would need to be generated as each is only valid for one use.
13. Navigate to the Security Server web page and verify that it is displayed as shown in the following screenshot. The page can be accessed using the URL `https://SecurityServerFQDN`; since we have not yet replaced the default self-signed SSL certificate, our web browser will likely display an error:

> **TIP**
> The procedure used to replace the Security Server self-signed SSL certificates is described in `Chapter 16`, *Managing Horizon SSL Certificates*.

14. Navigate to the **View Configuration** | **Servers** page within the Horizon Administrator console.
15. Select the **Security Servers** tab in the **Servers** window and verify that the security server is listed as shown in the following screenshot:

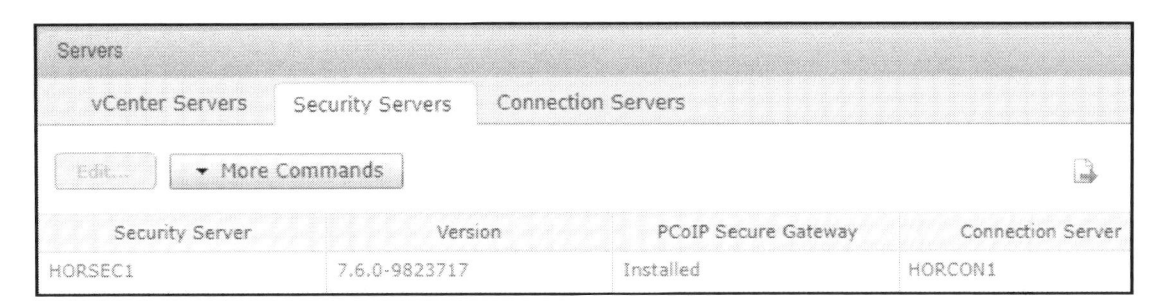

Security Server	Version	PCoIP Secure Gateway	Connection Server
HORSEC1	7.6.0-9823717	Installed	HORCON1

16. Repeat this process as needed to install additional Security Servers; you will also need to generate a new Security Server pairing password as well.

The final configuration steps will be completed in the Horizon Administrator console, and will be detailed in the next section.

> **TIP**: When the installation process has been completed, be sure to read the VMware Horizon `Read Me` file. By default, this file will be opened when you click **Finish** after the installation process. The `Read Me` file typically contains important information that you should know prior to placing your new or upgraded servers into production, and may save you wasted troubleshooting time later.

Updating the Horizon Security Server settings

Once paired to a Horizon Connection Server, the Security Server settings can be changed using the Horizon Administrator console. The following sections illustrate where within the console you update the Security Server Settings.

Horizon Security Server options

The following steps outline how to verify or update the Security Server options:

1. Log on to the Horizon Administrator console using an AD account that has administrative permissions within Horizon.
2. Open the **View Configuration** | **Servers** page within the console.
3. Select the **Security Servers** tab in the **Servers** window.
4. Highlight the Security Server you wish to update, and click on **Edit** to open the **Edit Security Server** window as shown in the following screenshot:

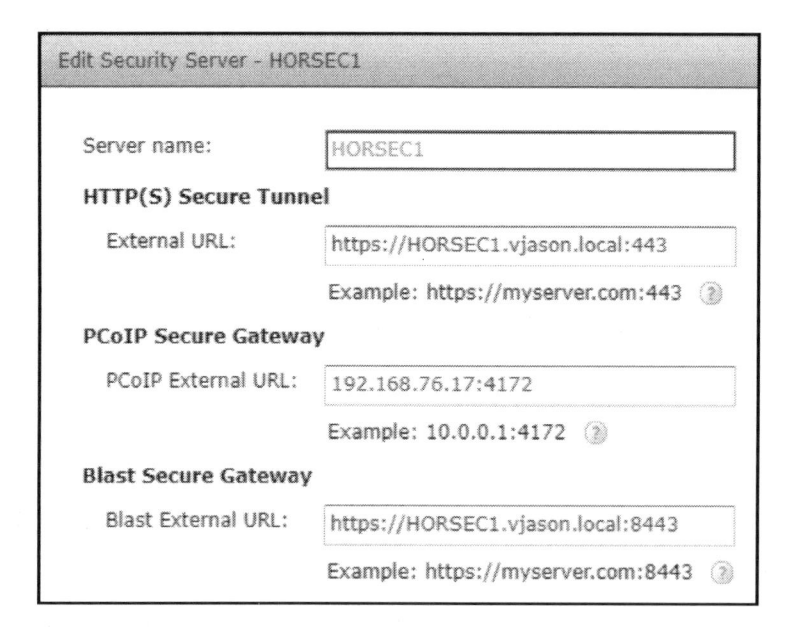

```
Edit Security Server - HORSEC1

Server name:            HORSEC1
HTTP(S) Secure Tunnel
    External URL:       https://HORSEC1.vjason.local:443
                        Example: https://myserver.com:443

PCoIP Secure Gateway
    PCoIP External URL: 192.168.76.17:4172
                        Example: 10.0.0.1:4172

Blast Secure Gateway
    Blast External URL: https://HORSEC1.vjason.local:8443
                        Example: https://myserver.com:8443
```

In the event that either the external URL or IP address of the Security Server is changed, it should be changed in this page to ensure that Horizon will function properly.

Horizon Security Server backup

A Horizon Security Server contains no information about the configuration of the Horizon installation, and therefore has no backup requirements. Assuming that the self-signed SSL certificate was replaced with one from a trusted internal or commercial certificate authority, it is important to maintain a backup of that certificate that includes the private key.

As the Horizon Security Server is a publicly accessible server, you may wish to backup the log files on a regular basis. These files are located in the same folder on every type of Horizon Connection Server: `%ALLUSERSPROFILE%\Application Data\VMware\VDM\logs`.

Horizon Security Server recovery or upgrade

The process used to recover a Horizon Security Server is almost identical to that used to perform an upgrade. The only difference is that when performing an upgrade the target server is typically in a usable state, and when doing a recovery a new server may be required. This section will provide one set of instructions that will cover both an upgrade or a recovery of a Horizon Security Server.

The simplest way to restore a Horizon Security Server is to simply reinstall the software using the steps provided earlier in this chapter, and re-pair the Security Server with the Horizon Connection Server.

The following steps outline how to restore a Horizon Security Server in a scenario where the previous one is unavailable, or how to upgrade an existing Security Server (steps that are specific to a recovery will be identified as such):

1. Generate a new Security Server pairing password using the process outlined earlier in this chapter.
2. Configure a new Security Server host using the same server name and IP address (only required for a recovery).
3. Log on to the Horizon Administrator console using an AD account that has administrative permissions within Horizon.
4. Open the **View Configuration** | **Servers** page within the console.
5. Select the **Security Servers** tab in the Servers window.

6. Verify which Security Server needs updating by reviewing the **Version** column. In the following screenshot, we can see that **VIEWSE02** is running an older version of the View Security Server software (highlighted in red) and needs updating (only required for an upgrade):

Security Server	Version	PCoIP Secure Gateway	Connection Server
VIEWSE01	7.0.0-3633490	Installed	VIEWCS02
VIEWSE02	6.2.0-3005368	Installed	VIEWCS02

7. Highlight the Security Server you wish to remove or upgrade, click on the **More Commands** option, and then click on the **Prepare for Upgrade or Reinstallation...** button as shown in the following screenshot:

Security Server	Version	PCoIP Secure Gateway
VIEWSE01	7.0.0-3633490	Installed
VIEWSE02	6.2.0-3005368	Installed

8. Click on **OK** in the **Warning** window shown in the following screenshot to remove the Connection Server IPsec rules in preparation for the upgrade or reinstallation:

Chapter 4

> **Warning**
>
> This Security Server is paired with the 'VIEWCS02' Connection Server instance using IPsec. If you continue, the IPsec rules that control communication between the security server and Connection Server instance will be removed. The current IPsec rules must be removed before you can upgrade or reinstall this security server and pair it again with the View Connection Server instance. Continue only if you intend to upgrade or reinstall.
>
> Warning: If you remove the IPsec rules for an active security server, all communication with the security server is lost until you upgrade or reinstall the security server.
>
> Click OK to remove the IPsec rules now. Otherwise, click Cancel.

> **TIP**: This process permanently dissociates the Security Server from the Horizon Connection Server. Once selected, the only way to restore the connection is to reinstall the Horizon Security Server software.

9. Install the Security Server software using the process outlined earlier in this chapter in the section titled *Installing a Horizon Security Server*. If performing an upgrade, the name of the Connection Server to pair with as shown in step 6 of that section should already be supplied.
10. Verify the Security Server settings in the Horizon Administrator console and test remote Horizon client connections.

Summary

In this chapter, we have been introduced to the VMware Horizon Security Server, a feature of Horizon that provides organizations with the ability to provide secure remote access to Horizon desktops or applications. We have learned what is required to deploy and configure a Horizon Security Server, what the limits of a Security Server are, and where the Security Server fits in within the Horizon infrastructure.

We also discussed which components of the Security Server need to be backed up, and which are custom SSL certificates, as well as the Security Server logs.

We concluded this chapter by discussing how to restore or upgrade a Horizon Security Server. In the next chapter, we will discuss Horizon Unified Access Gateway, which provides similar capabilities as a Horizon Security Server but is provided as a hardened, Linux-based virtual appliance.

Questions

1. Name the key functions of the Horizon Security Server.
2. Where is a Horizon Security Server typically installed within your network?
3. How many active sessions can a Horizon Security Server support?
4. A Horizon Security server can pair with how many Horizon Connection Servers?
5. Can a Horizon Connection Server pair with more than one Security Server?
6. How do you prepare a Horizon Connection Server so that it can pair with a new Security Server?
7. How do you prepare a Horizon Connection Server so that it can accept connections from a Horizon Security Server?
8. What tasks must be done before you upgrade a Horizon Security Server?

Further reading

The following resources may be used to learn more about the topics described in this chapter:

- VMware documentation:
    - VMware Horizon (https://docs.vmware.com/en/VMware-Horizon-7/index.html)
    - VMware vSphere (https://www.vmware.com/support/pubs/vsphere-esxi-vcenter-server-pubs.html)

5
Implementing Horizon Unified Access Gateway

VMware Horizon **Unified Access Gateway** (**UAG**), previously known as Access Point, is a core feature of the Horizon platform that enables secure remote access to applications and desktops, without the need to use a VPN connection or provide direct access from the internet to the Horizon Connection Server. The Horizon UAG is delivered as a hardened, Linux-based virtual appliance that serves as the connection point between external Horizon Clients and desktops or applications hosted on a private network.

This chapter will discuss the installation and configuration of the Horizon Unified Access Gateway.

In this chapter, we will look at the following topics:

- An overview of Horizon Unified Access Gateway
- The connection limits of Unified Access Gateway
- Unified Access Gateway network protocol and port usage
- Unified Access Gateway installation prerequisites
- How to configure Horizon Connection Servers to use with Unified Access Gateway
- How to deploy Unified Access Gateway
- How to troubleshoot Unified Access Gateway
- Updating the configuration of Unified Access Gateway

Horizon Unified Access Gateway overview

The Horizon Unified Access Gateway is a type of Horizon Connection Server that is designed to add an additional layer of security between remote Horizon Clients and Horizon resources that are located on a private network. Rather than providing remote clients with direct access to the Connection Server, organizations can deploy a Unified Access Gateway within a DMZ or other secure network to provide secure remote access to Horizon-managed resources. Some of the functions and features of the Horizon Unified Access Gateway include the following:

- Providing remote Horizon clients with their own dedicated connection broker, ensuring an optimal user experience
- Brokering connections between remote Horizon clients and internal Horizon-managed resources
- Authenticating user connection requests
- Supporting **RSA SecurID**, **RADIUS**, **Smart Cards**, and **Security Assertion Markup Language (SAML)**-based authentication to enable optional two-factor user authentication
- Ability to be placed in a DMZ to further isolate the Unified Access Gateway from the private network

> **TIP**: Horizon Unified Access Gateways perform the same tasks as Security Servers, but provide additional benefits such as being delivered as a virtual appliance, and they can work with more than one Connection Server at a time.

The following diagram shows the placement of a Horizon Unified Access Gateway in a simple Horizon environment. The **Horizon Unified Access Gateway** brokers access to a number of different components of the private Horizon infrastructure, each of which is shown in the diagram:

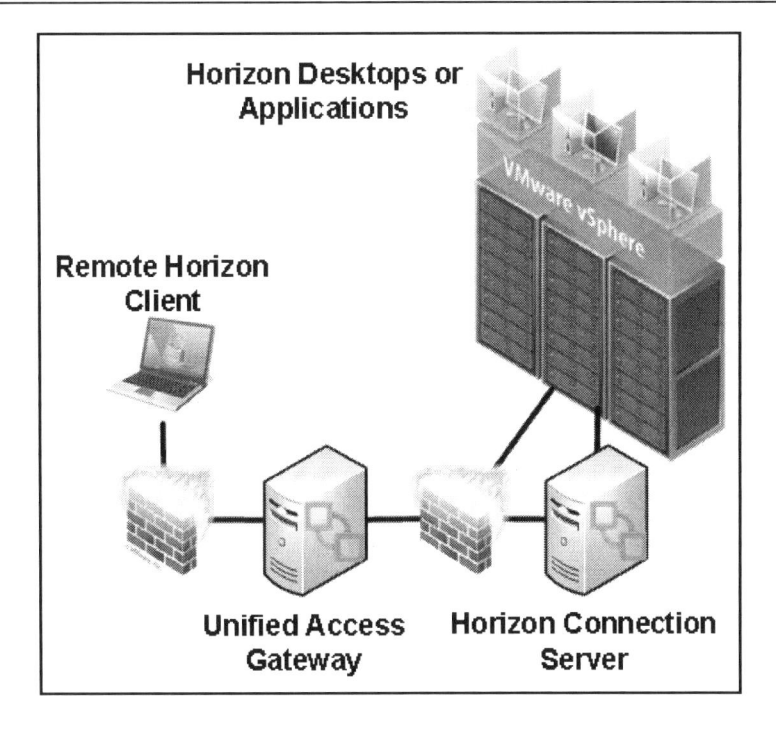

The Horizon **Unified Access Gateway** authenticates the clients by contacting the **Horizon Connection Server**, and then provides them with access to the entitled resources, including Horizon desktops or applications.

Horizon Unified Access Gateway limits

A **Horizon Unified Access Gateway** can be deployed in two different configurations, which support a maximum of 2,000 or 10,000 simultaneous Horizon client connections, depending on the deployment option chosen. Despite these limits, it is important to remember that multiple Unified Access Gateway appliances should be deployed to ensure both capacity and availability requirements are met.

Each Horizon Unified Access Gateway is a standalone instance; therefore, there is no specific guidance with regard to how many can be deployed. However, unlike a Horizon Security Server, a Horizon Unified Access Gateway can be used with multiple Connection Servers at once, although those Connection Servers must be placed behind a load balancer.

Horizon Unified Access Gateway additional considerations

The following are additional considerations that should be kept in mind when deploying a Horizon Unified Access Gateway:

- Like Horizon Connection and Security Servers, Horizon Unified Access Gateways have no native load balancing functionality. It is recommended to implement some sort of load-balancing functionality to help balance the client connections across all the Horizon Unified Access Gateways in your infrastructure. Refer to the *Load-Balancing Connection Servers* section in Chapter 2, *Implementing Horizon Connection Server*, for information about load-balancing options.
- As stated previously, a load balancer is also needed when you wish to use a Unified Access Gateway to connect to more than one Connection Server.
- When installed using the vSphere client **Deploy OVF Template** option, the Horizon Unified Access Gateway is configured with a self-signed SSL certificate that will not be trusted by Horizon clients. It is recommended to replace the self-signed certificate with one issued from an internal or commercial certificate authority that the Horizon clients will trust; in this chapter, we will do so during the deployment of the Unified Access Gateway using a PowerShell script that allows us to specify our own certificate at the time of deployment.
- Similarly to Horizon Security Servers, Unified Access Gateways require that the Connection Servers, client connection options are changed to a configuration not suitable for internal clients. Owing to this, dedicated Connection Servers are recommended when deploying Unified Access Gateways.
- VMware provides two distinct UAG OVA packages, the difference being that one is configured to be **Federal Information Processing Standards (FIPS)** compliant, and the other is not. If your organization is required to be FIPS compliant, be sure to download the proper OVA file.

High availability overview

When deploying Horizon Unified Access Gateways, it is important to understand how this impacts our high availability requirements. This section will provide an overview of what a highly available Horizon infrastructure that must service both internal and external clients might look like.

The following diagram illustrates a Horizon infrastructure that meets the following requirements:

- Internal Horizon clients use load balanced connections to Connection Servers.
- Remote Horizon clients use load balanced connections to Unified Access Gateways.
- Unified Access Gateways use load-balanced connections to Connection Servers.
- Unified Access Gateways must be installed in a DMZ.
- There must be dedicated Connection Servers for use with Unified Access Gateway appliances; these are configured with the settings outlined in this chapter.

The following diagram does not show the connections to the Horizon desktops or applications; it is only meant to illustrate the placement of load-balancing appliances, and show how true high availability might be achieved in an environment that includes multiple **Horizon Unified Access Gateways**. In addition, it shows that additional Connection Servers are being used for internal clients, as these servers do not require the same client connection settings as the ones used with Unified Access Gateways:

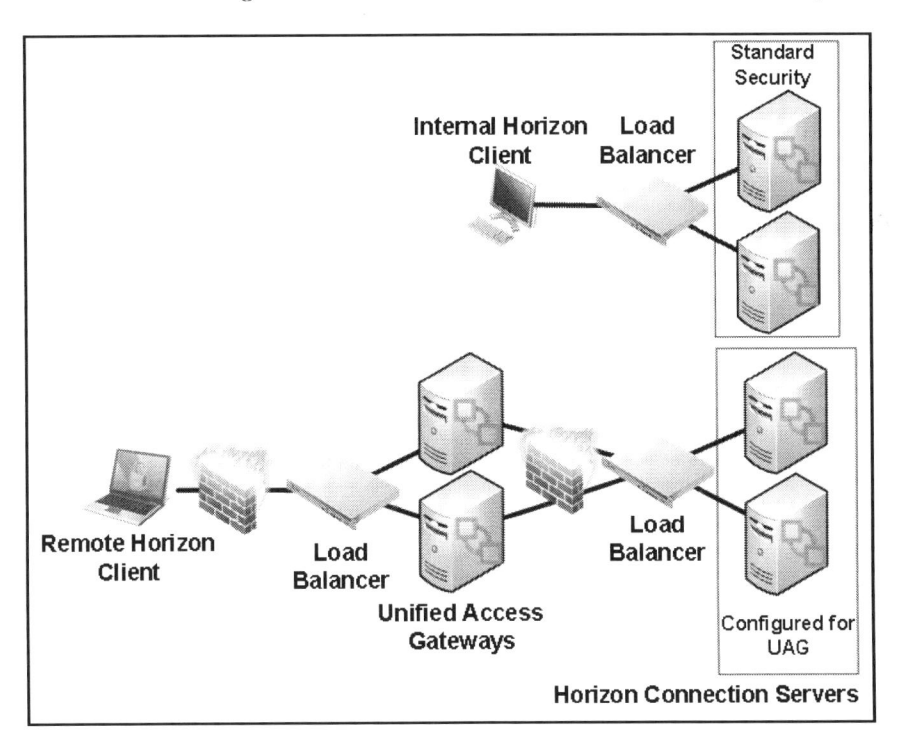

This Horizon architecture ensures that Horizon clients will be able to connect or reconnect if either of these two scenarios were to occur:

- Failure of any one of the four Connection Servers shown in the diagram
- Failure of any one of the Unified Access Gateways

> **TIP**
> When designing your Horizon infrastructure, you will want make all layers of it redundant, as this is the only way to ensure the high levels of availability and performance that your end users will require. If you do not have a load balancer, and are forced to pair your UAG appliances with individual Connection Servers, you will want to ensure you have at least two UAG appliances per Connection Server for redundancy purposes. If you have a load balancer, you don't need quite this many, since it can distribute client traffic among all available servers that it is balancing traffic for.

Load-balancing the Unified Access Gateways, and also their connection to your Connection Servers, ensures that your Horizon client connections will be maintained regardless of which server fails, be it a Unified Access Gateway or the Connection Server that it is paired to.

> **TIP**
> While not specifically mentioned, it is assumed that your load balancers are also redundant to ensure that the failure of any one of them will not impact Horizon client connections.

Horizon Unified Access Gateway network requirements

The following diagram illustrates how the primary protocols used by the Horizon Unified Access Gateway work with other components of the Horizon infrastructure. The diagram shows the following components of a Horizon infrastructure:

- Communication between the Horizon Unified Access Gateway and the Horizon desktops or applications
- Communication between the Horizon Unified Access Gateway and the Connection Servers

The arrows indicate the direction in which each protocol travels, assuming that the default settings are used:

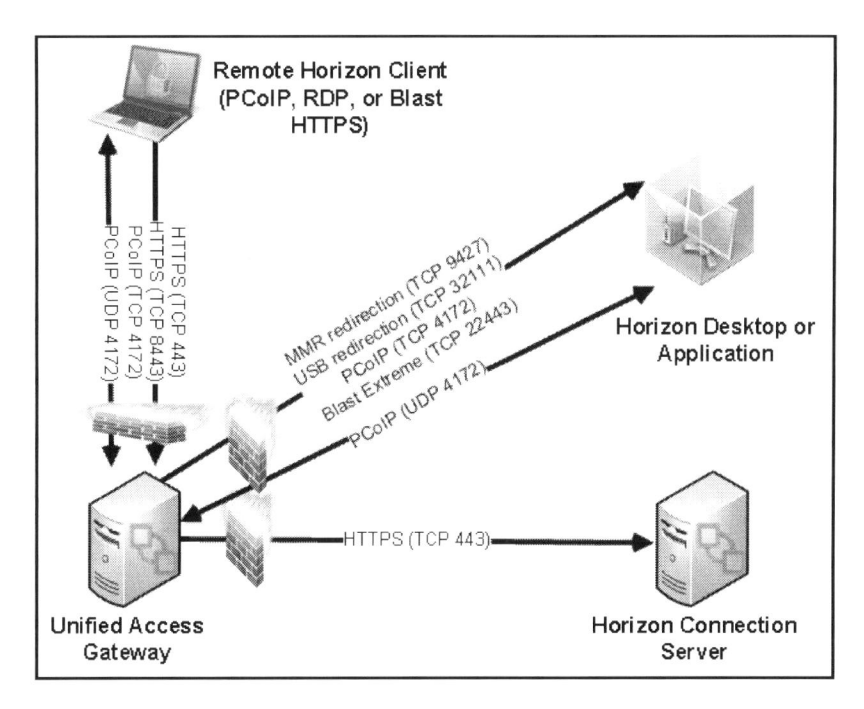

A list of ports used by the core components a outlined in the following table. Additionally, consult the *Firewall Rules for DMZ-Based Unified Access Gateway Appliances* section in the VMware document *Deploying and Configuring VMware Unified Access Gateway* (https://docs.vmware.com/en/Unified-Access-Gateway/index.html) for additional information concerning the function of each component, when the associated port is actually required to be opened in the firewall, and for information about other ports that may be required in more complex deployments:

Protocol or Service	Port	Notes
Blast Agent	TCP 22443	This is used to connect to the Blast (HTML Access) Agent on the desktop.
HTTP/HTTPS	TCP 80/443/8443	Port TCP 8443 is only used for HTML Access (web) clients.
MMR (Multimedia redirection)	TCP 9427	This is used alongside RDP; it uses client rather than server resources to render DirectShow-based media and codecs.
PCoIP	TCP/UDP 4172	
REST API and admin web interface	TCP 9443	Not shown; Horizon administrators use this port to connect to and configure a Unified Access Gateway after it has been deployed.

Implementing Horizon Unified Access Gateway

Syslog	UDP 514	Not shown; Unified Access Gateways can be configured to send Syslog events on this port.
USB Redirection for PCoIP and RDP	TCP 32111	TCP 32111 is used to support USB redirection to Horizon clients.

> **TIP**
> Consult the Horizon documentation (`https://docs.vmware.com/en/VMware-Horizon-7/index.html`) for a comprehensive list of all firewall ports required when implementing a UAG.

Preparing the infrastructure for a Horizon Unified Access Gateway

The installation and configuration process for the Horizon Unified Access Gateway requires quite a lot of preparation. This section will outline what is required prior to beginning the installation.

Installation prerequisites

There are a number of prerequisites that should be addressed prior to installing a Horizon Unified Access Gateway:

- Sufficient vSphere resources for each appliance, which includes 2.6 GB (thin provisioned) or 20 GB (thick provisioned) of disk space, and one, two, or three network interfaces:
    - The standard configuration of the appliance that supports up to 2,000 connections requires 2 vCPUs and 4 GB RAM.
    - The large configuration of the appliance that supports up to 10,000 connections requires 4 vCPUs and 16 GB RAM.
- The OVF file should automatically select the recommended values for disk capacity, CPU, and RAM; only the number of network interfaces should be changed.

- Three network interfaces are recommended for security purposes, as this allows us to separate internal facing, external facing, and management network traffic. If two network interfaces are selected, the internal and management traffic share the same interface; if just one is selected, all network traffic shares the same interface.
- At least one configured Horizon Connection Server with a license key installed.
- At least one Horizon pool to use to test the functionality of the Unified Access Gateway.

> Chapter 7, *Creating Horizon Desktop Pools*, and Chapter 9, *Performing Horizon Pool Maintenance*, discuss how to create pools that can be used to test the function of our Unified Access Gateways.

- Three static IP addresses in the DMZ for each Unified Access Gateway.

> While a Unified Access Gateway can be deployed with just one or two network interfaces, for security reasons and to make network traffic easier to analyze, I recommend three (one external facing, one internal facing, and one for administration).

- Firewall access between the internet and the Horizon Unified Access Gateways, and between those gateways and the necessary Horizon components on the private network.
- A URL and public IP address that will be used by external clients for connecting to our Horizon infrastructure.

> In Horizon production environments, the URL and IP address would typically point to a load balancer that is placed in front of two or more Unified Access Gateways.

- Firewall access between the internet and the Horizon Unified Access Gateways (and any load balancer used with them).

> Depending on your load-balancer configuration, it may or may not be necessary to provide access from the internet directly to the Unified Access Gateways themselves. Consult your load-balancer documentation to understand how client connections are maintained, specifically whether it tunnels the connections or hands them off to an available Unified Access Gateway.

[131]

- The SSL certificate **Thumbprint** for each of the Connection Servers that the Unified Access Gateways will connect to, obtained from the certificate Details tab, as shown in the following screenshot:

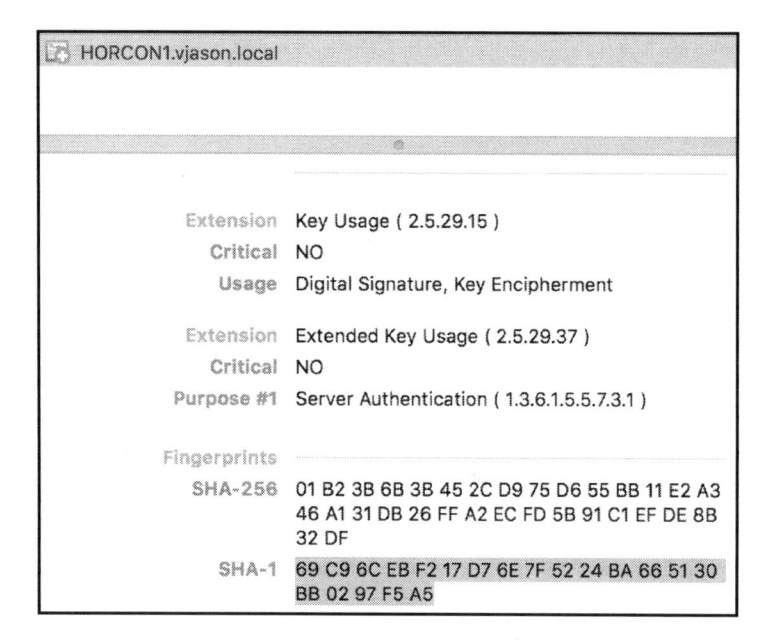

```
HORCON1.vjason.local

        Extension  Key Usage ( 2.5.29.15 )
         Critical  NO
            Usage  Digital Signature, Key Encipherment

        Extension  Extended Key Usage ( 2.5.29.37 )
         Critical  NO
       Purpose #1  Server Authentication ( 1.3.6.1.5.5.7.3.1 )

     Fingerprints
          SHA-256  01 B2 3B 6B 3B 45 2C D9 75 D6 55 BB 11 E2 A3
                   46 A1 31 DB 26 FF A2 EC FD 5B 91 C1 EF DE 8B
                   32 DF
            SHA-1  69 C9 6C EB F2 17 D7 6E 7F 52 24 BA 66 51 30
                   BB 02 97 F5 A5
```

- A SSL certificate chain in PFX format that includes a certificate for the Unified Access Gateway, as well as any root or intermediate certificate authority certificates involved in creating the certificate:
    - The certificate should include **Subject Alternative Names (SAN)** that include the external FQDN of the Unified Access Gateways (such as `horizon.vjason.com`).
- Obtain the following tools, which we will use during the installation process:
    - VMware vSphere PowerCLI 11.0.0 (`https://code.vmware.com/web/dp/tool/vmware-powercli/11.0.0`)
    - PowerShell Unified Access Gateway Deployment Scripts (`https://communities.vmware.com/docs/DOC-30835`)
    - VMware OVF Tool (`https://www.vmware.com/support/developer/ovf/`)

Chapter 5

> **TIP**: These tools are technically optional, but you'll find they make deployment much easier than using the native vSphere Deploy OVF Template feature and completing the configuration using the Unified Access Gateway REST API or even the UAG admin web interface.

Deploying a Horizon Unified Access Gateway

The procedure used to deploy a Horizon Unified Access Gateway can be broken down into the following stages:

- Infrastructure preparation, as outlined in the previous section of this chapter
- Using the Horizon Administrator console to reconfigure the Connection Server client settings
- Using the VMware PowerShell UAG deployment scripts to deploy the Unified Access Gateway appliances

Configuring the Connection Servers

A Horizon Unified Access Gateway provides secure gateway and tunneling capabilities for external client connections. For external Horizon client connections to connect to their destination desktops and Windows RDS servers on the internal network, it is necessary to disable these features on each of the Connection Servers used with our Unified Access Gateway appliances.

The following steps outline how to disable the tunneling and gateway features on our Connection Servers:

1. Log on to the Horizon Administrator console using an AD account that has administrative permissions within Horizon.
2. Open the **View Configuration** | **Servers** window within the console.
3. Click on the **Connection Servers** tab in the **Servers** window.

4. Click on the Connection Server that we intend to use with Unified Access Gateway, and then click the **Edit...** button shown in the following screenshot to open the **Edit Connection Server Settings** window:

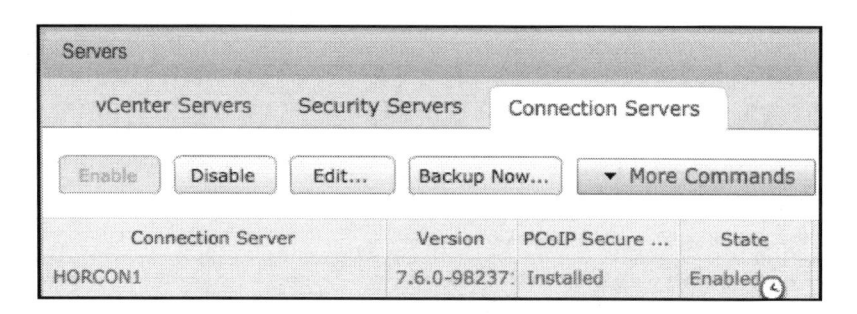

5. In the **Edit Connection Server Settings** window, uncheck the **HTTP(S) Secure Tunnel** and **Blast Secure Gateway** check boxes, as shown in the following screenshot, and then click **OK**:

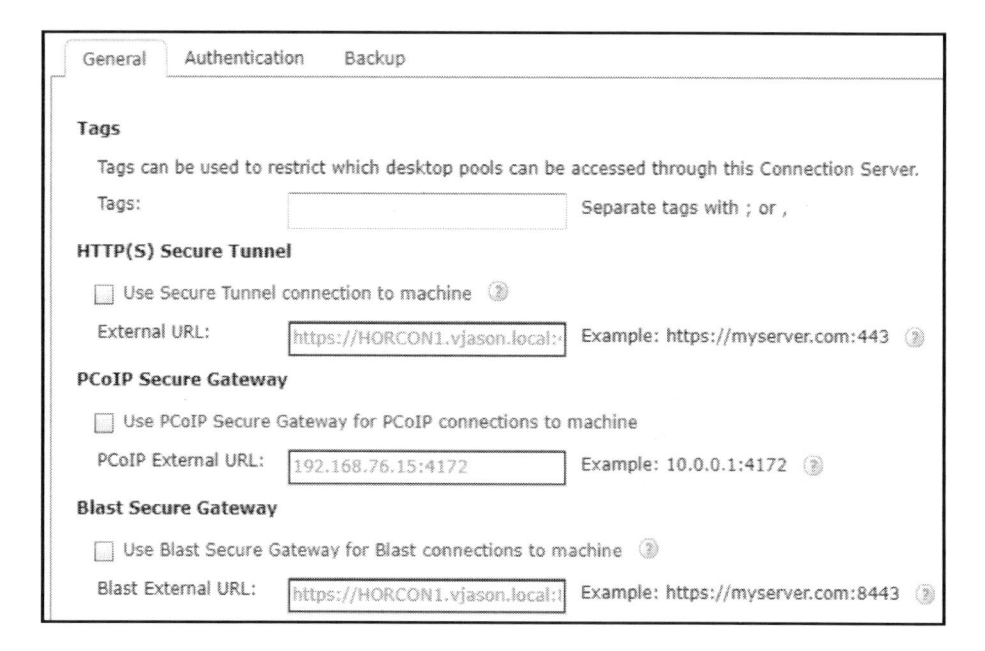

6. Repeat steps 4 and 5 for all other Connection Servers that will be used with the Unified Access Gateways.

Our Horizon Connection Servers are now ready for use with our Unified Access Gateways. The deployment of the Unified Access Gateways will be covered in the next section.

Deploying a Horizon Unified Access Gateway

The Horizon Unified Access Gateway software is delivered as a single **open virtual appliance (OVA)** file, named in a format similar to `euc-unified-access-gateway-x.x.x.x-yyyyyyy_OVF10.ova`. The following steps outline the deployment process:

1. If not already installed, install PowerShell, the VMware OVF tool, and VMware PowerCLI on the Windows-based computer you will use to deploy the Horizon Unified Access Gateway.
2. If not already extracted, extract the **VMware Unified Access Gateway Deployment Script** files.
3. Make a copy of the `uag2-advanced.ini` file named `uag1.ini`; you will customize the copied file for your Horizon deployment.
4. Customize the script as shown, using values specific to your Horizon infrastructure. The example provided is for a UAG appliance with 3 network interfaces, which is the recommended deployment:

```
[General]
name=UAG1
source=C:\Temp\euc-unified-access-gateway-3.3.1.0-9451788_OVF10.ova
target=vi://administrator@vsphere.local:Password123@192.168.76.40/Lab/host/Cluster1/
ds=ESXi01:Local1
diskMode=thin
netInternet=VM Network
netManagementNetwork=VM Network
netBackendNetwork=VM Network
defaultGateway=192.168.76.1
deploymentOption=threenic
ip0=192.168.76.90
netmask0=255.255.255.0
ip1=192.168.76.91
netmask1=255.255.255.0
ip2=192.168.76.92
netmask2=255.255.255.0
#routes0=192.168.1.0/24 192.168.0.1,192.168.2.0/24 192.168.0.2
#routes1=192.168.3.0/24 192.168.0.1,192.168.4.0/24 192.168.0.2
#routes2=192.168.5.0/24 192.168.0.1,192.168.6.0/24 192.168.0.2
dns=192.168.76.5
honorCipherOrder=true
sessionTimeout=39600000
[SSLCert]
pfxCerts=c:\temp\horizon.pfx
[SSLCertAdmin]
pfxCerts=c:\temp\horizon.pfx
```

```
[Horizon]
proxyDestinationUrl=https://192.168.76.15
proxyDestinationUrlThumbprints=sha1:69 c9 6c eb f2 17 d7 6e 7f 52
24 ba 66 51 30 bb 02 97 f5 a5
tunnelExternalUrl=https://horizon.vjason.com:443
blastExternalUrl=https://horizon.vjason.com:443
pcoipExternalUrl=192.168.76.90:4172
proxyPattern=(/|/view-
client(.*)|/portal(.*)|/appblast(.*)|/downloads(.*))
```

> **TIP**
> Note that `192.168.76.15` is the IP address of the destination Horizon Connection Server or Horizon Connection Server load balancer, the thumbprint provided was copied from the SSL certificate currently used on that server (or load balancer), and that `|/downloads(.*)` was added to the `proxyPattern` entry so that clients will download any needed Horizon clients directly from your Horizon servers rather than from the VMware website. While this example file does not contain any network routes (the default entries are commented out), be aware that in most cases your UAG appliance will be placed in a DMZ and you will need to customize the route entries so that it knows which network interface to use to reach Horizon resources on the internal network. Refer to the comments in the `ini` file to understand how to configure each value. The following example contains the minimum options required to deploy a fully functional UAG appliance with three network interfaces and a custom SSL certificate.

10. From within the folder containing the VMware UAG deployment scripts, use PowerShell to execute the following command: `uagdeploy.ps1 -iniFile uag1.ini`.

> **TIP**
> If this is the first time you are connecting to the vCenter Server specified in the `ini` file, you will be prompted to verify the server SSL thumbprint to continue. Verify the thumbprint when prompted to continue the deployment process.

11. Provide passwords for the UAG appliance root account and admin interface when prompted, select whether to join the VMware **Customer Experience Improvement Program**, and, if required, provide the password for the SSL certificates you are deploying with the appliance.

12. Monitor the deployment process for errors; a sample output is shown in the following screenshot:

```
Unified Access Gateway (UAG) virtual appliance deployment script
Enter a root password for UAG1: *************
Re-enter the root password: *************
Enter an optional admin password for the REST API management access for UAG1: *************
Re-enter the admin password: *************
Join the VMware Customer Experience Improvement Program?

This setting is supported in UAG versions 3.1 and newer.

VMware's Customer Experience Improvement Program (CEIP) provides VMware with information that enables VMware to
improve its products and services, to fix problems, and to advise you on how best to deploy and use our products.

As part of the CEIP, VMware collects technical information about your organization's use of VMware products and
services on a regular basis in association with your organization's VMware license key(s). This information does
not personally identify any individual.

Additional information regarding the data collected through CEIP and the purposes for which it is used by VMware
is set forth in the Trust & Assurance Center at http://www.vmware.com/trustvmware/ceip.html.

If you prefer not to participate in VMware's CEIP for UAG 3.1 and newer, you should enter no.

You may join or leave VMware's CEIP for this product at any time. In the UAG Admin UI in System Configuration,
there is a setting 'Join CEIP' which can be set to yes or no and has immediate effect.

To Join the VMware Customer Experience Improvement Program with Unified Access Gateway version 3.1 and newer,
either enter yes or just hit return as the default for this setting is yes.
Join CEIP for UAG1 ? (default is yes for UAG 3.1 and newer): no
Enter the password for the specified [SSLcert] PFX certificate file horizon.pfx: ****
Enter the password for the specified [SSLcertAdmin] PFX certificate file horizon.pfx: ****
Opening OVA source: C:\Temp\euc-unified-access-gateway-3.3.1.0-9451788_OVF10.ova
The manifest validates
Source is signed and the certificate validates
Opening VI target: vi://administrator%40vsphere.local@192.168.76.40:443/Lab/host/Cluster1/
Deploying to VI: vi://administrator%40vsphere.local@192.168.76.40:443/Lab/host/Cluster1/
Transfer Completed
Powering on VM: UAG1
Task Completed
Received IP address: 192.168.76.222
Completed successfully
Note that the IP addresses will be set to the specified IP addresses for each NIC
UAG virtual appliance UAG1 deployed successfully
```

13. Log on to the UAG admin web interface using the IP address provided for `ip1` in the INI file, using the following URL format: `https://192.168.76.91:9443/admin`. The admin web interface username will be `admin`, and the management access password will be the one you provided when running the deployment script.
14. Click the **Select** button under **Configure Manually** in the UAG admin web interface.

15. Click on the highlighted **Edge Service Settings** slider, then expand the options by clicking on the > icon. Verify that all settings are green, as shown in the following screenshot, indicating that the UAG appliance is able to successfully communicate with the Connection Server:

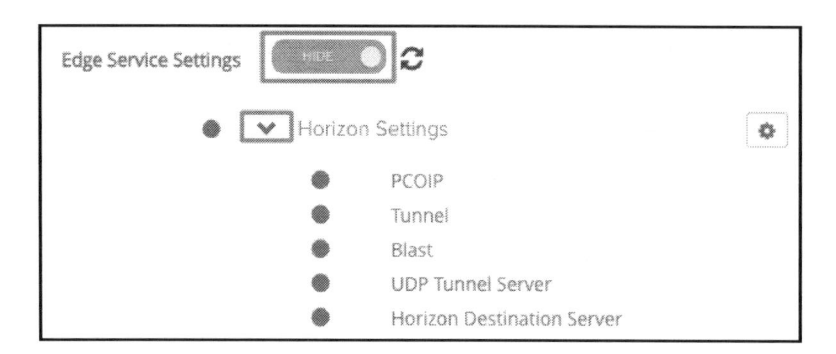

```
Edge Service Settings    [ HIDE  ⚪ ]  ⟳

        ● [ ⌄ ] Horizon Settings                        ⚙
                ● PCOIP
                ● Tunnel
                ● Blast
                ● UDP Tunnel Server
                ● Horizon Destination Server
```

16. To deploy additional UAG appliances, edit the script and provide unique values for the interface IP addresses, appliance `name`, and other values as required.

The Unified Access Gateway appliances have now been deployed, and you may implement load-balancing in front of the Unified Access Gateway appliances themselves if desired.

In the next section, we will review some of the resources that can be used to troubleshoot the deployment or functionality of Unified Access Gateway.

Troubleshooting a Horizon Unified Access Gateway deployment

While the actual process of troubleshooting a Horizon Unified Access Gateway deployment is likely to require research beyond the scope of what we can cover in this chapter, we can review the various options for obtaining the information needed to perform that troubleshooting:

- Review the output from the **PowerShell** window used to deploy the appliance in the previous section.
- A deployment log file used for general troubleshooting will be created in the directory the script was executed from; the text file name should match that of the appliance name (`log-UAG1.txt` in the example provided).

- A UAG appliance log file bundle can be downloaded from the UAG admin web interface referenced in the previous section of this chapter; to download the bundle, log into the admin web interface and then click on the **Log Archive** download icon shown in the following screenshot:

```
Support Settings

Log Archive                                              ⬇
```

It is important to remember that it only takes a few minutes to deploy a new Unified Access Gateway appliance. If a Unified Access Gateway stops working suddenly, it may be easier simply to delete it and use your saved `ini` file to quickly deploy a new appliance.

Updating the Horizon Unified Access Gateway configuration

The UAG admin web interface can be used to configure or reconfigure almost all aspects of the appliance configuration. Refer to the UAG documentation (`https://docs.vmware.com/en/Unified-Access-Gateway/index.html`) for instructions on how to configure the appliance using the admin web interface.

Additionally, you can submit **JSON** requests to the appliance REST API interface, which is also available on port `9443` of the appliance `ip1` interface. The Unified Access Gateway REST API specifications can be accessed by appending the UAG IP or fully qualified domain name with : `9443/rest/swagger.yaml`, or `https://192.168.76.91:9443/rest/swagger.yaml` for the appliance deployed in this chapter.

In this chapter, we used PowerShell, VMware PowerCLI, the VMware UAG deployment scripts, and the VMware OVF tool to configure all of the options needed when deploying the Unified Access Gateway appliance, so there is no need to perform any configuration using the REST API or admin web interface. The same cannot be said if you use just the vSphere Deploy OVF Template feature to deploy a Unified Access Gateway, as you will not be prompted for all of the possible settings, including those that virtually everyone would want, such as using a custom SSL certificate.

So, while you are welcome to use the REST API or admin web interface to make changes, never forget that it may be easier just to use the deployment utility to deploy a new appliance instead.

Summary

In this chapter, we were introduced to the VMware Horizon Unified Access Gateway, a feature of Horizon that uses a hardened, Linux-based appliance to provide Horizon customers with the ability to provide secure, remote access to Horizon desktops or applications.

We have learned what is required and how to deploy and configure a Horizon Unified Access Gateway, what the limits of a Unified Access Gateway are, and where the Unified Access Gateway fits within the Horizon infrastructure.

We have also discussed what resources are available to assist in troubleshooting a Horizon Unified Access Gateway, and how to obtain that information. We concluded the chapter by discussing the techniques used to update the configuration of a Horizon Unified Access Gateway.

In the next chapter, we will discuss how to deploy and configure a Horizon Cloud Pod, a feature of Horizon that enables us to create global Horizon entitlements that span multiple Horizon Pods.

Questions

1. Name the key functions of the Unified Access Gateway appliance.
2. Where is a Unified Access Gateway appliance typically installed within your network?
3. How many active sessions can a "large" Unified Access Gateway appliance support?
4. Name at least two differences between a Unified Access Gateway appliance and a Horizon Security Server.
5. Name at least one benefit of using Unified Access Gateway over Horizon Security Server.
6. How do you prepare a Horizon Connection Server so that it can be used with a Unified Access Gateway appliance?
7. What is the preferred method for deploying a Unified Access Gateway appliance?

Further reading

The following resources may be used to learn more about the topics described in this chapter:

- VMware documentation:
    - VMware Unified Access Gateway (`https://docs.vmware.com/en/Unified-Access-Gateway/index.html`)
    - Using PowerShell to Deploy Unified Access Gateway (`https://communities.vmware.com/docs/DOC-30835`)
    - VMware OVF tool (`https://www.vmware.com/support/developer/ovf/`)
    - VMware PowerCLI 11.0.0 (`https://code.vmware.com/web/dp/tool/vmware-powercli/11.0.0`)
    - VMware Horizon (`https://docs.vmware.com/en/VMware-Horizon-7/index.html`)
    - VMware vSphere (`https://www.vmware.com/support/pubs/vsphere-esxi-vcenter-server-pubs.html`)

6
Implementing a Horizon Cloud Pod

This chapter discusses how to enable, configure, and administer a VMware Horizon **Cloud Pod**. The Cloud Pod feature enables Horizon administrators to deploy multi-site, multi-pod view environments that support cross-Horizon pod user entitlements. Additionally, when deployed in a multi-pod configuration Horizon is capable of supporting up to 200,000 active sessions, or 20 times as many as a single Horizon pod. In this chapter, we will review the concepts behind a VMware Horizon Cloud Pod and cover key areas related to the Horizon Cloud Pod functionality.

In this chapter, we will cover the following topics:

- VMware Horizon Cloud Pod overview
- Cloud Pod port requirements and topology limits
- Configuring a Cloud Pod
- Configuring and associating users and groups to Horizon sites
- Creating Global Entitlements for Horizon desktop and application pools
- Updating Global Entitlements
- Determining the effective Horizon site for a user
- Monitoring connections to Cloud Pod Global Entitlements

Horizon Cloud Pod overview

A VMware Horizon Cloud Pod consists of an integrated set of Horizon pods, which may or may not be located within the same datacenter, and which clients are entitled to, and can, access as if it were a single pod. Prior to the introduction of the Cloud Pod feature, each pod was entitled and accessed separately, which made it difficult to deploy a multi-site Horizon architecture that appeared as a single pod to Horizon clients.

> **TIP**: Cloud Pods are mostly used with floating assignment desktop pools or application pools. If you use dedicated assignment pools, be aware that once a user has been assigned a desktop, they will always return to that desktop for subsequent client connections. This would negate most of the reasons why we use Cloud Pods, which are meant to provide access to Horizon resources across multiple sites or pods, using methods that are transparent to Horizon clients.

In a traditional VMware Horizon implementation, each pod is managed independently. With the Cloud Pod feature, you can join together multiple View pods to form a single Horizon implementation called a **Pod Federation**. While the Horizon pools are still managed at the pod level, Cloud Pod entitlements span all member pods, and Horizon clients can access any entitled pool from any member Connection or Security Server.

The terms **Cloud Pod** and **Pod Federation** will be used somewhat interchangeably in this chapter. You will also encounter this if you review the VMware document *Administering Cloud Pod Architecture in Horizon 7* (https://docs.vmware.com/en/VMware-Horizon-7/index.html).

A Cloud Pod can span multiple sites and offers the following benefits (among others) over the previous single-Horizon pod model:

- Centralized management of global entitlements to Horizon pools in up to five distinct sites.
- Cloud Pods can balance the Horizon client load across multiple datacenters using centralized rather than individual login portals:
    - While a Cloud Pod aggregates Horizon pools from multiple Pods into a Cloud Pod, Horizon can automatically route client connections to desktop or application pools located at their home site.

- Clients can be entitled to desktop or application pools in up to 25 Horizon pods across ten sites. Rather than selecting which pool to use when logging in to the Horizon client, the user is presented with only one pool, and the assignment of resources is handled automatically based on how the global entitlement is configured.
- Using Horizon Cloud Pods, we can enable native **Disaster Recovery** (**DR**) for the Horizon infrastructure.

The following diagram is an example of a basic Horizon Cloud Pod architecture:

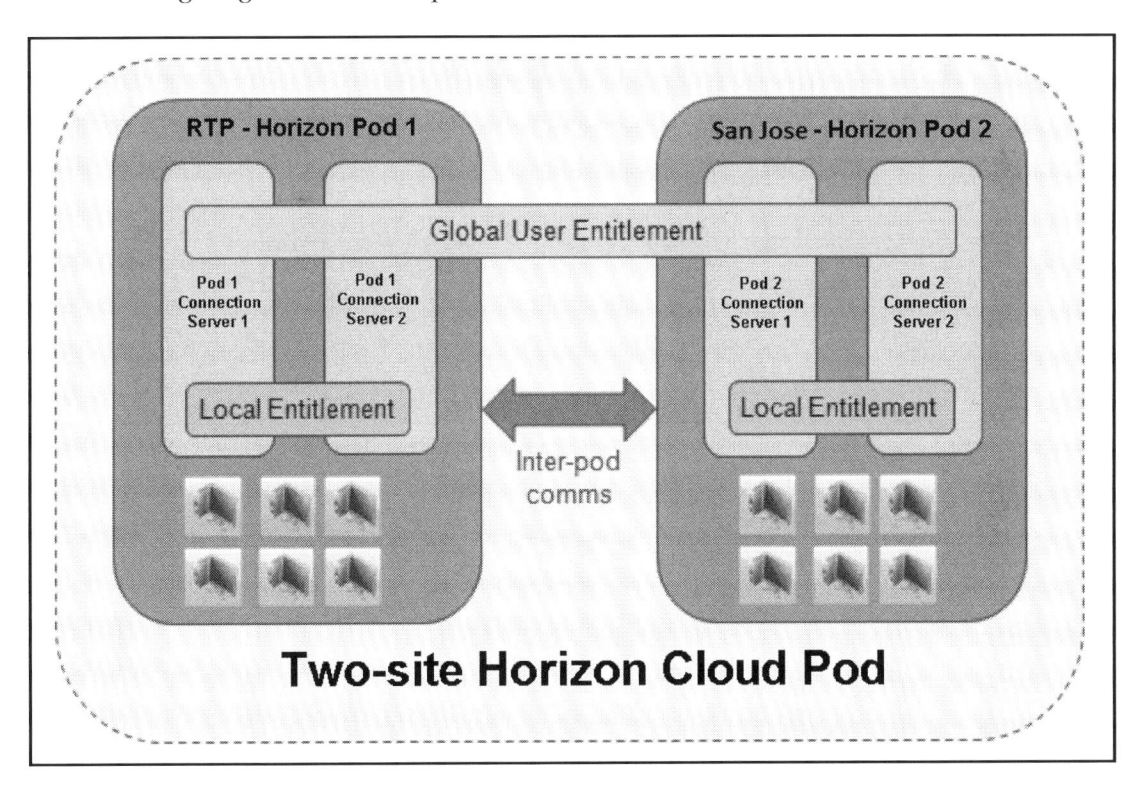

Two-site Horizon Cloud Pod

In the example topology, two previously standalone Horizon pods in different datacenters are joined together to create a **Pod Federation**. In a Pod Federation, an end user can connect to a Horizon Connection Server instance in the **Research Triangle Park** (**RTP**) datacenter and can be assigned a desktop located in a completely different Horizon pod located in the **San Jose** (**SJC**) datacenter.

> When a Horizon client connects and accesses a globally entitled Horizon pool within a Cloud Pod, and connection tunneling is required to maintain that session, the tunnel will be maintained by the Horizon Connection Server, Security Server, or Unified Access Gateway to which the client originally connected. Using the example provided, this means that a Connection Server, Security Server, or Unified Access Gateway in San Jose could conceivably manage a client session for Horizon pools located in RTP. By default, Horizon Connection Servers do not tunnel client connections and instead allow direct connections once a Horizon pool is selected. However, some organizations have unique security requirements, and as such enable connection tunneling for internal clients to allow for greater control over how those connections are maintained. Security Servers and Unified Access Gateways tunnel all Horizon client connections, which are required due to their typical placement within an organization's DMZ.

Sharing key data in the Horizon Cloud Pod Global Data Layer

The Horizon Connection Server instances in a Horizon Pod Federation use something called a **Global Data Layer** to share key data. The data that is shared includes information on the Pod Federation topology, user and group entitlements, Horizon policies, and other information concerning the configuration of the Pod Federation.

In a Horizon Pod Federation, the shared data is replicated between every member in the Horizon Connection Server instance. The entitlement and topology configuration information stored in the Global Data Layer determines where and how desktops are allocated across the Pod Federation.

When the Cloud Pod feature is enabled, or additional pods are added to an existing Pod Federation, the Global Data Layer is configured on each Horizon Connection Server instance.

Sending messages between Horizon pods

The Horizon Connection Server instances in a Pod Federation communicate using an inter-pod communications protocol called the **View InterPod API (VIPA)**.

Horizon Connection Server instances use the VIPA interpod communication channel to launch new desktops or applications, find existing desktops or applications, and share health status data and other information. The VIPA interpod communications channel is configured when the Cloud Pod feature is enabled.

Cloud Pod port requirements

A Horizon Cloud Pod uses two different network ports to replicate the data and status information. This communication occurs between Horizon Connection Servers located in different sites. The following table details the port numbers and their respective function within the Cloud Pod:

Port	Service	Description
8472	View Interpod API (VIPA) interpod communication channel	The shared data is replicated to every Horizon Connection Server instance within the Cloud Pod. Each Horizon Connection Server instance in a Cloud Pod runs a second LDAP instance to store this shared data.
22636	Global data layer LDAP	Horizon Connection Server instances use the VIPA interpod communication channel to launch new desktops, find existing desktops, and share health status data and other information.

Cloud Pod topology limits

The following table details the configuration limits of a Horizon Cloud Pod:

Component	Limit
Maximum active sessions per Cloud Pod	200,000
Maximum number of Horizon pods in a Cloud Pod	25
Maximum number of sites where Cloud Pod member Horizon pods can be located	10
Maximum number of Horizon Connection Servers instances in a Cloud Pod	175
Maximum number of recommended sessions per individual Horizon pod	10,000

It is important to note that while a single Horizon pod can support up to 10,000 (recommended) active sessions, a single Cloud Pod composed of up to 25 individual Horizon pods can support no more than 200,000 active sessions, even though (if not members of a Cloud Pod) those pods could support up to 250,000 active sessions.

> **TIP**
> The configuration maximums of a Horizon Cloud Pod are subject to change as new versions of Horizon are released. Consult the VMware Horizon documentation (https://docs.vmware.com/en/VMware-Horizon-7/index.html) for current information concerning platform limits.

Implementing a Horizon Cloud Pod

Admittedly, most readers of this book are not likely to be impacted by the architectural limitations of a Horizon Cloud Pod. Just know that while the feature does expand upon the limits of a single Horizon pod, it doesn't expand them linearly.

Configuring a Horizon Cloud Pod

A **Horizon Cloud Pod** is configured using the Horizon Administration console for each Pod that will be a member. In this section, we will create a Cloud Pod consisting of two Horizon pods.

> **TIP**: All Connection Servers within a Cloud Pod must have unique names, even if they are in different domains. Additionally, do not reboot or restart any services on Connection Servers while creating a Cloud Pod.

The following procedure outlines how to create a Cloud Pod:

1. Log on to the Horizon Administration console of the intended first member of the Cloud Pod using an AD account that has administrative permissions within Horizon.
2. Open the **View Configuration | Cloud Pod Architecture** window within the console.
3. Click on the **Initialize the Cloud Pod Architecture** feature link to open the **Initialize** window, as shown in the following screenshot. Click **OK** to proceed, and monitor the status window that will be displayed:

[148]

4. When the Cloud Pod feature has finished configuring, click **OK** in the **Reload** window to reload the console and refresh the **View Configuration | Cloud Pod Architecture** window, as shown in the following screenshot:

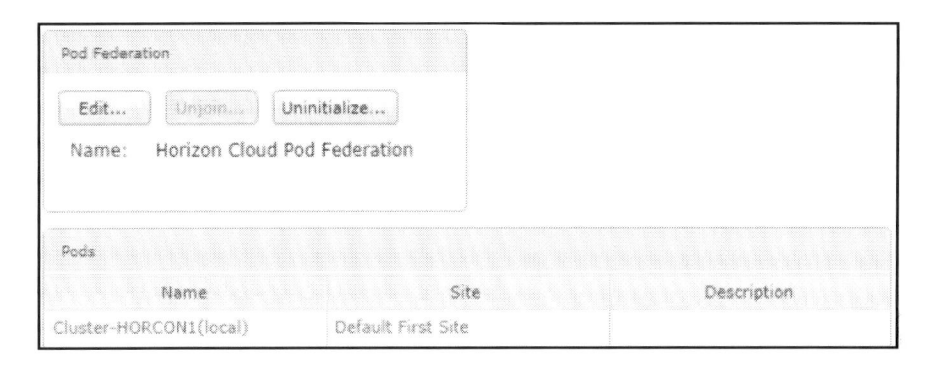

5. Log on to the Horizon Administration console of the intended second member of the Cloud Pod using an AD account that has administrative permissions within Horizon, and open the **View Configuration | Cloud Pod Architecture** window within the console.

6. Click the **Join the Pod Federation** link to open the **Join** window shown in the following screenshot. Provide the details for the Connection Server used in the previous steps, give the user name and password for an account with administrative permissions within Horizon, and then click **OK** to join the Pod Federation. Monitor the status window that will be displayed:

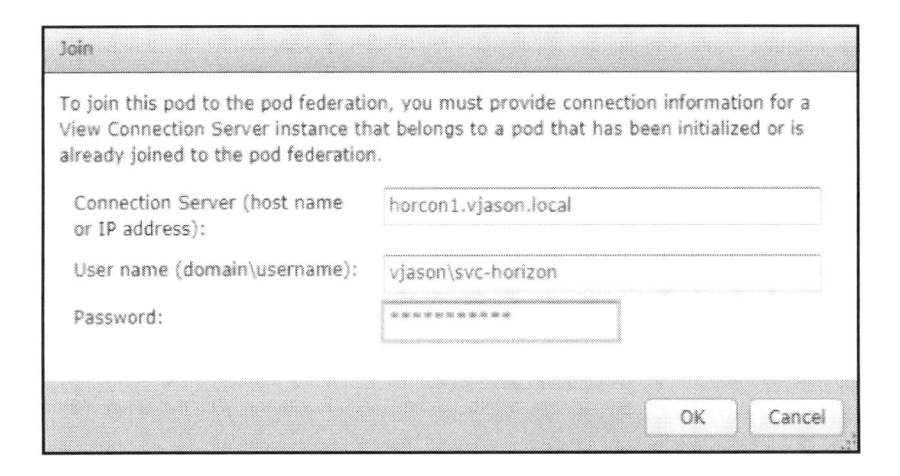

7. When the Cloud Pod feature has finished configuring, click **OK** in the **Reload** window to reload the console and refresh the **View Configuration | Cloud Pod Architecture** window, as shown in the following screenshot:

Name	Site	Description
Cluster-HORCON2(local)	Default First Site	
Cluster-HORCON1	Default First Site	

Pod Federation Name: Horizon Cloud Pod Federation

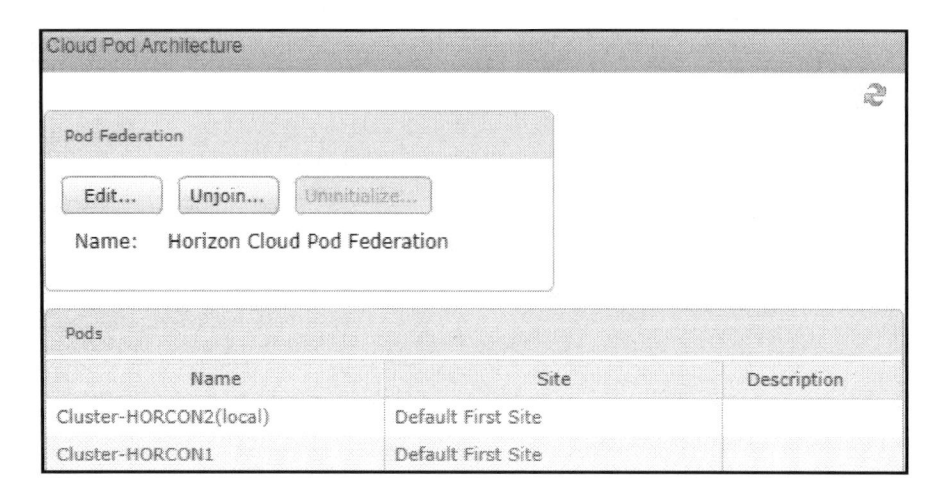

8. Repeat steps 5 through 7 as needed to add additional pods to the Cloud Pod.
9. Once finished, open the Horizon Administration console **Dashboard** and expand the **Remote Pods** section under **System Health,** as shown in the following screenshot. The status of all other pods in the Cloud Pod will be displayed here to make it easier to quickly identify whether there are issues that require further investigation:

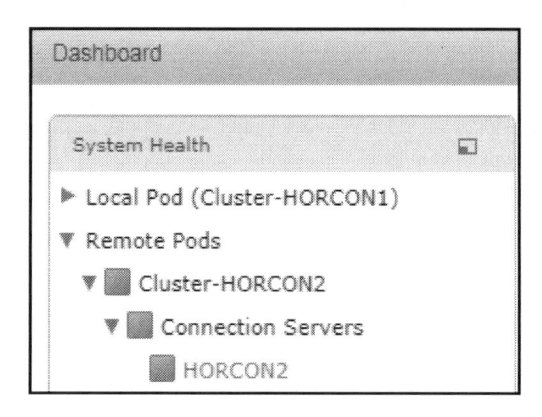

Dashboard — System Health
- ▶ Local Pod (Cluster-HORCON1)
- ▼ Remote Pods
  - ▼ Cluster-HORCON2
    - ▼ Connection Servers
      - HORCON2

The Horizon Cloud Pod is now configured, although we have not yet defined our Horizon **sites**. Horizon sites allow us to prioritize which Horizon pool a user is directed to, while retaining the ability to use any available resources within the Cloud Pod. The purpose and configuration of Horizon sites is described in the next section.

Configuring Horizon sites

A Horizon site is used to assign a Horizon pod to a location for the purpose of pinning users to it for Horizon resource prioritization. In many ways, it is similar to an Active Directory site, which (among other things) is used to automatically direct users to Active Directory resources in their immediate location.

Sites are most commonly used when your Horizon pods are located in the same physical or geographical location as your user base. For example, if you prefer users in your RTP office to use Horizon pools in that office, rather than the ones in San Jose, but in the event of maintenance or downtime in RTP, you want to retain the ability to use Horizon pools in San Jose, you can use a Horizon site.

It is important to note that creating Horizon sites does not by itself alter how users are assigned resources in a Cloud Pod. If and how sites are used is configured within a Horizon **Global Entitlement**, which we will configure in the next section. Additionally, you don't have to use sites with all users. In our example, we are only concerned about users physically located at those two sites, so we will only designate sites for them, and users located at other sites will be connected to Horizon pools at either site.

> **TIP**
> The example I'm using here is within the US, but feel free to think bigger. Sites are whatever you want them to be: continents, countries, states, cities, and so on. The most common reason for using sites is to not only to prioritize what resources specified clients use first, but also to preserve the capabilities of a Cloud Pod. Take your time, draw your proposed site configuration, and make sure it accomplishes what you are trying to do.

In this section, we will rename the default Horizon site to match one of our locations, create an additional site, and modify our Cloud Pod configuration to assign a Horizon pod to each:

1. Log on to the Horizon Administration console of any member of the Cloud Pod, using an AD account that has administrative permissions within Horizon.
2. Open the **View Configuration** | **Sites** window within the console.

3. Under the **Site** column, click on **Default First Site**, and then click the **Edit...** button to open the **Edit Site** window, as shown in the following screenshot. Rename the site as needed (RTP in the example provided), provide an optional description, and click **OK** to return to the **Sites** window. Right now, all existing Horizon pods are a member of this site; we will move them as needed after all sites are configured:

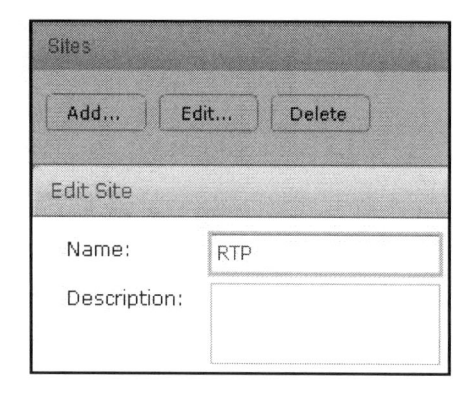

4. Click the **Add...** button to open the **Add Site** window. Provide a name for this second site (San Jose in this case), an optional description, and click **OK** to return to the **Sites** window.
5. Repeat step 4 as needed to add additional sites.
6. Under the **Pod** column, click on the Horizon pod you wish to associate with the new site you created in step 4 and then click the **Edit...** button to open the **Edit Pod** window, as shown in the following screenshot. Click on the **Site** drop-down menu, then click on the site the Horizon pod should be associated with, and then click **OK** to return to the **Sites** window:

Chapter 6

> **TIP**
> By default, Horizon pods are named for the first Connection Server that was installed, in the format `Cluster-HORIZONCSNAME`. The name of the pod is not visible to Horizon clients, and is typically only seen when working with Cloud Pods.

7. Repeat step 6 as needed to associate any additional Horizon pods with their associated sites.
8. Verify when finished that the **Sites** window shows each site required, and that each displays the correct number of associated pods, as shown in the following screenshot. You can click on a site to display what pods are associated with it; in the example provided, the **San Jose** site is associated with the **Cluster-HORCON2** pod:

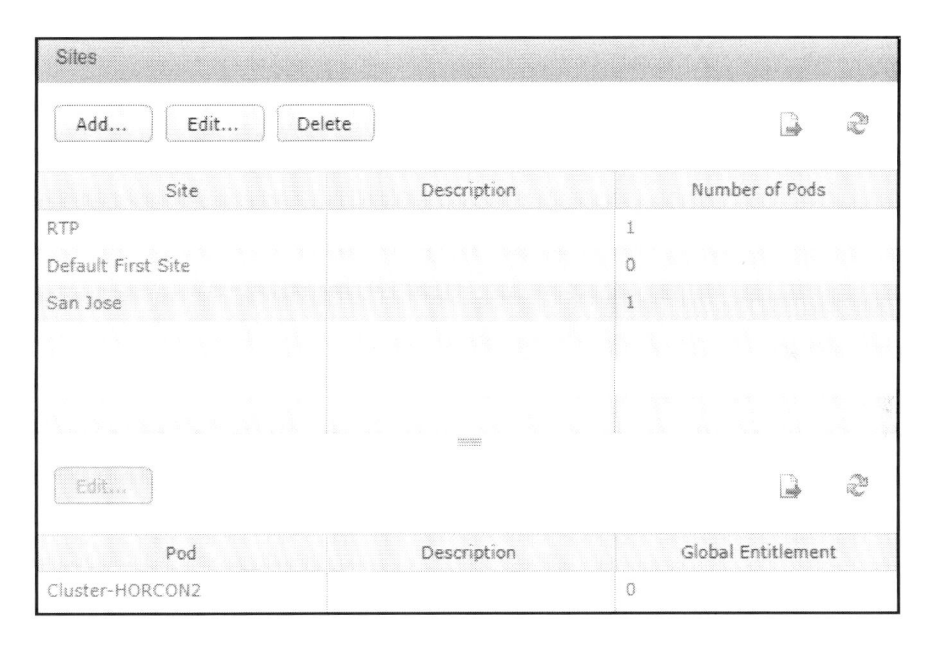

Site	Description	Number of Pods
RTP		1
Default First Site		0
San Jose		1

Pod	Description	Global Entitlement
Cluster-HORCON2		0

The Horizon sites are now configured, although we have not yet assigned users to their associated sites. The process used to assign Horizon sites is described in the next section.

Associating users with Horizon sites

In the previous section, we created and configured our Horizon sites, but until we associate users with them, they have no impact on how client sessions are distributed to the Horizon pools in our Cloud Pod. Our goal is to use Horizon site assignments to ensure that clients use locally hosted resources first, but will still be able to use resources in the other data centers if the local one is at capacity or otherwise unavailable.

In the example provided, we have created **Active Directory** (**AD**) security groups for the RTP and San Jose offices, and populated each with the accounts of the users who work in those offices. The following steps detail how to associate those security groups with their appropriate Horizon site:

1. Log on to the Horizon Administration console of any member of the Cloud Pod using an AD account that has administrative permissions within Horizon.
2. Click on **Users and Groups** under **Inventory**, and then click on the **Home Site** tab.
3. Click the **Add...** button to open the **Add Home Site** window, as shown in the following screenshot. Use the **Name** field to search for the AD security group you will associate with a site (Horizon_Homesite_SJC in the example provided), click the **Find** button, click on the group in the **Name** column, and click **Next** to continue:

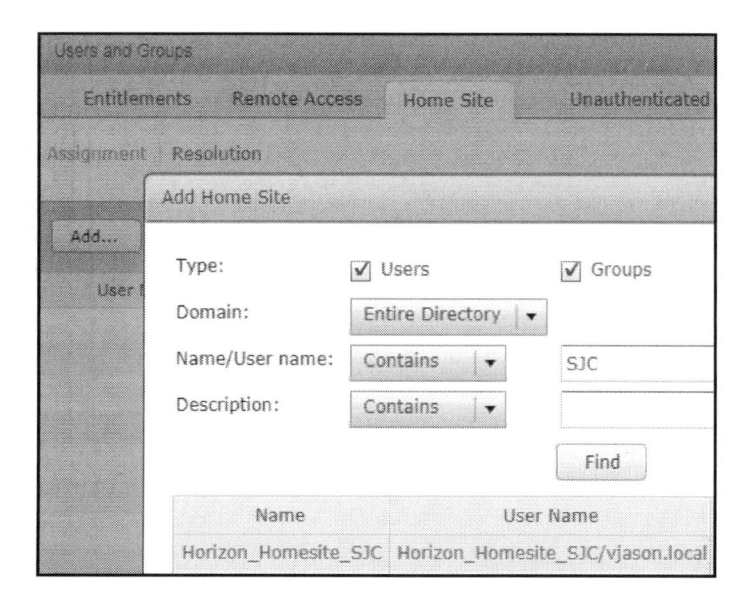

Chapter 6

> **TIP**
>
> You can also add individual users to a site, but I prefer security groups, as most organizations already have existing location-based security groups. By using those groups here, it ensures that users will automatically be added to those groups as needed, although, if not, you can still add them individually here.

4. Click on the **Home Site** drop down menu, select the Horizon site to associate the AD group with (**San Jose** in the example provided), as shown in the following screenshot, and then click **Finish**:

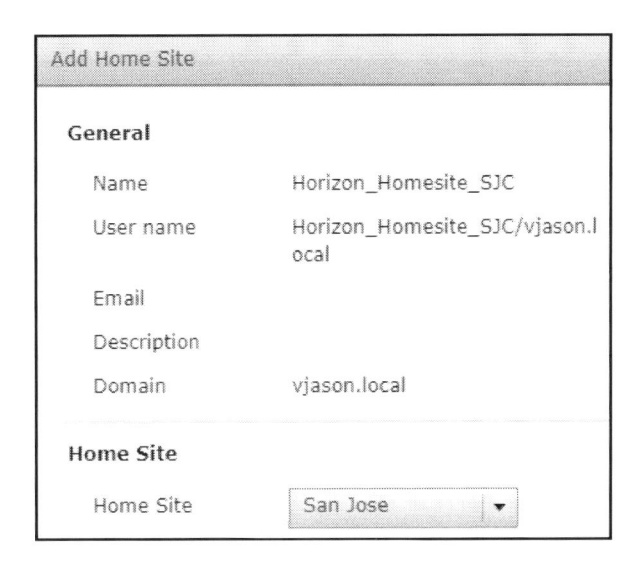

```
Add Home Site

General
    Name            Horizon_Homesite_SJC
    User name       Horizon_Homesite_SJC/vjason.l
                    ocal
    Email
    Description
    Domain          vjason.local

Home Site
    Home Site       San Jose ▼
```

5. Repeat steps 3 and 4 as needed to associate AD security groups with other sites, or additional groups with the same site.

[155]

6. From the **Users and Groups** window | **Home Site** tab shown in the following screenshot, verify that all required AD security groups or individual users have been associated with the desired Horizon site:

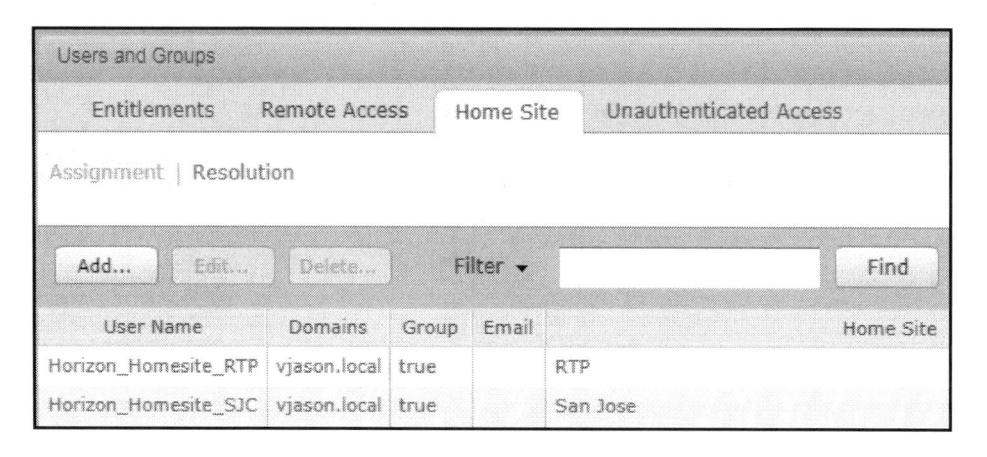

The AD security groups are now associated with Horizon sites. In the next section, we will create Horizon Global Entitlements, and see what option we must configure to ensure that our site assignments are used.

Creating Cloud Pod Global Entitlements

A Global Entitlement is unique to Horizon Cloud Pods, and is what we create in order to grant access to Horizon pools in two or more standalone pods. The process is somewhat similar to creating a Horizon pool, in that you specific some policy settings, but no actual pool is created as part of the process. You must create your Horizon pools individually in each pod that is a member of the Cloud Pod.

You do not specify the target Horizon pools when creating the Global Entitlement, only after, so it is not explicitly required to create them prior to creating the entitlement itself. For the examples provided in this section, we have already created both a desktop and application pool in each Cloud Pod member, and we will walk though creating and configuring a global entitlement for each.

> **TIP**
> From an end user perspective, a Global Entitlement appears as a desktop or application pool within the Horizon client. Owing to this, you should not individually entitle desktop or application pools within the standalone pods to users who will also be added to the Global Entitlement, as it would enable them to see and directly access those individual pools in the Horizon client, when we only want them to use the Global Entitlement. You are only required to entitle users to the Global Entitlement, and Horizon will automatically grant users the required access to the destination pool. This entitlement process is transparent; you will not notice any changes to the list of entitled users to the destination pools of the Cloud Pod members.

Creating and configuring a Global Entitlement for a Horizon desktop pool

The following steps detail how to create and configure a Global Entitlement for a Horizon desktop pool. The creation of the pools themselves will not be shown, only those steps required to create and configure the entitlement:

1. Log on to the Horizon Administration console of any member of the Cloud Pod, using an AD account that has administrative permissions within Horizon.
2. Open the **Catalog** | **Global Entitlements** window within the console. This window is only available if the Cloud Pod feature has been enabled in the pod.
3. In the **Type** tab, click the **Add...** button to open the **Add Global Entitlement** window, as seen in the following screenshot. We are creating a **Desktop Entitlement** in this section, so accept the default options and click **Next** to continue:

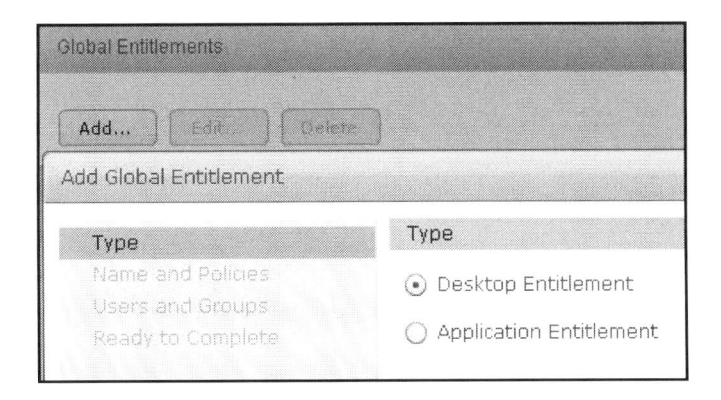

Implementing a Horizon Cloud Pod

4. In the **Names and Policies** tab, provide a **Name** for the Global Entitlement, select any options as required, and click **Next** to continue. In the example provided, we have selected a **Floating** user assignment, specified a **Scope** of **Within site** to ensure that users who do not have an assigned Horizon site access desktops in a pod local to their client connection if possible, selected **Use Home Site** to ensure that users with an assigned site use their local desktop pool if possible, instructed Horizon to **Automatically clean up redundant sessions** so clients do not have to prior to logging in, and clicked the **Allow users to reset their machines** and **HTML Access** checkboxes to enable those options. Review the descriptions of each option on the right side of the window as needed, and note that most can be changed later on if needed:

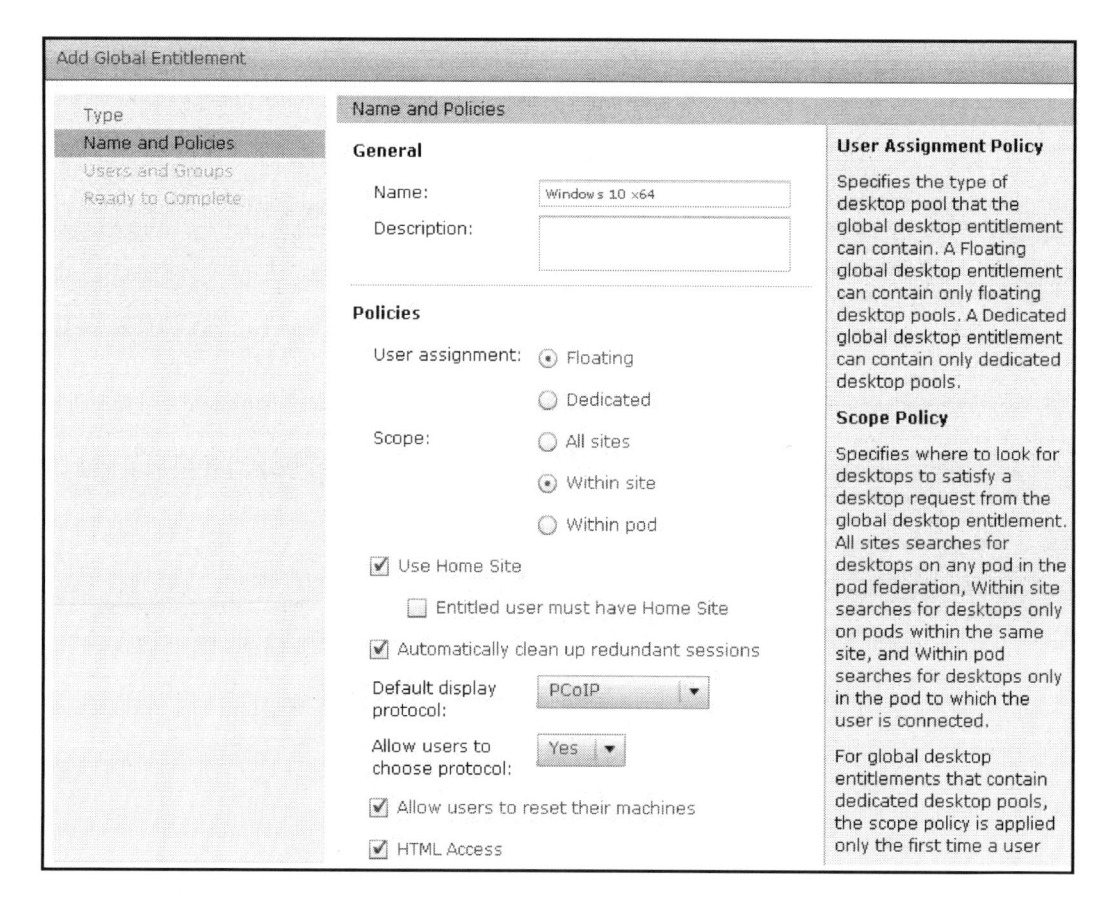

Add Global Entitlement		
Type	Name and Policies	
Name and Policies	General	**User Assignment Policy**
Users and Groups	Name: Windows 10 x64	Specifies the type of desktop pool that the global desktop entitlement can contain. A Floating global desktop entitlement can contain only floating desktop pools. A Dedicated global desktop entitlement can contain only dedicated desktop pools.
Ready to Complete	Description:	
	Policies	
	User assignment: ● Floating	
	○ Dedicated	**Scope Policy**
	Scope: ○ All sites	Specifies where to look for desktops to satisfy a desktop request from the global desktop entitlement. All sites searches for desktops on any pod in the pod federation, Within site searches for desktops only on pods within the same site, and Within pod searches for desktops only in the pod to which the user is connected.
	● Within site	
	○ Within pod	
	☑ Use Home Site	
	☐ Entitled user must have Home Site	
	☑ Automatically clean up redundant sessions	
	Default display protocol: PCoIP	
	Allow users to choose protocol: Yes	For global desktop entitlements that contain dedicated desktop pools, the scope policy is applied only the first time a user
	☑ Allow users to reset their machines	
	☑ HTML Access	

[158]

> **TIP**
> You will only be able to use Horizon pools with the Global Entitlement if you have the same settings as are configured here. For example, a dedicated assignment pool cannot be added to a floating assignment Global Entitlement. If clients experience errors logging in once the Global Entitlement is created, check the Horizon event logs to see if a mismatch in pool and Global Entitlement settings is the reason.

5. In the **Users and Groups** tab, use the **Add...** button to add users or security groups to the Global Entitlement, as shown in the following screenshot, and click **Next** to continue. This process is identical to that used to entitle Horizon pools:

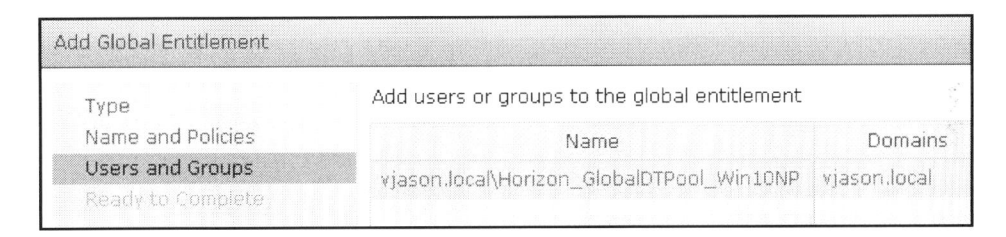

Add Global Entitlement		
Type	Add users or groups to the global entitlement	
Name and Policies	Name	Domains
Users and Groups	vjason.local\Horizon_GlobalDTPool_Win10NP	vjason.local
Ready to Complete		

6. In the **Ready to Complete** tab, review the Global Entitlement settings, make any changes needed using the **Back** button, and then click **Finish** to return to the **Catalog - Global Entitlements** window, as shown in the following screenshot. Note that at this time we have not yet associated any Horizon pools with the entitlement; additional steps are required for this:

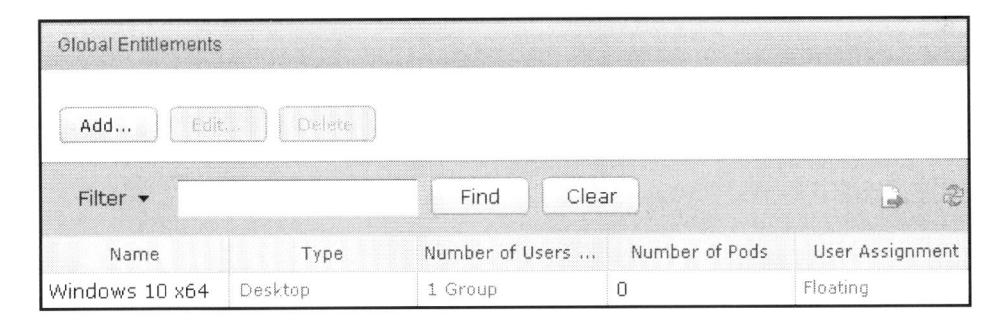

Global Entitlements				
Add... Edit... Delete				
Filter ▼ [ ] Find Clear				
Name	Type	Number of Users ...	Number of Pods	User Assignment
Windows 10 x64	Desktop	1 Group	0	Floating

> **TIP**
> You can also use this screen to delete Global Entitlements; simply click on the one you wish to delete and then click **Delete**.

Implementing a Horizon Cloud Pod

7. Double-click on the Global Entitlement we just created, click the **Local Pools** tab, and click the **Add...** button to open the **Assign Pools** window, as shown in the following screenshot:

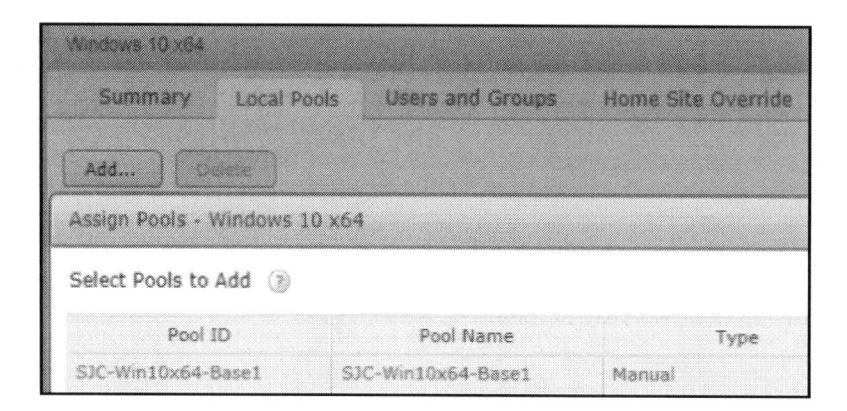

Pool ID	Pool Name	Type
SJC-Win10x64-Base1	SJC-Win10x64-Base1	Manual

Assign Pools - Windows 10 x64

> **TIP**: Only those pools that meet the requirements of the Global Entitlement will be shown. If no pools are available that meet the requirement, a popup will appear explaining this restriction.

8. Click on the desktop pool you wish to add to the Global Entitlement and then click **Add** to return to the **Local Pools** tab, as shown in the following screenshot. Note that only those pools in the Horizon pod you are logged in to will be shown:

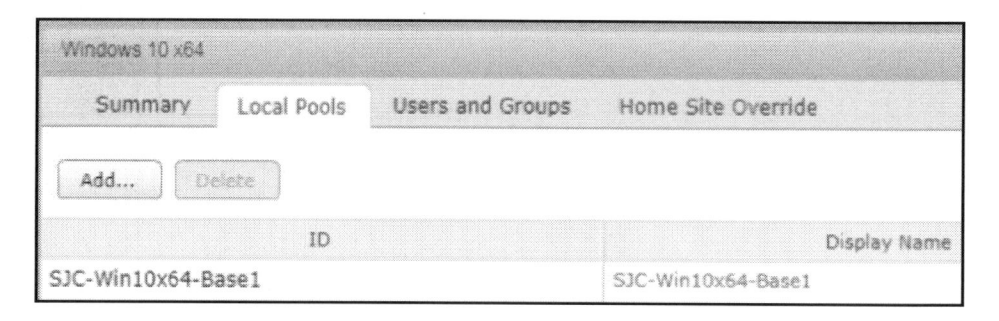

ID	Display Name
SJC-Win10x64-Base1	SJC-Win10x64-Base1

9. Repeat steps 7 and 8 using the Horizon Administration console of each member of the Cloud Pod that has pools you wish to grant the Global Entitlement.

The Horizon desktop Global Entitlement has now been created and configured, and entitled users will now be able to log in and access the target resources. The following screenshot shows what a Horizon client will see, which, as indicated earlier, looks no different than a pool hosted in a standalone Horizon pod. The screenshot also shows a Global Entitlement for a Horizon application pool, which we will create in the next section:

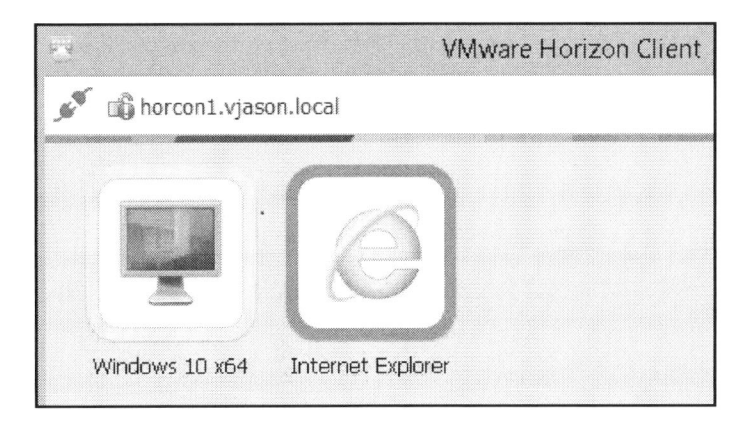

Creating and configuring a Global Entitlement for a Horizon application pool

The following steps detail how to create and configure a Global Entitlement for a Horizon application pool. The creation of the pools themselves will not be shown, only those steps required to create and configure the entitlement. All but one step of this differs from the procedure used to create a Global Entitlement for a desktop pool, so fewer screenshots will be shown:

1. Log on to the Horizon Administration console of any member of the Cloud Pod, using an AD account that has administrative permissions within Horizon.
2. Open the **Catalog - Global Entitlements** window within the console.
3. In the **Type** tab, click the **Add...** button to open the **Add Global Entitlement** window. Click the **Application Entitlement** radio checkbox, and click **Next** to continue.

4. In the **Names and Policies** tab, provide a **Name** for the Global Entitlement, select any options as required, and click **Next** to continue. In this example, where applicable, we used the same settings as the desktop Global Entitlement created in the previous section. Review the descriptions of each option on the right side of the window as needed:

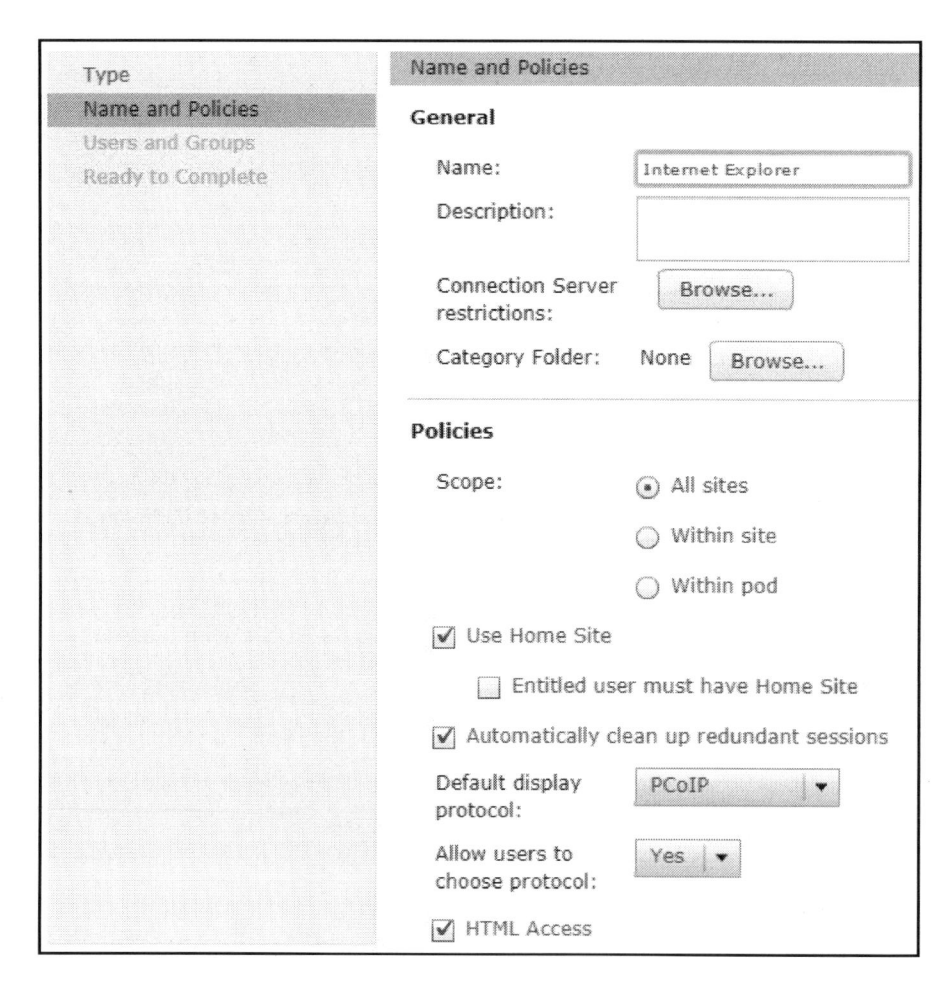

5. In the **Users and Groups** tab, use the **Add...** button to add users or security groups to the Global Entitlement, and click **Next** to continue.
6. In the **Ready to Complete** tab, review the Global Entitlement settings, make any changes needed using the **Back** button, and then click **Finish** to return to the **Catalog - Global Entitlements** window.

7. Double-click on the Global Entitlement we just created, click the **Local Pools** tab, and click the **Add...** button to open the **Assign Pools** window, as shown in the following screenshot:

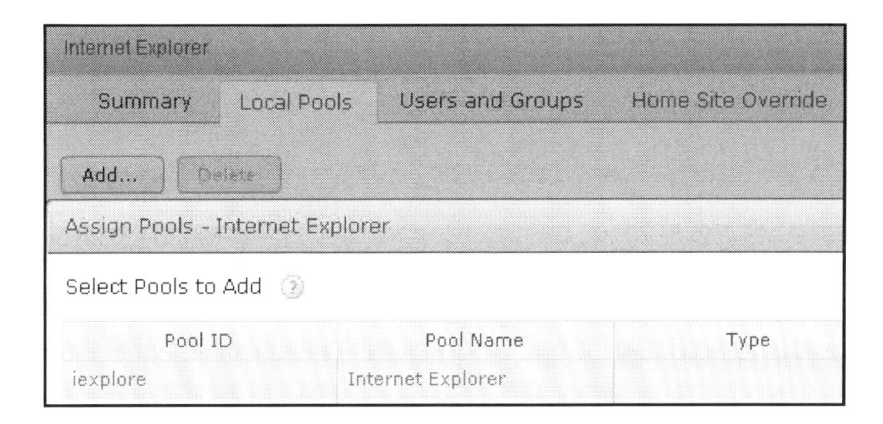

[screenshot: Assign Pools - Internet Explorer window showing Pool ID "iexplore", Pool Name "Internet Explorer"]

8. Click on the application pool you wish to add to the Global Entitlement and then click **Add** to return to the **Local Pools** tab.
9. Repeat steps 7 and 8 using the Horizon Administration console of each member of the Cloud Pod that has pools you wish to the Global Entitlement.

The Horizon application Global Entitlement has now been created and configured, and entitled users will now be able to log in and access the target resources.

Removing a Horizon pod from a Cloud Pod

The following steps outline how to remove a Horizon pod from a Pod Federation, and disable the Cloud Pod Architecture feature. You do not need to delete the individual pods' desktop or application pools as part of this, but you will need to remove them from any Global Entitlements they are part of:

1. Log on to the Horizon Administration console of the Horizon pod you wish to remove from the Cloud Pod.
2. Remove any desktop or application pools managed by this pod from the Global Entitlements; this is accomplished using the screen displayed in step 6 of the *Creating and configuring a Global Entitlement* sections of this chapter; simply click on the pool to remove and click **Delete** (this does not delete the pool itself; it simply removes it from the Global Entitlement).

Implementing a Horizon Cloud Pod

3. Open the **View Configuration** | **Cloud Pod Architecture** window within the console.
4. In the **Pod Federation** pane, click **Unjoin...**, click **OK** when prompted, and click **OK** again when promoted to reload the Horizon Administration console.

> **TIP:** This step is only performed if there are currently two or more members of the Cloud Pod.

5. In the **Pod Federation** pane, click **Uninitialize...**, click **OK** when prompted, and click **OK** again when prompted to reload the Horizon Administration console.

> **TIP:** To complete, remove the Cloud Pod, and repeat steps 1 through 5 on all Pods in the Cloud Pod until only one pod remains. For the final pod in the Cloud Pod, omit step 4 but perform all remaining steps.

The pod is now operating as a standalone Horizon pod, and the Cloud Pod feature and associated components have been disabled or removed as needed. The remaining members of the Cloud Pod will continue to function as before, even if only one pod remains in the Pod Federation.

Updating the settings of a Global Entitlement

Global Entitlements can be edited once created, much like desktop and application pools. Like desktop and application pools, some settings, such as the user assignment method cannot be changed without deleting and recreating the object in question.

The following Global Entitlement settings may be edited after deployment:

- General settings, as seen in step 4 of the sections where we created a Global Entitlement (excluding those that cannot be changed)
- Local pools that are members of the Global Entitlement, although remember that these changes must be made from the pod where the pool is hosted
- Users and groups who are entitled to use the pool

- **Home Site Overrides**, which allow us to set explicit overrides to any home site assignments:
    - The uses for a Home Site Override vary, but one example would be an employee who lives in one area, but for performance reasons prefers using applications or desktops in another.
    - You create a Home Site Override by identifying a user or group, and then by selecting a site you wish to explicitly designate as a home site. For example, in the following screenshot, we configured the listed user to explicitly use **San Jose** as their home site:

Editing the general settings of a Global Entitlement

To edit a Global Entitlement, open the **Catalog - Global Entitlements** window in the Horizon Administration console, double-click on the Global Entitlement you wish to edit, and click the **Edit** button shown in the following screenshot to open the **Edit Global Entitlement** window:

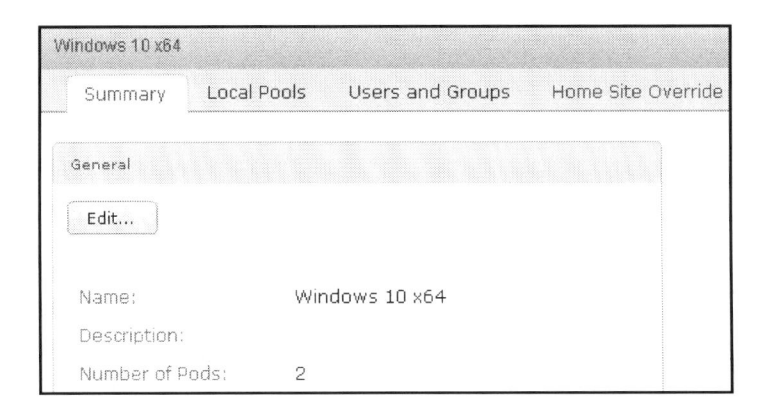

[165]

Implementing a Horizon Cloud Pod

Using the **Edit Global Entitlement** window shown in the following screenshot, we can edit most of the settings we first saw when initially creating the Global Entitlement:

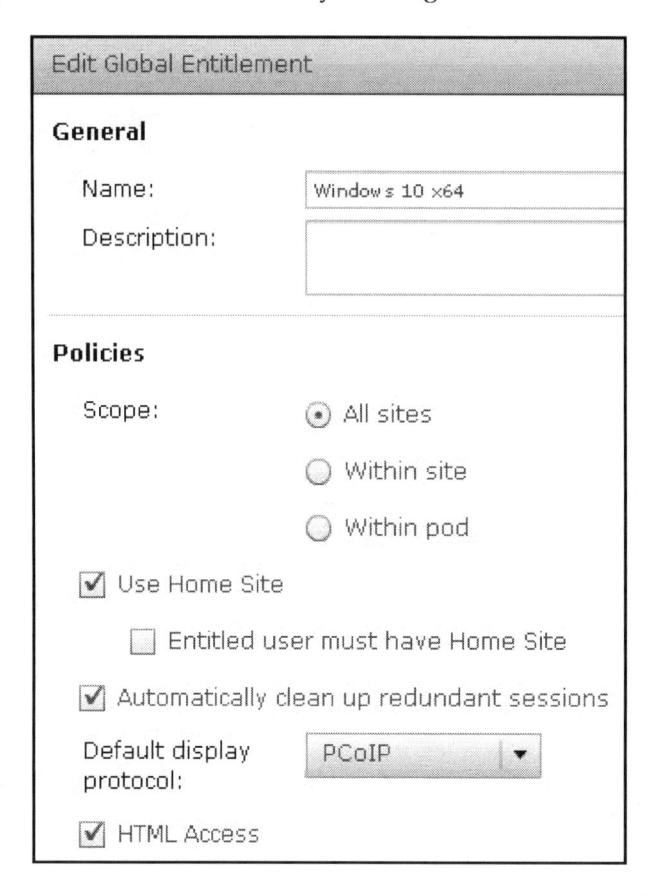

![Edit Global Entitlement window showing General section with Name "Windows 10 x64" and Description field, Policies section with Scope options (All sites selected, Within site, Within pod), Use Home Site checked, Entitled user must have Home Site unchecked, Automatically clean up redundant sessions checked, Default display protocol PCoIP, and HTML Access checked.]

Make changes as needed, and then click **OK** save the updated Global Entitlement.

[166]

Determining the effective home site of a user or security group

While the concept of a Horizon home site is easy enough to understand, owing to home site overrides and the fact that it is possible that a user can be assigned to multiple home sites at once, it is important to have a way to determine what the effective home site should be for a given user. We will use the Horizon home site resolution tool to determine the effective home sites for a user with the following characteristics:

- Member of **Horizon_Homesite_RTP** security group, which is assigned to the **RTP** home site.
- Home site override in place of the **Windows 10 x64** Global Entitlement that associates the user with the **SJC** home site.

The following steps outline how to use the Horizon home site resolution tool to identify which home site the user will be assigned in this case:

1. Log on to the Horizon Administration console of any member of the Cloud Pod using an AD account that has administrative permissions within Horizon.
2. Click on **Users and Groups** under **Inventory**, then click the **Home Site** tab, and finally click **Resolution,** as shown in the following screenshot:

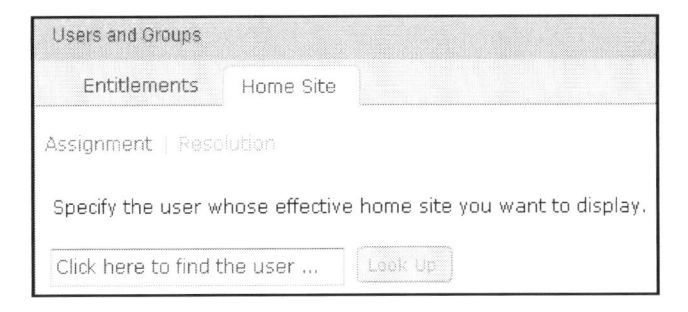

Implementing a Horizon Cloud Pod

3. Click on the field to the left of the **Look Up** button to open the **Find User** window. This window is similar to the one used to find users during the entitlement process, but in this case it can only find individual users and not security groups. Use the window to find the user you wish to investigate, and then click **OK** to return to the **Home Site** tab, as shown in the following screenshot:

```
Users and Groups

  Entitlements    Home Site

Assignment | Resolution

Specify the user whose effective home site you want to display.

vjason.local\Erik            Look Up
```

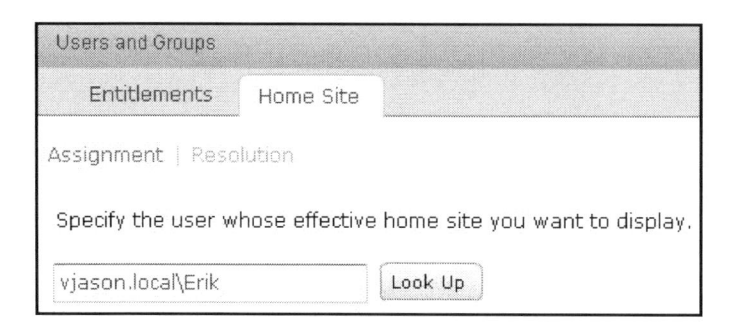

4. Click on the **Look Up** button to begin the resolution process; when it has finished, the **Home Site** tab will display the results, as shown in the following screenshot. When a user is assigned to a home site more than once, or is subject to a home site override (in this case both), a triangle will be displayed to the left of the Global Entitlement name. Click on the triangle to expand the results and see all home site assignments that the user was subject to. The effective home site will be displayed at the top of each list, and any others will be crossed out:

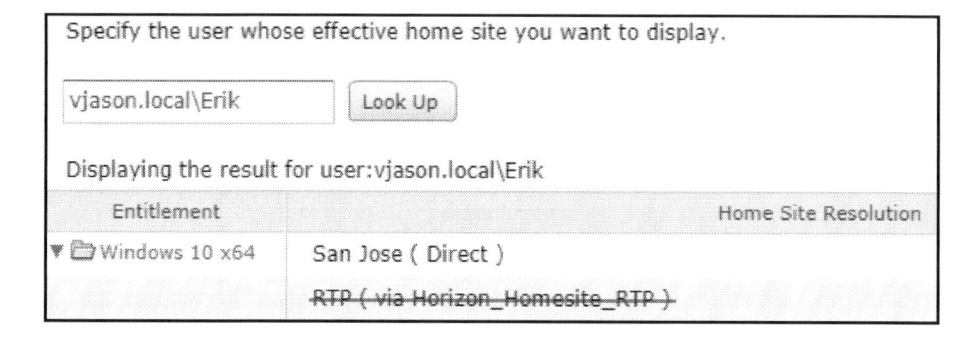

```
Specify the user whose effective home site you want to display.

vjason.local\Erik            Look Up

Displaying the result for user:vjason.local\Erik

Entitlement                              Home Site Resolution
▼ 📁 Windows 10 x64    San Jose ( Direct )
                       RTP ( via Horizon_Homesite_RTP )
```

> **TIP**
> In this case, we can see that the **San Jose** home site override of the **Windows 10 x64** Global Entitlement has precedence over all other home site assignments. Additionally, the direct assignment of the user account (identified as **Direct**) had precedence over the inherited assignment due to being a member of the **Horizon_Homesite_RTP** security group.

Monitoring Global Entitlement Horizon client sessions

Monitoring a Horizon client session to a Global Entitlement requires a slightly different approach, due to the fact that one Horizon pod could be brokering a connection for desktops in another. Consider the following scenario:

A user with the RTP home site assignment connects to the Horizon pod in San Jose, and is connected to a desktop in the RTP pod.

If you reviewed the **Monitoring - Sessions** window in the **RTP** pod, you might expect to see the connection to the desktop. This is not how it works in a Cloud Pod; the session data is maintained by the pod the user initially connected to, not the one where their desktop is hosted (we are assuming they are different for this example). Additionally, the **Monitoring - Sessions** window is not Cloud Pod-aware; unless you know where Horizon pools were actually located, you wouldn't know what Horizon pod a user is actually using for their desktop session.

The following screenshot was taken from the **RTP** pod, but the user is connected to a desktop in the **San Jose** pod. While the **Pool or Farm** or **DNS Name** identifies the actual location of the desktop the client is using, that is only because I integrated the site name into those values when creating the desktop pools. If I hadn't done that, I might not know the actual location of the desktop the user is connected to. As stated previously, the **Sessions** window in the **San Jose** pod will not have any information about this connection:

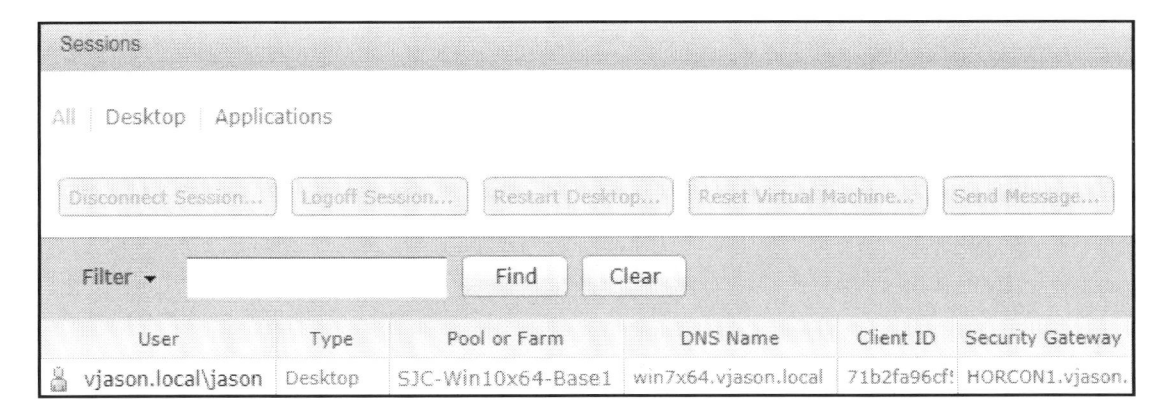

User	Type	Pool or Farm	DNS Name	Client ID	Security Gateway
vjason.local\jason	Desktop	SJC-Win10x64-Base1	win7x64.vjason.local	71b2fa96cf!	HORCON1.vjason.

> **TIP**: This is a good time to remind you that it is a good idea to build these types of identifying characteristics into your Horizon pools and desktop or RDS server names, even if you aren't deploying a Cloud Pod.

Implementing a Horizon Cloud Pod

The following steps outline how to view the full details of a Horizon client session on a Cloud pod:

1. Log on to the Horizon Administration console of any member of the Cloud Pod using an AD account that has administrative permissions within Horizon.
2. Click on **Search Sessions** under **Inventory** within the console, and then use the left drop-down menu to select **Brokering Pod,** as seen in the following screenshot. Click on the right drop-down menu to select the Horizon pod that is brokering the connections you wish to investigate:

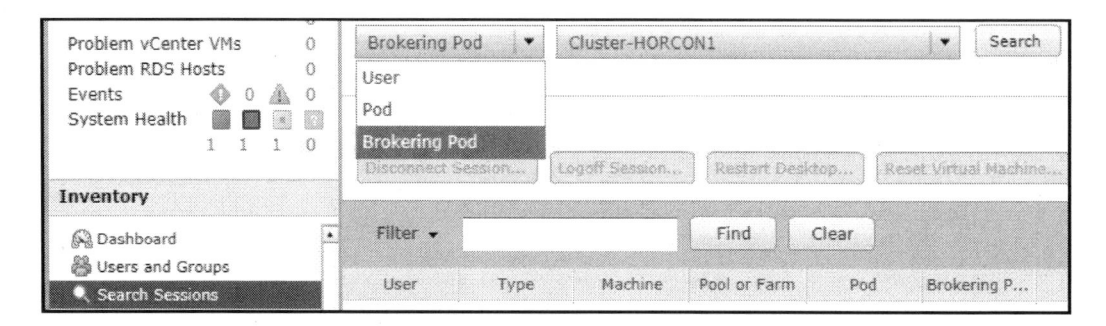

3. Click **Search** to display a list of connections the selected pod is brokering connections for, as seen in the following screenshot. Note that this screen is similar to the **Monitoring - Sessions** window, but adds columns for **Brokering Pod**, **Pod**, and **Site**, which allows us to easily identify the pod the user is connected to, the pod that contains the resources they are using, and their assigned site. Click on the client session if you wish to perform any of the available actions displayed in the screenshot:

Summary

In this chapter, we were introduced to Horizon Cloud Pods. We learned how to create a Cloud Pod, which enabled us to create a Cloud Pod Global Entitlement to entitle clients to pools in multiple Horizon pods at once, and allows those clients to log in to any Pod in the Cloud Pod and access the same Horizon pools (without having to know where those pools are).

We discussed the specifics of how a Cloud Pod works, and what the configuration maximums are. We then went through how to enable the Cloud Pod feature, which creates a Pod Federation, at which point we reviewed this to create a Global Entitlement.

We then learned how to use Horizon home sites to control how Horizon assigns desktops, which allows us to leverage a global desktop pool while still favoring specific desktop pools when possible. We finished by reviewing how we administer our Cloud Pod, including the various objects it contains, which is important should we need to modify settings after the initial configuration is complete.

In the next chapter, we will review how to create and manage Horizon Desktop Pools, which are used to provision and entitle access to virtual desktops.

Questions

1. Why would you want to implement a Horizon Cloud Pod?
2. What are the maximum number of sites supported by a single Cloud Pod?
3. What are the maximum number of pods that can be members of a single Cloud Pod?
4. What is the name of the Horizon entitlement you create to grant access to pools in a Cloud Pod?
5. Can you override the Cloud Pod site assignments for a user?
6. How do you determine the effective Cloud Pod site assignment for a user?
7. If you want to monitor a Horizon Cloud Pod client session, do you do that from the pod that contains the destination Horizon pool, or from the pod where the client originally connected?
8. If you try to add a Horizon pool to a global entitlement, but the pool is not displayed when you attempt to do so, what is the likely source of the problem?

Further reading

The following resources may be used to learn more about the topics described in this chapter:

- VMware documentation:
    - **VMware Horizon** (https://docs.vmware.com/en/VMware-Horizon-7/index.html)

Creating Horizon Desktop Pools

A **Horizon desktop pool** is a collection of desktops that users select when they log in using the Horizon client. A pool can be created based on a subset of users, such as finance, but this is not explicitly required unless you will be deploying multiple virtual desktop master images. The pool can be thought of as a central point of desktop management within Horizon: from it, you create, manage, and entitle access to Horizon desktops. This chapter will discuss how to create a desktop pool using the Horizon Administrator console, an important administrative task.

In this chapter, we will cover the following topics:

- An overview of Horizon desktop pools
- Desktop pool common terms
- How to create three different types of Horizon desktop pools
- How to monitor the provisioning of Horizon desktop pools
- Common problems encountered when provisioning a Horizon desktop pool
- How to manage entitlements to Horizon desktop pools

> Many storage array vendors have given their products the ability to provision desktops outside the Horizon environment and then register them directly within Horizon. If you choose to use this method to create your virtual desktops, you should review the vendor documentation carefully to understand the impact it has on managing your Horizon environment. For example, you will need to know how virtual desktop maintenance, discussed in `Chapter 9`, *Performing Horizon Pool Maintenance*, differs if the desktops are not deployed using Horizon.

Horizon desktop pool overview

Creating a Horizon desktop pool is commonly the final step in the process of deploying virtual desktops. In most cases, when you are ready to deploy your first desktop pool, you have done at least the following:

- Created the necessary infrastructure services needed for your virtual desktop deployment, such as DHCP, DNS, **Active Directory** (**AD**), and so on
- Deployed or identified the **vCenter** server you will use with Horizon
- Deployed at least one ESXi server to host your virtual desktops
- Deployed and configured at least one Horizon Connection Server
- If linked clones will be used, you will have deployed Horizon Composer either on the Horizon vCenter server (if using an older version of vSphere that supports a Windows-based vCenter server) or on a dedicated server
- Created a virtual desktop master image, as discussed in `Chapter 10`, *Creating a Master Virtual Desktop Image*

Each of these items will be required to deploy your first desktop pool. Prior to placing your Horizon environment into production, it is important to verify that you have deployed sufficient resources to meet your scalability and availability needs.

Desktop pool common terms

There are a number of options that must be selected when creating a Horizon desktop pool. Understanding what these options mean is important, as they will impact not only on how the desktops are deployed, but also on what options users have when they attempt to access those desktops.

Later on in the chapter, we will go through the deployment of two different desktop pools, but prior to that it is important to familiarize yourself with some of the terminologies that will come up during that process. Once you understand these terms, you will be able to create any type of desktop pool, which is something we cannot demonstrate in this book, due to the sheer number of options that exist:

Term	Definition
Access Group	Used to organize desktop pools within a Horizon pod, for reasons such as delegated administration.
Adobe Flash Settings for Sessions	Pool settings that control Adobe Flash's quality and throttling for Horizon clients, both of which affect connection bandwidth utilization.
Automated Desktop Pool	A pool that uses desktops provisioned using Horizon.
Automatic Assignment	Used with dedicated desktop assignment: If a user does not already have a desktop assigned, they will automatically be assigned a free one from the desktop pool.
Blackout Times	Used to set when the View Storage Accelerator and VM disk space reclamation will not run.
Connection Server Restrictions	Used to restrict what connection servers can be used to access a desktop pool: commonly used to assign pools to a connection server that has specific security settings.
Dedicated (assignment)	A desktop from the pool is assigned to a user, and from then on it is available only to that user, unless the assignment is manually removed.
Desktop Pool ID	The unique identifier for a desktop pool within a Horizon pod.
Display Name	The desktop pool name that will be displayed in the Horizon Client login window.
Disposable File Redirection	Used with a linked clone desktop to redirect disposable files to a non-persistent disk rather than the OS disk.
Floating (assignment)	Desktops are not assigned to any one user; if they are not in use, they are available to anyone that is entitled to access the desktop pool.
Full Virtual Machines (desktops)	Full virtual machine clones of a vCenter template created from the virtual desktop master image.
Guest Customization	The process of preparing a Horizon desktop for placement within an Active Directory domain.
Instant Clones	Instant Clone desktops share the same base virtual desktop master image as linked clones but can only be deployed using floating assignment pools. After every logoff, Instant Clone desktops are rapidly recreated using **vSphere VMFork** technology.
Manual Desktop Pool	A pool that uses desktops that already exist within vCenter, such as those configured using storage array-based cloning technologies.
Naming Pattern	Used by Horizon to generate names for the virtual machines that it creates.
Non-Persistent Disk	Optional part of a Horizon Composer-linked clone desktop: Used to store disposable files that will be deleted automatically when the user's session ends.

Persistent Disk	Optional part of a Horizon Composer-linked clone desktop: Used to retain user profile data during a Horizon Composer refresh, recompose, or rebalance operation.
QuickPrep	Similar to Microsoft Sysprep; optional method offered by Horizon for customizing and then joining linked clone desktops to an Active Directory domain.
Reclaim VM Disk Space	Reclaims blocks that are no longer being used by the virtual machine operating system.
Replica Disk	Part of a Horizon Composer-linked clone desktop; the replica disk is a read-only copy of the virtual desktop master image virtual hard disk that is shared among the desktops in the pool.
Storage Overcommit	Determines how Horizon places new VM on selected data stores. The more aggressive the setting, the more VM Horizon will place on the data store while reserving less space for sparse disk growth. Refer to the Horizon documentation (https://docs.vmware.com/en/VMware-Horizon-7/index.html) for specific details about the available overcommit levels.
RDS Desktop Pool	A pool that provides access to Windows RDS servers, which are typically used to host multiple simultaneous Horizon client sessions.
Transparent Page-Sharing Scope	Defines the level at which to allow **Transparent Page Sharing** (**TPS**), which frees up redundant memory pages on an ESXi host. Valid options are Pool, Pod, or Global.
Use Native NFS Snapshots (VAAI)	This feature eliminates the need for the **ESXi servers** to read and write data during the creation of Horizon Composer-linked clones by using the built-in capabilities of the storage array to create the virtual machines.
View Composer-Linked Clones	Clones of a virtual desktop master image that share the same base disk. Changes to linked clone desktops are written to a dedicated virtual hard disk attached to the linked clone virtual machine.
View Storage Accelerator	Uses up to 2 GB of ESXi server RAM to cache frequently used blocks of virtual desktop data.
VM Folder Location	The location where Horizon will place the virtual machines it creates in the vCenter VM and Templates view.

Horizon desktop pool options

There are multiple decisions that must be made prior to configuring your first desktop pool. These choices will have an impact on your infrastructure and how your virtual desktops work, which is why they must be considered in advance.

Horizon can provision three different desktop types: Horizon Composer-linked clones, Instant Clones, and full clones. From the perspective of an end user, each of these desktop types looks exactly the same, although their underlying configuration is quite different. The master image for both is prepared using the same tuning techniques discussed in `Chapter 10`, *Creating a Master Virtual Desktop Image*, but how that image is used differs greatly based on the type of desktop you choose to deploy.

Deciding on what type of clone type to use is not an easy task. While instant and linked clones have some definite advantages, which I will describe in detail, to maintain that advantage you must adopt new ways of performing desktop maintenance.

Horizon Composer-linked clones

Horizon Composer-linked clone desktops are created from a virtual desktop master image. While a full clone is created from a vSphere template, creating linked clones requires a virtual desktop master image that is in the standard virtual machine format. Once the image is ready for deployment, the only requirement is that it is powered down and a snapshot of the image is created. A snapshot is required so that Horizon Composer can create the replica of the virtual desktop master image. This replica will be used as the base image for all of the linked clone desktops in the pool.

In addition, as the virtual desktop master image has a snapshot, the Horizon administrator will be able to power it on and make changes to it, while still retaining the ability to deploy additional desktops based on the condition of the desktop when the snapshot was taken. When it is time to deploy the updated image, you would simply take a second snapshot and recompose the desktops using the techniques described in `Chapter 9`, *Performing Horizon Pool Maintenance*. Assuming you left the initial snapshot in place, you could even recompose the desktops to that snapshot as well as the second one that you created.

> The **Overview of VMware Horizon Composer** section of ;`Chapter 3`, *Implementing Horizon Composer* explains the underlying structure of a linked clone-based virtual machine.

Instant-clone desktops

Instant-clone desktops are very similar to linked clone desktops in that they are provisioned from and share the same virtual desktop master image. However, instant-clones are deployed using the vSphere VMFork technology, which utilizes a powered-on virtual desktop master image replica VM on each ESXi server so that the clones can copy its disk and memory state during the provisioning process. This enables instant-clones to be deployed or replaced in a matter of seconds, as they require no additional reboots to configure, while linked clones require multiple reboots to complete the customization process. Similar to linked-clones, the instant-clone replica image can be replaced at any time with an updated version, and App Volumes may be used to manage applications independent of the virtual desktop master image.

> Consult the VMware blog post **VMware Instant Clone Technology for Just-In-Time Desktop Delivery in Horizon 7 Enterprise Edition** (`https://blogs.vmware.com/euc/2016/02/horizon-7-view-instant-clone-technology-linked-clone-just-in-time-desktop.html`) for more information about how vmFork works, and why it is much faster than deploying using linked clones.

The following diagram shows the relationship between the memory and disk of an instant-clone-based Horizon VM and its parent VM. Instant-clones leverage a quiesced parent VM as their base, and copy any memory or disk blocks that need to be changed to their own deltas. This differs from Linked-clones, which can only refer to the virtual disk of their powered off parent virtual machine, and not the memory:

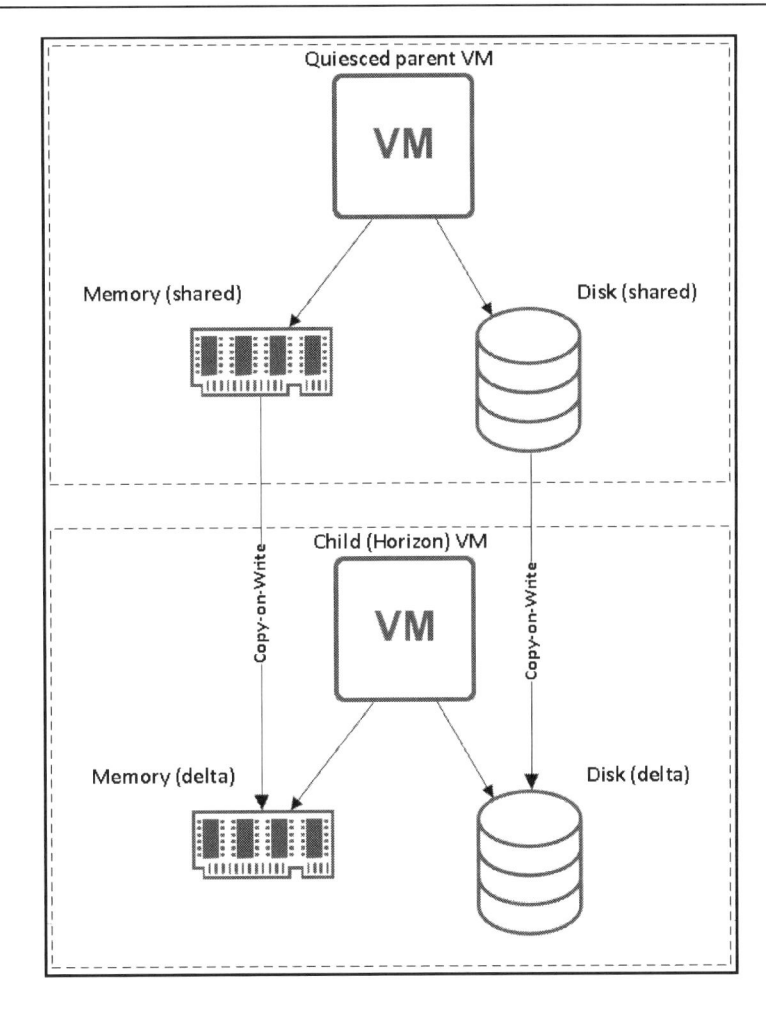

```
                    Quiesced parent VM
                           ┌────┐
                           │ VM │
                           └────┘
                          ↙      ↘
         Memory (shared)            Disk (shared)
            [memory]                  [disk]
─ ─ ─ ─ ─ ─ ─ ─ ─ ─ ─ ─ ─ ─ ─ ─ ─ ─ ─ ─ ─ ─ ─
                     Child (Horizon) VM
         ↑                                    ↑
      Copy-on-Write     ┌────┐         Copy-on-Write
                        │ VM │
                        └────┘
                       ↙      ↘
         Memory (delta)          Disk (delta)
            [memory]               [disk]
```

Instant-clone desktops differ from linked-clones in that they do not use Horizon Composer to deploy and manage the desktops, do not support dedicated user assignment, and there are no options for desktop persistence. All Instant-clone desktops utilize floating user assignment, and when the Horizon client logs off, the desktop is deleted and immediately deployed again using the vmFork functionality. If you require user persona data and personal files to persist, you must use tools such as User Environment Manager and folder redirection, discussed in Chapter 12, *Implementing User Environment Manager*. Similar to linked-clone desktop pools, a snapshot is required so that Horizon can create the replica of the master image.

Full-clone desktops

Full-clone Horizon desktops are created using a virtual desktop master image that has been converted to the vSphere template format. A full clone is an independent copy of that template, managed separately from other desktops and the template on which it was based. Aside from the fact that it was created from a template, from a conceptual standpoint it is very similar to the physical desktop that it may have replaced. As a result, the life cycle of the full clone desktop is typically managed using the same techniques used with a physical desktop.

Linux desktops

Horizon supports the use of Linux virtual desktops, although it contains no automated method to deploy them, and can only act as a connection broker for Horizon clients. Linux desktops must be deployed and managed outside of Horizon, and then added to **Horizon Manual Desktop Pools**. This process is much more complex than what is required to deploy Windows-based desktop pools, which makes it prohibitive to discuss further in this chapter.

The VMware document **Setting Up Horizon 7 for Linux Desktops** (`https://docs.vmware.com/en/VMware-Horizon-7/7.6/linux-desktops-setup.pdf`) provides examples of the scripts you can use to deploy and customize Linux desktops, and then register them with Horizon for use in manual desktop pools. Once the desktops have been deployed, configured, registered with Horizon, added to Horizon Manual Desktop Pools, and entitlements assigned, they will be available for use by Horizon clients.

Experience with both Linux and vSphere **PowerCLI** is a recommended prerequisite to deploying Linux desktops for use with Horizon.

QuickPrep versus Sysprep

Windows **Sysprep** is a utility included with the Windows operating system that is used to personalize a Windows image. Rather than install Windows on each machine individually, organizations can apply a preconfigured image to a machine and then use Sysprep to generate the identifiers that make that installation of Windows unique.

> Instant Clone desktop pools use a dedicated customization method called **ClonePrep**, which is similar to QuickPrep. There is no option to select Sysprep when creating Instant Clone desktop pools.

When deploying linked clone desktops, you have the option of using Sysprep or the included VMware **QuickPrep** tool to customize the operating system. The tools do not perform all of the same tasks, so it is important to understand what differs when you choose one over the other.

The following table details the differences between Sysprep and QuickPrep:

Task	QuickPrep	Sysprep
Change security identifiers on the parent image	No	Yes
Change the computer name	Yes	Yes
Join the new virtual machine to the domain	Yes	Yes
Remove local accounts	No	Yes
Remove parent image from the domain	No	Yes
Reuse preexisting AD computer accounts	Yes	Yes
Generate a new **System Identifier (SID)**	No	Yes
Update language, regional, data, and time settings	No	Yes
Reboots required	0	1
Requires a configuration file and Sysprep utility	No	Yes

> **TIP:** Like QuickPrep, ClonePrep retains the replica Windows OS SID and application **Globally Unique Identifiers (GUID)** during the cloning process. Unlike QuickPrep, ClonePrep cannot reuse existing AD computer accounts.

It is important to consider the differences between Sysprep and QuickPrep when determining which method to choose. In some environments, it may be that QuickPrep cannot be used because it does not generate a new SID for the guest operating system. In other environments, it may be that there are no issues with using QuickPrep. Generally speaking, QuickPrep enables faster desktop deployment, which affects not only desktop pool creation but recompose operations as well. Regardless of which method you choose, it is important to monitor the behavior of the desktop during a pilot program to ensure that the desktops are functioning as expected.

> **TIP:** You should use Microsoft **Key Management Services (KMS)** to license and activate your Horizon Desktops. This is particularly important when using linked clones, as nearly every Horizon Composer maintenance task will initiate a license activation request, regardless of whether ClonePrep, QuickPrep, or Sysprep was used. These requests would quickly exhaust ordinary **Multiple Activation Key (MAK)** license keys. Microsoft typically provides both KMS and MAK keys to organizations that purchase volume licensed versions of their Windows and Office products.

Advantages of Linked or Instant Clone desktops

Linked clone and Instant Clone desktops have a number of advantages over full clone desktops. Some of these advantages include the following:

- Linked clone and Instant Clone desktops share the same parent virtual disk for read operations; therefore, the amount of disk space they require is greatly reduced.
- Linked clone desktops can be recomposed, which is a process where their replica disks are replaced with an updated version that has software updates or other changes applied. Rather than apply updates to individual desktops, you can update the master image once, and then use a recompose operation to update the replica disks, which applies those changes to the entire desktop pool.
    - Instant Clone desktops support a similar operation named **Push Image**.
    - These procedures are described in `Chapter 9`, *Performing Horizon Pool Maintenance*.

> **TIP**
> Using a recompose to upgrade the operating system version is not supported.

- Linked clone desktops can be refreshed, a process that deletes the contents of the linked clone OS and disposable data disks, which returns them to the same state they were in when initially deployed. This enables you to discard any changes that were made after the desktop was deployed, allowing for tight control over the end user experience. Desktops can be refreshed at a specific time, when a specified amount of disk space has been used, or even after every logoff. The refresh process is described in `Chapter 9`, *Performing Horizon Pool Maintenance*.
    - Instant Clone desktops are automatically deleted every time a Horizon client logs off; manual refresh operations are not required.

- A linked clone desktop pool can be rebalanced, which redistributes linked clone storage evenly across data stores. Individual linked clone disk utilization will vary over time, leading to an imbalance in storage utilization across all the data stores. A rebalance operation addresses this by moving relocating linked clone storage. The rebalance process is described in `Chapter 9`, *Performing Horizon Pool Maintenance*.
    - Instant Clone desktop pools do not require or support a rebalance operation.

> **TIP**: Storage vMotion is not supported with linked clone desktops. You must use a rebalance operation to relocate or rebalance linked clone desktop storage.

Considerations for Linked and Instant Clone desktops

Owing to how linked and Instant Clone desktops work, it is important to remember that they should not be managed using the same techniques as a typical virtual machine. Some examples of this include the following:

- If you were to apply software patches to linked clones individually, rather than using a recompose operation, the linked clone virtual hard disks would grow significantly over time. This defeats the storage efficiency that is one of the primary reasons for choosing linked clones. Additionally, deploying patches to Instant Clone desktops would be pointless, as any changes are erased when the user logs off.
- Recompose, refresh, and rebalance operations all change the state of the linked clone virtual desktop, which can affect utilities such as indexing programs. If these operations lead to resource-intensive operations, such as a file index, every time they occur, it may be that they need to be disabled or have their behavior altered. This topic is discussed further in `Chapter 10`, *Creating a Master Virtual Desktop Image*.

Creating Horizon Desktop Pools

> **TIP**
> For performance reasons, Windows indexing features should be disabled in Instant Clone master images.

- Instant Clones currently support Windows 7 and Windows 10 only, require that **View Storage Accelerator** be enabled, and the **Instant Clone** option must have been selected during the Horizon agent installation process described in Chapter 10, *Creating a Master Virtual Desktop Image*.

Generally speaking, you should approach managing instant and linked clone desktops from the master image wherever possible as this enables you to realize most of the advantages of linked clones. If a proposed change can be done on the master image, and then rolled out to users using a recompose operation, that is the preferred method of working with linked clones, and the only way to work with Instant Clones. Chapter 9, *Performing Horizon Pool Maintenance*, will provide more information about how to manage linked and Instant Clone desktops.

Creating a Horizon desktop pool

This section will provide an example of how to create two different Horizon dedicated assignment desktop pools, one based on Horizon Composer-linked clones and another based on full clones. Horizon Instant Clone pools only support floating assignment, so they have fewer options compared to the other types of desktop pools. Also discussed will be how to use the Horizon Administrator console and the vSphere client to monitor the provisioning process.

> **TIP**
> The examples provided for full clone and linked clone pools created dedicated assignment pools, although floating assignments may be created as well. The options will be slightly different for each, so refer to the information provided earlier in this chapter, as well as the Horizon documentation (https://docs.vmware.com/en/VMware-Horizon-7/index.html), to understand what each setting means. Additionally, the Horizon Administrator console often explains each setting within the desktop pool configuration screens.

Creating a pool using Horizon Composer-linked clones

The following steps outline how to use the Horizon Administrator console to create a dedicated assignment desktop pool using Horizon Composer-linked clones. As discussed previously, it is assumed that you already have a virtual desktop master image that you have created a snapshot of. During each stage of the pool creation process, a description of many of the settings is displayed on the right-hand side of the **Add Desktop Pool** window. In addition, a question mark appears next to some of the settings; click on it to read important information about the specified setting:

1. Log on to the Horizon Administrator console using an AD account that has administrative permissions within Horizon.
2. Open the **Catalog - Desktop Pools** window within the console.
3. Click on the **Add...** button in the **Desktop Pools** window to open the **Add Desktop Pool** window.
4. In the **Desktop Pool Definition | Type** window, select the **Automated Desktop Pool** radio button as shown in the following screenshot, and then click on **Next >**:

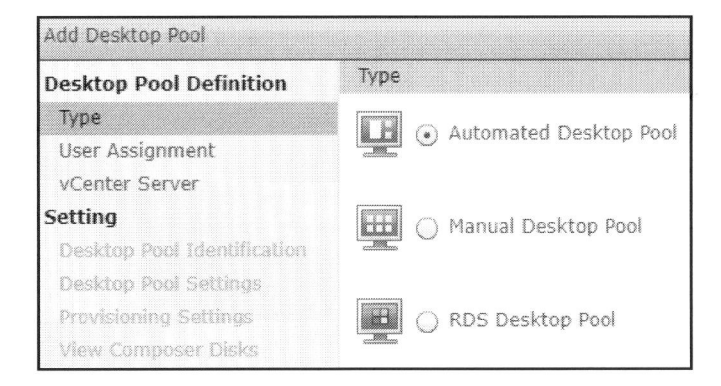

Creating Horizon Desktop Pools

5. In the **Desktop Pool Definition | User Assignment** window, select the **Dedicated** radio button and check the **Enable automatic assignment** checkbox, as shown in the following screenshot, and then click on **Next >**:

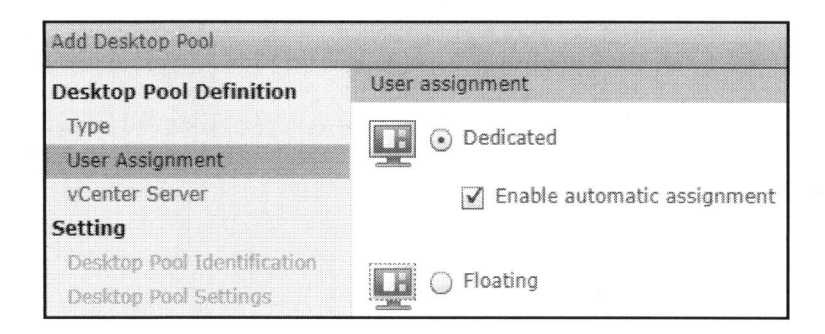

Add Desktop Pool	
Desktop Pool Definition	User assignment
Type	● Dedicated
User Assignment	
vCenter Server	☑ Enable automatic assignment
Setting	
Desktop Pool Identification	○ Floating
Desktop Pool Settings	

> **TIP**: Dedicated assignment pools assign a desktop to a single user permanently, although the Horizon administrator can remove the assignment. Floating assignment desktops are assigned to a user at logon, and unassigned when they log off. Floating assignment pools allow organizations to deploy only the number of concurrent desktops they need, rather than one per each user, although you must use tools such as persistent data disks, User Environment Manager, and so on, to ensure that user data and settings are retained when a user logs off.

6. In the **Desktop Pool Definition | vCenter Server** window, select the **View Composer linked clones** radio button, highlight the vCenter server, as shown in the following screenshot, and then click on **Next**:

Add Desktop Pool		
Desktop Pool Definition	vCenter Server	
Type	○ Instant clones	
User Assignment		
vCenter Server	● View Composer linked clones	
Setting	○ Full virtual machines	
Desktop Pool Identification		
Desktop Pool Settings	vCenter Server	View Composer
Provisioning Settings	vc-01.vjason.local(svc-horizon@vjason.local)	horcomp1.vjason.local
View Composer Disks		

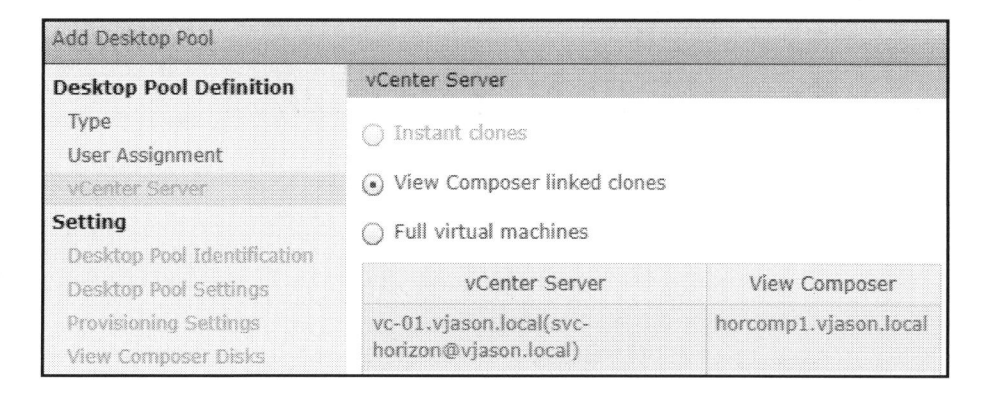

7. In the **Setting | Desktop Pool Identification** window, populate the pool **ID:**, as shown in the following screenshot, and then click on **Next**. Optionally, configure the **Display Name:** field. When finished, click on **Next**:

Add Desktop Pool - Win7x64-Base1	
Desktop Pool Definition	**Desktop Pool Identification**
Type	ID: Win7x64-Base1
User Assignment	
vCenter Server	Display name: Windows 7 LC Pool 1
Setting	Access group: /
Desktop Pool Identification	
Desktop Pool Settings	Description:

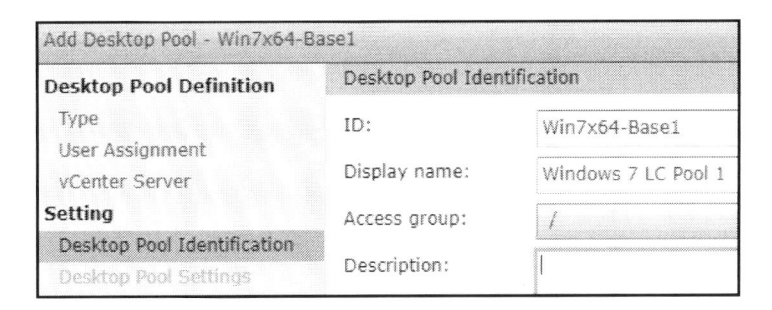

> **TIP**: The **ID** is used by Horizon internally to identify the pool; end users see only the **Display name**.

8. In the **Setting | Desktop Pool Settings** window, configure the various settings for the desktop pool. Many of these options are self-explanatory; those that are not are described in the *Desktop pool common terms* section of this chapter. These settings can also be adjusted later, if desired. When finished, click on **Next >**:

Add Desktop Pool - Win7x64-Base1		
Desktop Pool Definition	**Desktop Pool Settings**	
Type	**General**	
User Assignment	State:	Enabled
vCenter Server		
Setting	Connection Server restrictions:	None Browse...
Desktop Pool Identification		
Desktop Pool Settings	Category Folder:	None Browse...
Provisioning Settings	**Remote Settings**	
View Composer Disks		
Storage Optimization	Remote Machine Power Policy:	Take no power action
vCenter Settings		
Advanced Storage Options	Automatically logoff after disconnect:	Never
Guest Customization		

[187]

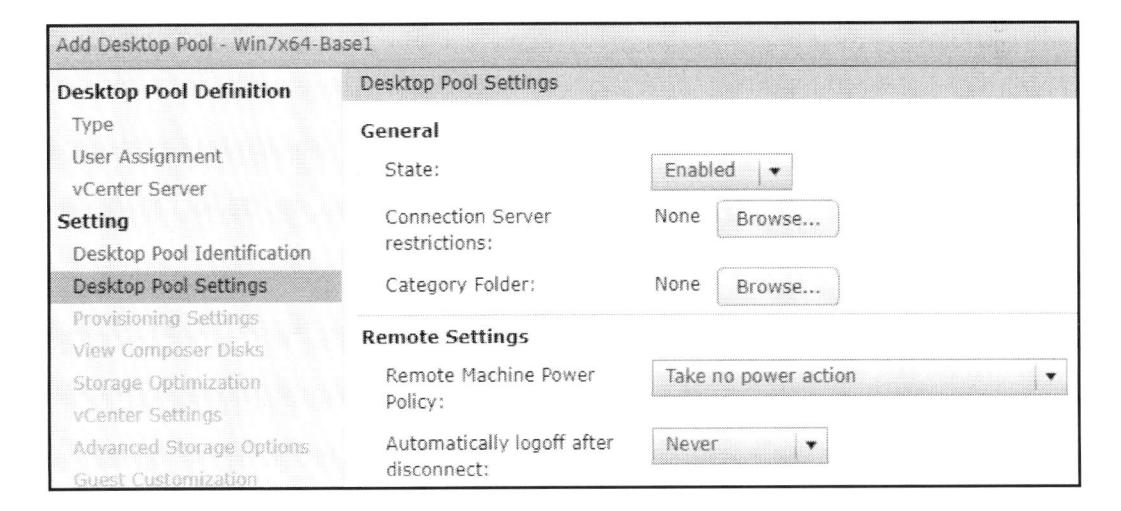

Creating Horizon Desktop Pools

9. In the **Setting** | **Provisioning Settings** window, configure the various provisioning options for the desktop pool that include the desktop-naming format, the number of desktops, and the number of desktops that should remain available during Horizon Composer maintenance operations. When finished, click on **Next >**:

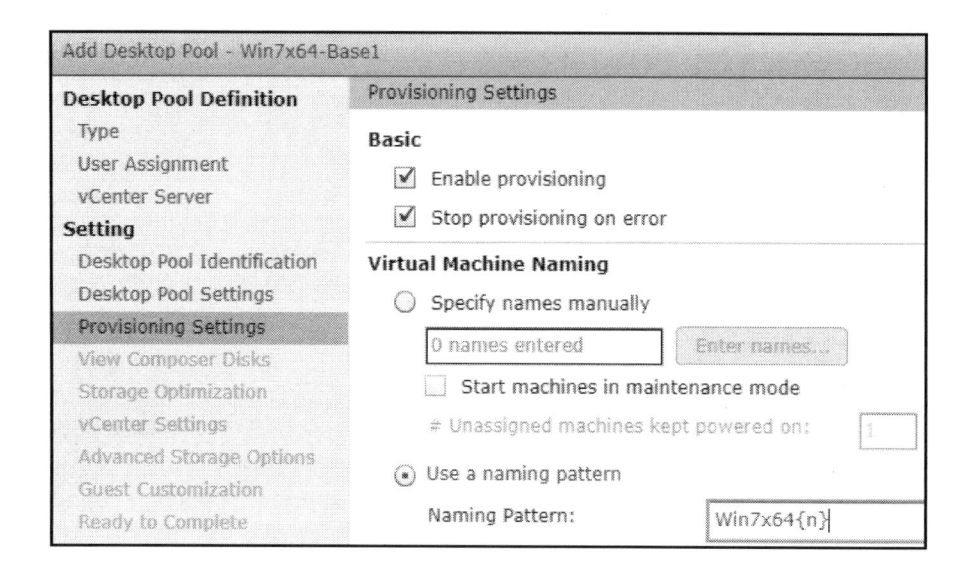

```
Add Desktop Pool - Win7x64-Base1

Desktop Pool Definition          Provisioning Settings
  Type                           Basic
  User Assignment                  [✓] Enable provisioning
  vCenter Server                   [✓] Stop provisioning on error
Setting
  Desktop Pool Identification    Virtual Machine Naming
  Desktop Pool Settings            ( ) Specify names manually
  Provisioning Settings
  View Composer Disks                  [0 names entered]     [Enter names...]
  Storage Optimization             [ ] Start machines in maintenance mode
  vCenter Settings                 # Unassigned machines kept powered on: [1]
  Advanced Storage Options
  Guest Customization              (•) Use a naming pattern
  Ready to Complete                    Naming Pattern:       [Win7x64{n}]
```

> **TIP**
> When creating a desktop naming pattern, use an {n} to instruct Horizon to insert a unique number in the desktop name. For example, using `Win7x64{n}`, as shown in the preceding screenshot, will name the first desktop `Win7x64-1`, the next `Win7x6-2`, and so on.

10. In the **Setting** | **View Composer Disks** window, configure the settings for your optional linked clone disks. By default, both a **Persistent Disk** for user data and a non-persistent disk for **Disposable File Redirection** are created. When finished, click on **Next >**:

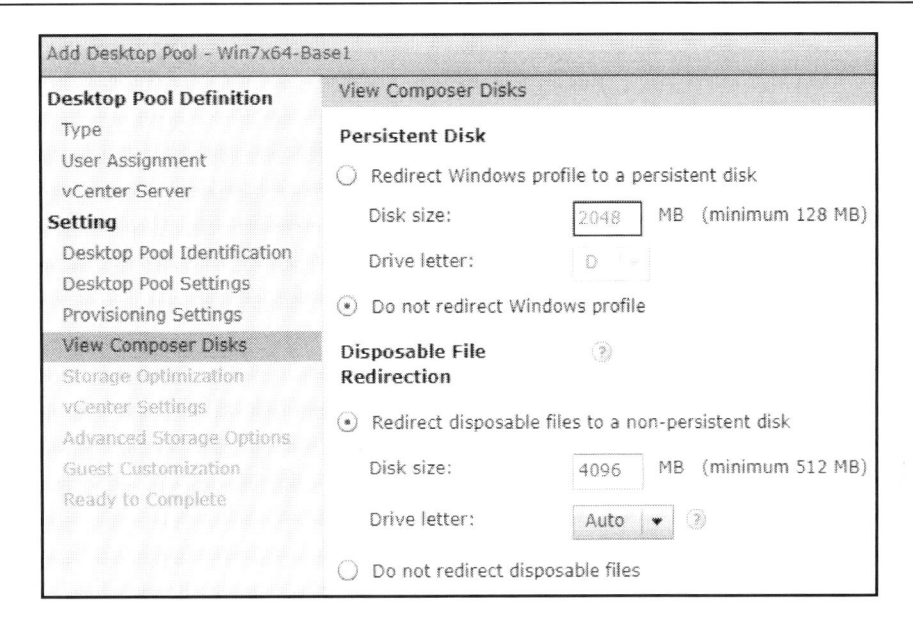

11. In the **Setting** | **Storage Optimization** window, we configure whether our desktop storage is provided by VMware Virtual SAN, and, if not, whether to separate our Horizon desktop replica disks from the individual desktop OS disks. In our example, VMware Virtual SAN is not available, so we will simply click **Next >**:

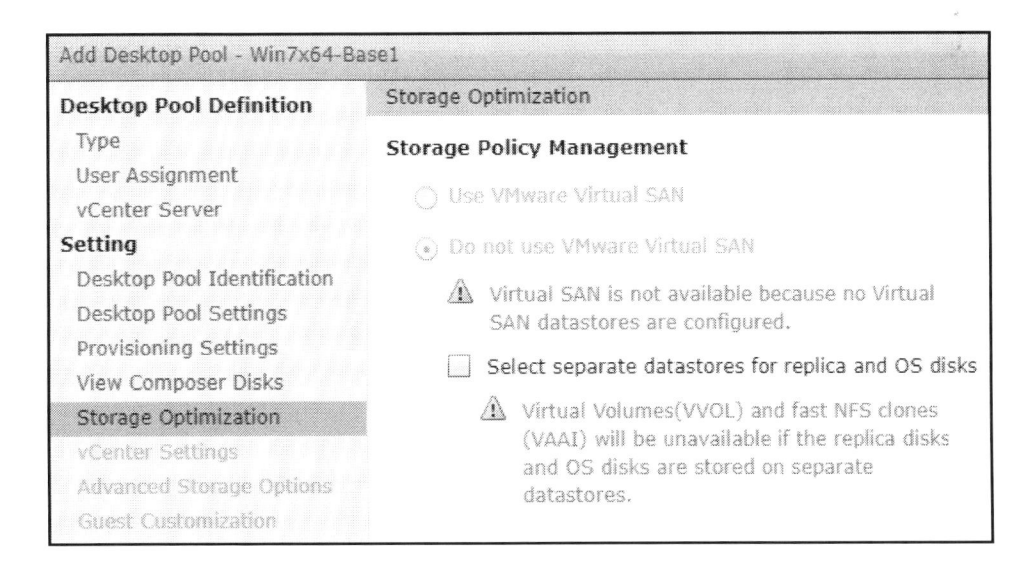

Creating Horizon Desktop Pools

> **TIP**
> As all-flash storage arrays or all-flash or flash-dependent **Software Defined Storage** (**SDS**) platforms become more common, there is less of a need to place the shared linked clone replica disks on separate, faster data stores than the individual desktop OS disks.

12. In the **Setting** | **vCenter Settings** window, we will need to configure six different options that include selecting the parent virtual machine, which snapshot of that virtual machine to use, what vCenter folder to place the desktops in, what vSphere cluster and resource pool to deploy the desktops to, and what data stores to use. Click on the **Browse...** button next to the **Parent VM:** field to begin the process and open the **Select Parent VM** window:

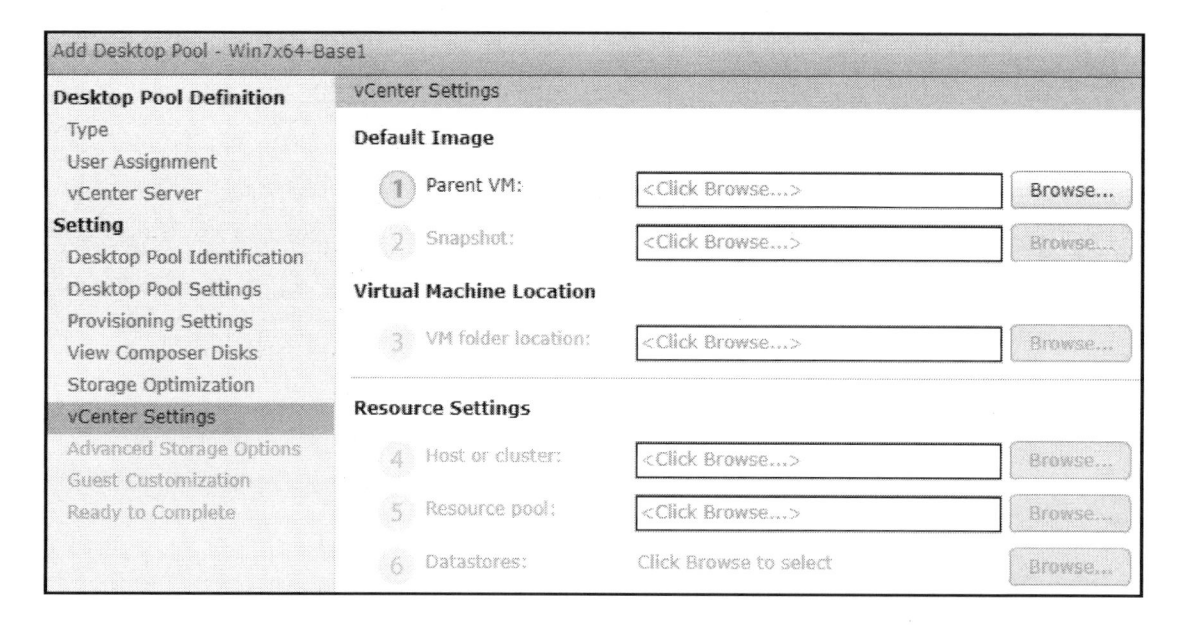

13. In the **Select Parent VM** window, highlight the virtual desktop master image that you wish to deploy desktops from, as shown in the following screenshot. Click on **OK** when the image is selected to return to the previous window:

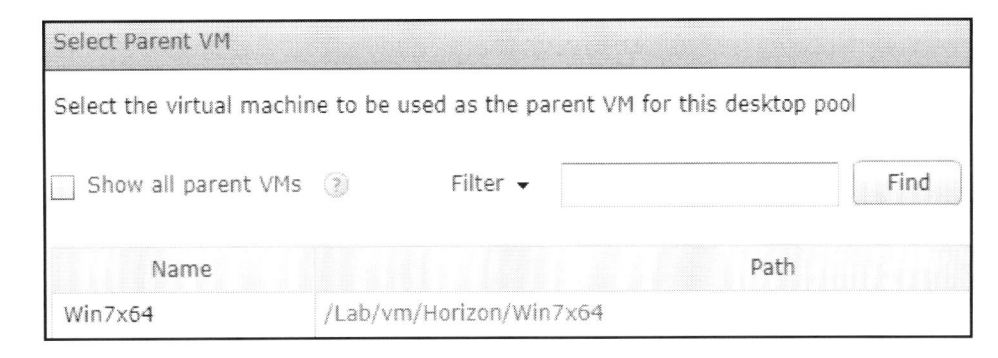

Select Parent VM	
Select the virtual machine to be used as the parent VM for this desktop pool	
☐ Show all parent VMs Filter ▼ [ ] [Find]	
Name	Path
Win7x64	/Lab/vm/Horizon/Win7x64

> **TIP:** The virtual machine will only appear if a snapshot has been created.

14. In the **Setting | vCenter Settings** window, click on the **Browse...** button next to the **Snapshot:** field to open the **Select default image** window. Select the desired snapshot, as shown in the following screenshot, and click on **OK** to return to the previous window:

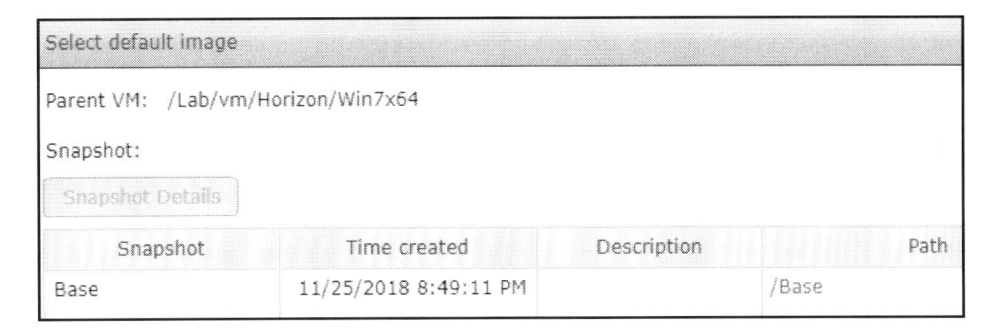

Select default image			
Parent VM: /Lab/vm/Horizon/Win7x64			
Snapshot:			
[Snapshot Details]			
Snapshot	Time created	Description	Path
Base	11/25/2018 8:49:11 PM		/Base

Creating Horizon Desktop Pools

15. In the **Setting** | **vCenter Settings** window, click on the **Browse...** button next to the **VM folder location:** field to open the **VM Folder Location** window, as shown in the following screenshot. Select the folder within vCenter where you want the desktop virtual machines to be placed, and click on **OK** to return to the previous window:

    VM Folder Location

    Select the folder to store the VM

    ▼ Lab
       Discovered virtual machine
       Horizon

16. In the **Setting** | **vCenter Settings** window, click on the **Browse...** button next to the **Host or cluster:** field to open the **Host or Cluster** window, as shown in the following screenshot. Select the cluster or individual ESXi server within vCenter where you want the desktop virtual machines to be created, and click on **OK** to return to the previous window:

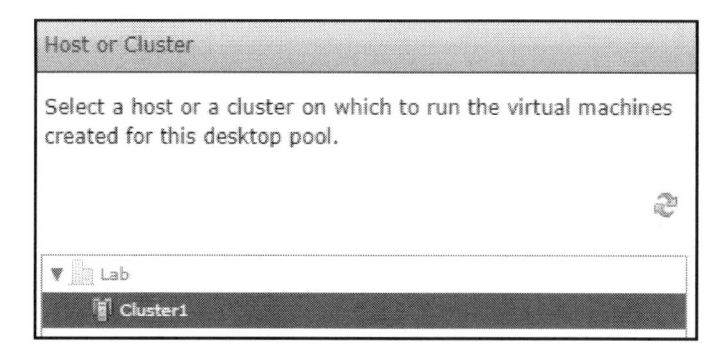

    Host or Cluster

    Select a host or a cluster on which to run the virtual machines created for this desktop pool.

    ▼ Lab
       Cluster1

17. In the **Setting | vCenter Settings** window, click on the **Browse...** button next to the **Resource pool:** field to open the **Resource Pool** window, as shown in the following screenshot. If you intend to place the desktops within a resource pool, you would select that here; if not, select the same cluster or ESXi server you chose in the previous step. Once finished, click on **OK** to return to the previous window:

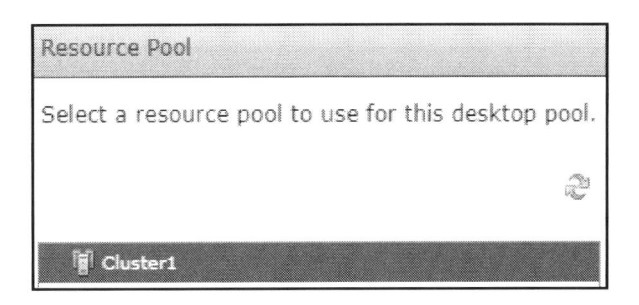

18. In the **Setting | vCenter Settings** window, click on the **Browse...** button next to the **Datastores:** field to open the **Select Linked Clone Datastores** window, as shown in the following screenshot. Select the datastore or datastores where you want the desktops to be created, their **Storage Overcommit** level, and then click on **OK** to return to the previous window:

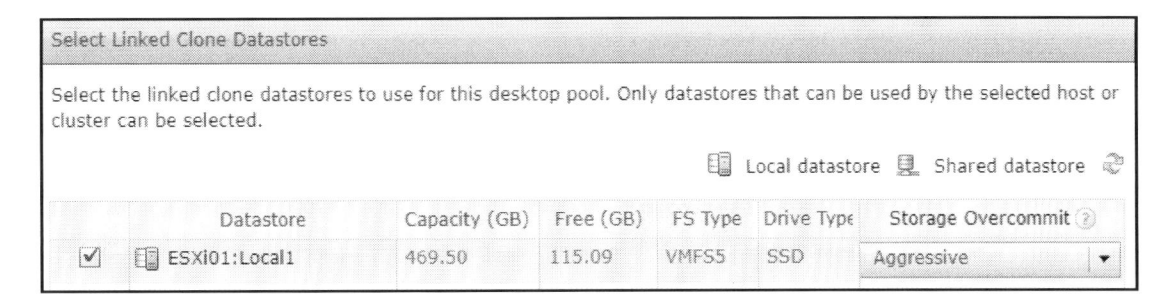

> **TIP**: If you were using storage other than VMware Virtual SAN and had opted to use separate datastores for your OS and replica disks in step 11, you would have had to select unique datastores for each here instead of just one.

19. The **Setting | vCenter Settings** window should now have all options selected, enabling the **Next >** button. When finished, click on **Next >**.

[193]

Creating Horizon Desktop Pools

20. In the **Setting | Advanced Storage Options** window, if desired, select and configure the **Use View Storage Accelerator** and **Other Options** check boxes to enable those features. In our example, we have enabled both the **Use View Storage Accelerator** and **Reclaim VM disk space** options, and configured **Blackout Times** to ensure that these operations do not occur between 08:00 and 17:00 on weekdays. When finished, click on **Next >**:

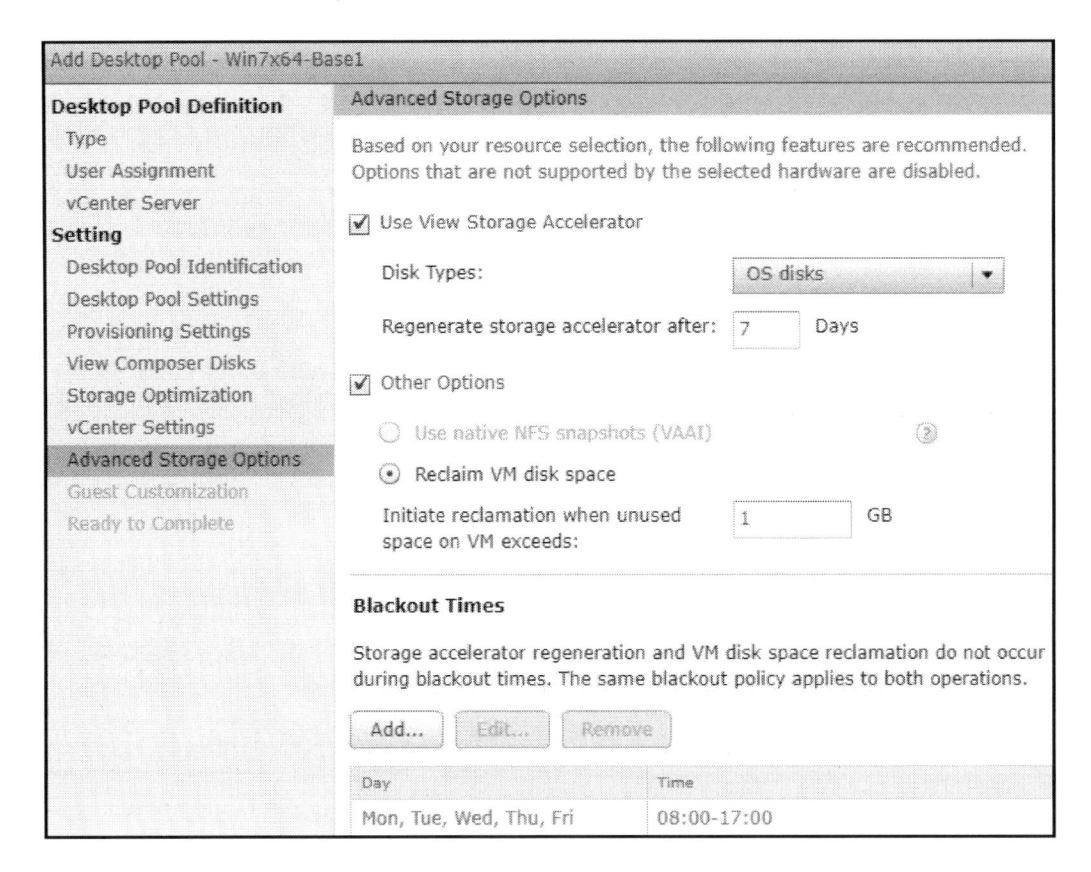

> The **Use native NFS snapshots (VAAI)** feature enables Horizon to leverage features of a supported NFS storage array to offload the creation of linked clone desktops. If you are using an external array with your Horizon ESXi servers, consult the product documentation to learn whether it supports this feature. If you were using VMware Virtual SAN, this and other options under **Other Options** are grayed out, as these settings are not needed. Additionally, if **View Storage Accelerator** is not enabled in the vCenter Server settings, the option to use it would be greyed-out here.

Chapter 7

21. In the **Setting** | **Guest Customization** window, select the **Domain:** where the desktops will be created, the **AD container:** (also known as **Organizational Unit**, or **OU**) where the computer accounts will be placed, whether to **Use QuickPrep** or **Use a customization specification (Sysprep)**, and any other options as required. When finished, click on **Next >**:

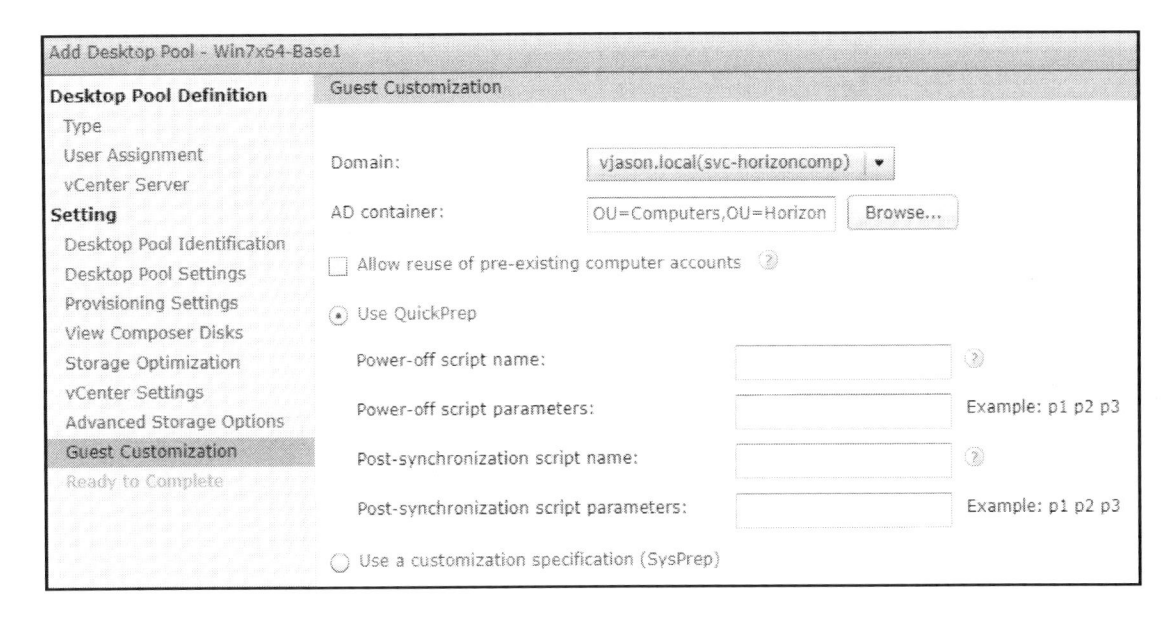

> You may want to create a unique OU for each of your Horizon pools. This allows you to develop and apply Windows group policies (be they for Windows, Windows applications, or Horizon itself) on a per-pool basis.

22. In the **Setting** | **Ready to Complete** window, verify that the settings we selected were correct, using the **< Back** button, if needed, to go back and make changes. If all the settings are correct, click on **Finish** to initiate the creation of the desktop pool.

The Horizon desktop pool and virtual desktops will now be created. To monitor the creation of the desktops, review the *Monitoring the desktop creation process* section of this chapter. Also located in this chapter is the *Managing Horizon Desktop Pool Entitlements* section, which outlines how to grant clients access to the desktop pools that we have created.

[195]

Creating a pool using Horizon Instant Clones

The process used to create an Instant Clone desktop pool is similar to that used to create a linked clone pool. As discussed previously, it is assumed that you already have a virtual desktop master image that has the Instant Clone option enabled in the Horizon agent, and that you have taken a snapshot of that master image.

> **TIP:** A master image can have either the Horizon Composer (linked clone) option or Instant Clone option enabled in the Horizon agent, but not both. To get around this restriction, you can configure one snapshot of the master image with the **View Composer** option installed, and a second with the **Instant Clone** option installed.

The following steps outline the process used to create the Instant Clone desktop pool. Screenshots are included only when the step differs significantly from the same step in the *Creating a pool using Horizon Composer linked clones* section:

1. Log on to the Horizon Administrator console using an AD account that has administrative permissions within Horizon.
2. Open the **Catalog | Desktop Pools** window within the console.
3. Click on the **Add...** button in the **Desktop Pools** window to open the **Add Desktop Pool** window.
4. In the **Desktop Pool Definition | Type** window, select the **Automated Desktop Pool** radio button, as shown in the following screenshot, and then click on **Next >**.
5. In the **Desktop Pool Definition | User Assignment** window, select the **Floating** radio button (mandatory for Instant Clone desktops) and then click on **Next >**.
6. In the **Desktop Pool Definition | vCenter Server** window, select the Instant clones radio button, as shown in the following screenshot, highlight the vCenter server, and then click on **Next >**:

Chapter 7

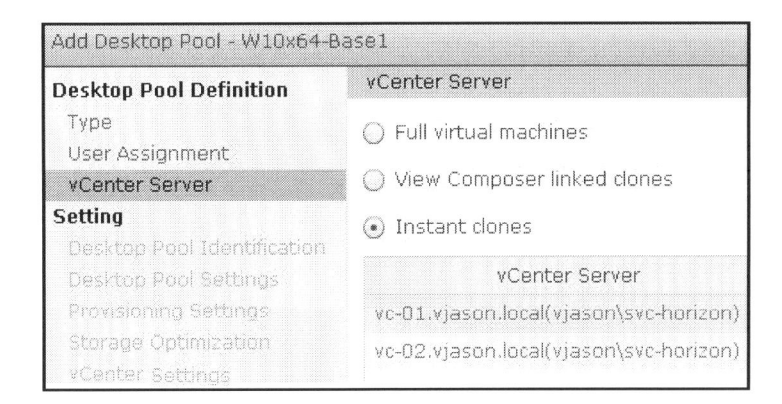

Add Desktop Pool - W10x64-Base1	
Desktop Pool Definition	vCenter Server
Type	○ Full virtual machines
User Assignment	
vCenter Server	○ View Composer linked clones
Setting	⊙ Instant clones
Desktop Pool Identification	
Desktop Pool Settings	vCenter Server
Provisioning Settings	vc-01.vjason.local(vjason\svc-horizon)
Storage Optimization	vc-02.vjason.local(vjason\svc-horizon)
vCenter Settings	

> **TIP**: If **Instant Clones** is grayed-out here, it is usually because you did not select **Floating** in the previous step.

7. In the **Setting | Desktop Pool Identification** window, populate the pool **ID:**, and then click on **Next >**. Optionally, configure the **Display Name:** field.
8. In the **Setting | Desktop Pool Settings** window, configure the various settings for the desktop pool. Many of these options are self-explanatory; those that are not are described in the *Desktop pool common terms* section of this chapter. These settings can also be adjusted later if desired. When finished, click on **Next >**.
9. In the **Setting | Provisioning Settings** window, configure the various provisioning options for the desktop pool, which include the desktop naming format, the number of desktops, and the number of desktops that should remain available during maintenance operations. When finished, click on **Next >**.

> **TIP**: Instant Clones are required to always be powered on, so some options available to linked clones will be greyed-out here.

10. In the **Setting | Storage Optimization** window, we configure whether or not our desktop storage is provided by VMware Virtual SAN, and, if not, whether to separate our Horizon desktop replica disks from the individual desktop OS disks. When finished, click on **Next >**.

Creating Horizon Desktop Pools

11. In the **Setting | vCenter Settings** window, we will need to configure six different options that include selecting the parent virtual machine, which snapshot of that virtual machine to use, what vCenter folder to place the desktops in, what vSphere cluster and resource pool to deploy the desktops to, and what datastores to use. Click on the **Browse...** button next to the **Parent VM:** field to begin the process and open the **Select Parent VM** window.
12. In the **Select Parent VM** window, highlight the virtual desktop master image that you wish to deploy desktops from. Click on **OK** when the image is selected to return to the previous window.
13. In the **Setting | vCenter Settings** window, click on the **Browse...** button next to the **Snapshot:** field to open the **Select default image** window. Select the desired snapshot, and click on **OK** to return to the previous window.
14. In the **Setting | vCenter Settings** window, click on the **Browse...** button next to the **VM folder location:** field to open the **VM Folder Location** window. Select the folder within vCenter where you want the desktop virtual machines to be placed, and click on **OK** to return to the previous window.
15. In the **Setting | vCenter Settings** window, click on the **Browse...** button next to the **Host or cluster:** field to open the **Host or Cluster** window. Select the cluster or individual ESXi server within vCenter where you want the desktop virtual machines to be created, and click on **OK** to return to the previous window.
16. In the **Setting | vCenter Settings** window, click on the **Browse...** button next to the **Resource pool:** field to open the **Resource Pool** window. If you intend to place the desktops within a resource pool you would select that here; if not, select the same cluster or ESXi server you chose in the previous step. Once finished, click on **OK** to return to the previous window.
17. In the **Setting | vCenter Settings** window, click on the **Browse...** button next to the **Datastores:** field to open the **Select Instant Clone Datastores** window. Select the datastore or datastores where you want the desktops to be created, and click on **OK** to return to the previous window.
18. The **Setting | vCenter Settings** window should now have all options selected, enabling the **Next >** button. When finished, click on **Next >**.
19. In the **Setting | Guest Customization** window, select the **Domain:** where the desktops will be created, the **AD container:** where the computer accounts will be placed, and any other options as required. When finished, click on **Next>**:

Chapter 7

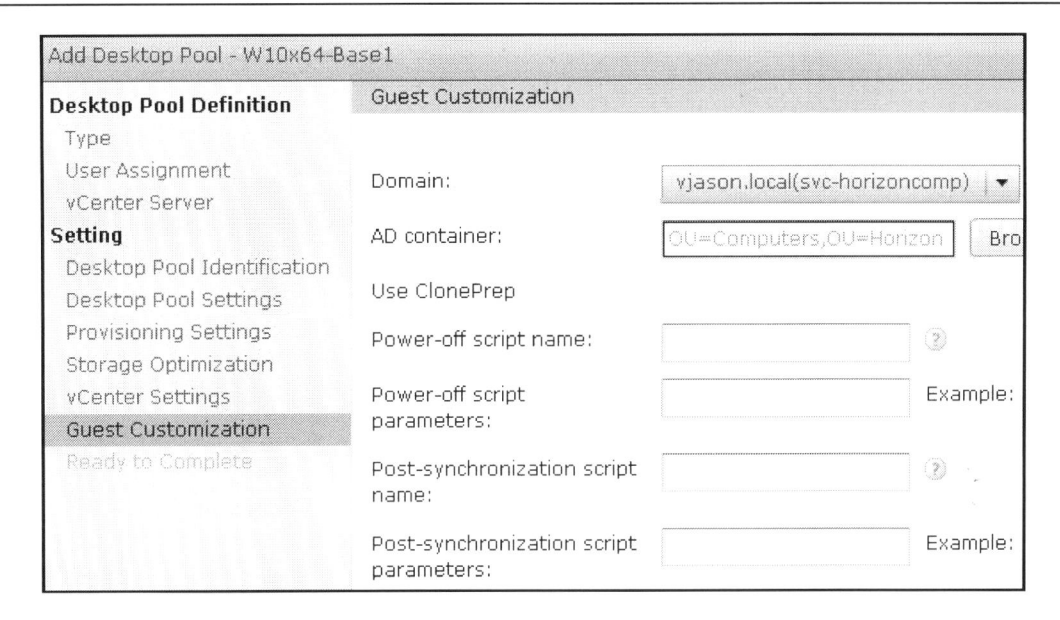

[Screenshot of "Add Desktop Pool - W10x64-Base1" dialog showing Guest Customization settings with Domain, AD container, Use ClonePrep, Power-off script name, Power-off script parameters, Post-synchronization script name, and Post-synchronization script parameters fields.]

> **TIP**: Instant Clones only support ClonePrep for customization, so there are fewer options here than seen when deploying a linked clone desktop pool.

20. In the **Setting** | **Ready to Complete** window, verify that the settings we selected were correct, using the **< Back** button if needed to go back and make changes. If all the settings are correct, click on **Finish** to initiate the creation of the desktop pool.

The Horizon desktop pool and Instant Clone virtual desktops will now be created. To monitor the creation of the desktops, review the *Monitoring the desktop creation process* section of this chapter. Also located in this chapter is the *Managing Horizon Desktop Pool Entitlements* section, which outlines how to grant users access to the desktop pools that we have created.

Creating a pool using full clones

The process used to create full clone desktop pools is similar to that used to create a linked clone pool. As discussed previously, it is assumed that you already have a virtual desktop master image that you have converted to a vSphere template.

Creating Horizon Desktop Pools

> **TIP**: The structure of a full clone Horizon desktop is no different than that of your typical virtual machine. Each one is created by doing a simple clone of a master image, and the resulting virtual machine is typically managed using the same techniques as physical desktops.

In addition, if you wish for Horizon to perform the virtual machine customization, you will need to create a Customization Specification using the vCenter Customization Specifications Manager. The Customization Specification is used by the Windows Sysprep utility to complete the guest customization process. Visit the VMware vSphere virtual machine administration guide (https://docs.vmware.com/en/VMware-vSphere/index.html) for instructions on how to create a Customization Specification.

The following steps outline the process used to create the full clone desktop pool. Screenshots are included only when the step differs significantly from the same step in the *Creating a pool using Horizon Composer linked clones* section:

1. Log on to the Horizon Administrator console using an AD account that has administrative permissions within Horizon.
2. Open the **Catalog | Desktop Pools** window within the console.
3. Click on the **Add...** button in the **Desktop Pools** window to open the **Add Desktop Pool** window.
4. In the **Desktop Pool Definition | Type** window, select the **Automated Pool** radio button and then click on **Next**.
5. In the **Desktop Pool Definition | User Assignment** window, select the **Dedicated** radio button, check the **Enable automatic assignment** checkbox, and then click on **Next**.
6. In the **Desktop Pool Definition | vCenter Server** window, click the **Full virtual machines** radio button, highlight the desired vCenter server, and then click on **Next**.
7. In the **Setting | Desktop Pool Identification** window, populate the pool **ID:** and **Display Name:** fields and then click on **Next**.
8. In the **Setting | Desktop Pool Settings** window, configure the various settings for the desktop pool. These settings can also be adjusted later if desired. When finished, click on **Next >**.
9. In the **Setting | Provisioning Settings** window, configure the various provisioning options for the desktop pool that include the desktop naming format and number of desktops. When finished, click on **Next >**.

10. In the **Setting | Storage Optimization** window, we configure whether our desktop storage is provided by VMware Virtual SAN. When finished, click on **Next >**.
11. In the **Setting | vCenter Settings** window, we will need to configure settings that set the virtual machine template, which vSphere folder to place the desktops in, which ESXi server or cluster to deploy the desktops to, and which datastores to use. Other than the **Template** setting described in the following step, each of these settings is identical to those seen when creating a Horizon Composer-linked clone pool. Click on the **Browse...** button next to each of the settings in turn and select the appropriate options.
    - To configure the **Template:** setting, select the vSphere template that you created from your virtual desktop master image as shown in the following screenshot, and then click **OK** to return to the previous window:

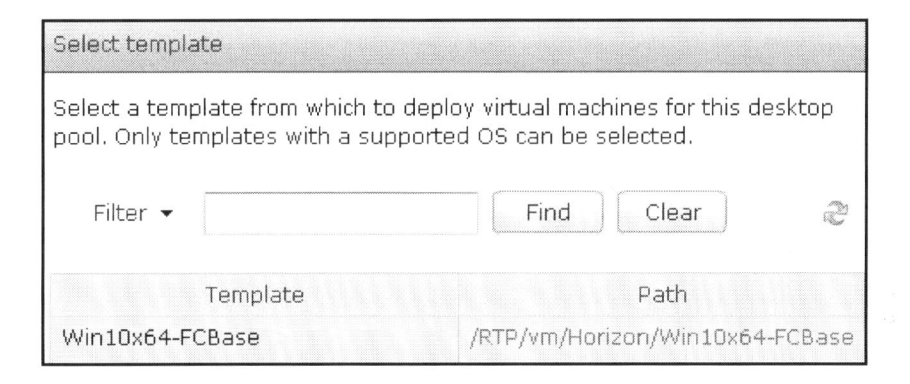

Template	Path
Win10x64-FCBase	/RTP/vm/Horizon/Win10x64-FCBase

Select template — Select a template from which to deploy virtual machines for this desktop pool. Only templates with a supported OS can be selected.

> **TIP:** A template will only appear if one is present within vCenter.

12. Once all the settings in the **Setting | vCenter Settings** window have been configured, click on **Next >**.
13. In the **Setting | Advanced Storage Options** window, if desired, select and configure the **Use View Storage Accelerator** radio buttons and configure **Blackout Times**. When finished, click on **Next >**.

Creating Horizon Desktop Pools

14. In the **Setting | Guest Customization** window, select either the **None - Customization will be done manually** or **Use this customization specification:** radio button, and if applicable select a customization specification. When finished, click on **Next >**. In the following screenshot, we have selected the **Win10x64-HorizonFC** customization specification that we previously created within vCenter:

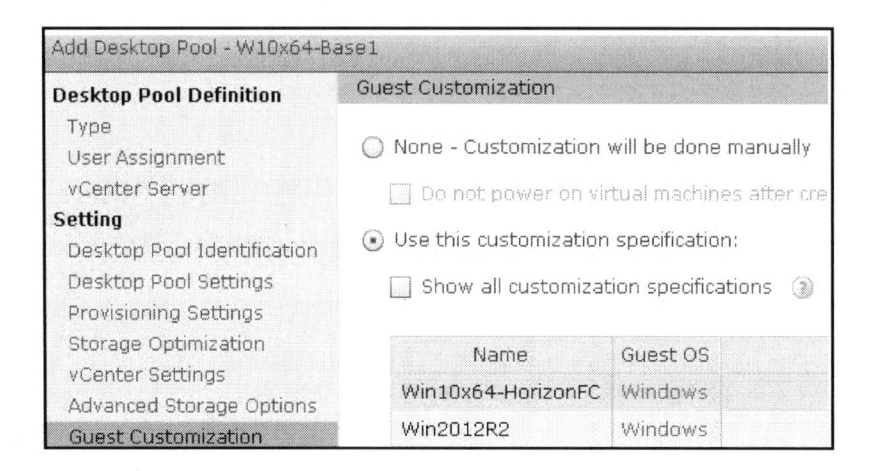

Add Desktop Pool - W10x64-Base1	
Desktop Pool Definition	**Guest Customization**
Type	
User Assignment	○ None - Customization will be done manually
vCenter Server	☐ Do not power on virtual machines after cre
Setting	
Desktop Pool Identification	● Use this customization specification:
Desktop Pool Settings	☐ Show all customization specifications
Provisioning Settings	
Storage Optimization	
vCenter Settings	
Advanced Storage Options	
Guest Customization	

Name	Guest OS
Win10x64-HorizonFC	Windows
Win2012R2	Windows

    > **TIP**: Manual customization is typically used when the template has been configured to run Sysprep automatically upon startup, without requiring any interaction from either Horizon or VMware vSphere.

15. In the **Setting | Ready to Complete** window, verify that the settings we selected were correct, using the **< Back** button if needed to go back and make changes. If all the settings are correct, click on **Finish** to initiate the creation of the desktop pool.

The desktop pool and virtual desktops will now be created. To monitor the creation of the desktops, review the *Monitoring the desktop creation process* section of this chapter. Also located in this chapter is the *Managing Horizon Desktop Pool Entitlements* section that outlines how to grant users access to the desktop pools that we have created.

Monitoring the desktop creation process

The amount of time it takes to create the desktop pool varies based on a number of factors. There are multiple locations within the Horizon Administrator console and the vSphere Client where you can monitor the progress of the desktop deployment.

Horizon Administrator console

Horizon desktops are displayed throughout the Horizon Administrator console as soon as they are initially created within vCenter. This section details two areas of the console where you can view the current status of the desktops:

- **Dashboard**: As desktops move through the deployment and configuration process, their status on the Desktop Status dashboard will change. The following screenshot shows how the Desktop Status dashboard window changes as desktops move from the Preparing stage (left) to the Prepared for use stage (right):

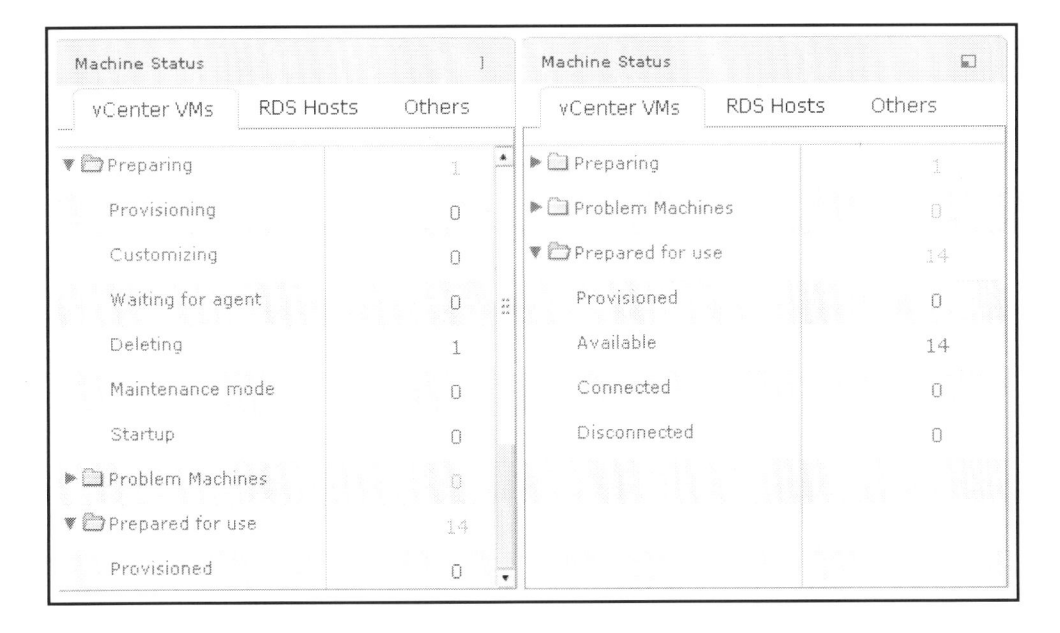

Machine Status			Machine Status		
vCenter VMs	RDS Hosts	Others	vCenter VMs	RDS Hosts	Others
▼ Preparing		1	▶ Preparing		1
Provisioning		0	▶ Problem Machines		0
Customizing		0	▼ Prepared for use		14
Waiting for agent		0	Provisioned		0
Deleting		1	Available		14
Maintenance mode		0	Connected		0
Startup		0	Disconnected		0
▶ Problem Machines		0			
▼ Prepared for use		14			
Provisioned		0			

Creating Horizon Desktop Pools

- **Desktops**: This option appears under **Inventory**. This window will display each of the Horizon desktops, along with their current status:

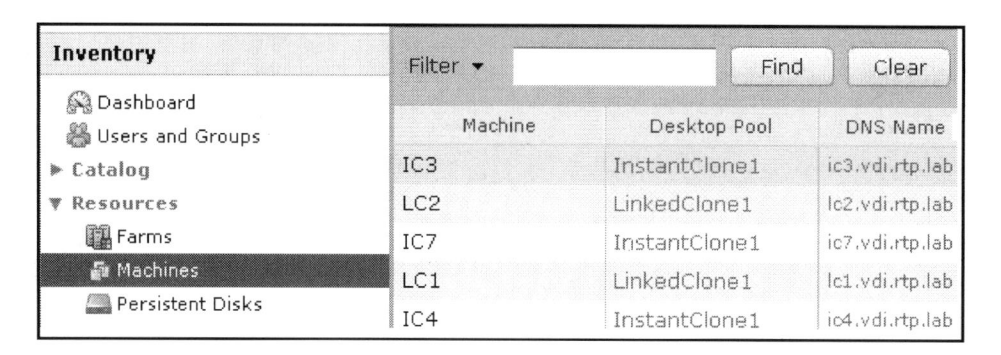

Inventory	Machine	Desktop Pool	DNS Name
Dashboard			
Users and Groups			
▶ Catalog	IC3	InstantClone1	ic3.vdi.rtp.lab
▼ Resources	LC2	LinkedClone1	lc2.vdi.rtp.lab
Farms	IC7	InstantClone1	ic7.vdi.rtp.lab
Machines	LC1	LinkedClone1	lc1.vdi.rtp.lab
Persistent Disks	IC4	InstantClone1	ic4.vdi.rtp.lab

The vSphere Web client task window

Creating virtual desktops will generate a number of vCenter tasks, during which the desktops will begin to appear within the vCenter Console. Monitor the following areas of the vSphere Web client to verify that the desktop pool is being created:

- **Task Console**: This window is shown in the following screenshot and will display the tasks associated with the creation and configuration of the virtual desktops:

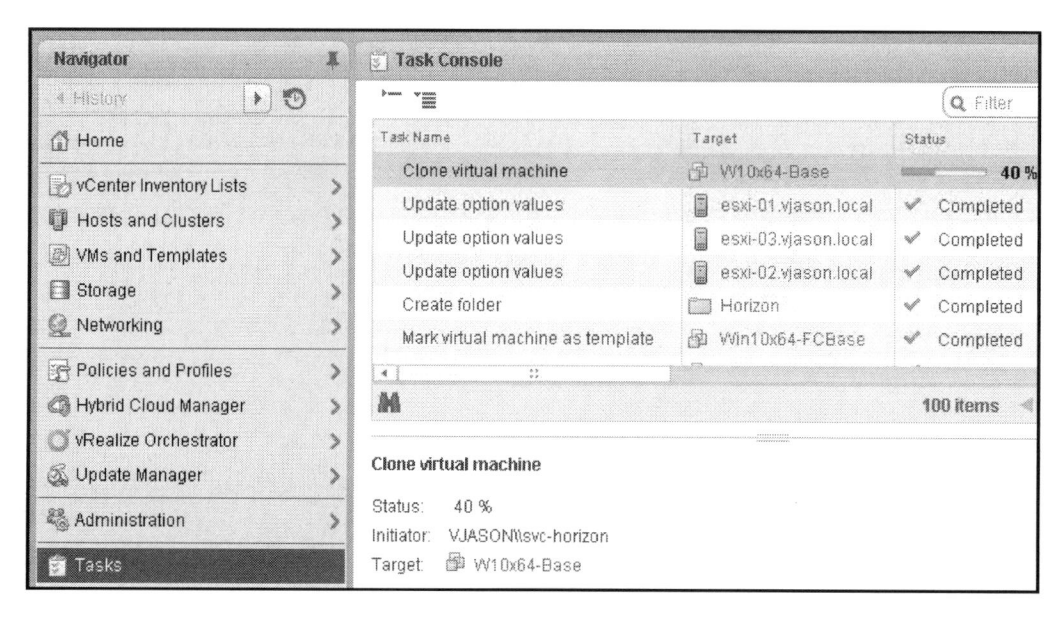

Task Name	Target	Status
Clone virtual machine	W10x64-Base	40 %
Update option values	esxi-01.vjason.local	✓ Completed
Update option values	esxi-03.vjason.local	✓ Completed
Update option values	esxi-02.vjason.local	✓ Completed
Create folder	Horizon	✓ Completed
Mark virtual machine as template	Win10x64-FCBase	✓ Completed

Clone virtual machine
Status: 40 %
Initiator: VJASON\svc-horizon
Target: W10x64-Base

- **VMs and Templates or Hosts and Clusters**: Horizon desktops will appear in these views of the vSphere client just as with any other virtual machine. The following screenshot shows Horizon desktops as seen in the VMs and Templates view, within the folder we specified during the creation of the desktop pool:

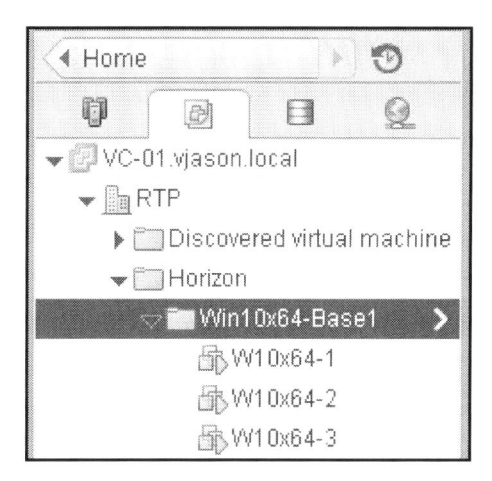

Common provisioning problems

There are a number of different issues that can arise during the deployment of desktop pools. While it is impossible to try and list them all, the following represent some of the more common issues that can occur:

- **Undersized or misconfigured DHCP address pool**: This is more common with linked clones, which change MAC addresses when redeployed; this can exhaust a DHCP pool. Linked clone environments typically work best when the DHCP lease time is very short. Desktops cannot complete the provisioning process without access to the network.
- **Issues with Windows operating system activation**: If Windows KMS services are not functioning within the domain, the provisioning process will fail.
- **Insufficient permissions within vCenter**: If the accounts used by Horizon and Horizon Composer do not have the required permissions within vCenter, the provisioning process will fail.
- **DNS not functioning properly**: DNS is integral to desktop provisioning. If the desktops cannot resolve the IP addresses or infrastructure services, including Active Directory and Horizon components, the provisioning process will fail.

The Horizon event log, located in the **Monitoring - Events** window of the Horizon Administrator console, contains detailed information that can be used to troubleshoot the provisioning process.

Managing Horizon Desktop pool entitlements

The following steps outline how to grant users or AD security groups access to a Horizon desktop pool, a necessary task, since no access is granted by default. This can be done while the pool is still being provisioned:

1. Log on to the Horizon Administrator console using an AD account that has administrative permissions within Horizon.
2. Open the **Catalog** | **Desktop Pools** window within the console.
3. Highlight the pool you wish to entitle, as shown in the following screenshot, and navigate to the **Entitlements...** | **Add entitlement...** to open the **Add Entitlements** window:

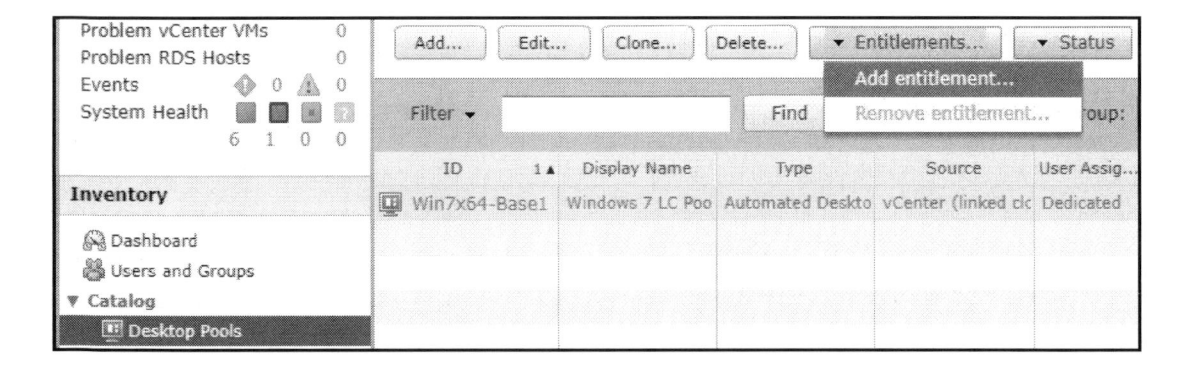

4. In the **Add Entitlements** window, shown in the following screenshot, click on the **Add...** button to open the **Find User or Group** window:

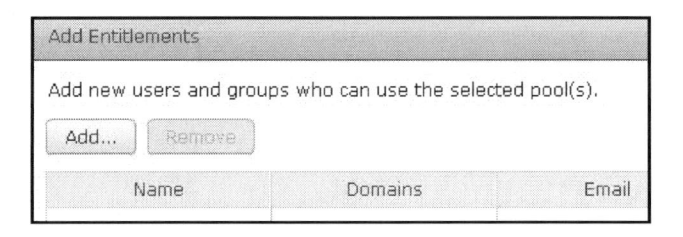

5. In the **Find User or Group** window, shown in the following screenshot, use the **Name/User name:** or **Description:** fields to search for the user or group to which you wish to grant access. In the following example, we used the **Find** button to search for a security group that was created specifically for a Horizon named **Horizon_DTPool_Win7NP**. Highlight the desired user or group, and click on **OK** to return to the **Add Entitlements** window:

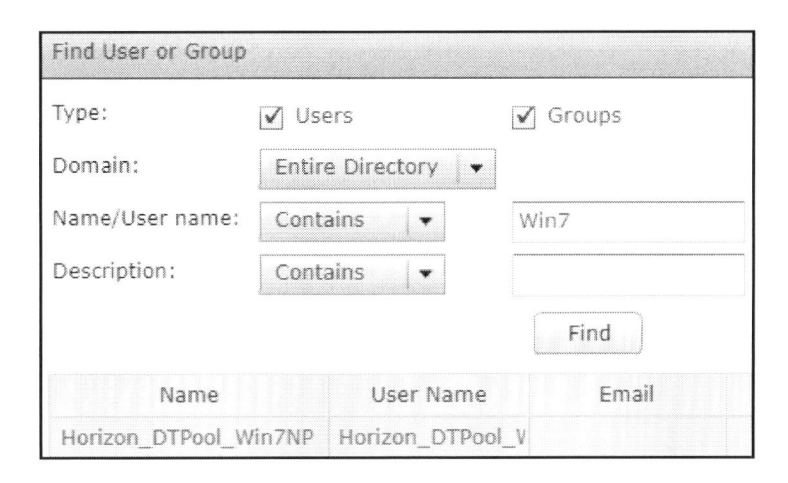

Find User or Group			
Type:	✓ Users	✓ Groups	
Domain:	Entire Directory ▼		
Name/User name:	Contains ▼	Win7	
Description:	Contains ▼		
			Find
Name	User Name	Email	
Horizon_DTPool_Win7NP	Horizon_DTPool_V		

6. Repeat steps 4 and 5 as needed to entitle additional users or groups.
7. If all the required users and groups have been added, click on the **OK** button in the **Add Entitlements** window to complete the action.

The selected users and groups now have access to the available desktops within the desktop pool. Now that we have entitled a user or group to do the desktop pool, the **Remove Entitlement...** option shown in step 3 will no longer be greyed-out, and we can use it to remove entitlements if needed.

Removing an entitlement to a dedicated assignment-linked clone or full clone desktop pool does not remove any assignments to the desktops themselves, which occur when a user logs in for the first time or when set manually by a Horizon administrator. To fully remove the entitlement, you must also highlight the desktop in the Horizon Administrator console **Resources - Machines** window, open the **More Commands** drop-down menu, as shown in the following screenshot, click **Unassign User...** to open the **Unassign User** window, and then click **OK**. The desktop will not be available for new logins until this is performed:

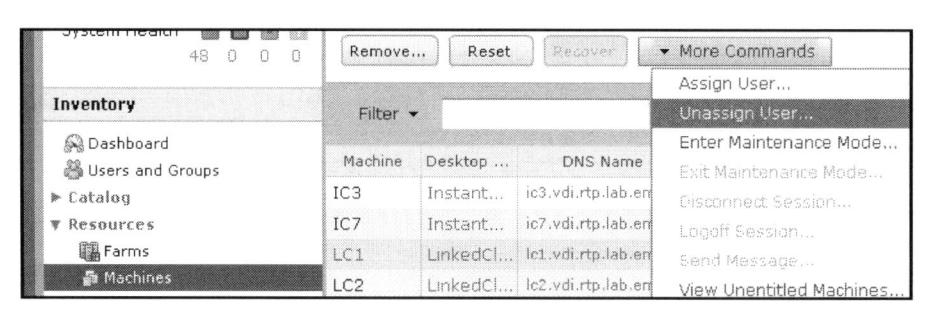

Alternatively, you may use the **Remove...** button to delete the desktop and force the creation of a new, unassigned desktop. Both methods require the entitlement to be removed as well; if this is not done, the user will be able to log in again and be assigned a new desktop.

Summary

In this chapter, we have learned about Horizon desktop pools. In addition to learning how to create three different types of desktop pools, we were introduced to a number of key concepts that are part of the pool creation process.

We discussed the differences between Instant Clone, linked clone, and full clone virtual desktops; how Sysprep differs from QuickPrep; how to monitor the provisioning of a Horizon desktop pool; the types of issues that can prevent a pool from provisioning successfully, and how to grant users or security groups access to desktop pools using desktop pool entitlements.

In `Chapter 8`, *Implementing Microsoft Remote Desktop Services Application and Desktop Pools*, we will examine how to create pools that can be used to stream applications using Microsoft Windows RDS servers.

Questions

1. What are the three different types of Horizon Desktop Pools?
2. What are the two different options for Desktop Pool user assignment?
3. What are the three types of virtual machines that Horizon can provision using vSphere?
4. What is the difference between a persistent and non-persistent desktop?
5. What is the function of a virtual desktop persistent disk?
6. You want your desktops to be named Windows1, Windows2, and so on; what would you enter in the Desktop Pool Naming Pattern field?
7. What does View Storage Accelerator do?
8. You create a new Desktop Pool, but when users log in to the Horizon Client, no pools are available for login. What is the first thing you should check?
9. You are attempting to create a new linked clone desktop pool, but when you go to select the Parent VM, no virtual machines are displayed. What is the first thing to check?

Further reading

The following resources may be used to learn more about the topics described in this chapter:

- VMware documentation:
    - VMware Horizon (https://docs.vmware.com/en/VMware-Horizon-7/index.html)
    - VMware vSphere (https://www.vmware.com/support/pubs/vsphere-esxi-vcenter-server-pubs.html)

8
Implementing the Microsoft Remote Desktop Services Application and Desktop Pools

VMware Horizon includes the ability to stream individual Windows applications or desktop sessions to clients using Microsoft Windows **Remote Desktop Services** (RDS), a feature formally known as Terminal Services. Application streaming is particularly useful to those clients that require access only to applications, as the application appears to them as it would if it were installed on their device, even if they are using a tablet-based Horizon client. For those clients, this is typically a much more efficient means of accessing their applications than navigating a traditional desktop GUI on a tablet device. While application streaming is not in itself a new feature, this feature enables individual applications to be accessed directly from the Horizon client.

> **TIP**
> In this book, the terms RDS and **Remote Desktop Session Hosts** (RD Session Hosts) are used interchangeably; they both refer to the same Windows server feature.

By installing the Horizon Agent directly onto a supported Windows server with the RDS feature installed, we can entitle applications and desktop sessions to users, just as we would entitle individual desktops. When streaming applications, an additional benefit is that on a per-client basis, for users that use a very small number of applications, or for a small number of applications concurrently, fewer resources will be required to deploy streamed applications compared to deploying individual desktops for each client.

In this chapter, we will review all the steps required to implement, configure, and administer the RDS application and desktop streaming using VMware Horizon. We will cover the following topics:

- Configuring a Microsoft RDSH server for use with Horizon
- Creating a linked clone-based RDS farm in Horizon
- Creating an RDS application pool in Horizon
- Creating an RDS desktop pool in Horizon
- Using the Horizon client to access RDS streamed applications
- Monitoring the status of RDS servers and Horizon client sessions
- Modifying an RDS application pool in Horizon
- Modifying an RDS farm or server in Horizon

Configuring a Microsoft RDSH server for use with Horizon

This section will outline the minimum steps required to configure Microsoft RDS to use with Horizon. For a more in-depth discussion on Microsoft RDS optimization and management, consult the Microsoft documentation page for Windows Server 2012 R2 (https://docs.microsoft.com/en-us/previous-versions/windows/it-pro/windows-server-2012-R2-and-2012/hh801901(v=ws.11))) or Windows Server 2016 (https://docs.microsoft.com/en-us/windows-server/index).

VMware Horizon supports the following versions of Window server for use with RDS:

- **Windows Server 2008 R2**: Datacentre, with SP1 or later installed
- **Windows Server 2012**: Datacentre
- **Windows Server 2012 R2**: Standard or Datacentre
- **Windows Server 2016**: Standard or Datacentre

The examples shown in this chapter were performed on Windows Server 2012 R2.

> If you intend to use Microsoft Office on RDS, note that it has specific licensing requirements for that use case. Consult Microsoft's **Licensing of Microsoft Desktop Application Software for Use with Windows Server Remote Desktop Services** document (https://download.microsoft.com/download/3/D/4/3D42BDC2-6725-4B29-B75A-A5B04179958B/Licensing-Windows-Server-2012-R2-RDS-and-Desktop-Apps-for-RDS.pdf) for additional information.

Microsoft RDS licensing

The Microsoft RDS feature requires a licensing server component called the **Remote Desktop Licensing role service**. For reasons of availability, it is not recommended that you install it on the RDS host itself, but rather on an existing server that performs some other function, or even on a dedicated server if possible. Ideally, the RDS licensing role should be installed on multiple servers for redundancy reasons.

The Remote Desktop Licensing role service is different from the Microsoft Windows **Key Management System** (**KMS**), as it is used solely for Microsoft RDS servers. Consult the Microsoft Windows IT Pro Center article, "Activate the Remote Desktop Services license server" (https://docs.microsoft.com/en-us/windows-server/remote/remote-desktop-services/rds-activate-license-server), for the steps required to install the Remote Desktop Licensing role service.

Microsoft RDSH Server recommended hardware configuration

The following resources represent a starting point for assigning CPU and RAM resources to Microsoft RDS servers. The actual resources that are required will vary based on the applications being used, and the number of concurrent users, so it is important to monitor server utilization and adjust the CPU and RAM specifications if required. The following are the recommended requirements:

- Four vCPUs to support a maximum of 50 RDS sessions (per server).

   > **TIP**: While it is possible to assign more vCPUs to support more sessions, this configuration offers a fairly predictable performance, regardless of the ESXi host server CPU configuration. If you decide to configure your RDS servers with more than four vCPUs, monitor the ESXi host **CPU Ready** statistics, which will reveal whether there are any delays in scheduling VM vCPU requests to the ESXi server CPU. A CPU Ready value of greater than 5% will usually impact performance of the VM, and the only way to alleviate this issue is to add more physical CPUs to the ESXi host, or remove vCPUs from the VM experiencing the issue.

- 24 GB RAM
- A minimum of 40 GB hard disk space for the RDS server itself, plus sufficient hard drive space to store RDS user profiles (if storing locally). Consider one of the following options to help better manage user profiles:

    - **VMware User Environment Manager (UEM)** may be used to manage profiles for users of Horizon application pools; refer to Chapter 12, *Implementing VMware User Environment Manager*, and the UEM documentation (https://docs.vmware.com/en/VMware-User-Environment-Manager/index.html) for further details.
    - **Horizon Persona Management**, which is not discussed in this book, is not supported for use with Microsoft RDS servers. Even if it were, owing to its more advanced capabilities, UEM is a better choice for user-profile management.

- Microsoft RDS includes multiple native options to control user-profile configuration and growth, including a RD user home directory, RD roaming user profiles, and mandatory profiles. For information about these and other options, consult the Windows IT Pro Center article, **Folder Redirection, Offline Files, and Roaming User Profiles overview** (`https://docs.microsoft.com/en-us/windows-server/storage/folder-redirection/folder-redirection-rup-overview`).

While the vCPU and RAM requirements might seem excessive at first, remember that to deploy a virtual desktop for each of these 50 users, we would need a bare minimum of 50 vCPUs, 100 GB of RAM, and 2 TB of hard disk space, which is much more than our single Microsoft RDS host requires.

By default, Horizon allows unlimited RDS user sessions for each Microsoft RDS host in the farm. Based on the RDS server specification provided, we will need to deploy multiple RDS servers if we anticipate having more than 50 connections, plus additional hosts for redundancy purposes. It is recommended that you set the default sizing to 50 as that is what recommended RDS server configuration has been optimized for.

Importing the Horizon RDS AD group policy templates

Some of the settings that are configured throughout this chapter are applied using AD group policy templates. Prior to using the RDS feature, these templates should be distributed to either the RDS servers, in order to be used with the Windows local group policy editor, or to an AD domain controller, where they can be applied using the domain. Complete the following steps to install the RDS group policy templates:

> When referring to VMware Horizon installation packages, `y.y.y` refers to the version number and `xxxxxx` refers to the build number. When you download packages, the actual version and build numbers will be in numeric format. For example, the filename of the current Horizon 7 GPO bundle is `VMware-Horizon-Extras-Bundle-4.0.0-3616726.zip`.

Obtain the `VMware-Horizon-Extras-Bundle-x.x.x-yyyyyyy.zip` file, unzip it, and copy the `en-US` folder, the `vmware_rdsh.admx` file, and the `vmware_rdsh_server.admx` file to the `C:\Windows\PolicyDefinitions` folder on either an AD domain controller or your target RDS host, based on how you wish to manage the policies. Make note of the following points when doing so:

- If you want to set the policies locally on each RDS host, you will need to copy the files to your RDS server master image.
- If you want to set the policies using domain-based AD group policies, you'll need to copy the files to the domain controllers, the group policy Central Store (described in the "How to create and manage the Central Store for Group Policy Administrative Templates in Windows" Microsoft support article: `https://support.microsoft.com/en-us/help/3087759/how-to-create-and-manage-the-central-store-for-group-policy-administra`), or to the workstation from which you manage these domain-based group policies.

The following steps outline the procedure to enable RDS on a Windows Server 2012 R2 host. Note that the host that's used in this section has already been connected to the domain, and has been logged in using an AD account that has administrative permissions on the server:

1. Open the **Windows Server Manager** utility and go to **Manage** | **Add Roles and Features** to open the **Add Roles and Features Wizard**.
2. On the **Before you Begin** page, click on **Next**.
3. On the **Installation Type** page, select **Remote Desktop Services** installation and click on **Next**, as shown in the following screenshot:

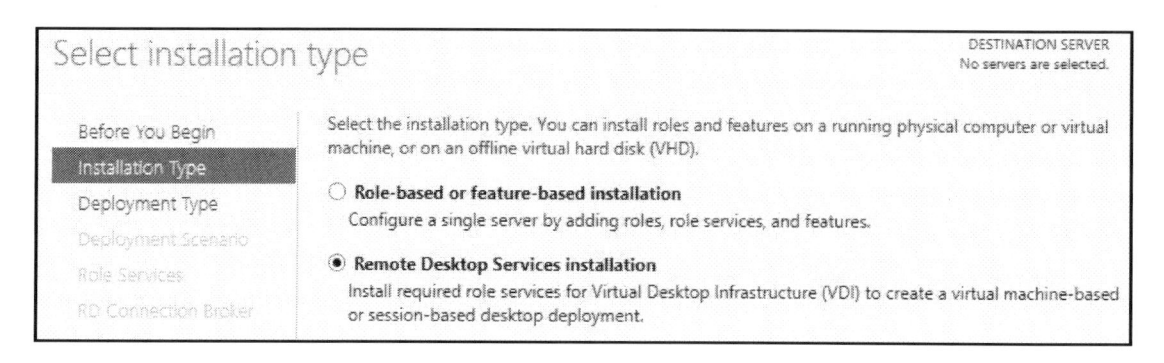

Chapter 8

4. On the **Deployment Type** page, select **Quick Start** and click on **Next**.

   > **TIP**: You can also implement the required roles using the standard deployment method outlined in the "Deploy the session virtualization" standard deployment section of the Microsoft TechNet article, "Remote Desktop Servers in Windows Server 2012 Test Lab" (`https://social.technet.microsoft.com/wiki/contents/articles/12934.remote-desktop-services-in-windows-server-2012-test-lab.aspx`). If you use this method, you will have completed the component installation and should proceed to step 9 in this section.

5. On the **Deployment Scenario** page, select **Session-based desktop deployment** and click on **Next**.

6. On the **Server Selection** page, select a server from the list under **Server Pool**, click the red, highlighted button to add the server to the list of selected servers, and then click on **Next**, as shown in the following screenshot:

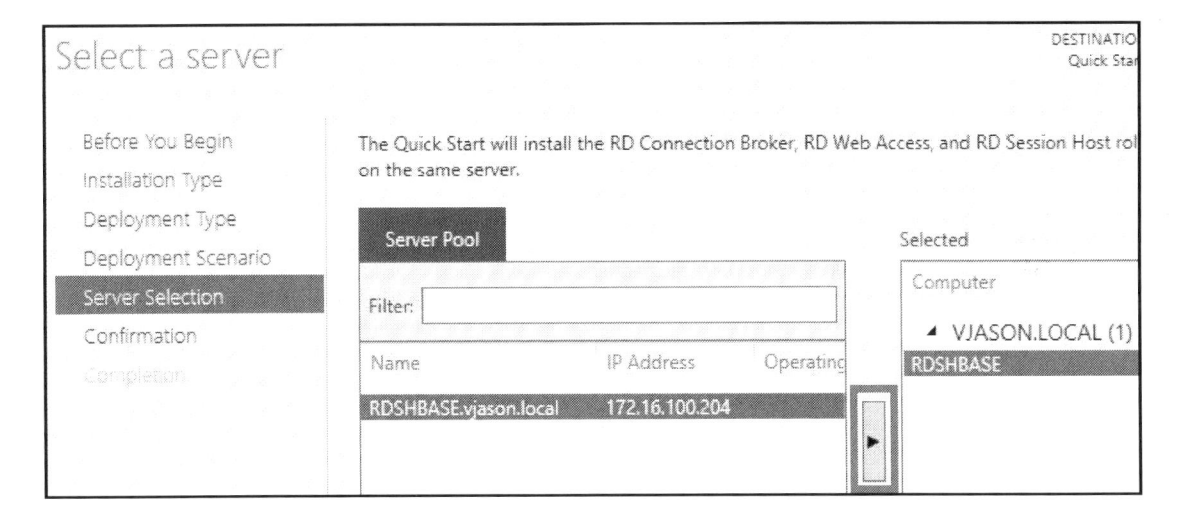

```
Select a server                                              DESTINATIO
                                                             Quick Star

Before You Begin        The Quick Start will install the RD Connection Broker, RD Web Access, and RD Session Host rol
Installation Type       on the same server.
Deployment Type
Deployment Scenario     Server Pool                          Selected
Server Selection                                             Computer
Confirmation            Filter:                              ▲ VJASON.LOCAL (1)
Completion              Name            IP Address  Operating   RDSHBASE
                        RDSHBASE.vjason.local  172.16.100.204
```

7. On the **Confirmation** page, check the box marked **Restart the destination server automatically if required** and click on **Deploy**.

8. On the **Completion** page, monitor the installation process and click on **Close** when finished to complete the installation. If a reboot is required, the server will reboot without the need to click on **Close**. Once the reboot completes, proceed with the remaining steps.

[217]

9. Set the RDS licensing server by using the `Set-RDLicenseConfiguration` Windows PowerShell command. In this example, we are configuring the local RDS host to point to redundant license servers (`RDS-LIC1` and `RDS-LIC2`) and are setting the license mode to `PerUser`. This command must be executed on the target RDS host. After entering the command, confirm the values for the license mode and license server name by answering `Y` when prompted. Refer to the following code:

```
Set-RDLicenseConfiguration -LicenseServer @("RDS-
LIC1.vjason.local","RDS-LIC2.vjason.local") -Mode PerUser
```

This setting may also be set using group policies that are applied either to the local computer or using **Active Directory** (**AD**). The policies are shown in the following screenshot, and you can locate them by going to **Computer Configuration** | **Policies** | **Administrative Templates** | **Windows Components** | **Remote Desktop Services** | **Remote Desktop Session Host** | **Licensing** when using AD-based policies. If you are using local group policies, there will be no `Policies` folder in the path:

Setting	State
Use the specified Remote Desktop license servers	Not configured
Hide notifications about RD Licensing problems that affect t...	Not configured
Set the Remote Desktop licensing mode	Not configured

10. Use local computer or AD group policies to limit users to one session per RDS host using the **Restrict Remote Desktop Services users to a single Remote Desktop Services session** policy. This policy is located at **Computer Configuration** | **Policies** | **Administrative Templates** | **Windows Components** | **Remote Desktop Services** | **Remote Desktop Session Host** | **Connections**, and should be set to **Enabled**.

11. Use local computer or AD group policies to enable **Time zone redirection**. This policy is located at **Computer Configuration** | **Policies** | **Administrative Templates** | **Windows Components** | **Horizon View RDS Services** | **Remote Desktop Session Host** | **Device and Resource Redirection** when using AD-based policies. If you are using local group policies, there will be no **Policies** folder in the path. To enable this setting, set **Allow time zone redirection** to **Enabled**.

12. Use local computer or AD group policies to enable **Windows Basic Aero-Styled Theme** to minimize the RDS server resources required to deliver each client session. This policy is located at **User Configuration | Policies | Administrative Templates | Control Panel | Personalization** when using AD-based policies. If you are using local group policies, there will be no `Policies` folder in the path. To configure the theme, set **Force a specific visual style file or force Windows Classic** to **Enabled** and set **Path to Visual Style** to `%windir%\resources\Themes\Aero\aero.msstyles`.

13. Use local computer or AD group policies to start `Runonce.exe` when the RDS session starts. This policy is located at **User Configuration | Policies | Windows Settings | Scripts (Logon/Logoff)** when using AD-based policies. If you are using local group policies, there will be no `Policies` folder in the path. To configure the logon settings, double-click on **Logon**, then click on **Add**, enter `runonce.exe` in the **Script Name** box, and then enter `/AlternateShellStartup` in the **Script Parameters** box.

The recommended AD group policies for the Microsoft RDS server have now been configured, and the server is ready for the Horizon agent software to be installed.

Installing the Horizon Agent on the Microsoft RDS host

The following steps outline how to install the Horizon Agent software on a Microsoft RDS host. These steps assume we will be deploying linked clone RDS servers, as described previously in this chapter. These steps should be performed on the RDS server master image, and the master image should be joined to the domain and have the RDS feature installed prior to beginning the agent-installation process:

1. On the Microsoft RDS host, double-click on the 64-bit Horizon Agent installer to begin the installation process. The installer should have a name similar to `VMware-viewagent-x86_64-y.y.y-xxxxxx.exe`. On the **Welcome to the Installation Wizard for VMware Horizon Agent** page, click on **Next**.
2. On the **License Agreement** page, select the **I accept the terms in the license agreement** radio check box and click on **Next**.
3. On the **Network protocol configuration** page, select your preferred protocol and click on **Next**.
4. On the **Custom Setup** page, enable the **VMware Horizon View Composer Agent** option to enable the deployment of linked clone RDS servers, make changes as needed to the other agent options, and click on **Next**.

5. On the **Ready to Install the Program** page, click on **Install** to begin the installation.
6. When the installation completes, reboot the server if prompted.

The RDS server is now able to be used to deploy linked clone-based Horizon application pools. Any applications that are needed may now be installed, and then the VM should be shut down and a snapshot taken.

vSphere customization specification for the Microsoft RDS servers

To deploy linked, clone-based Microsoft RDS servers using Horizon, you will first need to create a **customization specification** in vCenter. Customization specifications are used to customize the Windows OS during the deployment process, and include information such as the product key, local administrator passwords, and other basic information.

The VMware vSphere documentation section titled "Creating and Managing Customization Specifications" (https://docs.vmware.com/en/VMware-vSphere/6.7/vsphere-esxi-vcenter-server-671-virtual-machine-admin-guide.pdf) provides details on how to create and manage customization specifications in vCenter. The only customization specification setting explicitly required by Horizon in order to deploy RDS servers is the **Computer Name** setting; it should be set to **Use the virtual machine name**.

Additional resources related to using Microsoft RDS servers

The following resources provide additional information about the configuration of the RDS server master image:

- The Microsoft Windows IT Pro Center article titled "Set-RDLicenseConfiguration" (https://docs.microsoft.com/en-us/powershell/module/remotedesktop/set-rdlicenseconfiguration?view=win10-ps) provides the complete syntax of the PowerShell command that's used to configure the RDS licensing settings.

- The Microsoft Windows IT Pro Center article titled "Remote Desktop Services Client Access Licenses (RDS CALs)" (https://docs.microsoft.com/en-us/windows-server/remote/remote-desktop-services/rds-client-access-license) explains the different RDS license types and reveals that an RDS per-user **Client Access License** (CAL) allows our Horizon clients to access the RDS servers from an unlimited number of endpoints while still consuming only one RDS license.
- The Microsoft TechNet article titled "RD Licensing Configuration on Windows Server 2012" (https://blogs.technet.microsoft.com/askperf/2013/09/20/rd-licensing-configuration-on-windows-server-2012/) provides additional information on the group policies that are used to configure the RDS licensing options.
- The VMware Horizon documentation section titled "Enable Windows Basic Theme for Applications" (https://docs.vmware.com/en/VMware-Horizon-7/7.6/horizon-published-desktops-applications.pdf) explains that the Windows Basic aero-styled theme is the only theme supported by Horizon, and demonstrates how to implement it.
- The VMware Horizon documentation section titled "Enable Time Zone Redirection for RDS Desktop and Application Sessions" (https://docs.vmware.com/en/VMware-Horizon-7/7.6/horizon-published-desktops-applications.pdf) explains why timezone redirection is required, as it ensures that the Horizon client session will use the same timezone as the client device.
- The VMware Horizon documentation section titled "Configure Group Policy to Start Runonce.exe" (https://docs.vmware.com/en/VMware-Horizon-7/7.6/horizon-published-desktops-applications.pdf) explains why we need to add the `runonce.exe /AlternateShellStartup` command to the RDS logon script. This ensures that applications that require Windows Explorer will work properly when streamed using Horizon.

Creating a Microsoft RDS farm in Horizon

This section will discuss the steps that are required to create a linked, clone-based RDS farm in Horizon.

> **TIP**
> There are many additional options for creating RDS farms in Horizon, including the ability to deploy RDS servers as instant clones. Refer to the Horizon documentation (https://docs.vmware.com/en/VMware-Horizon-7/index.html) for a detailed listing of all available RDS farm deployment options.

Implementing the Microsoft Remote Desktop Services Application and Desktop Pools

An RDS farm is a collection of Microsoft RDS servers, and serves as the point of integration between the Connection Server and the individual applications that are installed on each RDS server. Additionally, key settings concerning client session handling and client-connection protocols are set at the RDS farm level within Horizon.

> **TIP**
> Many of the options that we will look at in this section are similar to those that are seen when we deployed linked clone desktops in Chapter 7, *Creating Horizon Desktop Pools*. Owing to this, not every setting will be explained like it was in that chapter. Refer to Chapter 7, *Creating Horizon Desktop Pools*, as well as the VMware Horizon documentation (https://docs.vmware.com/en/VMware-Horizon-7/index.html) for a more detailed explanation of the different options we will see in this section.

To create an RDS farm in Horizon, we need to have at least one RDS host master image configured using the steps that were described previously in this chapter. This includes taking a VM snapshot of that image once the configuration is complete; if this is not done, you will not be able to select the master image when creating the RDS farm. The following steps outline the procedure that's used to create a Microsoft RDS farm:

1. Log into the Horizon Administrator console using an account that has administrative privileges.
2. Navigate to **Resources** | **Farms** and click on **Add...**, as shown in the following screenshot:

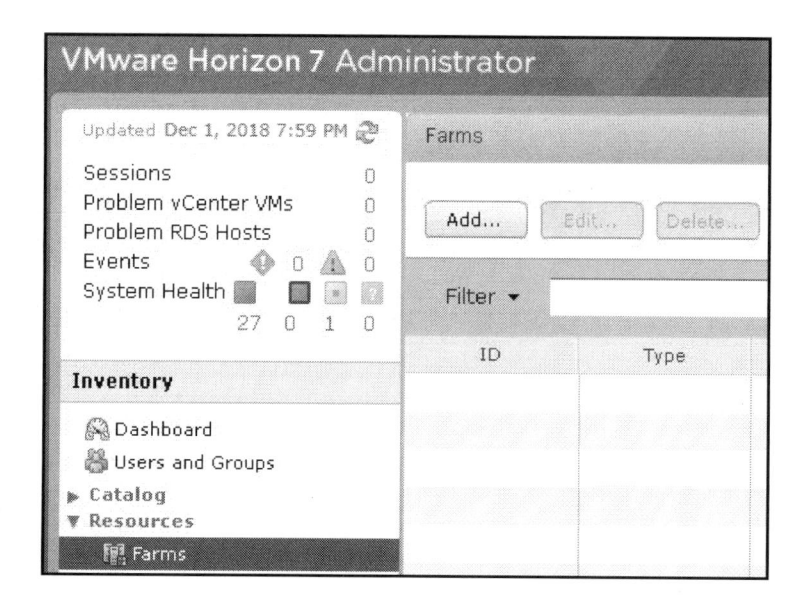

Chapter 8

3. On the **Add Farm | Type** page, click the **Automated Farm** radio button and then click **Next**.
4. On the **Add Farm | vCenter Server** page, click on the vCenter Server where the RDS master image resides and the RDS servers will be deployed, and then click **Next**.
5. On the **Add Farm | Identification and Settings** page, provide a farm **ID**, enter a **Description** if desired, make any desired changes to the default settings, and then click on **Next:**

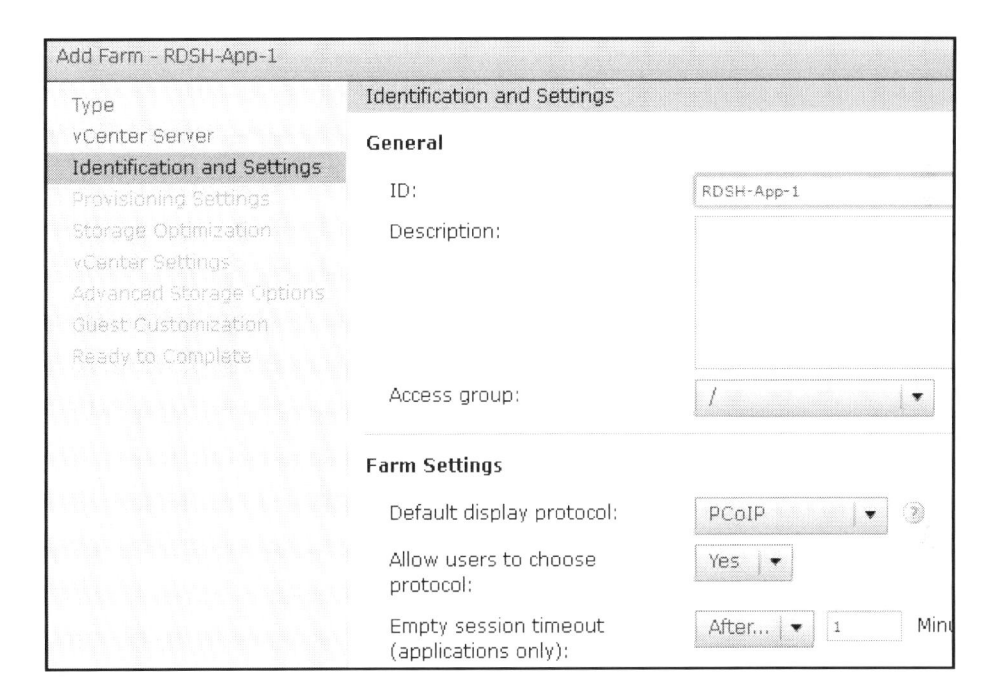

Add Farm - RDSH-App-1		
Type	**Identification and Settings**	
vCenter Server	**General**	
Identification and Settings	ID:	RDSH-App-1
Provisioning Settings	Description:	
Storage Optimization		
vCenter Settings		
Advanced Storage Options		
Guest Customization		
Ready to Complete		
	Access group:	/
	Farm Settings	
	Default display protocol:	PCoIP
	Allow users to choose protocol:	Yes
	Empty session timeout (applications only):	After... 1 Min

> **TIP**: These settings may also be edited after the application pool is created, as with desktop pools. Refer to the *Modifying Microsoft RDS farms* section later in this chapter for further details on how to modify existing RDS farms.

6. On the **Add Farm | Provisioning Settings** page, provide a desktop **Naming Pattern** and the **Max number of machines** (RDS servers) to deploy and click on **Next**:

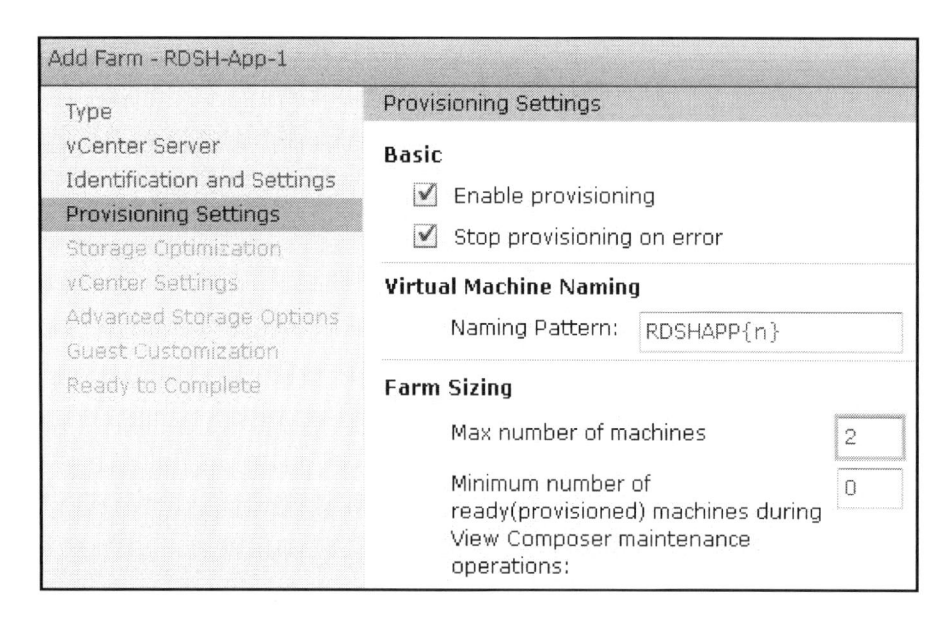

```
Add Farm - RDSH-App-1

Type                              Provisioning Settings
vCenter Server
Identification and Settings       Basic
Provisioning Settings                ☑ Enable provisioning
Storage Optimization                 ☑ Stop provisioning on error
vCenter Settings
Advanced Storage Options          Virtual Machine Naming
Guest Customization                  Naming Pattern:  RDSHAPP{n}
Ready to Complete
                                  Farm Sizing
                                     Max number of machines        2

                                     Minimum number of             0
                                     ready(provisioned) machines during
                                     View Composer maintenance
                                     operations:
```

You should deploy sufficient RDS servers so that you are able to accommodate RDS server-maintenance tasks or even unplanned outages.

> **TIP**: To add more RDS servers to the farm at a later date, you can edit the pool and update the value for **Max number of machines**. As is the case with desktop pools, as soon as you update that value, Horizon will provision the additional number of VMs required.

7. On the **Add Farm | Storage Optimization** page, edit the settings as required, selecting the **Use VMware Virtual SAN** radio button if applicable, and click on **Next**.

Chapter 8

8. On the **Add Farm | vCenter Settings** page, select the RDS server **Parent VM**, **Snapshot**, **VM folder location**, vSphere **Host or cluster**, **Resource pool**, and **Datastores**, as shown in the following screenshot. Then, click on **Next**:

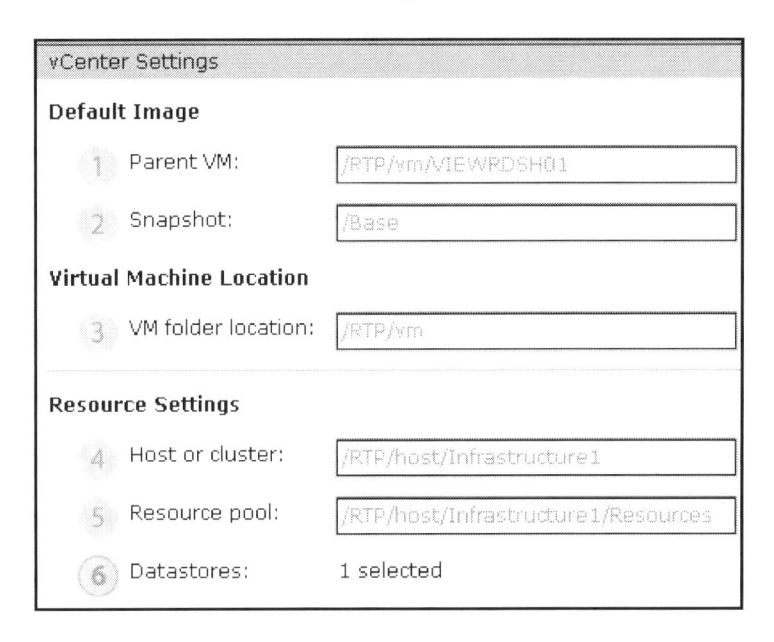

vCenter Settings	
Default Image	
1 Parent VM:	/RTP/vm/VIEWRDSH01
2 Snapshot:	/Base
Virtual Machine Location	
3 VM folder location:	/RTP/vm
Resource Settings	
4 Host or cluster:	/RTP/host/Infrastructure1
5 Resource pool:	/RTP/host/Infrastructure1/Resources
6 Datastores:	1 selected

9. On the **Add Farm | Advanced Storage Options** page, make any changes that are desired and click on **Next >**.
10. On the **Add Farm | Guest Customization** page, select an **AD container** for the RDS server computer accounts, the Customization Specification created for the RDS servers under **Using a customization specification (Sysprep)**, and then click on **Next >**.
11. On the **Add Farm | Ready to Complete** page, review the configuration and click on **Finish** to create the farm.

Implementing the Microsoft Remote Desktop Services Application and Desktop Pools

12. Once created, the farm will be listed in the Horizon Administrator console under **Resources | Farms**; click on it to bring up the summary page, as shown in the following screenshot:

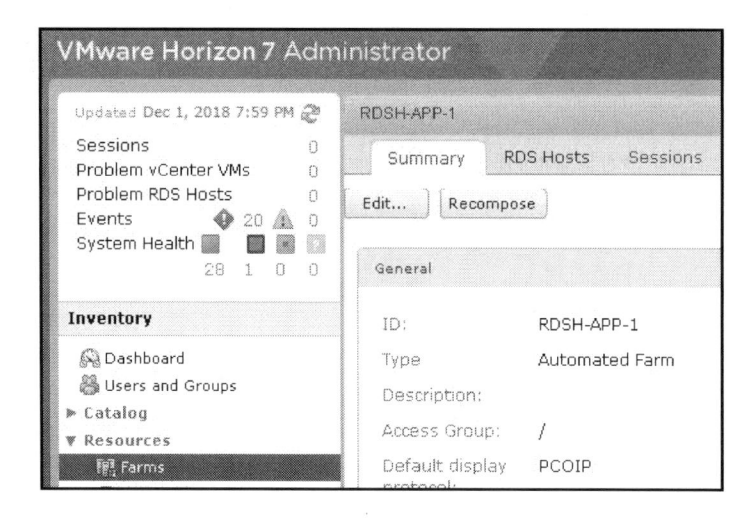

13. Click on the **RDS Hosts** tab to bring up a list of RDS servers that were deployed as part of the farm:

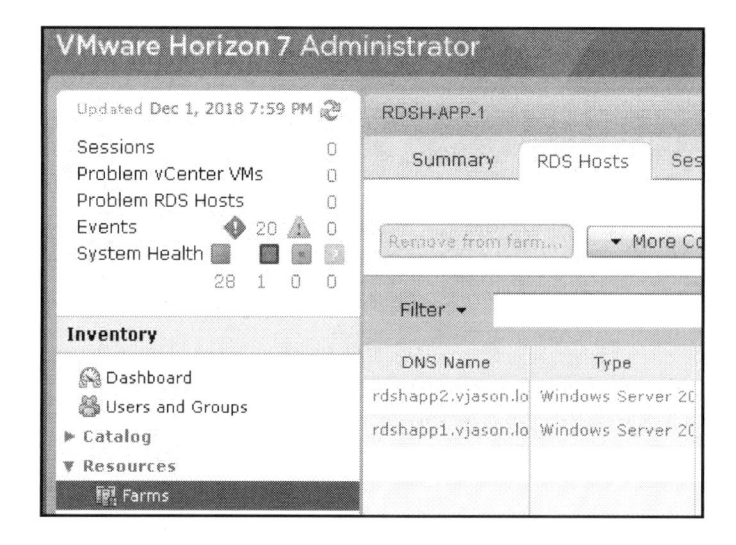

Now that the RDS servers have been deployed, we can create **Horizon application pools** to stream their applications to our Horizon clients. This process is described in the next section.

Creating a Horizon application pool

Horizon application pools are used to publish and entitle RDS streamed applications to Horizon clients. We must create an application pool for each application that we want to publish and, as in the case of desktop pools, we must entitle users to each application pool individually. Fortunately, we can create and entitle multiple applications at once, which simplifies the initial creation process. In this section, we will configure application pools for each of the core Microsoft Office applications that are installed on our Microsoft RDS servers.

To create an application pool in Horizon, we need to have at least one RDS farm configured in our pod. Assuming that the RDS farm creation process completed successfully in the previous section, we should see the farm in the Farms menu, under Resources, of our Horizon Administrator console.

The following steps outline the procedure for creating an RDS application pool. An RDS farm is required before you can create an application pool; in this example, we are using the farm that we created in the previous section:

1. Log into the Horizon Administrator console using an account that has administrative privileges.
2. Navigate to **Catalog** | **Application Pools** and click on **Add...**, as shown in the following screenshot:

Implementing the Microsoft Remote Desktop Services Application and Desktop Pools

3. On the **Add Application Pools** page, use the **Select an RDS farm** drop-down menu to specify the RDS farm to be used, and then click on the checkbox to the left of the application **Name** to add it to the application pool. Multiple applications may be selected; when finished, click on **Next**:

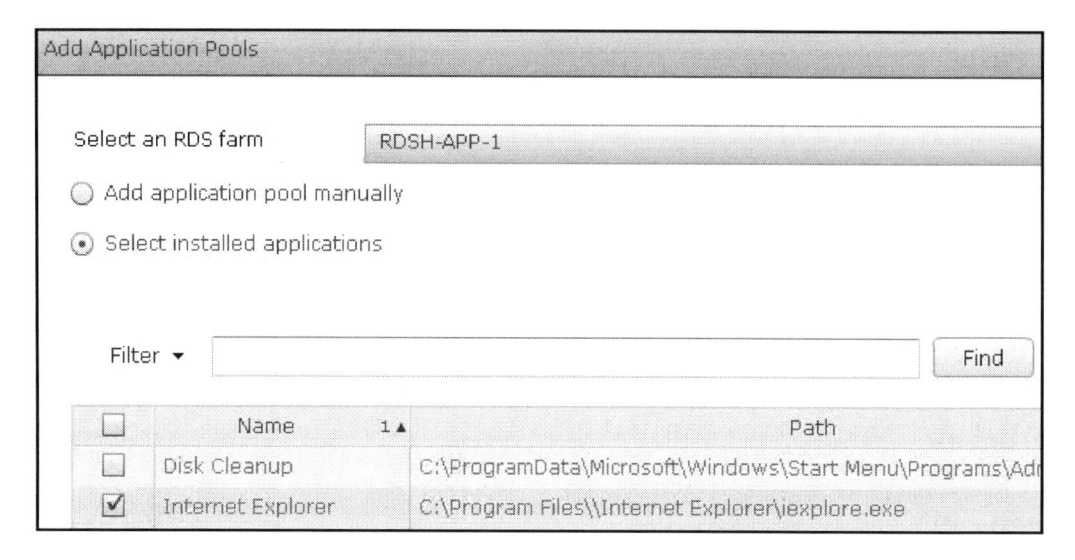

	Name		Path
☐	Disk Cleanup		C:\ProgramData\Microsoft\Windows\Start Menu\Programs\Ad
☑	Internet Explorer		C:\Program Files\\Internet Explorer\iexplore.exe

Select an RDS farm: RDSH-APP-1
○ Add application pool manually
◉ Select installed applications

4. On the **Add Application Pools** page, make any desired changes to the application **ID** or **Display Name**, then click on **Finish** to create the application pools and return to the **Catalog | Application Pools** window:

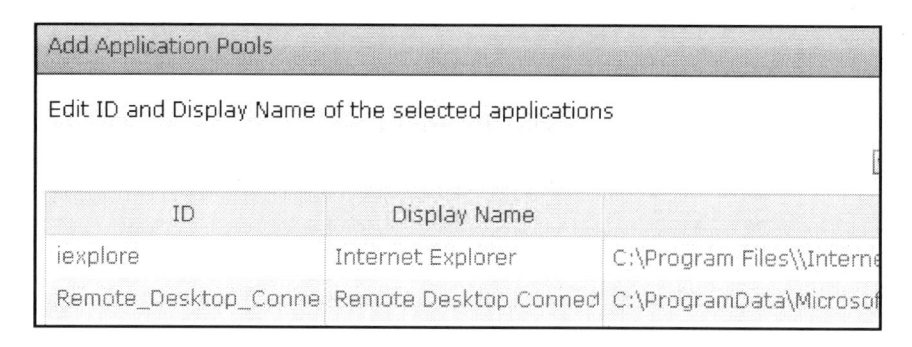

ID	Display Name	
iexplore	Internet Explorer	C:\Program Files\\Interne
Remote_Desktop_Conne	Remote Desktop Connec	C:\ProgramData\Microsof

> **TIP**
>
> These settings may also be edited after the Application Pool is created, as with Desktop Pools. Refer to the *Modifying a Horizon application pool* section later in this chapter for further details about how to modify existing Horizon application pools.

5. To entitle an Application Pool, click on it in the **Catalog | Application Pools** window, then click the **Entitlements...** drop-down menu, and then click **Add entitlement...** to open the **Add Entitlements** window. The remainder of the entitlement process is similar to that described in `Chapter 10`, *Creating Horizon Desktop Pools*.

> **TIP**
>
> You may also refer to the VMware Horizon documentation section titled "Entitling Users and Groups" (`https://docs.vmware.com/en/VMware-Horizon-7/7.6/horizon-published-desktops-applications.pdf`) for information about how to entitle desktop or application pools in Horizon.

The application pool has been created and entitled, and is now available to stream applications to Horizon clients.

Creating an RDS desktop pool

Horizon desktop pools are used to publish and entitle RDS-based desktops to Horizon clients. In this section, we will configure a simple desktop pool based on a pool of Microsoft RDS servers. To create an RDS desktop pool in Horizon, we need to have at least one RDS farm configured in our pod. Refer to `Chapter 9`, *Creating Horizon Application Pools*, for the procedures that are used to prepare and deploy an RDS farm.

The following steps outline the procedure for creating an RDS desktop pool. An RDS farm is required before you can create an application pool; in this example, we are using a farm that we created previously:

1. Log into the Horizon Administrator console using an account that has administrative privileges.
2. Navigate to **Catalog** | **Desktop Pools** and click on **Add...**, as shown in the following screenshot:

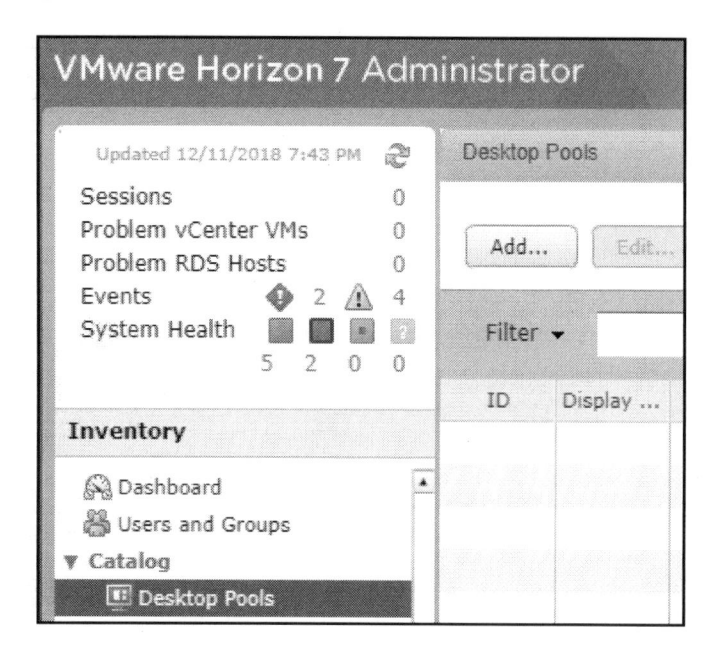

3. On the **Add Desktop Pool** page's **Type** tab, click the **RDS Desktop Pool** radio check box and then click **Next >**:

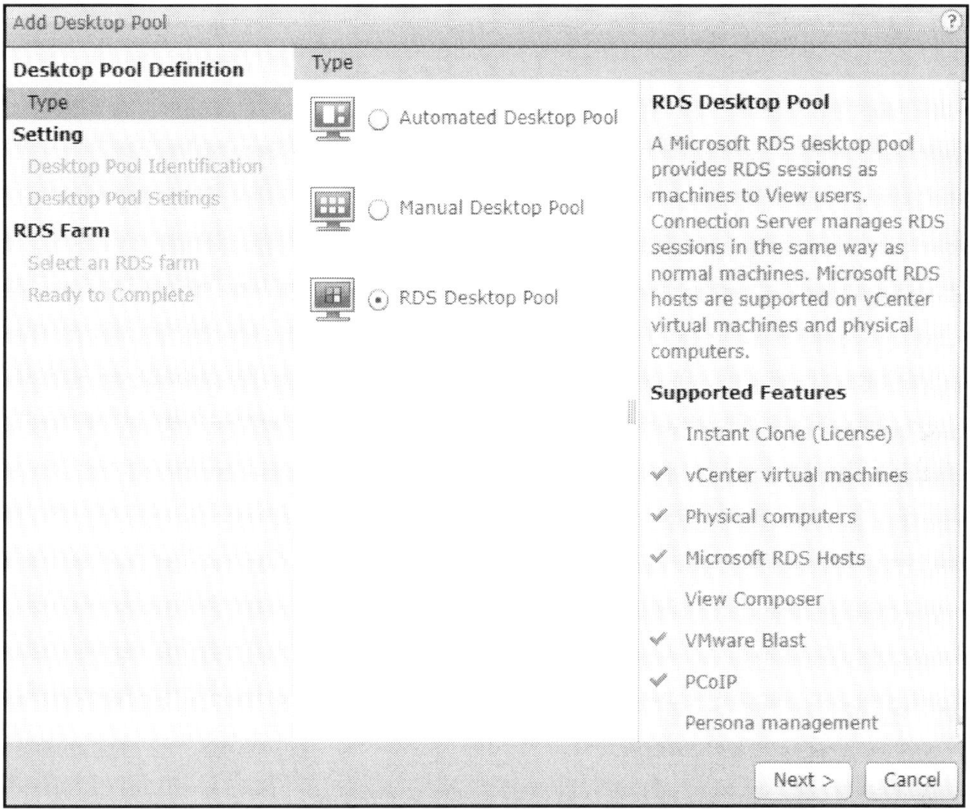

4. On the **Add Desktop Pool** page's **Desktop Pool Identification** tab, populate the **ID** and the optional **Display name** fields, and then click **Next >**:

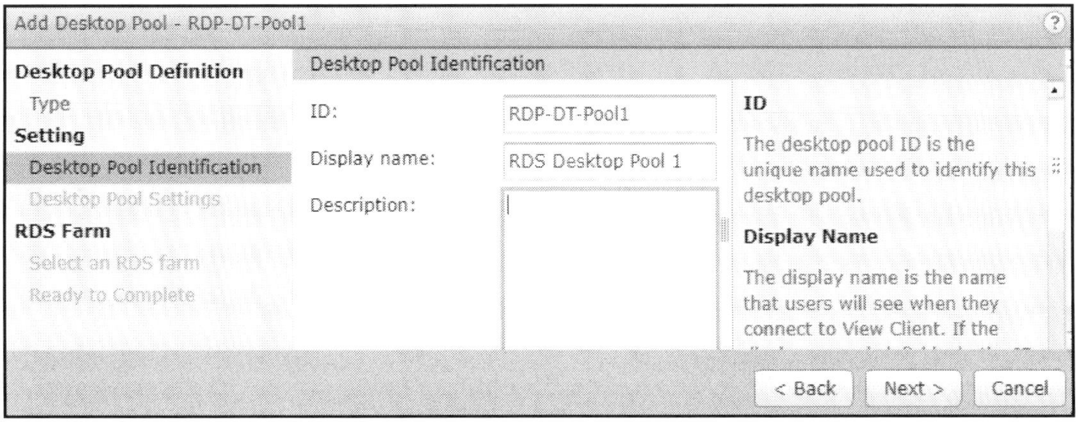

5. On the **Add Desktop Pool** page's **Desktop Pool Settings** tab, specify the options for the RDS desktop pool and then click **Next >**:

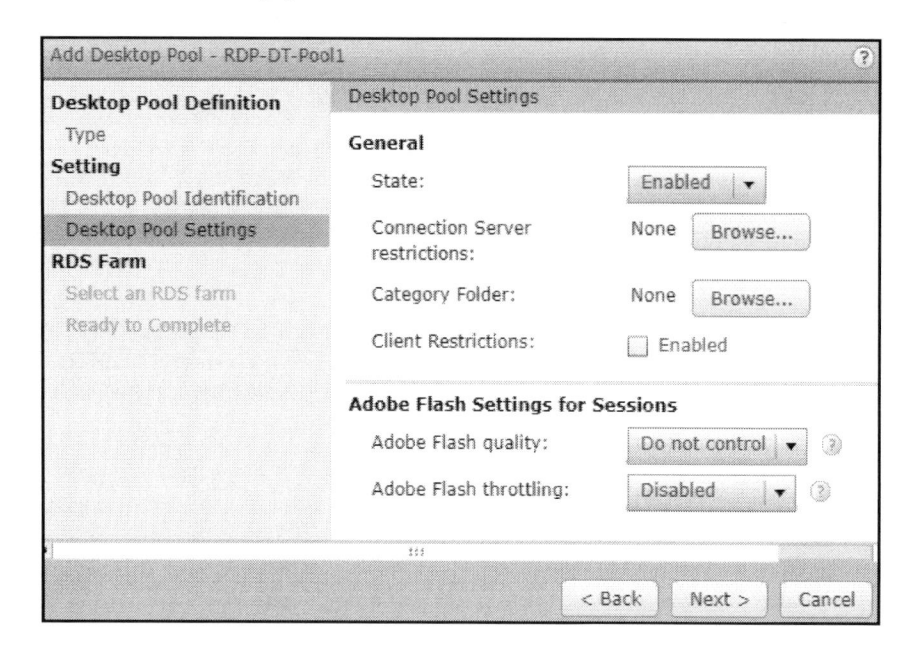

6. On the **Add Desktop Pool** page's **Select an RDS farm** tab, select the RDS farm you created and then click **Next >**:

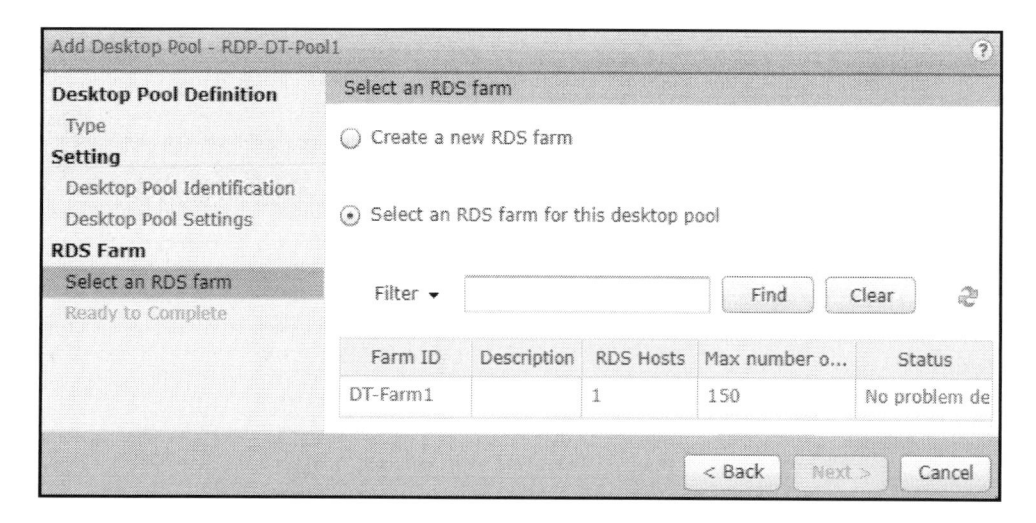

Chapter 8

7. On the **Add Desktop Pool** page's **Ready to Complete** tab, which is shown in the following screenshot, review the settings and then click **Finish**. You may also choose to check the **Entitle users after this wizard finishes** check box if you wish to immediately proceed with entitling access to the desktop pool:

> 💡 **TIP**
> These settings may also be edited after the RDS desktop pool is created, as with Desktop Pools. Additionally, you can refer to the VMware Horizon documentation section titled "Entitling Users and Groups" (`https://docs.vmware.com/en/VMware-Horizon-7/7.6/horizon-published-desktops-applications.pdf`) for information about how to entitle desktop or application pools in Horizon.

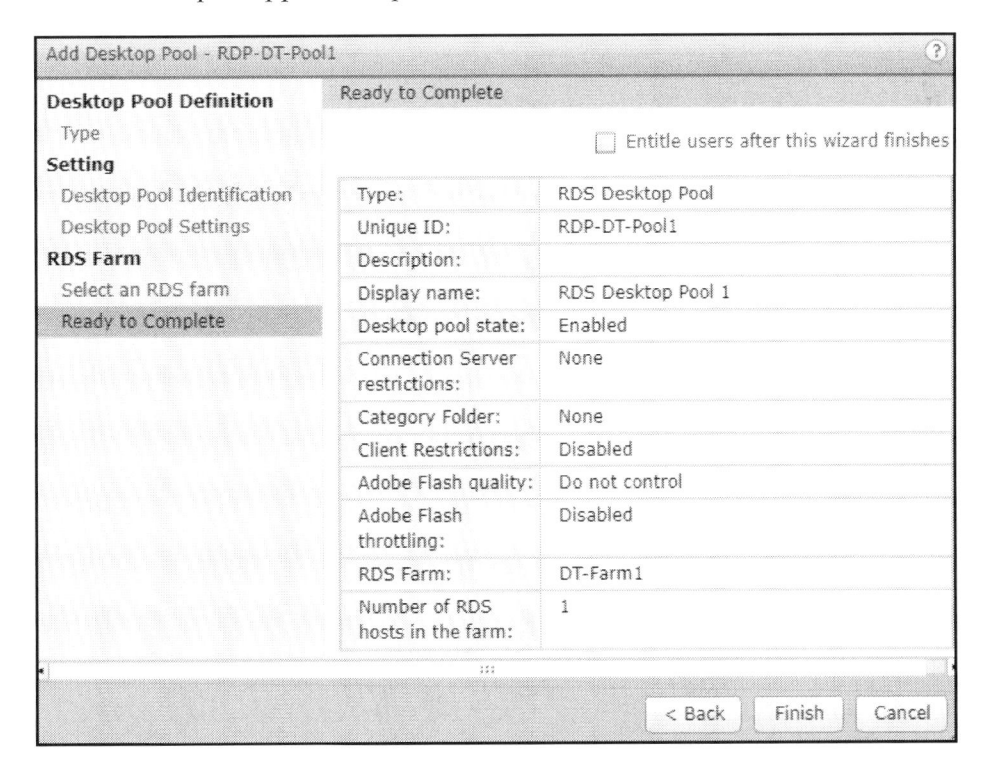

	Ready to Complete	
Desktop Pool Definition		
Type		☐ Entitle users after this wizard finishes
Setting		
Desktop Pool Identification	Type:	RDS Desktop Pool
Desktop Pool Settings	Unique ID:	RDP-DT-Pool1
RDS Farm	Description:	
Select an RDS farm	Display name:	RDS Desktop Pool 1
Ready to Complete	Desktop pool state:	Enabled
	Connection Server restrictions:	None
	Category Folder:	None
	Client Restrictions:	Disabled
	Adobe Flash quality:	Do not control
	Adobe Flash throttling:	Disabled
	RDS Farm:	DT-Farm1
	Number of RDS hosts in the farm:	1

The RDS desktop pool has been created and entitled, and is now available to the entitled Horizon clients.

[233]

Using the Horizon Client to access application pools

In this section, we will explore how RDS application streaming works from a Horizon client perspective. Unlike desktop pools, whose names are often created arbitrarily by the Horizon administrator, RDS applications appear much as they would in a Windows Explorer window.

> From a Horizon client perspective, an RDS desktop pool and traditional desktop pool provide virtually identical experiences. Therefore, this section only demonstrates how you can access RDS application pools.

The following steps outline how to use the Horizon Client to access application pools. In this example, we have already authenticated one of our Connection Servers using a user account that has been entitled to the application pool we created in the previous section. Perform the following steps:

1. Use the Horizon Client to authenticate one of the Connection Servers in the pod.
2. Click on one of the applications from the list presented in the Horizon Client window:

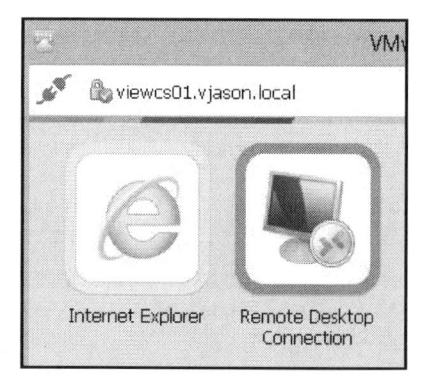

3. The application will appear just as it would if it were launched from the client's device; when finished, simply close it as you normally would.

We have now verified that RDS application streaming is working as intended. While a given user can only have one active session on a given RDS host, Horizon allows users to stream multiple applications using a single client session.

Monitoring the status of Horizon application pool clients and RDS servers

VMware Horizon includes multiple status pages for monitoring the status of Microsoft RDS servers and their client sessions. In this section, we will review the different status pages and review what each status page is used for. The following steps outline how to use the Horizon Administrator console to review the current status of our Microsoft RDS servers:

1. Log into the Horizon Administrator console using an account that has administrative privileges.
2. Navigate to **Resources** | **Machines**, click on the **RDS Hosts** tab, and review the status of each Microsoft RDS host, including the agent version, number of active sessions, and server availability:

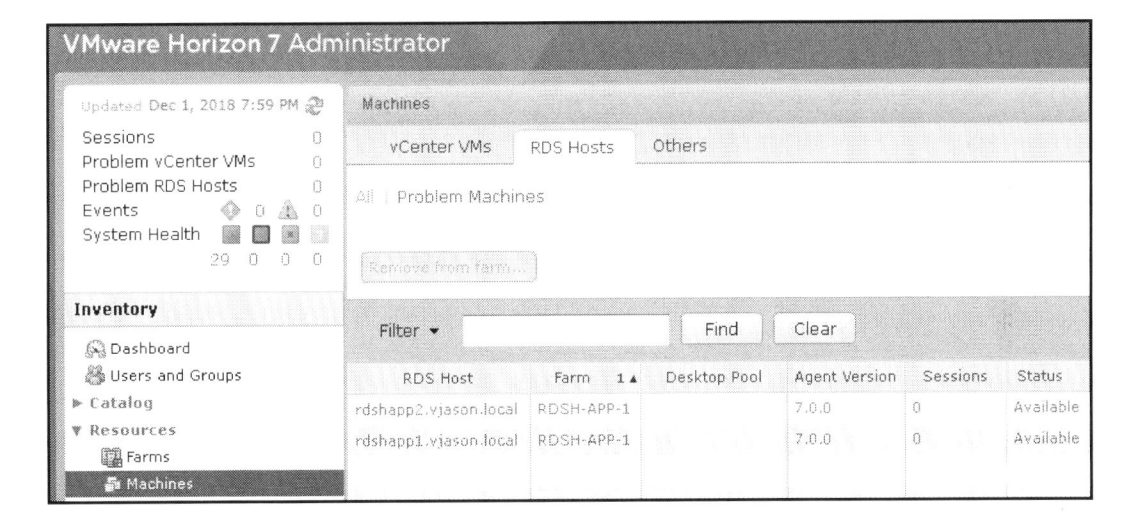

3. Navigate to **Monitoring | Sessions** and review the status of each client session. The **Desktop** and **Application** buttons can be used to control the types of clients that are displayed. Multiple pieces of information about the client connection are displayed, and other options are available, such as disconnecting or logging out of the session:

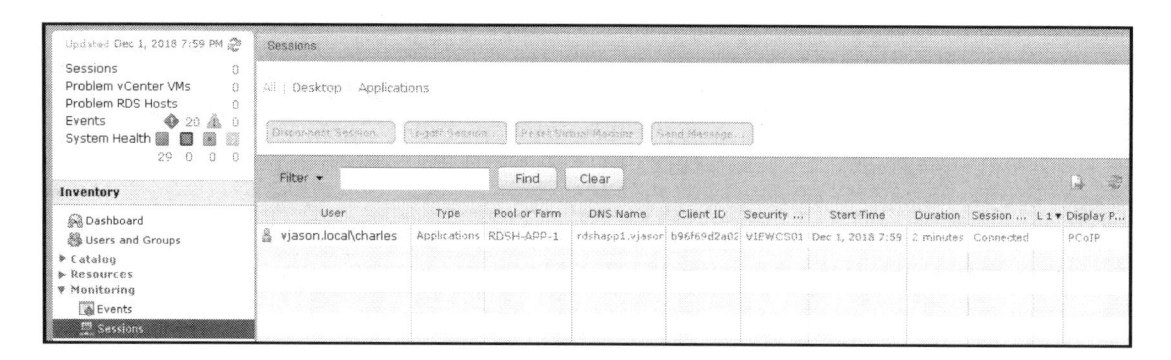

Modifying or deleting a Horizon application pool

This section will discuss the steps that are required to modify the configuration of an existing Horizon application pool. Limited options exist at the Application Pool level. This is because settings that impact Horizon client connections are edited at the farm level. This will be described in the next section.

> From a Horizon administrator perspective, managing the settings of and deleting an RDS desktop pool are similar. Therefore, this section only demonstrates how to edit or delete RDS application pools.

The following steps outline the procedure that's used to modify a Horizon application pool. Note that each individual application in Horizon is considered an Application Pool and, as is the case with desktop pools, they are managed independently of one another:

1. Log into the Horizon Administrator console using an account that has administrative privileges.
2. Navigate to **Catalog | Application Pools** and click on the application pool that you wish to update or delete. From here, there are several actions that can be performed.

[236]

3. To remove an application pool, click on **Delete**. The RDS servers themselves will not be impacted by this change.
4. To edit the application pool settings, click on **Edit...** (highlighted in red). Make changes as required to the fields shown, and then click on **OK**:

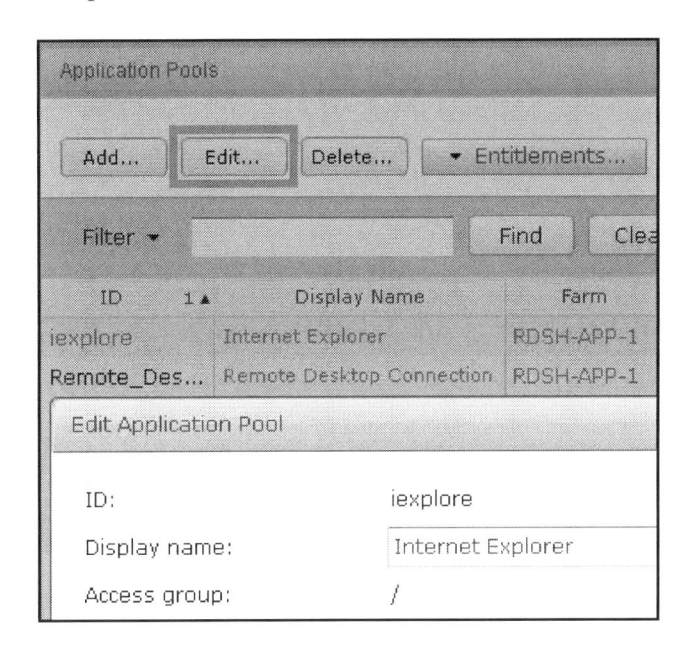

5. To add or remove an Application Pool entitlement, click on it in the **Catalog | Application Pools** window, then click the **Entitlements...** drop-down menu, and then click **Add entitlement** or **Remove entitlement...** to open the associated entitlement-management window. Perform the required changes and then click **OK**.

Managing a Horizon RDS farm or server

This section will discuss the steps that are required to modify the configuration of an existing Horizon Microsoft RDS farm or individual RDS server. These include key configuration items that impact the Horizon client connection protocol, session handling, and many other common pool settings.

The following steps outline how to edit the settings of an existing RDS farm. Individual RDS servers can only be disabled or deleted; no other configuration options exist.

1. Log into the Horizon Administrator console using an account that has administrative privileges.
2. Navigate to **Resources** | **Farms** and click on the RDS farm that needs to be updated.
3. Right-click on the farm and click on **Disable** to prevent additional clients from logging in; existing sessions will not be affected. This feature is typically used prior to performing farm-wide maintenance. From there, there are several actions that can be performed:
   - Click on a farm to open the farm **Summary** tab. Click **Recompose** to initiate a recomposition of the RDS servers in the farm; this feature works just like it does for linked clone desktops, which is to say that it allows us to replace the underlying RDS master image with one we have updated or modified:

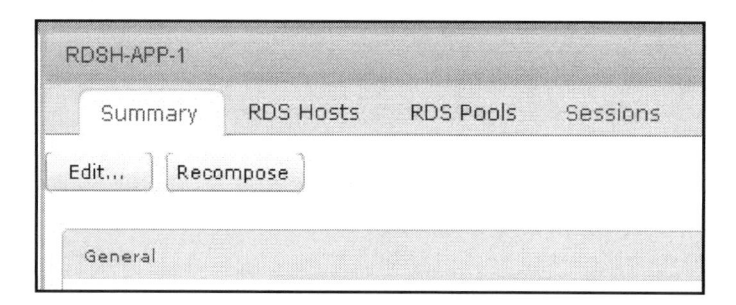

   > **TIP**
   > Note that unlike linked clone desktops, there is no option to perform a refresh, and RDS servers have no persistent data disk, so any user data saved on the RDS server will be lost. User-persona management features or folder redirection should be in place prior to using the recompose option.

4. From the **Resources** | **Farms** window, click on **Delete** to delete the RDS farm. Note that an RDS farm cannot be deleted unless any application pools it contains are deleted first.

Chapter 8

5. From the **Resources** | **Farms** window, click on **Edit...** to open the **Edit Farm** window. Update the farm settings as needed and click on **OK**. Note that most of these settings are identical to those seen when configuring desktop pools; a limited number of options, such as **Max sessions per RDS Host**, are unique to RDS farms. Consult the VMware Horizon documentation section titled "Creating Farms" (https://docs.vmware.com/en/VMware-Horizon-7/7.6/horizon-published-desktops-applications.pdf) for further details about the different options that are available when creating RDS farms:

Edit Farm - RDSH-APP-1				
Farm Settings	Provisioning Setti...	vCenter Settings	Guest Customizat...	Advanced Storage

General

ID:	RDSH-APP-1
Description:	
Access group:	/

Farm Settings

Default display protocol:	PCoIP
Allow users to choose protocol:	Yes
Empty session timeout (applications only):	After... 1 Minutes
When timeout occurs:	Disconnect
Log off disconnected sessions:	Never
Allow HTML Access to desktops and applications on this farm:	✓ Enabled — Requires installation of HTML Access.
Max sessions per RDS Host:	Unlimited

6. Click on a farm to open the farm **Summary** tab, and then click on the **RDS Hosts** tab to perform actions on individual RDS servers. The options include **Remove from farm...**, which will delete the selected server and force a new one to be created, and the **More Commands** drop-down menu, which offers us the ability to **Enable** or **Disable** hosts to perform maintenance. Actions performed here will not log off existing Horizon clients, but will prevent new sessions from connecting to the target RDS server:

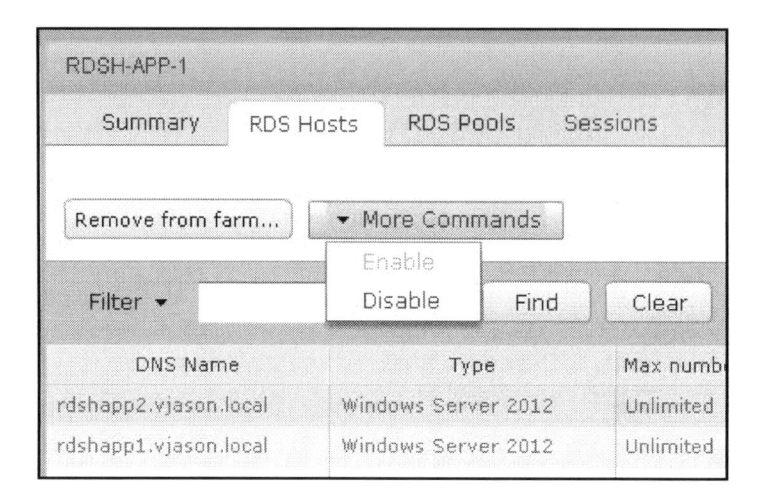

Summary

In this chapter, you were introduced to the Horizon Microsoft RDS application and desktop pools. You learned what versions of Windows server are supported, basic sizing information, and what is required to configure a Microsoft RDS server master image for use with Horizon, including the configuration of Windows and the installation of the Horizon Agent software.

We then discussed how to create a linked clone RDS farm, which functions like a linked clone desktop pool, in that each RDS server on a given datastore shares the same replica image.

Next, we discussed how to create and test Horizon RDS application pools, which enable Horizon clients to stream applications instead of full desktop sessions. Then, we discussed how to create Horizon RDS desktop pools, which enable Horizon clients to stream desktop sessions. We also reviewed how to monitor RDS servers, as well as Horizon application pool client sessions.

Finally, we learned how to manage existing RDS farms, application pools, and desktop pools once they have been deployed.

In the next chapter, we will discuss how to perform maintenance on Horizon pools.

Questions

1. What is the term for a collection of Microsoft RDS servers in Horizon used for streaming applications?
2. Which two of the following would you use to manage user personas/profiles when streaming applications? Windows Roaming Profiles, View Persona Management, VMware User Environment Manager.
3. What are the minimum requirements for a Microsoft RDS server you will use to stream applications?
4. What versions of Windows Server does Horizon currently support to stream applications?
5. What do you create to specify which applications you will publish for streaming to Horizon clients?
6. Configuring and maintaining a Horizon RDS desktop pool is similar to what other Horizon pool type?
7. From the perspective of Horizon clients, an RDS desktop pool is similar to what other type of Horizon pool?
8. What do you do to take a Microsoft RDS server offline for troubleshooting or maintenance?

Further reading

Check out the following resources to learn more about the topics that were covered in this chapter:

- VMware documentation:
    - **VMware Horizon:** `https://www.vmware.com/support/pubs/view_pubs.html`
    - **VMware vSphere:** `https://www.vmware.com/support/pubs/vsphere-esxi-vcenter-server-pubs.html`
- Microsoft documentation:
    - **Windows:** `https://docs.microsoft.com/en-us/windows/`

9
Performing Horizon Pool Maintenance

Maintaining desktops, or Windows RDS servers that are deployed using VMware Horizon, requires a different approach depending on what type of desktop you have selected. Full-clone desktops are typically managed using the same techniques as traditional physical desktops, as each is a fully independent virtual machine with dedicated underlying virtual hard disks. Many organizations choose full-clone desktops for this reason, as they can continue to manage them using tools and procedures that are already in place.

Linked-clone desktops are an entirely different matter, especially if you wish to minimize the amount of per-desktop storage that is required. If an organization were to manage its linked-clone desktops using the same traditional techniques that are used with physical or full-clone desktops, they would find that over time those desktops used more and more storage space, negating the benefits of using linked-clone desktops.

Instant-clone desktops are natively nonpersistent, so their maintenance is limited to updating the master image they are based on or deleting individual desktops.

This chapter will focus primarily on managing linked-clone and instant-clone desktops using the various features of Horizon itself.

This chapter will cover the following topics:

- An overview of Horizon instant-clone and linked-clone maintenance
- How to recompose a Horizon linked-clone desktop pool or single desktop
- How to refresh a linked-clone desktop pool or single desktop
- How to rebalance a linked-clone desktop pool or single desktop
- How to push a new parent image to an instant-clone desktop pool
- How to recover an instant-clone desktop
- How to manage Horizon Composer persistent disks

An overview of instant and linked clone maintenance

To understand why a linked clone desktop requires different techniques than a physical or full clone desktop, we must again understand what makes it different. The following diagram shows the relationship between the linked clone disk and the shared replica disk:

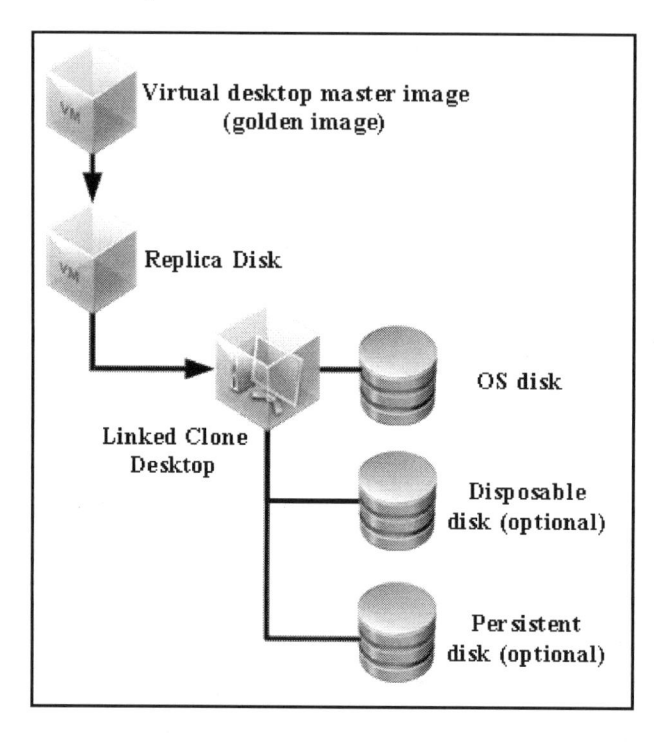

The replica disk is a read-only copy of the virtual desktop master image virtual hard disk; it is shared among as many as 1,000 desktops within a given Horizon desktop pool. The linked clone disk is used by the virtual desktop when it needs to write data; one virtual desktop is created for each linked clone desktop.

One of the primary advantages of linked clone desktops is that they require far less storage space than full clone desktops; this is made possible by the shared replica disk. This reduced storage utilization is certainly useful at the time the desktops are deployed, but to maintain this advantage over time, you must use Horizon's native recompose or refresh features.

> **TIP**
> Each of the maintenance operations described in this section requires the desktop to be powered off. Because of this and the storage I/O associated with each operation, it is recommended that you perform these tasks during off-peak hours. Each of these tasks can be scheduled, making it easier for Horizon administrators to accomplish this.

Instant-clone parent image update

An instant clone desktop is similar to a linked clone desktop in that it is dependent on a parent image, although, as we know, the desktops themselves function in two different ways. Instant clone desktop pools support a maintenance operation known as **push image**, which is similar to a linked clone recompose; however, instant clones also make use of the updated memory state of the new image. This is one of the characteristics of instant clone desktops that enables them to be deployed and configured much faster than linked clone desktops, albeit without the ability to maintain their state in-between Horizon client sessions.

Linked clone desktop refresh

A desktop refresh returns the desktop's linked clone disk—also known as the OS disk—to the original state and size as configured in the desktop pool options. If the desktop is configured with an optional persistent disk for storing user profile data, that data will be retained during the refresh operation. A refresh can be performed on either a desktop pool or an individual desktop. A desktop refresh provides the following benefits:

- A quick way of reducing linked clone storage utilization (the more time that has passed since the last refresh or recompose, the more storage capacity you are likely to reclaim)
- If a desktop develops software problems, a refresh can be used to restore it to the original state

A refresh operation is also performed during linked clone recompose and rebalance operations. A refresh operation typically requires less than 10 minutes of downtime per desktop, although the time required may vary depending on the performance capabilities of the Horizon infrastructure and the specified number of concurrent refresh operations allowed. Horizon Composer performs up to 12 concurrent refresh operations by default. Instructions on how to perform a desktop refresh operation are provided later in this chapter.

> **TIP**: Any maintenance task that includes a refresh operation will force the Windows desktop to reactivate the OS and Office software, if installed. Because of this, it is recommended that any organization that wishes to use linked clone desktops deploys a Windows KMS server to handle Windows and Office license activation. Windows MAK keys would be quickly exhausted in a linked clone desktop environment.

Linked clone desktop recompose

A desktop recompose is used to replace the existing linked clone replica disk, usually in response to a configuration change, software installation, or software update. A desktop recompose is the preferred method of updating the linked clone desktop, as the changes only affect the replica disk. Were the same updates or changes to be applied directly to the linked clone desktops themselves, each of the linked clone OS disks would increase in size by the amount needed to process the change.

The following example shows the difference between updating a virtual desktop master image and then using a recompose operation to deploy an updated replica disk, and installing the updates directly on the linked clone desktops.

In this example, it is determined that installing the updates on a single desktop requires 215 MB of additional space. In this case, the differences between the two methods will be as follows:

- If the virtual desktop master image is updated and a recompose operation is performed, only 215 MB of additional space will be required to update all 1,000 desktops in the pool
- If the linked clone desktops are patched individually, a pool of 1,000 linked clone desktops would require an additional 210 GB of storage, or 215 MB for each linked clone desktop

In addition to the additional storage required to install the patches directly on the linked clone desktops, the patches or software installed would not persist if any maintenance that requires a refresh operation were to be performed.

A desktop recompose operation consists of the following steps:

1. The Horizon administrator (or other responsible party) updates the virtual desktop master image with the required changes.
2. The Horizon administrator takes a new snapshot of the updated virtual desktop master image.
3. The Horizon administrator uses the Horizon Administrator console to initiate a recompose, selecting the updated snapshot. A new master image with a snapshot can also be selected, provided it is running on the same operating system.
4. Horizon Composer clones the selected virtual desktop master image and snapshot to a new replica disk. The original replica disk will remain until no more linked clones are associated with it.
5. Horizon Composer powers down the virtual desktop that will be recomposed.
6. Horizon Composer returns the existing linked clone OS disk to the original size and state (similar to a refresh operation), and associates it with the new replica disk. In addition, if the desktop has a persistent disk configured, it will be attached to the recomposed desktop at this point.
7. Horizon Composer powers on the recomposed linked clone and configures it using the Horizon agent.
8. The Horizon agent informs the Horizon connection server that it is available for use.

A recompose operation typically requires less than 10 minutes of downtime per desktop, and Horizon Composer performs up to 12 concurrent recompose operations by default. Instructions on how to perform a desktop recompose operation are provided later in this chapter.

Linked clone desktop rebalance

A desktop rebalance is used to rebalance linked clone desktop storage across existing datastores, including any new datastores that were added to the desktop pool configuration. As mentioned previously, it is important to remember that a rebalance operation will also refresh the desktop as part of the process.

A rebalance cannot be used to balance persistent disk storage as the persistent disk will remain in place until the desktop is deleted or the persistent disk is detached from the desktop and later deleted. Organizations that choose not to deploy a persistent disk may find that regular refresh or recompose operations are all that is required to maintain consistent desktop storage utilization throughout the life cycle of their linked clone desktops.

Managing Horizon maintenance tasks

Ongoing or scheduled refresh, recompose, or rebalance tasks can be paused, resumed from a pause, or canceled at any time using the Horizon Administrator console. When a maintenance task is canceled or paused, any operations currently underway will finish, but no new operations will start. When a paused task is resumed, the maintenance operation will continue. When managing these maintenance tasks, you should bear in mind the following two facts:

- The resources required to perform Horizon maintenance tasks may impact the performance of the Horizon infrastructure. If Horizon maintenance tasks are causing performance problems for Horizon desktops that are currently in use, or for other resources that share the infrastructure, simply pause the maintenance tasks. Resume the maintenance tasks during a period of reduced infrastructure utilization.
- I do not recommend canceling maintenance tasks, as this may leave the desktops in an inconsistent state; if the maintenance operation is causing performance issues, simply pause it until there is a more suitable time for it to be undertaken.

The following steps outline how to manage a task that is assigned to a desktop pool or an individual desktop:

1. Log in to the Horizon Administrator console using an **Active Directory** (**AD**) account that has administrative permissions within Horizon.
2. Go to **Catalog** and open the **Desktop Pools** window within the console.
3. In the **Desktop Pools** window, click on the pool that has the task that you wish to cancel. In our example, we will click on the pool called **AppVolumes-W10** to open the **AppVolumes-W10** window.

4. Under the **Tasks** tab of the **AppVolumes-W10** window (as shown in the following screenshot), highlight the task that you wish to update and click on **Cancel task...**, **Pause task...**, or **Resume task...**, as required. Since the sample task is not currently paused, the **Resume task** button is grayed out:

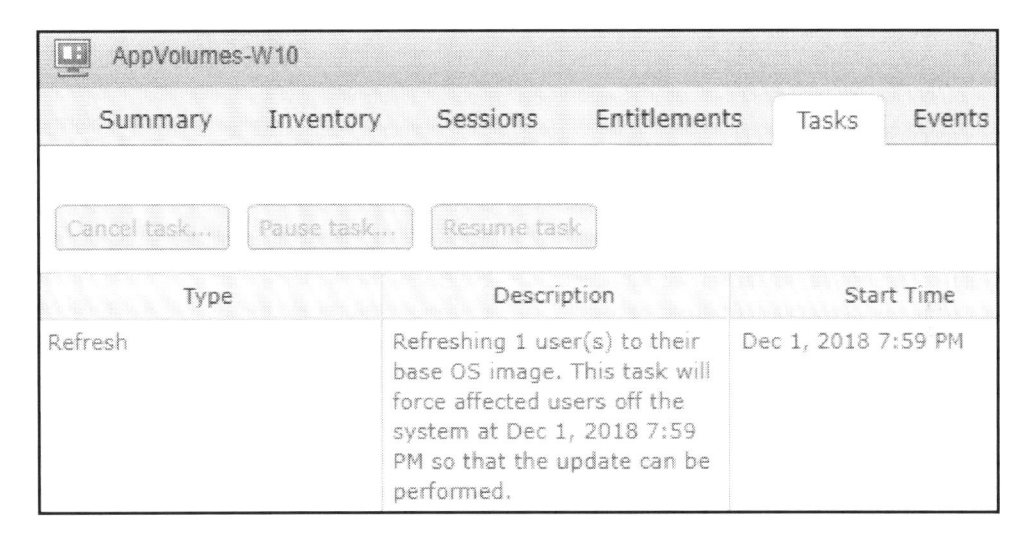

Type	Description	Start Time
Refresh	Refreshing 1 user(s) to their base OS image. This task will force affected users off the system at Dec 1, 2018 7:59 PM so that the update can be performed.	Dec 1, 2018 7:59 PM

> **TIP:** The **Tasks** tab will show the tasks that are assigned to individual desktops, as well as those assigned to the pool as a whole. The tasks are managed using the same process, regardless of their assignment.

Global settings for Horizon maintenance

There are multiple configuration options within Horizon's that affect Horizon refresh, recompose, and rebalance operations. This section will explain where those options can be found, and their purposes.

Logoff warning and timeout

When a Horizon administrator chooses to forcibly log the user off to perform a linked clone maintenance operation, the user is notified and the logoff proceeds after five minutes. The notification message and the timeout value can both be configured in the **Global Settings** window.

> **TIP**: If you choose to automatically log users off to perform desktop maintenance, your warning message will instruct them not to log in again until maintenance is complete. This will help prevent users from immediately trying to reconnect to their desktops after they have been logged off, which can interfere with the maintenance process.

The following steps outline how to update these global settings:

1. Log in to the Horizon Administrator console using an AD account that has administrative permissions within Horizon.
2. Open **View Configuration | Global Settings** within the console. Click on the **Edit...** button in the **General** section, as shown in the following screenshot:

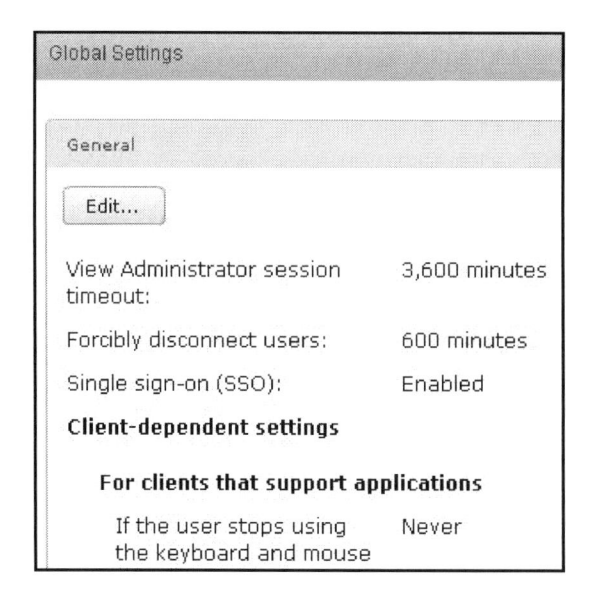

```
Global Settings

General

   [ Edit... ]

   View Administrator session          3,600 minutes
   timeout:

   Forcibly disconnect users:          600 minutes

   Single sign-on (SSO):               Enabled

   Client-dependent settings

      For clients that support applications

         If the user stops using       Never
         the keyboard and mouse
```

3. In the **General Settings** window, update the **Display warning before forced logoff** and **After warning, log off after:** settings as needed (as shown in the following screenshot). Click on **OK** to update the settings:

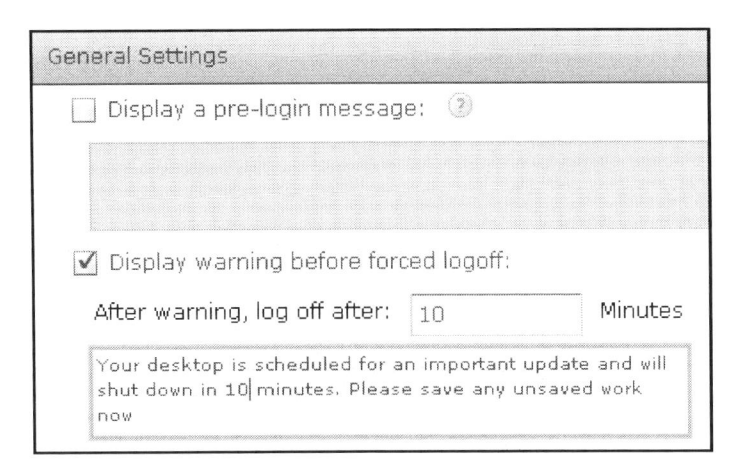

Concurrent maintenance operations

By default, Horizon Composer will perform no more than 12 maintenance operations at a time. While this is considered the optimal setting for this option, it is possible to increase or decrease the number if required. This number is set on a per-vCenter server basis, so if multiple vCenter servers are being used, each one will need to be changed individually.

The following steps outline how to update the number of concurrent maintenance operations that Horizon Composer will perform:

1. Log in to the Horizon Administrator console using an AD account that has administrative permissions within Horizon.
2. Open the **View Configuration** | **Servers** window within the console.

3. In the **vCenter Servers** tab of the **Servers** window (shown in the following screenshot), highlight the vCenter server you wish to update and click on the **Edit** button:

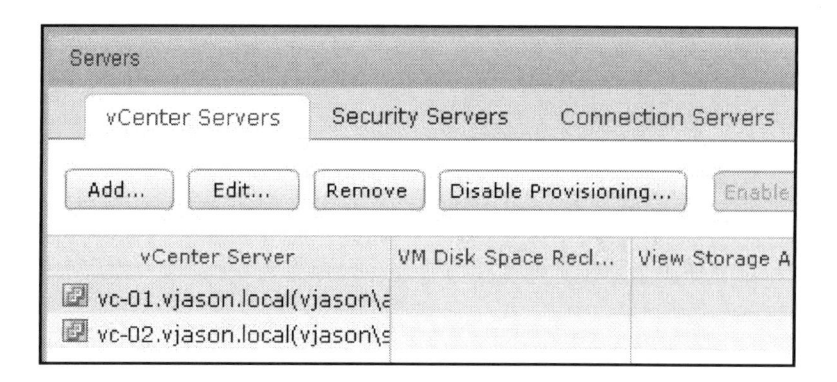

4. In the **Edit vCenter Server** window, click on the **Edit** button underneath the **vCenter Server Settings** section.
5. In the second **Edit vCenter Server** window, under the **Advanced Settings** section (shown in the following screenshot), update the **Max concurrent View Composer maintenance operations** value as needed. Click on **OK** twice to close both **Edit vCenter Server** windows and update the settings:

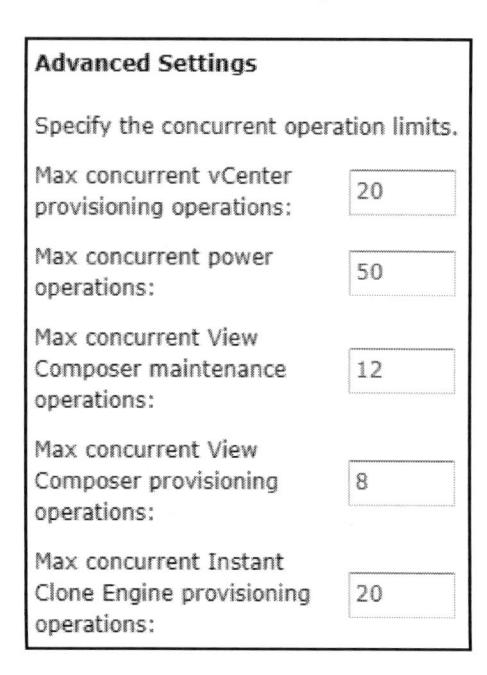

Advanced Settings

Specify the concurrent operation limits.

Max concurrent vCenter provisioning operations:	20
Max concurrent power operations:	50
Max concurrent View Composer maintenance operations:	12
Max concurrent View Composer provisioning operations:	8
Max concurrent Instant Clone Engine provisioning operations:	20

> **TIP:** The **Edit vCenter Server** window also allows you to change other settings that affect the speed at which Horizon desktops and Windows RDS servers are provisioned, deployed, and powered on. For each of these settings, the default value is considered optional and changes are not recommended.

Storage overcommit

Storage overcommit levels are configured on a per-datastore basis and affect how many linked clones Horizon Composer will provision on each datastore. Storage overcommit is typically configured when the desktop pool is created, but the settings can be updated at any time.

The following list shows the five different storage overcommit levels supported by Horizon. Each is calculated based on the size of the parent virtual machine:

- **None**: Storage is not overcommitted.
- **Conservative**: The default. Storage will be overcommitted up to 4 times the size of the datastore.
- **Moderate**: Storage will be overcommitted up to 7 times the size of the datastore.
- **Aggressive**: Storage will be overcommitted up to 15 times the size of the datastore.
- **Unbound**: Storage will be overcommitted without any limits, even if the datastore is filled to capacity.

Consider an example where the overcommit level is set to **Conservative**, the parent virtual machine uses a disk that is 12 GB in size, and linked clones will be configured on datastores that are 240 GB in size. In this situation, the following overcommit settings will be applied:

- *120 GB (datastore) X 4 (overcommit level) = 480 GB*
- *480 GB/12 GB (parent virtual machine size) = 40 linked clones*

Based on these figures, when using the default storage overcommit level, Horizon Composer will place up to 40 linked clones on each datastore at the time of the linked clone deployment or the rebalance operation.

Updating datastore storage overcommit settings

The following steps outline how to update the storage overcommit levels of an existing desktop pool:

1. Log into the Horizon Administrator console using an AD account that has administrative permissions within Horizon.
2. Go to **Catalog** and open the **Desktop Pools** window within the console.
3. In the **Desktop Pools** window, highlight the linked clone pool you wish to refresh. In our example, we will highlight the pool called **AppVolumes-W10**. Click on the **Edit** button that's shown in the following screenshot to open the **AppVolumes-W10** window:

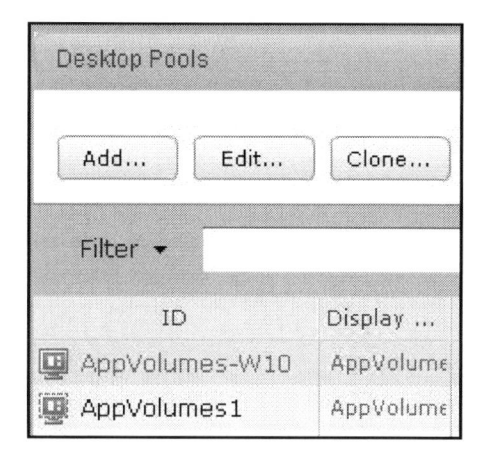

4. In the **AppVolumes-W10** window, click on the **vCenter Settings** tab.
5. In the **vCenter Settings** tab, click on the **Browse...** button next to the **Datastores** setting, as shown in the following screenshot. This will open the **Select Linked Clone Datastores** window:

6. In the **Select Linked Clone Datastores** window (shown in the following screenshot), open the **Storage Overcommit** drop-down menu next to each datastore to set the storage overcommit level. The level can only be changed for the datastores that are in use by the pool:

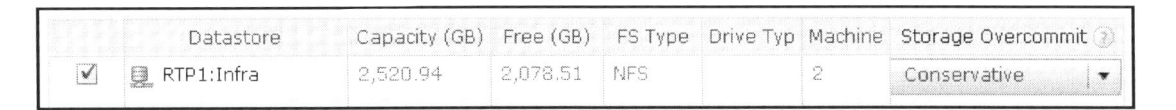

	Datastore	Capacity (GB)	Free (GB)	FS Type	Drive Typ	Machine	Storage Overcommit
✓	RTP1:Infra	2,520.94	2,078.51	NFS		2	Conservative

7. Click **OK** twice to close the **Select Linked Clone Datastores** and **Edit AppVolumes-W10** windows and implement the changes.

Changing the storage overcommit settings does not, by itself, initiate any desktop maintenance activities. To enforce the updated storage overcommit policies on an existing desktop pool, simply perform a desktop rebalance using the procedure that's described later in this chapter.

Performing linked clone desktop maintenance

In this section, we will look at the different techniques that are used to perform maintenance on linked clone desktop pools or individual linked clone desktops.

Refreshing linked clone desktops

The following steps describe how to refresh a linked clone desktop pool using the Horizon Administrator console:

1. Log into the Horizon Administrator console using an AD account that has administrative permissions within Horizon.
2. Go to **Catalog** and open the **Desktop Pools** window within the console.

Performing Horizon Pool Maintenance

3. In the **Desktop Pools** window (shown in the following screenshot), click on the linked clone pool you wish to refresh. In our example, we will click on the pool called **AppVolumes-W10** to open the **AppVolumes-W10** window:

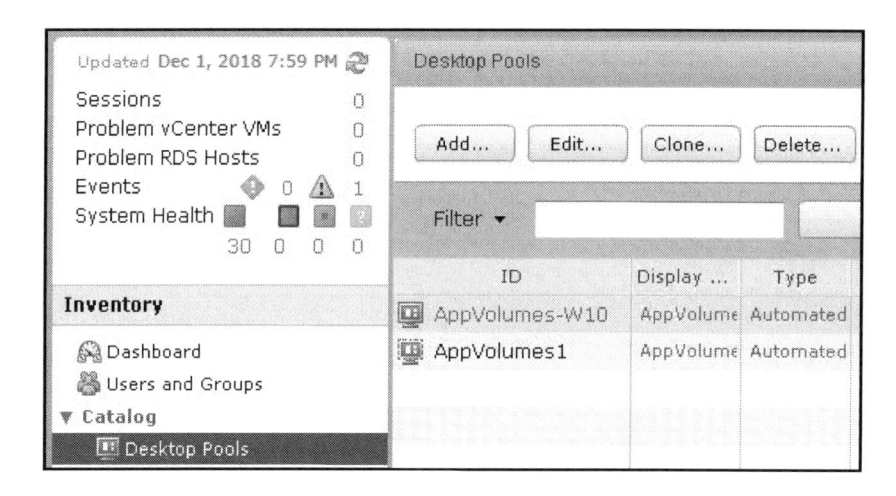

4. On the right-hand side of the **AppVolumes-W10** window (shown in the following screenshot), open the **View Composer** drop-down menu and click on **Refresh** to open the **Refresh** window:

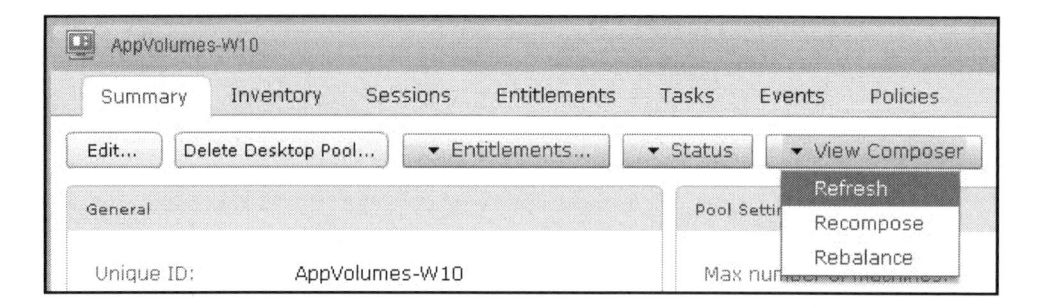

5. Go to **Refresh** and click **Scheduling**. In the **Scheduling** window (shown in the following screenshot), accept the default settings and click on **Next** to continue. If no changes are made, the refresh operation will begin immediately and users will be logged off from their desktops automatically after five minutes. The following are the optional settings:
    - The date and time that the refresh should start
    - Whether to force the users to log off or wait for them to log off

- Whether to stop the refresh if an error occurs
- Updates to the warning and grace period settings must be made in Horizon's global settings:

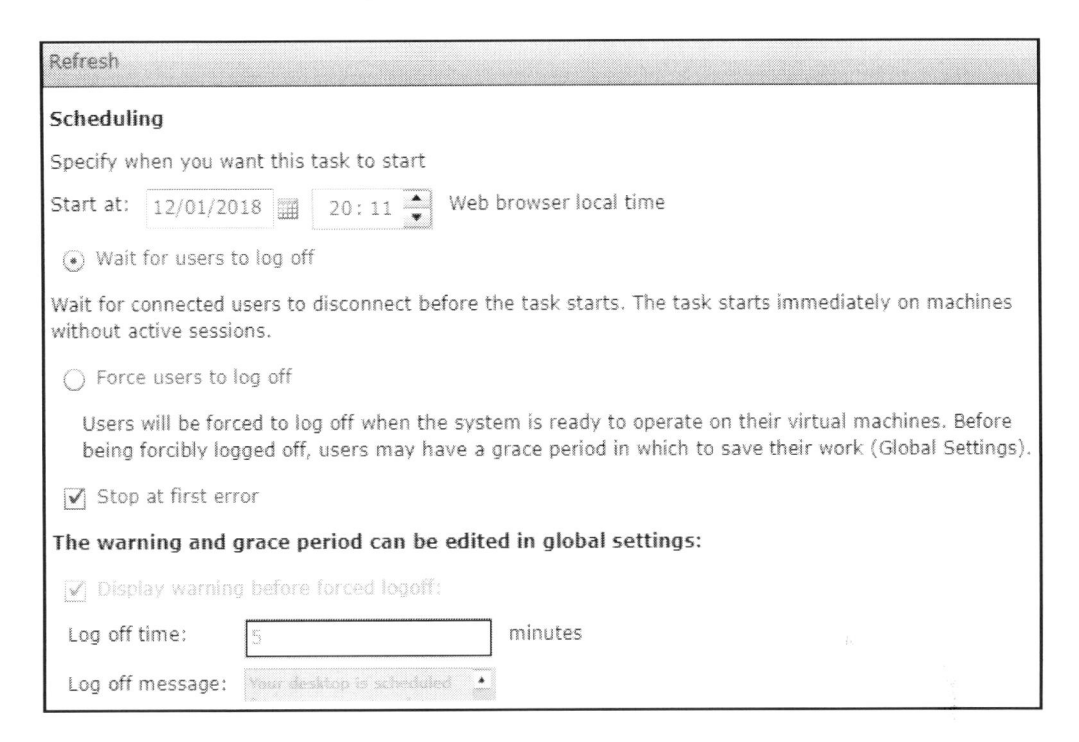

Refresh

Scheduling

Specify when you want this task to start

Start at: 12/01/2018 20:11 Web browser local time

◉ Wait for users to log off

Wait for connected users to disconnect before the task starts. The task starts immediately on machines without active sessions.

○ Force users to log off

Users will be forced to log off when the system is ready to operate on their virtual machines. Before being forcibly logged off, users may have a grace period in which to save their work (Global Settings).

☑ Stop at first error

The warning and grace period can be edited in global settings:

☑ Display warning before forced logoff:

Log off time: 5 minutes

Log off message: Your desktop is scheduled

6. Review the options in the **Refresh | Scheduling** window. If changes are required, click on the **Back** button to return to the previous screen. Click on **Finish** to begin or schedule the refresh operation, depending on what was configured in the previous step.

The time required to complete a linked clone desktop refresh operation varies, based on a number of different factors beyond that of the Horizon configuration itself. Generally speaking, under average circumstances, it will take no more than 10 minutes per desktop, starting from the time that Horizon Composer performs the initial powerdown of the desktop.

The status of the refresh operation can be viewed in the **Tasks** tab of the desktop pool.

Refreshing individual desktops

A refresh can also be performed on an individual desktop. This is often done in response to an event—such as a problem with the guest OS—that affects only the desktop that is to be refreshed. The following steps describe how to refresh a single linked clone desktop using the Horizon Administrator console:

1. Log into the Horizon Administrator console using an AD account that has administrative permissions within Horizon.
2. **Go to Catalog** and open the **Desktop Pools** window within the console.
3. In the **Desktop Pools** window, click on the pool that contains the linked clone desktop you wish to refresh.
4. In the window for the desktop pool you selected, click the **Inventory** tab.
5. Click on the linked clone desktop that you wish to refresh. In our example, we will click on the desktop named **APPV10-2** to open the **APPV10-2** window.
6. In the **APPV10-2** window, open the **View Composer** drop-down menu and then click on **Refresh** to open the **Refresh** window.
7. Complete the remaining steps to initiate the refresh operation.

Recomposing linked clone desktops

The following steps outline how to recompose a linked clone desktop pool using the Horizon Administrator console:

1. Log in to the Horizon Administrator console using an AD account that has administrative permissions within Horizon.
2. **Go to Catalog** and open the **Desktop Pools** window within the console.
3. In the **Desktop Pools** window, click on the linked clone pool you wish to recompose. In our example, we will click on the pool called **AppVolumes-W10** to open the **AppVolumes-W10** window.
4. On the right-hand side of the **AppVolumes-W10** window, open the **View Composer** drop-down menu and click on **Recompose** to open the **Recompose** window.

5. On the **Image** page of the **Recompose** window (shown in the following screenshot), highlight the updated snapshot that you wish to use with your desktops. You may also select a different parent VM and accompanying snapshot by clicking on the **Change...** button, as long as they use the same OS as the existing desktops. In our example, we have chosen a new snapshot of the existing parent VM. Click on **Next** to move to the next step:

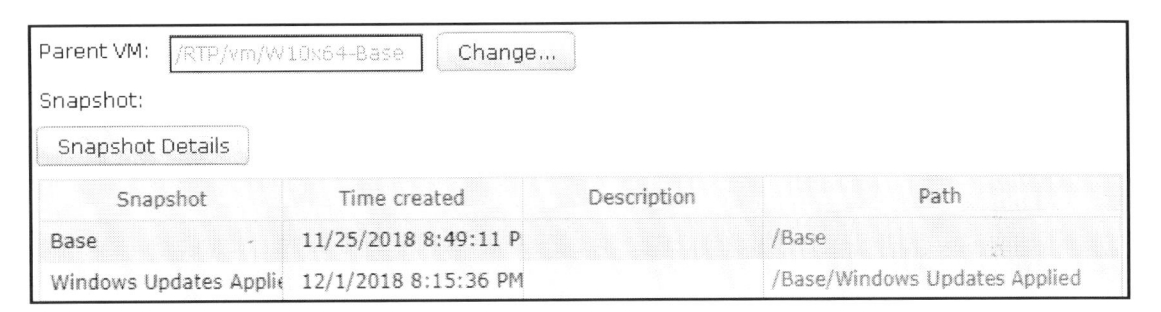

Snapshot	Time created	Description	Path
Base	11/25/2018 8:49:11 P		/Base
Windows Updates Applie	12/1/2018 8:15:36 PM		/Base/Windows Updates Applied

> **TIP**: By default, Horizon will use the selected snapshot when deploying new desktops within the desktop pool. Uncheck the **Change the default image for new desktops** checkbox to change this behavior and force new desktops to use the existing image.

6. On the **Scheduling** page of the **Recompose** window, select the desired scheduling options and click on **Next**. These are the same scheduling options that appear when performing a desktop refresh.
7. Review the options in the **Ready to Complete** page of the **Recompose** window. If changes are required, click on the **Back** button to return to the previous screen. Click on **Finish** to begin or schedule the recompose operation, depending on what was configured in the previous step.

The time required to complete a linked clone desktop recompose operation varies based on a number of different factors beyond that of the Horizon configuration itself. Generally speaking, under average circumstances, it will take no more than 15 minutes per desktop, starting from the time that Horizon Composer performs the initial powerdown of the desktop.

> If a desktop pool is configured to use Windows Sysprep for machine customization, a new Windows Machine **System Identifier** (**SID**) will be generated during a recompose operation. Consider any potential issues this may cause within your environment. The only alternative is to redeploy the desktops using VMware QuickPrep instead of Windows Sysprep. For more information about the differences between QuickPrep and System, consult the *Choosing QuickPrep or Sysprep to Customize Linked-Clone Machines* section of the VMware document, *Setting Up Published Desktops and Applications in View* (https://docs.vmware.com/en/VMware-Horizon-7/index.html).

The status of the recompose operation can be viewed in the **Tasks** tab of the desktop pool window.

Recomposing individual desktops

A recompose can also be performed on an individual desktop. One reason to do this might be because you need to test out an updated desktop configuration on a small number of users prior to recomposing all the desktops. The following steps describe how to recompose a single linked clone desktop using the Horizon Administrator console:

1. Log into the Horizon Administrator console using an AD account that has administrative permissions within Horizon.
2. **Go to Catalog** and open the **Desktop Pools** window within the console.
3. In the **Desktop Pools** window, click on the pool that contains the linked clone desktop you wish to recompose.
4. In the window for the desktop pool you selected, click the **Inventory** tab.
5. Click on the linked clone desktop that you wish to recompose. In our example, we will click on the desktop named **APPV10-2** to open the **APPV10-2** window.
6. In the **APPV10-2** window, open the **View Composer** drop-down menu and then click on **Recompose** to open the **Recompose** window.
7. Complete the remaining steps to initiate the recompose operation.

Rebalancing linked clone desktops

The following steps describe how to rebalance a desktop pool using the Horizon Administrator console. In this example, we will be adding additional datastores to our desktop pool, prior to the rebalance operation. These datastores will then be used for the rebalance:

1. Log into the Horizon Administrator console using an AD account that has administrative permissions within Horizon.
2. **Go to Catalog** and open the **Desktop Pools** window within the console.
3. In the **Desktop Pools** window, highlight the pool to which you wish to add the datastores and then rebalance. In our example, we will highlight the pool called **AppVolumes-W10**. Click on the **Edit** button to open the **Edit AppVolumes-W10** window.
4. In the **Edit AppVolumes-W10** window, click on the **vCenter Settings** tab.
5. In the **vCenter Settings** tab, click on the **Browse** button next to the **Datastores** setting. This will open the **Select Linked Clone Datastores** window.
6. In the **Select Linked Clone Datastores** window (shown in the following screenshot), click on the checkboxes next to the datastores you wish to add to the desktop pool. In our example, we will check the box next to the **RTP1:Infra2** datastore:

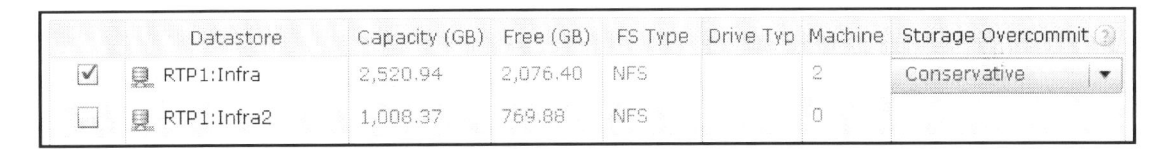

	Datastore	Capacity (GB)	Free (GB)	FS Type	Drive Typ	Machine	Storage Overcommit
✓	RTP1:Infra	2,520.94	2,076.40	NFS		2	Conservative
☐	RTP1:Infra2	1,008.37	769.88	NFS		0	

> **TIP**: By default, only datastores that are accessible by all hosts in the vSphere cluster will be shown.

7. Click on **OK** twice to close the **Select Linked Clone Datastores** and **Edit AppVolumes-W10** windows, implement the changes, and return to the **AppVolumes-W10** window.

Performing Horizon Pool Maintenance

8. On the right-hand side of the **AppVolumes-W10** window (shown in the following screenshot), open the **View Composer** drop-down menu and click on **Rebalance** to open the **Rebalance** window:

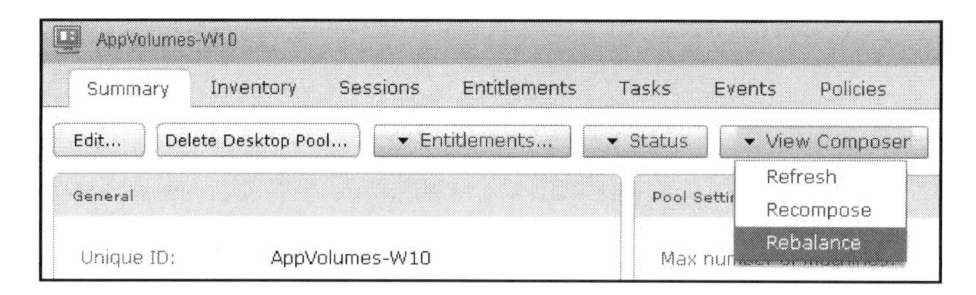

9. On the **Rebalance** page of the **Rebalance** window, review the message and click on **Next**.
10. On the **Scheduling** page of the **Rebalance** window, select the desired scheduling options and click on **Next**. These are the same scheduling options that appear when performing a desktop refresh or recompose.
11. Review the options on the **Scheduling** page of the **Rebalance** window. If changes are required, click on the **Back** button to return to the previous screen. Click on **Finish** to begin or schedule the rebalance operation, depending on what was configured in the previous step.

As with other Horizon maintenance operations, the time required to complete a linked clone desktop rebalance operation varies. Generally speaking, under average circumstances, it will take no more than 15 minutes per desktop, starting from the time that Horizon Composer performs the initial powerdown of the desktop.

The status of the rebalance operation can be viewed in the **Tasks** tab of the target desktop pool window.

Rebalancing individual desktops

A rebalance can also be performed on an individual desktop. This can be helpful in scenarios where only a small number of desktops need to be rebalanced rather than the entire desktop pool. Additionally, a rebalance can also be used to migrate desktops to different datastores-even ones on a different storage system. The following steps describe how to rebalance a single desktop using the Horizon Administrator console:

1. Log in to the Horizon Administrator console using an AD account that has administrative permissions within Horizon.

2. **Go to Catalog** and open the **Desktop Pools** window within the console.
3. In the **Desktop Pools** window, click on the pool that contains the desktop you wish to rebalance.
4. In the window for the desktop pool you selected, click the **Inventory** tab.
5. Click on the linked clone desktop that you wish to recompose. In our example, we will click on the desktop named **APPV10-2** to open the **APPV10-2** window.
6. In the **APPV10-2** window, open the **View Composer** drop-down menu and then click on **Rebalance** to open the **Rebalance** window.
7. Complete the remaining steps to initiate the rebalance operation.

Performing instant clone desktop maintenance

In this section, we will look at the different techniques that are used to perform maintenance on instant clone desktop pools or individual instant clone desktops.

Updating the instant clone desktop parent image

Because of the stateless nature of instant clone desktops, the process used to replace their base images is called push image rather than recompose. Since instant clone desktops do not save their state, all that is really performed during a push image operation is the base VM that the desktops are dependent on is replaced with an updated version.

A push image operation does require that the desktops be briefly powered off, but the operation can be delayed until the current user session ends. The following steps describe how to perform a push image operation on an instant clone desktop pool using the Horizon Administrator console.

> **TIP**
> Before you perform these steps, you should update the desktop master image and take a new snapshot. This is also typically done prior to recomposing a linked clone desktop pool.

1. Log in to the Horizon Administrator console using an AD account that has administrative permissions within Horizon.
2. **Go to Catalog** and open the **Desktop Pools** window within the console.

Performing Horizon Pool Maintenance

3. In the **Desktop Pools** window, click on the instant clone pool you wish to push a new image to. In our example, we will click on the pool called **InstantClone1** to open the **InstantClone1** window.
4. On the right-hand side of the **InstantClone1** window, open the **Push Image** drop-down menu, as shown in the following screenshot, and click on **Schedule** to open the **Schedule Push Image** window:

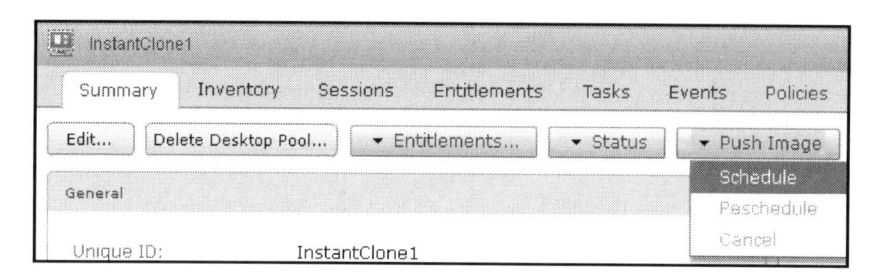

5. In the **Image** section of the **Schedule Push Image** window, as shown in the following screenshot, click on the updated snapshot and then click **Next**:

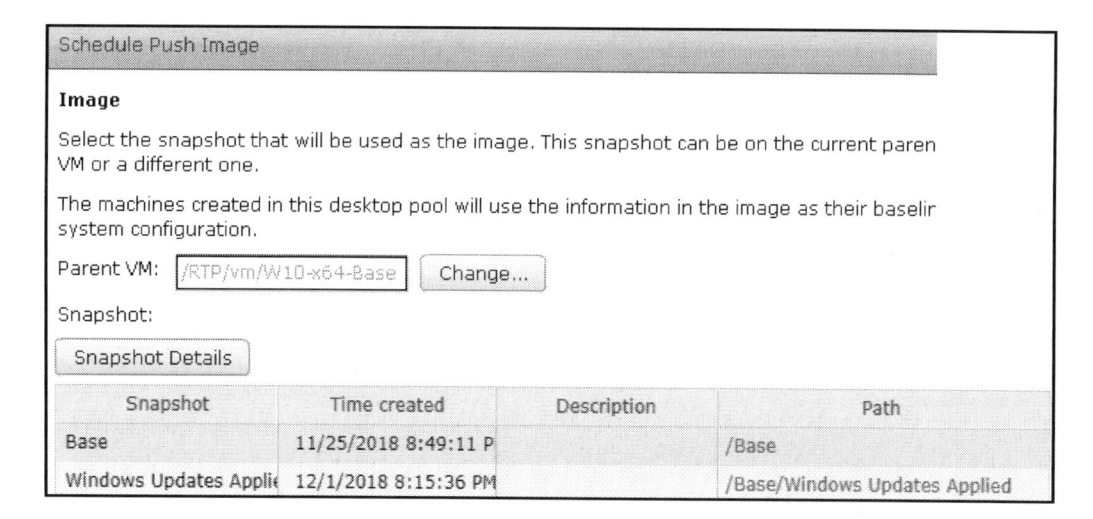

6. Go to **Schedule Push Image** and open the **Scheduling** window. Update the settings as needed and then click **Next**. This is the same screen that is displayed when performing any of the linked clone maintenance operations.
7. Go to **Schedule Push Image** and open the **Ready to Complete** window. Review the operation that will be performed, make changes if needed by clicking the **Back** button, and, when ready, click **Finish** to begin the push image operation.

The time required to complete an instant clone desktop push image operation varies depending on a number of different factors other than the Horizon configuration itself. That being said, once the updated replica disks have finished being cloned, the desktops themselves take only a few seconds to update. The status of the push image operation can be viewed in the **Tasks** tab of the target desktop pool window.

Recovering an individual instant clone desktop

Instant clone desktops have one additional maintenance operation that can be performed, known as **recover**. A recover operation deletes the desktop, at which point it is immediately replaced with a new one. This is the same operation that is performed when a user logs off a desktop session, but in some cases it may be necessary to perform this operation as part of troubleshooting Horizon, or for some other reason.

The following steps describe how to recover an individual instant clone desktop:

1. Log into the Horizon Administrator console using an AD account that has administrative permissions within Horizon.
2. Go to **Catalog** and open the **Desktop Pools** window within the console.
3. In the **Desktop Pools** window, click on the pool that contains the instant clone desktop you wish to recover.
4. In the window for the desktop pool you selected, click the **Inventory** tab.
5. Click on the instant clone desktop that you wish to refresh. In our example, we will click on the desktop named **IC2** to open the **IC2** window.
6. In the IC2 window, click the **Recover** button to open the **Recover Virtual Machine** window, shown in the following screenshot:

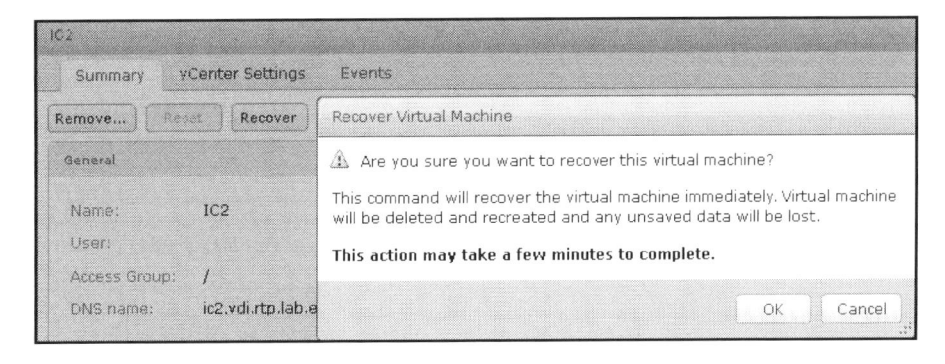

7. In the **Recover Virtual Machine** window, click **OK** to begin the recover operation.

The status of the recover operation can be viewed in the **Tasks** tab of the target desktop pool window. Because of the unique architecture of instant clone desktops, it should typically take less than a minute to recover a single desktop.

Managing Horizon Composer persistent disks

Horizon Composer persistent disks are used to store user profile data and enable it to persist during the Horizon Composer maintenance tasks described in this chapter. A linked clone is not required to have a persistent disk; features such as user profile folder redirection and User Environment Manager enable a linked clone desktop to appear to be persistent, even if it lacks a persistent disk.

Organizations that rely on Horizon Composer persistent disks to store critical user data should be familiar with how to manage them using the native features of Horizon. This section will provide examples of the different Horizon maintenance operations that involve Horizon Composer persistent disks.

> **TIP**
> Persistent disks will work only with the operating system version with which they were deployed. In the event that the original operating system is unavailable, and when the data on the disk must be accessed nonetheless, the persistent disks will need to be manually attached to a new virtual desktop and assigned a Windows drive letter. When attached this way, the persistent disks will simply appear as another hard drive.

Detaching persistent disks

Detaching the persistent disk from a desktop allows it to remain managed by Horizon while discarding the linked clone files that are no longer required. If the persistent disk is needed again at a later date, a desktop can be quickly deployed and the persistent disk is associated with it.

The following steps describe how to detach a persistent disk using the Horizon Administrator console:

1. Log into the Horizon Administrator console using an AD account that has administrative permissions within Horizon.
2. Go to **Resources** and open the **Persistent Disks** window within the console.
3. Highlight the persistent disk that you wish to detach. In the following example, we have highlighted the persistent disk associated with the **APPV10-1** desktop, belonging to the user called **vjason.local\Charles**. Click on the **Detach** button to open the **Detach Persistent Disk** window:

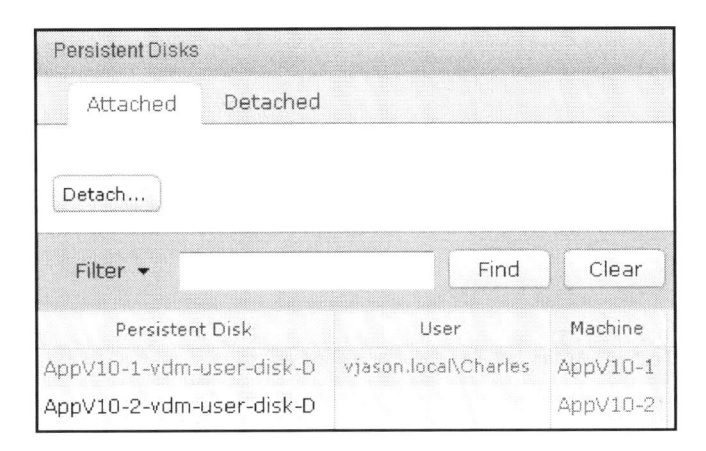

4. In the **Detach Persistent Disk** window (shown in the following screenshot), select where to store the persistent disk. In this example, we will leave it on the current datastore, although organizations may choose to move the disk elsewhere for organizational or archival purposes. Click on **OK** to detach the disk:

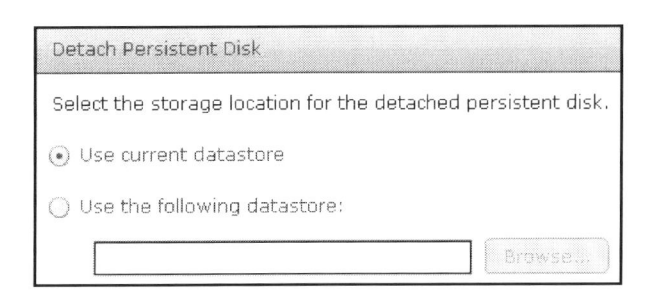

[267]

Performing Horizon Pool Maintenance

The persistent disk will be detached from the linked clone it was associated with, the linked clone will be deleted, and a new unassigned one will be deployed in its place. The detached persistent disk can be found under the **Persistent Disks** window's **Detached** tab, as shown in the following screenshot:

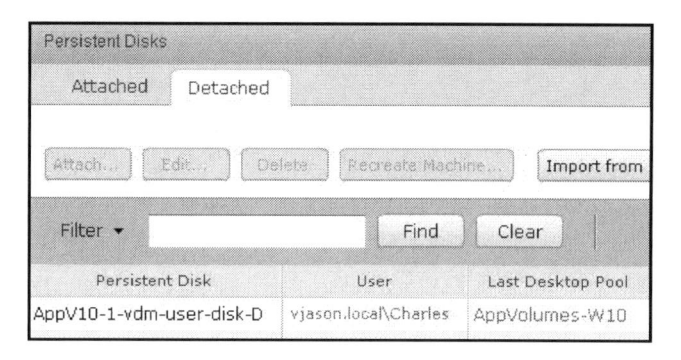

Horizon maintains the information required to quickly recreate the linked clone desktop, including the desktop pool and user it was assigned to.

Recreating a desktop using a persistent disk

The following steps describe how to recreate a linked clone desktop using a previously detached persistent disk:

1. Log in to the Horizon Administrator console using an AD account that has administrative permissions within Horizon.
2. Go to **Resources** and open the **Persistent Disks** window within the console. Click on the **Detached** tab.
3. Highlight the persistent disk you wish to use and click on the **Recreate Machine** button, as shown in the following screenshot:

4. In the **Recreate Desktop** window, review the information and click on **OK**.

Since Horizon retained information about the desktop pool to which the persistent disk was previously assigned, no further information is required to recreate the desktop.

Attaching a detached persistent disk to an existing desktop

Horizon provides the ability to attach a detached persistent disk to an existing desktop, enabling the user of that desktop to have access to that persistent disk, as well as his or her own disk. This can be useful in scenarios where someone needs quick access to the data of a departed user and you want to accomplish this task using only the Horizon Administrator console.

> Remember that linked clone virtual machines should never have their storage configuration changed from within vCenter, as this can render the desktop or Windows RDS server unmanageable by Horizon. Always use the Horizon Administrator console to make changes that affect the linked clone storage configuration.

The following steps describe how to attach the detached persistent disk to an existing desktop:

1. Log into the Horizon Administrator console using an AD account that has administrative permissions within Horizon.
2. Go to **Resources** and open the **Persistent Disks** window within the console. Click on the **Detached** tab.
3. Highlight the persistent disk that you wish to use and click on the **Attach...** button. This button is shown in the screenshot in step 3 of the previous section of this chapter.
4. In the **Attach Persistent Disk** window, select the desktop that you wish to assign the disk to and click on **OK**. Only desktops with assigned users will appear in the list of choices.

The persistent disk will be attached to the existing desktop and the contents will be accessible to the user whose desktop it was assigned to.

Importing a persistent disk

To support a wider range of recovery scenarios, Horizon supports importing persistent disks and using them to create a new desktop. An imported persistent disk will not have any owner or desktop pool information, so the Horizon administrator will have to choose a new owner and desktop pool. This can be useful in scenarios where an organization wishes to retain persistent disks offline or on secondary storage that is not attached to the Horizon infrastructure.

The following steps describe how to import persistent disks and use them to create a new desktop:

1. Log into the Horizon Administrator console using an AD account that has administrative permissions within Horizon.
2. Go to **Resources** and open the **Persistent Disks** window within the console. Click on the **Detached** tab.
3. Click on the **Import from vCenter...** button, as shown in the following screenshot:

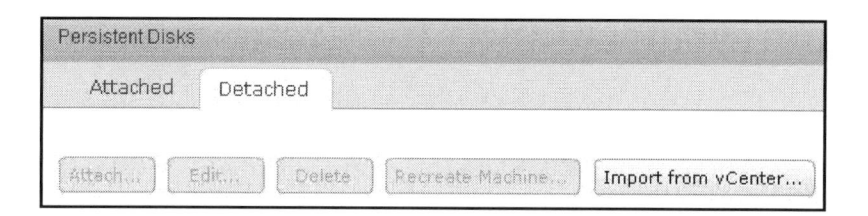

4. In the **Import Persistent Disk From vCenter** window (shown in the following screenshot), select the appropriate resources, including the following:
    - **vCenter Server**: Target vCenter Server
    - **Datacenter**: Target vCenter datacenter object
    - **Linked clone pool**: Pool where the linked clone will be created
    - **View Folder**: Optional—destination folder for the virtual machine object
    - **Persistent Disk File**: The file you will be importing
    - **User**: The user who will be assigned the desktop that will use the persistent disk:

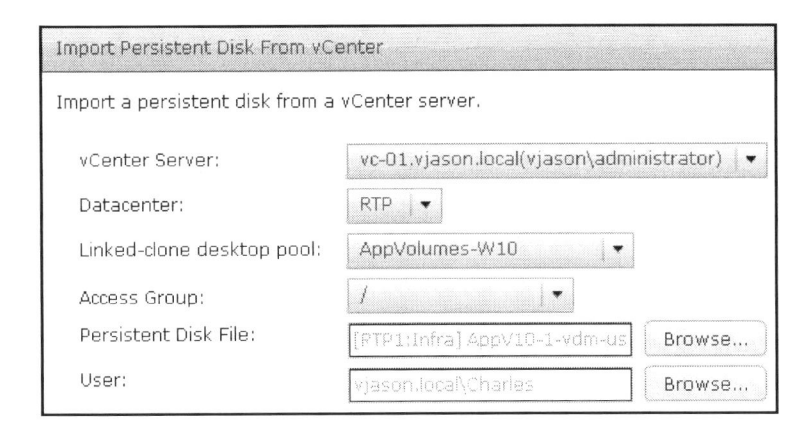

Import Persistent Disk From vCenter	
Import a persistent disk from a vCenter server.	
vCenter Server:	vc-01.vjason.local(vjason\administrator)
Datacenter:	RTP
Linked-clone desktop pool:	AppVolumes-W10
Access Group:	/
Persistent Disk File:	[RTP1:Infra] AppV10-1-vdm-us Browse...
User:	vjason.local\Charles Browse...

5. Click on **OK** to import the persistent disk and associate it with the linked clone desktop.

To access the data on the imported persistent disk, the user it was assigned to will need to log into the newly configured desktop.

Summary

In this chapter, we learned about different Horizon Composer instant and linked clone maintenance operations. We discussed each of these maintenance tasks and went through some examples of how they are used.

We learned about updating the instant clone parent image, and looked at the linked clone refresh, recompose, and rebalance operations. We learned about what they are for and what to be aware of concerning their use. We then went through the operation of each. We also learned about persistent disk maintenance, including how to detach them from existing desktops, how to reattach them, and how to use them to recreate a new linked clone desktop.

In the next chapter, we will discuss how to create a virtual desktop master image, an important task that requires careful consideration and planning.

Questions

1. Name the maintenance operations you can perform on instant clone and linked clone pools.
2. Explain the difference between a refresh and a recompose operation.
3. Name some of the reasons why you might refresh a linked clone desktop pool.
4. Name some of the reasons why you might refresh a single linked clone desktop.
5. When it comes to updating the master image, which are faster: instant clones or linked clones?
6. Explain how you can recreate a desktop using a detached persistent data disk.
7. Name all the things that occur during a desktop pool rebalance operation.

Further reading

The following resources may be used to learn more about the topics described in this chapter:

- VMware documentation:
    - **VMware Horizon** (https://docs.vmware.com/en/VMware-Horizon-7/index.html)
    - **VMware vSphere** (https://www.vmware.com/support/pubs/vsphere-esxi-vcenter-server-pubs.html)

10
Creating a Master Virtual Desktop Image

When designing your VMware Horizon infrastructure, creating a master virtual desktop image is second only to infrastructure design in terms of importance. The reason for this is simple: as ubiquitous as Microsoft Windows is, by default, it is not optimized for use as a virtual desktop.

The good news is that, with a careful bit of planning and a thorough understanding of what your end users need, you can build a Windows desktop that serves all your needs, while requiring the bare minimum of infrastructure resources.

A default installation of Windows contains many optional components and configuration settings that are either unsuitable for, or likely not needed in, a Horizon environment. Understanding the impact of these items and settings plays an important part in keeping the performance of the Horizon infrastructure consistent over time.

Uninstalling unnecessary components and disabling services or scheduled tasks that are not required will help reduce the amount of resources the desktop requires and ensure that the Horizon infrastructure can properly support the planned number of desktops, even as resources are oversubscribed.

> **TIP**
> Oversubscription is defined as having assigned more resources than are physically available. This is most commonly done with processor resources in virtualized environments, where a single-server processor core may be shared among multiple virtual machines. As the average desktop does not require 100 percent of its assigned resources at all times, we can share those resources between multiple desktops without affecting their performance.

This chapter, will focus on a number of different topics related to the planning and creation of a master virtual desktop image.

Creating a Master Virtual Desktop Image

In this chapter we will look at the following topics:

- The importance of optimizing a master virtual desktop image
- Sample Windows OS optimization results
- How to customize the master image filesystem cluster size
- Tasks to perform before optimizing Windows
- How to disable unwanted application-specific update features
- How to permanently remove Windows Store applications
- How to optimize the Windows OS
- The importance of customizing the default Windows-user local profile

The importance of desktop optimization

While nothing stops you from using a default installation of any OS or software package in a virtualized environment, you may find it difficult to maintain consistent levels of performance in Horizon environments where many of the resources are shared, and, in almost every case, oversubscribed in some manner. In this section, we will examine a sample of the CPU and disk I/O resources that could be recovered were you to optimize the master virtual desktop image.

> **TIP**
> Due to the technological diversity that exists from one organization to the next, optimizing your master virtual desktop image is not an exact science. The optimization techniques used and their end results will likely vary from one organization to the next, due to factors unrelated to Horizon or vSphere.

Optimization results – Horizon desktop IOPS

Desktop optimization benefits one infrastructure component more than any other: storage. Until all flash storage arrays achieve price parity with the traditional spinning disk arrays many of us use today, reducing the per-desktop **Input/Output Operations Per Second** (**IOPS**) required will continue to be an important part of any Horizon deployment.

> **TIP**
> On a per-disk basis, a flash drive can accommodate more than 15 times the IOPS of an enterprise SAS or SCSI disk, or 30 times the IOPS of a traditional desktop SATA disk. Organizations that choose an all-flash array may find that they have more than sufficient IOPS capacity, even without doing any optimization.

The following graph shows the reduction in IOPS that occurred after performing the optimization techniques described later in this chapter. This measurement was observed while testing the desktop using a user workload simulator:

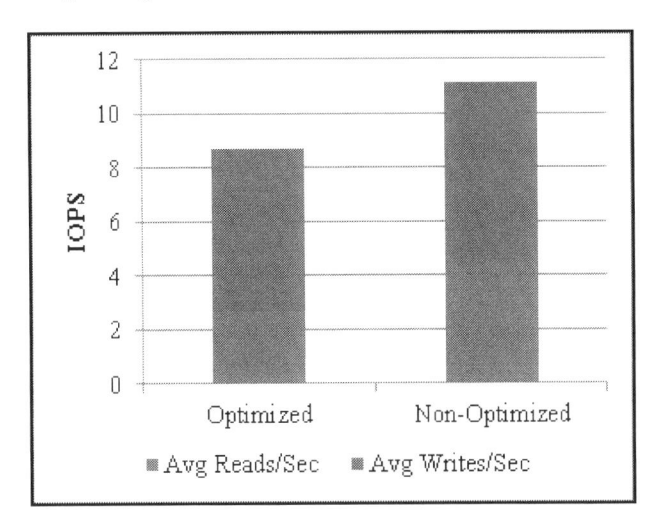

The optimized desktop generated 15 percent fewer IOPS during the user workload simulation. By itself, that may not seem like a significant reduction, but when multiplied by hundreds or thousands of desktops, the savings become more significant.

> **TIP**
> In an era where the cost of flash-based storage systems and flash-based or dependent **Software Designed Storage** (**SDS**) used in **Hyper Converged Infrastructure** (**HCI**) appliances seems to continually decrease, there is less of a concern to consider measures that focus on decreasing Windows desktop IOPS. Just know that optimizing your virtual desktop master image is about decreasing the total infrastructure resources it requires, and not just the storage itself.

Optimization results – CPU utilization

Horizon recommends a maximum of 8 to 10 desktops per physical CPU core. There is no guarantee that your Horizon implementation will be able to attain this high consolidation ratio, though, as desktop workloads will vary from one type of user to another. The optimization techniques described in this chapter will help maximize the number of desktops you can run per server core.

The following graph shows the reduction in ESXi server **% Processor Time** that occurred after performing the optimization techniques described later in this chapter:

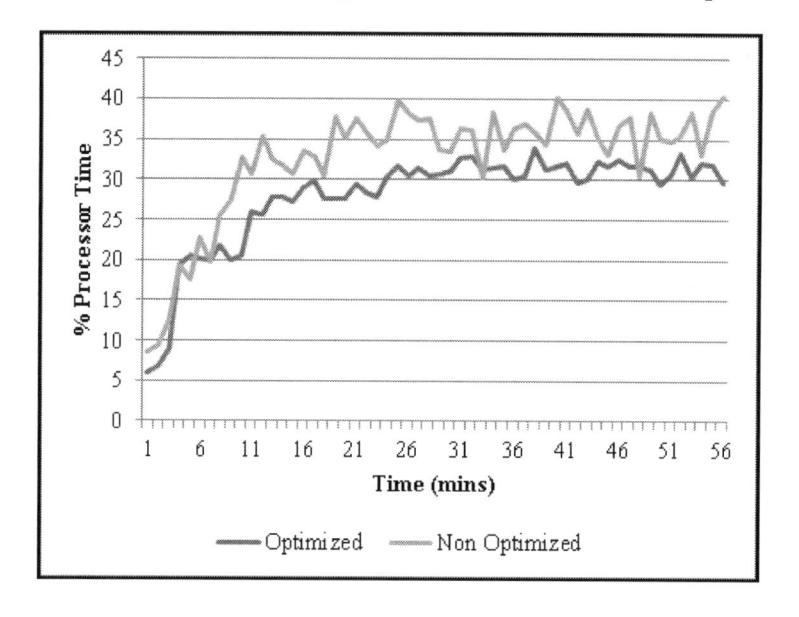

> **TIP**
>
> **% Processor Time** is one of the metrics that can be used to measure server processor utilization within vSphere. The statistics in the preceding graph were captured using the vSphere ESXTOP command-line utility, which provides a number of performance statistics that the vCenter performance tabs do not offer in a raw format that is more suited for independent analysis.

The optimized desktop required between 5 and 10 percent less processor time during the user workload simulation. As was the case with the IOPS reduction, the savings are significant when multiplied by large numbers of desktops.

Customizing the Windows desktop OS cluster size

Microsoft Windows uses a default cluster size, also known as an allocation unit size of 4 KB, when creating the boot volume during a new installation of Windows. The cluster size is the smallest amount of disk space that will be used to hold a file, which affects how many disk writes must be made to commit a file to disk. For example, when a file is 12 KB in size and the cluster size is 4 KB, it will take three write operations to write the file to disk.

The default 4 KB cluster size will work with any storage option that you choose to use with your environment, but that does not mean it is the best option. Storage vendors frequently do performance testing to determine which cluster size is optimal for their platforms, and it is possible that some of them will recommend that the Windows cluster size should be changed to ensure optimal performance.

Customizing the Windows cluster size during the installation process

The following steps outline how to change the Windows cluster size during the installation process; the process is the same for both Windows 8.1 and Windows 10. In this example, we will be using an 8 KB cluster size, although any size can be used, based on the recommendation from your storage vendor:

> **TIP**: The cluster size can only be changed during the Windows installation, and not after. If your storage vendor recommends the 4 KB Windows cluster size, the default Windows settings are acceptable.

1. Boot from the Windows OS installer ISO image or physical CD, and proceed through the install steps until the **Where do you want to install Windows?** window appears.
2. Press *Shift + F10* to bring up a command window.
3. In the command window, enter the following commands:

   ```
   diskpart
   select disk 0
   create partition primary size=100
   active
   format fs=ntfs label="System Reserve" quick
   create partition primary
   format fs=ntfs label=OS_8k unit=8192 quick
   assign
   exit
   exit
   ```

4. Click on **Refresh** to refresh the **Where do you want to install Windows?** window.

5. Select **Drive 0 Partition 2: OS_8k**, as shown in the following screenshot, and click on **Next** to begin the installation:

Name	Total size	Free space	Type
Drive 0 Partition 1: System Reserve	100.0 MB	88.0 MB	System
Drive 0 Partition 2: OS_8k	31.9 GB	31.8 GB	Primary

Where do you want to install Windows?

The System Reserve partition is used by Windows to store files critical to the boot process and will not be visible to the end user. These files must reside on a volume that uses a 4 KB cluster size, so we created a small partition solely for that purpose. Windows will automatically detect this partition and use it when performing the Windows installation.

> **TIP**
> Once Windows is installed, it is possible to move the boot files to the partition Windows was installed on and then remove the System Reserve partition, but only if the following four conditions are all met: the Windows partition is formatted using a **GUID Partition Table** (**GPT**) rather than a **Master Boot Record** (**MBR**), and the Windows partition uses a 4 KB cluster size; Windows BitLocker encryption is not enabled, and the Windows partition is a primary partition. If any of these items are untrue, the System Reserve partition must be left as is.

In the event that your storage vendor recommends a different cluster size from that shown in the previous example, replace the `8192` in the sample command in step 3 with whatever value the vendor recommends, in bytes, without any punctuation.

Permanently removing Windows Store applications

Windows 8.1 and later include a number of applications that may not be required in a Horizon environment. These applications are referred to as **Metro Apps** in Windows 8.1, but have since been renamed to **Modern Apps** with the release of Windows 10.

Some of these applications, such as ones that are weather- and news-related, are active even if they are not being used by the end user. The resources required to operate these applications place unnecessary load on the Horizon infrastructure, which is why the applications should be removed unless explicitly required.

The following procedure outlines how to remove some or all of the Online Windows Store packages, which are those that will be installed for all new users of the desktop image:

1. Open an elevated Windows PowerShell prompt.
2. To review the Windows store applications that will be installed for all users of the desktop image, as shown in the following screenshot, use the following PowerShell command:

   ```
   Get-AppxProvisionedPackage -Online | Select DisplayName, PackageName
   ```

   ```
   PS C:\> Get-AppxProvisionedPackage -Online | Select DisplayName, PackageName

   DisplayName                              PackageName
   -----------                              -----------
   Microsoft.BingFinance                    Microsoft.BingFinance_2014.
   Microsoft.BingFoodAndDrink               Microsoft.BingFoodAndDrink_
   Microsoft.BingHealthAndFitness           Microsoft.BingHealthAndFitn
   Microsoft.BingMaps                       Microsoft.BingMaps_2014.130
   Microsoft.BingNews                       Microsoft.BingNews_2014.221
   ```

3. To remove all Windows Store applications except the Windows Store itself, execute the following command, as shown in the following screenshot:

   ```
   Get-AppxProvisionedPackage -Online | Where-Object
   {$_.PackageName -notlike "*store*"} | Remove-
   AppxProvisionedPackage -Online
   ```

   ```
   PS C:\> Get-AppxProvisionedPackage -Online | Where-Object {$_.PackageName -notlike "*store*"} | Remove-AppxProvisionedPa
   ckage -Online

   Path            :
   Online          : True
   Restart Needed  : False

   Path            :
   Online          : True
   Restart Needed  : False
   ```

> **TIP**: Removing Windows Store is not recommended, as it is required for some features of Windows to function properly.

Creating a Master Virtual Desktop Image

4. To remove *a single* Windows Store application, using the information obtained in step 1 for the application **PackageName**, execute the following command:

```
Get-AppxProvisionedPackage -Online | Where-Object
{$_.PackageName -like "*BingFinance*"} | Remove-
AppxProvisionedPackage -Online
```

> **TIP:** When using the `-like` switch, along with wildcards, you can also use switches similar to `-like "*Bing*"` to remove all applications with "Bing" in the title.

Refer to the following Microsoft Windows IT Pro Center links for information about these and other PowerShell commands used to manage Windows Store applications:

- *Get-AppxPackage* (https://docs.microsoft.com/en-us/powershell/module/appx/get-appxpackage?view=win10-ps)
- *Remove-AppxPackage* (https://docs.microsoft.com/en-us/powershell/module/appx/remove-appxpackage?view=win10-ps)
- *Get-AppxProvisionedPackage* (https://docs.microsoft.com/en-us/powershell/module/dism/get-appxprovisionedpackage?view=win10-ps)
- *Remove-AppxProvisionedPackage* (https://docs.microsoft.com/en-us/powershell/module/dism/remove-appxprovisionedpackage?view=win10-ps)

Windows OS pre-deployment tasks

The following tasks are unrelated to the other optimization tasks that are described in this chapter, but they should be completed prior to placing the desktop into production.

Installing VMware Tools

VMware Tools should be installed prior to the installation of the Horizon Agent software. To ensure that the master image has the latest version of the VMware Tools software, apply the latest updates to the host ESXi server prior to installing the tools package on the desktop.

> **TIP:** The same applies if you are updating your VMware Tools software. The Horizon Agent software should be reinstalled after the VMware Tools software is updated to ensure that the appropriate Horizon drivers are installed in place of the versions included with VMware Tools.

Removing an unwanted application – native update features

A number of applications install their own updater utility, including the almost ubiquitous Adobe Acrobat Reader and the Oracle Java Runtime Environment. If `linked-clone` or `instant-clone` desktops are being used, and regular updates of the desktop master image are made, these updater utilities should be disabled to reduce the growth of the desktop OS disk. As for full-clone desktops, you may wish to leave these updaters enabled, unless the software will be updated by other methods.

The procedure used to disable or remove these components will vary based on the architecture of the individual application. The following are examples of how to disable the Adobe Acrobat Reader and the Java Runtime Environment application updaters. For other applications, consult with their vendors for instructions on how to control or otherwise disable similar features with their software packages.

Disabling the Adobe Acrobat Reader DC update feature

The following steps outline how to disable the Adobe Acrobat automatic updater:

> In the following instructions, the **Product Name**, **Product Version**, and **Product Code** registry keys will differ based on the version of Acrobat Reader that is installed. Simply select the installed version and make the remaining changes as instructed.

1. From an elevated Windows Command Prompt, load the `regedit.exe` application.
2. Navigate to **HKLM** | **SOFTWARE** | **Policies** | **Adobe** | **Product Name** | **Product Version** | **FeatureLockdown**.

Creating a Master Virtual Desktop Image

3. Update the `bUpdater` DWORD value to a value of 0, as shown in the following screenshot, which disables the updater and removes the updater-related user interface items. If this registry entry does not exist, create it as a DWORD value:

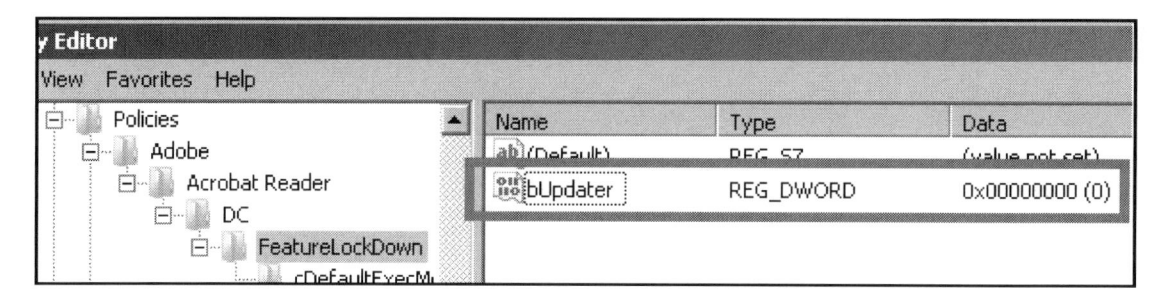

4. Navigate to **HKLM | SOFTWARE | Wow6432Node | Adobe | Adobe ARM | Legacy | Product Name | Product Code**.

5. Update the **Mode** DWORD value to a value of 0, as shown in the following screenshot, which prevents the download or installation of software updates. If this registry entry does not exist, create it as a DWORD value:

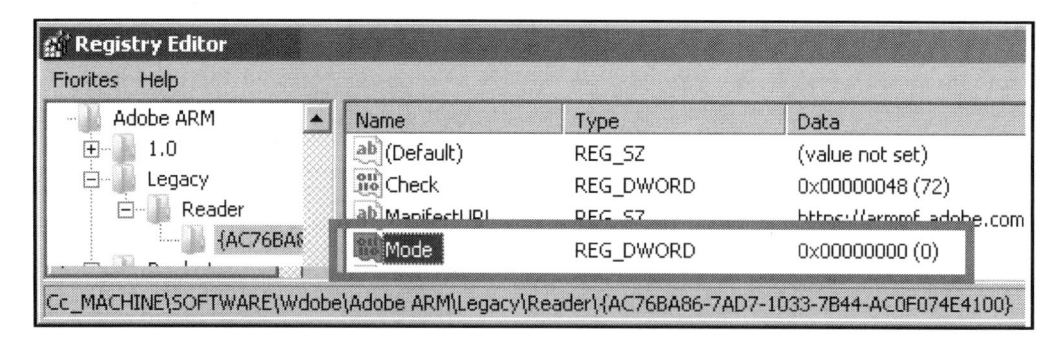

> **TIP**
> Step 4 is optional, and primarily used to configure the default updater settings, rather than disable them entirely using the procedure outlined in step 3. When configuring Horizon full-clone desktops, you may wish to skip step 3 and set the value of **Mode** to 4 in step 5, which automatically downloads and installs updates.

If you wish to prevent users from performing manual updates within the Acrobat Reader application itself, use the Adobe Acrobat Group Policy templates mentioned in the *Adobe Acrobat Enterprise Administration Guide* (https://www.adobe.com/devnet-docs/acrobatetk/tools/AdminGuide/index.html). These Group Policy objects enable you to completely disable the ability to update Acrobat Reader using the application menus.

Disabling the Java updater utility

The following steps outline how to disable the Java updater utility:

1. From an elevated Windows Command Prompt, load the `regedit.exe` application.
2. For 32-bit Windows versions, navigate to **HKLM | SOFTWARE | JavaSoft | Java Update | Policy**; for 64-bit Windows versions, navigate to **HKLM | SOFTWARE | Wow6432Node | JavaSoft | Java Update | Policy**.
3. Update the **EnableJavaUpdate** DWORD value to the value of 0, as shown in the following screenshot, which disables the updater:

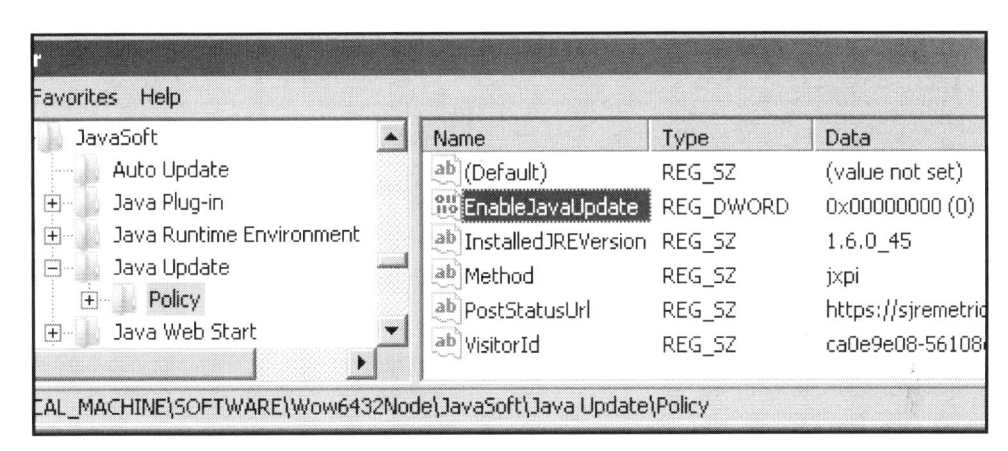

Windows OS optimizations

A default installation of Microsoft Windows contains a number of configuration settings, components, and scheduled tasks that may not be required or are not desirable in a Horizon environment. This section will detail these settings, and provide instructions on how to make the recommended changes.

> **TIP**
> A team of VMware engineers have created a tool that can be used to automatically apply (or remove) a number of different Windows desktop and server OS optimizations. The **VMware OS Optimization Tool** (https://labs.vmware.com/flings/vmware-os-optimization-tool) may be used to perform many of the optimizations detailed throughout the rest of this chapter, as well as additional ones not listed.

[283]

Many of these optimizations are implemented using Windows Group Policies, which can be applied to the master virtual desktop image prior to deployment, or by using domain-enforced Active Directory Group Policies. It is recommended to apply the majority of the policies directly to the master image when using linked clone and instant clone desktops. Doing this allows the Horizon pool maintenance operation to proceed more quickly, as the majority of the settings the desktop requires will already have been applied. Were the necessary policies to be applied using only domain-based Group Policy templates, a Horizon desktop or RDS server maintenance operation would be likely to take more time and resources to complete as each desktop must process the policy updates and make the necessary configuration changes. In addition, the desktops may require a reboot to fully implement the policy changes.

> Most of the information in this section applies to both Windows 8.1 and 10. If a specific recommendation applies only to Windows 8.1 or 10, it will be identified.

Disabling Windows Error Reporting

Windows Error Reporting compiles error reports that occur when an application crashes and, if configured to, forwards the information on to Microsoft. Linked clone and instant clone desktops are less likely to require this feature, as the underlying OS is likely to be updated on a regular basis. This feature may be needed when using full clone desktops, though, as those desktops generally have a much longer life cycle that may require occasional application troubleshooting. The following steps outline how to disable Windows Error Reporting:

1. Using the Group Policy console, edit the local desktop or domain-based Group Policy.
2. Select the **Computer Configuration** | **Administrative Templates** | **Windows Components** | **Windows Error Reporting** policy object.
3. Set **Disable Windows Error Reporting** to **Enabled**.

Disabling automatic updates

Linked clone and instant clone desktops are typically updated using a Horizon pool maintenance operation, which negates the need for the Windows update service. To prevent these desktops from installing updates, which would significantly increase the OS disk size, this Windows feature should be disabled.

> **TIP:** If your environment uses full clone virtual desktops, which are deployed using a vSphere template, you should regularly update the template with the latest Windows patches or other required configuration changes. This ensures that new desktops will require little or no additional configuration upon deployment.

The following steps outline how to disable Windows Update:

1. Using the Group Policy console, edit the local desktop or domain-based Group Policy.
2. Select the **Computer Configuration** | **Administrative Templates** | **Windows Components** | **Windows Update** policy object.
3. Set the **Configure Automatic Updates** to **Disabled**.

Delete the `C:\Windows\SoftwareDistribution\Download` folder to remove any update packages that may have already been downloaded to the desktop.

> **TIP:** Do not disable Automatic Updates if you are using `System Center Configuration Manager (SCCM)`; SCCM requires it to install Windows updates.

Removing unnecessary Windows components

There are a number of Windows components that are installed by default that may not be needed in a Horizon environment. To further reduce the resources required by the desktop, remove any Windows components that are not required. Some components that may not be required include the Indexing Service, Internet Printing Client, Media Features, Tablet PC Components, and Windows Search.

The following steps outline how to remove unnecessary Windows components:

1. Open the Windows Control Panel.
2. Navigate to **Programs** | **Turn Windows features on or off**.
3. Remove any unnecessary components.

Pre-compiling Microsoft .NET Framework assemblies

Microsoft .NET compiles framework assemblies on an as-needed basis when .NET-dependent programs are launched for the first time. This process can be both CPU- and disk-intensive, so you should pre-compile all .NET Framework assemblies on the master virtual desktop image prior to deployment.

> **TIP**: Microsoft .NET 3.5 is not installed by default on Windows 8.1. If it is required, it should be installed prior to completing the following procedure. Microsoft .NET 3.5 can be installed using the **Control Panel** entry **Programs | Turn Windows features on or off**.

The following steps outline how to pre-compile all versions of the .NET Framework assemblies:

1. Use Windows Update to download and install all available .NET updates, and reboot as needed.
2. Open an elevated Windows Command Prompt.
3. On 32-bit Windows computers, navigate to `C:\Windows\Microsoft.NET\Framework\v4.0.30319`; on 64-bit Windows computers, navigate to `C:\Windows\Microsoft.NET\Framework64\v4.0.30319`.
4. Type `ngen.exe executequeueditems` and hit *Enter*, as shown in the following screenshot. This process may require several minutes to complete; in the example provided, there were no additional assemblies to pre-compile:

> **TIP**: In some cases, a newer .NET Framework may be installed that has a higher version number than 4.0.30319. If step 4 fails, repeat step 3, but navigate to the directory created for that version and complete step 4 again.

```
Administrator: C:\Windows\System32\cmd.exe

C:\Windows\Microsoft.NET\Framework64\v4.0.30319>ngen executequeueditems
Microsoft (R) CLR Native Image Generator - Version 4.0.30319.34209
Copyright (c) Microsoft Corporation.  All rights reserved.
All compilation targets are up to date.

C:\Windows\Microsoft.NET\Framework64\v4.0.30319>
```

Disabling Windows hibernation

When the Windows OS goes into hibernation mode, a significant amount of write storage I/O is required to write the contents of the system's RAM to the `hiberfil.sys` file. An equivalent amount of storage-read I/O is needed to resume the desktop from hibernation. During periods of heavy use, this additional I/O may affect the performance of other desktops that share the same storage. In addition to that, the `hiberfile.sys` file requires disk space equivalent to that of the desktops, configured RAM, which further increases the amount of per-desktop space required. To reduce desktop storage utilization, hibernation should be disabled.

To disable hibernation, execute the following command from an elevated Windows Command Prompt:

```
powercfg /hibernate off
```

> **TIP:** If required, Horizon can manage workstation power states using native vSphere features. Desktops can be powered down or suspended as required, based on the configuration of the desktop pool. These settings are discussed further in `Chapter 7`, *Creating Horizon Desktop Pools*.

Disabling Windows System Restore

Windows System Restore is used to restore a Windows desktop to a previous state, a useful feature when using a traditional physical desktop. This feature is generally not required when using linked clone and instant clone desktops, though, as those desktops can be restored to their original state using Horizon maintenance operations.

> **TIP:** vSphere snapshots can be used in place of System Restore if you need the ability to quickly undo changes made to your master virtual desktop images or full-clone desktops. vSphere snapshots should not be used with linked clone and instant clone desktops, as the snapshot would prevent Horizon maintenance operations from completing successfully.

Generating Windows System Restore snapshots generates intermittent spikes in storage I/O, and also requires additional disk space. To minimize the per-desktop storage utilization, this feature should be disabled on all linked clone and instant clone desktops, as well as full-clone desktops unless the feature is explicitly required. The following steps outline how to disable system restore:

1. Right-click on **This PC** (Windows 8.1 and newer) and select **Properties**.
2. Select **Advanced system settings | System Protection**.
3. Click on the **Configure** button to open the **System Protection** window.
4. Under the **Restore Settings** section, click on the **Disable system protection** (Windows 8.1 or newer) radio button.

Sizing virtual machine RAM properly

The amount of RAM used for the desktop affects both the amount of storage space required and the likelihood that it will need to swap memory into the Windows page file.

Windows initially sizes the `C:\pagefile.sys` system file based on the amount of RAM the virtual machine is granted. From that point forward, the file expands as needed in response to Windows OS virtual memory requirements. The page file will also increase in size when the desktop RAM is increased.

The amount of RAM assigned to the virtual machine affects whether it is likely to need to utilize the Windows page file. Using the page file generates additional storage I/O, which we prefer to avoid in a Horizon environment where the storage is shared among multiple desktops. Using the techniques described in `Chapter 1`, *VMware Horizon Infrastructure Overview*, the desktop should be assigned sufficient RAM so that, under normal circumstances, it will not need to use the page file.

The Microsoft TechNet article **Pushing the Limits of Windows: Virtual Memory** (`https://blogs.technet.microsoft.com/markrussinovich/2008/11/17/pushing-the-limits-of-windows-virtual-memory/`) contains additional guidance about how to properly size Windows system RAM.

Setting the Windows page file to a fixed size

By default, Windows dynamically expands and shrinks the Windows page file as required. This leads to fragmentation of the page file and additional storage I/O. To minimize the storage I/O associated with page file operations, set the page file to a fixed size.

> Not every desktop configuration will require a page file. If you determine that a desktop pool has low per-desktop memory requirements, common when minimal applications are being used, you can disable the page file entirely.

The following steps outline how to configure a fixed-size page file:

1. Right-click on **This PC** (Windows 8.1 and newer) and select **Properties**.
2. Select **Advanced system settings | Advanced**.
3. Click on the **Settings...** button under **Performance** to open the **Performance Options** window.
4. In the **Performance Options** window, click on the **Advanced** tab.
5. In the **Advanced** tab, click on the **Change...** button.
6. Uncheck the **Automatically manage paging file size for all drives** checkbox.
7. Click on the **Custom size** radio button, and populate the **Initial size** and **Maximum size** fields with the same value in MB.
8. Click on the **Set** button to implement the changes, and then click on **OK** three times to complete the action. Reboot the desktop if prompted.

Refer to the Microsoft TechNet article *Pushing the Limits of Windows: Virtual Memory* for additional guidance about how to determine the fixed page file size.

Disabling paging the executive

By default, Windows writes kernel-mode drivers and system code to the Windows page file when not in use, which leaves more RAM available for the system. This action generates additional storage I/O, which we prefer to limit in a Horizon environment.

If the virtual machine is assigned sufficient memory, this feature is unnecessary and therefore should be disabled to reduce the per-desktop storage I/O. The following steps outline how to disable paging of the executive:

1. From an elevated Windows Command Prompt, load the `regedit.exe` application.
2. Navigate to **HKLM | System | CurrentControlSet | Control | Session Manager | Memory Management**.
3. Update the **Disable Paging Executive** DWORD to a value of 1 (from 0) to disable the feature.

Disabling Content Indexing of the desktop drive

Content Indexing creates storage I/O overhead, as it builds the content index cache for the desktop filesystems. If Content Indexing is not required, or if the desktop is a linked-clone or instant-clone, this feature should be disabled to reduce desktop storage I/O.

> **TIP**: Linked clone and instant clone desktops would require a Content Index after each Horizon pool maintenance operation, significantly increasing the storage I/O required to complete these operations. Content Indexing should be disabled when using these types of desktop.

The following steps outline how to disable indexing of the local disk:

1. Open the **This PC** (Windows 8.1 and newer) window, right-click on **C:**, and click on **Properties**.
2. On the **General** tab, clear the **Allow files on this drive to have contents indexed in addition to file properties** checkbox.
3. Click on **OK** to initiate the change, and click on OK again to update the indexing settings using the default option (**Apply changes to Drive C:\, subfolders and files**).

During the application of the new indexing settings, an error message stating that a file is in use may occur. If this happens, select **Ignore All**. If the desktop has additional hard disks, repeat this process for each of those disks.

Disabling Content Indexing for the remaining file locations

Windows indexes a number of system and user-specific folders by default. To reduce the storage I/O overhead associated with these indexing operations, remove any unnecessary folder locations from the index list.

> **TIP**: When using linked clone and instant clone desktops, it is suggested to uncheck all file locations from the **Indexed Locations** window.

The following steps outline how to disable the indexing of the remaining default locations:

1. Open the Windows **Control Panel**.
2. Navigate to **Indexing Options**.
3. Click on the **Modify** button to open the **Indexed Locations** window.
4. Deselect any locations or folders in the list that you do not want indexed and click on **OK**.

Disabling unnecessary services

There are multiple Windows services that are typically not useful in a Horizon environment and can be disabled to reduce desktop resource requirements. These services, a sample of which is listed in this section, can be disabled using the Windows Services MMC plugin. A description of each of these services is provided in the Services MMC plugin:

- Diagnostic Policy Service
- IP Helper
- Network Location Awareness
- Security Center
- Shell Hardware Detection
- SSDP Discovery
- SuperFetch (disable only when using non-persistent desktops; additional information about SuperFetch follows this section)
- Telephony
- Themes
- Touch Keyboard and Handwriting Panel Service

- Windows Defender Service (disable only when using alternative antivirus or anti-malware platforms)
- Windows Audio
- Windows Connect Now (Config Registrar; Windows 8.1 and newer only)
- Windows Update (optional for full clones; it should be disabled in linked and instant clones)
- WLAN AutoConfig
- WWAN AutoConfig

For a more detailed list of Windows services and configuration options, consult the *Windows 8.1 Service Configurations* and *Windows 10 Service Configurations* guides at www.blackviper.com.

SuperFetch

SuperFetch analyzes desktop usage patterns and pre-populates system RAM with the programs the user is most likely to use. When using non-persistent desktops, this results in unnecessary storage I/O, as the optimizations will not persist and will be repeated each time the desktop is used. Additionally, SuperFetch also allocates additional system RAM for its use, which increases the amount of per-desktop RAM required.

For persistent Horizon desktops that also have larger amounts of RAM, you should leave SuperFetch enabled so that Windows can optimize the disk layout of the prefetch data and proactively load user binaries into RAM. This will make the desktop more responsive, and, since the desktop is persistent, the SuperFetch optimizations will persist across Horizon client sessions.

Removing unnecessary scheduled tasks

Windows has a number of scheduled tasks that are either undesirable or not required in a Horizon environment. These tasks can be removed or disabled using the Windows **Control Panel | Schedule tasks** utility or an elevated Command Prompt. The following is a list of some of the tasks that should be reviewed to determine whether they are required within your Horizon environment; if not, they should be disabled or removed. Details about each task are available in the **Schedule tasks** Windows Control Panel utility:

- \Microsoft\Windows\Application Experience\ProgramDataUpdater
- \Microsoft\Windows\Application Experience\StartupAppTask—Windows 8.1 and newer only

Chapter 10

- \Microsoft\Windows\Autochk\Proxy
- \Microsoft\Windows\Bluetooth\UninstallDeviceTask
- \Microsoft\Windows\Customer Experience Improvement Program\Consolidator
- \Microsoft\Windows\Customer Experience Improvement Program\KernelCeipTask
- \Microsoft\Windows\Customer Experience Improvement Program\UsbCeip
- \Microsoft\Windows\Defrag\ScheduledDefrag
- \Microsoft\Windows\DiskDiagnostic\Microsoft-Windows-DiskDiagnosticDataCollector
- \Microsoft\Windows\FileHistory\File History (maintenance mode)—Windows 8.1 and newer only
- \Microsoft\Windows\Maintenance\WinSAT—Windows 8.1 and newer only
- \Microsoft\Windows\Mobile Broadband Accounts\MNO Metadata Parser—Windows 8.1 and newer only
- \Microsoft\Windows\Power Efficiency Diagnostics\AnalyzeSystem
- \Microsoft\Windows\Ras\MobilityManager
- \Microsoft\Windows\SpacePort\SpaceAgentTask—Windows 8.1 and newer only
- \Microsoft\Windows\SpacePort\SpaceManagerTask—Windows 8.1 and newer only
- \Microsoft\Windows\SystemRestore\SR
- \Microsoft\Windows\UPnP\UPnPHostConfig
- \Microsoft\Windows\Windows Error Reporting\QueueReporting
- \Microsoft\Windows\Windows Media Sharing\UpdateLibrary

To remove a task using an elevated Windows Command Prompt, use a command similar to the following example:

```
SCHTASKS /Delete /TN \Microsoft\Windows\Autochk\Proxy" /F
```

[293]

Creating a Master Virtual Desktop Image

Changing the Group Policy refresh interval

By default, all computers in an AD domain attempt to refresh their Group Policy settings every 90 minutes, with a 30-minute offset. This is extended to limit the peak amount of network bandwidth that is consumed when refreshing the Group Policies. By default, the Group Policy is also updated at every boot of the OS. The following steps outline how to change the Group Policy refresh interval:

1. Using the Group Policy console, edit the local desktop or domain-based Group Policy.
2. Select the **Computer Configuration | Administrative Templates | System | Group Policy** policy object.
3. Double-click on the **Group Policy refresh internal for computers** policy to open the policy properties window.
4. Click on the **Enabled** radio button to enable the policy.
5. In the **Options** area, configure how often the Group Policy will be applied to the computer by providing a value for the **Minutes** field.
6. In the same area, set the amount of random time to be added to the Group Policy refresh interval by providing a value for the **Minutes** field. This randomizes the policy refresh interval to prevent the desktops from refreshing the policies at the same time.

Disabling the Windows boot animation

Windows displays a start-up animation during the Windows portion of the boot process. This animation can only be seen when you are connected to the virtual machine console, and requires additional vSphere resources to display, which is why it should be disabled. The following steps outline how to disable the Windows boot animation:

1. From an elevated Windows Command Prompt, load the `msconfig.exe` application.
2. Select the **Boot** tab.
3. Under **Boot options**, check the **No GUI boot** and **Base video** checkboxes, as shown in the following screenshot. Click on **OK** to finalize the changes:

[294]

Optimizing the Windows profile

There are various Windows settings that cannot be changed using normal Group Policies or other post-installation customizations, such as those we have already described in this chapter. To implement these additional settings, we can customize the default Windows local user profile, implementing changes that will be applied to all users who log into the desktop for the first time.

In most cases, it is possible to create customized scripts or Group Policies that make these changes after a user has already logged into the account. This generally requires changes to the desktop system registry, and an in-depth understanding of how the settings are recorded and updated within Windows.

As we discussed earlier, and this is particularly the case with linked clone and instant clone desktops, it is preferable to apply as much of your customization as you can to the master virtual desktop image. This ensures that the desktops are prepared using the minimum system resources required and are fully configured prior to their use. Policies that apply after the desktops are deployed may require an additional reboot to fully implement, which is not ideal for a Horizon environment. The process used to customize the default local user profile is outlined in the Microsoft Windows IT Pro Center article **Create mandatory user profiles** (https://docs.microsoft.com/en-us/windows/client-management/mandatory-user-profile). The following settings, each of which helps reduce desktop resource utilization, are recommended to be made to the default local user profile.

> **TIP**
> The changes in this section will only apply to other desktop users if they are applied using the default user profile. The changes will not affect any profiles that are already present on the desktop image.

Adjusting for best performance

Some of the more advanced UI features, such as menu fading and animations, require additional desktop CPU and memory resources. The following steps outline how to disable these effects:

1. Right-click on **This PC** (Windows 8.1 and newer) and click on **Properties.**
2. Click on **Advanced system settings** to open the **System Properties** window.
3. In the **System Properties** window, click on the **Advanced** tab.
4. Under **Performance**, click on the **Settings** button.
5. Click on the **Adjust for best performance** radio button, and then click on **OK** twice to close the window and update the settings.

Turning off system sounds

System sounds require additional server and network resources and may not be required in every Horizon environment. If sounds are required, the Horizon administrator may want to configure a custom sound scheme based on the specific needs of the organization. The following steps outline how to turn off the system sounds:

1. Navigate to **Control Panel | Sound | Sounds**.
2. Set **Sound Scheme:** to **No Sounds**, or create and then select a custom sound scheme.

Disabling the Windows background and screen saver

Displaying a custom Windows wallpaper or screen saver requires additional server and network resources. The Windows wallpaper should be changed to either none or a solid color by choosing the appropriate option based on the version of Windows being used. The screen saver should be disabled, or set to a blank screen, by choosing the appropriate option based on the version of Windows being used.

Summary

In this chapter, we have learned about how to configure the master virtual desktop image and about what makes it different than configuring a traditional desktop.

We have discussed how to customize the Windows file system cluster size before beginning the installation process, how to permanently remove Windows store apps, disabling application native updaters, Windows optimizations that can reduce the desktop resource requirements, and when to use a custom Windows default user profile.

In `Chapter 11`, *Implementing App Volumes*, we will discuss how to deploy and configure the VMware App Volumes application-layering software.

Questions

1. Why is it important to optimize your master virtual desktop images?
2. Name at least five common Windows features that are most likely not needed when working with linked clone virtual desktops.
3. Name some application settings (not Windows itself) you would consider customizing when creating a virtual desktop master image.
4. Why do you typically disable Windows hibernation when working with virtual desktops?
5. Why do you typically disable features like Windows Update when working with linked clone virtual desktops?
6. Why do you typically disable any scheduled disk fragmentation when working with linked clone virtual desktops?
7. What is the benefit of using a default Windows profile?

Further reading

The following resources may be used to learn more about the topics described in this chapter:

- **VMware Horizon** (`https://www.vmware.com/support/pubs/view_pubs.html`)
- **VMware vSphere** (`https://www.vmware.com/support/pubs/vsphere-esxi-vcenter-server-pubs.html`)

11
Implementing App Volumes

VMware App Volumes is an optional component of VMware Horizon Enterprise Edition that extends two additional capabilities to virtual desktops:

- It delivers natively installed applications on demand, independent of the desktop image, using shared App Volumes AppStacks.
- It seamlessly roams user-installed applications between Horizon client sessions, even in non-persistent desktop environments using App Volumes Writable Volumes.

App Volumes uses vSphere VMDK files to enable transparent, on-demand, application portability without making any permanent changes to the virtual desktop. Applications are delivered and maintained using the App Volumes function and appear as if they were natively installed, because technically speaking they were. When used in combination with the software described in `Chapter 12`, *Implementing User Environment Manager*, you have the ability to provide a persistent desktop experience using non-persistent desktops, without having to buy any third-party software to do so.

This chapter will discuss the installation, configuration, backup, and recovery of the App Volumes manager servers and their associated AppStacks and user Writable Volumes.

By the end of this chapter, we will have covered the following:

- An overview of VMware App Volumes AppStacks, Writable Volumes, and the App Volumes Manager server
- App Volumes prerequisites
- How to install and configure an App Volumes Manager server
- How to add additional App Volumes Manager servers
- How to install the App Volumes Agent
- How to create and assign an AppStack to users
- How to update an AppStack
- How to assign Writable Volumes to users

- How to delete Writable Volumes
- Additional App Volumes resources for review

> **TIP**: This chapter is not meant to convey all possible App Volumes use cases or configurations. The goal is to help you stand up a basic App Volumes environment, and leverage its core features within your Horizon environment. I will provide several external resources that I recommend anyone intending to make heavy use of App Volumes in their organization ought to review.

App Volumes overview

Chapter 1, *VMWare Horizon Infrastructure Overview*, provided an overview of most of the key features of VMware App Volumes. To summarize that information, VMware App Volumes can be used to decouple applications from Horizon desktops and Windows RDS servers, be they user-installed or ones packaged and assigned by App Volumes administrators. The following diagram explains the conceptual relationship between the Horizon desktop and the Windows RDS server OS, the App Volumes Agent, and the AppStacks and Writable Volumes:

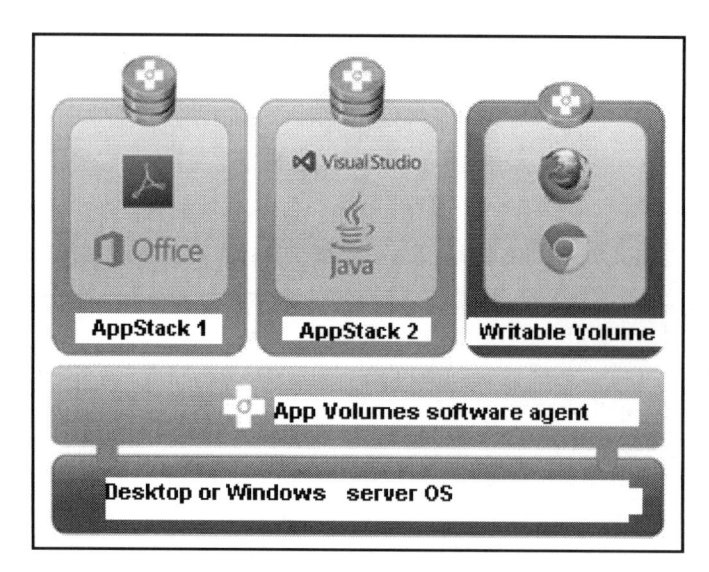

Chapter 11

> **TIP**
> RDS servers used with Horizon application streaming cannot use Writable Volumes, nor would they need them, since Horizon clients using that feature don't have the ability to install applications on the hosting server.

The capabilities enabled by App Volumes are transparent to the client, as shown in the following screenshot, which shows the client view from Windows Explorer for a Horizon desktop, next to the virtual desktop hard disk configuration as seen in the vSphere web client. In the web client, we see **Hard disk 4**, which is the writable volume, and **Hard disk 5**, which is a single App Volumes AppStack (the remaining disks are all part of the Horizon non-persistent desktop). These disks are silently and transparently integrated into the OS at login, and detached when the client session is ended:

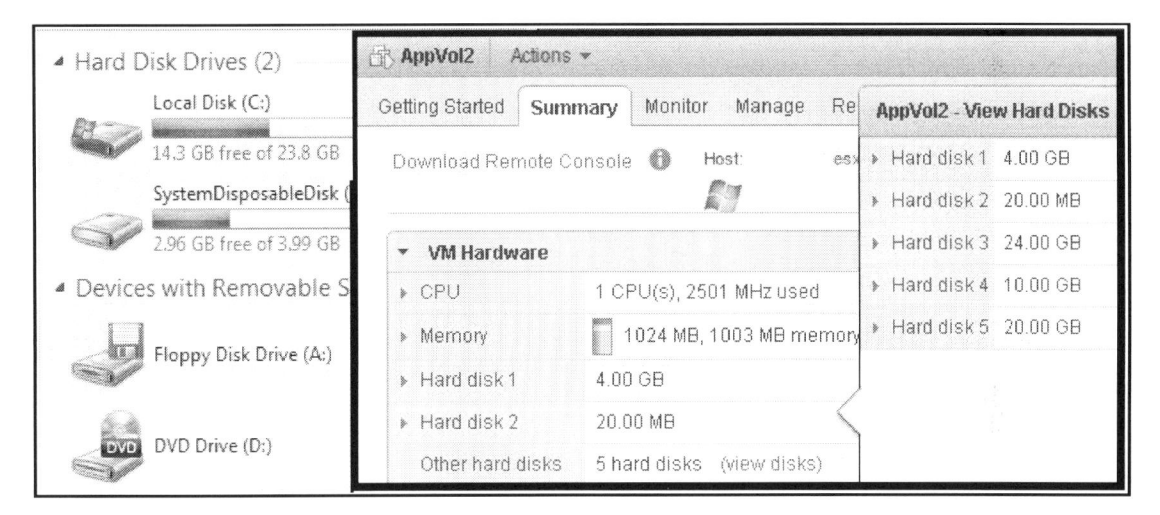

When combined with a user persona management solution, such as the one discussed in `Chapter 12`, *Implementing User Environment Manager*, App Volumes enables Horizon customers to provide a persistent desktop experience while leveraging non-persistent desktops (using Writable Volumes), and while also reducing the number of virtual desktop master images to support, since we have decoupled their applications (using AppStacks).

In the remainder of this chapter, we will learn how to implement and administer VMware App Volumes.

App Volumes prerequisites

A production installation of App Volumes will require the following items:

- App Volumes ISO file and license file.
- A Microsoft Active Directory domain at functional level 2003 or later.

> **TIP:** VMware recommends that you configure Active Directory for LDAP over SSL (LDAPS) or StartTLS (LDAP over TLS) to ensure secure communications between App Volumes and Active Directory, although you can configure App Volumes without it. The Microsoft Developer post entitled *Step-by-Step Guide to Setup LDAPS on Windows Server* outlines how to configure LDAPS (https://blogs.msdn.microsoft.com/microsoftrservertigerteam/2017/04/10/step-by-step-guide-to-setup-ldaps-on-windows-server/).

- A Microsoft SQL Server 2008R2 SP2 or later database and account with database owner permissions:
    - Consult the App Volumes documentation (https://docs.vmware.com/en/VMware-App-Volumes/index.html) for a complete list of supported SQL versions and patch levels
    - SQL Server Clustered Instances and Server Mirroring are also supported
    - In this chapter, we will use a database named `RTP_AppVolumes1` and a SQL user named `svc_appvolumes`
- vSphere 5.5.x or newer, including vCenter.
- Static IP addresses and pre-created DNS entries for each of the App Volumes Manager servers.
- App Volumes Manager-supported OSes and other requirements:
    - Windows 2008 R2 or newer
    - 4 GB RAM, 4 vCPU, 1 GB disk space
    - .NET 3.5 Framework
    - Accessible over TCP ports 80, 443, and 5985

- App Volumes Agent-supported OSes and hardware and configuration requirements:
    - Windows 7 SP1 or newer, excluding Vista (for use as a desktop OS, hot fix 3033929 required)
    - Windows 2008 R2 or newer (for use as an RDS server or as a desktop OS):
        - For desktops, disable the Control Read and Write Access to Removable Devices or Media group policy setting
    - 1 GB RAM, 1 vCPU, 5 MB disk space
- A provisioning computer, deployed as a virtual machine, running the same OS as the App Volumes clients; multiple provisioning computers will be required if you use more than one desktop or Windows RDS OS version.
- Two AD user accounts, or one account that has been granted both sets of the following permissions:
    - Read access to the Active Directory
    - vCenter permissions, as outlined in the next section of this chapter, entitled vCenter permissions
    - In the examples provided, we will use a single account named `svc-appvolumes`
- One AD group who you will grant administrative access to App Volumes. In the examples provided, we will use a group named `AppVolumes_Admins`.
- One AD group to assign AppStacks to. In the examples provided, we will use a group named `AppVolumes_NotepadPlus`.
- One AD group to create writable volumes for. In the examples provided, we will use a group named `AppVolumes_WV`.
- One vSphere datastore per 1,000 writable volumes. The default Writable Volume template is 10 GB in size, so these volumes could require as much as 10 TB of space each.
- One vSphere datastore for every 2,000 clients who will attach to AppStacks. The size of these AppStack datastores will vary based on the number of AppStacks that will be created.

> **TIP**
> The figures provided with regard to the number of App Volumes Manager appliances, and the number of users per vSphere datastore, is subject to change. Consult the VMware App Volumes product documentation (`https://docs.vmware.com/en/VMware-App-Volumes/index.html`) and other resources listed throughout this chapter for updated information on the recommended infrastructure configuration.

While not explicitly required, we will be using AD security groups to entitle users to AppStacks and Writable Volumes. It is possible to assign each directly to users using the same methods that will be demonstrated in this chapter.

vCenter permissions

The App Volumes vCenter service account (`svc-appvolumes` in the example provided) requires the following permissions to each of the Horizon vCenter Servers. These permissions may be granted using the same technique referenced in the *Create a vCenter role and grant permissions* section of `Chapter 2`, *Implementing Horizon Connection Server*:

- **Datastore**: Allocate space, Browse datastore, Low-level file operations, Remove file, and Update virtual machine files
- **Global**: Cancel task
- **Host**: Local operations—Reconfigure virtual machine
- **Sessions**: View and stop sessions
- **Tasks**: Create task
- **Virtual machine – Configuration**: Add existing disk, Add new disk, Add or remove device, Query unowned files, Change resource, Remove disk, Settings, and Advanced
- **Inventory**: Create new, Move, Register, Remove, and Unregister
- **Provisioning**: Promote disks

Installing App Volumes Manager server

The App Volumes Manager server software is deployed using the product ISO file, which is named in a format similar to `VMware_AppVolumes_vXXXX.iso`.

Chapter 11

The following steps outline the installation process:

1. Mount the App Volumes ISO on the App Volumes Manager host server.
2. From the server console, browse to the ISO **Installation** folder and then execute `setup.exe` to begin the App Volumes installation process.
3. In the **VMware App Volumes Installation Wizard** window, click **Next >**.
4. In the **License Agreement** window, accept the license agreement and then click **Next>**.
5. In the **App Volumes Install Screen** window, click the **Install App Volumes Manager** radio checkbox and then click **Install**.
6. In the **Choose a Database** window, click the **Connect to an existing SQL Server Database** radio checkbox and then click **Next >**.
7. In the **Database Server** window, enter the name of the database server that hosts the pre-created App Volumes database, enter the App Volumes database owner user credentials, click **Browse...** and select the App Volumes database, uncheck the **Overwrite existing database (if any)** checkbox, as shown in the following screenshot, and then click **Next >**:

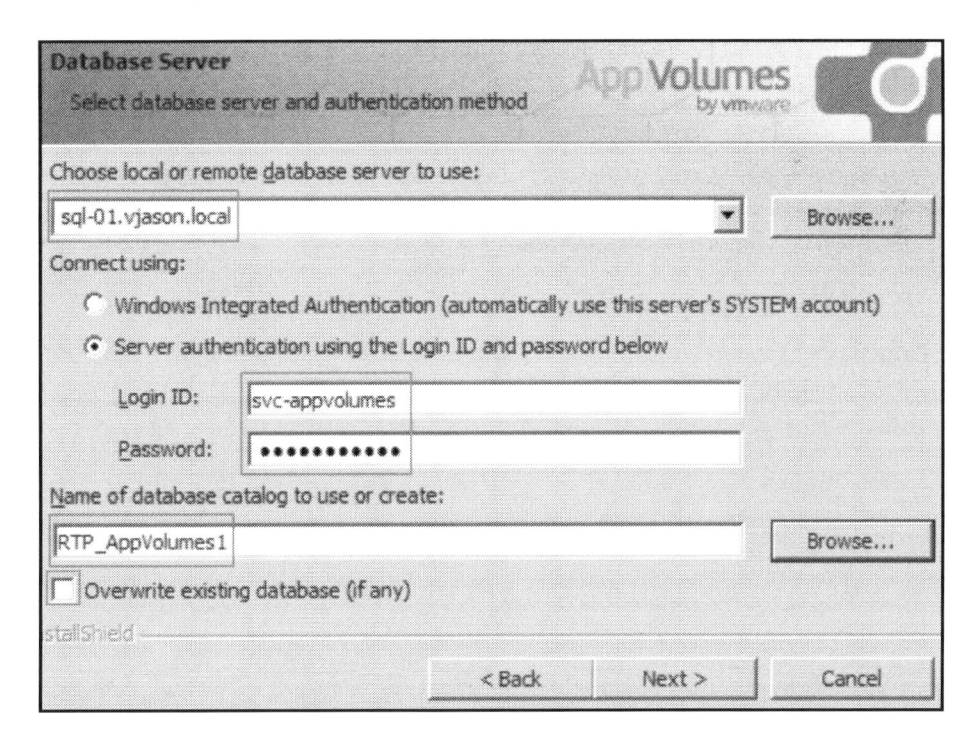

[305]

8. In the **Choose Network Ports and Security options** window, it is recommended to leave all options at their defaults and then click **Next >**.
9. In the **Destination Location** window, accept the default installation directory or make changes as needed and then click **Next >**.
10. In the **Ready to Install the Program** window, click **Install**.
11. In the **App Volumes Wizard Completed** window, click **Finish**. The App Volumes Manager shortcut shown in the following screenshot will have been placed on the server desktop as part of the installation process:

The App Volumes Manager appliance has been deployed, and is ready for final configuration steps. To replace the default self-signed SSL certificate, refer to the procedure found in the App Volumes Administration Guide (https://docs.vmware.com/en/VMware-App-Volumes/index.html).

Configuring App Volumes Manager

App Volumes is configured using a web-based GUI accessed on the App Volumes Manager server. For information about options not used, or otherwise referenced, during the configuration process, consult the *VMware App Volumes* documentation (https://docs.vmware.com/en/VMware-App-Volumes/index.html). The following steps outline the App Volumes configuration process:

1. Log in to the App Volumes Manager web console using the web browser, and the FQDN of the App Volumes Manager server or the shortcut on the desktop of the App Volumes Manager server. In the example provided, the URL is https://rtpappv01.vjason.local. No login is required during the initial configuration process.
2. On the **Welcome to App Volumes Manager** page, click **Get Started**.
3. In the **License** section of the configuration wizard, click **Edit** to enter your license information and then click **Next**. If you do not yet have a license, click **Next** to continue using the evaluation license.

4. In the **Active Directory Domains** section of the configuration wizard, populate the fields with your Active Directory information and the App Volumes service account ID and password, as shown in the following screenshot, and then click **Register**:

Active Directory Domain Name:	vjason.local	Fully qualified Active Directory domain name Example: vmware.com
Domain Controller Hosts:		This may be left blank (to use any Domain Controller) Example: adserver.vmware.com, 10.107.XX.XXX, 10.107.XX.XX
LDAP Base:		This may be left blank (to use all of Active Directory) Example: OU=engineering,DC=vmware,DC=com
Username:	svc-appvolumes	This may be a user with read-only access Example: administrator
Password:	•••••••••••	Password is stored encrypted
Security:	Secure LDAP (LDAPS) ▼ ☐ Disable certificate validation (insecure)	Requires corresponding ActiveDirectory configuration
Port:	636	This may be left blank (to use default port)

[Register]

> **TIP**: The default **Security:** setting is **Secure LDAP (LDAPS)**, but if your Active Directory does not have that configured, you will get an error when you click **Register**. You may need to change the setting to basic **LDAP**, which is unencrypted but should work.

5. In the updated **Active Directory Domains** section of the configuration wizard, click **Next**.

[307]

Implementing App Volumes

6. In the **Administrator Roles** section of the configuration wizard, search for the security group that contains the App Volumes admins, as shown in the following screenshot, and then click **Assign**:

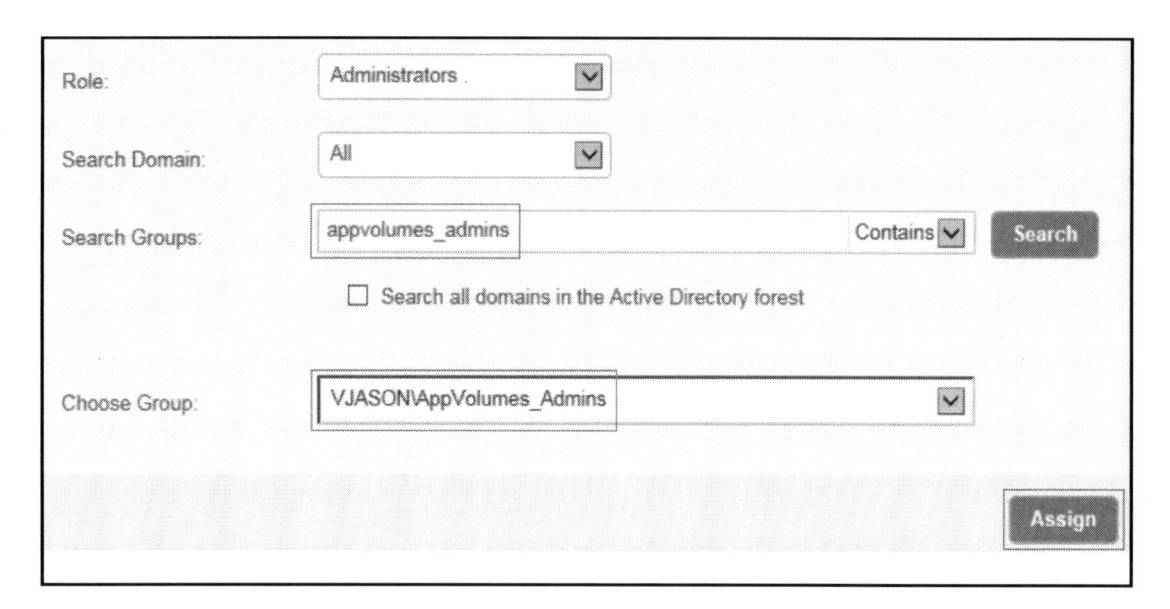

Role:	Administrators
Search Domain:	All
Search Groups:	appvolumes_admins — Contains — Search
	☐ Search all domains in the Active Directory forest
Choose Group:	VJASON\AppVolumes_Admins

Assign

7. In the updated **Administrator Roles** section of the configuration wizard, click **Next**.
8. In the **Machine Managers** section of the configuration wizard, provide the values for your vCenter Server, as shown in the following screenshot, and then click **Save**; you may review the various vCenter options and their purpose, but it is not necessary to change them at this time. In the following screenshot, we are connecting to that server using the `svc-appvolumes` account, which has only those vCenter permissions outlined previously in this chapter:

[308]

Chapter 11

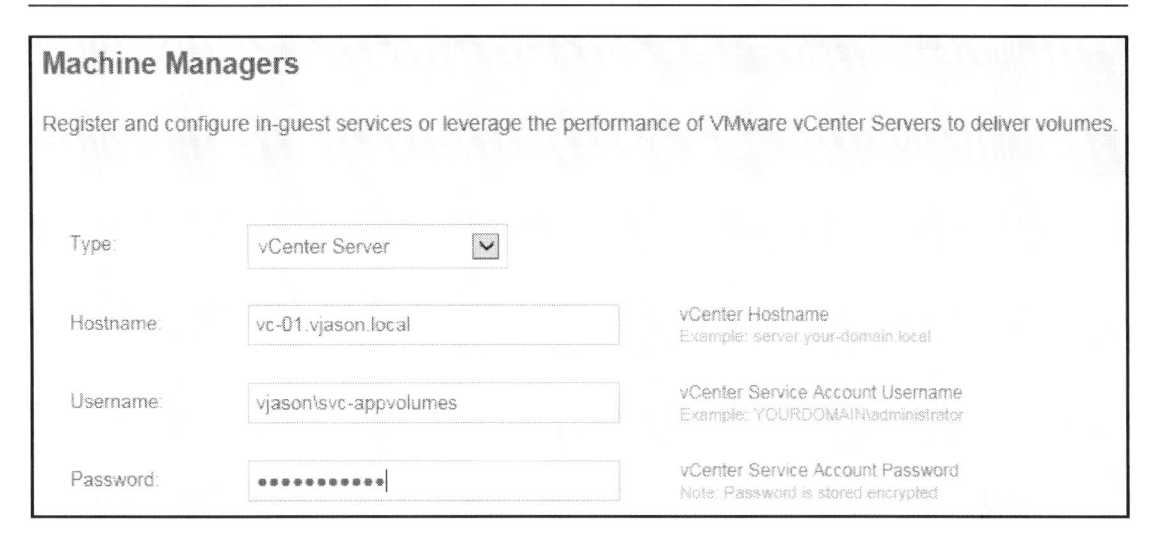

Machine Managers		
Register and configure in-guest services or leverage the performance of VMware vCenter Servers to deliver volumes.		
Type:	vCenter Server	
Hostname:	vc-01.vjason.local	vCenter Hostname Example: server.your-domain.local
Username:	vjason\svc-appvolumes	vCenter Service Account Username Example: YOURDOMAIN\administrator
Password:	●●●●●●●●●●●●	vCenter Service Account Password Note: Password is stored encrypted

> **TIP:** Additional vCenter servers may be added once the initial configuration is complete.

9. If your App Volumes Manager server does not trust the issuing certificate authority for your vCenter host, an **Untrusted Certificate** notification will appear next. Review the certificate details to ensure they are accurate and then click **Accept**.

> **TIP:** Refer to the App Volumes Administration Guide (https://docs.vmware.com/en/VMware-App-Volumes/index.html) for instructions on how to modify your App Volumes Manager server to trust certificate authorities.

10. In the updated **Machine Managers** section of the configuration wizard, click **Next**.

Implementing App Volumes

11. In the updated **Storage** section of the configuration wizard, use the **Default Storage Location** drop-down menus to select vSphere datastores that are accessible to all of your Horizon vSphere hosts. Leave the various **Path** locations at their defaults, as shown in the following screenshot, and then click **Save**:

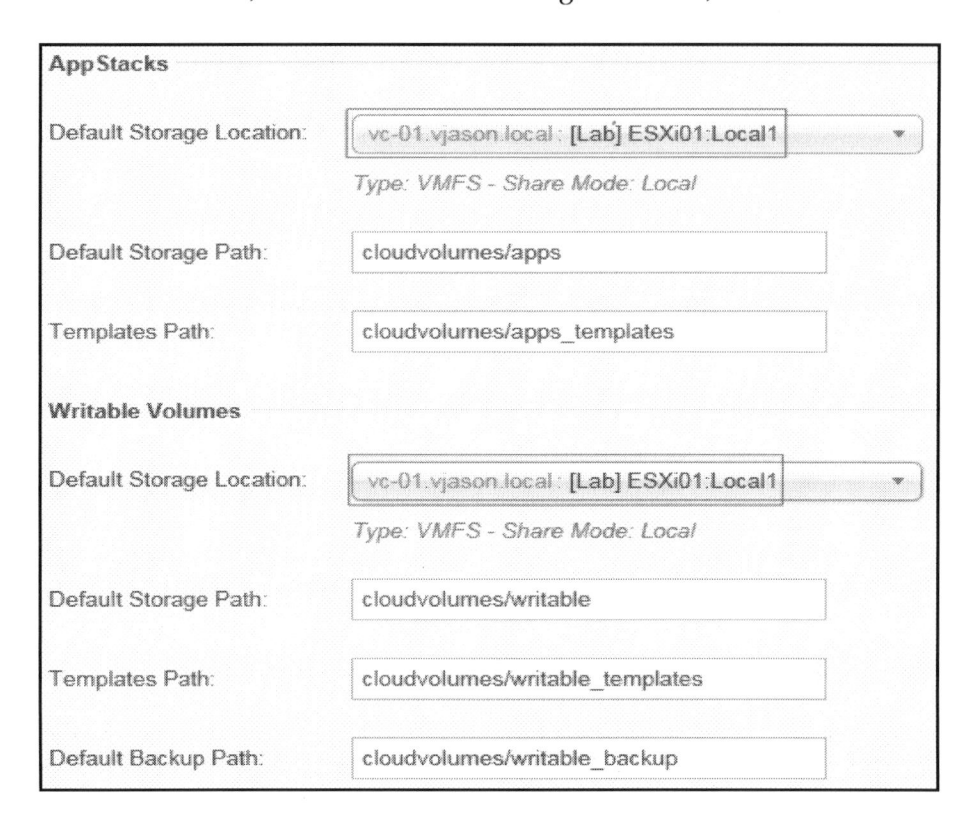

App Stacks	
Default Storage Location:	vc-01.vjason.local : [Lab] ESXi01:Local1
	Type: VMFS - Share Mode: Local
Default Storage Path:	cloudvolumes/apps
Templates Path:	cloudvolumes/apps_templates

Writable Volumes	
Default Storage Location:	vc-01.vjason.local : [Lab] ESXi01:Local1
	Type: VMFS - Share Mode: Local
Default Storage Path:	cloudvolumes/writable
Templates Path:	cloudvolumes/writable_templates
Default Backup Path:	cloudvolumes/writable_backup

> **TIP**: The example provided uses a single host with local storage; a production environment that uses VSAN or remotely mounted shared volumes will look slightly different.

12. In the **Confirm Storage Settings** pop-up window, click the **Import volumes immediately** radio checkbox and then click **Set Defaults**.
13. In the **Settings** section of the configuration wizard, review the different options for further customizing App Volumes. It is not necessary to make any further changes, but if you intend to use writable volumes, note the **Writable Volume Backups** settings, as shown in the following screenshot. Click **Save** when finished:

[310]

Writable Volume Backups	
Regular Backups:	⦿ Every 7 days (?)
Storage Location:	vc-01.vjason.local : [Lab] ESXi01:Local1 ▾
	Type: VMFS - Share Mode: Local
Storage Path:	cloudvolumes/writable_backup

Your App Volumes Manager server has been configured and is now available for use. It is recommended that you deploy at least one additional App Volumes Manager servers for load balancing and availability purposes. The following section outlines how to deploy additional App Volumes Manager servers.

Deploying additional App Volumes Manager servers

App Volumes Manager stores configuration information in the SQL database, so, to deploy additional App Volumes Manager servers, you only need to perform a small subset of the original installation steps. To deploy additional App Volumes Manager servers and enable them for use by clients, perform step 1, and either steps 2 or 3, from the following procedure:

1. Deploy and configure the new App Volumes Manager server using the steps outlined in the *Installing App Volumes Manager server* section of this chapter, and use the same database connection details as the first App Volumes Manager server that was installed.
2. Use a load balancer to distribute client traffic to all of the App Volumes Manager servers (optional; use if you do not want to modify the Windows registry on the App Volumes clients).
3. Modify the Windows registry on computers with the App Volumes agent installed so that they point to all available App Volumes Manager servers (optional; use if you will not be using a load balancer).

> **TIP:** This procedure is outlined in the *Configuring native load balancing for the App Volumes Agent software* section of this chapter.

You may repeat this procedure as required to ensure that your App Volumes infrastructure is sufficiently scaled to meet performance and redundancy requirements.

Installing the App Volumes Agent

The App Volumes Agent software is used to enable communication between App Volumes clients and the App Volumes Manager servers, and is typically installed in one of two places:

- Horizon desktop virtual desktop master image
- Horizon Windows RDS server master image

The agent installation files are located on the App Volumes ISO in the `Installation\Agent` folder, and should be copied to a location accessible to App Volumes clients. The installation process is the same regardless of where the agent software is being installed, so only one example will be provided.

The following steps outline the App Volumes Agent installation process:

1. Double-click the `App Volumes Agent.msi` agent installer to launch the **App Volumes Agent Installation Wizard**. Click **Next >** to proceed through the initial installation steps, including accepting the license agreement.
2. In the **Server Configuration** window, enter the FQDN for one of the local App Volumes Manager servers (`rtpappv01.vjason.local` in the example provided) and default port (`443`). If using the default App Volumes SSL certificate, check the **Disable Certificate Validation with App Volumes Manager** checkbox, and then click **Next >**.

> **TIP:** If you are going to use a load balancer with your App Volumes Manager servers, you should provide the load-balanced URL here instead. If you intend to use the native App Volumes Agent failover capabilities, you will need to add additional App Volumes Manager server addresses using the method outlined in the next section of this chapter.

3. In the **Ready to Install the Program** window, use the **< Back** button as needed to make any changes to the configuration, and then click **Install**.
4. In the **App Volumes Wizard Completed** window, click **Finish**.
5. If prompted, reboot the host.

The App Volumes Agent is now installed, and is ready for use with the App Volumes Manager server (or servers) named in step 3. In the next section, we will edit the agent software configuration so that the agent software can still use more than one App Volumes Manager server, an important step if a load balancer is not being used.

Configuring native load balancing for the App Volumes Agent software

The App Volumes Agent includes the ability to support low-level fault tolerance by utilizing more than one App Volumes Manager server. The primary difference between the agent-based load balancing, versus using a load balancer to transparently balance client connections, is that the agent-based method must wait for a timeout to occur to attempt to contact the next App Volumes Manager server.

Many dedicated load balancers can perform ongoing checks of downstream server availability, even when no client connections are occurring, ensuring that when an App Volumes client request is made, they will be immediately connected to a known functioning server.

The following steps outline the necessary registry changes that must be made to implement native App Volumes Agent load balancing:

1. Open the Windows Registry Editor on the computer that has the App Volumes Agent software installed.
2. Expand the computer registry to reach `Computer\HKEY_LOCAL_MACHINE\SYSTEM\CurrentControlSet\services\svservice\Parameters`.

Implementing App Volumes

3. Right-click on the **Parameters** registry key, and, in the menu that opens, click **New - String Value**. Name the string **Manager2**, and, in the **Data** field, provide the `FQDN:port number` for the second App Volumes Manager server, as shown in the following screenshot:

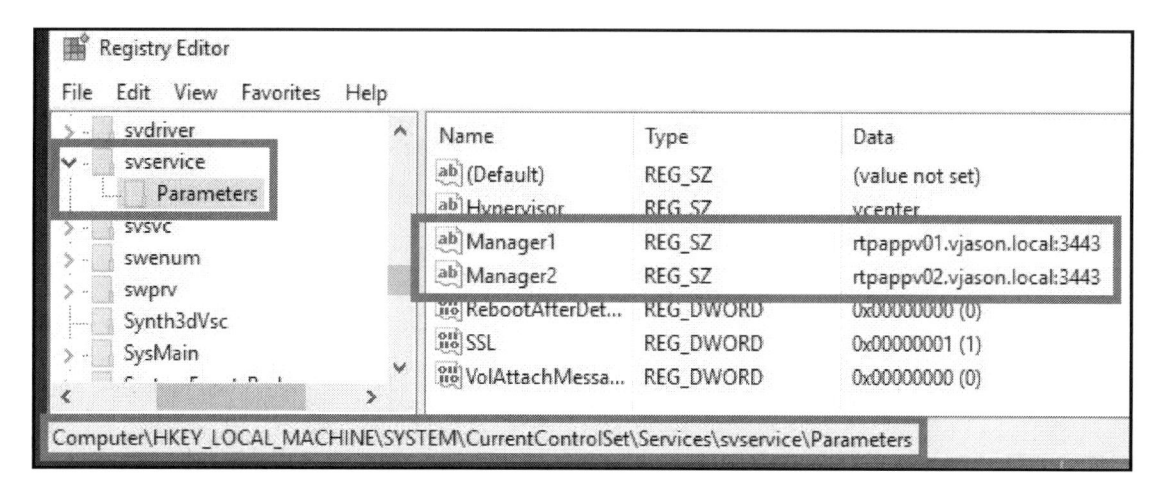

4. Repeat as necessary for additional App Volumes Manager servers, adding keys named **Manager3**, **Manager4**, and so on.

> **TIP**
> If you have multiple virtual desktop master images, use a different order for the App Volumes Manager servers in the `ManagerX` registry string values. For example, image 1 should use App Volumes Manager server 1 and 2 in that order, while image 2 would use them in the reverse order. This will help distribute the client load across all of your App Volumes Servers, instead of just a single one.

5. Reboot the computer or, alternatively, use the Windows **Services** management console to restart the **App Volumes Service**.

The load balancing settings may also be edited using AD Group Policies to add the required registry keys, or by importing the registry file (file with a `.reg` extension) with the updated settings, in a format similar to the following example:

```
Windows Registry Editor Version 5.00
[HKEY_LOCAL_MACHINESYSTEMCurrentControlSetservicessvserviceParameters]
Manager2=rtpappv01.vjason.local:3443
Manager3=rtpappv02.vjason.local:3443
```

[314]

Regardless of the method used to add the registry keys required, once finished, the App Volumes Agent will now be able to use each of the servers specified in the updated settings.

Creating an AppStack

App Volumes uses a very simple process to create an AppStack, requiring very little more from the administrator than executing a few commands and installing the target application. In this section, we will create an AppStack for **Notepad++**, although the process is similar for other applications, or even collections of applications.

> **TIP**
> Where possible, combine multiple applications in a single AppStack. The more AppStacks you assign to a user, the more likely it is that additional time will be required for them to log in due to the time required to attach multiple AppStack VMDK files.

The following steps outline the procedure used to create an AppStack. It assumes that the provisioning computer being used is running the same OS and patch level as the target App Volumes clients, has the App Volumes agent installed, is a member of the target Active Directory domain, and has not been used as an App Volumes client. Additionally, a snapshot of this computer should be taken prior to installing the application, as you will revert to this snapshot once the AppStack has been created:

> **TIP**
> For compatibility reasons, you should use multiple provisioning computers, one for each OS you intend to use with App Volumes. You will need to repeat the AppStack provisioning process on each of these computers, and only assign the resultant AppStack to Horizon desktops or RDS servers running the same OS.

1. Log in to the App Volumes Manager console (https://rtpappv01.vjason.local) using an account that has administrator permissions.
2. Click on the **Volumes** tab and then **AppStacks**.
3. Click the **Create** button to open the **Create AppStack** window.

Implementing App Volumes

4. Enter a **Name** for the AppStack; Notepad++ is used in the following screenshot. Leave the other options at their defaults, and then click **Create**:

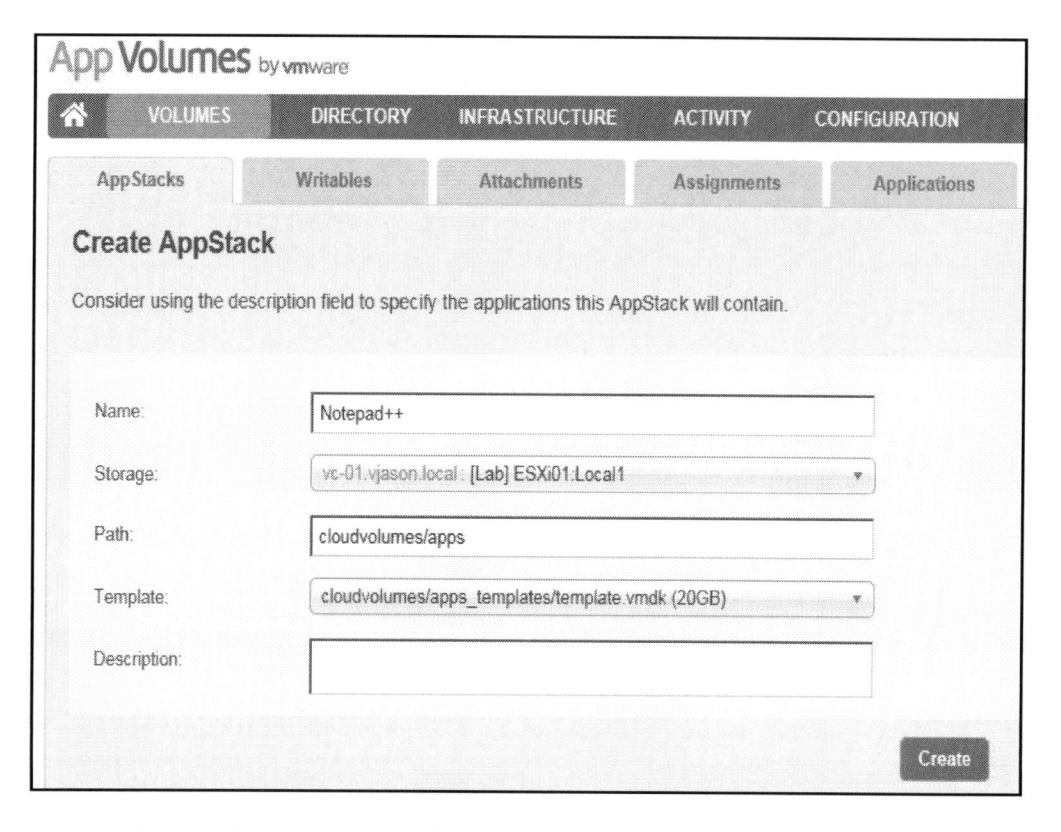

5. In the **Confirm Create AppStack** window, accept the default option of **Perform in the background** and then click **Create**.
6. You will be returned to the **AppStacks** window. Expand the **Notepad++** AppStack, as shown in the following screenshot, and then click **Provision**:

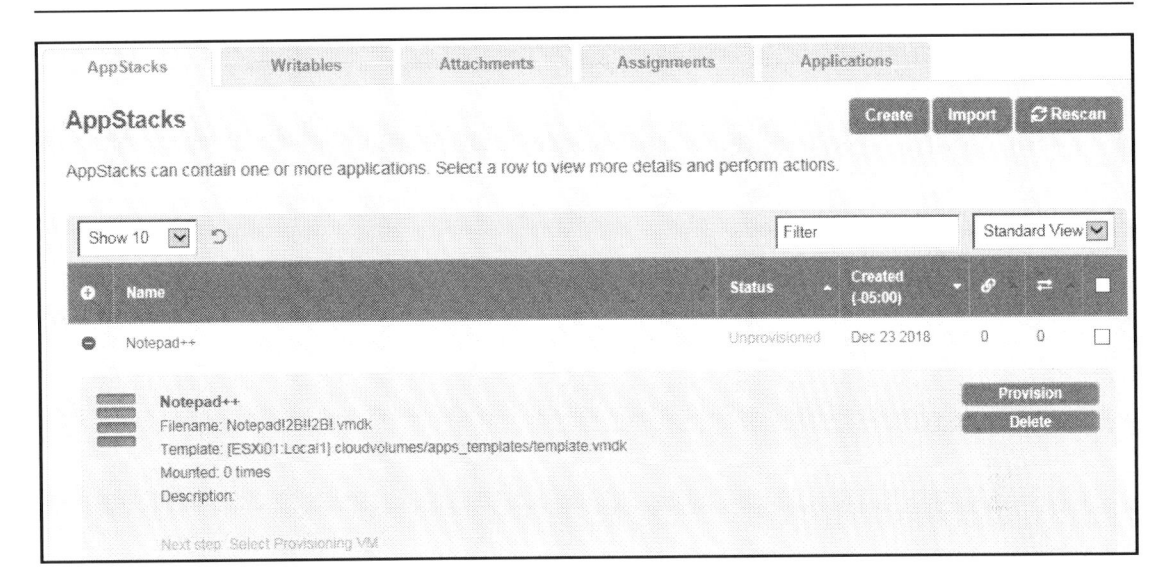

7. Search for the computer that you intend to use to provision AppStacks, click the radio checkbox to the right of it, as shown in the following screenshot, and then click **Provision**:

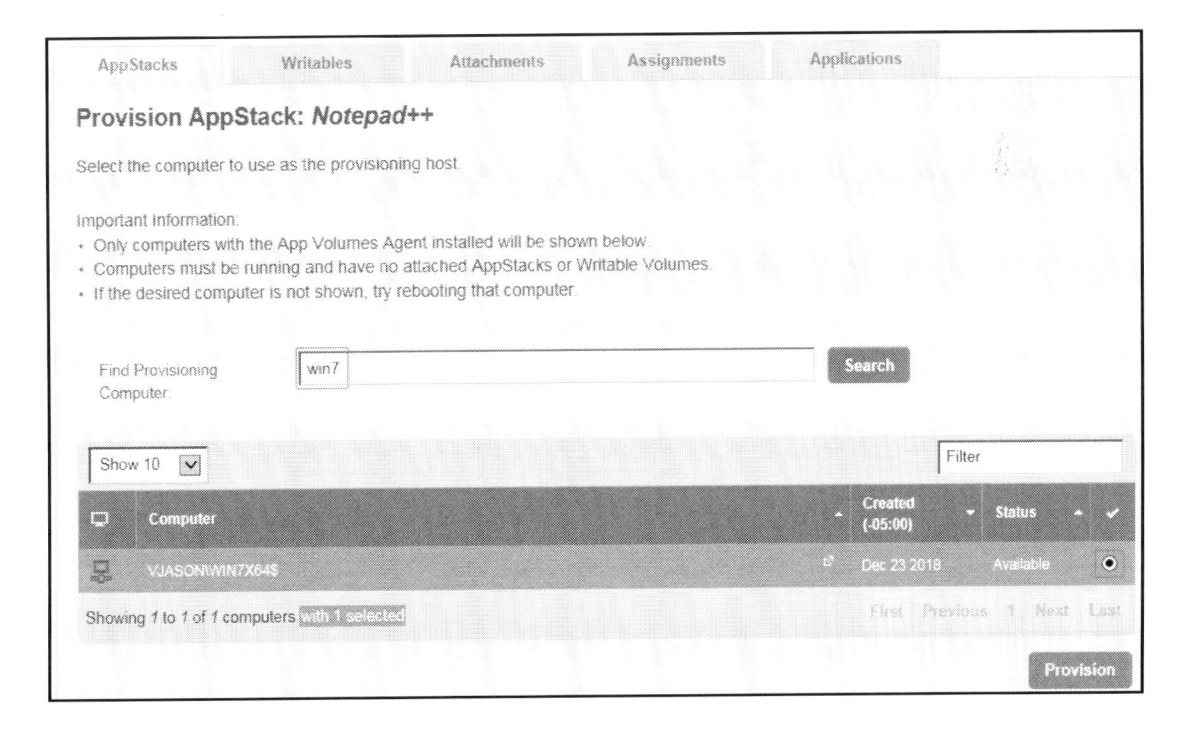

Implementing App Volumes

8. In the **Confirm Start Provisioning** window, shown in the following screenshot, click **Start Provisioning**:

> Confirm Start Provisioning
>
> Start provisioning for AppStack **Notepad++** on computer VJASON\WIN7X64$?
>
> Start Provisioning

9. Log in to the AppStack provisioning computer; you should see the dialog box shown in the following screenshot when you log in, which indicates that the computer is in provisioning mode:

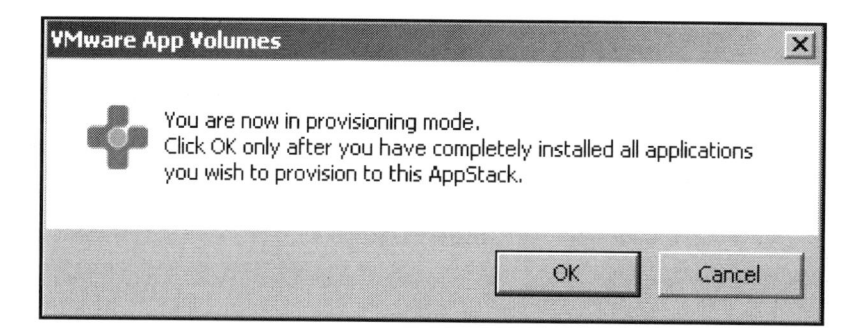

> VMware App Volumes
>
> You are now in provisioning mode.
> Click OK only after you have completely installed all applications you wish to provision to this AppStack.
>
> OK   Cancel

10. Install the application, or applications, as you would normally, making any specific customizations that you want applied to your `AppVolumes` clients. If you need to reboot the computer one or more times as part of the process, you may do so. When finished, return to the dialog box referenced in the previous step and click **OK**.

11. When prompted, as shown in the following screenshot, click **Yes** to continue:

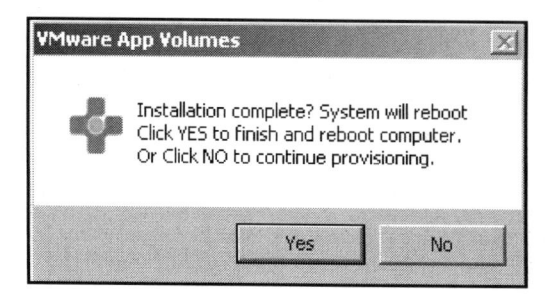

> VMware App Volumes
>
> Installation complete? System will reboot
> Click YES to finish and reboot computer.
> Or Click NO to continue provisioning.
>
> Yes   No

12. Click **OK** to begin the AppStack analysis, as shown in the following screenshot, and again to reboot the computer and continue the capture process:

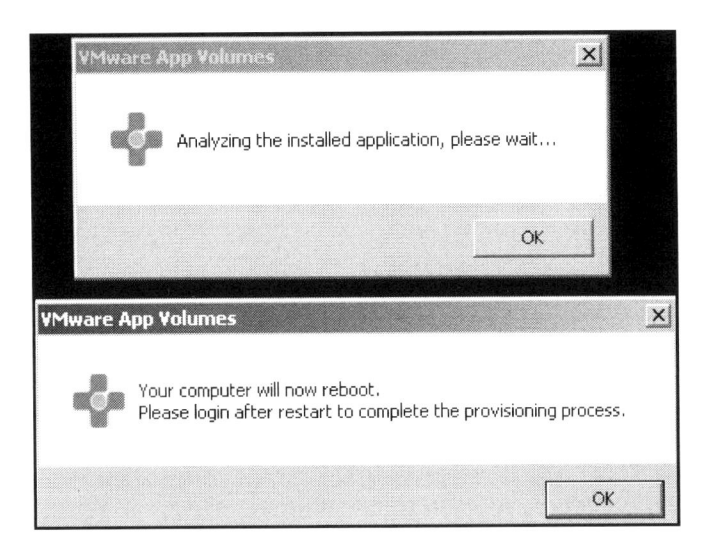

13. Log in to the AppStack provisioning computer; you should see the dialog box shown in the following screenshot when you log in, which indicates that the capture process is complete. As indicated, click **OK** before continuing; once that is done, you may revert the provisioning computer vSphere snapshot and return to the console in order to perform further tasks:

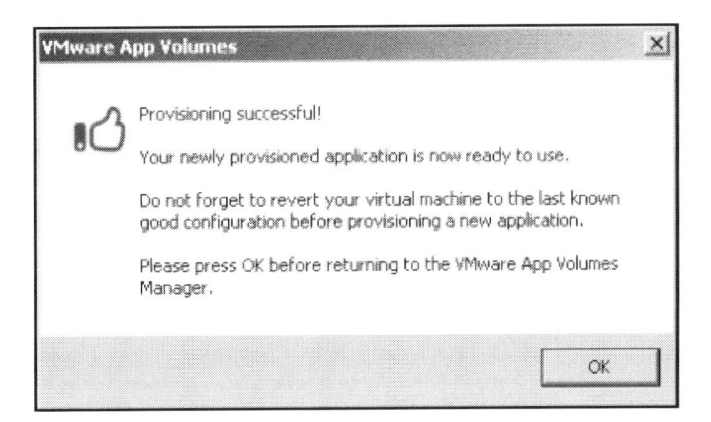

The AppStack creation process has now been completed. We can now assign the AppStack to your end users or associated AD security groups. The AppStack assignment process is outlined in the section of this chapter entitled *Assigning AppStacks*.

Implementing App Volumes

> **TIP**
> If you have an application captured using VMware **ThinApp** that has been packaged as a **Microsoft Installer** (**MSI**) file, you may use that to create an AppStack. Simply install the MSI as you would a normal application, and App Volumes will capture the application and the ThinApp virtualization layer. This is useful when you need the application virtualization capabilities of ThinApp, but want to leverage App Volumes in order to seamlessly, and transparently, deliver that application to your end users.

Updating an AppStack

The process used to update an AppStack is similar to that of creating one, with the exception that you will be making changes to an existing AppStack, rather than installing the software from scratch. When you initiate the AppStack update process, App Volumes clones the source AppStack so that you can go through the provisioning process again to make any needed changes, and, when finished, builds a new AppStack which you can then assign to your clients.

The following steps outline the procedure used to update an AppStack. It assumes that a snapshot was taken of the provisioning computer that it is now powered on, and that a user with local administrator privileges has logged in:

1. Log in to the App Volumes Manager console (https://rtpappv01.vjason.local) using an account that has administrator permissions.
2. Click on the **Volumes** tab, and then **AppStacks**.
3. Click the **+** button to the left of an AppStack to display additional information and options, as shown in the following screenshot, and then click **Update**:

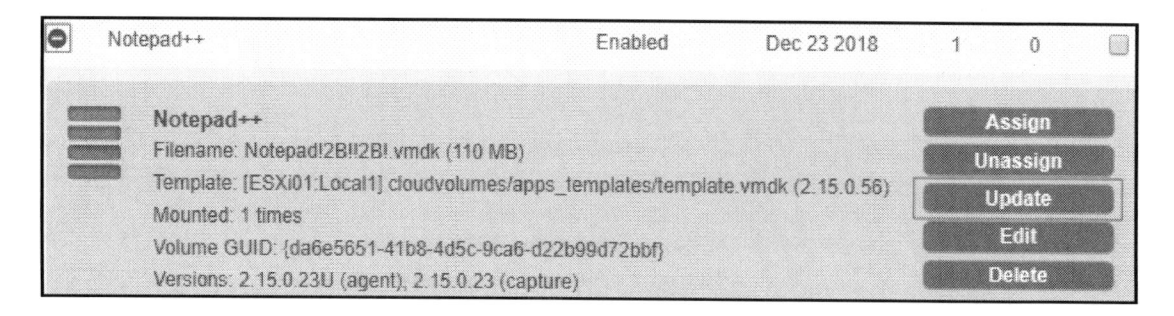

	Notepad++		Enabled	Dec 23 2018	1	0	
	Notepad++					Assign	
	Filename: Notepad!2B!!2B!.vmdk (110 MB)					Unassign	
	Template: [ESXi01:Local1] cloudvolumes/apps_templates/template.vmdk (2.15.0.56)					Update	
	Mounted: 1 times					Edit	
	Volume GUID: {da6e5651-41b8-4d5c-9ca6-d22b99d72bbf}					Delete	
	Versions: 2.15.0.23U (agent), 2.15.0.23 (capture)						

4. Enter a unique **Name** for the cloned AppStack; `Notepad++.v2` is used in the following screenshot. Leave the other options at their defaults, as shown, and then click **Create**:

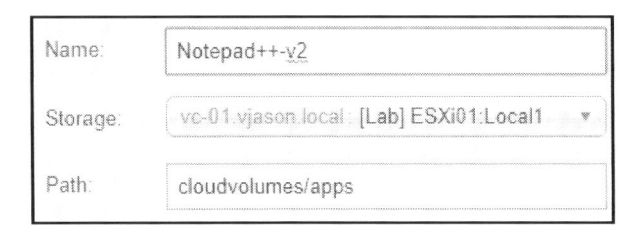

Name:	Notepad++-v2
Storage:	vc-01.vjason.local : [Lab] ESXi01:Local1
Path:	cloudvolumes/apps

5. Proceed with steps 5 and beyond from the *Creating an AppStack* section of this chapter to create the updated AppStack, being sure to select the new AppStack during those steps that instruct you to do so.
6. Assign the new (updated) AppStack to the target AppVolumes clients, and remove the older version.

The AppStack update process has now been completed.

Assigning AppStacks

App Volumes AppStacks may be assigned to individual users, AD security groups, or even AD organizational units. Additionally, the prefix of the computer name can be used to further restrict the AppStack assignments.

The following steps outline the procedure used to assign an AppStack:

1. Log in to the App Volumes Manager console (`https://rtpappv01.vjason.local`) using an account that has administrator permissions.
2. Click on the **Volumes** tab, and then **AppStacks**.

Implementing App Volumes

3. Click the + button to the left of an AppStack to display additional information and options, as shown in the following screenshot, and then click **Assign**:

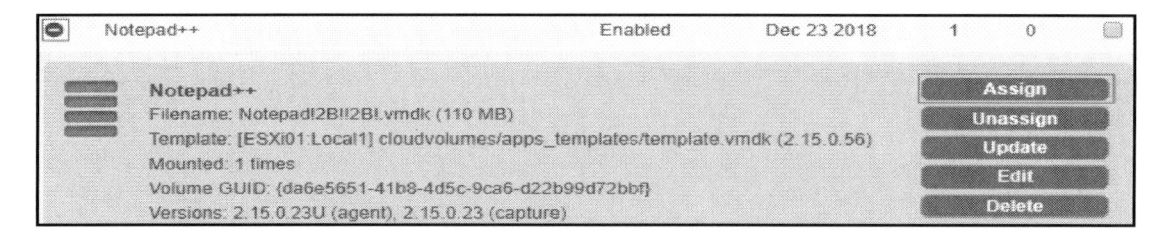

| | Notepad++ | | Enabled | Dec 23 2018 | 1 | 0 | |

Notepad++
Filename: Notepad!2B!!2B!.vmdk (110 MB)
Template: [ESXi01:Local1] cloudvolumes/apps_templates/template.vmdk (2.15.0.56)
Mounted: 1 times
Volume GUID: {da6e5651-41b8-4d5c-9ca6-d22b99d72bbf}
Versions: 2.15.0.23U (agent), 2.15.0.23 (capture)

Assign | Unassign | Update | Edit | Delete

4. Search for the object or objects you wish to assign the AppStack to, click the checkbox to the right of it (or them), and then click **Assign**. In the following screenshot, the `AppVolumes_NotepadPlus` AD group was selected:

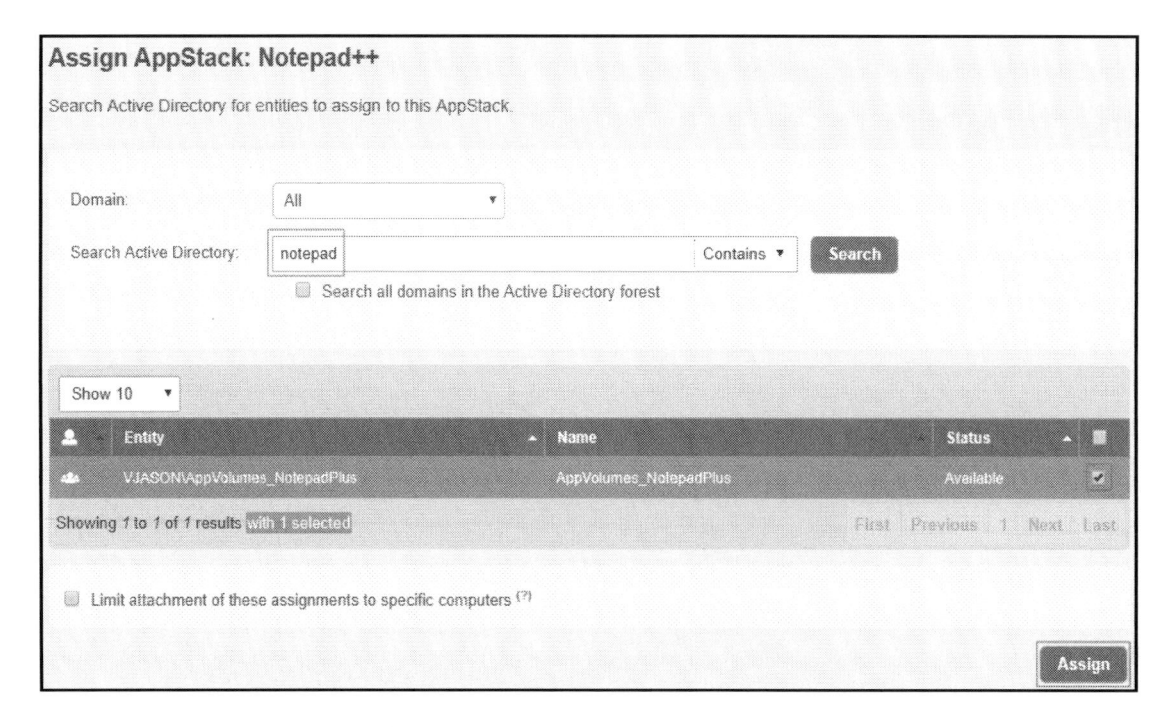

Assign AppStack: Notepad++

Search Active Directory for entities to assign to this AppStack.

Domain: All

Search Active Directory: notepad   Contains   Search

☐ Search all domains in the Active Directory forest

Show 10

Entity	Name	Status	
VJASON\AppVolumes_NotepadPlus	AppVolumes_NotepadPlus	Available	☑

Showing 1 to 1 of 1 results with 1 selected   First Previous 1 Next Last

☐ Limit attachment of these assignments to specific computers (?)

Assign

5. In the **Confirm Assign** pop-up window shown in the following screenshot, use the default option, **Attach AppStacks on next login or reboot**, and then click **Assign**:

[322]

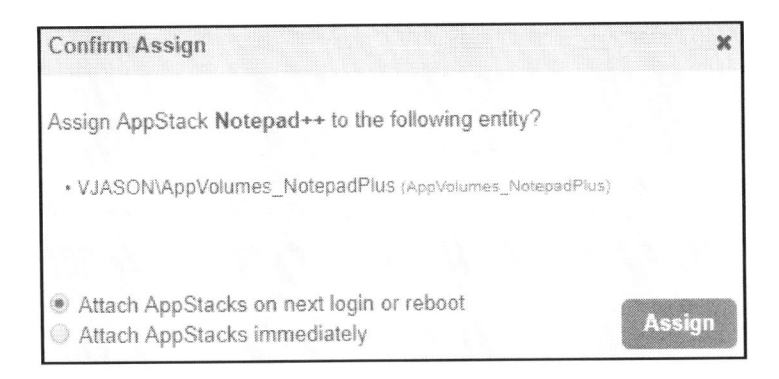

The AppStack assignment process has now been completed, and the selected clients will attach to the AppStack the next time they log in. In the next section, we will delete AppStacks assignments.

Deleting AppStacks assignments

The following steps outline the procedure used to delete an AppStack assignment:

1. Log in to the App Volumes Manager console (`https://rtpappv01.vjason.local`) using an account that has administrator permissions.
2. Click on the **Volumes** tab, and then **AppStacks**.
3. Click the + button to the left of an AppStack to display additional information and options, as shown in the following screenshot, and then click **Unassign**.
4. Click the checkbox to the right of the object or objects you wish to unassign the AppStack from, as shown in the following screenshot, and then click **Unassign**:

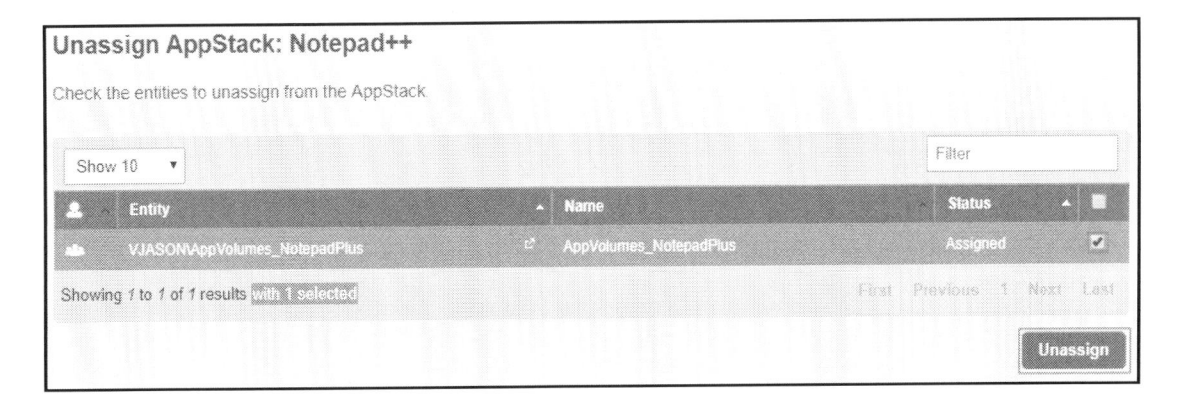

5. In the **Confirm Unassign** pop-up window shown in the following screenshot, use the default option, **Detach AppStacks on next logout or reboot**, and then click **Unassign**:

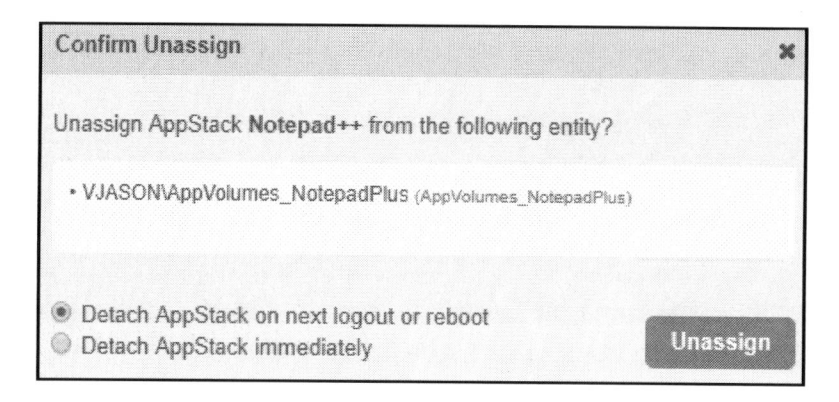

```
Confirm Unassign                                              ✕

Unassign AppStack Notepad++ from the following entity?

  • VJASON\AppVolumes_NotepadPlus (AppVolumes_NotepadPlus)

  ● Detach AppStack on next logout or reboot
  ○ Detach AppStack immediately                   [ Unassign ]
```

The AppStack has now been unassigned from the target object, and any currently connected clients will be detached from the AppStack the next time they log out.

Enabling Writable Volumes

App Volumes Writable Volumes offer the ability to capture user-installed applications so that they can persist across Horizon client sessions. A common use case for this is with non-persistent desktops, which, as you know, are disposed of when a user logs out. App Volumes provides Horizon administrators with another tool that allows them to leverage the efficiencies of non-persistent desktops, while still offering users the customization capabilities of persistent desktops.

> **TIP:** While writable volumes still offer options for capturing and persistent user profile data, VMware prefers you to use User Environment Manager for that task. This chapter will focus solely on capturing user-installed applications.

Writable volumes are assigned using a similar workflow to that of AppStacks. The following steps outline the procedure used to create a writable volume:

1. Log in to the App Volumes Manager console (`https://rtpappv01.vjason.local`) using an account that has administrator permissions.

2. Click on the **Volumes** tab, then **Writables**, and then click the **Create** button, as shown in the following screenshot:

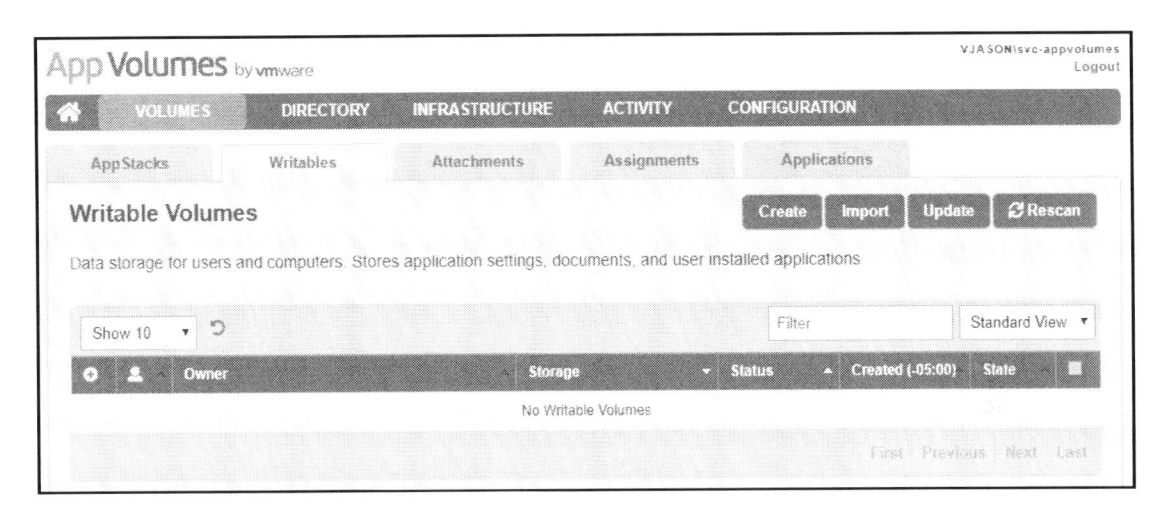

3. Search for the object or objects you wish to create writable volumes for, and then click the checkbox to the right of it (or them); in the following screenshot, the `AppVolumes_WV` AD group was selected:

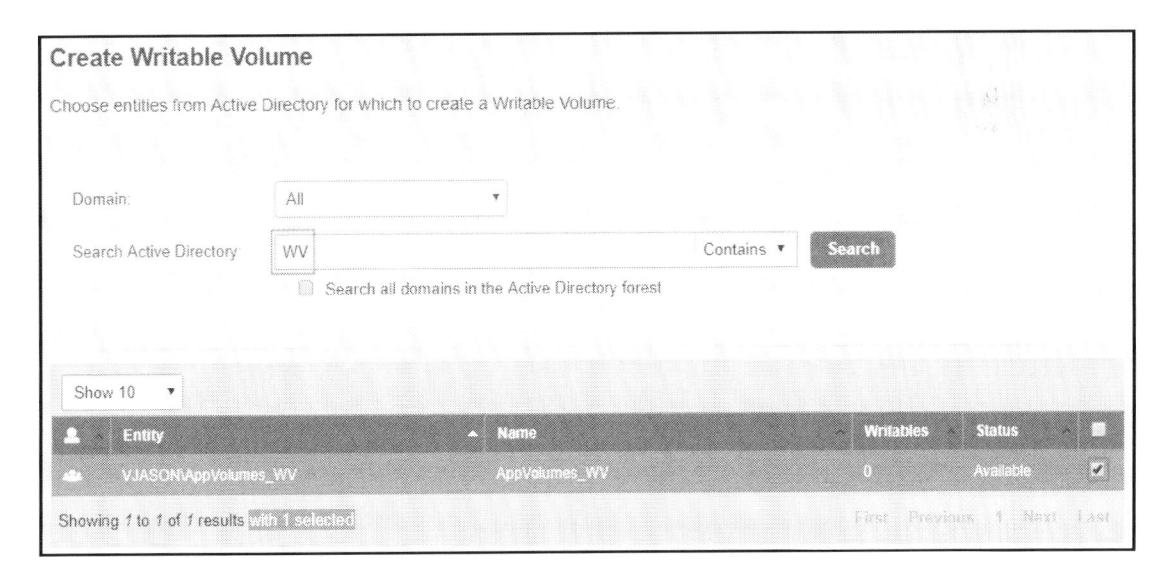

Implementing App Volumes

4. In the lower portion of the window from step 3, use the **Source Template:** drop-down menu to select the `template_uia_only.vmdk` template, as shown in the following screenshot, and then click **Create**:

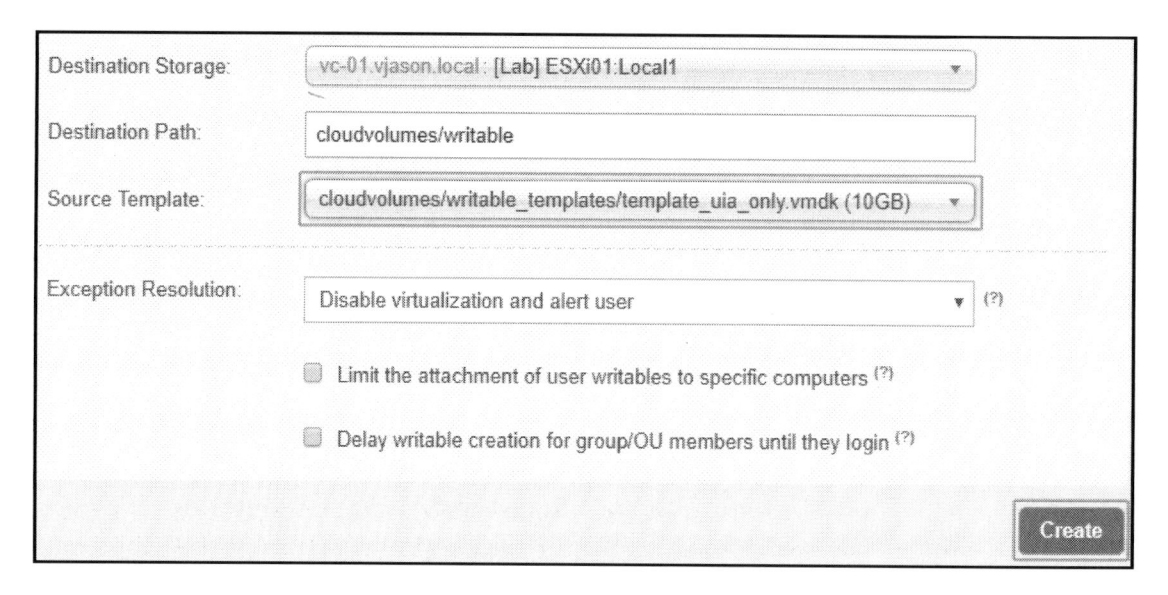

Destination Storage:	vc-01.vjason.local : [Lab] ESXi01:Local1
Destination Path:	cloudvolumes/writable
Source Template:	cloudvolumes/writable_templates/template_uia_only.vmdk (10GB)
Exception Resolution:	Disable virtualization and alert user (?)

☐ Limit the attachment of user writables to specific computers (?)

☐ Delay writable creation for group/OU members until they login (?)

[Create]

5. In the **Confirm Create Writable Volumes** pop-up window, as shown in the following screenshot, click **Create**:

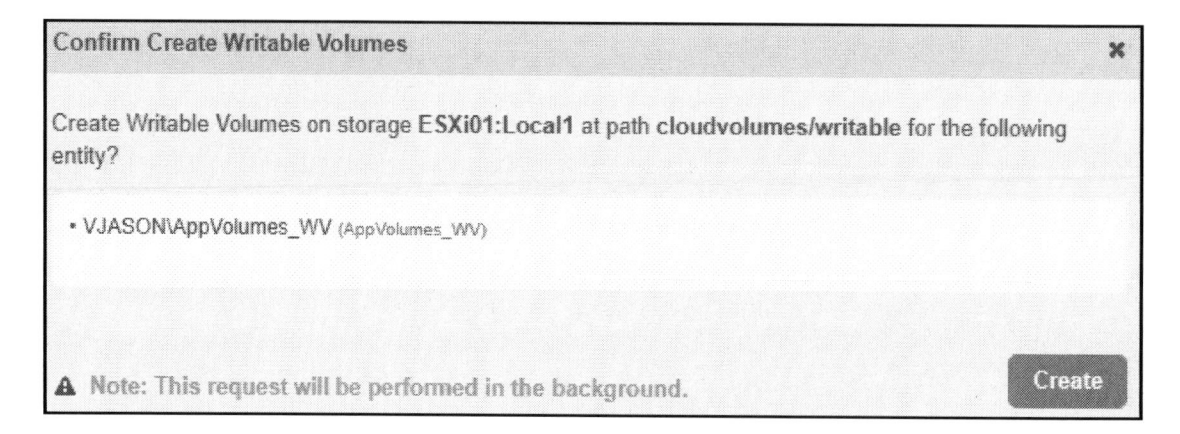

Confirm Create Writable Volumes   ✕

Create Writable Volumes on storage **ESXi01:Local1** at path **cloudvolumes/writable** for the following entity?

- VJASON\AppVolumes_WV (AppVolumes_WV)

⚠ Note: This request will be performed in the background.   [Create]

[326]

The writable volumes will now be created in the background. After a few minutes, you should be able to refresh the console window to see what was created. In the following screenshot, we can see that a writable volume was created both for the specified AD security group as well as the lone member of that group (**Erik**):

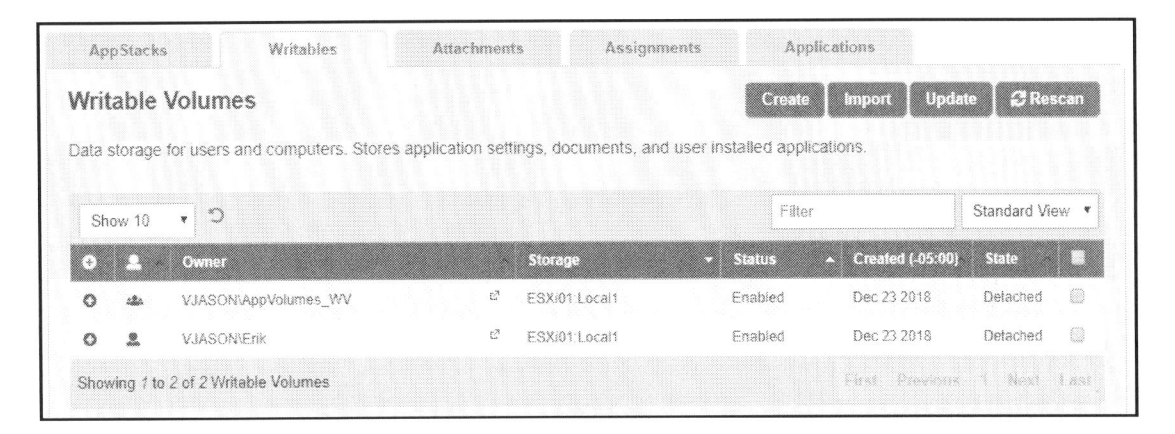

Owner	Storage	Status	Created (-05:00)	State
VJASON\AppVolumes_WV	ESXi01 Local1	Enabled	Dec 23 2018	Detached
VJASON\Erik	ESXi01 Local1	Enabled	Dec 23 2018	Detached

> **TIP**: Don't forget to back up your writable volumes. As discussed earlier, App Volumes can make copies of them for you, but that might not be sufficient for your data protection requirements.

Deleting Writable Volumes

The following steps outline the procedure used to delete a writable volume:

1. Log in to the App Volumes Manager console (`https://rtpappv01.vjason.local`) using an account that has administrator permissions.
2. Click on the **Volumes** tab, then **Writables**, and then check the box (or boxes) next to the objects whose writable volumes you wish to delete.

Implementing App Volumes

3. Click the **Delete Selected** button to begin the deletion process. Note the other options that exist for managing writable volumes, including disable, move, and backup:

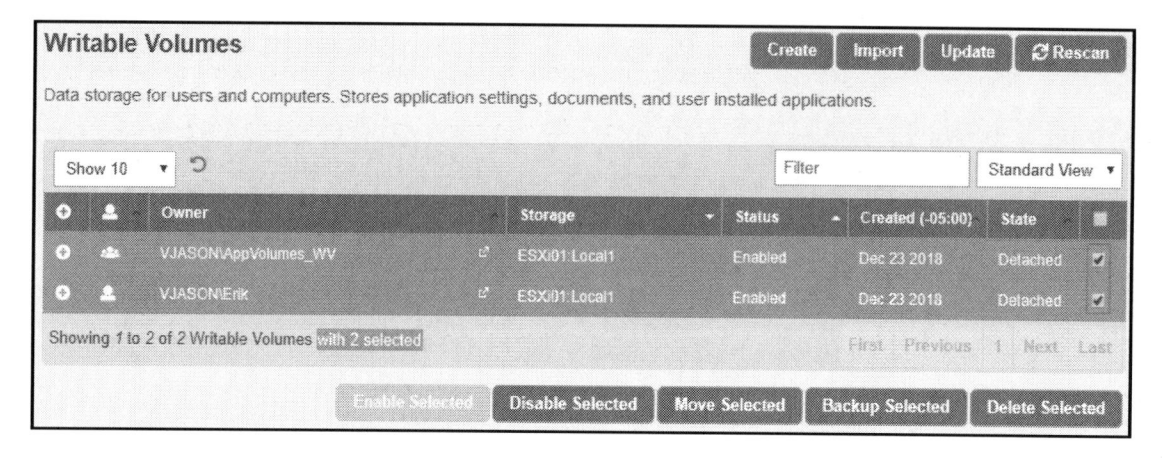

4. In the **Confirm Delete** pop-up window, as shown in the following screenshot, click **Delete**:

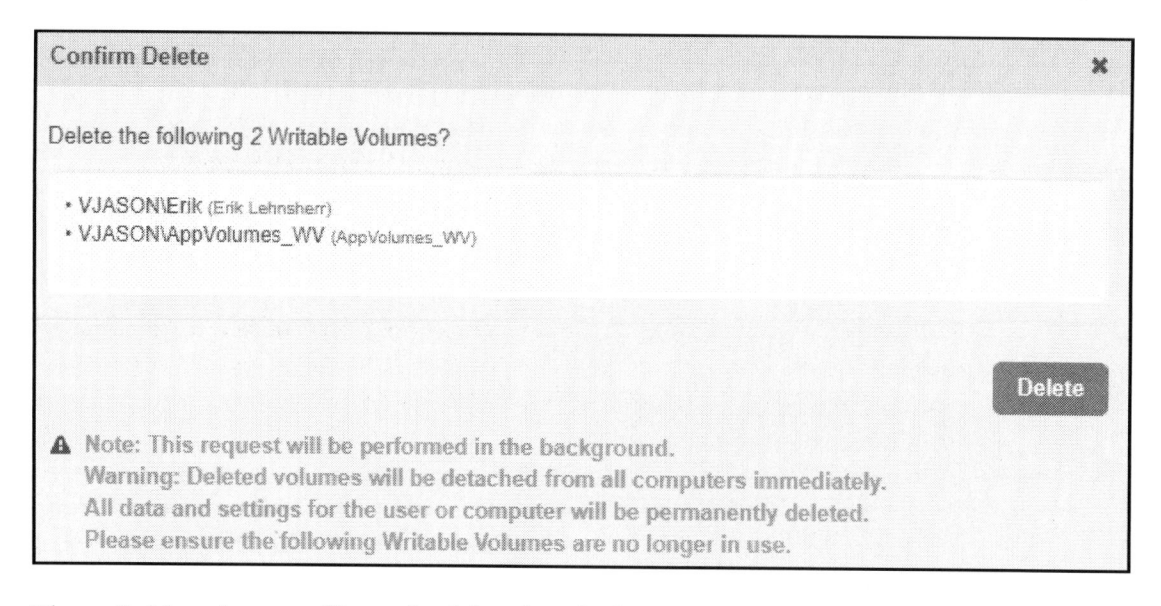

The writable volumes will now be deleted in the background. After a few minutes, you should be able to refresh the console window to confirm they were deleted.

App Volumes backup and recovery

App Volumes stores all configuration information in the App Volumes database, and the App Volumes Manager servers operate independently of one another. Owing to this, there is no critical information to back up on the App Volumes Manager servers themselves, although if custom SSL certificates were installed, you may wish to retain backups of those.

If your environment uses Writable Volumes, it is important to be able to recover the underlying storage configuration and contents. App Volumes manages writable volume assignments based on where the volume was first created, and, if those Writable Volumes are restored to an alternate location, their connection to the clients would be lost until they are imported and manually assigned.

What to back up

The following items should be backed up to ensure that App Volumes can be recovered in the event of a disaster or other scenario:

- App Volumes Manager servers appliances
- AppStacks can be backed up from and restored to anywhere; what is most important is getting a reliable backup
- App Volumes Writable Volumes, including their underlying storage configuration if possible
- App Volumes Manager server appliance custom SSL certificates (if used)

> VMware engineers have developed a utility that can be used to back up AppStacks and Writable Volumes. While the **App Volumes Backup Utility** (`https://labs.vmware.com/flings/app-volumes-backup-utility`) is not an official component of App Volumes, and offers no formal support, it may be useful for smaller environments that require a simple process for backing up critical App Volumes files.

Recovery process

The following provides a basic overview of App Volumes recovery. For more complex recovery scenarios, you will need to refer to the VMware App Volumes documentation (https://docs.vmware.com/en/VMware-App-Volumes/index.html), or, in some cases, even VMware product support. The following outlines the basic tasks that must be accomplished:

- If necessary, restore the Horizon vCenter Servers, and any other components of the Horizon infrastructure, including Horizon Connection Servers, desktops, and RDS servers
- Restore the AppStacks and Writable Volumes to their original locations
- Restore the App Volumes Manager servers

The steps will return most App Volumes installations to a fully functional state, assuming Horizon itself is functional. As previously mentioned, if the recovery is more complex, certain items may need to be reconfigured, or manually updated, either with the assistance of the App Volumes documentation or with VMware product support.

Summary

In this chapter, you have been introduced to a very useful component of Horizon: App Volumes. You learned what is required to deploy and configure App Volumes Manager servers and their associated client agent software, and how to build, deploy, and manage user access to AppStacks and Writable Volumes.

We then discussed how to create and assign Writable Volumes, which are used to enable the persistence of user-installed applications in linked and instant clone desktop-based Horizon environments.

Finally, we discussed what is required when backing up or recovering an App Volumes installation, including the AppStacks and Writable Volumes.

In the next chapter, we will discuss how to implement User Environment Manager, an optional Horizon component that can be used to configure and maintain user personas between client sessions.

Questions

1. What two key capabilities does App Volumes provide?
2. How does installing your second App Volumes Manager server differ from installing your first one?
3. Which is better – assigning a single large AppStack, or many small ones?
4. Why would you want to use writable volumes?
5. Describe in high-level terms how an AppStack works.
6. App Volumes is typically combined with what other VMware product when working with non-persistent desktops?
7. Name some reasons why you feel that AppStacks makes it easier to manage your applications.

Further reading

The following resources may be used to learn more about the topics described in this chapter:

- VMware documentation:
    - **VMware App Volumes Documentation** (https://docs.vmware.com/en/VMware-App-Volumes/index.html)
    - **VMware Community Forums for App Volumes** (https://communities.vmware.com/community/vmtn/appvolumes)
    - **VMware Horizon** (https://www.vmware.com/support/pubs/view_pubs.html)
    - **VMware User Environment Manager** (https://www.vmware.com/support/pubs/uem-pubs.html)
    - **VMware ThinApp** (https://www.vmware.com/support/pubs/thinapp_pubs.html)
    - **VMware vSphere** (https://www.vmware.com/support/pubs/vsphere-esxi-vcenter-server-pubs.html)

12
Implementing User Environment Manager

VMware **User Environment Manager** (**UEM**) is a standalone component of VMware Horizon Enterprise Edition that provides robust, contextual, and dynamic end-user persona management capabilities across different devices and locations. UEM can be used to provide a personalized and consistent desktop experience across Horizon desktops, physical computers, Windows RDS servers, and even virtual desktops managed by other virtual desktop platforms.

While UEM offers a significant number of different options for managing and customizing a user's persona, as we will show in this chapter, a basic installation capable of saving user persona data can be up and running in less than 30 minutes.

In this chapter, we will look at the following topics:

- The UEM pre-installation tasks, including file share and AD group policy requirements
- How to install the UEM agent
- How to use the UEM Easy Start feature to quickly configure a basic UEM environment
- How to configure UEM group policies
- How to implement profile folder redirection using UEM
- Some of the advanced UEM settings for user persona customization

> **TIP**
> The goal of this chapter is to help you set up a basic UEM version 9 installation for the purpose of managing user persona information within your Horizon infrastructure. Other components of UEM, such as **SyncTool**, **Application Profiler**, and the **Helpdesk Support Tool**, are not explicitly required to use UEM, and are sufficiently complex that they cannot be covered in this chapter. Consult the VMware UEM documentation (https://www.vmware.com/support/pubs/uem-pubs.html) for information about these UEM components; each has its own separate guide.

UEM overview

In early 2015, VMware acquired Immidio, the creators of UEM, and began offering their persona management product both as a standalone product and as part of Horizon Enterprise Edition. While Horizon already included a persona management utility, known as **Horizon Persona Management**, it represented an improvement over traditional Windows roaming profiles and was not a comprehensive user persona management solution with robust customization capabilities. **VMware UEM FAQ** (https://www.vmware.com/content/dam/digitalmarketing/vmware/en/pdf/products/user-environment-manager/vmware-user-environment-mngr-faq.pdf) states that the product easily scales to support more than 100,000 users, which is well beyond most Horizon infrastructure sizes.

While UEM improves on Horizon Persona Management in almost every way, it doesn't handle the management of user data, only the settings needed to enable a personalized user experience across UEM client sessions. This feature is certainly a benefit of Horizon Persona Management over UEM, but the truth is that, unless managed carefully, the movement of this user data by Horizon Persona Management between the remote file share and the Horizon desktop can cause frequent performance issues, particularly with profiles that have large amounts of user data.

> **Tip:** Already using Horizon Persona Management? While UEM and Persona Management aren't meant to be used side by side on an ongoing basis, migrating from Persona Management to UEM requires little more than running both at the same time for as long as is needed for all of your users to log in. VMware KB article 2118056 (https://kb.vmware.com/s/article/2118056) provides an outline of the steps required to migrate to UEM.

Like App Volumes, UEM provides the most benefit in non-persistent desktop environments. The combination of UEM and App Volumes enables users to leverage two of the most desirable architectural possibilities of VMware Horizon:

- **Non-persistent desktops**: UEM and App Volumes provide a persistent experience in a non-persistent environment. When compared to persistent desktops, non-persistent desktops typically require less effort to manage over the long term, as well as less physical storage.
- **Fewer virtual desktop master images with seamless migration between each**: UEM enables application personalization across Windows OS versions, while App Volumes decouples applications from the desktop image. The combination of both means that you only need one basic image for each Windows OS, which you can then customize using App Volumes, to then provide a personalized user experience using UEM, regardless of which OS they happen to log in to.

> **Tip:** Please note that App Volumes cannot roam user-installed applications between Windows OS versions; it will create distinct user-writable volumes for each. You will learn more about this in Chapter 11, *Implementing VMware App Volumes*.

The following diagram shows the combination of UEM and App Volumes layered on top of a Windows OS, presenting the user with a personalized experience while actually abstracting each of the components that make that personalization possible:

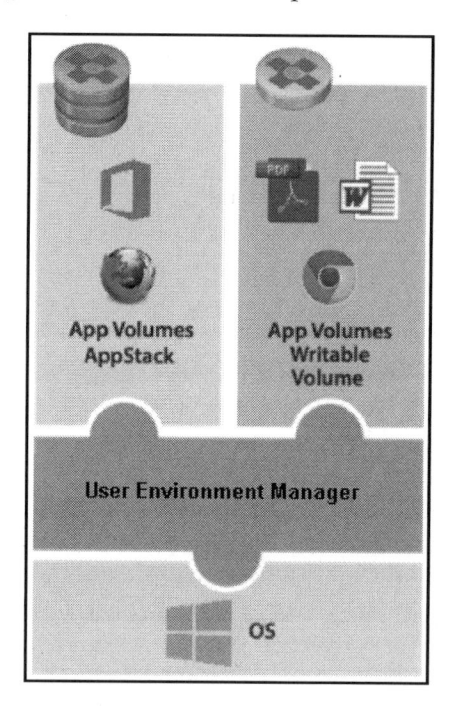

UEM pre-installation tasks

This section will outline what infrastructure resources are required prior to configuring UEM in your environment. For the purposes of this chapter, we will be using the following AD security groups and Windows file share names:

- **UEM administrators AD security group**: UEM_Admins
- **UEM users AD security group**: UEM_Users
- **UEM configuration file share location**: \\DC-01\UEM
- **UEM client persona data file share location**: \\DC-01\UEMUsers

While the purpose of each resource is in most cases self-explanatory, the specific function of each will be explained later on in this chapter.

Configuration share

UEM stores its configuration in a Windows-based file share. This share has minimal storage requirements, but must be accessible to all clients and any individuals who will use the UEM management console. The share and underlying folder requires the following permissions to be configured:

- Share-level permissions:
    - UEM administrators (`UEM_Admins`)—change
    - UEM users (`UEM_Users`)—read
- Folder-level permissions:
    - UEM administrators (`UEM_Admins`)—full control
    - UEM users (`UEM_Users`)—read and execute

> If you will be using the UEM Helpdesk Support Tool, additional share-level permissions will be required in order to for users of that tool. Consult the VMware *User Environment Management Helpdesk Support Tool Administrator's Guide* (`https://www.vmware.com/support/pubs/uem-pubs.html`) for details about the permissions required.

Persona share

UEM stores user persona data in a Windows-based file share, which must be accessible to all clients and any individuals who use the UEM management console. It is recommended to create a new share for this purpose and not attempt to use an existing file share used for general file storage.

> The amount of persona space required per user will vary greatly based on the UEM configuration, the amount of customization that was done, and the number of profile archives that are kept. It is suggested to start with at least 100 MB of storage per user during a pilot phase, and as the pilot progresses, monitor whether additional storage is required. The UEM share should be able to be expanded as needed if additional storage per user is required, as well as to support additional users.

The share and underlying folder requires the following permissions to be configured:

- Share-level permissions:
    - UEM administrators (`UEM_Admins`)—change
    - UEM users (`UEM_Users`)—change
- Folder-level permissions:
    - UEM administrators (`UEM_Admins`)—full control; apply to **This folder, subfolders and files**
    - UEM users (`UEM_Users`)—read and execute and **Create folders/append data**; apply to **This folder only**
    - Creator-owner (default Windows security principle)—full control; apply to **Subfolders and files only**

> **TIP**
> If you will be using the UEM Helpdesk Support Tool, additional folder-level permissions will be required in order for users of that tool. Consult the VMware *User Environment Management Helpdesk Support Tool Administrator's Guide* (`https://www.vmware.com/support/pubs/uem-pubs.html`) for details about the permissions required.

Windows user folder redirection share

Windows user profile folder redirection is not an explicit requirement of UEM, but for Horizon environments that require user data to be retained between non-persistent desktop sessions, it is one of multiple methods we can use. We will demonstrate folder redirection later on in this chapter, but only because many Horizon environments require some way to transparently persist user files across Horizon client sessions.

> **TIP**
> If you intend to use a single instance of UEM with Horizon pods across multiple sites, you will probably want to consider using AD **Distributed File System** (**DFS**) namespaces to ensure users are redirecting folders to file servers located within the same data centre as their UEM client. The Microsoft article titled *Deploy Folder Redirection with Offline Files* (`https://docs.microsoft.com/en-us/previous-versions/windows/it-pro/windows-server-2012-R2-and-2012/jj649078(v=ws.11)`) mentions some important things to consider when using DFS with folder redirection. Keep in mind, when reviewing that article, that our primary interest is using DFS and folder redirection together, as UEM itself will handle the task of actually implementing folder redirection.

The share and folder-level permissions for Windows-based file shares that will host redirected user folders should mimic those of any existing user home directories, which in most cases when created allow access only to the folder owner, along with any administrative and backup accounts. I am not providing specific permissions recommendations for these folders in this chapter, as each organization may have its own requirements for the security of the data of individual users, and given that these folders are used for exactly that, it is important that you determine what your own needs are.

> **TIP**
> Microsoft KB article 274443 (`https://support.microsoft.com/en-us/kb/274443`) provides examples of how to create shares to host-redirected folders that meet most common security requirements. Additionally, the share and folder-level permissions referenced in the *Persona share* section of this chapter may also be used as a reference to creating root file shares that automatically protect individual folders created within.

Group policy files

UEM is enabled at the client level using AD group policy objects, which are provided in the **XML-based GPO template** (**ADMX**) format. Six templates are provided by default for the following UEM components:

- **VMware UEM FlexEngine** (`VMware UEM FlexEngine.admx`)—used to enable UEM at the client level
- **VMware UEM Helpdesk Support Tool** (`VMware UEM Helpdesk Support Tool.admx`)—used to configure the UEM Helpdesk Support Tool, which provides for the management of UEM profile archives
- **VMware UEM Management Console** (`VMware UEM Management Console.admx`)—used to automatically configure the UEM environment settings in the management console, or to lock down what items the target users can access
- **VMware UEM SyncTool - Computer** (`VMware UEM SyncTool COMPUTER.admx`)—used to configure UEM SyncTool, which is designed to sync UEM profiles to physical clients who have only intermittent connectivity to the UEM shares; this GPO template is for AD computer objects
- **VMware UEM SyncTool - User** (`VMware UEM SyncTool USER.admx`)—same function as the UEM SyncTool—computer policy object, but for AD user objects
- **VMware UEM** (`VMware UEM.admx`)—Root UEM GPO folder object for the AD Group Policy Management Console; contains no configurable policies

Implementing User Environment Manager

The VMware UEM FlexEngine GPO template is the only one needed to enable UEM, and the only UEM GPO template we will use in this chapter. For information about the remaining policy templates and the features they enable, consult the VMware UEM documentation (https://www.vmware.com/support/pubs/uem-pubs.html).

Prior to performing the examples required in this chapter, the UEM ADMX files and their associated en-US directory were copied to the replicated PolicyDefinitions folder on the domain controller, located at c:\windows\sysvol\domain\Policies\PolicyDefinitions, which ensures that they will be replicated to and available on all domain controllers in the domain.

> **TIP**
> The Microsoft article **Managing Group Policy ADMX Files Step-by-Step Guide** (https://docs.microsoft.com/en-us/previous-versions/dotnet/articles/bb530196(v=msdn.10)) explains where to place ADMX files on a domain control to ensure they are accessible to remote users of the AD Group Policy Management Console.

Installing the UEM Agent

The UEM Agent software is used to enable UEM on client computers, which may include Horizon desktops, Windows RDS servers, physical computers, or desktops used with other VDI solutions. The installation process is the same regardless of where the agent software is being installed, so only one example will be provided.

The UEM installer files are provided by VMware as a single ZIP file; extract the files prior to beginning the installation process. The UEM Agent software is named in a format similar to VMware User Environment Manager X.y xYY.exe, where X.y is the current UEM version number, and xYY represents which processor type (x86 or x64) the installer is for. A UEM demo license is also available as a separate download; you will need that license or your permanent one during the installation of the UEM Agent software.

The following steps outline the UEM Agent installation process; this process should be performed on a virtual desktop or Windows RDS server master image prior to deployment, a linked or instant clone master image prior to being updated for redeployment or deployed to users for the first time, or, as stated previously, an existing or new physical computer:

1. Double-click `VMware User Environment Manager X.y xYY.exe` (32 and 64-bit versions are available) to launch the **VMware User Environment Setup** wizard. Click **Next** and proceed through the steps until you reach the **Choose License File** window, selecting a **Typical** installation when prompted.
2. In the **Choose License File** window, the installer should detect that it is being used with Horizon and allow you to move on to the next step by clicking on **Next**. If it does not and you are prompted for one, click **Browse...** to open the **Open** window, then select the UEM license file, and then click **Open** to return to the **Choose License File** window. Click **Next** to continue.
3. In the **Ready to Install VMware User Environment Manager** window, click **Install**, and, when completed, click **Finish**.

The UEM Agent software is now ready to use. The updated image is now ready to be deployed, although it will not function until we complete the steps outlined in the next section, *Configuring UEM*.

Configuring UEM

Assuming that we have configured the UEM shares and uploaded the GPO templates as described previously in the section of this chapter titled *UEM pre-installation tasks*, we are ready to configure UEM itself. In this section of the chapter, we will complete the initial configuration of UEM, which includes installing the UEM management console and implementing the required AD GPOs, and, while optional, we will also enable Windows folder redirection.

Installing the UEM management console

The UEM management console software may be installed wherever it is needed to facilitate UEM management. The actual UEM configuration is stored in the UEM configuration share; the console does nothing more than connect to and manage the UEM configuration data stored on it. In the examples provided in this chapter, administrative access to UEM is controlled using the `UEM_Admins` AD security group. Only members of that group have the necessary access rights to make changes to the UEM configuration share, which is what is required to administer UEM.

The following steps outline the UEM management console installation process. The console is installed using the same installer file as the UEM Agent. In the example provided, we are installing the console while logged in as a user who is a member of the `UEM_Admins` AD security group:

1. Double-click `VMware User Environment Manager X.y xYY.exe` to launch the **VMware User Environment Setup** wizard. Click **Next** to proceed through the initial installation steps, including accepting the license agreement.
2. In the **Destination Folder** window, accept the default software **Destination Folder**, or update as needed and then click **Next**.
3. In the **Choose Setup Type** window, click **Custom**.
4. In the **Custom Setup** window, uncheck the **VMware UEM FlexEngine** components and sub-components, check the **VMware UEM Management Console** component as shown in the following screenshot, and then click **Next**:

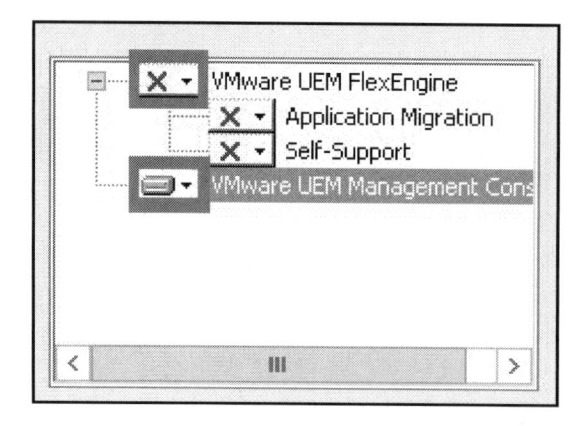

5. In the **Ready to Install VMware User Environment Manager** window, click **Install**.
6. When the install process completes, click **Finish**.

7. In the Windows **Start** menu, click the **VMware UEM** folder, and then click **Management Console** to open the UEM management console for the first time.
8. The UEM management console will open up the **UEM configuration share** window. Provide the FQDN **Location:** of the UEM configuration (`\\dc-01.vjason.local\UEM` in the example provided) share as shown in the following screenshot, and then click **OK** to return to the UEM management console main window:

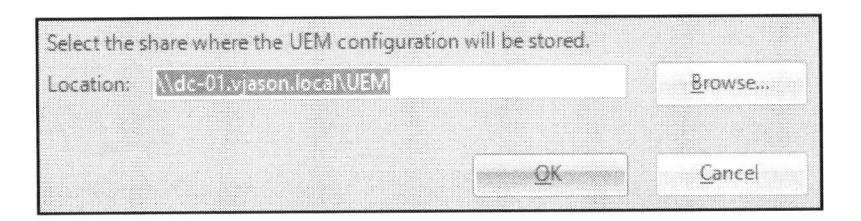

9. If this is the first time the UEM configuration share was accessed using the UEM management console, you will be prompted in the **Settings** screen to check which features you want to enable in the console. As shown in the following screenshot, enable all of the features and then click **OK**:

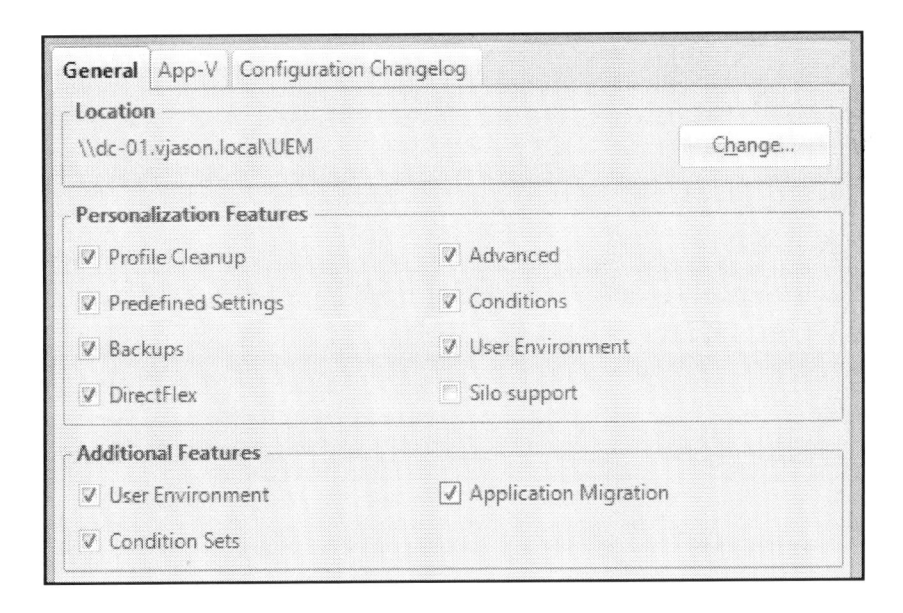

> **TIP:** These settings can be changed at any time using the **Configure** button in the UEM management console; this button is shown in the screenshot provided next.

The UEM management console is shown in the following screenshot and is ready to be used to customize the UEM installation. Since we have not yet configured the UEM client GPO objects, we are free to configure the UEM without the risk of impacting our clients:

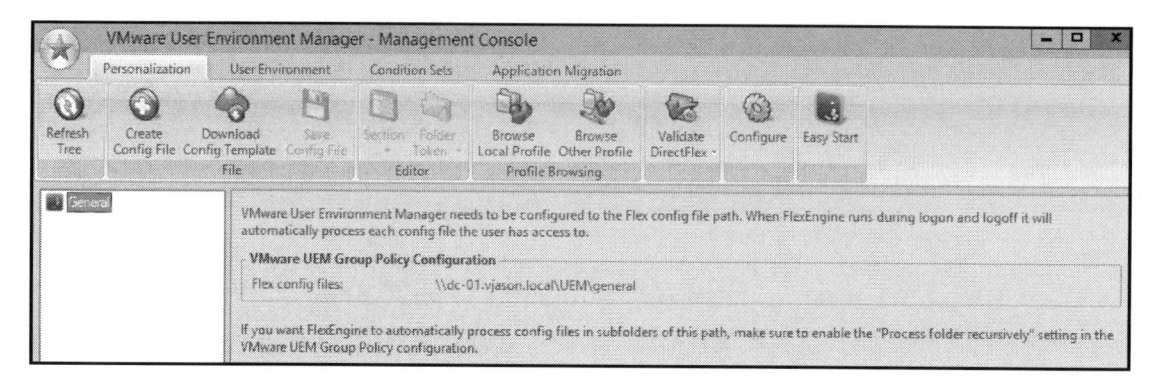

Easy Start configuration

The **Easy Start** feature of the UEM is used to quickly get it up and running, and is a good starting point for a basic installation. The following steps outline how to perform the initial UEM configuration using Easy Start:

1. Log in to a computer that has the UEM management console installed as a user who is a member of the `UEM_Admins` AD security group.
2. In the Windows **Start** menu, click the **VMware UEM** folder, and then click **Management Console** to open the UEM management console.
3. In the UEM management console, click **Easy Start** to open the **Easy Start** window.

4. In the UEM **Easy Start** window, shown in the following screenshot, click the versions of Microsoft Office you are using in your environment, and then click **OK**:

> Easy Start installs a default set of UEM configuration items, so you can quickly get a feel for the functionality. You can use these items as is, delete some of them, or just use this as a starting point for your own implementation.
>
> In addition to the default items, install UEM configuration items for the following Microsoft Office versions:
>
> ☐ Microsoft Office 2003
> ☐ Microsoft Office 2007
> ☐ Microsoft Office 2010
> ☑ Microsoft Office 2013
> ☑ Microsoft Office 2016

- The **Easy Start** window will now update to confirm a successful installation. Click **OK** to close the window and complete the initial configuration of UEM.
- UEM is now configured for use by clients; all that remains is to configure the required GPOs and instruct our users to log in as they normally would. In the next section, we will configure the GPOs needed to enable UEM.

Easy Start defaults

UEM Easy Start creates a number of sample items that are helpful in understanding the basics of how the software works, but should be removed prior to activating the software using the GPOs referenced in the next section of this chapter.

The UEM Easy Start setup configures a number of different Windows settings, but among those there are ones specific to users that will in most cases need to be removed before the UEM is placed into production.

The initial settings are created under the UEM management console **User Environment** tab, which is shown in the following screenshot and contains settings related to the Windows profile itself:

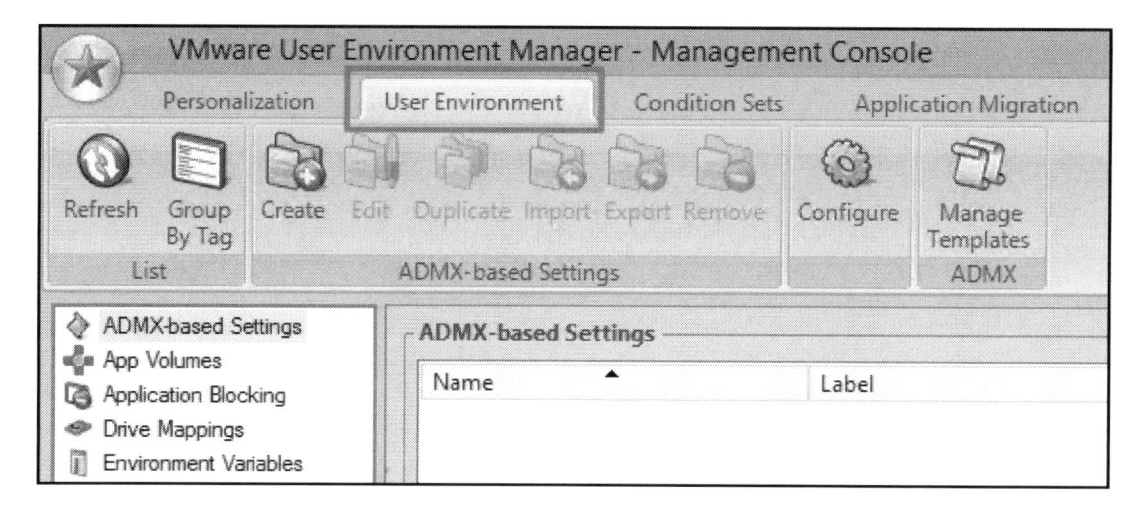

The following User Environment settings are among those configured by default, and are recommended to be removed or customized prior to placing the UEM into production:

- **Files and Folders**: Used to create the README file on the desktop and adds a VMware website entry to the Favorites folder
- **Registry Settings**: Used to create registry keys in `HKCU\Software\VMwareUEMDemo`
- **Shortcuts**: Used to create shortcuts for various default Windows applications, a shortcut to the VMware website, as well as UEM features such as Self-Support and User Environment Refresh
- **Triggered Tasks**: Used to display an information message when the user unlocks the computer

Consult the UEM documentation (`https://www.vmware.com/support/pubs/uem-pubs.html`) for information about the other settings available, and refer to the *Advanced configuration – examples* section of this chapter for examples of how some of these and other settings may be used in a UEM deployment.

UEM group policy settings

UEM is enabled and client options are set using GPOs applied at both the computer and user level. In the examples provided in this chapter, we will be using the following AD security groups and **Organizational Units** (**OUs**):

- `UEM_Users`: AD security group
- `Horizon`: Computers AD OU
- `Horizon`: Users AD OU

UEM user policies

The following steps will provide instructions on the configuration of the user AD GPOs needed to enable UEM:

1. While logged in as a user who has privileges to create and edit GPOs in the AD domain, open the AD **Group Policy Management Console (GPMC)**.
2. Create and link an AD GPO object to the **Horizon - Users** OU. In the example provided, we will name the AD GPO `UEM_Users`.
3. Edit the `UEM_Users` GPO object, and navigate to **User Configuration - Policies - Administrative Templates - VMware UEM - FlexEngine** as shown in the following screenshot:

> The full name of the `Administrative Templates` folder is actually `Administrative Templates: Policy definitions (ADMX files) retrieved from the central store`; to make the instructions easier to read, the shortened name will be used throughout this chapter.

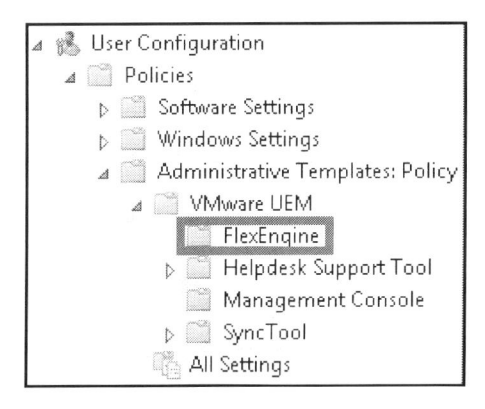

Implementing User Environment Manager

4. Configure the **Flex config files** policy as shown in the following screenshot. Provide the **Central location of Flex config files:**, check the **Process folder recursively** checkbox, and then click **OK**. In the example provided, the UEM Flex config file location is set to `\\dc-01.vjason.local\UEM\general`, where **general** is the default Flex config file folder created by the UEM management console during the initial configuration:

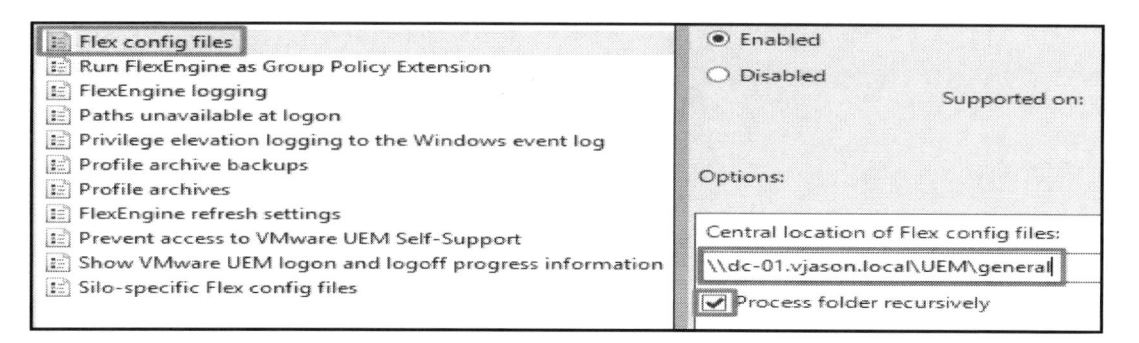

Setting	Options
Flex config files	● Enabled
Run FlexEngine as Group Policy Extension	○ Disabled
FlexEngine logging	Supported on:
Paths unavailable at logon	
Privilege elevation logging to the Windows event log	
Profile archive backups	Options:
Profile archives	
FlexEngine refresh settings	
Prevent access to VMware UEM Self-Support	Central location of Flex config files:
Show VMware UEM logon and logoff progress information	`\\dc-01.vjason.local\UEM\general`
Silo-specific Flex config files	☑ Process folder recursively

> **TIP**
> While not shown in the screenshot, when selected, each UEM GPO setting (along with almost every other GPO setting) is explained in detail within the AD GPMC itself. Refer to this information under **Help:** for a more detailed explanation of what it is you are configuring. You can also refer to the UEM documentation (`https://www.vmware.com/support/pubs/uem-pubs.html`) for information about the different UEM GPO settings.

5. Configure the **Profile archives** policy as shown in the following screenshot. Provide the **Location for storing user profile archives:**, check the **Compress profile archives** and **Retain file modification dates** checkboxes, and then click **OK**. In the example provided, the UEM profile archive file location is set to `\\dc-01.vjason.local\UEMUsers\%username%\Archives`, which will create it within the logged-on user's UEM profile folder:

Chapter 12

> **TIP**
> We won't be setting any of the hide folder options in any of these UEM GPOs, to make it easier to validate that UEM is functioning as intended. I recommend hiding both UEM folders and their shares by default in a production environment, to help prevent them from being discovered and subsequently modified, even by authorized users.

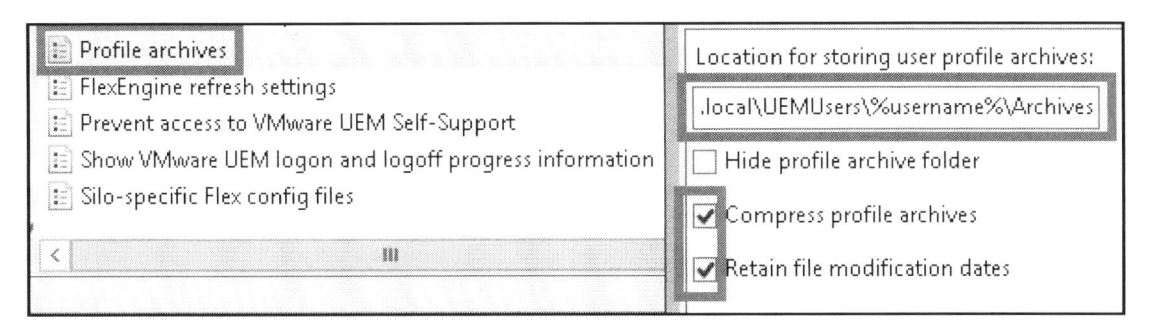

6. Configure the **Profile archive backups** policy as shown in the following screenshot. Provide the **Location for storing user profile archive backups:**, set the **Number of backups per profile archive:** to **1**, check the **Create single backup per day** checkbox, and then click **OK**. In the example provided, the UEM profile archive file location is set to `\\dc-01.vjason.local\UEMUsers\%username%\Backups`, which will create it within the logged-on user's UEM profile folder:

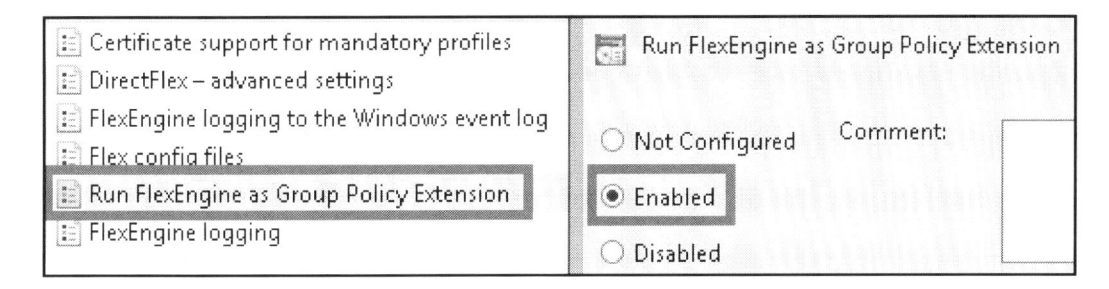

[349]

7. Click the **Run FlexEngine as Group Policy Extension** radio button, as shown in the following screenshot, and then click **OK**:

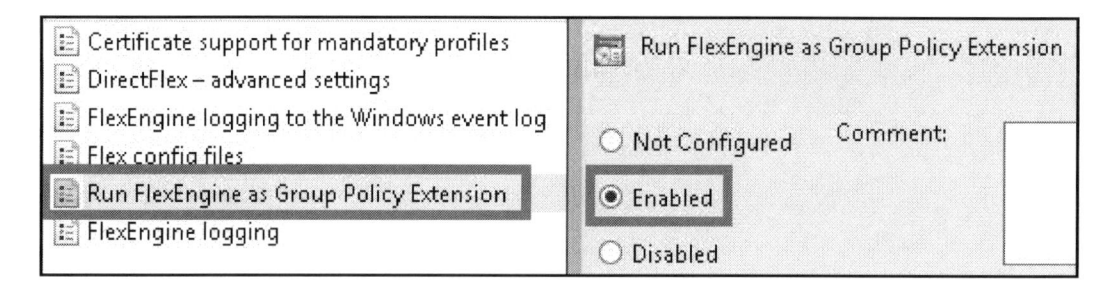

The UEM user GPOs have now been created. Proceed to the next section to create the required user GPOs.

UEM computer policies

The following steps will provide instructions on the configuration of the computer GPOs needed to enable UEM:

1. Create and link a GPO object to the Horizon - Computers OU. In the example provided, we will name the GPO UEM_Computers.
2. While logged in as a user who has privileges to create and edit GPOs in the AD domain, open the AD **GPMC**.

    > The policy we create here would need to be applied to all UEM client computers.

3. Edit the UEM_Computers GPO object, and navigate to **Computer Configuration** | **Policies** | **Windows Settings** | **Scripts** | **Logon/Logoff,** as shown in the following screenshot:

4. Double-click on **Logoff** to open the **Logoff Properties** window, and then click **Add...** to open the **Add a Script** window.
5. In the **Add a Script** window **Script Name:** field, type the full path to the `FlexEngine.exe` executable and, in the Script Parameters field, type **-s** as shown in the following screenshot. Click **OK** when finished, and **OK** again to close the **Logoff Properties** window:

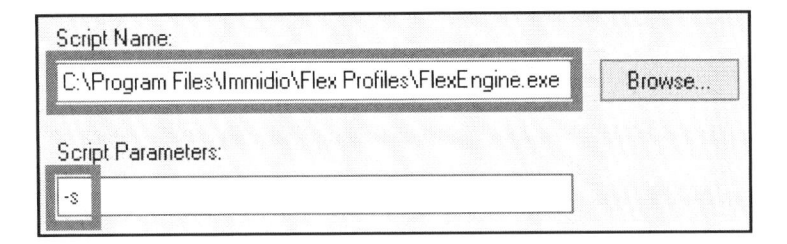

> **TIP**
> You may run the `FlexEngine.exe -s` command at logoff using other techniques if you wish; this isn't your only option for doing so.

6. Navigate to **Computer Configuration | Policies | Administrative Templates | System-Logon**.
7. Edit the **Always wait for the network at computer startup and logon** policy, and click the **Enabled** radio button, as shown in the following screenshot. Click **OK** when finished:

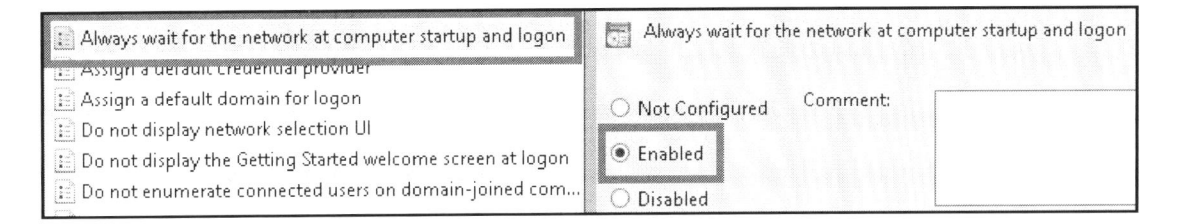

The UEM computer GPOs have now been created and, assuming the previous steps were completed successfully, UEM will now be activated within the client computers. In the next section, we will redirect some of the user profile directories.

[351]

Implementing User Environment Manager

Windows folder redirection

In this section, we will use UEM to enable Windows folder redirection. When deploying folder redirection in production deployments, it is recommended to use a dedicated share that meets your users' aggregate performance and capacity requirements for their data.

> **TIP**: As stated previously, folder redirection is optional and not required for UEM to function. In some cases, you may prefer to instruct users to save critical files to mapped network drives, rather than use the redirected profile folders. Folder redirection will not move existing data when enabled; if implementing within an existing environment, you must have a method to deal with any existing data on the target desktop or RDS server.

The following steps will provide instructions on configuring UEM to redirect user profile folders:

1. Log in to a computer that has the UEM management console installed as a user who is a member of the `UEM_Admins` AD security group.
2. In the Windows **Start** menu, click the **VMware UEM** folder, and then click **Management Console** to open the UEM management console.
3. In the UEM management console, click the **User Environment** tab, then the **Folder Redirection** section, as shown in the following screenshot, and then click **Create** to open the **Folder Redirection** window:

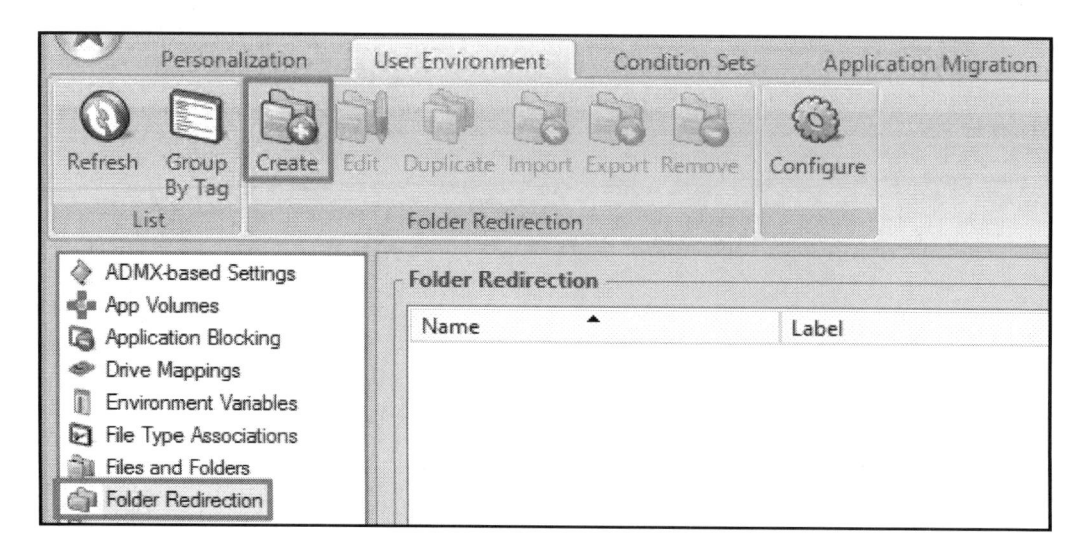

Chapter 12

4. Provide a **Name:** for the policy, and a **Remote path:** where the folders will be directed to. The path must include a variable for the user ID, such as `%username%`. In the example provided, our remote path is `\\dc-01.vjason.local\FolderRedir\%username%`. Click on the checkboxes next to the folders you want redirected, as shown in the following screenshot, and then click **Save**:

The UEM folder redirection settings have now been configured, and will apply to users the next time they log in to a computer that has the UEM agent installed. If data currently exists in the target folders on the computer, it will remain there and the user will be redirected to an empty folder. In the next section, we will review some of the different advanced configuration options for UEM.

Advanced UEM configuration examples

In this section, we will review each of the UEM management console configuration tabs, and provide examples of how some of the more common items are used. The configuration tabs are broken down into four sections:

- **Personalization**: Settings related to individual applications, Windows settings for various hardware devices (mouse, keyboard, and so on), or other system applications, such as the screensaver:
    - The **VMware Community forum for UEM Documents** page is regularly updated with new UEM Application Templates (`https://communities.vmware.com/community/vmtn/user-environment-manager/content?filterID=contentstatus[published]~objecttype~objecttype[document]`)
- **User Environment**: Settings related to a user's Windows profile configuration
- **Condition Sets**: Used to create conditions that control how and when a Personalization, User Environment, and Application Migration feature is used
- **Application Migration**: Used to enable UEM to migrate user settings between different versions of an application

> **TIP**: The Condition Sets and Application Migration features are considered advanced topics that are not discussed in this chapter; refer to the UEM documentation (`https://www.vmware.com/support/pubs/uem-pubs.html`) for details concerning these features.

Personalization

The UEM management console **Personalization** tab can be used to customize Windows application settings. By default, UEM includes templates for various default Windows applications, multiple versions of Microsoft Office, Adobe Acrobat, and WinZip. Additionally, the UEM Application Profiler can be used to generate templates for additional applications as needed.

> **TIP:** The VMware blog post titled *VMware User Environment Manager and Application Profile Settings* (https://blogs.vmware.com/consulting/2015/07/vmware-user-environment-manager-application-profile-settings.html) provides an example of how the Application Profiler tool is used.

Application profile Import/Export feature

One of the most common options that will be configured when using UEM within the application profile is the **Import/Export** feature, which determines which registry trees, folder trees, and even individual folders will be retained by UEM for use in subsequent client sessions.

The following screenshot shows the default **Import/Export** screen for Microsoft **Word** 2013, which is one of the application templates included by default with UEM. By default, no settings are retained which is, something we will change in the next screenshot:

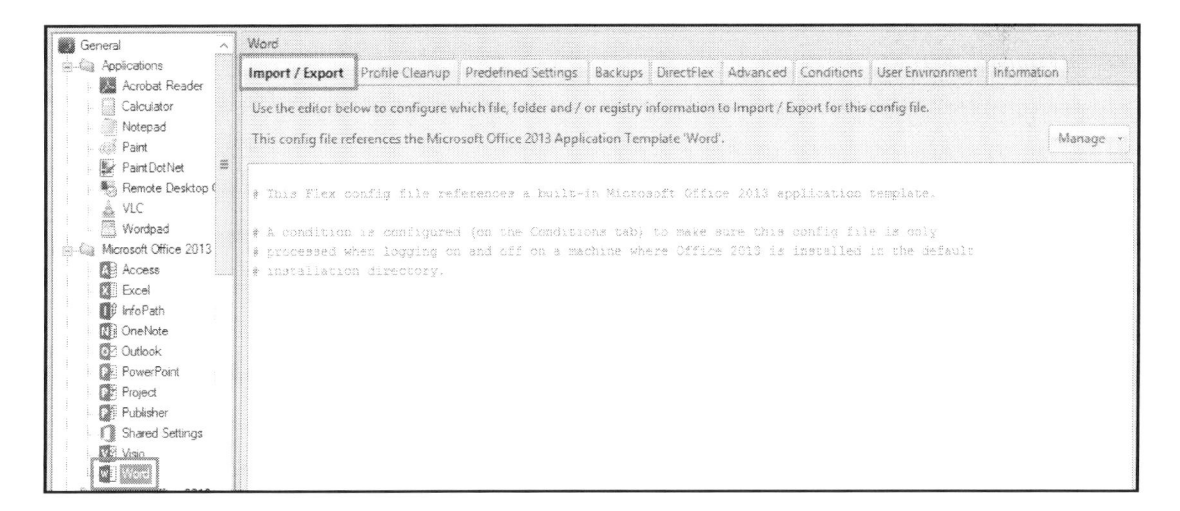

Implementing User Environment Manager

The following is what we must enter in the application template screen to retain the registry trees, folder trees, and files that we have determined we will need to retain across client sessions. To retain additional items, we would simply need to follow the same syntax and add those items to the template:

> Note that Windows environment variables are used, bracketed by < and > symbols instead of % signs, rather than providing full paths to any file references.

```
[IncludeRegistryKeys]
HKCU\Software\Microsoft\Office\Word
HKCU\Software\Microsoft\Office\15.0\Word
[IncludeFolderTrees]
<AppData>\Microsoft\Word
[IncludeFiles]
<LocalAppData>\Microsoft\Office\Word.officeUI
```

> **TIP**: Careful research and analysis is required to determine what, if any, registry settings or application files you need UEM to retain across client sessions. The VMware Community Forum for UEM is a good resource for this (https://communities.vmware.com/community/vmtn/user-environment-manager), but in some cases you may just need to experiment to get the results you want. Resist the temptation to copy every application configuration item you can find, and instead use Windows mandatory profiles or GPOs to set those values on a global basis so UEM isn't forced to manage more than it needs to.

UEM assists you in adding items to this screen by validating your entries whenever possible, be it by validating the text entry itself or by popping up a list of potential selections. The following screenshot shows the popup for the possible items to include or exclude, but a similar popup is displayed for user environment variables:

[IncludeFiles]
- IncludeRegistryTrees
- IncludeFolderTrees
- IncludeIndividualRegistryKeys
- IncludeIndividualRegistryValues
- IncludeIndividualFolders
- **IncludeFiles**
- IncludeFilesRecursively
- ExcludeRegistryTrees
- ExcludeIndividualRegistryKeys
- ExcludeIndividualRegistryValues

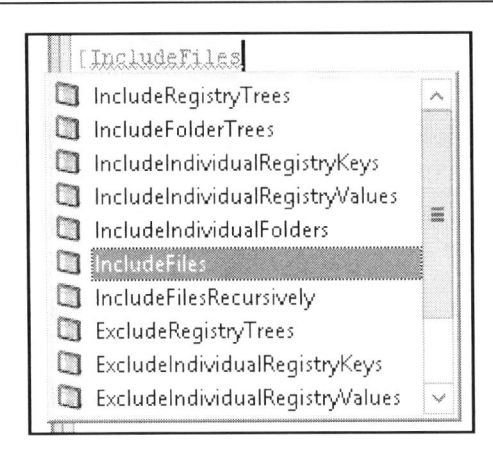

The following screenshot shows the completed entry. Click the **Save Config File** option to update the settings and apply them to UEM users. The next time the user logs off, the registry keys and files specified will be retained by UEM for use with subsequent client sessions:

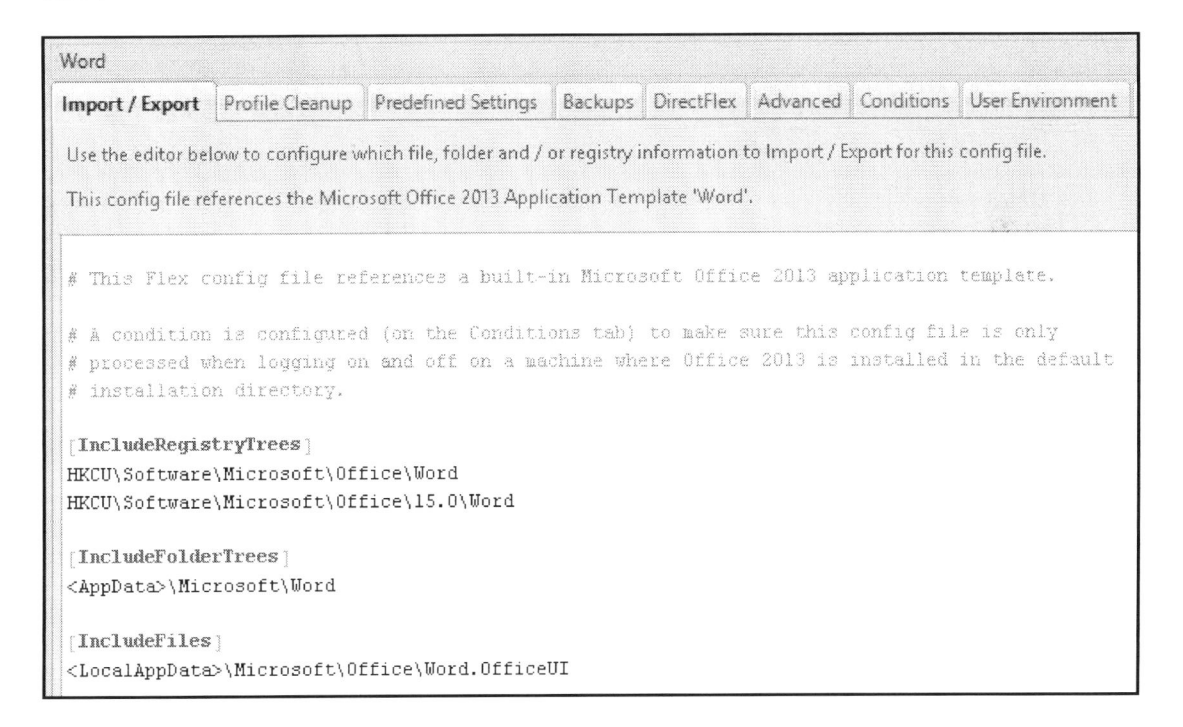

Word

Import / Export | Profile Cleanup | Predefined Settings | Backups | DirectFlex | Advanced | Conditions | User Environment

Use the editor below to configure which file, folder and / or registry information to Import / Export for this config file.

This config file references the Microsoft Office 2013 Application Template 'Word'.

```
# This Flex config file references a built-in Microsoft Office 2013 application template.

# A condition is configured (on the Conditions tab) to make sure this config file is only
# processed when logging on and off on a machine where Office 2013 is installed in the default
# installation directory.

[IncludeRegistryTrees]
HKCU\Software\Microsoft\Office\Word
HKCU\Software\Microsoft\Office\15.0\Word

[IncludeFolderTrees]
<AppData>\Microsoft\Word

[IncludeFiles]
<LocalAppData>\Microsoft\Office\Word.OfficeUI
```

As shown in each screenshot in this section, each application template has several options that control how and when it runs, sets limits that control what files are exported, and many other options. Consult the UEM documentation (https://www.vmware.com/support/pubs/uem-pubs.html) for information about these options, and how they can be used to enable even more granular control over the **Personalization** settings.

User Environment

The UEM management console **User Environment** tab can be used to customize user profile settings. UEM offers several different built-in options for managing the profile, as shown in the following screenshot, although, given that it includes the ability to update the registry virtually, any Windows option can be configured, assuming you know the proper syntax:

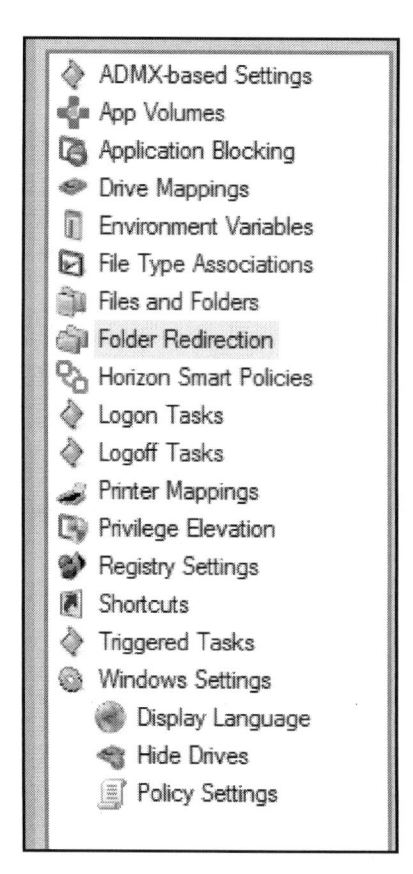

- ADMX-based Settings
- App Volumes
- Application Blocking
- Drive Mappings
- Environment Variables
- File Type Associations
- Files and Folders
- Folder Redirection
- Horizon Smart Policies
- Logon Tasks
- Logoff Tasks
- Printer Mappings
- Privilege Elevation
- Registry Settings
- Shortcuts
- Triggered Tasks
- Windows Settings
  - Display Language
  - Hide Drives
  - Policy Settings

Most of the settings are self-explanatory for anyone with basic Windows knowledge. These include **Drive Mappings**, **Environment Variables**, **File Type Associations**, **Logon Tasks**, **Logoff Tasks**, **Printer Mappings**, **Registry Settings**, **Shortcuts**, and common **Windows Settings**. Each of these represents items you can customize using traditional Windows GPOs, but the advantage of using UEM is that you don't need permissions in AD to configure these settings. The following remaining items can be set using the User Environment tab:

- **ADMX-based settings**: Using the Manage Templates button in the UEM management console, you can import AD ADMX files and use them to implement virtually any GPO setting using UEM.
- **Application Blocking**: Authorize or block applications within the desktop using detailed conditional policies, without the need to use an overhead of Windows group policies.
- **Files and Folders**: Copy files or folders to the UEM client, including items such as internet shortcuts.
- **Horizon Policies**: Apply common policies to Horizon desktops, including PCoIP bandwidth policies, USB redirection, and so on. When combined with the policy **Condition** tab, this enables very granular control over Horizon settings, without the need to use an overhead of Windows group policies.
- **Triggered Tasks**: Used to perform different tasks, including custom commands, when a UEM client computer is locked, unlocked, disconnected from, or reconnected to. You can also apply UEM Condition Sets to further control when these tasks are performed.

As stated previously, in many cases the actions these settings perform are something you can do using GPOs or even custom scripts, but the power of UEM is that it is all done from a central console, without the need to make changes to the AD domain itself. Additionally, given the power of features such as UEM condition sets, you can exercise complete control over how and when a given configuration item is applied.

Shortcut management feature

The following screenshot shows one example of the level of control provided by UEM. This is an example of a UEM-created shortcut, and you can see the different options that exist for where the shortcut is created; the **Conditions** tab, which allows us to control when it is created (if required); and other settings related to the application execution parameters and appearance:

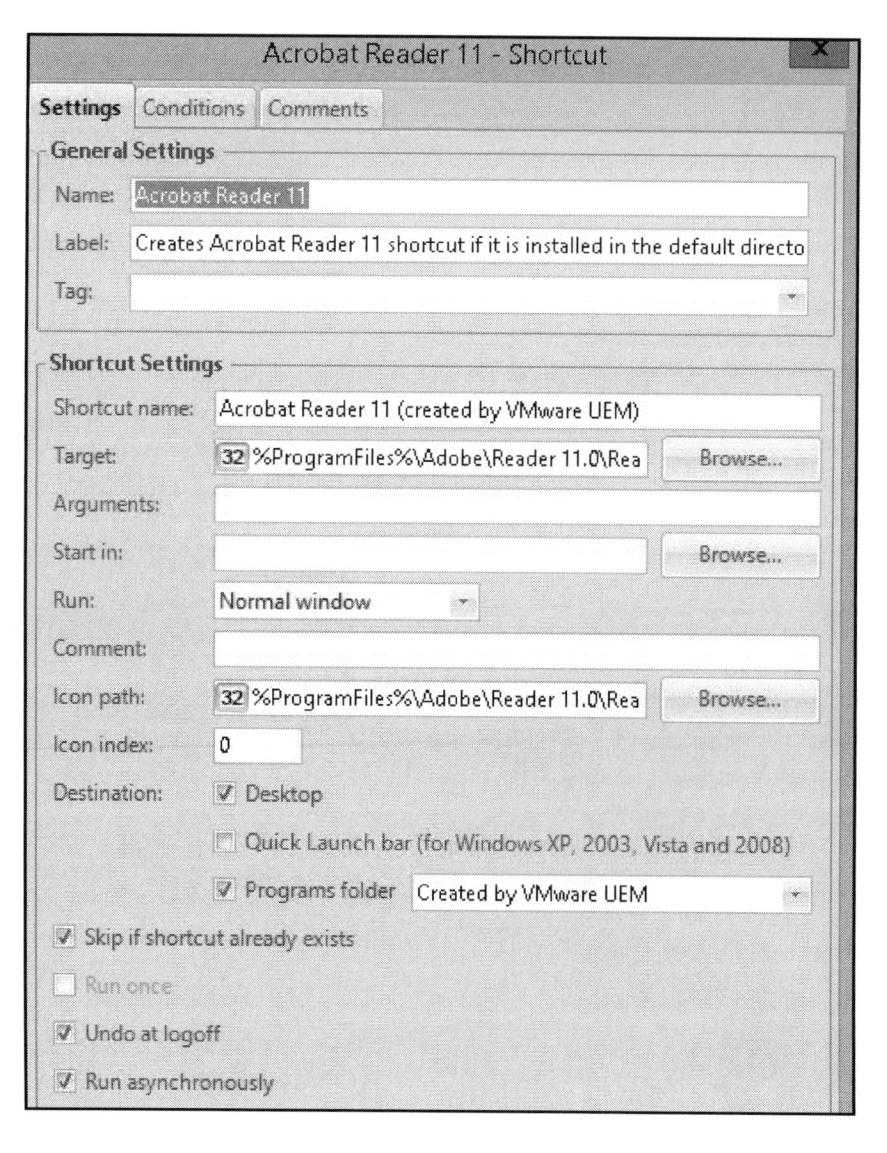

As shown in each screenshot in this section, each UEM has the ability to manage the entirety of a user's profile configuration without the need to make any changes to AD itself. Consult the UEM documentation (`https://www.vmware.com/support/pubs/uem-pubs.html`) for information about how to fully customize user profiles to suit your exact needs.

Summary

In this chapter, you have been introduced to a very useful component of Horizon: UEM. You learned what is required to deploy UEM and the UEM client agent, perform the initial configuration, and implement the AD GPOs required to enable the feature in the clients.

We then discussed UEM user profile folder redirection, which may be required in environments where you must be certain that user data files are retained across client sessions.

Finally, you were introduced to some of the more advanced features of UEM, which provide you with total control over user profile and Windows settings without the need to edit the existing AD GPO configuration.

In the next chapter, we will discuss the Horizon Just-in-Time Management Platform, which provides a whole new technique for managing the individual components that Horizon administrators bring together to provide end-user computing resources.

Questions

1. What is the purpose of VMware UEM?
2. What are some of the more typical use cases for UEM?
3. Explain one reason why you think UEM is a better product than Horizon Persona Management.
4. What types of Windows settings or data can UEM be used to capture?
5. What types of Windows settings or data should UEM not be used to capture?
6. What is the name of the UEM feature you can use to quickly begin capturing user persona data?

Further reading

The following resources may be used to learn more about the topics described in this chapter:

- VMware documentation:
    - **VMware User Environment Manager** (`https://docs.vmware.com/en/VMware-User-Environment-Manager/index.html`)
    - **VMware Horizon** (`https://www.vmware.com/support/pubs/view_pubs.html`)
    - **VMware vSphere** (`https://www.vmware.com/support/pubs/vsphere-esxi-vcenter-server-pubs.html`)
- Microsoft documentation:
    - **Windows** (`https://docs.microsoft.com/en-us/windows/`)

13
Implementing the Just-in-Time Management Platform (JMP)

The VMware Horizon **Just-in-Time Management Platform** (**JMP**), pronounced jump, is an optional component of an VMware Horizon infrastructure. The Horizon **JMP Server** provides for a single unified Horizon GUI that can assign instant-clone desktops, App Volumes AppStacks, and User Environment Manager persona settings to deliver personalized desktops and applications on demand, eliminating the need to maintain persistent desktops.

This chapter will discuss multiple topics surrounding the requirements, deployment, configuration, and use of the Horizon JMP Server.

We will cover the following topics:

- An overview of the Horizon Just-in-Time Management Platform
- The virtual machine and operating system requirements of a Horizon Connection Server
- Infrastructure, vCenter, and Horizon installation prerequisites
- Installing the Horizon JMP Server
- Configuring the Horizon JMP Server
- Creating a **JMP Assignment**, which uses a single wizard to entitle access to a Horizon pool and AppVolumes AppStacks, and select which UEM configuration options to apply
- Deleting, duplicating, or modifying a JMP Assignment

JMP Assignments make it much easier to grant access to Horizon resources. While veteran Horizon administrators may prefer using the individual administrative consoles to perform this task, you should ask yourself whether a JMP Server would make it easier for junior resources to create and administer end user workspaces.

An Overview of the Horizon Just-in-Time Management Platform

Horizon JMP combines features of Horizon, vSphere, User Environment Manager, App Volumes, and Workspace ONE to create an on-demand personalized desktop, without the need to use persistent desktops or multiple administration consoles to provision it all.

The following components work together to create a just-in-time personalized desktop:

- **User Environment Manager**: Stores user-specific desktop and application settings, persisting them across multiple devices, versions of Windows, and application instances.
- **User file share**: A file share that stores user data that is redirected from specific folders inside the VM. Redirecting folders reduces the need to copy files back and forth when a Horizon client starts or ends their session.
- **AppVolumes AppStacks:** Used to decouple applications from the virtual desktop master image, ensuring that users are only provided the applications that they need.
- **AppVolumes Writable Volumes**: Provides a destination for user-installed applications or for applications that require a local cache, since a writable volume appears as part of the local C: drive. Writable volumes allow these applications and their data to persist across Horizon client sessions, even when using Instant Clone desktops.
- **vSphere Instant Clones**: Used to rapidly clone both the memory and the disk of a running parent VM, allowing non-persistent desktops to be delivered on-demand with very little wait time. Since user-persona data, user files, and applications (both assigned and user installed) are decoupled from the desktop, there is no need to retain the contents of the desktop when the Horizon client logs off.

While Workspace ONE does not play a role in delivering Horizon infrastructure-hosted resources, it provides users a single workspace from which to access all of their applications or other critical resources.

Just-in-Time Management Server requirements

Like many other software services, Horizon JMP Server requires a minimum server configuration to ensure adequate performance. Additionally, specific versions of vSphere, Horizon, App Volumes, and User Environment Manager are required, as are a dedicated SQL server database. This section will provide details about these requirements.

Hardware requirements

The Horizon JMP Server has specific requirements with regard to the hardware specifications and host operating system.

The following table outlines the minimum hardware specifications of a Horizon JMP Server:

Hardware component	Minimum requirement
Processor	4 vCPUs
Memory	8 GB RAM
Hard disk capacity	100 GB

Like most other software platforms, the recommended guidelines should be followed to ensure that the Horizon JMP Server performs optimally.

Software requirements

Horizon JMP supports 64-bit Windows Server 2008 R2 SP1, 2012 R2, and Windows 2016 as the host operating system. Standard, Enterprise, and Datacenter editions of Windows Server 2008 R2 are supported, as well as Standard and Datacenter editions of Windows Server 2012 R2 and 2016.

General requirements

The Horizon JMP Server has the following additional requirements:

- You should consider replacing the default JMP Server certificate with one that is trusted by your infrastructure hosts and clients. Consult the Horizon JMP Server documentation for the procedure used to replace the default self-signed certificates (https://docs.vmware.com/en/VMware-Horizon-7/7.6/horizon-JMP-server-installation/GUID-FF922872-D60F-4A82-98F5-A717F489005E.html).
    - If you choose not to replace the JMP Server self-signed certificate, you will need to import the JMP Server certificate into the user **Trusted Root Certification Authorities** store on the workstation you use to configure the JMP Server.
- Active Directory must be at functional level of 2008 or later.
- Active Directory must be configured for **LDAP over SSL (LDAPS)** or **StartTLS (LDAP over TLS)**
    - You will also need a copy of the Active Directory SSL certificate, exported using the Windows certificates MMC as a **Base-64 encoded X.509 (.CER)** file named adCA.pem
        - You do not need to export the certificate private key
- A JMP Server service (user) account created in Active Directory that will be granted administrative permissions to your Horizon pod, App Volumes, and User Environment manager; in the examples provided we will use an account named svc-jmp.
- The Horizon JMP Server and Horizon Connection Servers must have their time synchronized.

Database requirements

Horizon JMP Server utilizes Microsoft SQL Server to store critical configuration data and JMP Assignments, which is the term used for combined resources you entitle using the JMP Server. The following versions of SQL are supported:

- SQL Server 2012 (SP1, SP2, SP3, and SP4)
- SQL Server 2014 (SP1 and SP2 with CU7 or later)
- SQL Server 2016 (SP1 with CU6 or later)

The database must be created prior to installing the JMP Server software. The following are the general requirements of the JMP Server database:

- The database name must not contain non-ASCII characters.
- You should determine whether your SQL Server supports SSL connections, as this is a JMP Server configuration option.
- Use the default values for the database and log file **Initial size** and **Autogrowth**.
- You may use either **SQL Server authentication** or **Windows authentication** for the database, and grant the account the following permissions:
    - The examples provided in this chapter will use a SQL account named `svc-jmp` and a database named `jmpdb`.
    - The account must have `db_owner` permissions in the target database.
    - The account must hold the `sysadmin` role on the hosting SQL Server instance.
- The JMP Server database should be backed up using a similar schedule to your Horizon pod and App Volumes Manager Server.

Consult the Microsoft SQL Server documentation (`https://docs.microsoft.com/en-us/sql/sql-server/sql-server-technical-documentation`) for additional information about creating databases and SQL user accounts, and granting access to SQL server instances and databases.

VMware infrastructure requirements

Horizon JMP Server relies on multiple VMware products in order to deliver just-in-time desktops. The following versions of these products are supported:

- vSphere 6.0 Update 2 or later (minimum requirement for Instant Clone functionality)
    - 6.5 or later recommended
- Horizon 7.5 or later (minimum requirement for JMP Server installation)
    - A Microsoft RDSH server or Windows desktop master image with a Horizon Agent with the Instant Clone option, App Volumes agent, and User Environment Manager FlexEngine service installed.

Implementing the Just-in-Time Management Platform (JMP)

- You will also need a copy of the Horizon Connection Server SSL certificate, exported using the Windows certificates MMC as a **Base-64 encoded X.509 (.CER)** file named `horizon.cert.pem`.
    - You do not need to export the certificate private key.
- The `svc-jmp` service account should be granted administrative permissions at the root level of the Horizon pod.
- You will need a floating assignment, Instant Clone-based desktop, or RDS Server pool to create a JMP Assignment.

- App Volumes 2.14 or later:
    - App Volumes should be configured as needed to attach AppStacks and, if required, writable volumes.
    - You will also need a copy of the App Volumes Manager server certificate, exported using a web browser connected to the server console, and saved as a `PEM` file named `av-selfsigned.cert.pem`.
    - The `svc-jmp` service account should be granted administrative permissions in App Volumes Manager.
    - If you wish to include AppStacks in your JMP Assignment, you will need to create them in advance.

> **TIP**
> While **JMP Assignments** will be used to assign AppStacks to users, writable volumes are still assigned using whichever method you prefer using the App Volumes Manager such as user, computer, security group, or organizational unit.

- User Environment Manager 9.2.1 or later:
    - UEM should be configured as needed to capture needed application settings and, if required, redirect user profile folders (documents, pictures, and so on).
    - The `svc-jmp` service account should be granted administrative permissions to the UEM configuration share.
    - If you wish to leverage UEM in your JMP Assignment, you will need to configure the settings you require in advance.
- Identity Manager 2.9.2 or later (for optional integration with VMware Workspace ONE)

> The deployment of Identity Manager and Workspace ONE, as well as their integration with the JMP server, are outside the scope of this book. Refer to the VMware Identity Manager (https://docs.vmware.com/en/VMware-Identity-Manager/index.html) and VMware Workspace ONE (https://docs.vmware.com/en/VMware-Workspace-ONE/index.html) documentation.

Deploying the JMP Server

The Horizon JMP Server software is delivered as a single executable (EXE) file, named in a format similar to `VMware-Jmp-Installer-x.x.x-yyyyyyyy.exe`. This installer is used for all three Horizon Connection Server types, which include Standard, Replica, Security, and Enrollment.

> You must make sure that your JMP Server database and user are prepared prior to installing the JMP Server software, and that you have exported the SSL certificates from your Horizon Connection Server, App Volumes Manager, and Active Directory domain controller.

Installing the JMP Server software

The following steps outline the installation process for the JMP Server software. They assume that you are already logged in to the server where you will install the JMP Server software, with a user account that has administrative permissions:

1. Double-click on the **Horizon JMP Server** installer EXE file to launch the installer.
2. In the **Welcome to the Install Shield Wizard for VMware Just-in-Time Manager Platform (JMP) Server** window, click on **Next>**.
3. In the **License Agreement** window, review the license agreement, click on the **I accept the terms in the license agreement** radio checkbox, and then click on **Next>**.
4. In the **Allow HTTP Traffic on Port 80?** window, it's recommended to leave the **Allow HTTP?** checkbox unchecked and then click **Next>**. HTTPS should be required for security purposes.

Implementing the Just-in-Time Management Platform (JMP)

5. In the **Database Server for JMP Server Platform Services** window, populate the fields for the **Database server that you are connecting to:**, **Connect using:**, and **Name of database catalog** sections, uncheck the **Enable SSL Connection ?** checkbox if your SQL Server does not support it, and then click **Next>**:

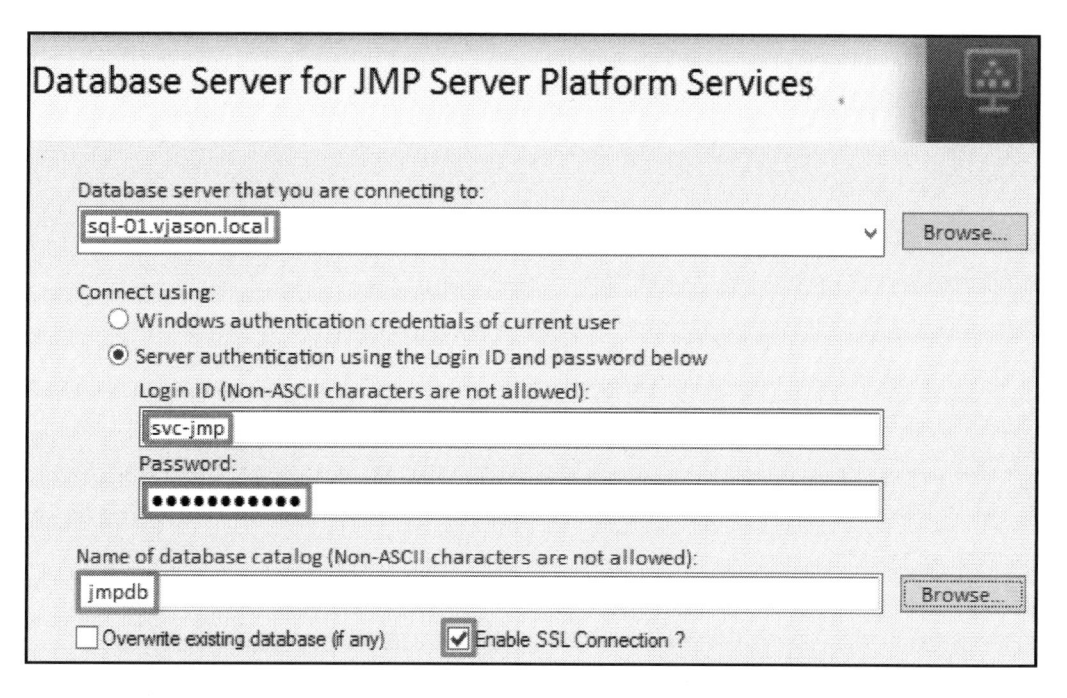

6. In the **Ready to Install the Program** window, click **Install**.
7. In the **Installation complete** window, click **Finish**.
8. If you decided to obtain a trusted SSL certificate for the JMP Server, back up the default Horizon JMP Server `key` and `crt` files (`jmp_self_vmware.com.key` and `jmp_self_vmware.com.crt`) located in the `C:\Program Files (x86)\VMware\JMP\com\XMS\nginx\conf` folder and shown in the following screenshot, and then replace them with the new trusted ones:

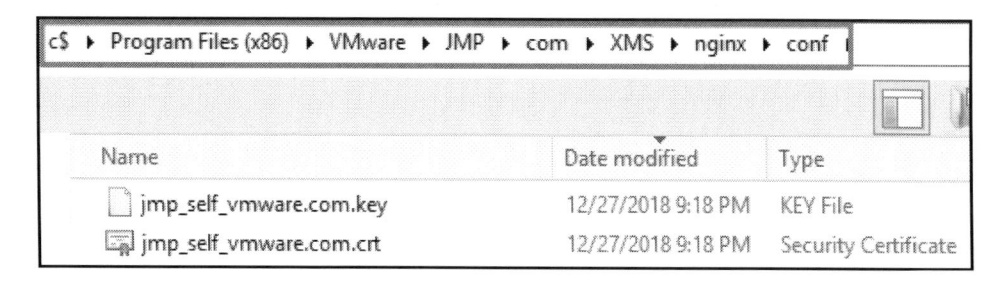

9. Copy the extracted and renamed Active Directory SSL certificate (`adCA.pem`) to the `C:\Program Files (x86)\VMware\JMP\com\XMS\config` folder:

Name	Date modified	Type
adCA.pem	12/29/2018 8:48 PM	PEM File

c$ ▶ Program Files (x86) ▶ VMware ▶ JMP ▶ com ▶ XMS ▶ config

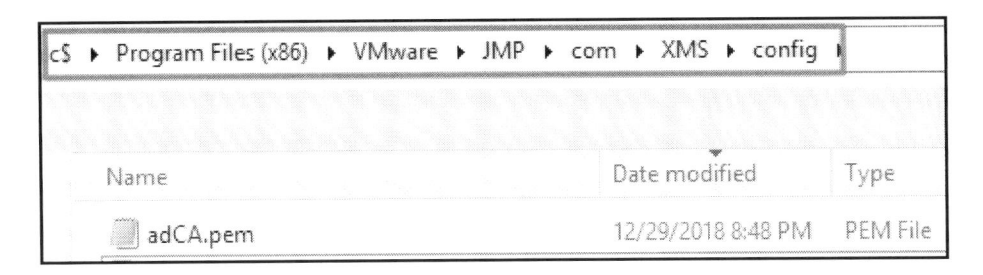

10. Copy the extracted and renamed Horizon Connection Server and App Volumes Manager Server SSL certificates (`horizon.cert.pem` and `av-selfsigned.cert.pem`, respectively) to the `C:\Program Files (x86)\VMware\JMP\com` folder:

Network ▶ horjmp1 ▶ c$ ▶ Program Files (x86) ▶ VMware ▶ JMP ▶ com

Name	Date modified	Type
av-selfsigned.cert.pem	12/27/2018 8:58 PM	PEM File
horizon.cert.pem	12/27/2018 8:53 PM	PEM File

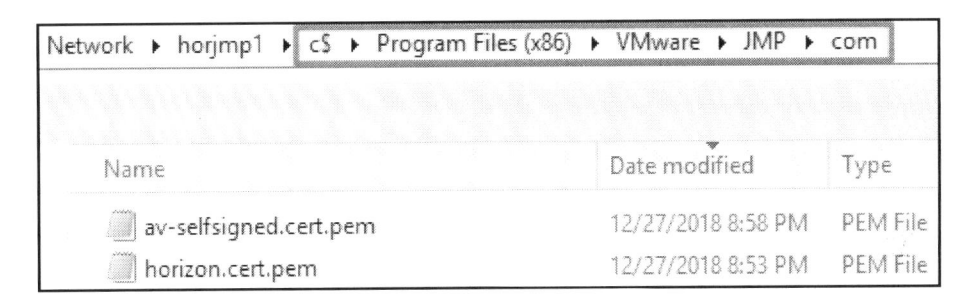

11. Restart the JMP Server to load all of the new and updated SSL certificates.

The Horizon JMP Server software is now installed, and ready to be integrated with the Horizon pod, App Volumes, and User Environment Manager.

> **TIP**: To ensure that you can recover the JMP Server in the event of a disaster, retain backups of the certificates that you copied to it, as well as a backup of the JMP Server database. If you are restoring all components of your Horizon infrastructure, all of the backups that will be used to perform the restore should have been performed as closely together as is possible.

Configuring the JMP settings

The Horizon JMP Server is configured using the **Horizon Console**, which is an alternative to the traditional Horizon Connection Server management interface that is both simpler in design and (also) the only location where you can enable various newer Horizon features such as the JMP Server.

> **TIP**
> If you did not replace the default JMP Server SSL certificate with one trusted in your environment, you will need to access the JMP Server web page using a web browser (https://horjmp1.vjason.local in the example provided) and import the self-signed certificate into the user **Trusted Root Certification Authorities** store on the workstation you will use to configure the JMP Server. Note that you cannot actually perform any tasks using the web page, you are just accessing it to import the SSL certificate.

The Horizon Console can be accessed by appending the Connection Server URL with /newadmin, such as https://horcon1.vjason.local/newadmin. The following steps outline the configuration process for the JMP Server:

1. Log in to the Horizon Console using an AD account that has administrative permissions. The following screenshot shows the login page for our sample Horizon Connection Server, which was accessed at the https://horcon1.vjason.local/newadmin URL:

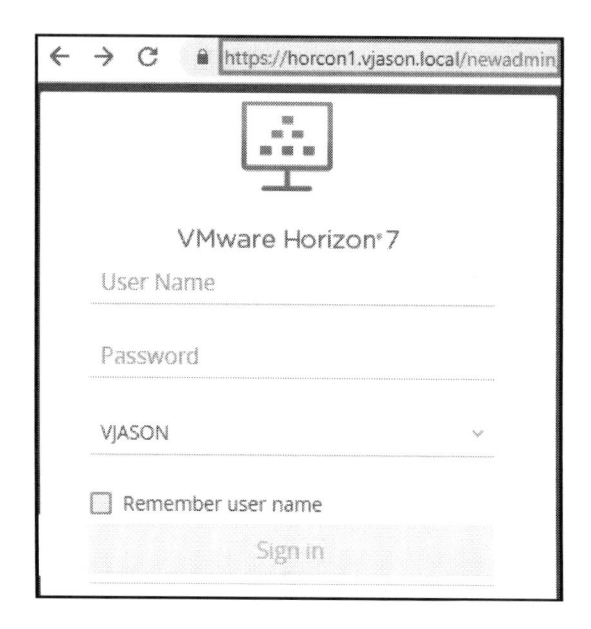

Chapter 13

2. Upon successful login, the dashboard will open to the welcome page:

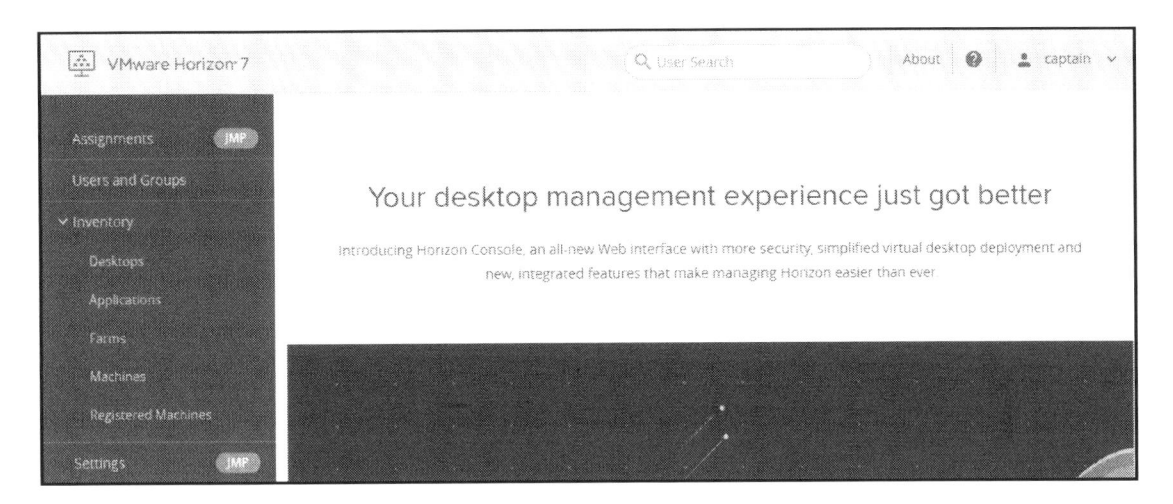

3. Click on **Settings**, then **Add JMP Server**, as shown in the following screenshot:

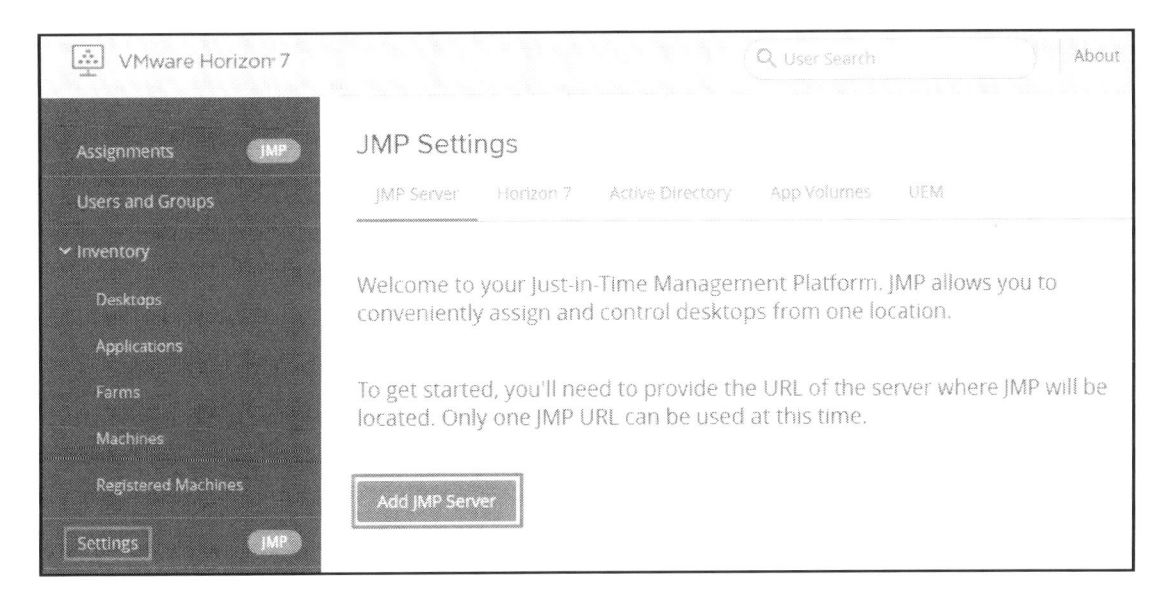

[373]

Implementing the Just-in-Time Management Platform (JMP)

4. Enter the **JMP Server URL** (`https://horjmp1.vjason.local`), and then click **Save**:

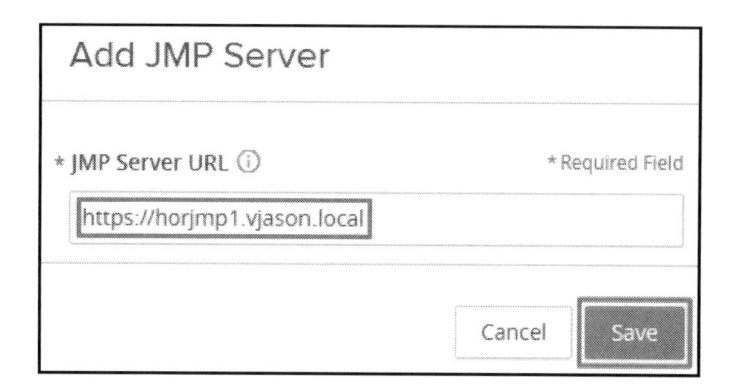

5. Verify that the **JMP server is validated!** message appears:

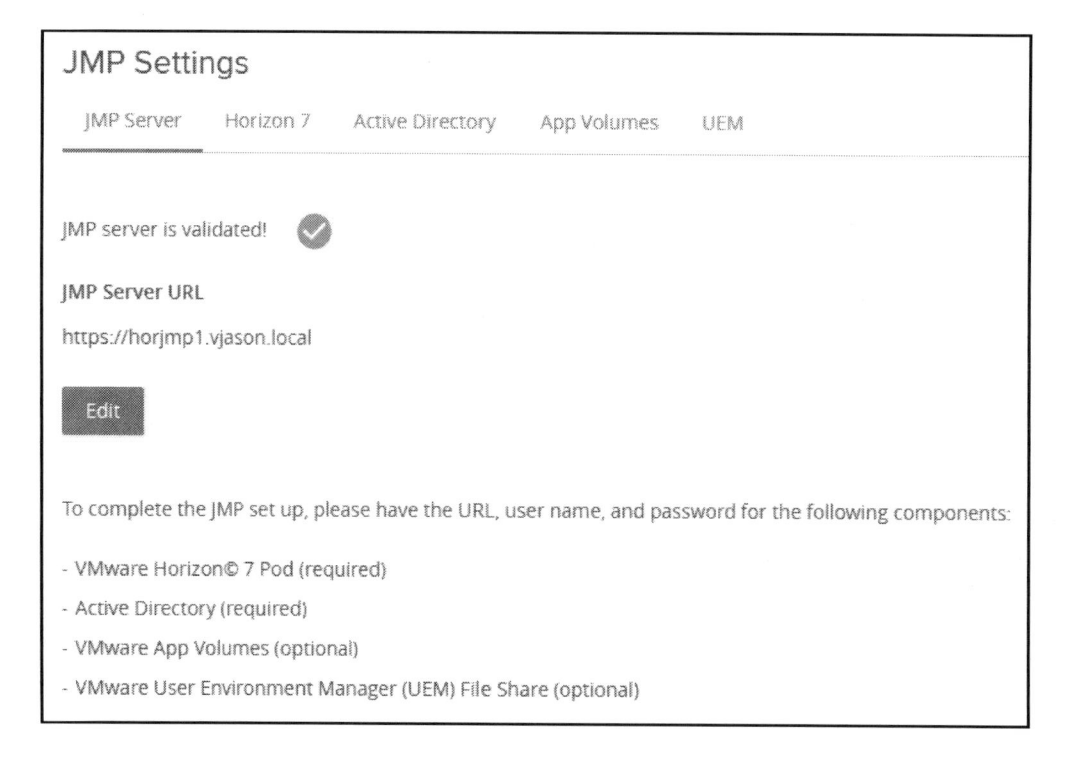

Note that other requirements are also displayed at this time; we will configure those next.

[374]

6. Click on the **Horizon 7** tab, then click **Add Credentials**:

JMP Settings

JMP Server | Horizon 7 | Active Directory | App Volumes | UEM

Add Credentials

Your Horizon service account is required for JMP. Click Add to enter the Horizon URL and service account credentials. The Horizon URL can't be changed once it's validated.

7. Enter the **Connection Server URL**, **Service Account User Name**, **Service Account Password**, and **Service Account Domain**, as shown in the following screenshot and then click **Save:**

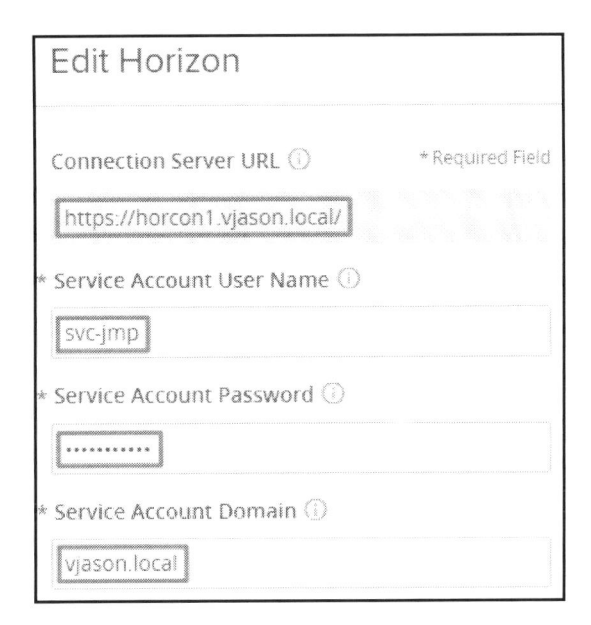

Edit Horizon

Connection Server URL   * Required Field

https://horcon1.vjason.local/

* Service Account User Name

svc-jmp

* Service Account Password

....

* Service Account Domain

vjason.local

Implementing the Just-in-Time Management Platform (JMP)

8. Click on the **Active Directory** tab, then click **Add**:

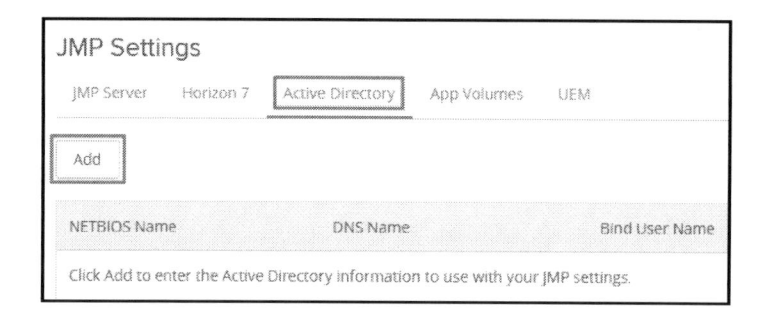

9. Enter the domain **NETBIOS Name**, **DNS Domain Name**, **Bind User Name** (JMP service account), and **Bind Password;** click on the radio checkbox for the **Protocol** to use when connecting to your domain controllers; edit the **Context** if needed (default is entire domain) as shown in the following screenshot; and then click **Save:**

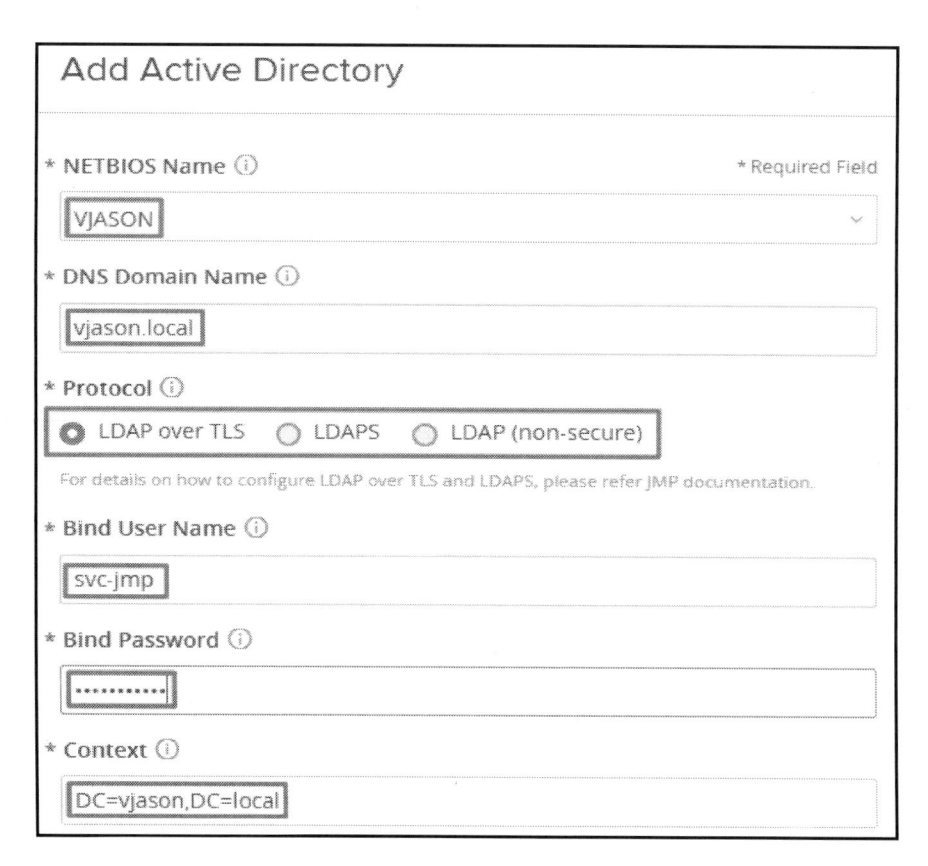

10. Click on the **App Volumes** tab, then click **Add**:

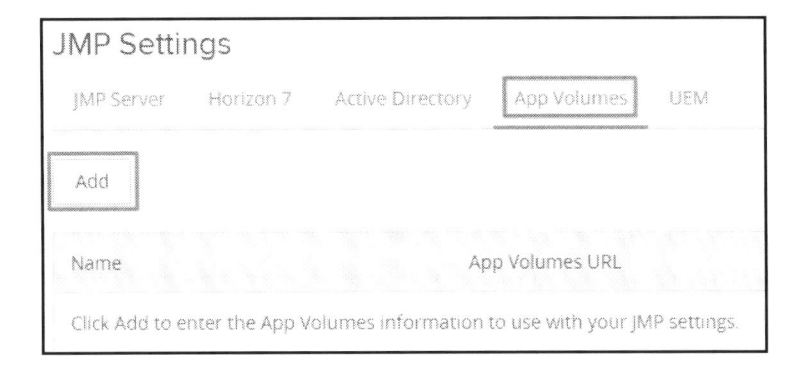

```
JMP Settings

  JMP Server    Horizon 7    Active Directory    App Volumes    UEM

  Add

  Name                                   App Volumes URL

  Click Add to enter the App Volumes information to use with your JMP settings.
```

11. Enter an identifying **Name** for the App Volumes instance, the **App Volumes Server URL**, the **Service Account User Name**, **Service Account Password**, and **Service Account Domain**, as shown in the following screenshot and then click **Save**:

```
Add App Volumes Instance

  Name                                     * Required Field
  [rtpappv01]

  * App Volumes Server URL
  [https://rtpappv01.vjason.local]

  * Service Account User Name
  [svc-jmp]

  * Service Account Password
  [············]

  * Service Account Domain
  [vjason.local]
```

> **TIP**: Remember that AppVolumes writable volumes are still assigned using App Volumes Manager directly.

[377]

Implementing the Just-in-Time Management Platform (JMP)

12. Click on the **UEM** tab, then click **Add**:

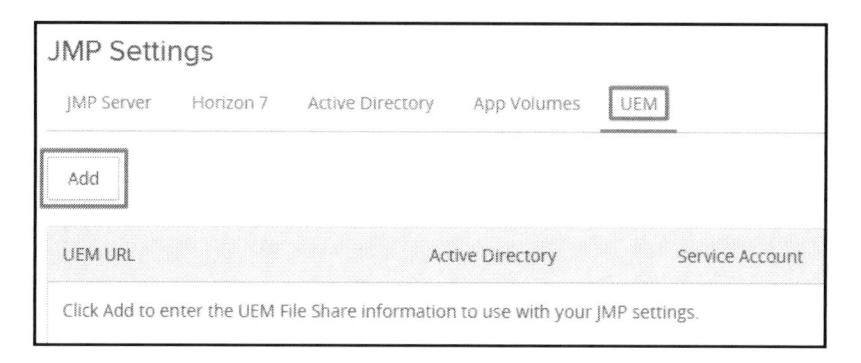

13. Enter the UEM Configuration **File Share UNC Path**, **User Name** (JMP service account), **Password**, and **Active Directory** NETBIOS domain name, as shown in the following screenshot, and then click **Save:**

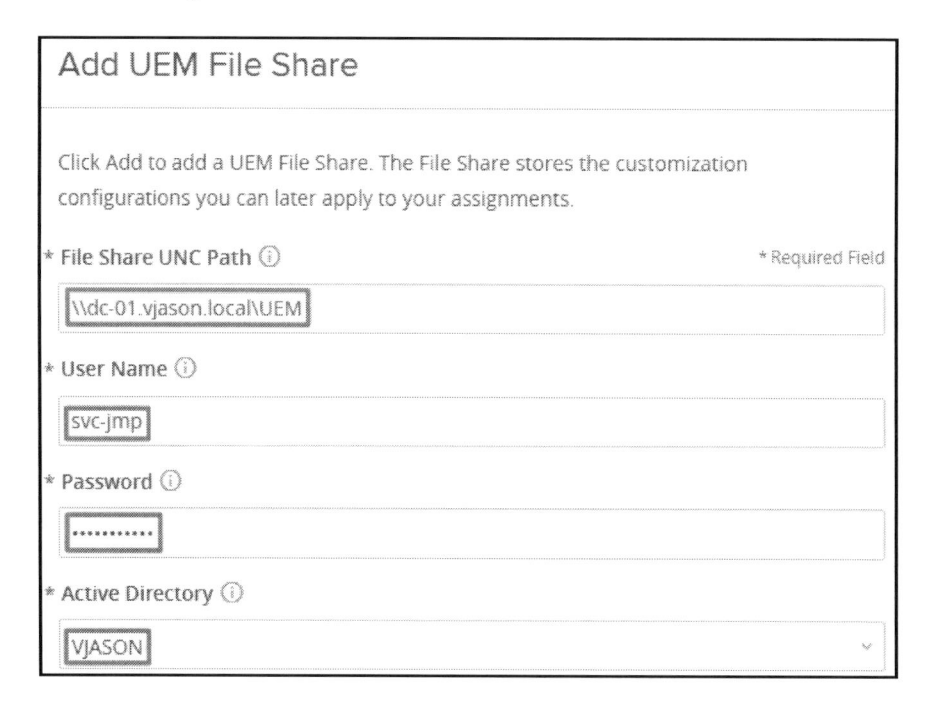

The JMP Server is now integrated with our Horizon pod, App Volumes Manager, and User Environment Manager. In the next section, we will create a JMP Assignment, which allows us to assign all of these resources to a user or group using a single wizard.

Managing JMP Assignments

JMP Assignments is the term used to describe the combination of Horizon pool entitlement, App Volumes AppStacks assignment, and specific UEM managed settings. The advantage of using a JMP Server to manage these assignments is that you can do all of it using a single wizard within the Horizon Console, rather than a combination of multiple management interfaces.

Creating a JMP Assignment

The following steps outline how to create a JMP Assignment using the Horizon Console:

1. Log in to the Horizon Console (`https://horcon1.vjason.local/newadmin`) using an AD account that has administrative permissions.
2. Click on **Assignments**, and then **New**:

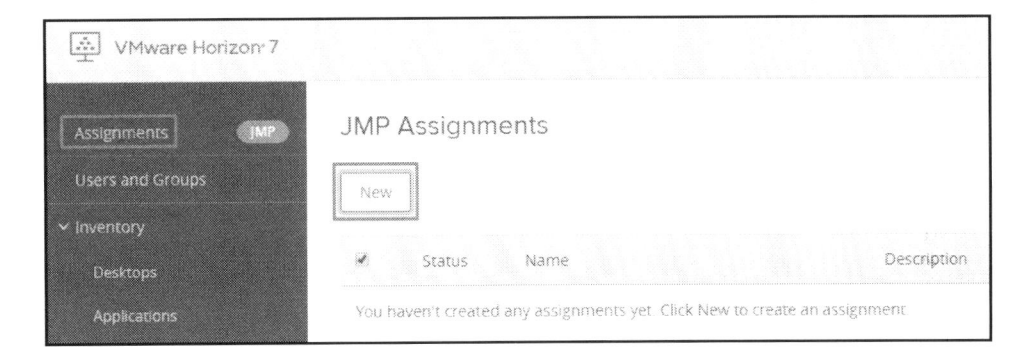

3. In the **Users** window, use the search field to select a user or group to create an assignment for. In the example shown in the following screenshot, we searched for and then clicked in a user named **Eric Lehnsherr:**

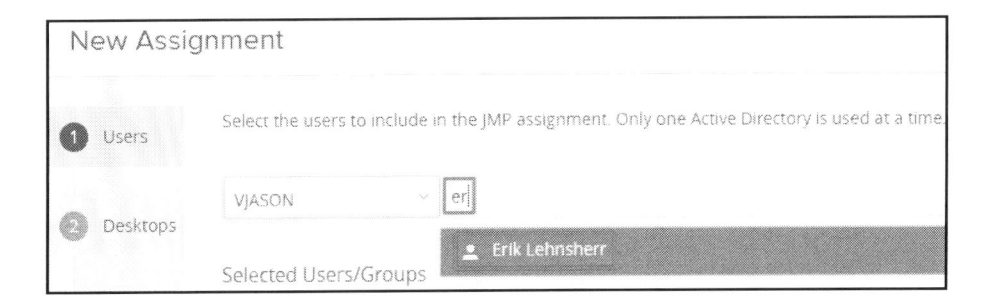

Implementing the Just-in-Time Management Platform (JMP)

4. Search for and add more users or groups if required, and then click **Next**:

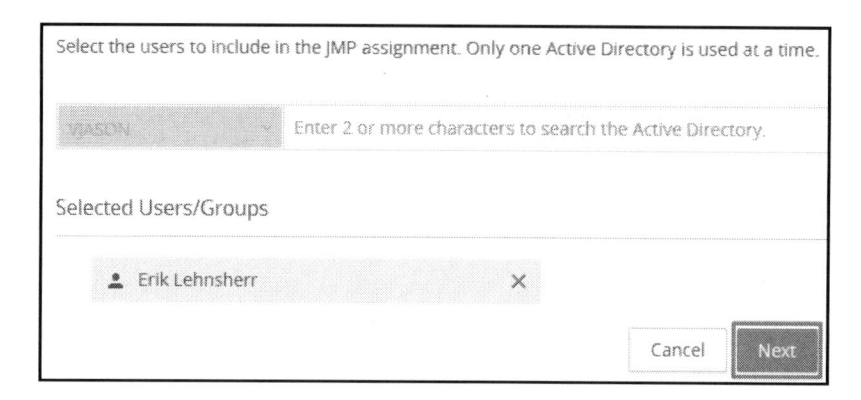

5. In the **Desktops** window, click on the Instant Clone-based Horizon pool that you will use with this assignment, and then click **Next**. The pool must be available prior to creating the JMP Assignment:

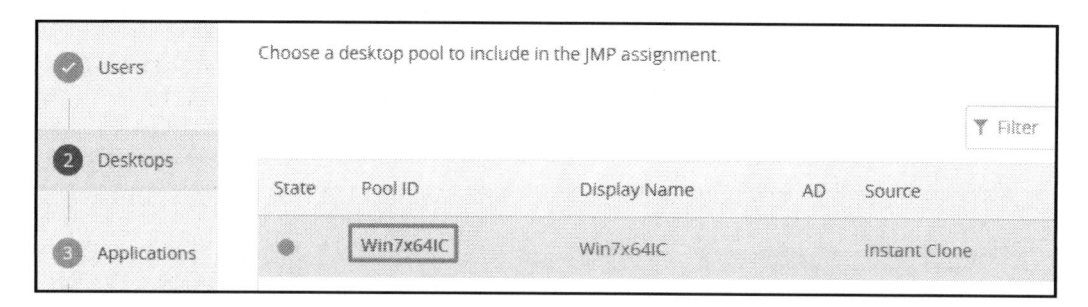

6. In the **Applications** window, click on the checkboxes for the AppVolumes AppStacks you wish to assign, and then click **Next**:

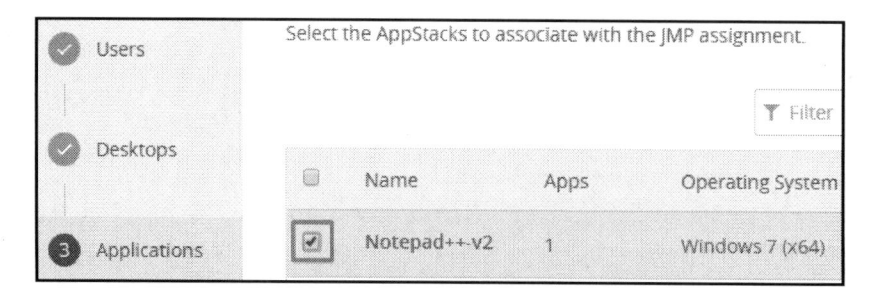

7. In the **User Environment** window, click on the checkbox or boxes for the UEM settings you wish to assign, and then click **Next**. Note that you may click on the **Disable UEM settings?** slider to disable UEM settings entirely:

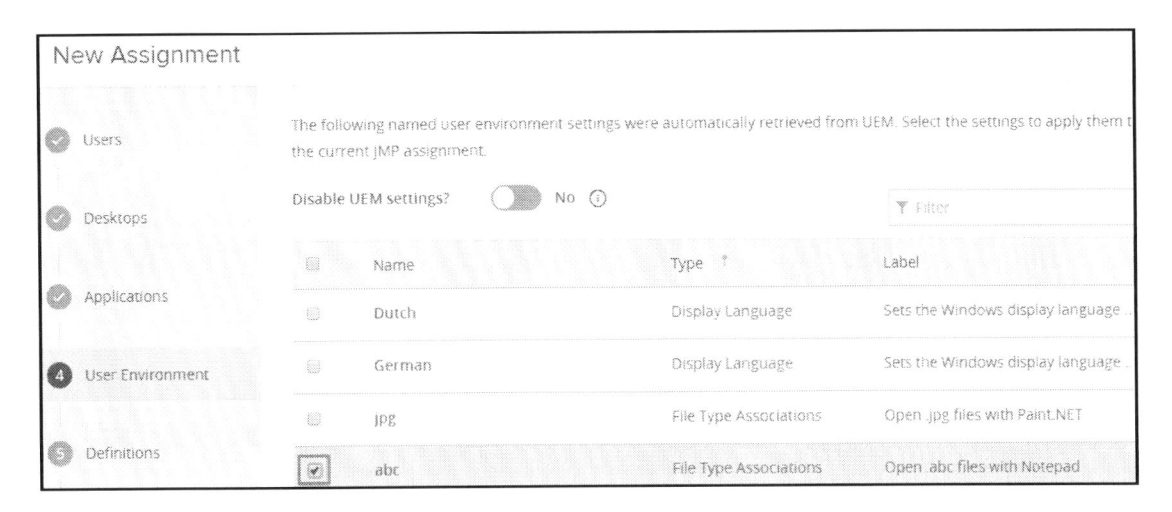

8. In the **Definitions** window, update the default JMP Assignment **Name** and change the **AppStack Attach** options (if desired), provide an optional description, and then click **Next**:

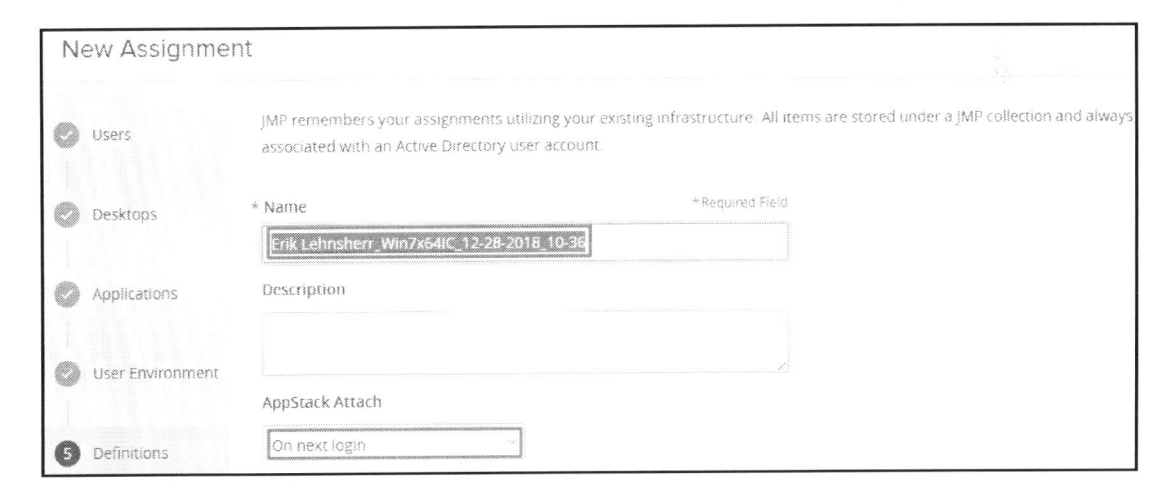

Implementing the Just-in-Time Management Platform (JMP)

9. In the **Summary** window, review the options selected, use the **Back** button if required to make changes, and then click **Submit** to create the JMP Assignment:

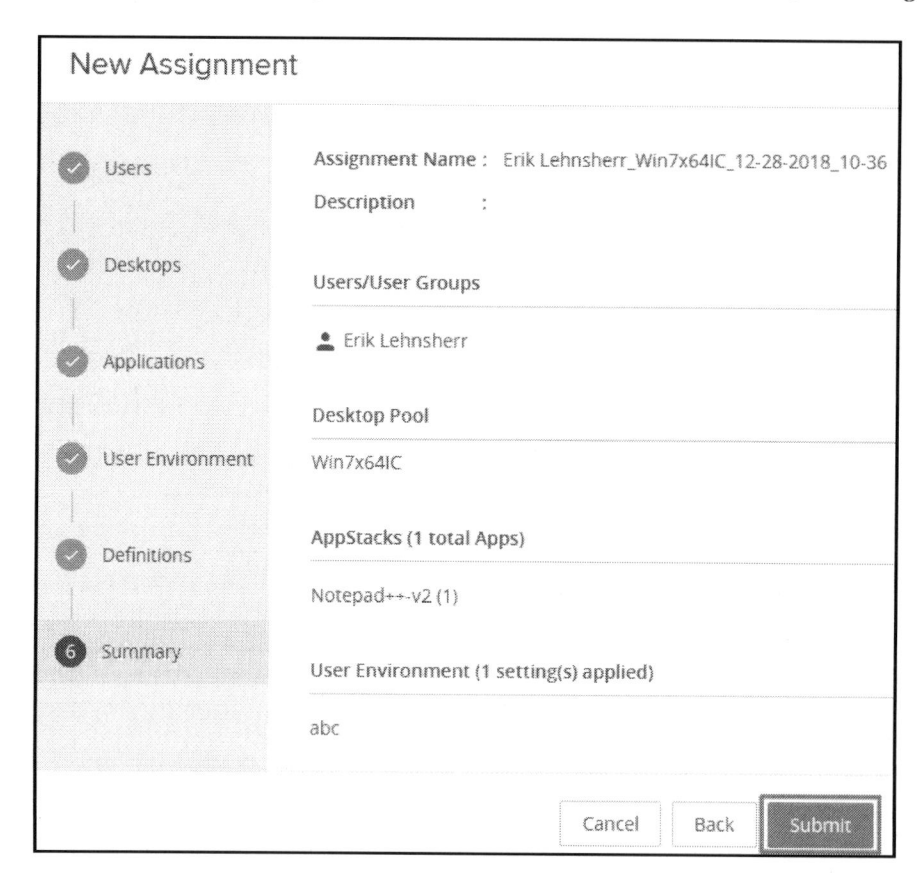

```
New Assignment

✓ Users           Assignment Name :  Erik Lehnsherr_Win7x64IC_12-28-2018_10-36
                  Description      :

✓ Desktops        Users/User Groups

                  👤 Erik Lehnsherr
✓ Applications
                  Desktop Pool

✓ User Environment   Win7x64IC

                  AppStacks (1 total Apps)
✓ Definitions
                  Notepad++-v2 (1)

6 Summary
                  User Environment (1 setting(s) applied)

                  abc

                                         Cancel    Back    Submit
```

The specified user has now been entitled to the selected Horizon pool, assigned the selected AppVolumes AppStacks, and will have the selected UEM settings enforced.

Deleting, duplicating, or editing a JMP Assignment

The following steps outline how to delete, duplicate, or edit a JMP Assignment using the Horizon Console:

1. Log in to the Horizon Console (`https://horcon1.vjason.local/newadmin`) using an AD account that has administrative permissions.
2. Click on **Assignments**.
3. Click on the checkbox to the left of a user or group you wish to perform an action on, and then click on one of the buttons in the following screenshot:
   - **Delete**: Deletes the JMP Assignment and removes the associated Horizon pool entitlements or AppStack assignments.
   - **Duplicate**: Creates another assignment that has the same configuration as this one.
   - **Edit**: Makes changes to the JMP Assignment settings:

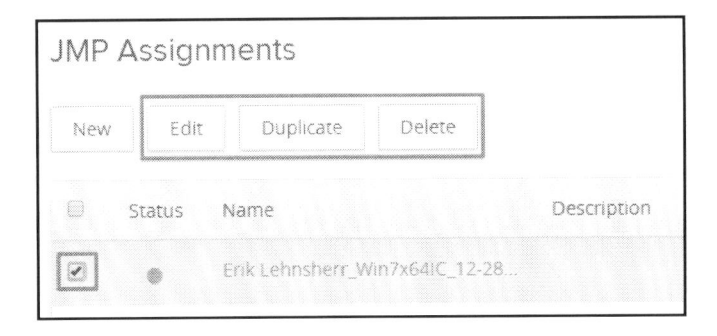

4. Complete any additional steps as needed, which will differ based on the action you want to perform.

Similar to when you created a JMP Assignment, the JMP Server will make the necessary changes to your Horizon pod or App Volumes Manager.

Summary

In this chapter, we discussed how to deploy the Horizon Just-in-Time Manager Server, which provides Horizon administrators a single wizard they can use to entitle access to Horizon pools, assign AppVolumes AppStacks, and specify which UEM settings to enforce.

We also learned how to use the Horizon Console, the next-generation Horizon administration portal, to create a Jment, which provides them with a persistent end user workspace that is built upon non-persistent Horizon pools.

In the next chapter, we will learn how to leverage VMware PowerCLI to administer Horizon resources, which is knowledge that can be used to automate many common Horizon tasks.

Questions

1. What VMware products can a JMP Server connect to so that it can assemble an end user workspace?
2. How do you access the Horizon console?
3. Why would you want to deploy a Horizon JMP Server?
4. What is the name of the object you create using a JMP Server that assigns users to their Horizon resources?
5. Which AppVolumes resource cannot be assigned using the JMP Server?
6. What must you extract and copy to the JMP Server before integrating it with your Horizon pod?
7. Of the three VMware products you integrate with the JMP Server, which is optional?

Further reading

Check out the following resources to learn more about the topics described in this chapter:

- VMware documentation:
    - **VMware Horizon:** `https://www.vmware.com/support/pubs/view_pubs.html`
    - **VMware vSphere:** `https://www.vmware.com/support/pubs/vsphere-esxi-vcenter-server-pubs.html`
- Microsoft documentation:
    - **Windows:** `https://docs.microsoft.com/en-us/windows/`

14
Using Horizon PowerCLI

In this chapter, we will learn how to enable remote management of our Horizon connection servers using PowerCLI, and then we will learn how to use PowerCLI to perform various tasks related to Horizon configuration, administration, and troubleshooting. The topics we will cover include the following:

- Enabling remote management on a Horizon connection server so that PowerCLI can be used remotely
- Establishing a remote PowerCLI session
- Viewing all the PowerCLI commands and their options
- Configuring the Horizon infrastructure
- Administering Horizon desktop pools
- Managing Horizon client entitlements and sessions
- Working with Horizon network label specifications
- Retrieving information about the Horizon infrastructure

VMware Horizon provides a number of different PowerShell commands that you can use to configure, manage, and monitor the Horizon environment. These commands form the Horizon PowerCLI tool, and they enable Horizon administrators to do everything from automating repetitive operations to using existing IT infrastructure management platforms in order to perform common Horizon tasks. While not every aspect of the Horizon environment can be managed or configured using Horizon PowerCLI, most of the common settings can be.

The Horizon PowerCLI commands can only be executed against a single Horizon pod at a time; if you have multiple distinct Horizon pods, you must use separate PowerShell sessions for each one. While each of these commands uses capital letters to identify individual words within the command, PowerCLI itself is not case sensitive—you do not need to capitalize any part of the PowerCLI commands or the command options.

Using the information provided in this chapter, you should be able to reduce the time you spend in the Horizon Administrator console by building scripts that can perform the actions more quickly, even automating tasks, if you wish.

Enabling remote management in Windows

Unlike vSphere PowerCLI, VMware Horizon does not include a standalone installer that is used to remotely manage Horizon using PowerCLI. The Horizon PowerCLI commands will only work when executed from a Horizon connection server. To enable remote management, we must enable Windows Remote Management (WinRM) on at least one Horizon connection server in each Horizon pod that we want to manage.

WinRM is based on the WS-Management protocol, which is a SOAP-based protocol that is used to enable interoperability between hardware and OSes from different vendors. We will use WinRM to establish remote PowerShell connections to a Horizon connection server; this will enable us to run commands from that server without actually having to log in to the server console.

Enabling WinRM

In this section, we will configure WinRM to use HTTPS for an added measure of security. This ensures that if we need to pass sensitive information over a WinRM session, it cannot be read in clear text. Consult Microsoft KB article 2019527 (found at http://support.microsoft.com/kb/2019527) for information on how to obtain the SSL certificate required to enable WinRM HTTPS connections.

The following steps describe how to enable WinRM in Windows in the event that it has not been previously enabled:

1. Log in to the Horizon connection server that you will use for your remote sessions.
2. Enable and start the Windows Remote Management (WS-Management) service. This service should be set to start automatically.
3. From an elevated Windows Command Prompt on the server, execute the following command in order to enable inbound WinRM requests over HTTPS:

    ```
    winrm quickconfig -transport:https
    ```

4. When prompted, answer `y` to approve the operation, and verify that the operation succeeded, as shown in the following screenshot:

```
C:\>winrm quickconfig -transport:https
WinRM service is already running on this machine.
WinRM is not set up to allow remote access to this machine for management.
The following changes must be made:

Create a WinRM listener on HTTPS://* to accept WS-Man requests to any IP on this
  machine.
Configure CertificateThumbprint setting for the service, to be used for CredSSP
authentication.

Make these changes [y/n]? y

WinRM has been updated for remote management.

Created a WinRM listener on HTTPS://* to accept WS-Man requests to any IP on thi
s machine.
Configured required settings for the service.
```

5. If the Windows firewall is enabled on the Horizon connection server, create a firewall rule that allows TCP port 5986 inbound. This is the port that is used when connecting to WinRM over SSL. If you wish to block WinRM over HTTP to ensure that only HTTPS can be used, then block TCP port 5985 inbound using an additional firewall rule.

WinRM should now be configured, and will be available to any users with local administrative access to the server.

Establishing a remote Horizon PowerCLI session

Once WinRM is enabled, you can connect to the Horizon connection server remotely over a PowerShell session. The following steps describe how to establish a remote PowerShell session and then enable the Horizon PowerCLI commands:

1. Open a PowerShell window on the computer that you will use to remotely manage VMware Horizon.
2. Use the following command to initiate a remote PowerShell session. You will need to provide the FQDN of the Horizon connection server—a user ID that has administrative access to both the Horizon and the connection server—and include the -UseSSL option:

```
Enter-PSSession -ComputerName "ConnectionServerFQDN" -UseSSL -
Credential "domain\username"
```

Using Horizon PowerCLI

3. The following screenshot shows an example of this command in our test environment:

```
PS C:\> Enter-PSSession -ComputerName "horcon01.vjason.local" -UseSSL -Credential "vjason\svc-horizon"
```

4. A Windows PowerShell credential request window will open, as shown in the following screenshot; provide the password for the user account specified in the -Credential option of the previous step and click on **OK**:

   Enter your credentials.
   User name: vjason\svc-horizon
   Password: ••••••••••••

5. The PowerShell window will now display a command prompt that includes the name of the Horizon connection server, as shown in the following figure. You will now be running a PowerShell session on this server from the local drive indicated in the console. You can change drives by selecting another drive letter exactly as you would if you were logged on directly using the console on the Horizon connection server:

```
[horcon1.vjason.local]: PS C:\Users\svc-horizon\Documents>
```

6. Switch to the following directory on the Horizon connection server; this folder path assumes that the Horizon connection server was installed in the default program `Files\VMware\VMware View\Server\extras\PowerShell` directory.
7. Execute the following command to run the script that will load the Horizon PowerCLI command:

   `.\Add-snapin.ps1`

Once the script has run completely, the text `Welcome to VMware View PowerCLI` should appear, as shown in the following screenshot. You should now be able to use PowerCLI to remotely manage the Horizon connection server.

Chapter 14

```
[horcon1.vjason.local]: PS C:\Program Files\VMware\VMware View\Server\extras\PowerShell> .\add-snapin.ps1
Loading VMware View PowerCLI

          Welcome to VMware View PowerCLI

[horcon1.vjason.local]: PS C:\Program Files\VMware\VMware View\Server\extras\PowerShell>
```

Viewing all the PowerCLI commands and their options

In this section, we will review all of the current VMware Horizon PowerCLI commands and provide examples of how they are used. The Horizon PowerCLI commands must be enumerated using either a local or remote PowerCLI session. To establish a remote session, refer to the *Establishing a remote Horizon PowerCLI session* section earlier in this chapter.

Listing all Horizon PowerCLI commands

The `Get-Command` PowerShell command is used to display all of the commands available in the specified PowerShell snap-in. To display a current list of PowerCLI commands available in the version of Horizon you are working with, use the following command:

`Get-Command -PSSnapin VMware.View.Broker | more`

VMware has not yet updated Horizon PowerCLI to include support for newer features, such as instant clone desktops, Windows RDS application pools, or cloud pods. When a new version of Horizon is released, in addition to reviewing the product documentation you can run this command to see what, if any, PowerCLI commands have been added.

Displaying the options for a single PowerCLI command

The `Get-Help` PowerShell command is used to display the command-line options for the specified PowerShell or Horizon PowerCLI command. To display a list of command options and examples, use the following command:

`Get-Help command | more`

To display more detailed information about any of the Horizon PowerCLI commands, append the `Get-Help` command with one of the following switches:

- **The `-detailed` switch:** This displays additional information about the command
- **The `-examples` switch:** This displays examples of how the command is used
- **The `-full` switch:** This displays additional technical information about the command

The following is an example of how these switches are used with the `Get-Help` command; replace command with the PowerCLI command you wish to get information on:

```
Get-Help command -full | more
```

Sample data for Horizon PowerCLI commands

The values in the following will be used to complete our example Horizon PowerCLI commands. Some portions of the text are in bold: these represent objects that are created automatically within vCenter, but that are not visible to the end user (such as vm or Resources) or objects that are unique to each environment (such as host, referring to a vSphere server hostname). These objects must be included in the PowerCLI command; otherwise, it will not work:

Configuration object	Example value
The AD domain name.	`vjason.local`
The AD group used for example commands.	`Engineering_Horizon_Users`
The AD user used for example commands.	`Charles Xavier (vjason\charles)`
The destination vCenter folder for Horizon desktops, including the path.	`/RTP/Desktops`
The linked clone OS disk storage.	`/RTP/host/HOR-Cluster1/DS1`
The linked clone persistent (user) data disk storage.	`/RTP/host/HOR-Cluster1/DS2`
The linked clone replica disk storage.	`/RTP/host/HOR-Cluster1/DS3`
For full clone desktops, each datastore serves the same role. We still need to specify a destination datastore for our desktops, but only one is explicitly required with full clones.	
Linked clone desktop parent VM, including the path.	`/RTP/vm/Master/Win10x32-LC`

The vCenter datacenter.	`RTP`
The vCenter server name.	`Vc-01.vjason.local`
The Horizon vCenter AD service account.	`vjason\svc-horizon`
The Horizon composer server AD account.	`vjason\svc-composer`
The Horizon composer AD domain.	`vjason.local`
The Horizon connection server used.	`Horcon1.vjason.local`
Horizon Engineering users AD group.	`Engineering_Horizon_Users`
The Horizon folder for the engineering desktop pool.	`Engineering`
Virtual machine snapshot 1 name.	`Base`
Virtual machine snapshot 2 name.	`UpdatesApplied`
The virtual machine template for full clone desktops with the path.	`/RTP/vm/Master/Win10x32-FC`
The vSphere cluster for desktops with the path.	`/RTP/host/HOR-Cluster1`
The vSphere resource pool for desktops with the path.	`/RTP/host/HOR-Cluster1/Resources`
vSphere Windows customization specification.	`Hor_Full_Clones`

Horizon PowerCLI commands not covered in this chapter

The following commands will not be covered in this chapter, as they are used to create and manage desktops and desktop pools for vSphere VMs that are managed by vCenter servers that are not linked to Horizon, VMs deployed on third-party virtualization platforms, or even physical computers. As such, these commands are not used in the majority of Horizon environments. Regardless, the syntax for these commands is very similar to the following commands, and any other information that we need can be obtained using the PowerCLI `Get-Help` command:

- `Add-ManualUnmanagedPool`: Used with VMs from any source, or even physical computers. The Horizon agent must be installed on these computers.
- `Get-DesktopPhysicalMachine`: Returns a list of physical desktops registered with Horizon that were added to a manual unmanaged pool.
- `Update-ManualUnmanagedPool`: Updates the configuration of a manual unmanaged Horizon desktop pool.

Using Horizon PowerCLI

The following commands will not be covered in this chapter as they are no longer supported by Horizon:

- `Add-TerminalServerPool`
- `Get-TerminalServer`
- `Update-TerminalServerPool`

Refer to VMware KB article 2124209 (found at `https://kb.vmware.com/selfservice/microsites/search.do?language=en_UScmd=displayKCexternalId=2124209`) for further details.

Configuring the Horizon infrastructure

In this section, we will look at several different commands that can be used to configure the Horizon infrastructure. These commands include those that are used for an initial configuration, as well as those that are used to modify existing settings.

Adding a vCenter server to Horizon

The `Add-ViewVC` command is used to add a VMware vCenter server to Horizon so that it can be used to manage and provision the Horizon desktops. The following example links the `Vc-01.vjason.local` vCenter server to Horizon:

```
Add-ViewVC -ServerName "Vc-01.vjason.local" -Username "vjason\svc-horizon" -Password "Password123" -CreateRampFactor 8 -UseComposer $true
```

The `Add-ViewVC` command requires several options to be specified in order to link a vCenter server to the Horizon environment. These include the following:

- `CreateRampFactor`: Maximum concurrent vCenter desktop provisioning operations.
- `Password`: Password for the `-Username` account. The password should be contained within quotes.
- `ServerName` or `Name`: FQDN of the vCenter server. Either option can be specified.
- `Username` or `User`: The user who has appropriate permissions within vCenter in the `domain\username` format. Either option can be specified.

Additional options can be specified. These include the following:

- `ComposerPort`: The port that needs to be used with the Horizon composer server.
- `DeleteRampFactor`: Maximum concurrent desktop power operations.
- `Description`: Description for vCenter server in the Horizon console. This value should be contained within quotes.
- `DisplayName`: Display name for vCenter server in the Horizon Administrator console. This value should be contained within quotes.
- `Port`: The port to be used with the vCenter server.
- `UseComposer`: Used when the Horizon Composer Server is installed on the vCenter server. The options are `$true` or `$false` (the default).
- `UseComposerSsl`: Enable SSL for the connection to the Horizon Composer server. The options are `$true` (the default) or `$false`.
- `UseSpaceReclamation`: Enable SeSparse space reclamation on vSphere hosts managed by the vCenter server. The options are `$true` or `$false` (the default).
- `UseSsl`: Enable SSL for the connection to the vCenter server. The options are `$true` (the default) or `$false`.

Options such as port numbers and whether or not to use SSL (enabled by default) will use their default values if not specified, and should not be changed under most circumstances.

A number of vCenter options cannot be configured when linking a vCenter server using PowerCLI. These include Horizon Storage Accelerator, standalone Horizon composer servers, dedicated users for the Horizon composer, the Horizon composer domains, and others. These options must be configured after using the Horizon Administrator console.

If your vCenter server or Horizon Composer Server SSL certificate is not trusted by the Horizon connection servers, the `Add-ViewVC` operation will fail. This is different from adding a vCenter server using the Horizon Administrator console, which allows you to accept an untrusted certificate. To use this command, you must replace the default vCenter server SSL certificate with one signed by a trusted certificate authority.

Updating the settings of the vCenter server that is linked to Horizon

The `Update-ViewVC` command can be used to update the settings of a vCenter server that is currently linked to Horizon. The following example command updates the `DeleteRampFactor` value as well as the `Description` of the vCenter server named `Vc-01.vjason.local`:

```
Update-ViewVC -ServerName "Vc-01.vjason.local" -DeleteRampFactor 10 -Description "VC-01 vCenter Server"
```

This command supports the same options as the `Add-ViewVC` command. You can specify the vCenter server to be updated using the `ServerName` or `Name` option, and then update the options as required.

Removing a vCenter server from Horizon

The `Remove-ViewVC` command can be used to remove a vCenter server that is currently linked to Horizon. The `Remove-ViewVC` requires only the vCenter server name in order to unlink it from Horizon. The vCenter server cannot be removed if desktops are currently deployed. The following example command will remove the `Vc-01.vjason.local` vCenter server from Horizon:

```
Remove-ViewVC -ServerName "Vc-01.vjason.local"
```

Updating the Horizon connection broker settings

The `Update-ConnectionBroker` command supports a number of options to configure Horizon connection brokers, which includes both connection servers and security servers. The following example command updates the external `PCoIP` URL of the Horizon security server named `HORSEC1`:

```
Update-ConnectionBroker -Broker_id "HORSEC1" -ExternalPCoIPUrl "192.168.0.1:4172"
```

The following options are supported when using the `Update-ConnectionBroker` command:

- `Broker_id`: Name of the Horizon connection broker.
- `DirectConnect`: Enable direct connections to the Horizon desktops. The options are `$true` or `$false` (the default).
- `DirectPCoIP`: Enable direct PCoIP connections to the Horizon desktops. The options are `$true` (the default) or `$false`.
- `ClearNodeSecret`: Clear the existing RSA SecurID node secret (if in use).
- `ExternalURL`: External URL for the connection server home page.
- `ExternalPCoIPUrl`: External URL for PCoIP access using the secure gateway.
- `LdapBackupFolder`: The folder that is used for the Horizon LDAP backups.
- `LdapBackupFrequency`: The frequency of LDAP backups. The options are `EveryHour`, `Every6Hour`, `Every12Hour`, `EveryDay` (the default), `Every2Day`, `EveryWeek`, `Every2Week`, and `Never`.
- `LdapBackupMaxNumber`: Maximum number of LDAP backups that need to be retained. The default is `10`.
- `LogoffWhenRemoveSmartCard`: Log off the Horizon client sessions when the clients' smart card is removed. The options are `$true` or `$false` (the default).
- `NameMapping`: Enforce RSA SecurID and Windows name matching. The options are `$true` or `$false` (the default).
- `SecureIDEnabled`: Enable RSA SecurID authentication. The options are `$true` or `$false` (the default).
- `SmartCardSetting`: Enable smart card authentication. The options are `Required`, `Off`, or `Optional` (the default).
- `Tags`: Set connection server tags, used to restrict connections to desktop pools to specific connection servers.
- `PCoIPBandwidthLimit`: Configure the per-session PCoIP bandwidth limit in Kbps.

Updating the Horizon global settings

The `Update-GlobalSetting` command can be used to update a number of different Horizon global settings. The following example command enables and configures the forced logoff and prelogin messages:

```
Update-GlobalSetting -DisplayPreLogin $true -PreLoginMessage "Unauthorized
users prohibited" -DisplayLogoffWarning $true -ForcedLogoffMessage "You will
be logged off"
```

Using Horizon PowerCLI

The following settings can be set using the `Update-GlobalSetting` command:

- `DisplayLogoffWarning`: Displays a warning to the Horizon client prior to a forced logoff. This value should be contained within quotes.
- `DisplayPreLogin`: Displays a login message prior to the Horizon client logging in to the connection server. This value should be contained within quotes.
- `ForceLogoffAfter`: Sets how long you need to wait in minutes after the warning message appears to force logoff the Horizon client.
- `ForceLogoffMessage`: The text for the force logoff message. This value should be contained within quotes.
- `MessageSecurityMode`: Sets the security level for communication between Horizon components. The options include `Disabled`, `Mixed`, and `Enabled` (the default).
- `PreLoginMessage`: The text for the prelogin message. This value should be contained within quotes.
- `ReauthenticateOnInterrupt`: Forces the Horizon client to reauthenticate after connection interruption. The options are `$true` or `$false` (the default).
- `SessionTimeout`: The timeout value in minutes for inactive Horizon client sessions.
- `UseSslClient`: Forces SSL Horizon client connections. The options are `$true` or `$false` (the default).
- `WidgetPolling`: Enables automatic status updates in the Horizon administrator. The options are `$true` (the default) or `$false`.

Configuring the Horizon license

The `Set-License` command is used to license a Horizon pod. The `Set-License` command requires only one option: `-key`. Do not remove the dashes from the license key, as shown in the following example command:

```
Set-License -Key "AAAAA-BBBBB-CCCCC-DDDDD-EEEEE"
```

Administering Horizon desktop pools

In this section, we will review the PowerCLI commands that are used to create Horizon desktop pools. This section assumes that you are familiar with Horizon pool configuration options, some of which are described in Chapter 7, *Creating Horizon Desktop Pools*.

As mentioned earlier in this chapter, if you need more information about a specific command you can use the PowerCLI `Get-Help` command in the format `Get-Help` command `-full | more`, replacing X with the command in question.

When creating linked clone desktop pools, you must specify the vCenter and Horizon composer domain in separate commands prior to beginning the command that actually creates the pool. This is done in the sample commands provided. The required text is shown in the following code:

```
Get-ViewVC -serverName "Vc-01.vjason.local" | Get-ComposerDomain -domain
"vjason.local" -username "vjason\svc-composer" | ...
```

The | character is used to feed the results of one PowerCLI command into the next command provided, which is an operation known as piping.

Creating a dedicated assignment persistent linked clone pool

In this section, we will create a dedicated assignment persistent linked clone Horizon desktop pool.

Not all of the values in the following example command are mandatory; the `FolderId`, `DataDiskLetter`, `DataDiskSize`, `TempDiskSize`, `VmFolderPath`, and `NetworkLabelConfigFile` values can all be omitted and the Horizon defaults will be used instead. The remaining values are all required in order to create a linked clone pool using the `Add-AutomaticLinkedClonePool` PowerCLI command:

```
Get-ViewVC -serverName "Vc-01.vjason.local" | Get-ComposerDomain -domain
"vjason.local" -username "vjason\svc-composer" | Add-
AutomaticLinkedClonePool -Pool_id "EngineeringLC1" -DisplayName "Engineering
Desktops" -NamePrefix "EngineeringLC{n:fixed=4}" -VmFolderPath
"/RTP/vm/Desktops" -ResourcePoolPath "/RTP/host/HOR-Cluster1/Resources" -
ParentVmPath "/RTP/vm/Master/Win10x32-LC" -ParentSnapshotPath "/Base" -
DatastoreSpecs "[Aggressive,OS]/RTP/host/HOR-
Cluster1/DS1;[Aggressive,data]/RTP/host/HOR-
Cluster1/DS2;[Aggressive,replica]/RTP/host/HOR-Cluster1/DS3" -MaximumCount
100 -MinProvisionedDesktops 25 -HeadroomCount 90 -MinimumCount 100 -
DataDiskLetter D -DataDiskSize 1536 -TempDiskSize 3072 -FolderId
"Engineering" -NetworkLabelConfigFile "d:\LCConfigFile"
```

Creating a floating assignment (non-persistent) linked clone pool

To create a floating assignment (non-persistent) linked clone desktop pool, the following changes would need to be made to the example command from the previous section of this recipe:

- Omit the options for `DataDiskLetter` and `DataDiskSize`
- The OS and data disks must be placed on the same datastore, so adjust the datastore specifications to read `[Aggressive,data,OS]`
- Add the `-Persistence NonPersistent` option

Based on these requirements, the updated command is as follows. The items that were added or changed are in bold; the items that were removed are not shown:

```
Get-ViewVC -serverName "Vc-01.vjason.local" | Get-ComposerDomain -domain
"vjason.local" -username "vjason\svc-composer" | Add-
AutomaticLinkedClonePool -Pool_id "EngineeringLC1" -DisplayName
"EngineeringDesktops" -NamePrefix "EngineeringLC{n:fixed=4}" -VmFolderPath
"/RTP/vm/Desktops" -ResourcePoolPath "/RTP/host/HOR-Cluster1/Resources" -
ParentVmPath "/RTP/vm/Master/Win10x32-LC" -ParentSnapshotPath "/Base" -
DatastoreSpecs
"[Aggressive,data,OS]/RTP/host/DTCluster1/DS1;[Aggressive,data,OS]/RTP/host
/HOR-Cluster1/DS2;[Aggressive,replica]/RTP/host/HOR-Cluster1/DS3" -
MaximumCount 100 -MinProvisionedDesktops 25 -HeadroomCount 90 -MinimumCount
100 -TempDiskSize 3072 -FolderId "Engineering" -Persistence NonPersistent
```

Creating an automatically provisioned full clone desktop pool

The `Add-AutomaticPool` command can be used to create Horizon full clone desktop pools. Some desktop pool options, such as Horizon Storage Accelerator, cannot be configured using PowerCLI. These settings must be configured after the pool has been created using the Horizon Administrator console.

Not all of the values in the following example command are mandatory; the `FolderID` and `CustomizationSpecName` values can both be omitted, and the Horizon defaults can be used instead.

The remaining values are all required in order to create a full clone pool using the `Add-AutomaticPool` PowerCLI command:

```
Get-ViewVC -serverName "Vc-01.vjason.local" | Get-ComposerDomain -domain
vjason.local" -username vjason\svc-composer" | Add-AutomaticPool -Pool_id
"EngineeringFC1" -DisplayName "Engineering Desktops" -NamePrefix
"EngineeringFC{n:fixed=4}" -VmFolderPath "/RTP/vm/Desktops" -
ResourcePoolPath "/RTP/host/HOR-Cluster1/Resources" -TemplatePath
"/RTP/vm/Master/ Win10x32-FC" -DatastorePaths "/RTP/host/HOR-Cluster1/DS1;/
RTP/host/HOR-Cluster1/DS2;/RTP/host/HOR-Cluster1/DS3" -MaximumCount 100 -
HeadroomCount 90 -MinimumCount 100 -FolderId "Engineering" -
CustomizationSpecName "Hor_Full_Clones"
```

Creating a manually provisioned desktop pool

Manually provisioned desktop pools are typically used when the Horizon desktops are created outside the Horizon environment, using tools such as vSphere or an array-based virtual machine cloning tool. These manually provisioned desktops must be available in vCenter in order for them to be added to the manually provisioned desktop pool.

VMware Horizon cannot deploy Linux desktops, so if you intend to use them as Horizon desktops then you will need to provision them manually and place them in a manually provisioned desktop pool.

Prior to creating the manually provisioned desktop pool, at least one supported virtual machine with the Horizon agent installed must be available within vCenter. This desktop must not be assigned to any existing Horizon desktop pools, as it will be added to the new manually provisioned desktop pool during the pool-creation process.

The following example command will create a manually provisioned desktop pool and add the virtual machine named `LinuxDT-01` to it:

```
Add-ManualPool -Pool_id "Manual1" -Id (Get-DesktopVM -Name "LinuxDT-01").id
 -Vc_name "Vc-01.vjason.local"
```

The `Get-DesktopVM` option was run within the command in order to obtain the value for the virtual machine ID (`id`). By placing the command within parentheses and appending it with `.id`, it returns the value we require in order to complete our `Add-ManualPool` command.

Manual desktop pools support most of the same configuration options as linked clone or full clone pools, as well as the following additional options:

- `Id`: vCenter machine ID for the virtual machine to be added to the pool
- `VC_name`: Hostname of the vCenter server that manages the pool VMs
- `Vm_id_list`: ID for multiple virtual machines to be added to the pool, separated by semicolons

The `Add-ManualPool` command requires at least the following options to be specified in order to create a pool: `Pool_id`, `VC_name` or `Vc_id`, and `Id`.

Updating the configuration of a Horizon desktop pool

The following two Horizon PowerCLI commands are used to update the configuration of a Horizon desktop pool. We will look at these two commands in this section:

- `Update-AutomaticLinkedClonePool`: Used to update the configuration of an existing Horizon linked clone pool.
- `Update-AutomaticPool`: Used to update the configuration of an existing Horizon full clone pool.

The majority of the Horizon pool configuration options can be modified after the pool has been deployed, regardless of whether they were specified during deployment. If you are unable to update a given configuration option, use the `Get-Help` command `-full | more` to verify whether the parameter in question is able to be updated. One example of this is the Horizon pool `Pool_id` value, which can only be set when the pool is first configured.

Updating a linked clone pool

In this example, we will update the linked clone desktop pool configuration using the `Update- AutomaticLinkedClonePool` command. The only option required is the value for `Pool_id`, along with any other options you wish to change, as shown in the following code:

```
Update-AutomaticLinkedClonePool -Pool_id "EngineeringLC1" -
AllowProtocolOverride $true
```

Updating an automatically provisioned full clone pool

In this example, we will update the full clone desktop pool configuration using the `Update- AutomaticPool` command. The only option required is the value for `Pool_id`, along with any other options you wish to change, as shown in the following code:

```
Update-AutomaticPool -Pool_id "EngineeringFC1" -DefaultProtocol PCOIP
```

Updating a manually provisioned pool

In the following example, we will update the manually provisioned pool configuration using the `Update-ManualPool` command. The only option required is the value for `Pool_id`, along with any other options you wish to change, as shown in the following code:

```
Update-ManualPool -Pool_id "Manual1" -FlashQuality HIGH
```

Refreshing a linked clone desktop or pool

The `Send-LinkedCloneRefresh` command is used to refresh either a specific Horizon linked clone desktop or an entire desktop pool. The following list shows two different ways the command is used:

- The following example command selects all the desktops in the `EngineeringLC1` pool and schedules them to refresh at the indicated time. In addition, the operation will continue even if an error occurs, but will not force users to log off:

```
Get-Pool -Pool_id "EngineeringLC1" | Get-DesktopVM | Send-LinkedCloneRefresh -schedule "2018-12-31 22:00" -StopOnError $false -ForceLogoff $false
```

- To refresh just a single desktop, you can use a simpler version of the command that requires only the machine ID and the schedule. This command will refresh only the desktop named `HorLC0001`, as shown in the following code:

```
Send-LinkedCloneRefresh -Machine_id (Get-DesktopVM -Name "HorLC0001").machine_id -schedule "2018-12-31 22:00"
```

Using Horizon PowerCLI

When using the `Send-LinkedCloneRefresh` command to refresh an entire pool, the command requires us to specify each desktop within the pool, so we will be piping the output of the `Get-Pool` and `Get-DesktopVM` commands into the `Send-LinkedCloneRefresh` command.

We must also specify the time to begin the refresh using the `-schedule` option in the `YYYY-MM-DD HH:MM` format using a 24-hour format for the hour. We must remember that any time specified will be executed based on the time on the Horizon connection server itself.

Other options for the command include `StopOnError`, which is enabled by default and halts the refresh if errors occur, and `ForceLogoff`, which is disabled by default and will force users to log off. Both of these options accept either `$true` or `$false` as options.

Recomposing a linked clone desktop pool

The `Send-LinkedCloneRecompose` command is used to recompose either a specific Horizon linked clone desktop or the entire desktop pool.

In the following example, we will be recomposing to a new snapshot of the same parent VM. The snapshot is named `UpdatesApplied`. Since this VM now has two snapshots, the `ParentSnapshotPath` will now be in the `/Base/UpdatesApplied` format, where `Base` is the name of the original snapshot used to create the pool. The remainder of the command follows a format that is similar to the `Send-LinkedCloneRefresh` command:

```
Get-Pool -Pool_id "EngineeringLC1" | Get-DesktopVM | Send-
LinkedCloneRecompose -ParentVMPath "/RTP/vm/Master/Win10x32-LC" -
ParentSnapshotPath "/Base/UpdatesApplied" -schedule "2018-12-31 22:00"
```

The command will recompose all desktops in the pool to the snapshot named `UpdatesApplied` at the indicated time. You can also select a different parent VM when performing a recompose, but remember that the VM must be running the same OS as the existing desktops.

You can also recompose a single desktop using the `-machine_id` option and the `Get-DesktopVM` command, as shown in the following code:

```
Send-LinkedCloneRecompose (Get-DesktopVM -Name "HorLC0001").machine_id -
ParentVMPath "/RTP/vm/Master/Win10x32-LC" -ParentSnapshotPath
"/Base/UpdatesApplied" -schedule "2018-12-31 22:00"
```

The `Send-LinkedCloneRecompose` command requires you to specify multiple options, including `Schedule`, `ParentVMPath`, and `ParentSnapshotPath`. The command also supports the `StopOnError` and `ForceLogoff` options.

Rebalancing a linked clone desktop pool

The `Send-LinkedCloneRebalance` command is used to rebalance either a specific Horizon linked clone desktop or an entire desktop pool. The following list shows two different ways the command is used:

- The following example command selects all the desktops in the `EngineeringLC1` pool and schedules them to rebalance at the indicated time:

    `Get-Pool -Pool_id "EngineeringLC1" | Get-DesktopVM | Send-LinkedCloneRebalance -schedule "2018-12-31 22:00"`

- To rebalance just a single desktop, you can use a simpler version of the command that requires only the machine ID and the schedule. The following command will rebalance only the desktop named `HorLC0001`:

    `Send-LinkedCloneRebalance -Machine_id (Get-DesktopVM -Name "HorLC0001").machine_id -schedule "2018-12-31 22:00"`

The `Send-LinkedCloneRebalance` command uses the same format as the other linked clone maintenance commands. All that is required is the desktop pool ID and the schedule. The command also supports the `StopOnError` and `ForceLogoff` options.

Resetting a Horizon desktop

The `Send-VMReset` command can be used to reset a Horizon desktop, for example, when it is in an unresponsive state. The following example command will reset the Horizon desktop named `HorLC0001`:

`Send-VMReset -Machine_id (Get-DesktopVM -Name "HorLC0001").machine_id`

The `Send-VMReset` command requires the machine ID in order to identify the desktop.

Managing Horizon client entitlements and sessions

In this section, we will review several different commands that can be used to manage Horizon client entitlements and sessions.

Adding desktop pool entitlements

Entitling is the act of granting AD users or groups access to the Horizon pools. In this section, we will review how to entitle both individual users as well as AD security groups. The following list shows how entitlements can be implemented:

- The following `Add-PoolEntitlement` command will entitle the `Engineering_Horizon_Users` group to the `EngineeringLC1` desktop pool:

    ```
    Add-PoolEntitlement -Pool_id EngineeringLC1 -sid (Get-User -Name
    "Engineering_Horizon_Users").sid
    ```

- To entitle individual users, simply provide the first and last name of the user, as shown in the following code:

    ```
    Add-PoolEntitlement -Pool_id EngineeringLC1 -sid (Get-User -Name
    "Charles Xavier").sid
    ```

The `Get-User` command accepts wildcards, but be careful while using them, as the wrong user might be returned. If in doubt, use the `Get-User` command by itself to verify that you are selecting the correct user.

Removing desktop pool entitlements

The `Remove-PoolEntitlement` command uses the same format as the `Add-PoolEntitlement` command; however, if you are removing the last entitlements from the desktop pool, you must add the `-ForceRemove $true` option for the command to succeed. This prevents you from accidentally removing all entitlements from a desktop pool. The following code shows how this can be correctly implemented:

```
Remove-PoolEntitlement -Pool_id "EngineeringLC1" -sid (Get-User -Name
"Engineering_Horizon_Users").sid -ForceRemove $true
```

The `Add-PoolEntitlement` and `Remove-PoolEntitlement` commands require you to specify the user or group AD system identifier (SID) in order to add or remove desktop pool entitlements. For this, use the `Get-User` command within the `Remove-PoolEntitlement` command. Despite the name, the `Get-User` command is used to obtain both AD users and groups.

Entitling or unentitling an individual desktop

Entitling an individual desktop is similar to entitling a desktop pool, except that, in this case, we need both the user SID and the machine ID. For the following example command, we will nest two commands, `Get-DesktopVM` and `Get-User`, within the two different `UserOwnership` commands:

```
Update-UserOwnership -Machine_id (Get-DesktopVM -Name
"HorLC0001").machine_id -Sid (Get-User -Name "Jason Ventresco").sid
```

The `Get-User` command accepts wildcards, but be careful while using them, as the wrong user might be returned. If in doubt, use the `Get-User` command by itself to verify that you are selecting the correct user.

The `Remove-UserOwnership` command requires only the desktop machine ID, as shown in the following code:

```
Remove-UserOwnership -Machine_id (Get-DesktopVM -Name
"HorLC0001").machine_id
```

Disconnecting the Horizon client session

The `Send-SessionDisconnect` command disconnects users based on the Horizon session ID. The following example command will disconnect the session belonging to the `vjason.local\charles` AD user:

```
Send-SessionDisconnect -Session_id (Get-RemoteSession -Username
"vjason.local\charles").session_id
```

The Horizon session ID is a really long value that is difficult to work with, so we will use the `Get-RemoteSession` command within the `Send-SessionDisconnect` command instead in order to disconnect the target user.

[407]

Logging off the Horizon client session

The `Send-SessionLogoff` command disconnects users based on the Horizon session ID. The `Send-SessionLogoff` command uses the same format as the `Send-SessionDisconnect` command. The following example command will log off the session belonging to the AD user `vjason.local\charles`:

```
Send-SessionLogoff -Session_id (Get-RemoteSession -Username
"vjason.local\charles").session_id
```

Retrieving information about the Horizon infrastructure

In this section, we will look at several different commands that can be used to display information about the Horizon infrastructure.

Retrieving Horizon composer server information

The `Get-ComposerDomain` command can be used to obtain the Horizon composer information using the `Vc_id`, `Domain`, or `Username` options.

The following example command retrieves the Horizon composer information that the vCenter server composer uses to link:

```
Get-ComposerDomain -Vc_id (Get-ViewVC -Name "Vc-01.vjason.local").vc_id
```

The `Get-ViewVC` command is run within the command to obtain the `vc_id` value, which is easier than attempting to type in the value manually, as it is a series of random letters and numbers. This technique will be used in many of the examples in this chapter, as it makes working with certain values much easier. Omit the options in order to retrieve a list of all Horizon composer server information.

Retrieving a list of the Horizon desktop pools

The `Get-Pool` command can be used to retrieve a list of all the Horizon pools or simply those that match the supplied specifications. The following command will retrieve a list of the Horizon pools that have the PCoIP protocol enabled:

```
Get-Pool -Enabled $true -Protocol PCOIP
```

Omit the options to retrieve a list of all the Horizon desktop pools. The `Get-Pool` command can be used to obtain information on desktop pools based on certain options: `Description`, `DisplayName`, `Enabled` (`$true` or `$false`), `Pool_id`, `PoolType`, `Protocol`, and `VcServerName`. The `VcServerName` option is simply the name of the vCenter server that hosts the desktop pools' virtual machines.

Retrieving the global Horizon configuration data

The `Get-GlobalSetting` command is used to retrieve information about the Horizon global settings. The command has no options; simply execute the command by itself in order to obtain the configuration data.

Retrieving the Horizon connection broker information

The `Get-ConnectionBroker` command is used to retrieve information about Horizon connection brokers, which include both connection servers and security servers. The following example command retrieves information about the `HORCON1` connection server:

```
Get-ConnectionBroker -Broker_id "HORCON1"
```

Retrieving a list of virtual machines managed by Horizon

The `Get-DesktopVM` PowerCLI command can be used to return a list of the Horizon virtual desktops that meet the specified criteria. The following example command retrieves a list of desktops that currently have a refresh operation scheduled.

Get-DesktopVM - ComposerTask refresh

You can omit the options in order to retrieve a list of all virtual machines. The `Get-DesktopVM` command supports multiple options that enable you to return desktops based on very specific criteria, including the following:

- **The `ComposerTask` option**: Retrieves desktops with the specified scheduled composer tasks. The options are `attachUdd`, `detachUdd`, `mkChkPoint`, `rebalance`, `refresh`, `replaceUdd`, and `resync`. The `Udd` term stands for user data disk. A full description of each of these options is available in the VMware document called *View Integration* (found at `https://docs.vmware.com/en/VMware-Horizon-7/index.html`).
- `GetNetworkLabel`: Retrieves the network label settings. The options are `$true` or `$false`.
- `IsInPool`: Retrieves desktops based on whether they are in a desktop pool. The options are `$true` or `$false`.
- `IsLinkedClone`: Retrieves desktops based on whether they are linked clones. The options are `$true` or `$false`.
- `Name`: Displays the name of the desktop in vCenter.
- `Pool_id`: The desktop pool ID.
- `PoolType`: Lists VMs that will work with the specified pool type; the only option is `Manual`.
- `Vc_id`: vCenter server ID.

Retrieving the AD user or group information

The `Get-User` command is typically used to pipe user or group names into other Horizon PowerCLI commands. The following example returns only those AD groups that start with Horizon:

```
Get-User -IncludeUser $false -Name "Horizon"
```

Omit the options to retrieve a list of all users and groups. The following options are available when using the `Get-User` command:

- `IncludeUser`: Specifies whether the results include AD user accounts. The options are `$False` and `$True` (the default).
- `IncludeGroup` **option**: Specifies whether the results include AD groups. The options are `$False` and `$True` (the default).

- `Name`: The name of the user or group to be returned. This value should be contained within quotes. If quotes are not used, partial matches are allowed based on the start of the name.
- `Domain`: Returns users or groups from a specific domain.

Retrieving information about user persistent data disks

The `Get-ProfileDisk` command can be used to retrieve information about the Horizon desktop persistent data disks that are registered with Horizon. The following example command will retrieve information about the persistent disk that belongs to a specified user:

```
Get-ProfileDisk -Username "vjason.local\charles"
```

Omit the `-Username` option in order to retrieve details about all of the persistent data disks registered with Horizon. The `Get-ProfileDisk` command supports the following options that can be used to retrieve information about the persistent disks registered with Horizon:

- `Name`: The name of the persistent disk.
- `Username`: The full domain\username of the owner of the persistent disk.
- `VmName`: The name of the VM that is using the persistent disk.
- `LastPool`: The desktop pool that contains the persistent disk.
- `DataStore`: The datastore where the persistent disk is stored.
- `Status`: The status of the persistent disk. The options include `In Use`, `Archiving`, and `Detached`.

Retrieving the Horizon event reports and their descriptions

The `Get-EventReportList` command is used to retrieve a list of Horizon event report names and their descriptions. The `Get-EventReportList` command has no options; simply execute the command by itself.

The `Get-EventReport` command is used to retrieve a list of Horizon events from the specified event report. The following example command retrieves all event data about user events:

```
Get-EventReport -ViewName user_events
```

Retrieving the Horizon infrastructure health monitors and their status

The `Get-Monitor` command is used to retrieve Horizon health-monitoring data from all or specific Horizon monitors. The following example command retrieves all the Horizon health-monitoring data for the `HORCON1` Horizon connection server:

```
Get-Monitor -Monitor_id "HORCON1"
```

Omit the options to retrieve a list of all of the Horizon monitoring data. The `Get-Monitor` command supports two different options, as shown in the following list:

- `Monitor_id` **option:** The ID of the monitor. You can provide the specific monitor ID itself, obtained using the `Get-Monitor` command, or you can specify a Horizon server name. All monitors for that server will be returned.
- `Monitor` **option:** The name of the monitor. The possible values include the following:
    - `CBMonitor`: Connection server monitor
    - `DBMonitor`: Horizon event database monitor
    - `DomainMonitor`: Domain connection monitor
    - `SGMonitor`: Security server monitor
    - `VCMonitor`: vCenter server monitor

Retrieving information about remote Horizon sessions

The `Get-RemoteSession` command is used to obtain information about any current Horizon sessions. The command supports several options that can be used to return only those sessions that match the specified criteria.

The following example command retrieves all the remote Horizon sessions for the `EngineeringLC1` desktop pool:

```
Get-RemoteSession -Pool_id EngineeringLC1
```

The `Get-RemoteSession` command supports multiple options for listing client connections. Only one option is required in order to retrieve session information. The options include the following:

- `Username`: The username is in the `FullDomainName\username` format—for example, `vjason.local\charles`
- `Pool_id`: The desktop pool ID—for example, `EngineeringLC1`
- `Session_id`: The horizon session ID
- `Duration`: Duration in the format "`dd day(s) hh hour(s) mm minute(s) ss second(s)`"—for example, `2 days 1 hour 15 minutes 1 second`
- `DnsName`: The DNS name of the virtual desktop
- `State`: The state of the desktop (`Connected` or `Disconnected`)
- `Protocol`: The protocol being used in the session (`PCOIP` or `RDP`)
- `StartTime`: The time at which the session was started, including the day, time, time zone, and year—for example, `Mon Dec 31 22:00:15 EST 2018`

Retrieving a list of the vCenter servers linked to the Horizon environment

The `Get-ViewVC` command retrieves the Horizon composer server information for the specified Horizon composer server. The following is an example of how the `Get-ViewVC` command is used:

```
Get-ViewVC -Name "Vc-01.vjason.local"
```

Omit the `-Name` option in order to retrieve a list of all vCenter servers.

Retrieving the Horizon license information

The `Get-License` command is used to retrieve the Horizon license status. The `Get-License` command has no options; simply execute the command by itself.

Reviewing the desktop pool entitlement

The `Get-PoolEntitlement` command can be used to review the AD users and groups that have been granted access to the specified pool ID. The `Get-PoolEntitlement` command supports only one option: `Pool_id`. The following example command retrieves the entitlement settings for the desktop pool with the `EngineeringLC1` ID:

```
Get-PoolEntitlement -Pool_id "EngineeringLC1"
```

Omit the options in order to retrieve a list of user entitlements for all desktop pools. If the pool does not have an entitlement, the command will return an exception.

Summary

In this chapter, we learned how to use Horizon PowerCLI to configure and administer VMware Horizon using the command line, which provides us the ability to script or automate various tasks.

We started out by learning how to enable SSL-encrypted remote management on our Horizon connection servers, which enables us to use Horizon PowerCLI remotely rather than needing to log on to the Horizon connection servers.

We continued by looking at each of the Horizon PowerCLI commands, seeing examples of how those commands are used to configure and manage the Horizon infrastructure, including the desktops, desktop pools, and the Horizon connection servers themselves.

In the next chapter, we will learn how to use the Horizon Windows group policy templates to configure various Horizon settings.

Questions

1. What tasks must you perform on a Horizon connection server in order to execute PowerCLI commands against it remotely?
2. How do you list all available Horizon PowerCLI commands?
3. How do you get help for an individual PowerCLI command?
4. Name the PowerCLI command used to link a vCenter server to a Horizon pod.
5. Name the PowerCLI command used to create a new desktop pool.
6. Name the PowerCLI command used to entitle a user to a Horizon pool.
7. Name the PowerCLI command used to refresh a linked clone-based desktop pool.

Further reading

The following resources may be used to learn more about the topics described in this chapter:

- **VMware documentation:**
    - **VMware Horizon:** https://docs.vmware.com/en/VMware-Horizon-7/index.html
    - **VMware vSphere:** https://www.vmware.com/support/pubs/vsphere-esxi-vcenter-server-pubs.html
- **Microsoft documentation:**
    - **Windows:** https://docs.microsoft.com/en-us/windows/

15
Implementing Horizon Group Policies

This chapter will discuss the Microsoft Active Directory Group Policy templates, which can be used to customize various aspects of the Horizon environment. The templates focus on the Horizon Agent, Client, Connection Server, PCoIP, and Blast settings, Microsoft RDSH servers, and other components of the Horizon software. Most organizations will use one or more of these templates to fine-tune various aspects of their Horizon environment.

In this chapter, we will cover the following topics:

- What are the names and the description of each Horizon ADM template file?
- Where are the Horizon ADM template files located?
- What is Group Policy Loopback Processing?
- Where are the Horizon group policies applied?
- What settings are contained within the 16 Horizon ADM template files?

Horizon Group Policy overview

Horizon includes 15 different Group Policy templates. Some of these templates are used with Horizon options that are not commonly used or those that are outside the scope of this book. Where noted, refer to the Horizon documentation (https://docs.vmware.com/en/VMware-Horizon-7/index.html) for additional information about these templates:

- `pcoip.adm`: Settings related to the configuration of the PCoIP display protocol
- `pcoip.client.adm`: Settings related to the configuration of the Horizon PCoIP client

Implementing Horizon Group Policies

- `urlRedirection-enUS.adm`: Used to redirect URLs to applications brokered by Horizon (running on desktops or Windows RDSH servers) or the Horizon client workstation; this template is less common and therefore not discussed in this chapter
- `vdm_agent.adm`: Settings related to the configuration of the Horizon Agent
- `vdm_agent_rtav.adm`: Settings related to realtime audio-video used with webcams; this template is less common and therefore not discussed in this chapter
- `vdm_agent_scanner.adm`: Settings related to redirecting Horizon client scanner output; this template is less common and therefore not discussed in this chapter
- `vdm_agent_serialport.adm`: Settings related to redirecting Horizon client serial port output; this template is less common and therefore not discussed in this chapter
- `vdm_blast.adm`: Settings related to the configuration of the Blast display protocol
- `vdm_client.adm`: Settings related to configuration of the Horizon Client
- `vdm_server.adm`: Settings related to the configuration of the Horizon Connection Server
- `vdm_common.adm`: Settings that are common to all Horizon Connection and Security servers
- `view_agent_direct_connection.adm`: Settings related to Horizon clients who connect directly to machines with the Horizon agent installed; this template is less common and therefore not discussed in this chapter
- `ViewPM.adm`: Settings used to enable and configure Horizon Persona Management; this template is less common and therefore not discussed in this chapter
- `vmware_rdsh.admx`: Settings related to Microsoft Windows RDSH servers; these templates are discussed in Chapter 9, *Performing Horizon Pool Maintenance*
- `vmware_rdsh_server.admx`: Settings related to Microsoft Windows RDSH servers; these templates are discussed in Chapter 9, *Performing Horizon Pool Maintenance*

The Group Policy template files are available for download from the VMware Horizon home page; obtain the `VMware-Horizon-Extras-Bundle-x.x.x-yyyyyyy.zip` file, unzip it, and copy the files to the `C:\Windows\PolicyDefinitions` folder on either an AD domain controller or to any folder on your AD administrative workstation.

The majority of the templates are provided in the **Administrative Template** (**ADM**) format, which allows them to be imported into an Active Directory Group Policy template. The templates used for Microsoft RDSH servers are provided in the newer **ADMX** format, which is functionally similar to the ADM format template and used in the same way. In this the remaining sections of this chapter, we will learn about the most commonly used templates, their general purpose, and what settings are contained within each.

Loopback processing for group policies

Horizon includes a number of user-based group policies that are only required when using a Horizon desktop, such as settings for the Horizon Agent. In addition, an organization may be using some user-based group policies that they don't want or shouldn't want applied to users when they are using Horizon desktops, such as policies that install software applications.

Group Policy **loopback processing** applies policies based solely on the location of the Active Directory computer object, discarding or lowering the priority of other user policies that may have been applied by other GPOs.

Loopback processing is an advanced Group Policy feature that should not be used without understanding how it will affect the group policies of Horizon desktop users. Since loopback processing will discard or reorder the application of other GPOs that apply to the user, before enabling it, research what policies are affected and plan your Horizon GPOs accordingly.

Implementing Horizon Group Policies

You can set the loopback policy in the Group Policy Object Editor snap-in by using the **Configure user Group Policy loopback processing mode** policy setting under **Computer Settings\Administrative settings\System\Group Policy**:

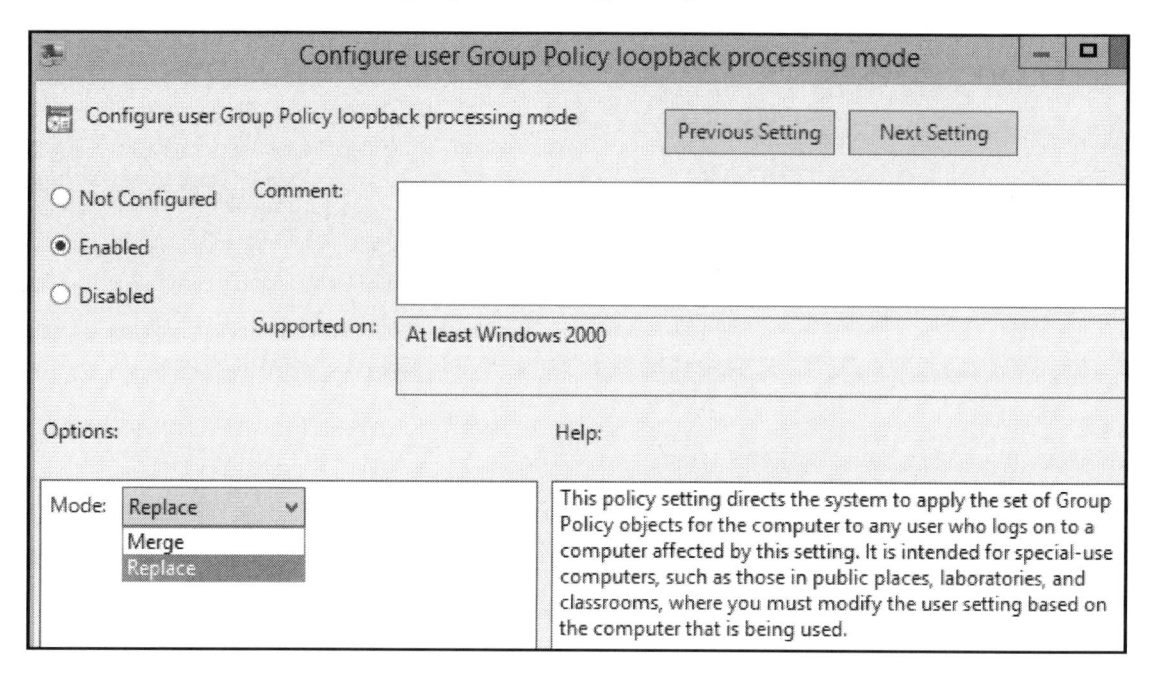

Two loopback processing modes are available:

- **Merge mode**: The list of user GPOs are gathered during the login process, followed by the computer GPOs. When the policies are applied, the computer GPOs are applied last, and as a result have higher precedence than the user GPOs.
- **Replace mode**: The other user GPOs are not gathered, only the computer GPOs. Only the user GPOs within the current policy itself are applied to the user. All Computer GPOs will be applied.

When you choose **Replace** mode, all other user policies are discarded. As a result, it is important to ensure that any domain-critical user policies are included in the GPO that has loopback processing enabled in Replace mode.

When enabling loopback processing on a GPO, ensure that the GPO has user policy settings enabled in the Details tab GPO Status drop-down menu. A setting of **Enabled** means that both user and computer policies in the GPO will be applied:

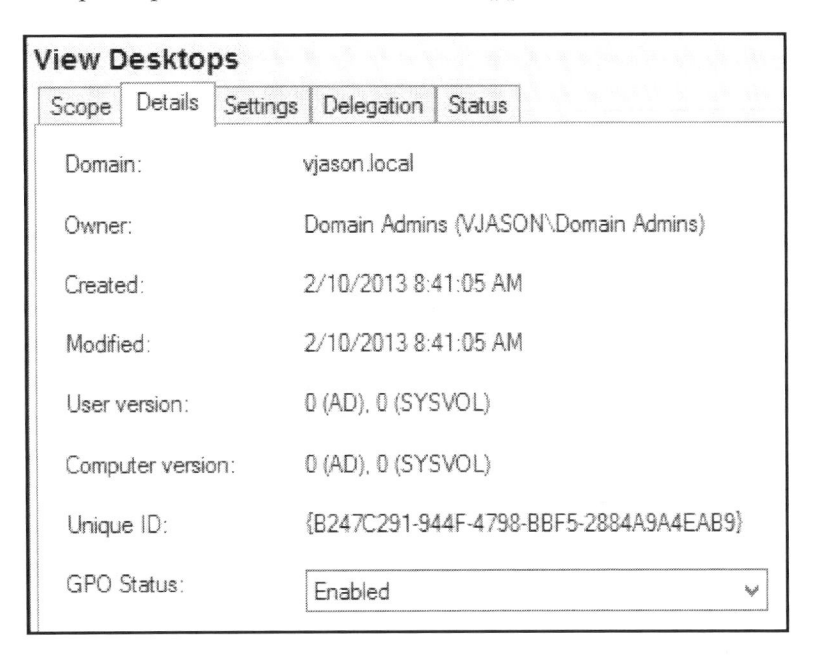

The Horizon Agent Configuration ADM template

The Horizon Agent Configuration ADM template file (`vdm_agent.adm`) contains policy settings related to the authentication and environmental components of Horizon Agent. Where applicable, the default values for the settings are provided.

The following sections of this policy deal with topics that are not covered in this book, so they will not be discussed in this section. Refer to the Horizon documentation (https://docs.vmware.com/en/VMware-Horizon-7/index.html) for details about the features that these settings are used with:

- Smartcard Redirection
- True SSO Configuration

Agent configuration base settings

The following settings apply to the base level of the Horizon Agent Configuration ADM template:

Policy	Applied to	Default value	Description
Recursive Enumeration of Trusted Domains	Computers	Enabled	This setting ensures that Horizon Clients will have access to all trusted AD domains when they attempt to log in. This setting should be enabled if the Horizon environment supports users in other domains or other trusted AD forests.

The Horizon Agent ADM template also includes USB Configuration policy settings. The same policies can also be applied to the Horizon Client using the Horizon Client ADM template. If the policies are applied using the Horizon Agent ADM template, the Horizon Client will download the USB policy settings from Horizon Agent and use them in conjunction with the Horizon Client USB policy settings to decide which devices it will allow to be available for redirection from the client computer. The USB policies are all computer configuration objects.

Viewing USB configuration settings

When configuring any setting that involves USB device families or specific devices, you have the option of overriding or merging the Horizon Agent setting with those of the Horizon Client. To override the Horizon Client setting, enter "O:" before the identifier; to merge the setting, enter "M:" before the identifier. The following examples all use the override option.

USB vendor and product IDs can be obtained from the device properties page in the Windows Device Manager. The following screenshot shows the USB hardware IDs obtained from the Details tab of the device properties:

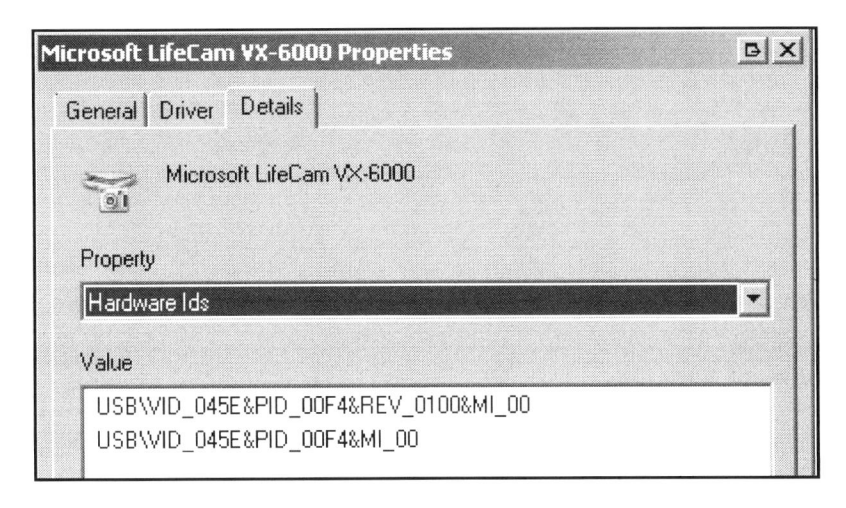

The portion of the vendor and hardware ID that will be used in the USB settings is `VID_045E&PID_00F4`. This value must be converted to a specific format for the USB policy setting. The following guidelines can be used to convert the ID into the value needed:

- The underscores should be replaced by dashes.
- The ampersand should be replaced by an underscore.

Using those guidelines, the new vendor and hardware ID will be `VID-045E_PID-00F4`. The `045E` represents the vendor ID, while the `00F4` represents the hardware ID. To specify all hardware devices made by that vendor, you can simply replace the hardware ID with `****`, which acts as a wildcard. The resultant ID would be `VID-045E_PID-****`.

USB device families are standardized names that are used by all vendors who sell USB devices. A full list of USB device names can be found in the VMware Horizon documentation (`https://docs.vmware.com/en/VMware-Horizon-7/index.html`).

[423]

Implementing Horizon Group Policies

The following settings apply to the **View USB Configuration** section of the Horizon Agent Configuration ADM template. Each of these settings is a computer configuration object, and undefined by default unless otherwise noted:

Setting	Description
Exclude All Devices	Prevents all USB devices attached to the Horizon Client from being forwarded to the Horizon desktop. Most Horizon environments allow some devices, such as a USB keyboard, mouse, or printer, to be forwarded, while disabling the forwarding of devices not needed in the Horizon desktops, such as Bluetooth or Smart Card readers. When set to either true or false, you can still use other policy settings to allow or prevent specific USB devices or families of USB devices to be forwarded. The default setting is false, which allows all devices. If set to true and the settings are passed to Horizon Client, this setting will always override the settings on Horizon Client.
Exclude Device Family	Prevents an entire family of devices from being forwarded to the Horizon desktop. This setting is used by organizations that want to allow USB devices in general to be forwarded, but prevent specific device families from being forwarded. To prevent Horizon-Client-attached storage devices and imaging devices from being forwarded, you would enter the following text in the policy setting field: O:storage;imaging Storage and imaging are the US device family names for mass storage devices and imaging devices. When using multiple device names, separate them with a semicolon.
Exclude Vid/Pid Device	Prevents devices with specific vendor and product IDs from being forwarded to the Horizon desktop. This setting can be used to prevent a specific device from being forwarded, while still allowing other devices within that family. To prevent the sample device referenced earlier in the chapter from being forwarded, you would enter the following text in the policy field: O: VID-045E_PID-00F4 To prevent all devices by that vendor from being forwarded, you would use the following: O: VID-045E_PID-****
Include Device Family	Specifies which device families can be forwarded to the Horizon desktop. This setting is often used in tandem with the Exclude All Devices setting, to enable the forwarding of specific device families. This setting is configured using the same format as the Exclude Device family setting.

| Include Vid/Pid Device | Allows devices with specific vendor and product IDs to be forwarded to the Horizon desktop. This setting is often used in tandem with the Exclude All Devices setting, to enable the forwarding of specific devices or devices from a specific vendor. This setting is configured using the same format as the Exclude Vid/Pid Device policy. |

Client Downloadable only Settings

The following settings apply to the **Client Downloadable only Settings** section of the Horizon Agent Configuration ADM template. While these settings exist within the Horizon Agent Group Policy template, they are only applied to the Horizon Clients when they connect. Each of these settings is a computer configuration object, and undefined by default unless otherwise noted:

Setting	Description
Allow Audio Input Devices	Allows audio input devices, such as microphones, to be forwarded to the Horizon desktop. The default setting within Horizon is to allow forwarding, which may not be desirable in environments where client bandwidth is tightly controlled.
Allow Audio Output Devices	Allows audio output devices, such as speakers, to be forwarded to the Horizon desktop. The default setting within Horizon is to block forwarding, which is recommended as the local Horizon Client audio output typically does not need to be forwarded to the Horizon desktop.
Allow Auto Device Splitting	Allows the automatic splitting of composite USB devices, such as a headset that has both headphones and a microphone. Splitting these devices allows the components to be managed individually using Horizon group policies, rather than as just one USB device. The setting should be enabled if an organization uses the Horizon USB policies to tightly control which USB devices can be forwarded to the desktop.
Allow HID Bootable	Allows input devices other than keyboards or mice that are available at boot time to be forwarded to the Horizon desktop. One common example is a keyboard or mouse that connects using a USB Bluetooth receiver. The default setting within Horizon is to allow forwarding, which ensures that these devices will be available to the desktop at all times.

Allow Other Input Devices	Allows input devices other than HID-bootable devices or keyboards with integrated pointing devices to be forwarded to the Horizon desktop. The default setting within Horizon is to allow forwarding, which ensures that these devices will be available to the desktop at all times.
Allow Keyboard and Mouse Devices	Allows keyboards with integrated pointing devices to be forwarded to the Horizon desktop. The default setting within Horizon is to block forwarding, although organizations that use these devices may wish to enable this option.
Allow Smart Cards	Allows Smart Card devices to be forwarded to the Horizon desktop. The default setting within Horizon is to block forwarding, which is recommended unless the Smart Card readers are required for logging into the Horizon desktop.
Allow Video Devices	Allows video devices to be forwarded to the Horizon desktop. The default setting is to allow forwarding, which is the recommended setting.
Exclude Vid/Pid Device From Split	Excludes a specific composite USB device from splitting. This setting is used when Auto Device Splitting is allowed, but only when you need to prevent specific devices from splitting so that you can manage them as a single USB device. To enable the policy, use the same format as Exclude Vid/Pid Device policy, which uses the USB vendor and product IDs to identify the device.
Split Vid/Pid Device	Used to allow a specific composite USB device to split even when Allow Auto Device Splitting is disabled. To enable the policy, use the same format as Exclude Vid/Pid Device policy, which uses the USB vendor and product IDs to identify the device.

Agent Configuration settings

The following settings apply to the **Agent Configuration** section of the Horizon Agent Configuration ADM template:

Policy	Applied to	Default value	Description
AllowDirectRDP	Computers	Enabled	Allows anyone to directly connect to a Horizon desktop using the Microsoft RDP. This setting should be disabled if you wish to prevent direct access to Horizon desktops for security purposes. Do not disable this setting if your environment has Horizon Clients running on Mac OSX as this will prevent their normal Horizon sessions from connecting successfully.
AllowSingleSignon	Computers	Enabled	Enables passing through your Horizon Client logon credentials to the Horizon desktop, allowing you to log in automatically. When this setting is disabled, users will be required to log in again at the Horizon desktop Windows login screen.
CommandsToRunOnConnect	Computers	Undefined	Specifies a list of commands or scripts to be run when a Horizon Client session is first connected. This setting is similar to a traditional login script, and can be used to run commands that are only required when logging into Horizon desktops.

CommandsToRunOnDisconnect	Computers	Undefined	Specifies a list of commands or scripts to be run when a Horizon Client session is disconnected.
CommandsToRunOnReconnect	Computers	Undefined	Specifies a list of commands or scripts to be run when a Horizon Client session is reconnected. These commands will only run if the user session is still active within the desktop when the user attempts to reconnect.
ConnectionTicketTimeout	Computers	900 seconds (Horizon default)	Specifies the amount of time in seconds that the Horizon connection ticket is valid. Horizon clients use a connection ticket for verification and SSO when connecting to Horizon Agent on the Horizon desktop. For security reasons, the ticket is valid for a limited amount of time. If authentication of the Horizon Client does not complete within the connection ticket timeout period, the logon session times out.

CredentialFilterExceptions	Computers	Undefined	Specifies the executable files that are not allowed to load the agent Credential Filter, preventing those executables from accessing the Horizon Client SSO login information. Filenames must not include a path or suffix, and use a semicolon to separate multiple filenames. This setting is often left at the default to ensure that all components on the desktop function properly.
Disable Time Zone Synchronization	Either	Disabled	Determines whether the timezone of the Horizon desktop is synchronized with that of the Horizon Client. When set to enabled, the setting only applies if the Disable timezone forwarding setting of the Horizon Client Configuration policy is not set to disabled. This setting should be left at the default to ensure that the desktop time matches that of the Horizon Client.

Implementing Horizon Group Policies

Enable multi-media acceleration	Computers	Enabled	MMR is a Microsoft DirectShow filter that forwards multimedia data from specific codecs on the Horizon desktops directly through a TCP socket to the client, where it is decoded and played. MMR should be disabled if the Horizon Client has insufficient resources or lacks the support for local multimedia decoding.
Force MMR to use software overlay	Computers	Disabled	Enabling this setting forces MMR to use a software overlay on all monitors, required in multi-monitor systems where only the primary monitor would normally support it. This setting should only be enabled if multi-monitor MMR support is required.
ShowDiskActivityIcon	Computers	Enabled	Displays the disk activity icon in the Windows system tray. This setting should be disabled if the disk activity icon is not required.
Single sign-on retry timeout	Computers	5000 ms (Horizon default)	Specifies the time in ms after which the agent will retry SSO.

| Toggle Display Settings Control | Computers | Enabled | Determines whether to disable the Settings tab in the Display Windows control panel when a Horizon Client session uses the PCoIP display protocol. This setting should remain enabled to ensure that the Horizon desktops use the display settings that are configured in the desktop pool. |

Agent Security settings

The following settings apply to the **Agent Security** section of the Horizon Agent Configuration ADM template:

Policy	Applied to	Default value	Description
Accept SSL encrypted framework channel	Either	Undefined	Determines whether the Horizon Agent will accept an SSL encrypted framework channel from the Horizon Client. If legacy Horizon Clients need to connect to the Horizon infrastructure, this setting may need to remain at the default, which allows those legacy clients to connect without SSL while using SSL for newer clients.

Unity Touch and Hosted App settings

The following settings apply to the **Unity Touch and Hosted App** section of the Horizon Agent Configuration ADM template:

Policy	Applied to	Default value	Description
Enable system tray redirection for Hosted Apps	Either	Enabled	Specifies whether remotely connected hosted apps will redirect their system tray actions.

| Enable Unity Touch | Either | Enabled | Specifies whether to enable the Horizon Agent Unity Touch feature. |
| Enable user profile customization for Hosted Apps | Either | Disabled | Specifies whether to generalize a user profile and the associated customization when using hosted applications. |

> At the time of publication, an error with the Horizon ADM files places the User version of these settings within the **Agent Security** section of the template.

VMware FlashMMR Settings

The following settings apply to the **VMware FlashMMR** section of the Horizon Agent Configuration ADM template:

Policy	Applied to	Default value	Description
Enable flash multi-media redirection	Computers	Disabled	Specifies whether to redirect flash content for specified URLs (provided in another policy setting) to the Horizon client. This setting typically reduces CPU and network utilization on the Horizon infrastructure.
Hosts URL list to enable Flashmmr	Users	Undefined	Specifies which URLs to redirect using the Flastmmr feature. The URLs must include either a http:// or https:// prefix; wildcards are supported using an *.
Minimum rect size to enable FlashMMR	Computers	320,200 (Horizon default)	Specifies minimum size (width, height) in pixels to enable FlashMMR.

The Horizon Client Configuration ADM template

The Horizon Client Configuration ADM template file (`vdm_client.adm`) contains policy settings related to the Horizon Client configuration. Where applicable, the default values for the settings are provided.

Client Configuration Base settings

The following settings apply to the base level of the Horizon Agent Configuration ADM template:

Policy	Applied to	Default value	Description
Default value of the "Hide the selector after launching an item" checkbox	Computers	Disabled	Specifies whether the selector is hidden after launching an item.
Delay the start of replications when starting the View Client with Local Mode	Computers	900 seconds (Horizon default)	Specifies the number of seconds to delay the start of the replication of Local Mode desktop data after the Horizon Client with Local Mode starts. Replication will begin after the delay period, based on the replication schedule, as configured in local mode policies in the Horizon Manager Admin console.
Disable desktop disconnect messages	Either	Enabled	Determines whether to display the default messages that are shown upon desktop disconnection.
Disable time zone forwarding	Computers	Undefined	Determines whether timezone synchronization between the Horizon desktop and the Horizon Client is disabled. This setting should be left at the default to ensure that the desktop time matches that of the Horizon Client.

Disable toast notifications	Either	Undefined	Determines whether to disable toast notifications from Horizon Client, such as the warning for when a Horizon Session is nearing timeout. This setting should be left at the default to ensure that the Horizon Client receives important status messages.
Enable relative mouse	Either	Disabled	Determines whether to use relative mouse mode with PCoIP desktops, which is typically recommended for certain graphics applications.
Redirect smart card readers in Local Mode	Computers	Enabled	Determines whether Smart Card readers are redirected to the Horizon local mode desktops. When enabled, the readers will be shared with the client system. This setting should be left at the default if Smart Cards are required for authentication to the local mode desktop.
Tunnel proxy bypass address list	Computers	Undefined	Specifies a list of tunnel IP addresses, which are IP addresses that should be accessed directly and not through a proxy server. Use a semicolon (;) to separate multiple entries. This setting should be enabled if specific IP addresses should be accessed directly.
URL for View Client online help	Computers	Undefined	Specifies an alternate URL from which the Horizon Client can retrieve help pages, such as an internal help desk page. This setting should be used when an organization has created a custom internal web page for Horizon Client support.
Always on top	Users	Enabled	Ensures that the Horizon Client window is always the topmost window, preventing the Windows taskbar from obscuring a full-screen Horizon Client window. This setting should be left at the default, but can be enabled if the Horizon Client needs ongoing access to locally installed applications.

Chapter 15

Default Exit Behavior For Local Mode Desktops	Users	Shutdown	Controls the default exit behavior of Horizon local mode desktops. The default setting is optimal in most environments, as it ensures that the desktop will be powered down when not in use.
Don't check monitor alignment on spanning	Users	Disabled	By default, the Horizon Client desktop will not span multiple monitors if the screens do not have the same height (when beside one another) or width (when positioned top and bottom). This setting should be left at the default to ensure that spanned displays display properly.
Enable multi-media acceleration	Users	Undefined	Determines whether MMR is enabled on the Horizon Client. If MMR is disabled in the Horizon Agent, this setting has no effect. This setting is often used when the desktops have MMR enabled, but a subset of the Horizon Clients should not due to performance or support concerns.
Enable the shade	Users	Enabled	Determines whether the Horizon Client shade menu bar is visible. This setting should be left at the default to ensure that the Horizon Clients have access to the menu bar commands.
Pin the shade	Users	Enabled	Determines whether the pin on the Horizon Client shade menu bar is enabled, which prevents the menu bar from auto-hiding. This setting should be left at the default to ensure that the share menu is displayed by default.

Scripting definitions settings

The following settings apply to the **Scripting definitions** section of the Horizon Client Configuration ADM template. Each of these settings can be applied to either a user or computer, and are undefined by default:

Setting	Description
Automatically connect if only one launch item is entitled	Determines whether a user will automatically connect to an application or desktop if they are only entitled to one object.
Connect all USB devices to the desktop on launch	Determines whether all of the available Horizon Client USB devices are connected to the Horizon desktop upon login. This setting should be left at the default, as the Horizon Agent USB policies allow for more granular control over what devices are forwarded to the Horizon desktop.
Connect USB devices to the desktop when they are plugged in	Determines whether Horizon Client USB devices are connected to the Horizon desktop when they are plugged in. This setting should be left at the default, as the Horizon Agent USB policies allow for more granular control over what devices are forwarded to the Horizon desktop.
DesktopLayout	Specifies the layout of the Horizon Client window when logging into a Horizon desktop. This setting should be configured based on the needs of your environment. In environments where a user will do all of their work within the Horizon Client, the preferred setting is Full Screen.
DesktopName to select	Specifies the desktop pool that Horizon Client will use during login. This setting eliminates the need for the Horizon Client to select the desktop pool, and can be useful when an environment has a large number of pools.
Disable 3rd-party Terminal Services plugins	Determines whether the Horizon Client disables third-party Terminal Services plugins. This setting does not affect Horizon-specific plugins, such as USB redirection. Third-party plugins are enabled by default, which ensures that they will be available if required. This setting can be disabled if none of the Horizon clients uses the RDP protocol.
Locked Guest Size	Determines the screen resolution of the Horizon desktop, disabling the auto-fit functionality. Supports values between `640x480` through `4096x4096`.

Logon DomainName	Specifies the NetBIOS name of the AD domain that Horizon Client uses during login. This setting can be used to preselect the AD domain name to further simplify the Horizon Client login process.
Logon Password	Specifies the password that Horizon Client will use to log in. The password is stored in plain text by Active Directory; for security reasons, this setting should not be used under most circumstances.
Logon UserName	Specifies the username that Horizon Client will use to log in. This setting can be used to populate the AD username to further simplify the Horizon Client login process.
Server URL	Specifies the URL that the Horizon Client will use to log in. This setting can be used to populate the Horizon Connection Server URL name in the Horizon Client, eliminating the need for users to memorize it.
Suppress error messages (when fully scripted only)	Determines whether Horizon Client error messages are hidden during the login process. This setting applies only when the login process is fully scripted, meaning that all information needed to complete the login was provided by a script or Group Policy settings. This setting is only required when your environment includes clients that use fully automated logins.

Security Settings

The following settings apply to the **Security Settings** section of the Horizon Client Configuration ADM template:

Policy	Applied to	Default value	Description
Allow command-line credentials	Computers	Disabled	Determines whether the Horizon Client allows user credentials to be provided using command-line options. If this setting is enabled, when users execute the Horizon Client using the command line, the SmartCardPIN and password options will be accepted. The default setting is disabled, which is preferred as it prevents users from creating scripts or batch files to log in which include their password or Smart Card PIN.
Certificate verification mode	Computer	Undefined	Configures SSL certificate checking settings on the Horizon Client, which affects how the client handles connections to untrusted certificates. The default setting is Warn But Allow, which is acceptable for new Horizon deployments but not the ideal configuration. This setting allows clients to connect to the untrusted certificate after accepting a warning. Where possible, the Horizon Connection and Security Servers should be given trusted certificates, and the policy set to Full Security. This allows Horizon Clients to connect only to servers with trusted certificates.
Configures SSL protocols and cryptographic algorithms	Either	See policy	Configures the Horizon client cipher list. This is used to restrict which cryptographic algorithms and protocols may be used.

Default value of the "Log in as current user" checkbox	Either	Disabled	Specifies the default value of the Horizon Client "Log in as current user" checkbox, and will override the default value specified during Horizon Client installation. Enabling this setting ensures that SSO will be used to log into the Horizon Client, unless the user manually unchecks the checkbox.
Display option to Log in as current user	Either	Enabled	Determines whether the Horizon Client "Log in as current user" checkbox is visible. When the checkbox is visible, users can select or deselect it, overriding its default value. When the checkbox is hidden using the policy, users cannot override its default value. This policy, when combined with the Default value of the Log in as current user checkbox policy, can be used to force the Horizon Client to use SSO to log in.
Enable jump list integration	Computer	Enabled	Determines whether a Windows jump list appears in the Horizon Client icon in the taskbar of Windows 7 and later systems. A jump list lets users quickly connect to recent Horizon Connection Server instances and Horizon desktops. The default setting is enabled, which is recommended to enable quick logins to frequently-used Horizon Connection Servers.
Enable Single Sign-On for smart card authentication	Computer	Undefined	Determines whether SSO is enabled for Smart Card authentication when logging into the Horizon Client. When SSO is disabled, the Horizon Client does not display a custom Smart Card PIN dialog. This setting is often left at the default in order to support SSO when using Smart Cards.

Enable SSL encrypted framework channel	Either	Undefined	Determines whether the Horizon Client will accept an SSL-encrypted framework channel from the Horizon Agent. If your Horizon Agents all have full support for Horizon 5.2 or later, SSL encryption should be enforced. Assuming your Horizon Clients and Horizon Desktops are all running the current versions of their respective Horizon software components, this setting should be set to Enforce to ensure that only SSL connections are used.
Ignore certificate revocation problems	Either	Disabled	Determines whether Horizon Client errors associated with a revoked SSL certificate will be ignored. This setting should be left at the default, which ensures that any errors will be communicated to the Horizon Client.
Servers Trusted For Delegation	Computer	Undefined	Specifies which Horizon Connection Servers will accept the user credentials that are passed when a user selects the Log in as current user checkbox. If you do not specify any Horizon Connection Server instances, all Horizon Connection Servers will accept the login information. All servers are trusted by default, which is the typical setting for most environments. If you do not want to use SSO in your environment, or for specific Horizon Connection Servers, you can use this setting to restrict it.

RDP Settings

The following settings apply to the **RDP Settings** section of the Horizon Client Configuration ADM template. These settings apply only to Horizon Clients who are using the RDP protocol. Each of these settings is a user configuration object, and undefined by default unless otherwise noted:

Setting	Description
Audio redirection	Determines whether the audio played within the Horizon desktop is redirected. By default, the audio is redirected to the Horizon Client, which is the most common setting.
Bitmap cache file size in	Specifies the size of the bitmap cache, in kilobytes or megabytes, to use for specific bits per pixel (bpp) bitmap color settings. Increasing the bitmap cache provides more storage on the client for image data, potentially reducing the need retransmit that data when it needs to be displayed again, which may reduce the bandwidth required for the connection. Separate versions of this setting are provided in different unit and bpp combinations. This setting should not be altered without measuring the impact at both the Horizon desktop and the Horizon Client to ensure that performance is not affected.
Bitmap caching/cache persistence active	Determines whether persistent bitmap caching is enabled on the Horizon Client. Persistent bitmap caching can improve performance by reducing the amount of image data that is transmitted between the Horizon desktop and the Horizon Client, but it requires additional disk space. This setting should not be altered without measuring the impact at both the Horizon desktop and the Horizon Client to ensure that performance is not affected.
Color depth	Specifies the display color depth. This setting is often used in limited use cases when an organization wishes to reduce the display color depth in order to help minimize the bandwidth required by the Horizon Clients.
Cursor shadow	Determines whether a mouse cursor shadow appears. This setting can be disabled as part of a larger effort to optimize Horizon desktop performance. By itself, this setting does not have a significant impact on desktop performance.

Setting	Description
Desktop background	Determines whether the Windows desktop background will appear. This setting helps minimize the bandwidth required to display the Windows desktop background. This setting can be disabled as part of a larger effort to optimize Horizon desktop performance.
Desktop composition	Determines whether Windows desktop composition, also known as Aero, is enabled. Unless explicitly required, desktop composition should be disabled to optimize the performance of the Horizon desktop.
Enable audio capture redirection	Specifies whether the default Windows audio input device is redirected. This default setting is disabled, which is the preferred setting unless audio capture is explicitly required.
Enable compression	Determines whether RDP data is compressed, which reduces the amount of bandwidth required for the RDP session. The default setting is enabled, which is the optimal setting for Horizon environments that use the RDP protocol.
Enable Credential Security Service Provider	Specifies whether the Horizon desktop RDP connection uses Windows **Network-Level Authentication** (**NLA**), a more secure authentication method for the RDP protocol. This setting must be enabled if Windows has been configured to require NLA authentication.
Enable RDP Auto-Reconnect	Determines whether the RDP client component of the Horizon Client will attempt to reconnect to a Horizon desktop after an RDP protocol connection failure. This setting has no effect if the "Use secure tunnel connection to desktop" option is enabled in the Horizon Manager Admin console. The default setting is disabled. If RDP auto-reconnect is desired, this setting should be enabled.
Font smoothing	Determines whether anti-aliasing is used when displaying fonts. This setting causes a slight increase in resources used by the Horizon desktop, but provides a superior user experience.
In-memory bitmap cache in KB for 8 bpp bitmaps	Specifies the size, in KB, of the RAM bitmap cache for the 8 bpp color setting. This setting should not be altered without measuring the impact on both the Horizon desktop and the Horizon Client to ensure that performance is not affected.

Menu and window animation	Determines whether animation for menus and windows is enabled. This setting helps eliminate the resources and bandwidth required to render and transmit display updates that involve menu and window animations. This setting can be disabled as part of a larger effort to optimize Horizon desktop performance.
Redirect clipboard	Determines whether the Horizon Client clipboard information is redirected. This setting can be used to control whether clipboard data on the Horizon Client can be pasted within the Horizon desktop. Most organizations allow this, but depending on security concerns, you may wish to disable this option.
Redirect drives	Determines whether local disk drives on the Horizon Client are redirected. By default, local drives are redirected from the Horizon Client to the Horizon desktop. If this is not desired, this feature should be disabled.
Redirect printers	Determines whether local printers on the Horizon Client are redirected. By default, local printers are redirected from the Horizon Client to the Horizon desktop. If this is not desired, this feature should be disabled.
Redirect serial ports	Determines whether COM ports on the Horizon Client are redirected. COM port redirection is only required if the Horizon clients use serial port devices whose input must be forwarded to the Horizon desktop, as is found in some point-of-sale (POS) platforms.
Redirect smart cards	Determines whether Smart Cards on the Horizon Client are redirected. If Smart Card redirection is not required in your environment, this feature should be disabled.
Redirect supported plug-and-play devices	Determines whether local **Plug-and-Play** (**PnP**) and POS devices on the Horizon Client are redirected. This setting is often enabled to allow these devices to connect. If specific restrictions are required, they can be applied using the Horizon Agent USB policies.

Implementing Horizon Group Policies

Shadow bitmaps	Determines whether Windows bitmaps are shadowed when using the Horizon Client in anything less than full-screen mode. Shadow bitmaps may be disabled to reduce Horizon desktop resource utilization as part of a larger effort to optimize Horizon desktop performance. By itself, this setting does not have a significant impact on desktop performance.
Show contents of window while dragging	Determines whether the folder contents appear when users drag a folder to a new location. This setting can be disabled to help reduce Horizon desktop resource utilization as part of a larger effort to optimize Horizon desktop performance. By itself, this setting does not have a significant impact on desktop performance.
Themes	Determines whether Windows themes appear. Windows Themes should be disabled unless explicitly required. This ensures that the Horizon desktops have a similar base resource requirement, while still providing optimal performance.
Windows key combination redirection	Determines whether Windows key combinations are applied at the Horizon Client or Horizon desktop. This setting should be configured based on the needs of your organization.

Horizon USB Configuration settings

The Horizon USB Configuration section of the Horizon Client Configuration ADM template contains the same settings as the *Horizon USB configuration* and *Client Downloadable only settings* sections of the Horizon Agent ADM template. Refer to that section for information about those settings.

Settings not configurable by Agent

The following settings apply to the **Settings not configurable by Agent** section of the Horizon Client Configuration ADM template. Each of these settings is a computer configuration object, and undefined by default unless otherwise noted:

Policy	Description
Allow Device Descriptor Failsafe behavior	Allows devices on the Horizon Client to be redirected, even if config/device descriptors could not be read. This setting is often enabled when troubleshooting issues in regards to devices not redirecting when expected.

Disable Remote Configuration	Prevents the download of Horizon Client configuration settings from the Horizon desktop. Horizon Client configuration settings are downloaded by default. Enabling this setting prevents those configuration settings from being applied, which may be useful for troubleshooting purposes.
Exclude Path	Used to prevent specific USB hub or port paths from being redirected. To configure this setting, the path must be specified in the following format, where 0 is the USB Bus, and 01 is the USB port number: bus-0_port-01 All values should be in hexadecimal format. The device numbers can be found in the Windows device properties window under Details – Bus number, and the port numbers under Details – Location information for a device plugged into the given port. This setting has very limited use since the USB Bus and port values will vary on a platform-by-platform basis. Wildcards are not supported when using this setting.
Include Path	Used to identify specific USB hub or port paths that can be redirected. This setting is configured using the same format as that of the Exclude Path setting.

The Horizon Common Configuration ADM template

The Horizon Common Configuration ADM template file (`vdm_common.adm`) contains policy settings common to all Horizon components. Each of the settings in this section is computer configuration settings, and undefined by default. Where applicable, the default values for the settings are provided.

Common Configuration Base settings

The following settings apply to the base level of the Horizon Common Configuration ADM template. These settings apply to all Horizon components:

Policy	Description
Disk threshold for log and events in megabytes	Specifies the remaining disk space threshold in MB for Horizon server logs and events. When the specified value is met, event logging stops. The default is 200 MB, which should prevent the Horizon server from filling up the disk with event and log data.
Enable extended logging	Determines whether the Horizon log files include trace and debug events. This setting should be enabled when performing advanced troubleshooting of the Horizon environment.
Override the default View Windows event generation	Specifies which Horizon events will be recorded in the Windows event log, overriding the default settings.

Log Configuration settings

The following settings apply to the **Log Configuration** section of the Horizon Common Configuration ADM template:

Policy	Description
Number of days to keep production logs	Specifies how long the Horizon log files will be retained. If no value is set, the log files will be kept for seven days. This setting is often increased for auditing and troubleshooting purposes.
Maximum number of debug logs	Specifies the maximum number of debug log files to retain. When a log file reaches its maximum size, a new log file is created. When the number of log files reaches the value of this setting, the oldest log file is deleted. This setting is often increased for auditing and troubleshooting purposes.
Maximum debug log size in Megabytes	Specifies the maximum size of a debug log in MB. Once this limit is reached, the log file is closed and a new one is created. This setting should be left at the default to make the log files easier to review.

Log Directory	Specifies the full path to the log file directory. If the specified location is not writeable, the default location will be used. An extra directory with the client name will be created for client log files. For Horizon servers, this setting is often updated to redirect the log files to a location where they cannot impact the operation of the server itself, such as an alternate hard disk.
Send logs to a Syslog server	Specifies whether to send Horizon Connection Server logs to a syslog server. Note that this data is sent unencrypted.

Performance Alarm settings

The following settings apply to the **Performance Alarms** section of the Horizon Common Configuration ADM template. These settings apply only to Horizon Connection Servers and desktops running the Horizon Agent software:

Policy	Description
CPU and Memory Sampling Interval in Seconds	Sets the CPU and memory polling interval, which determines how often their usage is measured. If the value is set too low, a large amount of log data will be generated. This value should be kept to the minimum required to properly monitor resource utilization.
Overall CPU usage percentage to issue log info	Sets the threshold at which the overall CPU utilization of the system will be logged. When multiple processors are available, this percentage represents the combined usage of those processors. This value should be used to reduce the amount of log data that is recorded by only monitoring CPU utilization above a certain level.
Overall memory usage percentage to issue log info	Sets the threshold at which the overall committed system memory use will be logged. This value should be used to reduce the amount of log data that is recorded by only monitoring memory usage above a certain level.
Process CPU usage percentage to issue log info	Sets the threshold at which the CPU usage of specific processes will be logged. This setting is often useful for troubleshooting purposes.

Process memory usage percentage to issue log info	Sets the threshold at which the memory usage of specific process will be logged. This setting is often useful for troubleshooting purposes.
Process to check, comma separated name list allowing wild cards and exclusion	A comma-separated list of queries that correspond to the name of one or more processes to be examined by the Process CPU and memory monitoring policies. The following example shows how to specify two different processes: • `McTray.exe` • `winlogon.exe` You can filter this list by using wildcards within each query.

Security Configuration settings

The following settings apply to the **Security Configuration** section of the Horizon Common Configuration ADM template:

Policy	Description
Type of certificate revocation check	Sets the type of certificate revocation check that the Horizon servers will perform. The default setting is WholeChainButRoot, which checks all the certificates in the certification chain, except for the root certificate. Any setting is acceptable for this policy as all will yield the same revocation check results.
Only use cached revocation URLs	Specifies whether certificate revocation checking will use only cached URLs. The default setting is false, which allows the service to check both cached and non-cached URLs. This is the preferred setting.
Revocation URL check timeout milliseconds	Specifies the cumulative timeout across all certificate-revocation URL wire retrievals in ms. The default is 0, which informs the server to use the default value in Windows. This setting is typically not altered.

The Horizon Server Configuration ADM template

The Horizon Server Configuration ADM template file (`vdm_server.adm`) contains policy settings related to the Horizon Connection Servers. Each of the settings in this section is a computer configuration setting, and undefined by default. Where applicable, the default values for the settings are provided.

The Server Configuration Base template

The following settings apply to the base level of the Horizon Server Configuration ADM template:

Policy	Default Value	Description
Enumerate Forest Trust Child Domains	Enabled	Enables the enumeration of child domains within a trusted AD forest.
Recursive Enumeration of Trusted Domains	Enabled	Used to enable Horizon Clients access to all trusted AD domains when they attempt to log in. This setting should be enabled if the Horizon environment supports users in other domains or other trusted AD forests.
Windows Password Authentication Mode	KerberosOnly (Horizon default)	Used to specify the Windows password authentication mode.

The PCoIP Session Variables ADM template

The Horizon PCoIP Session Variables ADM template file (`pcoip.adm`) contains policy settings related to the PCoIP display protocol, and is used to apply settings to Horizon Connection Servers. Each of the settings in this section is a computer configuration setting and undefined by default. Where applicable, the default values for these settings are provided.

> **TIP**: Many of the settings in the `pcoip.adm` ADM template can be set on a per-Horizon client basis using the `pcoip.client.adm` ADM template. The **Client** column in the table in the next section will note which settings can be controlled using this template.

Implementing Horizon Group Policies

The settings can be configured as not overridable, or overridable by an administrator. If a policy is overridable, users with local administrator permissions can make changes to the settings. To configure the policies, simply choose them from the following subfolders based on which option you prefer:

- Overridable Administrator Defaults
- Not Overridable Administrator Settings

Each subfolder contains the same policy items; the only difference is whether they can be overridden.

PCoIP Session Variables Base settings

The General Session Variable Group Policy settings are used to configure general session characteristics, such as PCoIP image quality, USB devices, and network ports.

The following settings apply to the base level of the Horizon Common Configuration ADM template. Each of these settings is a computer configuration object and undefined by default unless otherwise noted:

<td">Specifies the maximum PCoIP session bandwidth that can be used for audio (sound) playback.The default value is 500 kilobits per second, which provides acceptable quality in most cases.

Policy	Client	Description
Configure clipboard redirection		Determines whether the Horizon Client clipboard information is redirected. This setting can be used to control whether clipboard data on the Horizon Client can be pasted within the Horizon desktop. The default setting is "Enabled client to server only", which you may wish to disable depending on security concerns.
Configure frame rate vs image quality preference		Controls whether to favor image quality or frame rate during Horizon client connections. The higher the value, the higher the preference on image quality. The default setting is 50, which provides an equal preference to both.

[450]

Configure PCoIP client image cache size policy	Client template only	Used to specify the size in MB of the PCoIP client image cache, which stores previously transmitted images and reduces the amount of data that must be transferred to clients over time. The default client image cache size is 250 MB.
Configure PCoIP event log cleanup by size in MB	Yes	PCoIP event logs larger than the specified size in MB will be deleted at client-session startup. The default value is 100 MB.
Configure PCoIP event log cleanup by time in days	Yes	PCoIP event logs older than the specified number of days will be deleted at client-session startup. The default value is 7 days.
Configure PCoIP event log verbosity	Yes	Specifies the PCoIP event log verbosity, which affects how much data is recorded in the logs. The default setting is 2, but may be increased to 3 when performing advanced PCoIP troubleshooting.
Configure PCoIP image quality levels		Controls how PCoIP renders images during periods of network congestion. The Minimum Image Quality (default value of 40, range of 30 to 100), Maximum Initial Image Quality (default value of 80, range of 30 to 100), and Maximum Frame Rate (default value of 40, range of 1 to 120 frames per second) values work in tandem to provide granular control in environments where network bandwidth is limited.
Configure PCoIP session encryption algorithms	Yes	Controls the encryption algorithms that will be advertised by the Horizon PCoIP Client during session negotiation. This policy is typically updated to enable or disable a particular algorithm for security purposes. The default settings enable the `Salsa20-256round12` and `AES-128-GCM` algorithms.
Configure PCoIP USB allowed and unallowed device rules		Specifies which USB devices are allowed or not allowed for PCoIP sessions that are initiated from a zero client running the Teradici firmware. By default, all devices are allowed, which ensures that all devices will be supported. Devices are specified using class or device IDs as described in the Horizon Agent USB policy settings.

Implementing Horizon Group Policies

Configure PCoIP virtual channels	Yes	Specifies which virtual channels can or cannot operate over Horizon PCoIP Client sessions. Virtual channels are used for operations such as USB or clipboard redirection. All channels are enabled by default. When specifying channels, you must separate them with a |, and if the channel name contains a | or \, you must place a \ before them. The following are examples of possible policy settings based on these rules: • sample1|sample2 • sam\\|ple3\\sample4 This setting is often left at the default unless you have specific security policies that you must enforce.
Configure SSL connections to satisfy security tools	Yes	Specifies how the Horizon Client SSL session negotiation connections are established. This setting is often enabled when testing the Horizon desktops with port scanner utilities. This setting should otherwise be left at the default.
Configure SSL protocols	Yes	Specifies which SSL protocols are enabled for Horizon agents and clients. The default value is TLS1.1:TLS1.2. This setting is typically changed due to specific encryption requirements within an organization.
Configure the Client PCoIP UDP port	Client only	Specifies the UDP client port that is used by software-based Horizon PCoIP Clients. The UDP port value specifies the base UDP port to use. The UDP port range value determines how many additional ports to try if the base port is not available. The base port is 50002 and the port range is 64 by default. These values should not be changed unless the client ports are being used for other applications.
Configure the maximum PCoIP session bandwidth	Yes	Specifies the PCoIP session maximum bandwidth, in kilobits per second. The bandwidth includes the imaging, audio, virtual channel, USB, and control PCoIP traffic. The default value is 900,000 kilobits per second, which can be adjusted as needed based on bandwidth availability.

Configure the PCoIP session audio bandwidth limit		
Configure the PCoIP session bandwidth floor	Yes	Specifies a lower limit, in kilobits per second, for the bandwidth reserved by the PCoIP session. The default value is 0 (no minimum). The default setting is often changed when you wish to provide a guaranteed minimum bandwidth to Horizon PCoIP Clients.
Configure the PCoIP session MTU	Yes	Specifies the **Maximum Transmission Unit** (**MTU**) size in bytes (B) for UDP packets within PCoIP session. The default value is 1,200 bytes, which is not typically changed.
Configure PCoIP transport header	Yes	Configures the Horizon PCoIP transport header to support QoS, which is used by supported network devices to prioritize traffic when experiencing network congestion. The default setting is enabled, which ensures that QoS enables networking equipment to prioritize Horizon Client traffic (when configured to do so).
Configure the TCP port to which the PCoIP host binds and listens		Specifies which TCP server port will be bound to by software-based PCoIP hosts. The default TCP port is 4172 and the port range is 1, neither of which is typically changed.
Configure the UDP port to which the PCoIP host binds and listens		Specifies which UDP server port will be bound to by software PCoIP hosts. The default UDP port is 4172 and the port range is 10, neither of which is typically changed.
Disable sending CAD when users press *Ctrl + Alt + Del*		When this policy is enabled, users must press *Ctrl + Alt + Insert* rather than *Ctrl + Alt + Del* (CAD) to send a **Secure Attention Sequence** (**SAS**) to the desktop during a Horizon PCoIP session. *Ctrl + Alt + Del* is enabled by default. Enable this setting if you want CAD sequences to be sent Horizon desktop only.

Enable access to a PCoIP session from a vSphere console		Allow a vSphere Client console to display an active PCoIP session, and allow input to be sent to the Horizon desktop. The default setting is disabled, which is recommended to prevent vSphere Clients from interrupting active Horizon Client sessions.
Enable/disable audio in the PCoIP session	Yes	Enable or disable audio within PCoIP sessions. Both endpoints must have audio enabled or the policy will have no effect. Audio is enabled by default, but can be disabled for those environments that do not require audio within their PCoIP sessions.
Enable/disable microphone noise and DC offset filter in PCoIP session		Enable or disable the microphone noise and DC offset filter for microphone input during PCoIP sessions. The default setting is enabled, which is recommended to ensure optimal quality of microphone input.
Turn off Build-to-Lossless feature		Disable the build-to-lossless feature of the PCoIP protocol. Build to lossless uses PCoIP bandwidth to build the display to a lossless state over time, meaning that the Horizon Client display represents the exact state of the remote Horizon desktop display. This default setting is enabled, which is the optimal setting for environments with bandwidth constraints. Build-to-lossless is often used for desktops that require maximum image quality, such as those in the medical or design fields.
Turn on PCoIP user default input language synchronization		Synchronize the default input language for the user in the PCoIP session with the default input language of the PCoIP client. The default setting is disabled, which ensures that no errors will be encountered if a client were to attempt to connect to a Horizon desktop that doesn't have the appropriate input language installed. This setting should only be enabled if the Horizon desktops support all input languages that could possibly be required.

Use alternate key for sending Secure Attention Sequence		Specifies an alternate key to be used when sending a **Secure Attention Sequence** (**SAS**). The default setting uses the *Ctrl + Alt + Insert* key sequence. This setting is typically updated when the *Ctrl + Alt + Insert* SAS is already in use by some other operation.

The Blast Session Variables ADM template

The Horizon Blast Session Variables ADM template file (vdm_blast.adm) contains policy settings related to the Blast display protocol, and is used to apply settings to Horizon Connection Servers. Each of the settings in this section is a computer configuration setting, and undefined by default.

The settings described in this section should be left at their defaults unless advanced tuning of Blast sessions is being performed.

Blast Session Variables settings

The General Session Variable Group Policy settings are used to configure general session characteristics, such as image quality, bandwidth, and frame rate:

Policy	Description
Max Session Bandwidth	Used to set the total maximum bandwidth in kilobits per second for each Horizon Blast session.
Min Session Bandwidth	Used to set the total minimum bandwidth in kilobits per second for each Horizon Blast session.
Max Frame Rate	Used to set the maximum number of frames per second for each Horizon Blast session.
UDP Protocol	Used to enable the UDP protocol for Blast sessions. This is the default is to use the TCP protocol.
H264	The default Blast encoding standard; set to Disable to use JPEG/PNG encoding.
Screen Blanking	By default, the local virtual machine console displays a blank screen; set to Disable to display the active session in the virtual machine console.
Session Garbage Collection	Specifies how often the Horizon Connect Server will scan for and then delete abandoned Blast client sessions.

Image Quality	Specifies the image quality for the Blast client; different values may be set for the low profile (frequent screen updates) and the high profile (infrequent screen updates).
HTTP Service	Specifies the port that's used for the Blast HTTP service.
Audio playback	Specifies whether to enable audio playback; this setting is enabled by default.
Configure clipboard redirection	Specifies the clipboard redirection settings; this setting allows Blast-client-to-server-clipboard redirection by default.

Summary

In this chapter, we learned about the different Group Policy templates that are included in VMware Horizon. We discussed what Group Policy Loopback Processing was, and why an organization might need to use it as part of their Horizon Deployment. We also went into detail about each of the Horizon Group Policy templates, including what they are used for and the meaning of each policy setting.

In the next chapter, we will discuss how to manage SSL certificates for the various components of the Horizon infrastructure.

Questions

1. What does loopback processing do?
2. Where do you copy the Horizon ADMX and related files to on your Active Directory server?
3. What Horizon ADMX file contains policy settings for Horizon Connection Server?
4. What Horizon ADMX file contains policy settings for all Horizon components?
5. What Horizon ADMX files contain policy settings for Horizon connection protocols?
6. What Horizon ADMX file contains policy settings for Remote Desktop Services?
7. What Horizon ADMX file contains policy settings for the Horizon Agent?
8. What Horizon ADMX file contains policy settings for the Horizon Client?

Further reading

Check out the following resources to learn more about the topics that were covered in this chapter:

- **VMware Horizon:** `https://docs.vmware.com/en/VMware-Horizon-7/index.html`
- **VMware vSphere:** `https://www.vmware.com/support/pubs/vsphere-esxi-vcenter-server-pubs.html`

16
Managing Horizon SSL Certificates

VMware Horizon, similar to many other applications that require SSL-based encryption, installs self-signed SSL certificates by default. A self-signed certificate is one that is signed by the creator, in this case the VMware Horizon component that is being installed. While self-signed certificates do enable secure communications, by default they will not be trusted by any client or server who connects to them. An untrusted certificate leads to the familiar "*There is a problem with this website's security certificate*" message in Microsoft Internet Explorer, or the "*The host name in the certificate is invalid or does not match*" message in the VMware Horizon client.

In addition, the default self-signed SSL certificates may have a smaller key length than what is required within your organization; this is something that can only be addressed by replacing them after the installation has completed.

While it is possible to add exceptions that will make the default Horizon SSL certificates trusted by the different components of the Horizon infrastructure, and the Horizon clients themselves, it is preferable to replace the certificates with those signed by a commercial or private certificate authority. A number of commercial certificate authorities are supported by many OSes by default, and organizations can distribute their own root certificate from a private certificate authority, which will enable trusted connections to any resource using certificates issued by that authority.

This chapter will show how to replace the default SSL certificates installed by each of the components of Horizon. We will use Microsoft **Active Directory** (**AD**) Certificate Services to issue the certificates, although the process would be similar if you were to use a commercial certificate authority.

Managing Horizon SSL Certificates

In this chapter, we will be covering the following topics:

- How to create a Local Computer Certificates console
- How to request a certificate using Microsoft AD Certificate Services
- How to request a certificate with Subject Alternative Names using Microsoft AD Certificate Services
- How to replace the Horizon Connection Server certificate
- How to replace the Horizon Security Server certificate
- How to replace the Horizon Composer certificate
- How to replace the Horizon Unified Access Gateway appliance certificate

Creating a Local Computer Certificates console

The Local Computer Certificates **Microsoft Management Console** (**MMC**) will be used to replace the certificate on the Horizon Connection, Security, and Composer servers:

> **TIP**
> It is not necessary to create this console on each of the Horizon servers. The same console can be created on a remote server and, in step 5 in the following procedure, a remote connection is made rather than a local one.

1. From the Windows Start menu, open the MMC by searching for and opening the `mmc.exe` application.
2. In the MMC console window, open the **File** menu and select **Add/Remove Snap-in...** to open the **Add or Remove Snap-ins** window.
3. In the **Available snap-ins:** section of the **Add or Remove Snap-ins** window, select **Certificates** and click on **Add >** to open the **Certificates snap-in** selection window.

4. In the **Certificates** snap-in window, click the **Computer account** radio button, and then click on **Next >** to move to the **Select Computer** window:

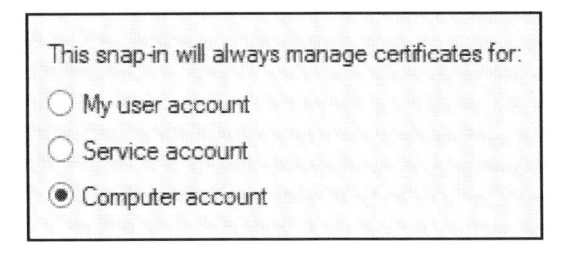

   This snap-in will always manage certificates for:
   - ○ My user account
   - ○ Service account
   - ⦿ Computer account

   > **TIP**: Note the option to select **My user account**; we will use that option in the next section of this chapter to export newly created certificates.

5. In the **Select Computer** window shown in the following screenshot, if the computer is not already selected, click on the **Local computer:** (the computer this console is running on) radio button, and then click on **Finish** to return to the **Add or Remove Snap-ins** window.

6. Click on **OK** to close the **Add or Remove Snap-ins** window and return to the MMC console window. The console will now include the **Certificates (Local Computer)** snap-in, as shown in the following screenshot:

   File Action View Favorites Window Help

   Console Root
   ▲ Certificates (Local Computer)
     ▷ Personal

   Name
   Certificates (Local Computer)

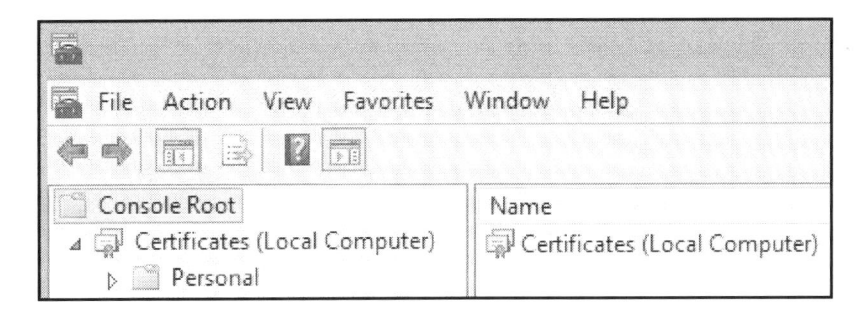

7. If you also wish to add a certificate manager snap-in for your logged-on user account, repeat steps 2 through 6, this time selecting **My user account** in step 4. This will create a single console that can be used to manage certificates for both the local computer and, currently logged-on user, as shown in the following screenshot:

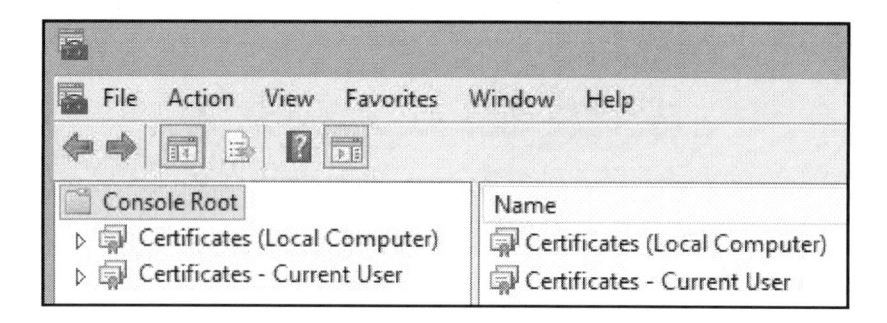

The **Local Computer Certificates** console is now ready for use. To create a shortcut for the console, open the **File** menu and click on **Save As** to open the **Save As** window. Provide a name and location for the shortcut and click on **Save**. This shortcut can be used to access the console without having to reconfigure it again.

Requesting a certificate using Microsoft AD Certificate Services

Microsoft AD Certificate Services is an optional component of the Windows Server OS that enables organizations to create their own private certificate authority. Similar functionality is available with alternative OSes, but many organizations that have a large Windows infrastructure often already rely on AD Certificate Services to provide a number of different client and server certificates.

We will use AD Certificate Services to request certificates for each of the Horizon components. The process is the same for each, although Horizon Security Servers and Horizon Unified Access Gateways may require additional information to be provided in step 5 in the following procedure. Consult the next section of this chapter for instructions on how to add additional DNS names and IP addresses, known as **Subject Alternative Names (SAN)**, to a certificate request.

Chapter 16

> **TIP**
> If you wish to configure a certificate suitable for multiple private or public FQDNs (or both), or one that includes IP addresses, and intend to use Microsoft AD Certificate Services to issue the certificate, you will need to enable support for SAN on an AD Certificate Services server. Consult the Microsoft Certificate Services documentation (`https://docs.microsoft.com/en-us/windows/desktop/seccrypto/certificate-services`) for instructions on how to configure support for SANs.

In this section, we are focusing on using the AD Certificate Services website to request a certificate, rather than using the Certificate MMC we configured in the preceding section. The advantage of using the console is that you can use it from the Horizon Connection Server, and the certificate will be placed directly in the appropriate certificate store. This differs from using the Certificate Services website, which places it in the logged-on user's Personal certificate store, which requires us to export the certificate and then import it into the local computer's Personal store.

> **TIP**
> You cannot use the Certificate console to request a certificate on a Horizon Security Server because those servers are typically not members of a domain that has Microsoft AD Certificate Services installed.

The reason we use the website in this chapter is that we can use it to request certificates for all Horizon components, not just the Connection Servers. If you are interested in using the Certificates MMC console to request a certificate, the Microsoft TechNet Wiki article titled *Create a Certificate Request using the Microsoft Management Console (MMC)* (`https://social.technet.microsoft.com/wiki/contents/articles/10377.create-a-certificate-request-using-microsoft-management-console-mmc.aspx`) details the procedure used to do so.

The following steps may be performed from any available computer that has access to the AD Certificate Services website. We will export the certificate when we are finished with the request, which is required for later import in the destination server:

1. From a web browser, open the Microsoft AD Certificate Services website. The URL for the site is typically in the format `https://FQDN of the server/certsrv`. If prompted, provide credentials for a user with the ability to request certificates from the certificate authority.

Managing Horizon SSL Certificates

> **TIP**
>
> To access the Microsoft AD Certificate Services website remotely, it must be configured with an SSL certificate. If your Certificate Services server has not been configured with an SSL certificate, you can only access the Certificate Services website from a web browser on the Certificate Services server itself, using HTTP instead of HTTPS. This section assumes that you can access the Certificate Services server remotely.

2. In the Microsoft AD Certificate Services **Welcome** page, click on **Request a certificate.**
3. On the **Request a Certificate** page, shown in the following screenshot, click on **advanced certificate request**:

Request a Certificate

Select the certificate type:
   User Certificate

Or, submit an advanced certificate request.

---

4. In the **Advanced Certificate Request** window (shown in the following screenshot), click on **Create and submit a request to this CA**:

Advanced Certificate Request

The policy of the CA determines the types of cert

   Create and submit a request to this CA.

   Submit a certificate request by using a base-6 using a base-64-encoded PKCS #7 file.

Chapter 16

5. In the **Advanced Certificate Request** window (shown in the following screenshot), use the **Certificate Template:** drop-down menu if required to select a web server template that allows the certificate keys to be exported, provide any remaining information needed to complete the request, and click **Submit >**:

> **Advanced Certificate Request**
>
> Certificate Template:
>
> [Web Server-Export ▼]
>
> Identifying Information For Offline Template:
>
> Name: horizon.vjason.com
> E-Mail: jason@vjason.com

> 💡 **TIP**
> The **Name:** field must always be populated with the FQDN of the target server. This field is the same as the **Common Name** field you see when using the Certificates MMC to request a certificate, and is also used in various other SSL certificate-related resources.

6. In the **Web Access Confirmation** window, review the message and click on **Yes** to complete the certificate request.

> 💡 **TIP**
> If Microsoft AD Certificate Services is configured to approve web server requests automatically, the certificate will be available immediately. If not, the certificate administrator must approve the request to create the certificate.

> 💡 **TIP**
> This section assumes that the certificate request will automatically be approved and available for immediate download. If you need to wait for the certificate administrator to approve the certificate request, simply return to the certificate services website after the request has been approved, and select **View the status of a pending certificate request to download the certificate**.

Managing Horizon SSL Certificates

7. In the **Certificate Issued** page, click on **Install this certificate** to install the certificate in the logged-on user's **Personal** certificate store, as shown in the following screenshot:

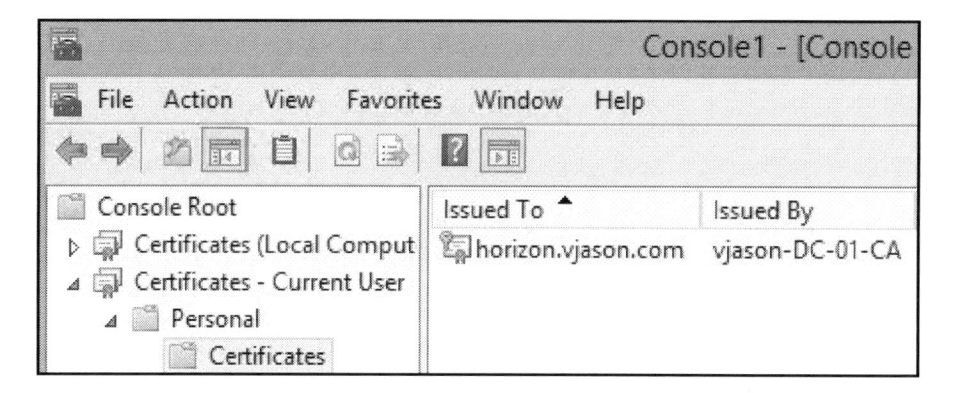

8. Right-click on the certificate shown in the following screenshot and click **Export...** to open the **Certificate Export Wizard**:

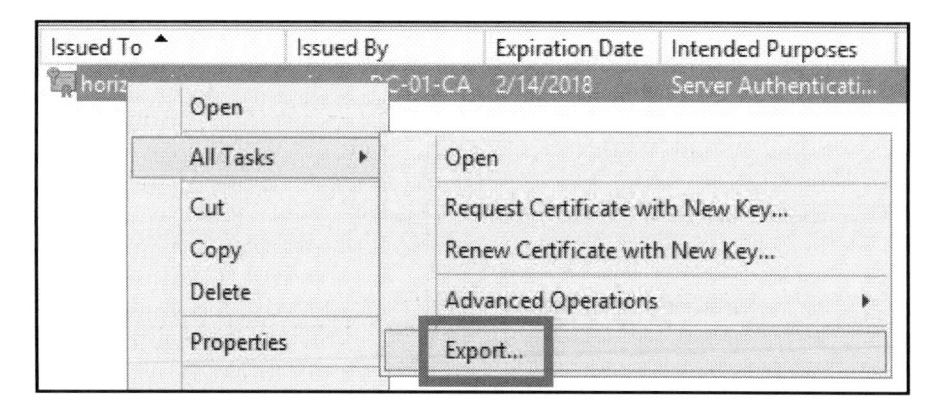

9. In the **Certificate Export Wizard** welcome screen, click **Next**.

[466]

10. In the **Certificate Export Wizard | Export Private Key** screen, shown in the following screenshot, click the **Yes, export the private key** radio button and then click **Next**:

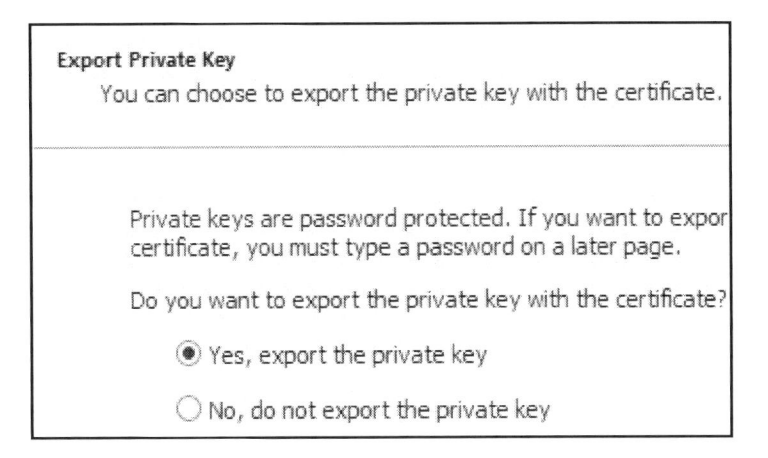

> **Export Private Key**
> You can choose to export the private key with the certificate.
>
> Private keys are password protected. If you want to export certificate, you must type a password on a later page.
>
> Do you want to export the private key with the certificate?
>
> ⦿ Yes, export the private key
> ◯ No, do not export the private key

11. In the **Certificate Export Wizard | Export File Format** screen, shown in the following screenshot, check the options shown under **Personal Information Exchange - PKCS #12 (.PFX)** and then click **Next**:

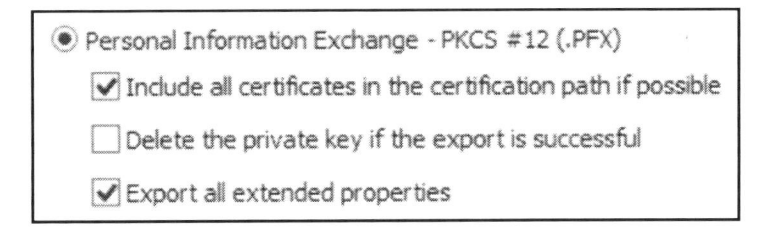

> ⦿ Personal Information Exchange - PKCS #12 (.PFX)
> ☑ Include all certificates in the certification path if possible
> ☐ Delete the private key if the export is successful
> ☑ Export all extended properties

12. In the **Certificate Export Wizard | Security** screen shown in the following screenshot, click the **Password:** checkbox, provide a password for the certificate, and then click **Next**:

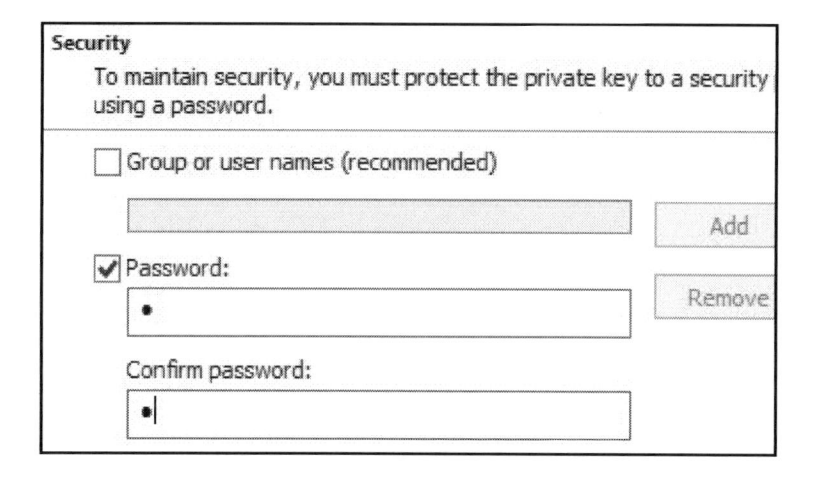

13. In the **Certificate Export Wizard | File to Export** screen, provide a name and destination location for the exported PFX file and then click **Next**.
14. In the **Certificate Export Wizard | Completing the Certificate Export Wizard** screen, review the settings and then click **Finish** to complete the export process.

New certificates should be copied and archived to a secure location, prior to being imported into their destination certificate stores. This enables the certificates to be reused if any of the Horizon servers ever need to be rebuilt.

Requesting a certificate with SANs

A certificate's SAN is often used on servers that have only one web service running, but are accessed from multiple DNS names. A Horizon Security Server or Unified Access Gateway are examples of this, as they are often accessed using a publicly known name such as `horizon.vjason.com`, as well as a private (internal) name such as `horsec1.vjason.local`.

> **TIP:** VMware security guidelines recommend that you do not supply IP addresses as SSL SANs, preferring that Horizon clients use FQDNs when accessing Horizon resources.

While a certificate will work regardless of what DNS name was used to connect to it, if the DNS name used to access it is not present as a SAN in the certificate, the client will receive an error that the certificate name does not match. To prevent these errors from occurring when requesting the certificate, we simply need to provide a list of the different DNS names that will be used to connect to the server.

In this section, we will request a certificate with SAN from our AD Certificate Services server. As mentioned previously, you will need to enable support for SAN on your AD Certificate Services server or the SAN will not be added to the certificate.

To request a certificate with SAN, all that is needed is to provide additional information in step 5 of the preceding section, *Requesting a certificate using Microsoft AD Certificate Services*. As shown in the following screenshot, we will use the **Attributes:** section of the **Advanced Certificate Request** window to request the SAN:

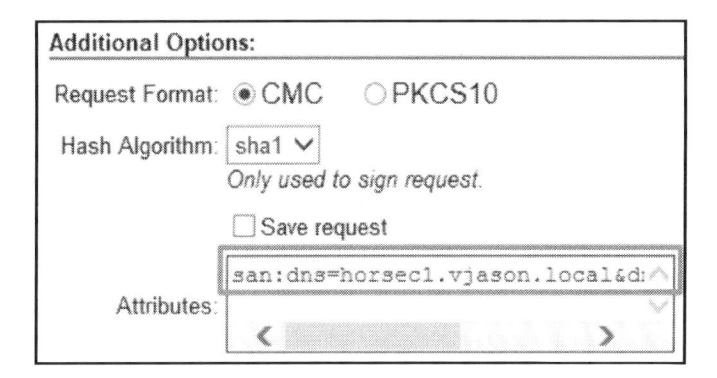

Using the examples provided in this chapter, the following text should be added to the **Attributes:** field to add SAN to the certificate request. You must add all possible alternative server names to this option, including the name used with the certificate request:

    san:dns=horsec1.vjason.local&dns=horizon.vjason.com

If additional SANs are required, simply append the text with an ampersand (&), and then the additional DNS names or IP addresses in the format `dns=my.domain.com`.

Managing Horizon SSL Certificates

The following screenshot shows the properties of a certificate that has multiple SANs, which was created using the example text provided earlier. When SANs are added to a certificate, a new property **Subject Alternative Name** is created under **Field** in the **Details** tab, and the additional DNS names or IP addresses are added. This certificate enables the destination server to be accessed using any of the four DNS names shown, without any errors about a certificate-to-host name mismatch (were the DNS name used not listed among the SAN):

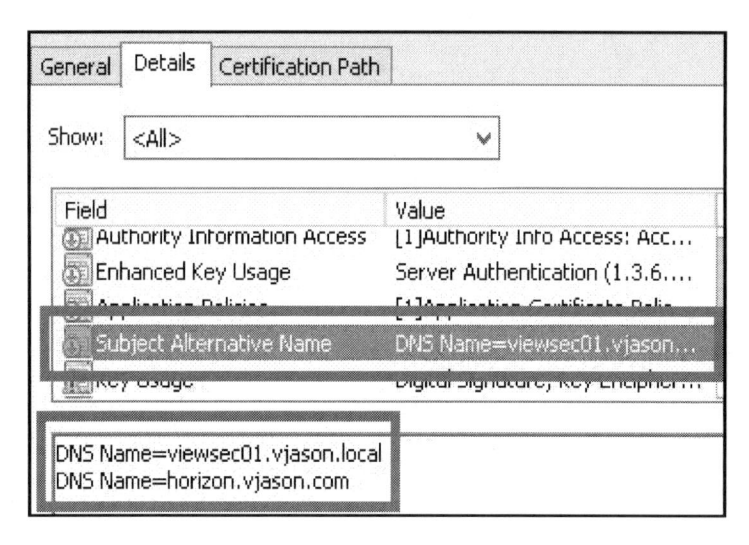

The rest of the certificate request process is the same; once the request has been approved, save the certificate to the local computer for later import into the Windows certificate store.

Replacing a Horizon Connection Server certificate

The following steps outline how to replace the certificate on the Horizon Connection Server, and assume that you have already obtained the replacement certificate using the steps outlined in *Requesting a certificate using Microsoft AD Certificate Services*. The Horizon Connection Server will be unavailable while the certificate is being replaced, so plan for downtime accordingly:

1. Using the Services MMC, stop the **VMware Horizon View Connection Server** service. This will also stop other Horizon-related services.
2. Open the Local Computer Certificates MMC you created in the *Creating a Local Computer Certificates console* section.
3. Right-click on the existing Horizon Connection Server certificate (shown in the following screenshot) and click on **Properties** to open the **Properties** window. This certificate is easily identified as it has a **Friendly Name** of **vdm**:

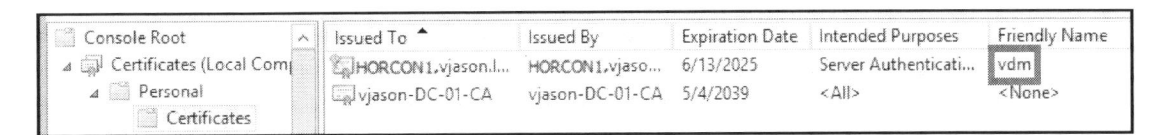

4. In the certificate's Properties window, append the friendly name of the certificate with `-original`, as shown in the following screenshot, and click on **OK** to return to the Local Computer Certificates MMC:

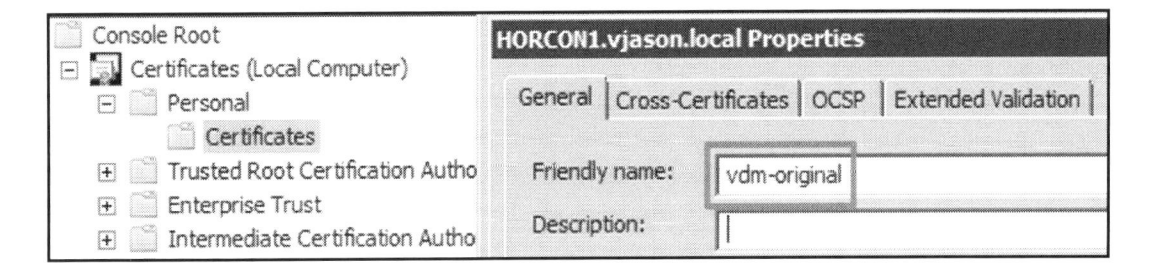

Managing Horizon SSL Certificates

5. In the **Local Computer Certificates** MMC, go to **Certificates (Local Computer)** | **Personal**. Then, right-click on the **Certificates** folder and click on **All Tasks** | **Import...** as shown in the following screenshot. This will open the **Welcome to the Certificate Import Wizard** window:

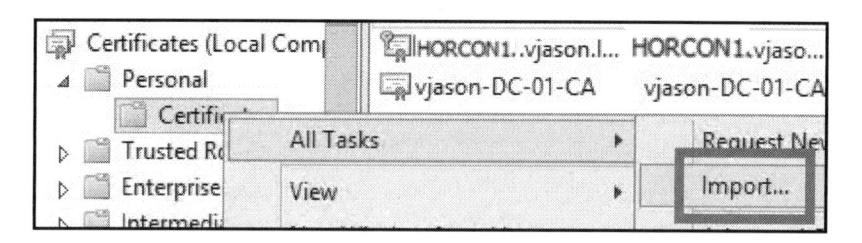

6. In the **Certificate Import Wizard** window, click on **Next**.
7. In the **Certificate Import Wizard** | **File to Import** window, click on the **Browse...** button, use the file type drop-down menu to show **All Files (*.*)**, select the certificate file that you obtained from your certificate authority, and click on **Next**.
8. In the **Certificate Import Wizard** | **Private key protection** window, type the certificate password used when the certificate was exported, and then click **Next**.
9. In the **Certificate Import Wizard** | **Certificate Store** window (shown in the following screenshot), the **Place all certificates in the following store** radio button should already be selected. Select the **Personal** store and click on **Next**:

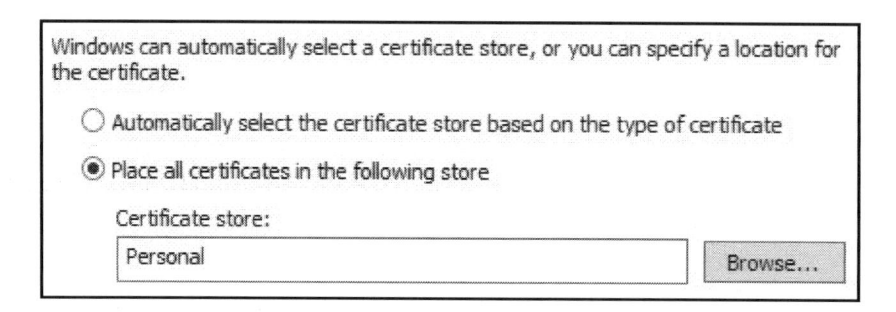

10. In the **Certificate Import Wizard** | **Completing the Certificate Import Wizard** window, review the settings and click on **Finish** to close the **Certificate Import Wizard** window. If changes are required, click on the **Back** button and make the changes where necessary.
11. The **Certificate Import Wizard** will open an additional window to confirm the successful import of the certificate. Click on **OK** to close this window.
12. The new certificate will appear alongside the existing certificate, as shown in the following screenshot. Note that the certificate was issued by our internal certificate authority, and not the local server itself like the default certificate:

HORCON1.vjason.local	HORCON1.vjason.local	9/24/2028
horcon1.vjason.local	vjason-DC-01-CA	12/16/2020
PCoIP Security Gateway	VMware Horizon View Ga...	9/24/2028

13. Right-click on the new certificate and click on **Properties** to open the **Properties** window. This certificate is easily identified as it has no friendly name.
14. In the certificate's **Properties** window, set the friendly name of the certificate to vdm and click on **OK** to return to the Local Computer Certificates MMC.
15. Import the following Windows registry information into the Connection/Security server; it instructs the PCoIP Secure Gateway component to use the new SSL certificate rather than the separate, default SSL certificate created during the installation process:

```
Windows Registry Editor Version 5.00
[HKEY_LOCAL_MACHINE\SOFTWARE\Teradici\SecurityGateway]
"SSLCertWinCertFriendlyName"="vdm"
```

> **TIP**: The Horizon Connection and Security Server software identifies what certificate to use by the value of the friendly name, which should be vdm.

16. Using the Services MMC, start the **VMware Horizon View Connection Server** service.

17. From a web browser, access the Horizon Connection Server using HTTPS and the FQDN. As shown in the following screenshot, verify that no SSL errors are shown, the new certificate is being used, and the certificate is trusted:

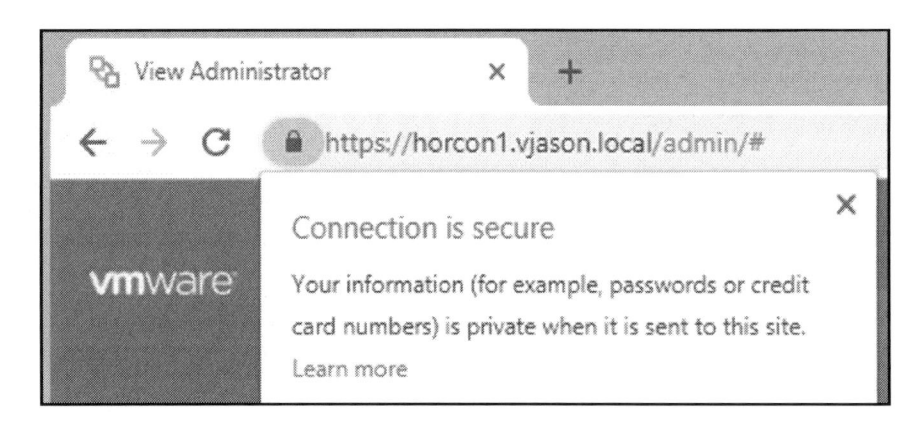

The same process should be repeated for any additional Horizon Connection Servers, using unique certificates for each one.

Replacing a Horizon Security Server certificate

The process used to replace the certificate on a Horizon Security Server is nearly identical to that of the Horizon Connection Server. This section will detail which steps from the preceding section differ when replacing the certificate on a Horizon Security Server. The Horizon Security Server will be unavailable while the certificate is being replaced, so plan for downtime accordingly.

These updated steps assume that you have already obtained the replacement certificate using the steps outlined in *Requesting a certificate using Microsoft AD Certificate Services*. Follow the steps outlined in the *Replacing the certificate in a Horizon Connection Server* section, replacing steps 1, 14, and 15 as follows:

- **Step 1**: Using the Services MMC, stop the **VMware Horizon View Security Server** service. This will also stop other View-related services.
- **Step 14**: Using the Services MMC console, start the **VMware Horizon View Security Server** service.

- **Step 15**: From a web browser, access the Horizon Security Server using HTTPS and all of the FQDNs that are defined in the SAN certificate. Verify that no SSL errors are shown, the new certificate is being used, the certificate is trusted, and the expected SANs are present.

The same process should be repeated on any additional Horizon Security Servers, using unique certificates for each one.

Replacing a Horizon Composer certificate

Horizon Composer uses a default certificate that is not trusted by the Horizon Connection Server. While an exception can be made to trust this certificate when Composer is enabled, replacing the certificate with one that is trusted is straightforward, and enables Composer to be trusted without an exception being made.

The following steps outline how to replace the Horizon Composer SSL certificate, and assume that you have already obtained the replacement certificate using the steps outlined in *Requesting a certificate using Microsoft AD Certificate Services*. Horizon Composer will be unavailable while the certificate is being replaced, so plan for downtime accordingly:

> This process should be done before any linked-clone desktops are deployed. This isn't a requirement; however, if any problems occur with Horizon Composer, it is much easier to rebuild if no linked-clone desktops are deployed.

1. Open the Local Computer Certificates MMC.
2. In the Local Computer Certificates MMC, go to **Certificates (Local Computer)** | **Personal**, right-click on the Certificates folder, and click on **All Tasks** | **Import...**. Complete the steps to import the certificate.
3. The new certificate will appear alongside the existing certificate. Unlike the certificates for the Horizon Connection and Security Servers, you do not need to change the certificate's Friendly Name.
4. Open the Services MMC and stop the **VMware Horizon 7 Composer** service.

Managing Horizon SSL Certificates

5. Open Windows Command Prompt and change to the `\Program Files (x86)\VMware\VMware View Composer` directory, as shown in the following screenshot:

```
c:\Program Files (x86)\VMware\VMware View Composer>dir *.exe
 Volume in drive C has no label.
 Volume Serial Number is 0217-149C

 Directory of c:\Program Files (x86)\VMware\VMware View Composer

11/29/2015  10:34 PM           327,384 SviConfig.exe
11/29/2015  10:34 PM            40,664 SviWebService.exe
11/29/2015  10:34 PM            81,920 zip.exe
               3 File(s)        449,968 bytes
               0 Dir(s)  27,883,098,112 bytes free

c:\Program Files (x86)\VMware\VMware View Composer>
```

6. Enter the following command and press the *Enter* key. The `delete=false` option leaves the existing certificate in place, allowing us to use it again if ever required:

   `SviConfig -operation=replacecertificate -delete=false`

7. Type in the number for the new certificate from the list provided and press the *Enter* key. As shown in the following screenshot, we will select certificate **2** as that is the newly issued certificate that we wish to enable. The output of the `SviConfig` command should verify that the operation completed successfully:

```
c:\Program Files (x86)\VMware\VMware View Composer>SviConfig.exe -operation=repl
acecertificate -delete=false
Select a certificate:

1. Subject: C=US, S=CA, L=CA, O=VMware Inc., OU=VMware Inc., CN=HORCOMP1, E=sup
port@vmware.com
      Valid from: 10/4/2018 5:37:03 PM
      Valid to: 10/4/2020 5:37:03 PM
      Thumbprint: F079D288B46E84ADEDD53F518593B969626F4072

2. Subject: CN=horcomp1.vjason.local
      Valid from: 12/17/2018 12:08:41 AM
      Valid to: 12/17/2020 12:18:41 AM
      Thumbprint: 901CA2E28D145E3F4EE04F5ECEC9863DCD9BC863

3. Subject: C=US, S=CA, L=CA, O=VMware Inc., OU=VMware Inc., CN=HORCOMP1, E=sup
port@vmware.com
      Valid from: 11/25/2018 8:20:40 PM
      Valid to: 11/25/2020 8:20:40 PM
      Thumbprint: 52DCAF9F8A0D21B8F6304F506D7E3451A11768A6

Enter choice (0-3, 0 to abort):
```

8. Open the Services MMC and start the **VMware Horizon 7 Composer** service.
9. To verify that the certificate is trusted by the Horizon Connection Servers, open the Horizon Administrator console.
10. In the Horizon Administrator console dashboard, under **System Health**, expand the **View Composer Servers** object.
11. Click on the Horizon Composer Server you wish to check, to open the **View Composer Server Detail**s window as shown in the following screenshot. Verify that the SSL Certificate field is shown as **Valid**:

View Composer Server Details	
Name:	https://horcomp1.vjason.local:18443
Version:	7.6.0.45796
Status:	No problem detected.
SSL Certificate:	Valid

The same process should be repeated on any additional servers that host Horizon Composer, using a unique certificate for each.

Replacing a Horizon Unified Access Gateway certificate

Horizon **Unified Access Gateway** (**UAG**) SSL certificates can be replaced using the default administrative interface. You should use a certificate with SAN that includes the FQDN of the individual UAG appliance, the FQDN used on any load balancers in front of the UAG (if applicable), and the UAG appliance IP address (or addresses). Using the method outlined in *Requesting a certificate with SANs*, that would require a certificate attributes string similar to this:

```
san:dns=uag1.vjason.local&dns=horizon.vjason.com
```

Managing Horizon SSL Certificates

The following process outlines the steps required to replace the certificate on a Horizon Unified Access Gateway, and assumes that you have already obtained the replacement certificate with the appropriate SAN string, that the certificate is in a PFX format with the private key, and that you know the private key password:

1. Log on to the UAG administrative web interface; in this book our UAG admin interface could be accessed using the following URL: `https://192.168.76.91:9443/admin`.
2. Click the **Select** button under **Configure Manually** in the UAG admin web interface.
3. Click on the gear icon to the right of **TLS Server Certificate Settings**.
4. Upload the certificate and then complete the options as shown: click the checkboxes for **Admin interface** and **Internet interface**, use the **Certificate Type** drop-down menu to select **PFX**, and then supply the password for the certificate private key. Click **Save** when you are finished updating the certificate settings:

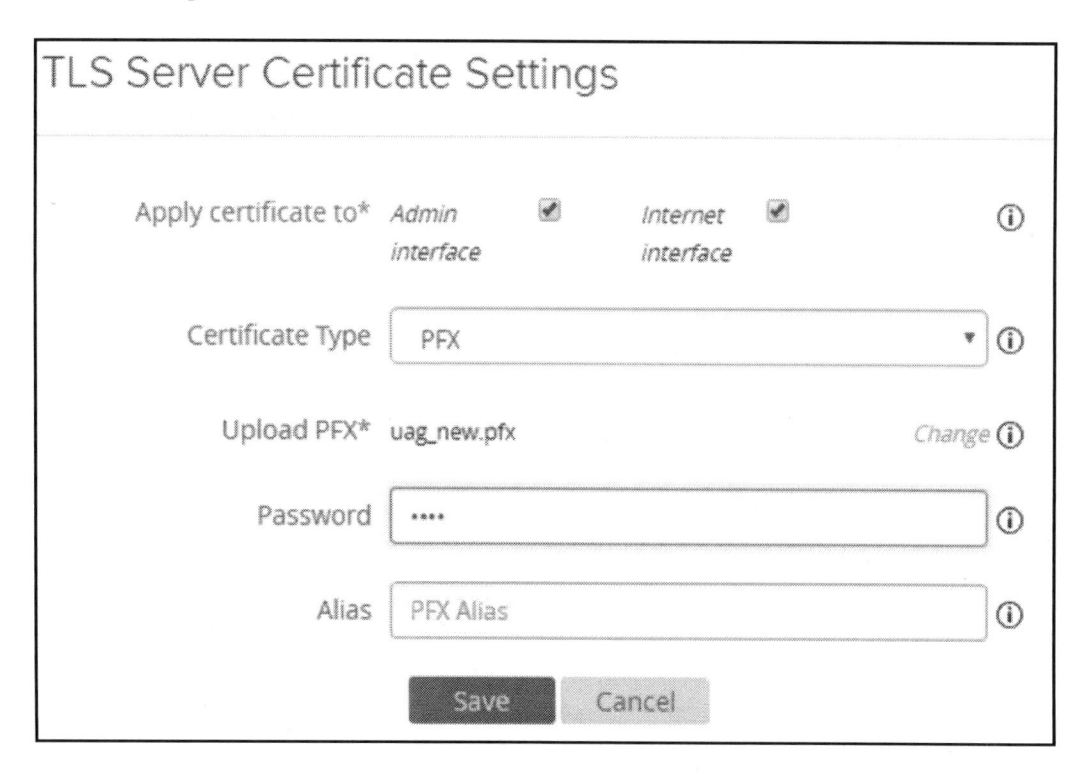

TLS Server Certificate Settings	
Apply certificate to*	Admin interface ☑ Internet interface ☑
Certificate Type	PFX
Upload PFX*	uag_new.pfx *Change*
Password	••••
Alias	PFX Alias
	Save Cancel

5. Close and reopen the UAG administrative interface web page.

6. View the properties of the UAG administrative interface web page SSL certificate to verify that the new certificate is being used; the following example shows the certificate SAN values that match those submitted in the certificate request:

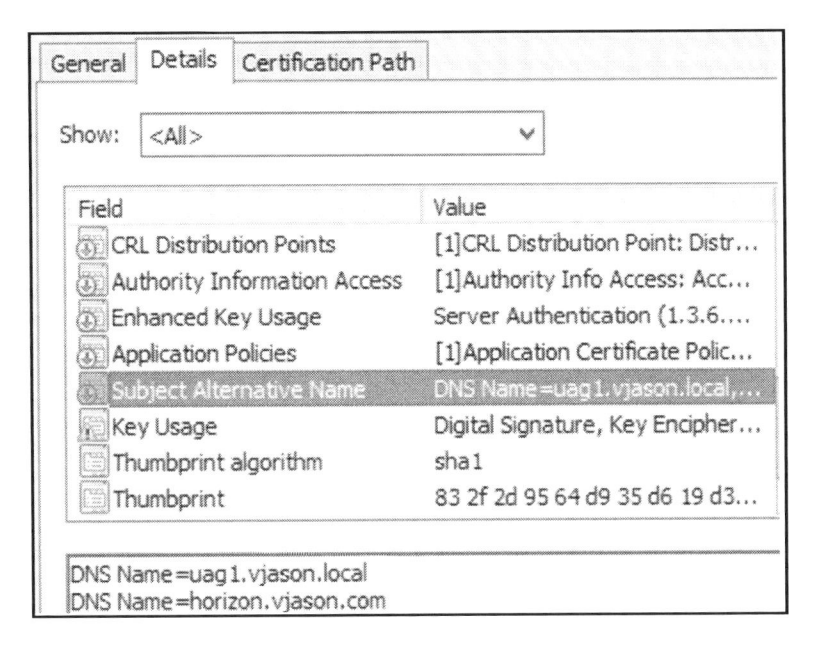

7. Open the UAG Horizon client login web page and verify that the new certificate is also being used there.

The Horizon Unified Access Gateway appliance is now updated with the new certificate.

Summary

In this chapter, we discussed how to use native Windows OS features to create certificate requests and generate certificates, and how the new certificates are imported and enabled.

We also learned how to request a certificate with SANs, which allows us to add additional DNS names and even IP addresses to a certificate, an option typically required for Horizon Security Servers, and Unified Access Gateway appliances.

Finally, we learned how to replace the SSL certificates in each of the Horizon servers, as well as the Unified Access Gateway appliances.

Questions

1. What are some of the reasons why you might want to replace the default Horizon certificates?
2. Name what is different about the Horizon client experience if your SSL certificates are untrusted.
3. How does the Horizon Connection Server know what certificate to use in the local Windows certificate store?
4. What is the term for an SSL certificate that has more than one hostname associated with it?
5. Do you need to back up SSL certificates?
6. Name at least one value VMware recommends you do *not* include as a SSL certificate SAN.

Further reading

The following resources may be used to learn more about the topics described in this chapter:

- VMware documentation:
    - VMware Horizon (https://www.vmware.com/support/pubs/view_pubs.html)
    - VMware vSphere (https://www.vmware.com/support/pubs/vsphere-esxi-vcenter-server-pubs.html)
- Microsoft documentation:
    - Windows (https://docs.microsoft.com/en-us/windows/)

Assessments

Chapter 1, VMware Horizon Infrastructure Overview

1. Administer the Horizon software, broker client connections, and integrate with other components of a Horizon infrastructure such as VMware vSphere and Active Directory.
2. Create and manage linked clone-based virtual machines.
3. VMware Product Interoperability Matrices and the Horizon documentation.
4. Easy, OVA-based deployment, and it has the ability to broker connections to multiple Horizon Connection Servers.
5. vSphere 6.0.0 and later.
6. Maintains user persona settings across multiple platforms and OS versions, provides context-aware customization of the user session, and works with natively installed and virtual applications.
7. Liquidware Labs Stratusphere UX, Login VSI, and Lakeside SysTrack.
8. Linked clone desktops share the base virtual disk of a virtual desktop master image and are created by Horizon Composer. Instant clones share the quiesced virtual disk and memory of a virtual desktop master image, and are created by Horizon Connection Server using the vSphere VMFork feature.
9. 10,000.
10. Client connection protocol, amount and frequency of display change, application characteristics, and multimedia usage.

Chapter 2, Implementing Horizon Connection Server

1. Windows 2008 R2 SP1, Windows 2012 R2, Windows 2016 (all x64).
2. Standard, Replica, Security, and Enrollment.

Assessments

3. 25.
4. 4vCPU, 10 GB RAM.
5. Standard.
6. Replica.
7. 4,000.
8. Add the group to the local administrators group on the Horizon Connection Server(s).

Chapter 3, Implementing Horizon Composer

1. Ability to create a manage linked clone-based virtual machines.
2. Ability to install Horizon Composer on the vCenter Server.
3. Oracle and Microsoft SQL.
4. Backup the Horizon Composer SSL certificate.
5. Yes.
6. Deploy a compatible Windows server host, and create a supported database and database user with the required permissions.
7. Edit the properties of the linked vCenter Server.

Chapter 4, Implementing Horizon Security Server

1. Broker external Horizon client connections to resources located on a private network.
2. DMZ.
3. 4,000.
4. 1.
5. Yes.
6. From the **View Configuration** | **Servers** menu, click on the target Connection Server, then click on the **More Commands** drop-down menu, select **Specify Security Server Pairing Password**, and then provide a pairing password.

7. From the **View Configuration | Servers** menu, click on the target Connection Server, then click **Edit**. On the Connection Server **General** tab, check the box next to **Use PCoIP Secure Gateway for PCoIP connections to machine**. Also, ensure **HTTP(S) Secure Tunnel** and **Blast Secure Gateway** are enabled.
8. From the **View Configuration | Security Servers** menu, click on the target Security Server, then click on the **More Commands** drop-down menu, and then select **Prepare for Upgrade or Reinstallation**.

Chapter 5, Implementing Horizon Unified Access Gateway

1. Broker external Horizon client connections to resources located on a private network.
2. DMZ.
3. 2,000.
4. Linux-based virtual appliance, can broker connections to multiple Connection Servers.
5. It can broker connections to multiple Connection Servers.
6. From the **View Configuration | Servers** menu, click on the target Connection Server, then click **Edit**, and then uncheck all three secure gateway options. Also, disable **Origin Check on the Connection Servers**.
7. Using three NICs (one external facing, one internal facing, one for management).

Chapter 6, Implementing a Horizon Cloud Pod

1. Create a Horizon deployment that spans multiple sites, or supports more connections than are possible with a single pod.
2. 10.
3. 25.
4. Global Entitlement.
5. Yes.

Assessments

6. Use the Horizon home site resolution tool.
7. The pod where the connection originated from.
8. The pool you are trying to add does not use the same settings as the Global Entitlement, such as floating or dedicated assignment.

Chapter 7, Creating Horizon Desktop Pools

1. Automated, Manual, and RDS.
2. Floating or Dedicated assignment.
3. Full clone, linked clone, and instant clone.
4. The persistent desktop state is retained when a user logs off; it is not for non-persistent desktops.
5. Persist data across Horizon client sessions.
6. Windows{n}.
7. Copies frequently-used Horizon virtual machine data to a cache on the ESXi host where it can be accessed much more quickly.
8. That you are entitled to use the pool.
9. That a snapshot has been taken of the virtual desktop master image.

Chapter 8, Implementing Microsoft Remote Desktop Services Application and Desktop Pools

1. RDS Farm.
2. Windows Roaming Profiles and VMware User Environment Manager.
3. 4 vCPU, 24 GB RAM, and 40 GB disk space.
4. Windows Server 2008 R2, 2012 R2, and 2016.
5. Application Pool.
6. Linked clone desktop pool (or instant-clone, if using that option).
7. Regular desktop pool.
8. Disable it under **Resources | Farms - More Commands**.

…
Chapter 9, Performing Horizon Pool Maintenance

1. **Instant-clone**: Push image; Linked clone: Recompose, refresh, or rebalance.
2. A recompose replaces the underlying virtual desktop master image, while a refresh simply erases all changes made to a desktop since it was deployed.
3. Reduce storage utilization, revert to a known desktop state.
4. Resolve issues with that specific desktop.
5. Instant clones.
6. In Horizon Administrator, select **Resources | Persistent Disks**. From the **Detached** tab, select the persistent disk and click **Attach**, then select a linked clone virtual machine to which to attach the persistent disk, select **Attach as a secondary disk**, and then click **Finish**.
7. Desktops are powered off, then refreshed, then the persistent data disks are balanced among the available datastores, and then the desktop are powered off (assuming the pool policies specify that).

Chapter 10, Creating a Master Virtual Desktop Image

1. Potentially reduce per-desktop infrastructure resource requirements, optimize performance, and eliminate specific known issues related to using the target OS as a virtual desktop.
2. Hibernate, disk defragmentation, automatic updates, Windows error reporting, and Windows System Restore.
3. Disable native application update features, perform any required software activation or activation workarounds, and optimize application settings
4. Causes unneeded disk IO when writing Windows RAM contents to disk, and leads to slower login times when reading RAM contents back into memory when the user logs in again.
5. Linked clones are typically updated by updating the master image, then recomposing users to that new image. If you applied an update directly to a link clone, the space it requires would increase significantly since its configuration would no longer match the virtual desktop master image.

Assessments

6. Defragmentation would increase space utilization since any moved blocks would be written to the link clone disks.
7. Since Windows does not have to create a new profile from scratch, user login times are typically reduced as fewer infrastructure resources are required to process the users' first logins.

Chapter 11, Implementing App Volumes

1. Decouple applications from the underlying virtual desktop master image where they can be attached to a desktop on demand, and persist user-installed applications even when using non-persistent desktops.
2. You will use the same database that the first one uses, but be sure you do not erase it when performing the installation.
3. A single large AppStack.
4. Persist user-installed applications across Horizon client sessions.
5. The application and any integration points it has with Windows are captured and exported to a separate virtual disk file. Once extracted, the resulting disk file can be attached to multiple virtual desktops at once.
6. User Environment Manager.
7. Applications can be updated independently of the virtual desktop master image, multiple versions of an application can be deployed at the same time, the virtual desktop master image is often easier to maintain since it has fewer applications to install, and AppStacks can be added to a virtual desktop at any time, even if a user is currently logged on.

Chapter 12, Implementing User Environment Manager

1. Persist user persona settings across Horizon client sessions and enforce Windows and application settings as required.
2. Used with non-persistent desktops to provide a persistent-like experience.
3. UEM provides far more capabilities for customizing desktops and is far more efficient than Horizon Persona Management.
4. Folder redirection, implement custom Windows registry entries, and configure user profile options.

5. Settings that should be implemented using Windows default profiles, user files, and settings that are not persisted across Horizon client sessions.
6. Easy Start.

Chapter 13, Implementing the Just-in-Time Management Platform (JMP)

1. Horizon, AppVolumes, User Environment Manager.
2. `https://HorizonConnectionServerFQDN/newadmin`.
3. Enable a single wizard to use to assign desktops, applications, and user persona settings.
4. JMP assignment.
5. Writable volumes.
6. SSL certificates from the Horizon Connection Server and App Volumes Manager Server.
7. User Environment Manager.

Chapter 14, Using Horizon PowerCLI

1. Execute the `winrm quickconfig -transport:https` command on the Connection Server, and if present, also create a firewall rule to allow TCP port `5986` inbound.
2. Execute the `Get-Command -PSSnapin VMware.View.Broker | more` PowerShell command.
3. Execute the `Get-Help` command | more PowerShell command.
4. `Add-VicwVC`.
5. `Add-AutomaticLinkedClonePool`.
6. `Add-PoolEntitlement`.
7. `Send-LinkedCloneRefresh`.

Chapter 15, Implementing Horizon Group Policies

1. Applies a consistent set of policies to all users that log in to a particular computer, regardless of where their account is located in Active Directory
2. `%systemroot%\PolicyDefinitions`
3. `vdm_server.admx`
4. `vdm_common.admx`
5. `pcoip.admx and pcoip.client.admx`
6. `vmware_rdsh_server.admx`
7. `vdm_agent.admx`
8. `vdm_client.admx`

Chapter 16, Managing Horizon SSL Certificates

1. To prevent Horizon clients and admins from receiving errors or alerts about untrusted certificates.
2. They will receive an error message stating that the certificate name does not match the hostname, or that the certificate is not trusted.
3. The certificate has the Friendly Name set to `vdm`.
4. **Subject Alternative Names (SAN)**.
5. Yes.
6. Potential security concerns since the certificate contains additional hostnames that do not match the server name; that certificate could be used elsewhere and clients would trust it.

Other Books You May Enjoy

If you enjoyed this book, you may be interested in these other books by Packt:

VMware vSphere 6.5 Cookbook - Third Edition
Abhilash G B, Cedric Rajendran

ISBN: 978-1-78712-741-8

- Upgrade your existing vSphere environment or perform a fresh deployment
- Automate the deployment and management of large sets of ESXi hosts in your vSphere Environment
- Configure and manage FC, iSCSI, and NAS storage, and get more control over how storage resources are allocated and managed
- Configure vSphere networking by deploying host-wide and data center-wide switches in your vSphere environment
- Configure high availability on a host cluster and learn how to enable the fair distribution and utilization of compute resources
- Patch and upgrade the vSphere environment
- Handle certificate request generation and renew component certificates
- Monitor performance of a vSphere environment

VMware NSX Cookbook
Bayu Wibowo, Tony Sangha

ISBN: 978-1-78217-425-7

- Understand, install, and configure VMware NSX for vSphere solutions
- Configure logical switching, routing, and Edge Services Gateway in VMware NSX for vSphere
- Learn how to plan and upgrade VMware NSX for vSphere
- Learn how to use built-in monitoring tools such as Flow Monitoring, Traceflow, Application Rule Manager, and Endpoint Monitoring
- Learn how to leverage the NSX REST API for management and automation using various tools from Python to VMware vRealize Orchestrator

Leave a review - let other readers know what you think

Please share your thoughts on this book with others by leaving a review on the site that you bought it from. If you purchased the book from Amazon, please leave us an honest review on this book's Amazon page. This is vital so that other potential readers can see and use your unbiased opinion to make purchasing decisions, we can understand what our customers think about our products, and our authors can see your feedback on the title that they have worked with Packt to create. It will only take a few minutes of your time, but is valuable to other potential customers, our authors, and Packt. Thank you!

Index

A

Active Directory (AD) 43, 154, 459
Administrative Template (ADM) 419
ADMX format 419
Adobe Acrobat Reader DC update feature
  disabling 281, 282
advanced UEM configuration examples
  about 354
  Personalization tab 355
  User Environment tab 358, 359
Amazon Web Services (AWS) 10
App Volumes Agent
  installing 312, 313
  native load balancing, configuring 313
App Volumes Backup Utility
  reference 329
App Volumes Manager servers
  deploying 311
App Volumes Manager
  configuring 306, 309, 311
  reference 306
  server, installing 304, 306
App Volumes
  backup process 329
  overview 300
  prerequisites 302, 303
  recovery 329
  recovery process 330
  reference 302, 330
  vCenter permissions 304
application pools
  accessing, Horizon client used 234
Application Profiler 334
AppStack
  adding 321, 323
  assignments, deleting 323
  creating 315, 319
  updating 320

B

Blast Secure Gateway 111
Blast Session Variables ADM template
  about 455
  General Session Variable Group Policy settings 455

C

certificate
  requesting, with Microsoft AD Certificate Services 462, 464, 468
  requesting, with SAN 468, 470
Client Access License (CAL) 221
ClonePrep 180
Cloud Pod 144
Cloud Pod Global Entitlements
  configuring, for Horizon application pool 161, 162, 163
  configuring, for Horizon desktop pool 157, 159
  creating 156
  creating, for Horizon application pool 161, 162, 163
  creating, for Horizon desktop pool 157, 159
components, for creating just-in-time personalized desktop
  AppVolumes AppStacks 364
  AppVolumes Writable Volumes 364
  User Environment Manager 364
  user file share 364
  vSphere Instant Clones 364
components, VMware Horizon
  about 10
  Horizon Agent 16
  Horizon Client 16

Horizon Composer 16
Horizon Connection Server 12
Horizon Enrollment Server 14
Horizon Security Server 12
Horizon Unified Access Gateway 13
VMware App Volumes 17, 18
VMware ThinApp 19
VMware User Environment Manager 18
VMware vCenter Server 15
VMware vSphere 14
custom SSL certificate
   Horizon Composer, restoring with 97

D

default SSL certificate
   Horizon Composer, restoring with 96
delta disk 71
Demilitarized Zone (DMZ) 12
desktop creation process
   monitoring 203
desktop optimization
   CPU utilization 275
   Horizon desktop IOPS 274
   significance 274
desktop pools
   datastore storage overcommit settings, updating 254, 255
desktop
   recreating, persistent disks used 268
detached persistent disk
   attaching, to desktop 269
Disaster Recovery (DR) 145
Distributed File System (DFS) 338
Domain Name System (DNS) 22
Dynamic Host Configuration Protocol (DHCP) 22

F

Federal Information Processing Standards (FIPS) 126
full clone Horizon desktops 180
full clones
   used, for creating pool 199, 200, 201, 202
fully qualified domain name (FQDN) 53

G

Get-AppxPackage
   reference 280
Get-AppxProvisionedPackage
   reference 280
Gigabit Ethernet (GbE) 28
Global Data Layer 146
Global Entitlement Horizon client sessions
   monitoring 169, 170
Global Entitlement
   about 151, 164
   general settings, editing 165
   settings, updating 164
global settings, Horizon maintenance
   about 249
   concurrent maintenance operations 251, 252
   logoff warning 250, 251
   storage overcommit 253
   timeout 250, 251
Globally Unique Identifiers (GUID) 181
GUID Partition Table (GPT) 278

H

Helpdesk Support Tool 334
Home Site Overrides 165
Horizon AD LDS 39
Horizon AD LDS database
   backing up 64
Horizon Administrator console
   about 203
   Dashboard 203
   Desktops 204
Horizon Agent Configuration ADM template 421
   Agent Configuration settings 427
   Agent Security settings 431
   base settings 422
   Client Downloadable only settings 425
   Unity Touch and Hosted App settings 431
   USB configuration settings, viewing 422
   VMware FlashMMR settings 432
Horizon Agent
   about 16
   installing, on Microsoft RDS host 219
Horizon application pool clients

status, monitoring 235, 236
Horizon application pool
  creating 227, 228, 229
  deleting 237
  modifying 236
Horizon Client 16
Horizon Client Configuration ADM template
  about 433
  Client Configuration Base settings 433
  Horizon USB Configuration setting 444
  RDP settings 441
  Scripting Definitions setting 436
  security setting 438
  Settings not configurable by Agent section 444
Horizon client entitlements
  desktop pool entitlements, adding 406
  desktop pool entitlements, removing 406
  individual desktop, entitling 407
  individual desktop, unentitling 407
  managing 406
  session, disconnecting 407
  session, logging off 408
Horizon client sessions 406
Horizon client
  used, for accessing application pools 234
Horizon Cloud Pod
  about 143, 148
  configuring 148, 149
  Global Data Layer, key data sharing 146
  messages, sending 146
  overview 144, 145
  port requisites 147
  site, configuring 151, 152, 153
  topology limits 147
  users, associating 154, 156
Horizon Common Configuration ADM template
  about 445
  Common Configuration Base setting 446
  Log Configuration settings 446
  Performance Alarm settings 447
  Security Configuration setting 448
Horizon Composer certificate
  replacing 475, 477
Horizon Composer database
  about 85

backing up 92
restoring 94
Horizon Composer recovery 94
Horizon Composer SSL certificates
  backing up 93, 94
  restoring 96
Horizon Composer, in AD
  permissions, delegating 82, 83
Horizon Composer-linked clone
  about 177
  advantages 182
  considerations 183, 184
  pool, creating 185, 186, 187, 188, 189, 190, 192, 193
Horizon Composer-linked clones
  pool, creating 194, 195
Horizon Composer
  about 16, 71
  AD permissions 82
  backing up 92
  configuring 88, 89, 90, 92
  deploying 86
  hardware requisites 77
  installation prerequisites 78
  installing 87
  limitations 78
  linked clone desktops, recomposing 76
  linked clone desktops, refreshing 75
  overview 72, 73
  permissions, granting 81
  persistent disks, managing 266
  restoring, with custom SSL certificate 97
  restoring, with default SSL certificate 96
  service account 79
  vCenter permissions 80
  vCenter role, creating 81
Horizon Connection Server certificate
  replacing 471, 473, 474
Horizon Connection Server
  about 12, 36
  AD LDS database, restoring 67
  backing up 63
  configuring 50, 54, 55
  deploying 47
  hardware requisites 38

Horizon AD LDS database, backing up 64
installing 47
limitation 39, 40
load balancing connection servers 40
process, upgrading 62
recovering 65
removing 66
requisites 38
restoring 66
software requisites 39
vCenter database, restoring 67
vCenter Server database, backing up 63
vCenter Server requisites 41, 42
Horizon Console
  reference 383
Horizon desktop IOPS 274
Horizon Desktop pool
  entitlements, managing 206, 207
Horizon desktop pools
  about 173
  administering 398
  automatically provisioned full clone desktop pool, creating 400
  automatically provisioned full clone pool, updating 403
  configuration, updating 402
  creating 184
  dedicated assignment persistent linked clone pool, creating 399
  floating assignment (nonpersistent) linked clone pool, creating 400
  inked clone desktop or pool, refreshing 403
  linked clone desktop pool, rebalancing 405
  linked clone desktop pool, recomposing 404
  linked clone pool, updating 402
  manually provisioned desktop pool, creating 401
  manually provisioned pool, updating 403
  options 175, 176
  overview 174
  provisioning problems 205
  resetting 405
Horizon Enrollment Server 14
Horizon Group Policy
  overview 417
  reference 417

Horizon home site
  determining, security group 167, 168
  determining, user group 167, 168
Horizon infrastructure
  about 408
  AD user/group information, retrieving 410
  ComposerTask refresh 410
  desktop pool entitlement, reviewing 414
  global Horizon configuration data, retrieving 409
  health monitor status, retrieving 412
  health monitors, retrieving 412
  Horizon composer server information 408
  Horizon connection broker information, retrieving 409
  Horizon desktop pool list, retrieving 409
  Horizon event reports, retrieving 412
  license information, retrieving 413
  linked vCenter servers, retrieving 413
  remote Horizon session information, retrieving 413
  user persistent data disk information, retrieving 411
  virtual machines managed by Horizon, retrieving 409
Horizon installation
  event database 46
  infrastructure 43
  permissions, granting 43, 44, 45
  prerequisites 42, 43
  SQL Database Tutorials 47
  vCenter role, creating 43, 44, 45
Horizon Instant Clone Engine
  configuring 55
  Instant Clone Engine AD user account, configuring 56
  Instant Clone Engine Domain Administrator setting, updating 56, 57
Horizon Instant Clones
  pool, creating 196, 197, 199
Horizon maintenance tasks
  managing 248, 249
Horizon maintenance
  global settings 249
Horizon Manual Desktop Pools 180
Horizon Persona Management 214, 334
Horizon pod

removing, from Cloud Pod 163, 164
Horizon PowerCLI commands
  about 393
  options 391
  sample data 392
  viewing 391
Horizon RDS AD group policy templates
  importing 215, 216, 218, 219
Horizon RDS farm
  managing 237, 238, 240
Horizon Replica Connection Server
  backing up 61
  deploying 58
  Horizon AD LDS database 61
  Horizon event database 61
  Horizon vCenter databases 61
  installing 58
  prerequisites, prerequisites 61
  prerequisites, upgrading 60
  upgrading 60
Horizon Security Server certificate
  replacing 474
Horizon Security Server
  about 12
  backup 119
  Blast/PCoIP Secure Gateway, enabling 111
  considerations 104
  deploying 110
  high availability overview 105
  installation prerequisites 108
  installing 108, 113, 114, 115, 116, 117
  limitations 103
  network requisites 106, 107
  options 118
  overview 102
  pairing password 109, 110
  recovery 119, 120
  settings, updating 117
  upgrade 119, 120, 121
Horizon Server Configuration ADM template
  about 449
  Server Configuration Base Template 449
Horizon Unified Access Gateway certificate
  replacing 477, 479
Horizon Unified Access Gateway
  about 13
  configuration, updating 139
  connection servers, configuring 133, 134
  considerations 126
  deploying 133, 135, 136, 138
  deployment, troubleshooting 138
  high availability 126, 127
  infrastructure, preparing 130
  installation prerequisites 130, 131
  limitations 125
  network requisites 128
  overview 124
Horizon
  connection broker settings, updating 396
  global settings, updating 397
  infrastructure, configuring 394
  license, configuring 398
  Microsoft RDS farm, creating 221, 222, 223, 224, 225, 226
  vCenter server settings, updating 396
  vCenter server, adding 394
  vCenter server, removing 396
Hyper Converged Infrastructure (HCI) 275

I

individual desktops
  rebalancing 262
  recomposing 260
  refreshing 258
individual instant clone desktop
  recovering 265
Input/Output Operations Per Second (IOPS) 274
instant clone desktop maintenance
  performing 263
instant clone desktop parent image
  updating 263, 264
instant clone desktop
  about 243
  parent image update 245
Instant Clone desktops
  about 178
  advantages 182, 183
  considerations 183, 184
Instant Clone Engine AD user account
  configuring 56

Instant Clone Engine Domain Administrator 35
Instant Clone Engine Domain Administrator setting
  updating 56, 57
Internet Protocol (IP) 22

J

Java updater utility
  disabling 283
JMP Assignment
  creating 379, 381
  deleting 383
  duplicating 383
  editing 383
  managing 379
JMP Server
  deploying 369
  settings, configuring 372, 377
  software, installing 369
Just-in-Time Management Platform (JMP) 363, 364
Just-in-Time Management Server
  database requisites 366
  general requisites 366
  hardware requisites 365
  infrastructure requisites 367
  requisites 365
  software requisites 365

K

Key Management Services (KMS) 71
Key Management System (KMS) 213

L

Lakeside Software SysTrack
  reference 26
LDAPS
  reference 302
license levels, VMware Horizon 19, 20
linked clone desktop maintenance
  performing 255
linked clone desktops
  about 243
  overview 244, 245
  rebalance operation 247, 248
  rebalancing 261, 262
  recompose operation 246, 247
  recomposing 258, 259
  refresh operation 245, 246
  refreshing 255, 256
linked clone disk
  with replica disk 244
Linux desktops 180
Liquidware Labs Stratusphere UX
  reference 26
load-balancing appliances 41
Local Computer Certificates console
  creating 460, 462
Login VSI
  reference 26
loopback processing
  for group policies 419
  merge mode 420
  replace mode 420

M

Master Boot Record (MBR) 278
Maximum Transmission Unit (MTU) 453
Metro Apps 278
Microsoft Active Directory Lightweight Directory
    Services (MS LDS) 38
Microsoft AD Certificate Services
  used, for requesting certificate 462, 464, 468
Microsoft Installer (MSI) 319
Microsoft KB article 274443
  reference 339
Microsoft Management Console (MMC) 460
Microsoft RDS farm
  creating, in Horizon 221, 222, 223, 224, 225, 226
Microsoft RDS host
  Horizon Agent, installing on 219
Microsoft RDS licensing 213
Microsoft RDS optimization and management
  reference 212
Microsoft RDS server
  resources 221
  status, monitoring 235, 236
  vSphere customization specification 220
Microsoft RDSH server
  configuring, for usage with Horizon 212

recommended hardware configuration 214
Microsoft SQL Server documentation
  reference 367
Modern Apps 278
Multiple Active Key (MAK) licenses 71

N

native update features 281
Network Load Balancing (NLB) 40
Network-Level Authentication (NLA) 442
non-persistent desktops 17

O

Open Virtualization Format (OVF) 13

P

PCoIP Secure Gateway 111
PCoIP Session Variables ADM template
  about 449
  Base setting 450, 453
persistent disks
  detaching 267
  importing 270
  managing 266
  used, for recreating desktop 268
Personalization tab, advanced UEM configuration example
  application profile Import / Export feature 355, 356
Plug-and-Play (PnP) 443
Pod Federation 144, 145
pool
  creating, full clones used 199, 200, 201, 202
  creating, Horizon Composer-linked clones used 185, 186, 187, 188, 189, 190, 192, 193, 194, 195
  creating, Horizon Instant Clones used 196, 197, 199
PowerCLI commands
  Get-Help PowerShell command 391
  listing 391
PowerShell Unified Access Gateway Deployment Scripts
  reference 132
Product Interoperability Matrices

reference 21
push image 245

Q

QuickPrep
  versus Sysprep 180, 181

R

RDS desktop pool
  creating 229, 231, 233
RDS server
  managing 237, 239, 240
Remote Desktop Licensing role service 213
Remote Desktop Services (RDS) 211
Remote Desktop Session (RDS) 10
Remote Desktop Session Hosts (RD Session Host) 211
remote Horizon PowerCLI session
  establishing 389
remote management
  WinRM, enabling 388
Remove-AppxPackage
  reference 280
Remove-AppxProvisionedPackage
  reference 280
replicas 35
Research Triangle Park (RTP) 145
Resource Record (RR) 22
RSA SecureID 14

S

Service Record (SRV) 22
Single Sign-On (SSO) 14
Software Designed Storage (SDS 275
SQL Database tutorials
  reference 86
Subject Alternative Names (SAN)
  about 132, 462
  used, for requesting certificate 468, 470
SuperFetch 292
SyncTool 334
Sysprep
  versus QuickPrep 180, 181

T

templates, UEM components 339
Terminal Services 211
Transparent Page Sharing (TPS) 176

U

UEM Agent
  installing 340, 341
UEM group policy settings
  about 347
  UEM computer policies 350
  UEM user policies 347, 349
  Windows folder redirection 352, 353
UEM management console
  installing 342, 343
UEM pre-installation tasks
  about 336
  configuration share 337
  persona share 337, 338
  Windows user folder redirection share 338, 339
Unified Access Gateway (UAG) 13, 477
unwanted application
  removing 281
User Environment Manager (UEM)
  about 18, 214, 333
  benefits 18
  configuring 341
  Easy Start configuration 344, 345
  Easy Start defaults 345, 346
  overview 334
User Environment tab, advanced UEM configuration example
  about 358
  shortcut management feature 360

V

vCenter Server requisites 41, 42
View InterPod API (VIPA) 147
Virtual Machine Disk (VMDK) file 18
Virtual SAN (vSAN) 15
virtual Storage Area Network (SAN) 15
VMware App Volumes
  about 17, 18
  features 17

VMware Community forum, for UEM Documents page
  reference 354
VMware Compatibility Guide
  reference 21
VMware document Horizon 7 Architecture Planning
  reference 28
VMware Horizon 6.2 13
VMware Horizon Connection Server
  overview 36, 37
VMware Horizon core infrastructure requirements
  about 21
  database requirements 23
  Horizon Agent-supported operating systems 24
  Microsoft infrastructure requirements 21
  operating system requirements 22
  vCenter Server requirements 23
VMware Horizon design
  overview 25
  sufficient Horizon Client bandwidth, providing 28
  Virtual Desktop resource requirements, measuring 25, 26
  VMware Horizon pilot 29
  vSphere reserve capacity 26, 27
VMware Horizon pilot
  about 29
  performance 31
VMware Horizon product page
  reference 10
VMware Horizon
  components 10
  license levels 19, 20
VMware Identity Manager
  reference 368
VMware KB article 2118056
  reference 335
VMware OS Optimization Tool
  reference 283
VMware OVF Tool
  reference 132
VMware resources
  references 20
VMware ThinApp
  about 19, 319
  reference 19

VMware Tools
  installing 280
VMware UEM 339
VMware UEM documentation
  reference 334
VMware UEM FAQ
  reference 334
VMware UEM FlexEngine 339
VMware UEM Helpdesk Support Tool 339
VMware UEM Management Console 339
VMware UEM SyncTool - Computer 339
VMware UEM SyncTool - User 339
VMware vCenter Server 15
VMware vSphere 14
VMware vSphere PowerCLI 11.0.0
  reference 132
VMware Workspace ONE Identity Manager 14
VMware Workspace ONE
  reference 368
vSphere customization specification
  for Microsoft RDS servers 220
vSphere installation
  reference 42
vSphere VMFork technology 175
vSphere Web client task window 204, 205

W

Windows background
  disabling 296
Windows cluster size
  customizing, during installation process 277
Windows desktop OS cluster size
  customizing 276
Windows OS optimizations
  about 283
  automatic updates, disabling 284, 285
  Content Indexing, disabling for remaining file locations 291
  Content Indexing, disabling of desktop drive 290
  Group Policy refresh interval, modifying 294
  Microsoft .NET Framework assemblies, pre-compiling 286
  paging the executive, disabling 289, 290
  unnecessary scheduled tasks, removing 292
  unnecessary services, disabling 291
  unnecessary Windows components, removing 285
  virtual machine RAM, sizing properly 288
  Windows boot animation, disabling 294
  Windows Error Reporting, disabling 284
  Windows hibernation, disabling 287
  Windows page file, setting to fixed size 289
  Windows profile, optimizing 295
  Windows System Restore, disabling 287, 288
Windows OS
  pre-deployment tasks 280
Windows profile
  adjusting, for best performance 296
  system sounds, turning off 296
Windows screen saver
  disabling 296
Windows Store applications
  removing, permanently 278, 279
Windows System Restore 287
Windows
  remote management, enabling 388
WinRM
  enabling 388
writable volumes
  deleting 327
  enabling 324, 327

X

XML-based GPO template (ADMX) 339

Printed in Poland
by Amazon Fulfillment
Poland Sp. z o.o., Wrocław